The Family Roe

ALSO BY JOSHUA PRAGER

The Echoing Green

Half-Life

100 Years
(with Milton Glaser)

THE
FAMILY
ROE

An American Story

JOSHUA PRAGER

W. W. NORTON & COMPANY
Independent Publishers Since 1923

For information about permission to reproduce selections from this book,
write to Permissions, W. W. Norton & Company, Inc., 500 Fifth Avenue,
New York, NY 10110

For information about special discounts for bulk purchases, please contact
W. W. Norton Special Sales at specialsales@wwnorton.com or 800-233-4830

Manufacturing by Lakeside Book Company
Book design by Daniel Lagin
Production manager: Julia Druskin

ISBN 978-0-393-24771-8

W. W. Norton & Company, Inc., 500 Fifth Avenue, New York, N.Y. 10110
www.wwnorton.com

W. W. Norton & Company Ltd., 15 Carlisle Street, London W1D 3BS

1 2 3 4 5 6 7 8 9 0

To my treasures,
Ella Vita and Eden Max

Be it said . . . see how elastic our stiff prejudices grow when love once comes to bend them.

Herman Melville, *Moby-Dick*

Contents

The Family Roe

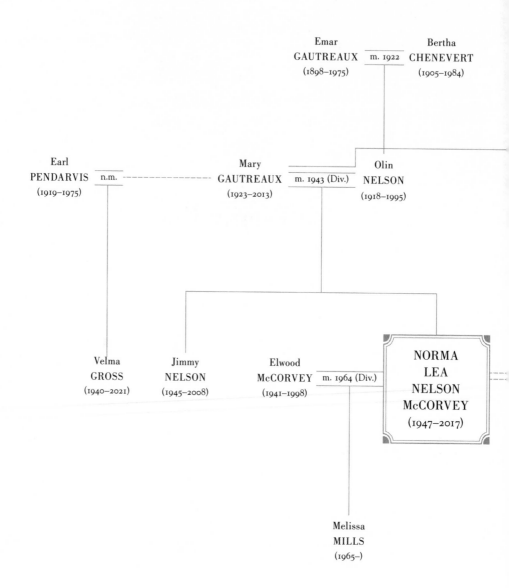

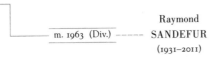

Raymond
m. 1963 (Div.) SANDEFUR
(1931–2011)

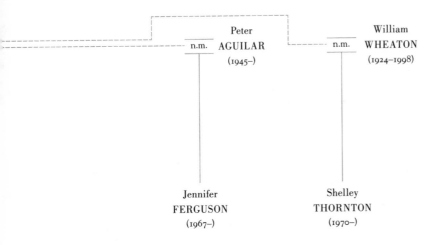

Peter   William
n.m.   AGUILAR   n.m.   WHEATON
(1945–)   (1924–1998)

Jennifer   Shelley
FERGUSON   THORNTON
(1967–)   (1970–)

This tree only includes family members who feature prominently in the book.

PROLOGUE

On January 22, 1973, the Supreme Court decided *Roe v. Wade*, granting women the right to an abortion "free of interference by the State."

The Court was undecided at first where in the Constitution to ground that right. It settled on the Fourteenth Amendment, ruling that it guaranteed Americans a right to privacy, and that a right to privacy secured a right to have an abortion.

There were some, even among the pro-choice, who assailed *Roe*'s reasoning. The feminist icon Ruth Bader Ginsburg would later argue, in an article she wrote while a member of the DC Circuit appeals court, that the right to abortion ought to be grounded in equality, not privacy. But others applauded *Roe*'s logic and its author, too, the Nixon appointee Harry Blackmun. Six of his eight fellow justices joined his opinion, and its longevity was assumed; when nearly three years later Gerald Ford nominated John Paul Stevens to the Supreme Court, the Senate did not even ask the judge his opinion of it.

But the fault line that is abortion in America began then to slip and heave, to produce tremors not only of politics and law but of religion and sex, the stuff that quakes the puritanical foundations of this country like little else. And today, to hear both pro-life and pro-choice tell it, the confirmation hearings of Supreme Court nominees are above all referenda on *Roe*.

Roe has come to dictate far more than judicial appointments. It is, as the legal philosopher Ronald Dworkin wrote, "undoubtedly the best-known case the United States Supreme Court has ever decided." More, it is the most enduringly divisive. There is no surer indicator of political affiliation in America than *Roe*, the ruling a Rorschach test and a rallying cry, a means not only to party consensus but donor dollars—millions determined to uphold it, millions determined to overturn it.

Today, fifty years after the Court first heard arguments in *Roe*, the decision is hanging by a thread. Whether it falls or not, the American divide on abortion will remain. "Any victory, no matter how sweeping, will simply trigger a new round of fighting," writes Mary Ziegler, a law professor expert on the American abortion debate. She adds: "the abortion conflict is a tale of hopeless polarization, personal hatreds and political dysfunction."

Indeed, ours is a nation divisible by *Roe*. And as Blackmun noted in his preamble to the ruling, it is often personal experience—"exposure to the raw edges of human existence"—that determines which side of that divide one is on. The justice might have added that four years before he joined the Court, his daughter Sally had found herself unhappily pregnant in college.

———

ROE V. WADE WAS so named for its pseudonymous plaintiff, Jane Roe, and its defendant, Dallas district attorney Henry Wade. But at its heart, the case did not pit Roe against Wade; it pitted her against the fetus she was carrying. And the Court's ruling alluded, if only obliquely, to the existence of the child that fetus became. Wrote Blackmun: "the normal 266-day human gestation period is so short that the pregnancy will come to term before the usual appellate process is complete."

Blackmun was making a simple legal point: it did not matter that the gestation of a lawsuit is longer than the gestation of a baby. The case had not been rendered moot because its plaintiff was no longer pregnant. But Blackmun did not write that Jane Roe had given birth. And the public was left to assume that Jane Roe—whoever she was—had gotten the abortion made legally available to her.

Normally, a plaintiff is required to use her real name. The Federal Rules of Civil Procedure demand it. But, owing to the stigma of abortion, an exception was made in *Roe*, and Blackmun addressed it. "Despite the use of the pseudonym," he wrote, "no suggestion is made that Roe is a fictitious person."

Jane Roe was real. Her name was Norma McCorvey. And when, in 2010, I read an article that mentioned that *Roe* had been decided too late for Norma to have an abortion, I wondered about the baby she'd placed for adoption forty years before. I decided to look for her.

Months after Norma gave birth to that child in 1970, she met her lifelong partner, Connie Gonzales. Norma had just left Gonzales when, in June 2010, I visited Gonzales at her Dallas home. She told me that the stories Norma had told about herself were not true.

Gonzales's home was due to be foreclosed on when I returned to see her the next year. She pointed me to a cache of papers that Norma had left behind in the garage and did not want. Looking through her speeches and letters, her holy cards and sheet music, I wondered not only about the *Roe* baby but about the other two daughters Norma had let go. I wondered also about Norma. Lifting a picture of Norma as a toddler atop a pony, I looked at the little house behind her up on piers and wondered, too, about her family rooted there on the banks of a Louisiana river.

PART I

Sex and Religion

Chapter 1

The Atchafalaya River flows south from a small Louisiana town called Simmesport, where, in the fifteenth century, it branched off the Mississippi. The river runs to the Gulf of Mexico, traveling 137 miles through a triangle of Louisiana locals call Acadiana. The name recalls Acadia, the bygone French colony in northeastern North America. There, starting in 1755, thousands of French exiles were driven from their homes. They began, nine years later, to settle along a Louisiana river two thousand miles to the southwest.

No locks or levees or dams yet harnessed the young river. And the Acadians—as those early Americans would be called—though they dug furrows and ditches beside the river and set their huts atop blocks of cypress, often found themselves in water. If the river flooded, it also bore crawfish and silt, the sediment feeding crops of soybean and indigo. More crops followed: tobacco, cotton, maize, molasses, sugar. The Acadians soon owned plantations and people, too—Africans working their fields, breastfeeding their young. Their community grew; by the early nineteenth century, there were roughly five thousand Acadians in Louisiana. They gave its marshes and bayous and prairies French names: Prairie Basse, Prairie des Femmes, Prairie des Coteaux.

Francophone and Catholic, the Acadians took to the South—to its fiddles and faith healers, its Spanish moss and slavery. By 1860, forty-nine Acadians owned more than fifty slaves each. But they were no patriots. Flags changed; the Acadians had already seen the French, Spanish and Americans govern this land. When the Confederate Army conscripted their men, the Acadian soldier was all but indifferent to the cause. Some surrendered. Some deserted.

When the war ended, the Acadians had lost their slaves and infrastructure, and many became fishermen or trappers or lumberjacks. But having previously filled steamboats and trains with produce for export, they now struggled to feed their own. Poverty took hold. Starvation was endemic. Alcoholism, too. More and more, as historian Carl Brasseaux noted, Acadians came to be thought of as primitive, as ignorant, as "Cajun"—the word a derisive variant of "Acadian."

Reconstruction did little to lift the Acadian parishes. They remained in a deep recession well into the twentieth century.

———

AMONG THE FIRST to leave Acadia for Acadiana was a newlywed from the Nova Scotian community of Grand-Pré named Amand Gautreaux. He arrived in Louisiana in the 1760s and began farming along the Mississippi. His son Jerome moved to the banks of the Atchafalaya, and it was there that generations of his progeny remained: Jerome's son Joseph and Joseph's son Jerome and Jerome's son Francois and Francois's son Emar—who in 1922 was suddenly in a fix.

Emar worked on a plantation just east of the river, tending at age twenty-three to fields of cotton and corn and sugarcane. His foreman, a diabetic French-Canadian named Joseph Chenevert, had a wee, brown-eyed daughter named Bertha who fed the farmhands, beans and rice mostly. But she gave Emar more. And she had just turned seventeen when she found herself pregnant.

It did not occur to the young couple to prevent the birth of a child. Both were Catholic and knew well the disallowance of contraception. Besides, abortion was not safe. Those tonics and hairpins that could end a pregnancy could also end the life of a prospective mother. And when on January 12, 1923, a black midwife named Mary Posey helped to deliver a fair girl with blue eyes named Mildred, the baby was born to a man and woman who had been married just six months. Neither would ever confess to Mildred their indiscretion.

The young family settled on the west bank of the Atchafalaya, renting the first floor of a shack in a bean field that passed for a town called Woodside. A Pentecostal preacher named Brother Richmond lived upstairs. It wasn't long before the family Gautreaux was Pentecostal too, leaving behind the sacraments of their church for the ecstasies and ululations of a movement no older than they. A couple come together in sin had been born again.

Emar had to follow the crops, to move with wife and child to those farms where there was cotton to be picked. And in every block of cypress and cement in which they lived, he and Bertha made sure to do as Brother Richmond had: to host prayer meetings, nights of speaking in tongues, of receiving the Holy Ghost, of ridding them and their fellow Pentecostals of demons while the children hid behind the door.

The young couple beseeched Jesus for rain—and, in 1927, for the rain to stop. The Mississippi had flooded, and Emar and Bertha hurried to higher ground, pitching a tent atop a levee for themselves and their three kids.

The 1927 flood displaced more than half a million others, too. Dense as cities, their camps fostered disease and pregnancy. "Many illegitimacies," one priest noted. "Relatives take the child and then compel the couple to marry." Emissaries from the American Social Hygiene Association, come south from New York, spoke to the displaced in the language of the land, likening the consequences of indiscretion to those of a leaking levee. The Catholic church was not pleased. As one local priest put it: "We hope this is not anything on birth control."

But the church had little need to worry. The homeless, among them some 100,000 Acadians, heeded its proscriptions. It did not matter that uncontrolled birth was impoverishing or that, all through the coming decade, the Acadian community would remain, as the historian Brasseaux noted, "too poor to notice the Great Depression." In the Acadian home, birth was often biennial, and by 1938, Emar and Bertha had had eight kids in sixteen years, contraception as taboo as the mere suggestion of sex. "You wouldn't even say someone was pregnant in front of the children," recalls their daughter Sandra Guilbeau. Adds her niece Velma Gross: "when a girl had her monthly, you stayed in your room till that time was done."

BACK IN 1897, Theodore Roosevelt had asserted that American schools ought to conduct classes in "English, and no other language." The idea gained traction with the start of the First World War. Wanting to Americanize its Acadians, Louisiana banned French from its schools in 1921. And so, in their classroom atop a levee in little Innis, the Gautreaux kids learned to read and write in English. Their parents spoke French and were illiterate; both had left school by the second grade. It fell to Mildred, their eldest, to read for her mama and papa—a passage from the Bible, a letter, or a contract, as when the family bought a bay mule for $125 with the written understanding that it was not warrantied "against sickness, accident and death."

Mildred was a happy child—"outgoing, laughing, cutting-up," says her childhood friend Julia Saucier. But after sixth grade, she had to leave school for the cow and plow, the fields of corn and cotton. Her light brown hair plaited in pigtails, Mildred learned to pull those fibrous white puffs from the sharp open bolls that bled her fingers.

Her brothers were also in the fields—Milbin, Murphy, Hilman, L.F. and Freddie, dusting acres of cotton, from atop their black mare, with fertilizer and 3–5-40 that killed the boll weevil and burned their legs, too. They worked hard. But not as hard as their father, who also picked cotton and drove a gravel truck and captained a ferry and raised a garden of tomatoes and snap beans and cowhorn okra. And not as hard as their mother, who made meals from those vegetables along with the chickens she killed and the fifty-pound sacks of rice and beans she bought and the coffee beans she ground and the rice kernels she stripped and the blocks of yeast she turned with warm water and strong forearms to biscuits and bread. Bertha also had to mind the broom and mop and slop bucket and washboard. And, of course, there were the ten bodies she had to clothe with the cotton she sewed and starched and ironed and washed and recycled—flour sacks turned to aprons, clothes turned to quilts after too many scrubbings of dust and mud left them threadbare.

The dust blew through the windows, a fine brown mist. And the mud, gray and wet with water risen from the Atchafalaya, was underfoot. It softened the Louisiana sod and clay, the fields and forests of palmettos and pecans and oak and hackberry. Everywhere, it pooled in slate puddles—in the sunken gutters of dirt roads, in the riverine tracks between lines of crop, around the blocks and tires that held up home and car, Emar stepping in rubber boots from his yellow Ford after every long day.

It was a hard life. Still, the tall and thin farmer was God-fearing and sober save his taste for muscatel wine. Wife Bertha, meantime, was strict, ready with a switch of sycamore to "burn our legs," says daughter Sandra, if, say, Sandra and her sisters neglected to scrub the holed plank in the outhouse. But Bertha was also warm. She saw to it that, come 1940, the family still spent its days together, mama and papa and the kids gathering Sunday afternoons beneath the sycamore and chinaberry trees to scoop ice cream from broken mugs. Says Sandra: "It makes you want to cry."

———

ON APRIL 25, 1940, a woman named Ruth Lambert arrived in little Letts-worth, at the Gautreaux home. The house, on State Lane, was like any other along the Atchafalaya—of cypress and cement, kerosene lamps and moss mattresses. It cost four dollars a month to rent, and the family made it pretty, adhering a floral paper to the walls with a homemade paste of flour and water.

Lambert was a census taker, and Bertha told her about her husband who'd worked all fifty-two weeks that year and earned fifty-plus dollars, and about the eight children aged three to seventeen who filled their home.

But then, suddenly, there were nine children. For Mildred, seventeen and unmarried, was pregnant. And something had to be done.

Mildred did not want to be pregnant. But whether a woman wanted to be pregnant was immaterial in 1940. Abortion was illegal throughout the country.

Bertha had been in the same strait eighteen years before. She did not want the daughter she had birthed out of wedlock to do as she had, to marry in shameful haste. Nor did she want her to deliver a bastard to be homilized by Brother Deshotels, a preacher who rode through town on horseback. No. She wished for her daughter to leave.

"If a girl got pregnant, she'd go away—they wouldn't let you stay home," remembers Mildred's friend Julia. "It was a hush-hush thing."

Mildred went off to her aunt Odessa and uncle Kaiser in Baton Rouge. "It seemed like [she left] overnight," recalls Julia. "She's gone." As her belly grew sixty miles southeast from all who knew her, Bertha and Emar told folks that their eldest had moved to the city to earn a better wage. Mildred did indeed get a job, working as a cashier at a Walgreen's right up until September, when she gave birth to Velma Jean and brought her home. Emar and Bertha met them on a Saturday at the bus station in New Roads.

Bertha was thirty-five years old. She was now a grandmother. But a secret had to be kept. The standing of the family depended upon it. And so, grandparents became parents, mother became sister, an only child became one of nine and then ten when, three years later, Bertha gave birth to her daughter Sandra.

A day would come when Bertha would almost confess the truth. She would, recalls Velma, tell her granddaughter: "'I can tell you something that would hurt you but I won't tell you.'"

But secrets emerge over time. And Velma's aunt turned sister, Esther Rae, would one day tell her of the afternoon she, Velma, had arrived as a baby from Baton Rouge, wrapped in blankets. Mildred would come clean, too. She told Velma that when she was pregnant, Velma's biological father had followed her to Baton Rouge, but Uncle Kaiser had turned him away while she hid under a bed.

Those reckonings, however, were decades away. For now, mama and papa would say nothing. They would confide only in the Bible—writing in the Good Book the dates and names of the family births and marriages, testaments to unions both holy and profane.

Emar kept the Bible in the armoire and forbade all from touching it. Only after farmer and housewife had died did a daughter-in-law open its black leather cover.

———

FOR SEVENTEEN YEARS, through flood and poverty and communal neglect, the family Gautreaux had remained intact even as it grew ever larger and moved from shanty to shack. But sex had done what crisis and poverty had not. It had separated a piece from the whole. Mildred remained apart. Cast off, her maternity erased, she soon boarded a bus back to Baton Rouge. "That pregnancy changed her whole life," says Velma. "She was the only one who left and left in shame."

Mildred wished to be reborn. And just as Pentecostalism had rid her parents of their premarital sin, the teenager now reclaimed the virginal name given her at birth—Mary. She also took a job waitressing at a bus station. Soon after, at a sandwich counter in a Walgreen's, she met Olin Nelson, an electronics repairman with a drawl and black hair and a wide smile. He went by "Jimmy."

Nelson was twenty-two, the eldest of four from a broken home in a small Texas town. His father, William, had been estranged from his family when he died a decade before, and his mother, Alma, was a palm reader whose business peaked every fall when the grounds opposite her home in East Dallas welcomed the state fair. Alma had divorced a second time when, in 1941, her son Olin said goodbye to his girlfriend Mary and enlisted in the military. Alma was readying to marry a fourth time when, two years later, on March 6, 1943, her son, a sergeant on leave from his station in Panama, wed Mary in a double ceremony in Baton Rouge on the west bank of the Mississippi.

The U.S. Army Corps of Engineers would soon determine that the river's flow to Baton Rouge (and, just downriver, New Orleans) was in jeopardy. The river's distributary, the Atchafalaya, had begun to absorb the Mississippi, widening and deepening at its expense. If nothing was done, the Atchafalaya would capture the Mississippi, the river from which it flowed, at Simmesport—the little Louisiana town where the two rivers parted, and where now Mary settled with Olin.

One year later, in 1944, Mary got pregnant. She now had a husband and a new name, and so stayed in Simmesport. There, one month after the radios Olin fixed told that the war was over, Mary gave birth to a boy she named Jimmy.

Mary, though, was not at peace. Her firstborn was just over the river. Though Mary doted on her—Velma "always wondered why," she says—Mary could not call her her own. It wasn't long before Mary began serving drinks in the local bars, and then began to drink, too, the waitress partial to whiskey.

Mary was soon pregnant a third time. On September 22, 1947, she entered the door reserved for whites at the clinic of her doctor, Winfield Plauche. At ten o'clock, Norma Lea Nelson was born, four ounces shy of seven pounds.

It was the last night of summer. Mary would never forget the storm that raged as she labored, wind and rain beating the Atchafalaya.

Chapter 2

Mary had returned to the wetlands with her secret intact: none knew that the ninth Gautreaux child was hers. But all knew what had become of Mary. "We just heard the gossip," says her friend Julia Saucier. "That she turned to alcohol, kind of a wild life."

Olin heard the gossip too. He knew that it was true—that his wife, like his mother, had a taste for alcohol and men. He took to leaving home, going off on long solitary drives with a pack of cigarettes. But in 1950, he took his wife and kids with him, off to Texas in search of a new start. Olin soon pledged himself to Jehovah, the better to reform his wayward wife.

Norma would not remember Louisiana; she was a toddler when the family packed the Studebaker and drove west. Her first memory would be of Texas, of fig trees that grew in an empty lot off Shoreham Street near her Houston home. The trees were straight except for one. And like her reborn father, who began now to find homilies in the everyday, Norma would tell years later of that one crooked tree that drew her.

TO BE A Jehovah's Witness is to be certain that Armageddon is imminent. But doctrine tells that the end of days will spare 144,000 non-sinners. And after Mary shed her Pentecostalism and was a Witness, too, the family Nelson took to the road, off on Sundays in their new Chevy

wagon to minister to those few who might be saved. Quiet six days a
week, on the seventh Olin preached, in the Kingdom Halls about east
Texas, of Jehovah and salvation and sin.

Norma and Jimmy watched their father turn red with zeal. They helped
him, too, knocking on doors with stacks of *The Watchtower*, peddling in their
Sunday best its "thou shalt not"s: abortion, war, the transfusion of blood,
the saluting of flags, the celebration of Christmas and birthdays. When, on
September 22, 1955, Norma turned eight, she blew out no candles.

Still, the little girl was spirited—a half-pint with curly brown hair
and olive eyes running about in shorts and T-shirts. And when the
school year at Berry Elementary ended, she headed to Louisiana, off
to the green shack on the west bank of the Atchafalaya where she had
lived her first two years. Her grandparents had bought the home from
Olin and Mary—the first they had ever owned. Having shared its lone
bedroom with their four youngest children, they had since built on two
more, and had room enough for another little girl.

Norma had fun with her family. She explored the levees with
uncles and jitterbugged with aunts. She listened to the stories Grandpa
told from his rocker, and bought Coke and candy with nickels from
Grandma, sitting out front of Uncle Bob's Store on the plank that locals
called the "nigger bench" because, her aunt Sandra says, "that's where
they would sit."

Norma was happy on the river. But, come fall, she returned to a family fervent with Jehovah. She "resented the teachings," recalled Mary.
Norma was angry, for example, when she got sent to the principal for
refusing, as her parents had instructed, to salute the flag. And she was
nine when, back beside that crooked fig tree, Norma took for herself
an imaginary friend, a blond girl her age she named Janie who told her
what to wear. "She was the opposite of me," said Norma. "Very smart,
very reserved." Added Norma: "She knew when bad things happened."

Janie thus knew when Norma got her first bra and was unsure how
to put it on and her mother called her, said Norma, a "stupid little imp."
And Janie knew when one day Norma lost her footing while climbing a
tree and decided to let go of the branch she'd grasped. "Why not fall?"
she thought. She was, she said, owing to her mother, "always sad in my
heart." Norma was not hurt.

Janie filled a void; she was the sister Norma wanted but did not have. Norma, though, *did* have a sister—the older half-sister she thought was her aunt. And in early 1958, Velma came to live with her after learning that she was pregnant.

Velma's predicament was familiar to her family; both her grandmother and her mother (whom she knew, respectively, as her mother and her sister) had also gotten pregnant when they were seventeen and unmarried. Velma's sister-in-law Wavia suggested that Velma leave town at once, that she go to a "girls' home" in Shreveport where her baby could be born and placed for adoption. But Emar—the grandfather Velma believed was her father—had already disappeared one daughter. Months shy of sixty, he wondered to what end. If the family name had been preserved, it had been sullied just the same when Mary, bereft, had turned to alcohol and sex. What's more, Mary had suffered. If sex had consequences, so did religion and the fear of rebuke.

And so, Emar intervened. "He said 'no!'" recalls Velma. "She's staying right here!" The family would remain whole.

Velma relaxed. But six weeks pregnant, she soon wished to leave home, wished to go live with her beloved sister Mary. Says Velma: "I felt a bond with her always." Velma took the bus from Lafayette to Houston, leaving Louisiana for the first time.

Mary doted on her lost daughter. She took her, along with little Norma and Jimmy, to movies and parks. Velma in turn "kept house," she says, cooking and taking care of the kids when Olin and Mary were at work. When Velma returned to Louisiana after four months, Norma went with her, the girl of ten eager for another summer on the river.

Mary had said nothing to Velma of their true relation. And, spared her emotional burden, Velma remained no less close to her parents or to God, turning to the Bible she'd gotten as a girl with coupons clipped from *True Story* magazine.

Mary, meantime, was less apt to look for truth in scripture than in palms or coffee grinds. And as Velma's belly grew big with two boys, Norma returned to a family that was tiring of Jehovah. They soon moved from Houston to Dallas, settling into an apartment one flight above McKinney Avenue.

The apartment was small; the shower was in the hallway. But the

Nelsons stayed apart—Olin happiest in his shop, Mary at her bar, Jimmy in his science fiction, Norma out back with Janie. Norma was no more at home at school; her grades at William B. Travis Elementary were rarely higher than a two out of four. When at age twelve, in 1960, she took an intelligence test, she placed in the twelfth percentile. Her teachers at Travis noted that Norma was "absent on slightest excuse" and "not interested in school work."

Norma was interested in cigarettes and beer; she began to smoke like her dad and drink like her mom. She returned to Louisiana that summer a changed child—smoking and drinking and darting after a local boy. "Norma was a handful," remembers Velma. "She was wild. . . . I was always in the streets looking for her."

Back in Dallas, no one looked for her. School had started up again when Norma and a friend boarded a bus to Oklahoma City. The girls checked into a motel, lay in bed and kissed.

Norma knew what sex was. She had seen her mother "lay out with men," she said, had heard talk of banishing her pregnant aunt. Sex was caustic. It was illicit, too; having heard her father preach against forbidden relations, she was beginning to see Jehovah in the dark spaces. When one schoolday on a softball field she bled from between her legs, she knew, said Norma, that God was punishing her.

And so, it made sense to her when the police arrived and her friend alleged, said Norma, "that I tried inappropriate things with her." The police returned Norma to a mother enraged by her lesbianism. After the Juvenile Court of Dallas declared Norma "a delinquent child," her father paid forty dollars a month to enroll her in a Catholic boarding school in southwest Dallas.

Mount St. Michael was of a more genteel world than the one Norma knew—of beanies and saddle shoes, beef stew and school plays; Norma played a Polynesian peasant in a production of *South Pacific*. But Norma was soon in trouble. When she refused to take catechism class, she landed in detention. And when, on laundry duty, she cursed at a nun who asked her to iron a shirt a second time, she got kicked out. Norma was thirteen.

Years later, Norma would tell of a great trauma she suffered in Catholic school, of being raped in a shower by a nun named Veronica.

But there never was a Sister Veronica on staff at Mount St. Michael. There was instead, as Norma confided only privately, an older student named Barbara who, three nights before she was to vow to become a nun, had lain beside her in her cot, uninvited but welcome, and touched her.

Norma had reimagined herself as not a sinner but a victim. In time, she would do so over and over again, and most often regarding sex— that which in the Nelson home was profane, extramarital. Indeed, upon returning home from school, she found that her mother had begun seeing a man she'd met in a bar, a trucker named Raymond Sandefur. In February 1961, Mary and Olin divorced.

That same month, the Texas Youth Council placed Norma in a local elementary school. She stopped going to class, and turned from beer and cigarettes to whiskey and marijuana. Mary struggled to mother her. "She lost all control of me," said Norma. Norma had shaved her eyebrows when, in April 1962, she fell into the custody of the state, "committed to an institution."

That institution was the Gainesville State School for Girls, a cluster of brick buildings on fields of grass just south of the Oklahoma border. The state agency that oversaw the school would soon refer to it as "one of the best training facilities for delinquent girls in America today." And Norma was not unhappy at Gainesville. She enjoyed her classes: photography and upholstery and science. She liked her fellow students, too, a white and Latina sorority of truants and offenders. (The school would not integrate for four more years.) If Norma still broke rules— pouring acid, for example, onto the coat of a teacher—she was at roll call at 6:30 every morning.

It did Norma good to be away from her family. And she began to feel differently about those two great cross-currents that had long guided it: sex and religion.

━━━

SEX AND RELIGION are not by nature opposed. Hinduism, for example, sanctifies sex and sensual pleasure, while Judaism considers sex sacred even as it forbids various relations. "The pre-Christian world generally thought of sex as a natural and positive part of human experience," wrote the constitutional scholar Geoffrey Stone. "It did not see sex as predominantly bound up with questions of sin, shame, or religion."

Jesus said little on the matter. But decades after His crucifixion, the Apostle Paul declared that "it is good for a man not to touch a woman." Celibacy was best. And it was a celibate Christian convert named Augustine who, centuries later, extended that notion, positing that sex was sinful and that "man by his very nature is ashamed of sexual desire." It was lust, not disobedience, wrote Augustine, that had expelled Adam from Eden. It was through sex that Adam had transmitted his original sin to all humanity.

The church would canonize Augustine and adopt his dogma. More than a millennium after his death, Augustine, as Professor Stone noted, "helped shape traditional American views of sexuality."

Those views in turn shaped an American family. In the forty years since Mary had been born to Bertha, her family had viewed religion and sex in terms of consequences. Sin led to hell as surely as pregnancy did to marriage—or banishment. But Norma had come to see her mother as less devout than hypocritical. And she now dismissed her and Jehovah, too, celebrating her newfound atheism with three dots inked by a fellow student into the fold of skin between her left thumb and forefinger. "It was explained to me," said Norma of her tattoo, "that it was for someone who didn't believe in God or love."

Norma, though, *did* believe in love. She was sixteen and besotted with her fellow Gainesville girls, who bunked with her in brick cottages the school had named for women of the Bible: Sarah and Rebecca and Hannah and Naomi. Norma was less than pretty, with a high forehead and a sunken chin. But she was fun and rowdy, and soon had a run of girlfriends—the cosmetology student who did Norma's brown curly hair, the Latina named Lydia who called her "mi cuata," slang for twin.

Norma had been at Gainesville nineteen months when, in the middle of upholstery class, President Kennedy was shot dead just south, in Dallas. One year later, Norma headed home to her family in that same grief-stricken city.

The family had come to include Raymond. The trucker had married Mary in March, and moved with her and her son Jimmy into a two-family home on Vickery Boulevard. But his bride, forty years old, continued to cheat, and Raymond turned now to her daughter for answers. "He said," recalled Norma, "'what's been going on every day when I've been going to work?'" Norma said nothing.

Mary offered no apologies. Even decades later, she looked past her own indiscretions to those of her daughter, to the alcohol and marijuana and sex that Norma enjoyed. "She drank and she took dope and she slept with women," Mary recalled from the lobby of a Dallas nursing home, her yellow hands tightening about the silver arms of a wheelchair. The last, Norma's lesbianism, repulsed Mary. Looking back with clouded blue eyes at the memory of an impenitent daughter, she mouthed a confession. Said Mary: "I beat the fuck out of her."

———

IT HAD BEEN liberating for Norma to discover at school sex different than she had known at home, sex open and reciprocal and gay; it was girls she desired, she later reflected, they who were "soft and gentle." But she was sixteen now and she told herself that it was time to marry. She had just taken a job as a waitress on skates at a Dallas drive-in when a little man in a big Ford pulled up.

Norma took him in. He had brown eyes and a black pompadour. He ordered a Coke and a "furburger," and asked Norma to come for a ride in his black Fairlane. She did.

His name was Elwood McCorvey. He was twenty-one and new to Texas. He had come south from a Catholic home in Brooklyn, where he and his younger brother had helped their parents run a bakery.

Back in Brooklyn, Elwood had spent his days off from work on the family boat in Canarsie. He had enjoyed movies, too. And he was at a cinema on Kings Highway when he met a girl from Manhattan Beach named Carol. The two were soon a couple, Elwood, fifteen, sharing his life with the girl one year his junior: boat rides and homemade pasta and church dances and midnight Mass. Carol, though, was Jewish. Wanting to end the relationship, her mother sent her to school in Connecticut. Elwood joined the navy.

Elwood was home from a stint in the Mediterranean when Carol graduated from high school. She got back in touch. She was eighteen and a day when, in November 1960, she and Elwood married. Carol, however, wished to go off to college, and soon wished, too, that she was single. When Elwood returned from his next tour aboard the USS *Allagash*, docking in Rhode Island, she handed him divorce papers.

Elwood was distraught. He left the navy and turned to cars, passing his days calling out from a Camaro or a Mustang or a hot rod to every young woman he saw—some of whom hopped in for a ride that would last a few days or weeks or months until, says his cousin Tony, "they got rid of him."

Elwood needed a job. His aunt Zell told him to go work for his cousins in Texas and he did, driving a truck for their sheet metal plant outside Houston. He welded, too, able to wriggle his five and a half feet into ducts and pipes. But the little man who now went by "Woody" was "hotheaded," says Tony. He would quit and drive off and look for women.

Woody had now found a brunette named Norma. After driving her around town a few nights, the gearhead and the carhop slept together at the Shangri-La Motel, where Norma had moved in.

Norma did not like having sex with Woody. "It was overkill," she said. But she liked him. On June 17, 1964, Norma wed Woody at the Dallas County courthouse, a bride in black. She was sixteen.

Waitressing could wait, Woody said. Sheet metal, too. It was time for them to hit it big. For Norma loved to perform; she was quick to recite the one snippet of schooling she recalled by heart, couplets from *Macbeth* about the poor player strutting his hour upon the stage. Woody had the thought that Norma could become a singer. So the couple drove to Hollywood and sold their Ford and moved into a rooming house and put their hands in the concrete depressions of stars. But Norma had never really sung much, and she and Woody soon stopped speaking of the records she would cut. Then they just stopped speaking. Money wired from family got them an Oldsmobile which they drove east to a city called El Monte, where Woody found work in sheet metal. Norma was lonely. And she had just turned seventeen—the age at which her grandmother and mother and half-sister had all first gotten pregnant—when she began to feel sick.

It was the manager of the pink stucco building where she lived who told Norma why she was sick. Norma was stunned. She was excited, too. "I really wanted this baby," she said. "I wanted to be the first of my friends to be married and have a baby. I wanted everything to fall in line the way it should."

But a poor marriage does not accommodate a pregnancy. Norma had not yet given birth when the marriage ended, and she flew back to Texas, to the family, and the pier and beam house, that she had wished to leave forever.

Norma would later write that Woody had suspected she was pregnant with another man's child and had beaten her. But the little man had run from physical altercation all his life. And long before Norma alleged that he had beaten her, she'd confided in a reporter that she had in fact left her husband after finding him in bed with another woman.

Back in Dallas, Norma took a job waitressing nights; she served food until two and drinks until six. And though her tips grew along with her belly, Mary and Raymond felt for Norma, the stepfather putting money in the tip jar she brought home, the mother taking her to an obstetrician and then to a courthouse to file for divorce.

Mary took Norma to a bar, too. Norma was mindful, she said, not to drink "to excess"—a temptation that grew after she found her way to a gay bar on Haskell. It was the first of thousands of nights Norma would spend in the comfort of lesbian bars, in the comfort of her people—the unfettered, the disapproved of, the drunk. Some looked at her belly and spoke of motherhood. Some bought her a beer. Months later, Norma was at a gay bar called the Numbers when her water broke. A cab took her to Dallas Osteopathic Hospital. At 6:27 a.m. on a May morning in 1965, Norma McCorvey became a mother.

Chapter 3

N orma held her daughter. She was happy to have a girl and pondered the names Michelle, Misty, Melissa. She chose the last—the baby, chubby with brown eyes and brown curls, the youngest in a family that reached back five generations to a Louisianan named Lodo Jeansonne, a woman of eighty-three who was mother to Bertha, grandmother to Mary, great-grandmother to Norma and, now, great-great-grandmother to Melissa.

Norma returned with her baby to Mary and Raymond, and set Melissa in a crib beside her bed. But she found that she had no desire to care for her. She wished only to be back at work. Six weeks later she was, a teenager once again serving drinks to girls she hoped to bed while her mother, and Raymond too, cared for little Melissa—seeing to her formula and cloth diapers and the pouch of asafetida they hung from her crib to keep the spirits away. Says Mary: "We took good care of that child."

If Norma was aloof from Melissa, Woody was absent. He had not met his daughter when a judge decreed in September that he set aside for her ten dollars a week. Woody did not do so. Weeks later, he got married a third time.

That same fall, in 1965, a woman eyed Norma from the far end of a bar. Her name was Diane Hyman. She was thin with short brown hair and a sweet round face that, in her twenty-three years, she had rarely made up. There was no need to prettify, to posture. She was who she was—a child of rural Texas, a lapsed Baptist, a lesbian. She was a hard worker, too, and had planned on a degree in Phys Ed until a car crash broke her jaw and hip and got her nine thousand dollars and redirected her toward nursing. But after rent, a car, a jag through Europe and a year of tuition, she was running out of money and left nursing for respiratory therapy. It paid just ninety-eight dollars every two weeks. Still, there was money left for beer. And raising a bottle of Bud to her thin lips, Diane now approached the brunette at the bar five years her junior. "She was real cute," recalls Diane. "Dark curly hair. Thin."

Norma beheld Diane, her blue jeans and brown eyes. She was enchanted, and so was Diane—no less so when Norma mentioned that she had a daughter four months old. The women began to drink and then kiss and dance, and a stranger asked if they wished to marry. Gay marriage was illegal but so what; they answered yes. After a boozy night, they drove off to a motel in Oklahoma. "We went on a honeymoon," says Diane. "Love at first sight."

The honeymoon continued back in Dallas, where Norma left her daughter and moved with Diane into a garage off Greenville Avenue. It was spare. Diane hadn't grown up with much—her childhood home had an outhouse—and she cared little for possessions save her four-door Rambler. Norma, meantime, owned nothing but clothes, and the couple got by on bologna, Budweiser and Marlboros. Still, to lower their bills, they moved into an apartment with roommates, then moved again when one of them fell for Norma, and again when a bedroom wall was too thin.

The couple landed in an old brick building near Baylor University Medical Center, where Diane got a job. She enjoyed the work, all respirators and chest physiotherapy. She had the thought that Norma might enjoy it too, and she got her a spot in a Baylor training course. Norma took to it, proud in her lab coat.

The future seemed bright, and Norma liked to tell Diane how one day the spotlight would find her. She decided to balance her work with classes at a high school named Crozier Tech. Norma was much older than her tenth-grade classmates, yet fell behind them. When a math teacher noted to the class that it was her second attempt at a diploma,

Norma, embarrassed, left school for good, again passing her hours in the bars she loved.

Norma was happiest with a drink in a crowd; she liked to flirt. But she loved Diane and would speak to her of all that had brought them together, from Jehovah to her mother, Mary, who, Norma said, got shots from an osteopath after every extramarital screw, the better to guard against venereal disease.

That same mother was now raising Norma's daughter. But baby Melissa had not yet turned one when Mary made clear that it was time for Norma to care for her child herself. "Ms. Sandefur wanted Norma to be responsible and take the baby," recalls Diane of Mary. "She insisted."

Norma acquiesced. But she was just seventeen years older than her baby. And when, as babies do, Melissa cried at night, Norma turned away. "Norma wasn't very responsible," says Diane. "I was the one who got up and took care of her . . . I remember feeding her, sitting on the couch." So it went for a month until, says Diane, "Norma wanted to send her back." Mary proposed that she adopt Melissa. Norma agreed. Recalls her half-sister Velma: "Mary adopted her because Norma didn't want her."

Norma would later reject that discomforting fact, alleging first that she had relinquished Melissa under "intense pressure from her parents," and then that her mother had "kidnapped" Melissa. It was a galling lie, not only because Norma had beseeched her mother to take Melissa from her but because Mary herself had been made to relinquish a child to *her* mother. Yet the truth remained (recorded in state records), and Norma began to drink more. She was impetuous when drunk; one sodden night, she had green-blue arches tattooed where her eyebrows had been.

―――――

NORMA HAD BEEN with Diane a year when, in the fall of 1966, outside an elevator at the Baylor hospital, a man walked up to her and sniffed. He asked her the name of her perfume.

His name was Pete Aguilar. He was twenty-one, and had come to Dallas from a Catholic home in the railroad town of Sweetwater, where his grandparents had settled after emigrating from Mexico. He wore the white coat of a vocational nurse. But his avocation was sex. "I was always flirting," he says. "That was my key thing, of getting them in bed."

Pete had been bedding girls since he had had sex with a neighbor at thirteen. But when, the next year, he got drunk for the first time, he found himself looking at men. That he did so upset him; Bible school had made clear that homosexuality was taboo, and Pete feared that to sleep with a man would damn his soul. So he slept with more women, beginning at sixteen to travel on weekends to Ciudad Acuña, a Mexican town two hundred miles south where a prostitute could be had for two dollars. Pete enjoyed the sex. But years of heterosexual indulgence south of the border did not curb his desire for men. As he neared the end of high school, it was only fear for his soul that kept him from them.

Three years later, Pete was a licensed vocational nurse at Baylor when he spotted Norma. He liked what he saw. Norma did, too—Pete was a little man three inches taller than she with brown skin, bright brown eyes and a wide smile. Norma answered his question: she wore patchouli.

Pete and Norma had lunch in the hospital cafeteria. Neither was single. Says Pete: "I was going with three girls." Norma was the fourth and she quickly distinguished herself. "She knew all the right moves," says Pete of Norma. "We'd screw all night."

Pete had never slept with a man. But he liked that Norma slept with women and was excited, he says, that she was cheating. Their affair had gone undetected a few months when, in early 1967, Norma traveled with Pete to Oklahoma for a friend's wedding. Diane ended the relationship, and Norma had not yet moved out when Diane found her in bed with Pete. Diane was enraged. She cut up his clothes with scissors and then headed for the bed with a butcher knife. She swung at Pete. "I dodged it," he says. He ran from the house with his keys, naked and drunk on scotch.

Diane phoned Mary to come get Norma. Mary did so and Norma returned to her mother and daughter and bartending, too, leaving her job at the hospital to pour drinks at a lesbian pub called the White Carriage.

———

NORMA TENDED BAR alongside a broad-shouldered Louisianan of twenty-four named Andi Taylor. Norma soon lived beside Andi too, leaving her daughter Melissa again, and moving with her black cat into a green garage just behind Andi's home on Myrtle Springs Road.

Andi drank while she worked—up to twenty Coors a night. She had grown up with a father who drank. Alcohol left him violent. It had also left a wife and four daughters incredulous that there was such a thing as a good man. The five women would suffer through twelve husbands. One of them had been Andi's, and anyway, she preferred the company of women.

So did Norma. Nicknamed "Pixie" by Andi, she was soon at the heart of a sorority that included Jinx and Billy Joe and Lynn and Judy and Be-Bop, women bound above all by their sexuality and the ways it had bled them. That a mother had beaten Norma because she was gay was no more remarkable than that Andi had watched the police load her friends into a paddy wagon outside a bar called Mercy Mary's. Indeed, to be gay in Texas in 1967 was to be subject to all manner of hurt. The women needed to hide.

"We couldn't tell anyone we were gay—our jobs, our families," says Andi. "If we went to straight places we had to dress straight, had to wear earrings. We couldn't wear pants or a fly front."

The women found release where they could. Says Andi: "What'd we do besides shoot pool, drink beer, and fuck?" At nineteen, that can be enough. And every night at the White Carriage was a night Norma hoped might end in someone's bed. "She'd come to work and bring a dress and Levi's," says Andi. "If it was a feminine girl, she'd put on her jeans." The dress was for "a cute butch."

Norma slept with many women. But she'd also slept with Woody and Pete. And in early 1967, a month or so after leaving Pete, she began to feel sick.

Norma did not want another child. One had been inconvenience enough, responsibility and expense she'd been eager to shed. But her doctor confirmed that she was pregnant and Norma phoned Pete. He asked if she was certain. She was. He asked if she wanted to marry. She phoned back to say no thanks.

Nineteen years old, Norma knew little of abortion. At her next doctor's appointment, she asked a nurse what it was. "I said," recalled Norma, "I've heard of a way that they take your baby but I can't remember what the word is." The nurse spoke the word but told her that abortion was illegal.

And her doctor, an osteopath named Richard Lane, spoke to Norma of adoption instead. Lane had arranged adoptions before, working together with a Dallas lawyer named Henry McCluskey. "I would deliver the baby," recalls Lane. "He would then pick up the baby and deliver it to the adoptive parents." The doctor cautioned Norma not to drink while carrying her baby, and then approached a colleague who wanted a child.

His name was Setrag Kebabjian. He was an anesthesiologist. He had a bedside manner as calming as the drugs he administered; not for nothing did the stitching on his white coat read "Dr. Wonderful." He loved children, too. But he was infertile. And having adopted the daughter his wife Donna had had during a failed first marriage, he now told Donna that he wished to adopt this baby as well. She agreed, and the couple phoned McCluskey. Soon after, Norma went to meet him.

McCluskey was twenty-four, with a thin face and a wide smile. He was kind and straightforward, and asked Norma if she was drinking. Norma said no—though she later recalled that she was drinking more than she had during her first pregnancy. She did, though, tell the lawyer that she was gay.

McCluskey was, too. But he did not say so. Gay sex was illegal and it was wise to be cautious.

Norma asked McCluskey the name of the family adopting her child. McCluskey refused to tell and Norma stormed off. But Norma liked McCluskey, and the adoption proceeded. "I can never recall seeing him without a smile on his face or in a good mood," she reflected. "I considered him a friend."

———

AT NINE IN THE MORNING, on October 11, 1967, Norma gave birth to a little girl. The baby weighed just five pounds, and had tan skin that recalled her father. Norma was not supposed to see the child but got a forbidden glimpse when her friend Jinx, an aide at Dallas Osteopathic, brought the baby to her. Norma got a second look when a nurse mistakenly brought the baby back. Said Norma: "She fucked up." But then, the baby was gone. Norma seemed unperturbed, and, standing at her bedside, her friend Andi struggled to relate. "I never been around that before," says Andi. "My mother would've killed to keep us kids."

The next day, Norma phoned Pete. "She told me she had a little baby girl," he recalls. "I said, well, what do you want to do?" Norma told him that she wanted the child to be gone from them both. Pete felt a flash of anger; he wished to have had a say in whether he might raise his child. But then he told himself that it was just as well. And he sent Norma a dozen yellow roses. "I wonder," he says, "if she ever got them."

Chapter 4

The lawyer McCluskey had heard good things about the Kebabjians. "Their integrity and moral character is unquestionable," a note from a neighbor attested. "The Kebabjians," it added, "have a very stable marriage and their home atmosphere is always pleasant."

The couple had come to Texas from different worlds—Setrag raised by Armenian immigrants in New York, Donna the youngest of ten kids born to Mormon parents in Utah. They had met at their Dallas hospital, a doctor and nurse's aide. And after a decade of marriage, they were happiest at home, living in beautiful Richardson with their daughter, Cindy. All was well save for their want of a second child. Now they had one, a girl they named Jennifer Marie. Four days after she was born, they welcomed her to their big brick house, setting her in a crib in a yellow room just down the hall from their own.

Donna was a great cook, making from scratch pizzas and cakes, stuffed grape leaves and baklava. But the newest Kebabjian contented herself with formula, fattening up on bottles of Similac. Older sister Cindy was overjoyed to have little Jennifer at the table; she'd wanted a sibling near all her thirteen years. Every morning, after her father whistled to wake her up, Cindy dressed and fed Jennifer. Says Cindy: "She was like my real-life baby doll."

Cindy did not care that that doll was of unknown parentage. So too, in part, was Cindy, her biological father a policeman her mother would not speak of.

Donna would say nothing, either, of the woman who'd birthed her younger daughter. But she knew who she was. ("I remember the name Norma," Donna allowed decades later.) But no matter. In the fall of 1967, no one was asking; the Kebabjians were just another family in Richardson raising kids with privilege and love, driving them about the manors and pools in a Lincoln Town Car as "Pleasant Valley Sunday" played from every radio.

TEN MILES TO THE SOUTH, baby Jennifer's half-sister was living with her grandmother in that two-family home in Dallas. Little Melissa had been moved over and over during her two years of life. Come 1968, she was off again, moving with Mary and Raymond to the banks of the Atcha-falaya, where nine generations of her family had grown like so many palmettos.

The river no longer threatened the Mississippi. The U.S. Army Corps of Engineers had built a system of floodgates, spillways, levees and channels which ensured that the Mississippi could continue east-ward toward New Orleans rather than be pulled south into the head of the Atchafalaya. It was there, at Simmesport, that Mary settled into a trailer to raise the girl whom she had led to believe was her daughter.

Mary, though, still drank and caroused. She struggled to parent. And she now asked her brother Millburn if he would adopt Melissa. He said yes. Mary, though, "didn't follow through," says her sister Sandra. And so, Velma—the daughter Mary had lost to her mother—stepped forward.

Velma had long since married a farmer, a man named Robert with whom she was raising beans and corn and three kids. Velma wished now to add a fourth; it upset her to see little Melissa exposed to the men and drunkenness Mary brought home. She asked Mary if she could have custody of the child.

Mary didn't tell Velma that she was her mother, not her sister. She didn't tell Velma that Norma was her sister, not her niece. She didn't tell Velma that it was only because she'd been sent away at seventeen that Velma had been allowed to stay home. And she didn't tell Velma that she might have been a better mother to Norma—and a grandmother to Melissa—if she'd been allowed to mother her.

Instead, Mary told Velma that she could not adopt Melissa but could take her home. "She said," recalls Velma, "'I will let you keep her and raise her.'"

Melissa moved into the little cypress house where Velma and her family lived on a muddy riverbank called Yellow Bayou. The little girl ate the fowl and potatoes that Velma fried in Crisco. She kept warm by the stoves that Robert filled with logs of pecan and ash. She bathed in the metal basin out back, and peed in the "slop drawer" that pulled out from beneath her bed. Oblivious to the poverty of her family, the girl of three thrived, there beside the Atchafalaya where a day was a predictable thing. Melissa soon formed what would be her first memory: playing in a makeshift pool beside Mary's trailer across the river, amidst pecan trees, chickens, ducks and ponies.

"It was real peaceful out in the country," says Melissa. "Quiet. It smelled good. I was happy."

———

A GENERATION BEFORE, Melissa's actual mother had also found peace in the company of Cajun cousins. That peace, however, had been short-lived, and Norma had long since escaped into the numb comfort of barrooms and bedrooms. When now, at age twenty-one, she served a woman a drink at a club called Sultan's Harem, and the woman offered her black pills in turn, Norma swallowed a helping of speed, and then took from the woman LSD. She began tripping at work.

Norma liked being high. "It was fun," she said. When then she was fired, she simply went to work for her dealer, selling acid and amphetamines from home. Some of her clients were prostitutes, women who worked on Cedar Springs Road, a stretch of tobacco shops, strip joints and gay clubs in central Dallas. Norma soon went to work with them. "I started seeing her on Cedar Springs," recalls Patti Milford, who'd met Norma at a gay bar called the Highland Lounge. A prostitute named Carolyn Ham confirmed to Patti that Norma was walking the street. Andi had figured as much. "It's one of those things that you kind of thought," she says, "but didn't pursue." Asked years later of her work as a prostitute, Norma was coy. "I'm not denying it," she said, "but I wouldn't admit it."

Norma was apart from her family. She felt a sudden desire to be with her father and found him in Old East Dallas repairing televisions and living on San Jacinto Street. Norma moved into an apartment nearby. They reconnected, passing the hours with cigarettes and coffee and talk of the women they hoped to bed. Still, Norma was increasingly depressed. She turned to diazepam. "Valium was the answer then," she said. "They'd say, this is for your nerves. It will make you relax. You won't be able to think."

But Norma did think. And a thought came to mind. Recalled Norma: "Why the hell should I live?" It was the same thought that had come upon her as a little girl when she decided to let go of that branch. She was still selling her body when she tried to hang it from a rope that she tied to a pipe overhead. She fell to the ground.

It wasn't long after her attempted suicide that Norma stopped selling drugs and prostituting herself, and returned to the life she had only just left, back to the White Carriage and her bed in that green garage where she slept beside her cat and a carousel of women. Along the way, Norma slept with a few men, too—a carnie named Eric, a mute biker named Carl, and, come 1969, a newlywed alcoholic named Bill.

———

WILLIAM KENNETH WHEATON was a generation older than Norma, born in 1924 to a housewife and a Freemason in Columbus, Ohio. They were Lutherans and patriots, and Wheaton and his brother Jack enlisted to fight in the Second World War. He became an infantryman and rose to the rank of lieutenant—an officer with brown eyes and strawberry hair. When the war ended, he had lost his teeth to gum disease but found a wife, an army nurse named Irene he met and married in 1946 while stationed in Vienna.

Back in the States, Wheaton hoped to remain a military man. But after being decommissioned, he went to school—off to Ohio State on the GI bill, and then to Western Reserve University to study law. The tuition, though, was beyond him, and he dropped out, finding a job scouting locations for gas stations in Pennsylvania. He and Irene then moved east, to northern Virginia, where he sold commercial property.

The couple had two boys and two girls. And the children came to know a father who smoked menthol cigarettes and played the harmonica and gambled and cheated, leaving the family for a time after an affair in 1960. He was crass, too; when his younger daughter matured early, he commented uncomfortably on her body. She would later claim to the family that he molested her.

It was his alcoholism, however, that most bled the family. Wheaton had begun to drink during the war. When drunk, he subjected a wife and four kids to humiliations and abuse; one boozy night in 1966, he broke a plate over his wife's head. Daughter Wendy grabbed a knife, a girl of thirteen forcing her father from the house. Wheaton was soon gone for good, divorced from Irene on July 3, 1968, on grounds of "desertion."

Wheaton wed again the next month, his bride a telephone company worker named Ann Dovalosky. She was sixty, sixteen years his senior. It was her first marriage.

The couple had met when Wheaton sold her a house. They'd not been married a year when, facing financial trouble, he talked Ann into selling that house and moving to Texas. The couple settled in the Oak Cliff neighborhood in Dallas, where Wheaton took a job as a machinist. Soon after, he injured his right index finger. A man he played pool against recalled that it was cut off at the joint.

Wheaton was not a great pool player. But he was one to think he could game the system, and he chose opponents he could beat. Norma took note, eyeing Wheaton at the White Carriage in the spring of 1969. Norma shot pool, too, and organized tournaments at the bar, collecting bets. She and Wheaton were soon partners. They made money at clubs and Norma called him "honey" and he bought her a black dress. Though she was less than half his age, she began to sleep with him. "All I knew is that I liked him and he was good in bed and that he liked to have fun," said Norma. "We stayed drunk and stoned most of the time."

NORMA HAD NEVER seen fit to use protection during sex. "When you're in a hurry, you're in a hurry," she said. She speculated, besides, that douching was protection enough. But when, in September 1969, she began to feel a familiar soreness in her breasts, she was distraught. Despite all attempts at erasure, that she had birthed and given up two girls remained an open wound. And she no more desired to relinquish a third child than to become a mother.

But abortion remained illegal. Her doctor, Richard Lane, would not perform one. Though Norma soon found an unlicensed doctor who would, she could not afford his $500 fee. She was scared, besides, she later recounted, "to turn my body over to him." Norma had begun to show when, at the start of 1970, a lesbian couple approached her in a bar and asked if she would give them her baby. Norma told them she was unsure if she was having it.

"They were so highfalutin, the type that thinks they're better than everyone," said Norma. "This butch says, 'But Norma, we can give this baby a home, we can educate it.' I told them to jump up my ass. And Bill came over and kissed me on the back of my neck."

Norma and Wheaton did not speak of the future. And they spoke little of their pasts. "I think he had been married and I think he had had one or two kids," recalled Norma. "We didn't discuss things like that."

Still, on occasion, Norma looked back at her life, at the daughters who were no longer hers. And she now told Wheaton that she wished to visit the one who remained within reach. "I really wanted to see Missy," she said of Melissa.

The couple liked car trips—"so that we could drink and drive," laughed Norma. (Wheaton had been arrested for driving drunk and would be again.) They headed east, Wheaton driving Norma in her Plymouth to Louisiana, off to see the girl of four who was waiting for them with her grandmother.

Melissa greeted Norma. And then Norma—she whom Melissa believed was her sister—left the little girl by herself. "I remember her leaving me in the car, in the rain, in the dark," says Melissa.

"All the doors were locked. They were in the trailer getting high or drunk."

Wheaton and Norma soon parted. He would never know that his Texas affair would spawn one of the most divisive legal rulings in American history.

Chapter 5

Norma was at a loss. Having carried two pregnancies to term, she was desperate to end her third. But in January 1970, abortion was illegal in Texas except to save the life of a pregnant woman. Norma's doctor, Richard Lane, would not break the law.

There was reason to think that the law might soon change; in the coming months, Alaska, Hawaii, New York, and Washington would legalize abortion. Still, abortion was as yet legal in just Oregon and California, and not explicitly illegal in Washington, DC. And while it was available to nonresidents in the latter two, Norma had no money to board a plane.

Her predicament was common. Many women in the United States wanting abortions had no access to a doctor who would perform one. But had Norma lived in a different time and place—in, say, ancient Greece—she would have had no problem ending her pregnancy. The doctor Hippocrates forswore the specific use of pessaries to cause abortions, but Aristotle expressed the prevailing Greek view when he wrote: "When couples have children in excess, let abortion be procured before sense and life have begun." (Sense and life began, he wrote, at forty days for boys, twice that for girls.)

The Bible was no more protective of the unborn. It ignored the matter altogether. As the New Testament scholar Richard Hays flatly notes: "The Bible contains no texts about abortion."

Indeed, in all the Old and New Testaments, just one verse addresses even the *inadvertent* loss of fetal life; the book of Exodus declares that if a man accidentally causes a woman to miscarry, he is not killed but is made to pay her husband a fine. It is not the rights of the fetus at issue but the loss of offspring, of property. As the book *Abortion in Judaism* notes, Jewish law regards the matter "as a tort, rather than a homicide." Indeed, the next verse in Exodus states that only if the pregnant woman dies along with her fetus is the offending man put to death.

The Septuagint, however—the original Greek translation of the Bible—mistranslated a Hebrew word at the heart of those verses: *ason*. There is rabbinic consensus that the word means harm or injury, and refers to the pregnant woman. But the Septuagint translated *ason* as *exeikonismenon*, meaning a fetus already "fully formed." And it thus followed that the two punishments meted out in Exodus—fiscal fine and death—were not for killing, respectively, a fetus and a pregnant woman, but a fetus unformed and formed.

That mistranslation, coupled with the Aristotelian distinction between the killing of a fetus early or late in pregnancy, came to inform the Christian view of abortion. Writing in the fifth century of those same verses in Exodus, Augustine of Hippo, a Christian theologian in Africa, posited that to kill an unformed fetus—"non formatum puerperium"—could not be called homicide "because it cannot yet be called a living soul in that body which lacks sensation."

The Catholic church agreed. In 1211, Pope Innocent III introduced that same distinction into canon law, writing of a priest who had impregnated a woman and then caused her to miscarry. The priest, wrote the pope, would not be defrocked unless the dead fetus had already been "vivificatus"—moving in the womb.

Canon law thus held that abortion could be ruled a homicide (and the woman who had one excommunicated) only if it was performed after "quickening"—the point in a pregnancy, at roughly sixteen weeks, when movement of the fetus is discernible. The law would remain unchanged for all but three of the next 658 years, until 1869, when Pope Pius IX included a brief statement on abortion in a papal bull. Any woman who procured an abortion, he wrote, would be censured by ordinary clergy or a bishop.

Ten years later, a priest and canon lawyer named Thomas Carr, tasked by the Irish church to clarify the bull, determined that what little the pope had written of abortion negated the distinction between aborting fetuses "animatus" and "inanimatus." *All* abortion would henceforth be punishable by censure. A 1917 papal codification of canon law confirmed this interpretation, which rested on the belief that the unborn were, from conception, no less ensouled than the pregnant woman. As Pope Pius XI wrote in 1930: "The life of each is equally sacred."

—————

IF THE CATHOLIC CHURCH no longer distinguished between abortions early and late, other systems did. The first law regarding abortion in the United States, an 1821 statute in Connecticut, made it illegal to poison the fetus of a woman already "quick with child." Texas made no such distinction when, in 1854, it criminalized abortion except to save the life of the pregnant woman. The guilty doctor faced two to five years in prison.

What the guilty woman faced, well into the twentieth century, was "death and publicity," as the author Leslie Reagan put it. For the drugs and instruments used to end pregnancy were apt not only to kill a fetus but to cause hemorrhage or infection, and newspapers often wrote of those women who died having abortions—some two to three thousand annually all through the Depression.

Many more women survived abortion—hundreds of thousands each year. And on it went in the U.S.—abortion illegal and hazardous but *ordinary*, performed by physicians and midwives and housewives, too. A naturopath named Ruth Barnett, for example, performed thousands of abortions in Oregon for decades with little resistance, while in New York City, there were three blocks of brownstones peopled with abortion providers. As a law review article about abortion later put it: "There is a significant disparity between what the law commands and what people do."

But then the nation changed. Lifted by a world war, it could afford to grow, and there was a postwar "push for maternity and domesticity," wrote Reagan. Police began to raid clinics, enforcing laws long overlooked, while hospitals created committees to oversee "therapeutic" abortions, thereby limiting their number. Abortion went back underground.

Even so, it was growing safer. Medical doctors now performed some 90 percent of illegal abortions, men like George Timanus in Maryland and Robert Spencer in Pennsylvania seeing thousands of women referred to them by hundreds of doctors. Coupled with the advent of penicillin—the first American to receive it was battling septicemia following a miscarriage in 1942—the number and rate of abortion-related deaths continued to drop. According to the National Center for Health Statistics, there were 284 confirmed deaths in 1959, down from 985 in 1944.

Such totals, however, were undoubtedly low; owing to stigma, doctors attributed many abortion-related deaths to septicemia, poison and other causes, says Stanley Henshaw, a sociologist who long did abortion research at the Guttmacher Institute. Still, he says, by the close of the 1950s, the annual total of abortion-related deaths was very likely under a thousand. It continued to drop; in 1968, the National Center for Health Statistics would report just 133 abortion-related deaths.

Abortion was not simply growing safer. Recent events—an outbreak of rubella, and the ingestion by some pregnant women of a tranquilizer called thalidomide—suggested to the public that abortion could spare women the grief of delivering babies with severe birth defects. And in 1967, a New York minister named Howard Moody formed a national abortion referral network. The network, which grew to include more than a thousand clergymen, connected women to abortion providers around the country. (The pro-choice activist Lawrence Lader had recently compiled a list of "skilled abortionists" in twenty-nine states and the District of Columbia.)

Meantime, as the sixties drew to a close, abortion was being viewed increasingly through the prism of sex. "Our society," wrote the retired Supreme Court Justice Tom Clark in 1969, "is currently in the midst of a sexual revolution which has cast the problem of abortion into the forefront of religious, medical, and legal thought."

Abortion, of course, was already in the forefront of feminist thought. Men had proclaimed women inferior for millennia, and traced that inferiority to the womb. The word "hysterical," fraught and gendered, derived from the ancient Greek for womb, and Plato posited that a barren womb became "extremely frustrated" and moved within

the body, causing a variety of illnesses. It was thus imperative that a
woman bear children. And men had long sought to control the reproductive capacity of women. (The psychologist Steven Pinker would list
the tools men used: "chaperones, veils, wigs, burkas, niqabs, chadors,
segregation by sex, confinement, foot-binding, genital mutilation, chastity belts, restrictions on birth control, double standards for adultery,
violent sexual jealousy and laws and customs that make a woman the
property of her husband.") Restricting abortion was but another tool in
that tradition, which meant that providing it gave women agency. Feminists, building on the work of Mead and Kinsey and Friedan—renegades
who had broadened views of female sexuality and seen women in terms
beyond reproduction and domesticity—fought to make abortion every
bit as available as the pill. Advocacy organizations were born, among
them the National Organization for Women and the National Association for the Repeal of Abortion Laws.

NOW and NARAL—founded, respectively, in 1966 and 1969—
took aim at a system designed by men, and that left men in control of
abortion. Lawmakers outlawed anyone but doctors from performing
what few abortions were legal—and, unlike midwives or herbalists, for
example, doctors were mostly men. (The American Medical Association had excluded women for sixty-nine years.) As the sociologist Kristin Luker wrote: "Abortion was murder if performed by women, but a
therapeutic measure if performed by [men]."

The procedure they performed was dilation and curettage, or D &
C. By 1970, it was clinical and routine: the vaginal walls separated with
a speculum, the cervical nerves numbed, the cervix dilated with a series
of metal rods, the lining of the uterus scraped away with a spoonlike
scalpel called a curette. Legal abortion, in fact, was now safer than birth.

Abortion was less safe where it was not legal. (The CDC would
report that in 1972, illegal abortion accounted for nearly twice the
number of maternal deaths as did legal abortion.) To highlight the
consequences of laws banning abortion, Lawrence Lader, who had
helped to form NARAL, collected some thousand testimonials of
recent "non-hospital" abortions—handwritten letters laying bare what
awaited a woman like Norma if she sought out what her obstetrician
would not provide.

Many of these women had gotten pregnant not because they had failed to use birth control but because the birth control they used had failed. Among them was Woman #144—a mother at age twenty-nine of six children, the youngest of whom was unplanned. "The contraceptive was faulty," she explained to Lader. "I had used it in good faith."

She was a Protestant in Ohio. Pencil on paper, she confided her predicament. "Family doctor was very sympathetic," she wrote, "but said his hands were tied due to present laws, said it would be impossible to even get a legal abortion which I asked him to do on the grounds that my last child has epileptic seizures. One other doctor said he would try to get me the name of someone who would do operation but he came up with a blank."

The woman concluded: "All the doctors I talked to were sympathetic but they are all scared to death of this word—ABORTION."

Indeed, in 1970, the average obstetrician would not perform one, would not risk going to jail, even as he saw firsthand what the law did to women. "They were getting illegal abortions in someone's backyard," recalls Dr. Frank Bradley, who delivered Norma's second child. "They were getting very sick and ending up in the hospital." He adds: "It seemed to me that there ought to be legality set to it."

The American Medical Association disagreed. The illegality of abortion empowered the AMA; only doctors could determine the few instances when abortion was legal, as when, for example, a pregnancy threatened the physical health of a woman. But in 1967, the law had begun to change. On the suggestion of a *legal* body, the American Law Institute, a few states had begun to legalize abortions that safeguarded the mental well-being of women (as well as the abortion of fetuses not developing properly and those conceived by rape or incest).

The medical monopoly on abortion had been broken. Having crusaded against abortion for the better part of the previous century, the AMA now changed course, instructing its members in June 1970 to defer to state laws.

The shift in policy made no legal difference. But some doctors were livid nonetheless. The duty of a doctor, they said, was to preserve life, not end it.

Among them was a transplanted Texan who, this same spring,

spoke out against abortion at the biannual meeting of the Massachusetts Medical Society. The doctor made an impression; she was vehement, spellbinding, striking besides. And when a group of doctors drafted a petition objecting to the new AMA policy, they sought out her signature. The doctor liked to sign her name in full: Mildred Fay Jefferson.

PART II

Three
Texans

Chapter 6

Mildred Jefferson was born on April 6, 1927, in a speck of a town
called Pittsburg—three square miles in the northeast corner
of Texas. She soon moved a few specks south into the pine
home of her grandparents in Walnut Grove, after her mother, Gurthie,
took a job teaching in a local school.

Father Millard did not make the move. He and Gurthie had just
married, wedding in Waco some ten months before the birth of their
child. But he was the pastor of the local Methodist church and wished to
live among his congregation. He would never rejoin his wife and child.

Mildred nonetheless enjoyed the warmth of family. She and her
mother and her grandparents, George and Fannie Roberts, shared their
one-story house with an uncle and a cousin. The last would soon be
Mildred's closest companion, a tongue-tied girl named Fannie Lou. A
year apart, the girls skipped rope and played with dolls. And they ran
about the family farm, fields of mustard and beans and potatoes and
watermelon and sugarcane and peas and collard greens and corn and
cotton, the last sold to gins to be spun into dresses and jumpers like
those the two girls wore, pure white on black skin.

To be black in Texas was to be set apart; come 1932, it was only from
the balcony of the theater in nearby Carthage that Mildred took in *Little
Orphan Annie*. But the girl of five did not, as a rule, see color, did not
accommodate it. When townsfolk gathered round the family wagon
to buy the catfish and trout and perch that her grandfather caught and

sold, the little girl struck up conversations with near all of them—even the white folks. Recalls Fannie Lou: "She had *nerve*."

Among those folks was the town doctor, Charlie Baker. Mildred asked if she might accompany him on house calls. The white doctor said yes and the black girl confided that she wished to be a doctor too. Dr. Baker responded: "Why don't you?"

Mildred had decided on medicine after reading of Elizabeth Blackwell, who in 1849 became the first female doctor in the country. The little girl had already begun her training. "When they killed a hog," recalls Fannie Lou, "she would get the intestines and liver . . . and talk to me about it." Mildred routinely dissected frogs, fish and butterflies. She even asked her cousin to open wide, Mildred snipping with a scissors the frenum beneath a human tongue. The surgery worked—Fannie Lou tongue-tied no more—and Mildred, all of seven years old, looked to the future. Recalls Fannie Lou: "She would always say, 'I'm going to be a doctor and go to Texas College.'"

First, however, was elementary school. So as to harness her smarts and precocity, her mother and grandmother, teachers by trade, schooled Mildred at home. "They had a bulletin board upside the fireplace," recalls Fannie Lou. "I'd be looking in."

The curriculum was rigorous. And even when class (and piano lessons from Aunt Velma) was out, Mildred remained in her books. Says Fannie Lou: "I would be down there playing mud cakes and she'd be up there reading."

Among her books was the Bible. Mildred was schooled in it by her Baptist grandfather and, on rare occasions, by her Methodist father, when he visited from his pulpits in Arkansas, Louisiana, Michigan. Says Fannie Lou: "She knew God."

Indeed, Mildred had been baptized in a nearby creek. She went to a Baptist church on Sundays. And by age eight, she was apt to reflect upon the Sunday sermon, that weekly juxtaposition of scripture and sin, in which adultery might be invoked but never abortion. For no one spoke of abortion, recall Fannie Lou and her cousin Kirthel Roberts. No one, they say, even knew anyone who'd had an abortion. Safety and principle aside, the procedure was too expensive.

Birth, however, was much talked about. It took place in the home, and young Mildred had discussed it through and through with her great-aunt Josephine, who was a midwife. Birth intrigued the little girl. All big things did—death and life after death, too. These were the mortar of her father's sermons, and Mildred prevailed upon her mother to take her to hospitals so that she could sit beside the dying. "I always wanted to see the soul leave the body," Mildred recalled years later. "But I never saw it."

The mother encouraged Mildred's curiosity. She encouraged her to aspire, too. Gurthie's father was named George Washington and her husband was named Millard Fillmore, and she rooted in her daughter the foundational message that self-determination could hurdle any impediment.

Mildred burned with determination—both her own and that of her parents. They had both graduated from college, and intended, eight decades after their grandparents had been slaves, for their only, and ever more exceptional, child to continue the family rise. This Mildred did. She was ten when she left her homespun classroom for Center Point, the all-black school in Pittsburg where her mother taught. There, she skipped grades as other kids skipped rope.

That Mildred was petite and pretty, with a bright smile, high cheekbones and eyes agleam, helped endear her to her classmates. Despite her drive, says Fannie Lou, they rooted her on, proud when, on occasional Sundays, she shared thoughts on the Bible from the pine pulpit in church, proud when in 1942 she and her 138 IQ graduated from Carthage Colored High at the age of fifteen.

Mildred had no boyfriends. Romance was distraction. To learn, to achieve, to become a doctor, was all. Besides, she was ill-suited to partnership, a teenager stubborn and inflexible, particular and pedantic. She permitted only close relatives to call her Millie, and listed her height as 5 feet 3¾ inches, adamant that others be as precise as she. "If you told her something," says Fannie Lou, "you made sure to tell her the truth."

It was truth and knowledge that Mildred sought when, months after graduating from high school, she left for college, driven south to Carthage on the dirt lane that passed for Route 4.

Mildred arrived in the town of Tyler and took in the bricks and roses of Texas College. A group of Methodist ministers had formed the school back in 1894 so that black students inadmissible elsewhere might have a place to learn. Learn Mildred did; days after turning eighteen in the spring of 1945, she graduated summa cum laude with majors in biology and Spanish.

Mildred was not only the top student among her class of fifty-one, and its youngest, but its conscience, too. "You'd never say a bad word in front of her," her classmate Margaret Surry-Fingal recalled. "She always said the right thing and did the right thing." That included chorus and a science club and a health club and a sorority and a journal and a Christian group. Still, it was medicine Mildred most esteemed, and she knew where she wished to study it. As Mildred later said: "No other medical school but Harvard would do."

It was more than excellence that attracted her to Harvard. Her father had enrolled there, graduating from its U.S. Army Chaplain School in 1943 before heading to South Korea. More important still, Harvard was north. That a young black woman wished to leave the South was no surprise. She was, as her mother put it, "a jewel too costly for its setting."

But if race closed fewer doors up north, gender closed just as many; in 1945, Harvard had yet to admit a woman to its medical school. Still, Mildred headed to Massachusetts, beginning a masters in biology at Tufts, moving in with her mother, who had settled in the Roxbury neighborhood of Boston.

That same fall, Harvard admitted a first handful of women to its medical school. And after a year of A's at Tufts, Mildred applied to join them. She intended, she wrote to Harvard, to use her medical education to help "all mankind."

Months later, in January 1947, Mildred became the first black woman accepted to Harvard Medical School. The acceptance was national news. Read a headline in the *Cleveland Herald*: "Harvard Admits Race Woman to Medical School." There was more good news: a local synagogue, Brotherhood of Temple Israel, would pay her tuition and a cash stipend besides.

Mildred received the grant because she was black. But she'd been accepted to Harvard because she was brilliant. When a local paper intimated otherwise, she jotted her displeasure atop the newsprint, adding that its chosen term for her, "negress," was "most revolting."

To have black skin in 1947 demanded that it be thick. And as Jackie Robinson stepped a first time onto a big league field that same spring, Mildred mustered only pleasantries for the press. "Americans are coming to realize," she said, "that given the opportunity, the colored people can contribute much to this nation's greatness."

School began and Mildred took in the city—ballet and bridge, music and art and theater. She placed in the top third of her class. And in 1951, the first black woman to graduate from Harvard Medical School became the first woman with a surgical internship at Boston City Hospital.

Mildred was no mere doctor. She was a star. The press was on hand that summer to watch her perform an emergency appendectomy, writing in breathless prose of she who was not only an MD at twenty-four but also a beauty who wrote fiction and recited *Henry V* and was a ten handicap on the links and asserted with a smile that race was no barrier.

Mildred was happy with herself. She told the *Boston Sunday Post* that achievement was simply "a willing of the right thing to happen." She added that she hoped someone would give her a no-interest loan of ten thousand dollars—money to be lent, she said, "in the interest of science and medicine."

Having been the top, the first, all her life, Mildred had come to expect accommodation as an artist might a patron. A doctor soon loaned her twelve hundred dollars.

The money ought to have sufficed. Mildred had no tuition to repay or rent due; she lived with her mother in a home owned by her father, who was now a captain with an anti-aircraft battalion in Washington state. But she spent great sums on clothing, on suits and dresses of the highest make—Hattie Carnegie, Ceil Chapman, Adele Simpson, Christian Dior. Though she found herself in debt, she continued to spend, taking up skiing and cricket. And in 1955, months before she was to complete her residency—and months after she took out a small loan to buy from her father the Roxbury home—the hospital suspended its pioneer.

Mildred was twenty-eight. She wrote to a professor that the

suspension was "the first real defeat of my entire life." She acknowledged in her letter "serious personal problems," and wrote that she
feared prison or litigation. Yet she alleged that her suspension, which
likely owed to some financial misstep, was the result of misogyny. "It
may be that I shall join the small percentage of medical women who
do not practice," she now wrote the *Harvard Bulletin*, "but the only
reason will be that I have perished at the roadblock erected by my
colleagues-in-pants."

That women doctors encountered discrimination was clear. Mildred's professor wrote to her of her "girlish whims," while her superiors at Boston City Hospital had assigned her with a smirk to the male
urological service. Surgery in particular was held to be the province of
men; Mildred would recall being told that the post of chief resident was
"too precious to waste on a woman"—let alone a black woman. Indeed,
Mildred was doing her residency at Boston City Hospital when her
supervisor, a surgeon named A. J. A. Campbell, told her, he recalled,
that if she remained at the hospital, "she would run into problems . . .
because she was a black female and this may be resented by some of the
doctors and nurses that she would have to deal with."

Mildred had black friends in whom to confide—a friend from Tufts
named Gloria Bowens, who was a public school teacher, and the tennis
great Althea Gibson, whom Mildred had met through Hazel Wightman,
another tennis star who lived close by in Chestnut Hill. There were also
the twenty or so members of the Progressives, a support group for black
working women in Boston which Mildred had joined, along with her
hairdresser and dry cleaner.

Still, Mildred had little choice but to leave the hospital, and she
applied for and accepted fellowships in New Hampshire and then back in
Boston. But board certification still did not follow. In the spring of 1957,
behind on her mortgage payments, she took a job in cancer research.

The job was in Boston, and her supervisor was Sidney Farber, the
pioneering pathologist. Farber had taught Mildred at Harvard and was
delighted to have her at the institute that would later bear his name.
She was, he recalled, "a superb doctor." The problem, he said, was that
doing research on tissue transplant and chemotherapy would not help
her to become a surgeon.

Mildred moved back to Roxbury, to her room on the second floor of her wooden house with her mother and her books and a pear tree out back. A block away were kid cousins who revered Mildred as had Fannie Lou back home. But Mildred spent little time with family. She didn't join them at home for holidays or at church on Winthrop Street. And she spent little time dating, though men flocked to her. A doctor she met on a train would soon write her a poem.

That April of 1957, Mildred turned thirty, and headed off on her birthday to a New Hampshire inn to ski. She was alone and a naval officer approached. His name was Shane Cunningham. He was all of twenty-one and on leave from his station aboard the USS *Leyte*, an aircraft carrier patrolling the Atlantic coast for Soviet subs. Come north this spring Saturday to ski with a shipmate, he was smitten with Mildred, recalling almost sixty years later her intelligence and beauty.

Mildred was taken in turn. The sailor was lean and handsome, with black hair and blue eyes. And he was open to the world, the son of a diplomat who'd grown up in Brazil, Paraguay and Costa Rica. "As with everything else," recalls Mildred's friend Anne Fox, "she carefully picked what she thought was the best."

The black doctor and the white sailor began to correspond. He called her Jeff. By the time he shipped off to Spain two years later, he also called her "My Muse" and "Locus of all My Points" and "Emoción de mi Vida" and "Luz de mi Vida," endearments that began the letters he typed on his Hermes while at sea.

The couple met where they could—back at the inn, and in Europe, Mildred flying to Paris in 1960. But always they slept in separate beds. "Our relationship was correct in the clinical sense," says Shane. "We did not cohabitate." Her abstention was absolute. Says Shane: "she was an extraordinarily persevering person."

The issue was not desire. Mildred was in love. But she feared for her career, feared that extramarital sex might doom it. "The term was 'moral turpitude,'" says Shane.

There was the matter of race, too. For though Mildred did not wish to say so publicly, the confinements of color in midcentury America were severe. Whereas extramarital sex could cost her a job, marital sex could land her in prison; when in 1957 she met Shane, miscegenation was a felony, illegal in half of the forty-eight states.

Interracial marriage was, however, legal in her adopted home. Shane suspected this was why Mildred was staying in Massachusetts even as her one consuming goal, to become a board-certified surgeon, was not taking root in it. She whose social circle was white wished to widen her path to marriage. That path led now to Shane. Come 1962, the sailor left his ship for National Shawmut Bank, there to evaluate the credit of Latin Americans—and be close to Mildred.

The couple wished to marry. But before they did, there was something Mildred wished Shane to know.

Not many years before, Mildred had looked out at the world with eyes bright beneath French bangs and long lashes, and seen only promise. Achievement, she had said, was a mere matter of will. But in the decade since, money had complicated her circumstances, gender her career, race her relationships. And she had come to believe that there was a consequence to sex even more grave than joblessness or prison. That consequence was conception. To live, she now told Shane, was to experience hypocrisy, discrimination, "extreme unfairness." And she, a black woman, would not, she told him, conceive a child only to subject it to such injustice. Her boyfriend assented, even agreed. But not without lament. Says Shane: "She would have been a wonderful mother."

———

IN APRIL 1962, the couple eloped to New Hampshire, the relationship consummated five years and a day after it began.

The newlyweds settled into a one-bedroom apartment in the Back Bay of Boston. They were happy, a husband and wife, twenty-six and thirty-five, indulging in walks and restaurants and concerts and conversation. Shane was apt to analogize in deep and unhurried voice, Mildred to stake out opinions as incisive as they were informed. But the doctor was ever more standoffish, cynical. When her alma mater, Texas College, asked its prize alumna to commend its incoming class, she refused even to wire good wishes. And when she left her job in research, she reflected to a friend upon her stalled career: "It is still traditional," she wrote, "that I must be excluded."

Mildred excepted herself in turn. If ever a journalist came calling, she volunteered nothing, not even her date of birth. And walking with her mutt and shepherd along the bay, Mildred hid herself in an old coat and floppy hat, carried a club too. She would protect herself.

Thus did the woman Mildred was thought publicly to be, and the woman she was, begin to diverge—one sociable and meticulous, one distrustful and cluttered, none but Shane there to see his wife ceding their home to piles of books and papers. "If a newspaper went unread," says Shane, "she would hold it to read it later. You know how that works." Shane prevailed upon his wife to sell the mounting stacks as wastepaper, paid for by the pound. But new stacks rose.

Mildred still yearned to practice surgery. Yet certification remained out of reach.

Before her marriage, Mildred had left her job in cancer research in the hope of getting work at Massachusetts General Hospital. But when she applied for a surgical internship at the hospital, she was rejected— "partly because she was a woman, partly because she was black, partly because she was Mildred Jefferson," the surgeon Claude Welch would recall. Another surgeon, named Clement Darling, allowed Mildred to observe him on rounds and in surgery. Over the coming years, a trio of other surgeons at Mass General did too. Still, come 1967, Mildred remained uncertified at forty—a shadow, not a surgeon.

FROM TIME TO TIME, Mildred attended meetings of the Massachusetts Medical Society. It was at one such meeting in 1967 that two doctors, Joseph Stanton and Barbara Rockett, spoke of their distress over the growing movement to legalize abortion.

Growing up, Mildred had given the issue little thought. Abortion had been all but unavailable in Texas—unaffordable and undiscussed besides. Still, the girl had known of it. "I was aware," she would later recall, "that sometimes people were doing things to interfere with pregnancies because every so often girls would turn up dead with no real good explanation."

But if once Mildred had taken note of those who died because abortion was illegal, she had come in the years since to think more of those who would die if it were not. She listened quietly as Stanton and Rockett spoke.

Rockett in particular had her ear. For she was a woman and a working surgeon. But Rockett was white. And the American Board of Surgery had yet to certify a single black woman. But now, finally, in 1968, the board did certify a black woman, a surgeon in Los Angeles named Hughenna Gauntlett. That barrier finally breached, Boston University School of Medicine promptly hired Mildred as chief surgical resident. Mildred performed well, the picture of composure besides. "Her manners were tops," recalled Dr. Farber, "and she carried herself with grace."

Mildred was less composed at home. Her apartment at 279 Beacon was choked with papers and belongings—walkways narrowed, clothing piled in the bath. Her husband had left banking for the management of property but he struggled to manage his own. "There would be little aisles," says Shane. "I tried to remove stuff, which upset [Mildred] greatly." Shane was forced to shower at the office, returning home, he says, only to sleep.

Mildred's stacks continued to grow, her newspapers and clothes and assorted impedimenta rising thigh-high. In 1970, they forced Shane from his home. "How can you live," he asks, "where you can't get in?" Shane moved into a building he was managing on Marlborough Street just across the alley out back, converting the empty front end of its first floor into an apartment.

Shane tried to understand his wife; perhaps in holding tight to her belongings, she was holding tight to herself. "If you are subconsciously aware that you're being rejected," he would later reflect, "would you take steps to ensure that the things you don't want to lose would not be thrown out?"

———

IN THE SPRING OF 1970, Mildred had been chief resident nearly a year when, at a medical society meeting, the conversation again turned to abortion, and the various state laws legalizing it.

Mildred knew where she stood. She had come to conclude that a fetus was a life that ought not to be ended. That conclusion, says Shane, was "part of her intellectual evolution of wanting to be a doctor." It owed to her father, too—the pastor who'd long since seeded in her the want to channel, as he had, says Shane, "the voice of God."

Millard Jefferson had slipped from his daughter's life. The two were estranged. (Mildred had not even told Shane that her father was living when Shane had assumed him dead.) Still, his memory was a comfort to Mildred; she would later remark, in only slight jest, that "only my father, in this world, understood that I was perfect; my mother never did learn that." And, says Shane, even in absence, Millard's influence on Mildred remained "profound." As Mildred would soon assert in the first article she would ever write on abortion: "The male parent has an interest in the new being whether he claims or acknowledges it or not."

And so, three years after Mildred had first listened to her fellow doctors discuss abortion, she now spoke, decrying it with the imperativeness of a prophet. The room was in thrall. "I was amazed," says Dr. Rockett. "She was terrific." Here was a potential asset. One month later, in June 1970, the neurosurgeon Rockett sought Mildred out, handing her a petition in protest of a new AMA directive that required doctors to defer to their state laws on the matter of abortion.

Mildred might have resisted; she wished to join the establishment, not buck it. But what marked her most was principle. And she was ever more absolute. She had resolved to never partake of tobacco or alcohol or coffee. She had told Shane that she would never drive because she'd read that doctors were poor drivers. She had told him, too, that she would never speak Spanish because it should only be spoken if spoken perfectly. And having told her husband that she would never have a child, she now made clear her belief that neither should a child, once conceived, ever be prevented from being born.

The doctor signed the petition. And though she yearned still to become a board-certified surgeon, she began to wonder if she might save more lives with her words than her scalpel—those millions imperiled by a new lawsuit filed back home by a plaintiff called Roe.

Chapter 7

If there was at least one doctor in 1970 who would not perform abortions despite the law, there was another who, despite the law, would. His name was Curtis Boyd.

Boyd had been born on an east Texas farm in 1937, seven miles of dirt road from the closest town of Athens. His father was an accountant, his mother a farmer raising two boys and acres of cantaloupe and corn, hogs and hay—harvesting and breeding with the stamina, says Boyd, of any man. Theirs was a country life, of kerosene lamps and well water and a school bus that drove scores of miles to collect enough kids to fill the small brick schoolhouse in Cross Roads.

The Boyds were Primitive Baptists. They believed that God predetermined the lot of every soul, and prayed that their lots were to be saved. When the local pastor ran a church service each month in nearby Rhome, the family washed its feet in basins of water in imitation of Jesus before the Last Supper.

Christ was alive to the young Boyd; the boy had little to read but farming magazines and the Bible. He knew the son of God to be a wellspring of love. That Christ also righted wrongs—overturned the tables of money-changers—was better still.

It was thus confusing to Boyd that his school of Christians was segregated, that white people all about him, he says, called black people "nigger." The boy struggled, he says, "to square this with the Bible, with the teachings of Jesus."

Boyd was in tenth grade when he fell for Virginia, a pretty and jovial girl with a beautiful voice one grade below. He helped her out with algebra. And he was hoping to ask her to sing at an event he was running for the Future Farmers of America when a friend told him that the captain of the football team had gotten her pregnant. Recalled Boyd years later: "My great suggestion was met with silence."

Boyd was deeply upset. "The fact that he had fucked her made him a big man on campus," says Boyd. But it made Virginia a pariah, a schoolgirl excluded from school events for having had sex outside of marriage. "Virginia was a sinner," says Boyd. "She was condemned."

Boyd got to thinking about sex and religion and the law and what it was to be a woman. "Every act of intercourse," says Boyd, "she risked ruination."

Still, Boyd loved religion, its scripture and prescriptions. His paternal grandmother, a heavyset and happy midwife, decided that her grandson was a prophet. After all, Curtis not only knew Bible chapter and verse but was empathetic and smart, the top student at school and the "Most Courteous." She told him to preach.

Boyd did as prompted; he was ordained a minister at age sixteen. Looking out through horn-rimmed glasses, Boyd gave monthly sermons, a pubescent at the pulpit—skinny and tall with a buzz cut and a lupine nose—instructing his elders, he says, on "how we should live our lives." Boyd, however, was suddenly less sure how to live his own. For he learned now that the Bible he knew was a translation. This startled Boyd, unsteadied him, took from him the literality of scripture, of those many chapters he summoned by heart. Still, when in 1955 high school ended and Boyd left home to study biochemistry at Texas A & M, he continued to preach.

A & M was all-male. One had to leave campus to meet girls, and Boyd was a junior behind the wheel of a 1957 Plymouth when a carhop named LaMerle took his order. She was a senior at Palestine High, a Methodist with blue eyes. Boyd wrote her a letter and the following winter they wed, moving soon after to a federal housing project in Dallas beside Southwestern Medical School, where Boyd enrolled.

The couple got along well. But Christianity was soon a point of divide. "I learned that he had been rethinking religion and that he didn't believe some of the things he was preaching," recalls LaMerle. Among them, says Boyd, was the belief that "God came down and impregnated a young woman."

It was less apostasy that upset LaMerle than the fact that Boyd kept his changed thoughts to himself. She asked him to be forthright with his parents. But Boyd wished to make no waves, to drift quietly from his conservative church and family, to simply pray less, put down his Bible, cease to preach.

Boyd did not confide in his best friend either. His name was Ben Johnson. The men had only just met but shared a love of religion and family, country and medicine, kindred cadets in the ROTC who moved into neighboring houses with their young Christian brides.

"We were both devout Christians," Johnson recalled years later. "And we just walked together and knew that we would enjoy practicing together."

First, though, was school. To earn money for tuition, the friends spent their first summer as medical students peddling hardbound Bibles door to door through the towns of northeast Texas, revelation just $29.95.

Boyd said nothing of his lapsed faith. He had come to see faith, whether in religion or in the law, as ill-served. Both were fallible. The law had barred the Negro from white water fountains. And religion—the sanctification of pregnancy—had, those many years before, turned his pregnant schoolmate into a sinner.

Still, Boyd hoped to reconcile his changed beliefs with his abiding love of the church. And so, he became a Unitarian, joining a congregation in Dallas that was predicated, he says, on humanism and justice and reason.

———

BOYD HAD BEEN a young teen when a profane pregnancy attuned him to the consequences of sex. He was a young man when now he encountered the consequences of illegal abortion, dangerous bleeding that Boyd and his fellow medical students were taught to stanch.

The lesson extended beyond dilation and curettage. The students were told to report such women to the police.

Boyd was in a bind. He had come to believe in a right to abortion. But he wished to follow rules and so, now, he reported a patient. A detective harassed the woman and Boyd resolved never to do so again. Says Boyd: "I was embarrassed."

Boyd was in his third year of medical school when LaMerle got pregnant. Young and overwhelmed, the couple looked for a doctor to perform an abortion, says Boyd. They failed to find one; their son was born in 1963.

Boyd graduated third in his class, and the family of three moved back to Athens, where he and Ben Johnson opened the practice they had long envisaged. The two young doctors treated infections, accidents, the flu. They also delivered a thousand or so babies.

"He was the native son, the hometown boy who makes good," LaMerle recalled years later. "And all of a sudden, he changed."

Indeed, with the zeal Boyd had long reserved for religion, he now embraced civil rights. And he made certain that everyone in his Protestant town saw his newfound liberalism clear as the hair and beard he grew long. Among much else, the doctor sought to institute a class on sex in the local schools. Much of the town was irate.

Boyd was in California protesting war and segregation when he met groups of women who spoke to him of another blight: the disenfranchisement of their gender. The doctor was already mindful of what Betty Friedan had recently termed "the problem that has no name"— that of the woman discontented with domesticity, wanting, she wrote, "something more than my husband and my children and my home." But the women Boyd met now went further, telling him that the place of women in society could not be bettered until they controlled if and when to have a child.

Boyd listened. He began to think less of the babies he was delivering and more of the women birthing them. There were, it struck him, many Virginias—women whose lives were derailed by pregnancy.

A few years later, in 1967, "a simple, young country woman" told Boyd, he recalls, that she wanted an abortion. The doctor told the woman that he couldn't provide one. The law forbade it. But the woman pleaded and said that she had three kids at home and couldn't feed them and that their father was gone.

Boyd stepped from the room. He told himself that the woman was destitute and desperate, that she was not more than ten weeks along, that abortion ought to be legal. And then he put an instrument into her uterus and "just sort of moved it around," he says. He admitted her to the local emergency room and wrote in her chart that she'd miscarried.

Never before had Boyd broken a law. Never before had he felt so right.

———

BOYD WAS NOW, IN 1967, a father of three. And every Sunday, he drove his kids and wife to the Unitarian church in Tyler where, some forty miles east of home, they prayed and spoke and ate potluck meals with like-minded liberal folk. Among them were clergymen Boyd had met in medical school, who told him now of an abortion referral network based at Southern Methodist University. The network paired women in want of abortions with doctors willing to perform them. Twenty-nine states, plus the District of Columbia, had at least one such provider, and the network asked Boyd if he was willing to join them.

Boyd agreed to help the network find doctors who would perform abortions. Such doctors were few and far between. The clergy soon asked Boyd if he would perform them himself.

The doctor understood the risks. "I knew it was illegal," says Boyd. "I knew I could lose my medical license and go to prison." But, thirty years old, he wished to do something *important*. As he later told his son, performing abortions would enable him, he felt, to "strike a blow for human freedom."

Boyd joined the referral network. Over the coming months, he terminated some ten pregnancies, none more than ten weeks along. The procedure had two steps: blocking the cervical nerves, and curetting the uterus. (Boyd had learned to do dilation and curettage in medical school to help women who'd miscarried or had uterine bleeding.) After every abortion, he sent the woman to the ER where her uterus could be emptied fully, and where it could be assumed that she had miscarried.

Boyd began to worry he'd be found out. A woman could have second thoughts upon arriving at the ER. Or she could have medical complications and alert the police. Or she could die. "Then," says Boyd, "you get charged with murder." Indeed, as Article 1194 of the Texas Penal Code put it: "If the death of the mother is occasioned by an abortion so produced or by an attempt to effect the same it is murder."

Boyd decided that admitting patients to the hospital was too risky. He would need to complete each abortion himself—to fully curette the uterus, empty it so that its lining was again smooth and thin. To do so, he would need to dilate the cervix first. This he now did, ready for each patient with an array of metal instruments he ordered by mail: thin rods to measure the depth of the uterus, curved rods to dilate it, curettes to empty it, a tenaculum to grasp the cervix.

Boyd learned as he went. When once he could not empty a uterus and his patient bled, he sent her to the ER and issued himself a warning: "Do not have complications. You must get very good at doing this." This he did, better and better the more abortions he performed, able within a few months to end pregnancies up to twelve weeks along—the entirety of the first trimester. "I became quite a master at dilating the cervix," says Boyd. He adds: "I did not know how far I could go, how far I *should* go."

It was then, in 1969, that a young Sioux woman beginning her second trimester came to see Boyd. She was on scholarship at the University of Chicago, the first in her family to go to college. And she was desperate. Boyd performed the abortion.

Boyd began using a small forceps to extract slightly bigger fetuses than he had before, taking on patients at fourteen and then sixteen weeks. There was pain and bleeding. "It was scary at first," allows Boyd. "But I saw I could do this."

Boyd was on his own. "The second-trimester field did not exist," he says. Later that same year, Boyd began using a vacuum aspirator, the first such machine in Texas, he says. Boyd studied its parts, its pump and cannulas which could suck the uterus empty of a fetus up to thirteen weeks old.

Every advance in abortion technology elicits condemnation. Norman Mailer, for example, in his 1971 screed against women's liberation, *The Prisoner of Sex*, derided the safety of suction. The writer was nostalgic for "the days of honest abortion," he wrote, "when the fingernails of the surgeon were filthy and the heart of a woman went screaming through a cave as steel scraped at the place where she touched the beyond." Boyd disagreed. "I thought," he says, "this is fabulous."

There were others in Texas who, for many hundreds of dollars, it was said, would end a pregnancy—an old woman in Oak Cliff, an old man in Malakoff. Boyd was different. "I was the only one doing it somewhat openly," he says. "The only one getting referrals from the clergy. They knew who they were coming to."

Boyd did not want to hide. He had his name on the door and took pride that twenty-five women a day—some six hundred a month—found their way to the glass and brick building at 3620 Fairmount where, for one hundred dollars and, later, one hundred and fifty, the bespectacled doctor offered reprieve.

All types found Boyd; among his patients, he says, were the girl-friends, daughters and wives of legislators, judges and politicians, powerful men who sought in private what in public they condemned. Such men were "scoundrels," says Boyd. Still, the great bulk of his patients were college students, a caravan of Volkswagen Bugs driving to little Athens from all over Texas, Oklahoma, Louisiana, Arkansas. And if, says Boyd, the police had their suspicions, "they couldn't take any action because there were no complaints." He adds: "Someone's got to accuse you of a crime."

———————

SIX YEARS AFTER graduating from medical school, Boyd practiced no medicine save abortion. And though he performed roughly half of them at no cost, the work paid well. In 1969, he earned some $100,000, payment he took in cash so as to ensure patient confidentiality.

His partner, Ben Johnson, was desperate for Boyd to stop. And when one day a pregnant patient accidentally came to him instead of to Boyd, Johnson could no longer pretend not to know of his work. He wrote Boyd a letter informing him that owing to career, family and religion, the doctors had to split. Boyd burned the letter. "It was too painful," he says. "I cried over that."

Another doctor might have set aside his curettes. But, forced to choose between a procedure and a best friend, Boyd chose abortion. "Once you start doing this," he says, "it starts to take over your life."

LaMerle had hoped her husband would choose otherwise. Mother to their three young kids, she struggled with the prospect of his imprisonment, the two to five years to which he could be sentenced. More, their town had made clear that there was little room in it for an *abortionist*, a hippie besides. When Boyd began to raise funds for a benefit in defense of students expelled by the local college for having long hair, the local upset boiled over. Recalls LaMerle: "The town went wild." The benefit was approaching when the local hardware store began encouraging customers to buy guns. Boyd called the benefit off. And in late 1969, after a nurse in his office told Boyd that she could not abide the taking of prenatal life and that he had best leave town, he did, saying goodbye to Athens and to his parents and moving with his family to Dallas, seventy miles northwest.

Boyd rented from a dentist the ground floor of a small brick building beside a bus stop in Oak Lawn. As before, he would rely upon chaplains to screen his patients, to put out fires should a complication arise. He would keep no records lest they be subpoenaed, would work with no other doctors lest one testify against him.

It was a relief to leave town for city. Still, Boyd needed help. He invited a woman he'd met through the Unitarian church to be his aide. "I believe in this," Eva Cox recalls telling Boyd. "You can train me."

Cox was well matched with Boyd. She too had grown up on a farm in a tiny East Texas town—five square miles home to a hundred people and three churches and a light that blinked at the intersection of two highways. She too had lived a life centered on a fundamentalist church. First Baptist of New Summerfield had taught her to walk like Christ. The story of the virgin birth, however, had confused the young Cox. The girl nicknamed Reggie was still at a loss when at age twelve she was baptized. "You're sitting in a little wooden church and being taught that this man came forth," she recalls. "Well, *how* did he come forth?"

Cox knew nothing of sex, let alone of birth control or abortion. Menstruation was a mystery, too, no more clear when her mother, busy with four kids and a job digging potatoes, gave her a booklet from Kotex. Says Cox: "I didn't understand half of the words."

Still, come adolescence, there was Cox, tall and thin with brown hair and green eyes, spooning with boys in the graveyard and at the drive-in. When she got pregnant at seventeen, her mother was clear with instruction, telling her youngest to leave school and marry. This she did, moving with her husband to Tyler, where she gave birth prematurely to twin girls who soon died. After a son was born on her nineteenth birthday, her husband moved north to seek a job. Soon after, they divorced.

Cox had been a single mother for four years when, in 1968, she happened upon a newspaper ad for a Unitarian church that cast doubt on the notion of heaven and hell. Cox had come to question the afterlife. She joined the church, and felt at home among members like Curtis Boyd. Theirs was a gospel of unity and compassion; when a member of the church got arrested for selling marijuana, Cox went to the sentencing to comfort his parents. Their son got five years and Cox got fired, let go by the doctor she worked for after he heard that she had sat beside Mr. and Mrs. Oliphant. Recalls Cox: "He used the word 'nigger.'"

Cox remarried and moved to Dallas. There, in 1970, she reconnected with Boyd. She agreed to be his right hand.

Boyd gave Cox a white coat and responsibility, teaching her, she says, "how to draw blood and to do pap smears, blood pressure, pulse." He taught her as well to give each patient not only juice and crackers but counseling, to talk through abortion and birth control and pregnancy. Most important, he taught her to maintain an air of calm. When a man phoned the clinic daily to say that he would shoot Boyd and Cox dead, the doctor and his aide, fellow farm-bred Unitarians, were undeterred.

Boyd made clear that the greatest danger he and Cox faced was the law. Abortion was illegal and they were but one complaint or emergency away from arrest. When a coed from Austin, sixteen weeks pregnant, went into cardiac arrest on the table before them, one thought leapt to Boyd's mind: manslaughter. "It's all over," he recalled thinking. "I'm in prison."

But Boyd resuscitated the woman; she returned to college and he to work. And if the police had never confirmed their suspicion that Boyd was performing abortions, neither did the great majority of women wanting abortions know of his work. Among them, right there in Dallas, was Norma McCorvey.

In 1970, when the second trimester of her third pregnancy began, Norma knew of no legitimate doctor who would end it.

Chapter 8

Norma had not wanted to return to Henry McCluskey. Though the lawyer was kind and had found her second child a good home, Norma did not wish to deal with another adoption. She wanted an abortion. But her obstetrician had made clear that abortion was not possible. And so now, in the first month of a new decade, Norma headed back downtown to see McCluskey. He greeted her, and she said, "Oops!" After they laughed, Norma told him that she wanted an abortion and was angry with the law.

McCluskey understood that anger. He was gay in a state where gay sex was illegal.

Months before, McCluskey had filed a suit to fight the sodomy statute in Texas. He had turned to another lawyer, named Linda Coffee, for help. She had told McCluskey that she wished to overturn a second set of laws, too—the four articles of the Texas Penal Code that criminalized abortion. But she needed a plaintiff.

McCluskey told this to Norma. Norma asked what a plaintiff was and he said it was someone who brought a lawsuit.

Norma also asked if becoming a plaintiff would enable her to have an abortion. McCluskey did not know. He called Coffee.

LINDA NELLENE COFFEE was born in Houston on Christmas Day in 1942. After a younger sister was born, the family of four moved to Dallas.

There, every Sunday, they prayed at the large Southern Baptist church on Gaston Avenue, where Linda's grandfather was a deacon.

The church was a hearth, home to more than prayer. It was where little Linda went for Sunday school and softball and choir, an alto in a dress.

Coffee liked the organ; in time, Bach would give her goosebumps. But after watching the band at Stonewall Jackson Elementary march into the school auditorium, she chose at age nine to play the clarinet.

The second-grader's first choice had been drums. "Something real physical and fun," says Coffee. Dad had said no. But he said yes to softball; he coached the team. And so, his firstborn played shortstop and then catcher, crouching in mask and Jerry Coleman glove, writing her address in black marker on the back of its pocket: 5711 Anita.

Home on her lawny lane in suburban Dallas, Mary Coffee was too nervous and displeased to watch her daughter play; a girl ought not to squat. The housewife had long envisaged a daughter more like her—neat and conservative and feminine. Mary prettied her house and was at the beauty parlor every week. But her daughter hated housework almost as much as the bonnets her mom had once made her wear. The girl was not girly.

Coffee instead resembled her father, a quiet engineer. She was shy but unafraid; she walked on stilts and killed the scorpion that scared the other girls at Baptist camp. She was absentminded but cerebral. Come high school, she joined the Latin and science clubs, tutored math and took college-level physics. The teachers at Woodrow Wilson High told the Coffees how smart she was. They had but one lament. Says Coffee: "I needed to participate more in class."

Coffee did not want to. She knew the answers. And she was happy to keep to herself; save Smokey her dog, she had few friends, went on few dates. "When I had to call up some guy to go to a dance or something, it was just awful," she says. "I hated it!" The teenager preferred to play ball or clarinet, she says—"to do something fun instead of just being a pretty object."

Coffee *was* pretty—thin with high cheekbones, her brown hair in a soft bob. She was also "pretty chaste," she says. After reading a book in high school about a young woman who chooses to have an abortion, it struck her as important for "women to control their fertility." She wondered why it was acceptable for a man, but not a woman, to have sex before marriage.

Coffee had not yet had a boyfriend when she began her junior year. Her mother was upset and let her know it. "I was beginning to think that our house was too small," says Coffee. "I needed to be gone." Linda was seventeen when, in 1960, she left on a student exchange program, bound by steamship from San Francisco to New Zealand.

The students, twenty-eight teens selected by the American Field Service, were meant to represent the U.S., and among the items that Coffee, the lone Southerner, presented to her hosts was a Sears Roebuck catalogue and a Confederate flag. But her nine months abroad opened her eyes to new points of view; Labour governments, she decided, were not all bad. And when in 1961 Coffee enrolled at Rice University, she peered down career paths that her mother—housewife, census taker, secretary—had not taken, like math and medicine and German literature, Coffee studying the last, one summer in Tuebingen, Germany, on a Ford Foundation grant.

None of those careers, however, seemed a good fit. Coffee found the slide rule in calculus cumbersome. Medical school was too expensive and took too many years. And though Coffee loved Goethe and Mann, she hated Kafka and Schiller. Even secretarial work seemed a stretch, she says, after she "failed a typing test miserably." By graduation, the only job she'd had was as a carhop at Prince of Hamburgers. Mother was displeased. Says Coffee: "I sort of did it to spite her."

As a last resort, Coffee took the LSAT. High-minded yet practical, she found that the law suited her, and she began to study it at the University of Texas at Austin. Coffee had joined the Human Rights Research Council, a national organization of law students devoted to "the protection of individual and civil liberties," when, in 1967, she graduated with high honors.

Coffee thought she might go into domestic relations law; she'd interned at a legal aid society in Austin, helping disadvantaged women to get out from bad marriages. But in 1968, few law firms hired women; a woman needed the backing of a man just to rent an apartment. Not one firm made Coffee an offer. She went to work at the Texas Legislative

Council, paid six hundred dollars a month to help legislators draft statutes. She found the work boring.

It was then that her mother heard through a lawyer at the Baptist
General Convention that Sarah Hughes, the first female federal judge
in Texas, wished to hire another clerk.

Hughes was famous for having sworn in President Lyndon Johnson aboard *Air Force One*. But long before Kennedy was assassinated,
Hughes had been known for her feminism—fighting to secure women
equal pay and the right to serve on a jury. When Coffee applied for
the clerkship and the judge phoned to invite her to the courthouse
for an interview, Coffee was overwhelmed. "My voice," she says,
"was shaking."

Coffee had little need to worry. The *Dallas Morning News* happened to print the bar results the April morning of her interview, and
Hughes let Coffee know that she'd seen her score—87, second highest
in the state. The interview went well until the judge asked her would-
be clerk which presidential candidate she wished to see elected. Coffee answered Hubert Humphrey but added that Nelson Rockefeller
would be fine. "Her tone changed," says Coffee. "She said she was not
interested hiring anyone who didn't vote Democratic." Coffee made
clear that she understood that politics mattered: "I said, 'Oh yes!'"
She got the job and was soon making her way through a backlog of
civil motions.

Hughes appreciated Coffee; she told her clerk, says Coffee, that
her work "was most satisfactory." Still, Hughes expected more.
Law school had taught Coffee to argue both sides of a case; Hughes
wished her clerks to take stances. The judge aspired to legal progress commensurate with the seriousness of the times, and in 1968,
America was convulsing—Martin Luther King and Robert Kennedy
assassinated, the Democratic National Convention shadowed by violent protest.

Coffee was stirred. But as her clerkship wound down, she again saw,
as after law school, all the good jobs going to men. "'Oh, we'd only hire
a woman for [debt] collection,'" Coffee recalled the firms telling her.
"'We'd never hire a woman to be a partner.'" Adds Coffee: "Just overt
discrimination . . . I was panicked."

IN APRIL 1969, Coffee's clerkship was winding down when Henry McCluskey visited her at her desk in the jury room of the federal courthouse.

The two had met years before as young classmates in Sunday school at the church on Gaston. The boy was tall and kind, like all his family, a gentle Baptist. And like Coffee, he kept to himself. "We didn't have to have friends," says his older sister Barbara, "because we had each other."

Like Coffee, too, the young McCluskey was taken with music and sport; he arrived in junior high playing bass fiddle and rooting for the Cowboys. Still, the two had not been in touch since high school when, these many years later, McCluskey reached out. He had heard that Coffee was a lawyer in Dallas just like him, and Coffee assumed, she says, "that he was hoping that I could help him. I obviously knew certain things having worked for a federal judge."

On this spring day, however, it was McCluskey who tried to help Coffee. She said she needed a job, and he suggested that she buy the law practice of a woman he knew who was getting married. The practice, though, was nothing but collections and defaults, while Coffee—who thought she might want to become a prosecutor—hoped to get a job with the Dallas district attorney, Henry Wade. Says Coffee: "I wanted to get experience trying cases." She had applied for a job with the DA when McCluskey invited her to dinner with his parents and a friend who knew Wade. The friend liked Coffee, and spoke to Wade about her. The DA then interviewed Coffee and told her that she'd impressed him, too. But the only job he had for a woman, he said, was collecting child support from delinquent dads. Coffee turned it down. She had landed at a small bankruptcy firm in Dallas when McCluskey asked her to help him defend a defrauded man. She did so. He then asked for help on a very different matter.

Sodomy was illegal in Texas. It had been since 1860, the Texas General Laws criminalizing sex that might not result in pregnancy—anal sex, and sex between man or woman and beast. The law became binding in 1879. Ninety years later, McCluskey wished to fight it, and had put an ad in a local gay newspaper seeking a plaintiff. He had found one—a man twice convicted of having consensual oral sex with another man. But McCluskey needed help with his suit.

The case concerned matters of privacy, the fact that police spied on locations where men met for sex. "You have the government in the bedroom," says Coffee. "I thought, that's awful! That's just horrible! They would just sit there watching people using the bathrooms!" Coffee was keen to help her friend. Says Coffee: "I wrote some kind of brief and drafted a complaint for him."

The suit, *Buchanan v. Batchelor*, did not mention her name. "I wasn't about to touch that publicly," says Coffee. "I would not have enough nerve to even be the counsel of record."

McCluskey filed suit in May 1969 and appeared before the three-judge federal court in Dallas to argue it.

McCluskey had graduated from Baylor magna cum laude and had been the case notes editor of the *Baylor Law Review*. But he failed to impress, and a law clerk named Randy Shreve, who knew that Coffee was helping McCluskey, phoned her. "The clerk was desperate," she recalls with a laugh. "He couldn't understand what [McCluskey] was saying . . . what his argument was." The court asked McCluskey for a brief after his oral argument. Coffee wrote the brief and gave it to the clerk who gave it to the court which eventually ruled that, as Coffee suggested, the law was unconstitutional at least with respect to married couples. Says Coffee: "I analyzed it right."

The work on privacy gratified Coffee in a way that bankruptcy did not. She helped McCluskey over and over again that summer of 1969, a Cyrano content to go unrecognized. The lawyers, meantime, got along well. They had much in common, both twenty-six and single and living with their parents. They began seeing each other outside of work, McCluskey taking Coffee out on what seemed like dates—to the bar at the Adolphus Hotel, to his high school reunion. Their relationship, says Coffee, was soon "somewhere between friendly and more than that."

That both lawyers were gay went unspoken. But, says Coffee, McCluskey started taking her to places that might communicate what he dared not to—a club for swingers, a gay club for men, a street corner where he alerted her to a man who, he said, was "hustling." Still, she says, "it seemed that he wanted a straight life." She adds: "he was having gender—some sort of confusion."

If Coffee was closeted, she was not confused. She'd upended stereotype from the start, preferring drums to clarinet, math to typing, comfort to fashion, work to the prospect of a family. She'd never had a boyfriend, and retained, she would soon tell a reporter, "a live and let live attitude about marriage." She added that "we [working women] would like to try it but we just don't have time for everything at once."

SEPTEMBER 1969 HAD arrived when Coffee came upon mention, in the Southern Methodist University library, of *People v. Belous*, a case that only days before had exonerated a California doctor for referring a woman to an illegal abortion provider. Coffee's mind raced. Here was a ruling that rendered a state abortion law void on grounds that it was constitutionally vague, that it violated the due process clause of the Fourteenth Amendment. Surely the abortion law in Texas was vulnerable, too. "I just thought, my goodness!" recalls Coffee. "The same logic would apply!"

The thought had not occurred to Coffee before. But suddenly it consumed her, the idea, as she later explained, that "process" aside, laws that deprive a person of "some important fundamental liberty"—such as privacy—are in and of themselves impermissible.

Coffee was a feminist, a member of Women for Change and the National Organization for Women and the Women's Equity Action League. Long mindful that birth control was unreliable at best, and that the illegality of abortion, says Coffee, "seemed to be something that held women back from achieving their full potential," she now saw that the Texas law enforcing that illegality was weak—a legal relic out of step with the fact, she says, that "if a woman self-aborted, she was guilty of no crime, not even a misdemeanor."

In a few days, the abortion rights lawyer Roy Lucas would file in New York the first suit against a state abortion law. Coffee told McCluskey over lunch at the Adolphus that she wished to do the same. There was, she said, just one problem: "I couldn't figure out how I could find a pregnant woman who was willing to come forward."

Four months later, in January 1970, McCluskey phoned Coffee with word of a woman who'd come to his office wanting an abortion.

PART III

Roe v. Wade

Chapter 9

It was still January when Norma and McCluskey met Coffee downtown in her office at Palmer, Palmer & Burke, where, for $450 a month, Coffee waded through petitions for bankruptcy.

Coffee was intense, incapable of small talk, pale and unkempt besides. All at once, Norma was ill at ease beside her. She looked, said Norma, "like she got out of bed and forgot to comb her hair."

Looking back at Norma, Coffee saw a small woman with a big belly. Says Coffee: "She looked really pregnant."

Exactly how far along Norma was could not be known. In 1970, gestational age could only be estimated, and estimates could be off by up to four weeks. "We weren't using ultrasound at that time," explains Frank Bradley, the Dallas obstetrician who delivered Norma's second child. Instead, he says, doctors used pelvic exams and menstrual history to "try to figure it out best they could."

It was more than likely that Norma had reached at least her twentieth week. And she had thus reached the legal limit at which any doctor in the U.S.—even where abortion was legal—could perform an elective abortion. In January 1970, abortion was legal only in Oregon, where residents were permitted to abort through the first 150 days, and in California, where nonresidents too could abort through twenty weeks. Abortion was also not illegal in the District of Columbia. (A federal district court had recently declared the anti-abortion law in DC unconstitutional, and the appellee in that case performed abortions until at least the twentieth week.)

Coffee thus knew that it was almost certainly too late for Norma to get an abortion. "It was my opinion," the lawyer soon recalled, "that, very likely, the suit would not solve her immediate problem." It was not too late, however, for Norma to file suit. Indeed, it would be of no legal consequence if the suit Norma filed came to term after she did. "There were fairly established principles that that doesn't moot the case," says Coffee. (Among them was the category of cases deemed "capable of repetition yet evading review"—which meant, in essence, that the issue was a recurring one, but in each instance would pass before the courts had time to fully address it.)

Coffee told Norma what she knew. "I remember saying," she recalls, "that I thought she was probably too far along to have an abortion under the protection of the federal court." But Norma had nowhere else to turn. Coffee was her last hope.

Coffee told Norma that if she filed suit, she might have to testify. Norma agreed—never mind, says Coffee, that she "likely had no idea what that would entail." Coffee sensed that Norma had little idea what filing suit even meant. "I could tell she didn't have a lot of education," says Coffee. "Maybe she was being a little too cooperative . . . Most people would ask more questions if they were thinking about filing a lawsuit over something of that magnitude." Norma only asked if filing suit would cost her money. It would not; Coffee would do the case pro bono. Norma agreed to file and left.

Coffee marveled. McCluskey had come through. She had a plaintiff. And that plaintiff was perfect. As Coffee later told a reporter: "It had to be a pregnant woman wanting to get an abortion. She couldn't have the funds to travel to California . . . for a legal abortion. And we had to have someone who could take the publicity. We weren't able to guarantee her anonymity."

Still, Coffee would try to keep Norma anonymous. Alone in her office, she fashioned for her would-be plaintiff a pseudonym, combining Jane, which was suitably common, she says, with Roe, which was standard legal vernacular and already the surname of two plaintiffs (alongside two Hoes, two Poes and a Doe) in a 1959 lawsuit on contraception. "In my mind," says Coffee, "I considered her being Jane Roe as soon as I got an actual woman being ready to file."

Coffee picked up the phone. There was one person she wanted to alert at once.

———

COFFEE HAD STUDIED LAW at the University of Texas alongside a woman named Sarah Ragle. The women were not friends, says Coffee. But they were two of just five women in the entering class of 1965, and both had thrived in law school only to be rejected by every firm.

Both women had since found their footing. Ragle had been hired by one of her professors to help draft the ethical standards of the American Bar Association. But misogyny remained rooted in Texas and beyond. And in the fall of 1968, a group of women in Austin, some twenty current and former students at U of T, began meeting to discuss the issues they faced.

Among these was abortion. The women began referring women wanting abortions to those few clinicians they deemed safe. But the women were circumnavigating the law. And in November 1969, they approached a young lawyer they knew—the former Sarah Ragle, who had since married a law student named Ron Weddington. As the author David Garrow later phrased their question: "Would open and above-board provision of referral information leave the project volunteers vulnerable to arrest?"

Weddington seemed an odd person to ask. That she was smart was undeniable; she'd skipped two grades, graduated college magna cum laude besides. "I have received very few B's in my whole life," she later recalled. But at twenty-four years old, Weddington was hardly counter-cultural. She was the daughter of a Methodist minister, had headed her high school chapter of the Future Homemakers of America, and had been assistant house mother for her Delta Gamma sorority. She was middle-class and married.

Weddington, though, fervently believed in the need for abortion reform. Unbeknownst to the group, she had found herself pregnant the year before she was to marry and had traveled to a clinic south of the border in a town called Piedras Negras to have an abortion.

Prim in her ponytail and pantsuits, Weddington had kept her abortion secret. But when approached by the group of UT alumnae, she agreed to investigate their question at no cost. And in late November, she let the women know that she had found no clear answer; the law was ambiguous. The group then wondered if the Texas abortion law could be challenged in federal court. Weddington thought so. Asked if she might file suit, Weddington balked.

Weddington was confident. Her parents had raised her and her younger siblings to believe, she later recalled, that they "could do whatever they wanted," and so she had—from soloing in the church choir to serving as secretary of her college student body. But her body of legal work was sparse—a few divorces and wills, an adoption. She suggested that the group hire a lawyer in a firm, she recalled, "with research and secretarial backup."

The women, however, wanted Weddington. So back to the library she went, comforted by the thought, she later wrote, that any suit she filed would simply back the growing number of suits that already contested abortion laws in other states.

Still, the drafting of documents was daunting. Weddington again wondered if the case might be better handled by a lawyer with knowledge of federal courts and procedure. A former classmate turned clerk leapt to mind. On December 3, she phoned Linda Coffee.

Coffee was delighted. She'd arrived at this same juncture and simply needed a plaintiff. Weddington suggested that Coffee file suit on behalf of the alumnae group in Austin. Coffee agreed and typed Weddington a letter the next day. "Would you consider being co-counsel in the event that a suit is actually filed?" she wrote. "I have always found that it is a great deal more fun to work with someone on a law suit of this nature." Weddington phoned to accept.

Coffee worried, however, that because the Austin group was not a pregnant woman, it might not have standing in the eyes of the court. Besides, only a case filed in Dallas could land on the sympathetic desk of Coffee's mentor, Judge Hughes. The search for a plaintiff thus continued, extending into late January, when an exultant Coffee phoned Weddington to tell of the pregnant woman who'd just left her office.

———

DAYS LATER, NORMA was all belly and blue jeans when she met the two lawyers for pizza in a restaurant popular with SMU students. Seeing Coffee again made Norma anxious. But Norma was taken with Weddington, strawberry-blonde and curvy and just two years older than she. "She was wholesome and robust and had things happening!" said Norma. "I fell in love with Sarah. She had all this hair."

Over a tablecloth of red and white gingham, talk turned to the inalienable rights of women. The lawyers asked, recalled Norma, if it was not a good thing that women could smoke in public, could vote. Norma agreed that it was, and then that women ought to have the right to an abortion, too.

Still, it was not conviction that had led Norma to Columbo's Pizza Parlor this winter afternoon; it was happenstance, the fact that her doctor happened to know McCluskey who happened to know Coffee. And Norma again made clear that she did not want to further a cause; she wanted an abortion. Weddington repeated what Coffee had said, about her probably being too far along. "I'm not saying I misunderstood," said Norma. "But I thought we were all real clear on what I really wanted."

Had Coffee and Weddington really wanted to help their potential client get an abortion, they might have at least tried. As Victoria Foe, a biology student who worked with Weddington on the referral network in Austin, recalled: "in desperate situations, women up to twenty weeks were not turned away." And the lawyers might have taken Norma to a doctor for an X-ray so as to better gauge how far along she actually was. If there *was* time to end her pregnancy, they might have asked a judge to issue a temporary restraining order to prevent state officials from enforcing the law against their client. Or they might have sent Norma to a clinic in their network—be it in Piedras Negras, just over the Mexican border (where both Weddington and Foe had had abortions), or in California, where every Friday a group of Texas women flew. "American

[Airlines] was the plane," Weddington recalled decades later. "About ten women every Friday went to California and then they were back late on Sunday."

But the lawyers did none of those things. It didn't matter that only months before, Weddington had helped to write the American Bar Association's code of ethical standards, which instructed that every lawyer must work "solely for the benefit of his client." Weddington and Coffee had interests of their own. They wished to file a lawsuit. And, as the law professor Kevin McMunigal later noted, they now set aside Norma's desire for an abortion "in favor of the collective interests of the abortion rights cause."

It remained possible that Norma might yet spurn her lawyers. She had considerations beyond theirs. And so, in January 1970, Coffee and Weddington decided to file a second suit on behalf of a second plaintiff Coffee had found that same month. Her name was Marsha King. She was unlike Norma in almost every way.

King had a graduate degree in physics, a job as an engineer, a husband. She'd been in poor health the previous summer—her vision and muscles and mood faltering. A doctor had suspected birth control was to blame, and forgoing her pills did help. But when, in October, King got pregnant (despite using a diaphragm), she was distraught. For she still felt ill—and ill-prepared to have a child. An abortion in Mexico was successful but traumatic.

The experience had left King, at age twenty-six, deeply committed to abortion reform, and in January, she gave a talk about it to a women's group at a Dallas Unitarian church. Coffee spoke to the same group, and King told the lawyer that she and her husband were willing to file suit. Coffee was delighted; the Kings were impassioned and smart. They were not, however, pregnant, and Coffee worried that a court might find that they did not have standing because they would not have a personal stake in the outcome of a trial.

Coffee and Weddington nonetheless decided to file suit on behalf not only of Jane Roe but of Mary and John Doe too. And in February—weeks before McCluskey took Norma to see *Swan Lake* at Fair Park in Dallas, a pink dress tight over her big belly—Coffee sat down in the SMU library to prepare the legal ground upon which her lawsuits would stand.

THE U.S. CONSTITUTION says nothing explicit about sex or its consequences. It does not mention conception or birth, contraception or abortion.

But, as Coffee looked now for a constitutional basis for abortion, she knew that the Constitution did not have to expressly address an issue to say something about it. A legal right could be *inferred*. The job of the lawyer was to justify that inference.

To do so, a lawyer looked for precedent, for some previous analogous ruling that might help her to persuade the court that the Constitution also protected whatever right it was she sought to defend. Regarding abortion, this was difficult. In its 180 years, the Supreme Court had not once addressed the issue.

The Court had, however, addressed contraception just five years before. Coffee believed that that 1965 ruling, in *Griswold v. Connecticut*, was the precedent she needed. *Griswold* had, by a 7–2 vote, overturned a state ban on the use of contraceptives, on grounds that the ban violated the constitutional right to privacy.

Back in 1888, a Michigan judge named Thomas Cooley had written of "the right to be let alone." Louis Brandeis then championed that right—both in an article he co-authored at Harvard Law School and in a dissent he wrote in 1928 as a Supreme Court justice, calling it "the most comprehensive of rights and the right most valued by civilized men." Coffee agreed. More, it now seemed to her that the right to privacy ought to encompass not only contraception but abortion, that what held for the prevention of pregnancy might hold for its termination.

Pinning a case to privacy had its challenges. For one thing, privacy is less obviously implicated by a medical procedure than by the use of contraception in "the sacred precincts of marital bedrooms," as the Court had put it in *Griswold*. For another, nowhere does the Constitution actually mention a right to privacy. At a loss, the *Griswold* Court had situated that right, as Justice William Douglas wrote, in the "penumbras" and "emanations" of the Bill of Rights.

Still, *Griswold* was the closest the Supreme Court had ever come to the abortion right Coffee sought to establish. And, readying to write her memos, she resolved to do what Justice Douglas had not: be clear about where in the Constitution the right to privacy lay, that is, about exactly which amendments the Texas abortion law violated.

Her first thought was the First Amendment. "At that time," says Coffee, "if you could file the right you were asserting under the First Amendment, the courts were much more likely to not say that you had to go to the state courts." (Coffee hoped to have her case heard in federal court both because that was where Judge Hughes sat and because a federal court was thought more likely to declare a state law unconstitutional.) But other amendments could support privacy, too. The Ninth, for example, allowed for rights beyond those enumerated in the Constitution, while the Fourteenth limited the state's ability to deprive people "of life, liberty, or property, without due process of law."

In time, Coffee decided to rely on six amendments, to argue that the Texas statute violated not only the First, Ninth and Fourteenth amendments, but the Fourth, Fifth and Eighth too. As February turned to March, Coffee, who'd failed a typing class, began to hunt and peck her way through her memos on *Roe* and *Doe*.

The memos said little about their plaintiffs. (Coffee described Roe simply as unmarried and pregnant and poor and wanting an abortion she couldn't obtain.) The memos centered instead on the law, Coffee asserting over eight pages that the Texas statutes not only violated a right to privacy but were "vague" and "unconstitutionally broad," and thus infringed upon the "fundamental right of all women to choose whether to bear children."

"You almost had to argue on the basis of common sense," says Coffee, noting how little precedent there was for her to summon. She adds, "It was pretty easy . . . The law was so obviously unconstitutional."

Coffee was done. It was time to submit her work. But, she says, her co-counsel hesitated to attach her name to it. "Sarah didn't want to sign it at first," says Coffee. "I think she was just cautious."

Only months before, it had been Coffee who was cautious, the lawyer preferring that her work on *Buchanan*, on sodomy, go unrecognized. But regarding abortion, Coffee was unabashed, happy to be counsel of record, to take aim with *Roe* and *Doe* at another law that bound sex to procreation.

On March 3, 1970, Coffee delivered her petitions to the federal courthouse on North Ervay Street, paying thirty dollars (with two personal checks) to have them filed, signing them in black ink. She named Henry Wade as defendant—the Dallas DA she'd hoped to work for less than a year before.

———

WADE WAS AN INSTITUTION. He'd been the district attorney of Dallas nearly twenty of his fifty-six years. And he knew everybody, had spoken not only with LBJ and JFK but Lee Harvey Oswald and Jack Ruby, prosecuting the last.

In turn, everybody knew Wade. They knew that he chewed cigars and had two working farms and kept his phone number listed (TA3–6955). They knew that he was fierce; Wade would in time seek thirty death sentences and secure all but one.

The DA was nonetheless considered by most to be fair. The son of a judge, the whole of his allegiance was to the law. (When his older brother, Ney Wade, drove drunk, Henry put him in jail.) And, capital punishment aside, if he had a political or judicial leaning, it was decidedly left, a worldview informed by his pastor, W. B. J. Martin, a progressive Welsh theologian with a penchant for poetry. "My father was open-minded," recalls his son Kim, a lawyer and former Assistant U.S. Attorney in Texas. "Kind of a closeted liberal democrat."

Wade was happy to go unrecognized. (Working for the FBI after law school, he'd posed in Ecuador as a journalist.) And that a Texas DA would keep his liberalism quiet made sense. Crime and convictions kept him employed. Says his son Kim: "I don't think his liberal tendencies would have helped him get elected."

Those tendencies extended to abortion. Unknown to everyone, Henry Menasco Wade was pro-choice.

Wade would never say so publicly. But almost twenty years after a lawsuit had pitted him in perpetuity against Roe, he would confide in his son—as they drove east in a Chevy pickup toward the family farm in Sachse—that he had disagreed with the abortion statutes it had been his charge to defend. Says Kim: "he was not anti-abortion."

Wade had generally looked past the statutes; his few prosecutions regarding abortion had sought less to protect the unborn than the women carrying them, the DA targeting only the most reckless of practitioners. But no longer could he do so. For Coffee, the young and brilliant lawyer who'd once sought to work for him, had named him the defendant in *Roe*.

That was actually a mistake. Coffee had sought to enjoin *all* the district attorneys in Texas from enforcing the abortion statute, not merely Wade. She ought to have named the Texas attorney general, Crawford Martin, as defendant. But the court did not instruct Coffee and Weddington to amend their complaint, and Wade's office readied to work together with the office of the Texas AG.

Roe v. Wade and *Doe v. Wade* were now part of the U.S. legal system. But when Coffee let Norma know, the plaintiff was unmoved. She was due to give birth in three months and had come, by March, to grasp that her suit would not end her pregnancy. It was, however, poised to end many others, after Coffee and Weddington amended *Roe* to make it a class action suit on behalf of their plaintiff and, they wrote, "all other women similarly situated."

The lawyers laid out their plaintiff's predicament, filing an affidavit in late May. Little more than two pages, and ostensibly written by Norma, it contained a few small errors. (Fewer than five years, for example, not six, had passed since Norma's divorce.) Its central claims, however, were true. Jane Roe had chosen to remain anonymous to avoid the "notoriety occasioned by the lawsuit." She considered "the decision of whether to bear a child a highly personal one." She had not traveled to where abortion was legal because she was poor. And the abortion providers she could afford were both illegal and, potentially, dangerous.

Still, one assertion at the heart of the affidavit was not true. It was neither the economic strain of pregnancy nor the stigma of birthing an "illegitimate" child that had led Jane Roe to want an abortion. She simply did not want another child.

Norma, though, was going to have one. She was due any day.

Chapter 10

Once filed, *Roe v. Wade* no longer needed its plaintiff. And Jane Roe and Norma McCorvey had parted ways.

Norma was aloof from her suit. Her mind was on a baby that, wanted or not, had to be delivered. Jane, meantime, had landed in the friendly arms of Sarah Hughes and two Dallas federal court colleagues.

———

BACK IN MARCH, Fifth Circuit Judge John R. Brown had decided that a three-judge federal panel would hear the *Roe* and *Doe* cases together. A third case had then joined the docket, that of a doctor who'd been arrested for performing abortions just north of Dallas.

The hearing was slated for May 22. Coffee and Weddington were ready. They had amended their complaint as needed, filed briefs and affidavits, prepared for the courtroom. Jane Roe was in good hands.

The state's case was in the hands of one of Wade's attorneys, a Notre Dame graduate named John Tolle, who would work together with a lawyer from the office of the Texas AG named Jay Floyd.

Tolle handled cases concerning federal civil rights. (It was he who'd argued opposite Henry McCluskey over sodomy.) Readying now for *Roe*, the lawyer understood its potential importance not only because he was Catholic and "very much opposed to abortion," he says, but because the case had been filed by Coffee, a lawyer he respected. "She thought she had a case," he says. And so, Tolle did, too.

Tolle knew that the anonymous plaintiff was pregnant. The father of two found himself wondering about the baby not yet born, speaking of it to an older lawyer in the office named Wilson Johnston. "We knew that baby as Fetus Roe," says Tolle. "That's what we called it."

The *Roe* hearing began at 2 p.m. on May 22, Coffee addressing, on the fourth floor of the Dallas federal courthouse, the procedural points of jurisdiction and standing; Jane Roe, she said, had the right to file suit. Weddington then moved on to the less arcane contention that the plaintiff also had the right to choose whether to have children. She spoke of privacy and precedent and personhood.

The lawyers representing Texas countered. Floyd argued that Jane Roe did not have standing. The abortion statutes at issue, he said, were aimed at doctors who performed abortions, not at women who wanted them. He added that as it was no doubt too late for the plaintiff to get an abortion, her suit was moot. His co-counsel Tolle then asserted that a fetus's right to life was more important than a woman's right to privacy. Neither side presented a witness.

The panel did not address the question of mootness. And weeks later, on June 17, it declared the abortion statutes in Texas unconstitutional. The right of a woman to have an abortion, it said, was embedded within the Ninth Amendment, within the right to privacy. Read the front page of the *Dallas Morning News*: "Texas Abortion Law Void."

Coffee exulted. "Quite a victory," she told the press.

It was, however, an incomplete victory. The panel had found that Mary and John Doe (who were not expecting a child and might never be) did not have standing. More, owing to sensitivity about federal-court interference in state processes, it had declined to order Texas not to enforce the very laws it deemed unconstitutional.

Coffee petitioned the judges to reconsider, telling of officials at a local hospital who, fearing the law, would not end the pregnancy of a girl of fifteen raped by her father. The ruling, though, remained, and Coffee readied to file an appeal. Tolle did too.

Tolle was soon off the case; the Texas AG was taking over. Yet Tolle still found himself thinking of what he had months before called "Fetus Roe." And the day after the *Roe* ruling, Coffee told the press that her plaintiff was due to give birth in just a few weeks.

Norma had in fact already given birth. Her baby had been born early, two weeks before, at 6:51 a.m. on June 2.

———

THE *ROE* BABY was four months old when, in October 1970, Coffee filed her appeal. Coffee explained to Weddington what the abortion rights lawyer Roy Lucas had explained to her—that because the panel had found a state law unconstitutional while granting no injunction against enforcing it, they could appeal directly to the Supreme Court. This she did.

Back when Coffee filed *Roe*, she had not imagined her case could reach the Supreme Court. "Never in a million years!" she says. Even now, the odds were long. At least eight times, the Court had chosen not to review decisions involving anti-abortion laws.

The Court had, however, earlier that year, decided at last to address abortion. The case, *United States v. Vuitch*, concerned a DC law that banned abortion except when "the mother's life or health" was at stake. On April 21, 1971, the Court ruled that health included mental health, and that the law was not unconstitutionally vague.

Still, it is one thing to challenge the vagueness of a law, and quite another to assert that a woman has a constitutional right to choose to have an abortion. And weeks later, on May 3, the Supreme Court agreed to hear *Roe*, coupling it with a similar case from Georgia, *Doe v. Bolton*. Coffee and Weddington exulted.

It was Coffee who had found their plaintiff and filed their suit and attached her name to it, Coffee who had conceived its legal grounding and presented half its oral argument and appealed the ruling to the Supreme Court. The lawyer would continue to bring other successful suits, too (including *Johnston v. Luna*, which would soon void a new state law requiring political candidates to pay a filing fee).

But if Coffee was brilliant, she was bedraggled. Several of her clients would express concern that she made a poor impression in court. Recalls Peggy Clewis, the secretary at her firm: "They were embarrassed." And so, facing a second oral argument, the two lawyers decided that Weddington would present the whole of it. Optics mattered. "She was younger than I was," says Coffee of Weddington. "She was blond, blue-eyed." More, Weddington enjoyed the limelight as much as Coffee disliked it.

Weddington got to work. The previous spring, she'd hesitated to affix her name to *Roe*. But she now committed to it fully, working with her husband tirelessly through the summer on the legal brief the high court required—doing research in New York and DC, using both moot courts and mirrors to hone her arguments, the latter "to see," she later noted, "how you were getting your message across."

Coffee helped, of course. "Linda worked with me some," Weddington later recalled. So did others—the activist Roy Lucas providing legal direction, an heiress named Ruth Bowers and an industrialist named Thomas Cabot footing many bills. Then there were the amici curiae, "friends of the court" who submitted briefs in support of every legal or medical or psychiatric or religious point that might serve the plaintiff.

That plaintiff was uninvolved, unseen by her lawyers in the year since Coffee had come to her apartment at 4706 San Jacinto with an affidavit to sign. *Roe* had left Norma behind.

That was fine with Weddington. Plaintiffs, she later wrote, were merely "vehicles for presenting larger issues." But then, suddenly, Weddington needed Norma. Only Norma could decide who would represent her in court, and Lucas made clear that he intended to do so. "The clients in a case have the final say-so about who argues," Weddington later explained. And so, as Norma recalled: "Sarah got in touch with me, for the first time in a long time."

Weeks later, on December 13, 1971, it was Weddington who stood at a mahogany lectern in the Supreme Court. She was all of twenty-six. Looking up at the seven robed men looking down at her—their number depleted by two September retirements—Weddington suddenly wondered, she recalled, how best to return their gaze, how best to "respond in a personal way to their obviously sort of looking me over." "Do I smile and wink? Or do I look demure?"

Weddington wore a suit, heels and pearls. The courtroom sketch artists took note. "She was rather attractive," recalled the artist Betty Wells. Harry Blackmun agreed. So as to better recall the argument of every lawyer come before him, the justice jotted a quick physical description of him or her. As Weddington began now to speak of pregnancy and fetuses, of precedent and state interest, of the lengths women traveled to end their pregnancies, he made himself a note. Wrote Blackmun: "large blond hair, rather pretty, plump."

Weddington was prepared and poised. Seated to her side at their counsel table—in a skirt and jacket and ribboned blouse that she could never quite tie—Coffee listened, another lawyer in a crowd that included supporters from Planned Parenthood and NARAL but not her parents. "Since I wasn't arguing," says Coffee, "they didn't come." That she was a spectator suited Coffee. Despite her uncomfortable clothing, she could relax, could take in the figures of Menes and Moses and Muhammad carved in marble above, take in the seven justices seated at the mahogany bench before her.

Of the seven, it was William Brennan whom Coffee most esteemed. He wrote, she says, "elegant opinions for the minority," opinions most often in the service of individual rights that the justice supported with an expansive view of the Constitution and its Fourteenth Amendment.

It was that same amendment, with its ostensible guarantee of privacy, that Weddington had come to determine offered *Roe* its best chance. Before concluding her argument this Monday morning, she asserted the constitutional right of all people "to determine the course of their lives."

As after every oral argument, Blackmun now graded the lawyer who made it. He was ungenerous: C+. Jay Floyd approached the bench.

To argue opposite a woman was a rare thing; Weddington was just the eighth in twelve months to argue before the Court. (The lawyers' lounge did not even have a ladies' room.) And representing Texas, his speech deliberate and drawled, Floyd began with a joke: "When a man argues against two beautiful ladies like this, they are going to have the last word." No one laughed.

Floyd moved on. The plaintiff, he said, "is no longer pregnant." As such, her case was moot. Justice Potter Stewart made clear that he disagreed, and Floyd, after assertions about maternal responsibility and fetal life, closed by saying that the Constitution did not address abortion. It was a matter, he said, for lawmakers, not judges. Blackmun gave Floyd a B, noting that he was "squarely built, nice looking."

The judges convened three days later. Five of the seven determined that the Texas law was unconstitutional. Among them was Blackmun. Home in his living room, the junior justice confided to his wife and three daughters that he hoped the case might fall to him. "I remember him saying," recalls his eldest daughter, Nancy, "'I'd give my eyeteeth to write that opinion!'"

Blackmun did not say why he wanted to author *Roe*. But Nancy had a thought. As she would observe almost thirty years later in eulogizing her father: "Dad saw at close range what it was like for a woman alone in the world."

Indeed, he had. Blackmun was a boy in St. Paul, Minnesota, when his aunt Annette was left alone to raise two children after her husband went to jail for embezzlement. He was a teenager at Harvard studying math and working odd jobs when he befriended one of the university maids everybody knew as "goodies." ("She was a single mom," says Nancy. "They were in touch the rest of her life.") He was past forty when, after years of practicing copyright and tax law, he became counsel at the Mayo Clinic and observed the back-alley abortions that landed women at St. Mary's Hospital. And he was a Minnesota judge nearing sixty when, in 1966, it was his own daughter undone by circumstance—Sally became pregnant while a sophomore in college. In short order, she dropped out of school, married, miscarried and divorced.

Blackmun had come to understand that law is not a theoretical science. At his confirmation hearing in May 1970, after President Richard Nixon nominated him to the Supreme Court, the judge was clear when asked if he viewed the Court "as the protector of our most basic liberties." Yes, said Blackmun. His opinions revealed "in the treatment of little people, what I hope is a sensitivity to their problems." The Senate confirmed the judge without opposition.

Come to DC, Blackmun remained his Midwestern Methodist self. He ate breakfast with his clerks, talking baseball over raisin toast and a scrambled egg. He wore patched sweaters, and told the uninitiated that he was "a lawyer in Washington." At the close of every term, he and his wife Dottie drove back to Minnesota in his VW Bug.

Blackmun was the second Minnesotan on the Court; he'd grown up six blocks from Warren Burger, who'd been appointed Chief Justice the previous June. The two Republicans were dubbed the Minnesota

Twins. And on December 17, days after discussing *Roe* (and its companion *Doe*) with their five colleagues, Burger assigned both cases to the friend he'd met in Sunday School back in 1914.

Blackmun was unsure why. Perhaps Burger had in mind his medical background. Or perhaps, as the clerks had it, he thought he could influence an old friend. "The insider speculation," recalls George Frampton, a Blackmun clerk, "was that he would want to manipulate the opinion."

Blackmun, sixty-three, started in on *Roe* that very day. "Would your well-stocked library have anything about the history of abortion?" he wrote a former colleague at the Mayo Clinic. "You can imagine why I ask."

———

AMONG THOSE HANGING on the fortunes of *Roe* was Curtis Boyd, the Dallas doctor violating Texas law with nearly every abortion he performed.

Abortion consumed Boyd. Since performing his first almost four years before, it had driven him from his hometown, his best friend, his medical practice. And since reading, on the front page of the *Dallas Morning News* in the spring of 1970, that *Roe* was bound for the Supreme Court, he'd wondered if it would drive him further. For though a three-judge federal panel had found that women had a right to have an abortion and that doctors had a right to perform one, it had not enjoined Henry Wade from prosecuting those same people. The DA took note. "Apparently, we're free to try them," Wade had told the press, "so we'll still do that."

Boyd had phoned an attorney to ask what it all meant. The lawyer, recalls Boyd, was clear: "Don't bet your safety on this."

Up to that point, Boyd had been careful. He had kept no records, worked with just one partner, seen only patients screened by his referring clergy, relocated from town to city. And yet, he lived in fear. Says Boyd: "A police car would pull up behind me and my heart rate would accelerate."

The following September, in 1971, the retirements of Justices Hugo Black and John Harlan II left *Roe* in the hands of a court that would carry four Nixon appointees. Certain that the court would vote *Roe*

down, Boyd decided that it was time to move again. He knew where
he would go.

Eight years before, the American Law Institute, a body of lawyers,
professors and judges, had proposed legalizing, among others, abortions that it termed "therapeutic"—those that safeguarded the physical
or mental well-being of the woman. Twelve states had since adopted all
or part of the ALI proposal. One was New Mexico.

Boyd knew that other states had more liberal policies. (Alaska,
Hawaii, New York and Washington had legalized all abortions performed by doctors in early pregnancy.) He knew that even in New Mexico, the majority of the abortions he performed would fall outside the
law. But Boyd wished to work where the women of Texas could reach
him, and New Mexico lay just to the west.

Boyd turned to his wife. He was no longer the man LaMerle had
fallen for—a Baptist with cropped hair who aspired to doctor in his
hometown. He now wished to use his medical degree for just one
thing—ending the pregnancies of women unable to end them elsewhere.
He told LaMerle that he could better do so out of state.

LaMerle listened. She respected her husband. She believed in his
cause. But if he lived in fear of arrest, she feared most what his arrest
would do to their kids. She beseeched him to return to general medicine. But come fall, Boyd drove west in a U-Haul loaded with the gear
of his three procedure rooms: exam tables and lamps, curettes and cannulas. The family followed, settling with Boyd a few hundred miles west
in an adobe house on a dirt road beside the Santa Fe River.

New Mexico law required that abortion be performed in a hospital.
But Boyd wished to work only with his trusted aide, and Cox helped
Boyd resettle their clinic into the home she rented in the Atalaya Hills.
Soon after, she set off to the Albuquerque airport, there to gather the
first of the women the clergy sent their way.

So as to find each other, Cox and the women had agreed to wear
something red—a blouse or shoes or coat or flower in the hair. They
then piled into the yellow Ford wagon with room for nine that Boyd had
bought to transport his patients from airport to clinic.

The trip was sixty miles. The women spoke en route, telling of
the diaphragms that had failed in Shreveport and San Antonio, of the

grandfathers who had molested them in St. Louis and Denver, of the families of five in Houston and Oklahoma City that simply could not afford a sixth. And when, along Interstate 25, morning sickness took hold of a passenger, Cox gave her a basin and told her what awaited—the sedative and the pelvic exam and the doctor in the white coat who would end any pregnancy through its sixteenth week.

Boyd didn't think of his work as the termination of something. He had come to see abortion, he says, as a means of fulfillment, of self-preservation. Still, one hemorrhage could land him in prison. And, says Cox, "he was meticulous." He was lucky, too. When once a woman lied to him about the stage of her pregnancy and the doctor accidentally perforated her uterus, bringing down a piece of bowel, he rushed her to a hospital where a doctor he knew performed surgery and kept his secret. The woman recovered.

Such emergencies were rare. Nearly all who made the trek to Boyd flew home only hours later, no longer pregnant and thankful for the doctor who for $300 had let them resume their lives. "And then," says Cox, "the women were gone forever."

Months passed and Boyd did his work undisturbed. He was happy to have left Texas. He would keep his eye on *Roe*.

———

BLACKMUN LIKED TO WORK in his chambers, to look out at a favorite cherry tree from behind his mahogany desk in the southeast corner of the high court building. It was a soothing space, light blue walls rising about a cranberry rug. But the office had its distractions: a secretary, clerks, a phone. And often, the justice carried his colored pencils and perforated pads up two flights of marble steps to the library, where, of all the justices, only he worked.

The work was urgent; in the coming term, the Court would rule, for example, on the death penalty. And the hours were long; save for lunch and calisthenics in the afternoon, Blackmun took no breaks, returning home at 6:30 to continue working until Dottie rung a bell to call him for dinner.

Blackmun enjoyed his dinners at home. They were a time for the father "to throw some question out," says daughter Nancy. And it was over dinner, toward the close of 1971—days before Lewis Powell and William Rehnquist joined the Court—that Blackmun asked his wife and three daughters about abortion. The four women, though, were of four minds, and the judge was exasperated. "You people don't understand me at all!" Nancy recalls her father saying. He threw down his napkin.

It had been left to Blackmun to address the laws at stake in *Roe* and *Doe*, and the constitutional issues behind them. He returned to the library, reading of law and abortion in a green reclining chair, his loafered feet up. But the justice was uncertain where to find in the Constitution legal grounds for abortion, uncertain when in the course of a pregnancy those grounds might expire.

It was thus with self-doubt that, on May 18, 1972, Blackmun circulated a memo on *Roe* to his colleagues. Its seventeen pages did not address whether there was a constitutional right to abortion. They merely argued that the Texas abortion law was unconstitutionally vague, or, as Blackmun put it, "insufficiently informative to the physician to whom it purports to afford a measure of professional protection." Blackmun called his memo "a first and tentative draft," and added that he was "still flexible as to results."

The justices were not impressed. They had wanted, as William Brennan now wrote to Blackmun, "a disposition of the core constitutional question." And so, they made two decisions. First, *Roe* and *Doe* would be reargued in the fall (before a full complement of judges). Second, Blackmun would have another go at his memos.

Blackmun turned to a clerk for help. Recalls John Rich: "The *Roe* case came to me."

Rich had come to the Court six months before, at the age of twenty-eight. Like the judge, the clerk had studied math at Harvard, devoting a subsequent year to philosophy. Law, though, had long been an interest; Rich wrote in high school about the Fourteenth Amendment, and in college about the Fifth. Eager to commit himself, in an era of civil rights, to something less abstract than math, he had applied to law school, studying at Yale and then Oxford before clerking for a judge whose work on the insanity defense Blackmun admired. Blackmun phoned Rich himself to offer a clerkship.

Back in December, Rich had helped Blackmun to ready for *Roe*, writing a bench memo that distilled the issues at play, chief among them whether the Texas abortion statutes were unconstitutional or vague. The clerk now typed up another memo, fourteen pages of suggestions small and large—a different word to describe the relationship of pregnancy to nonmootness ("justification"), a different justification for the Does' lack of standing.

Blackmun had also to absorb the briefs filed by the opposing parties—one of which sought to humanize the fetus (that which "requires only nutrition and time to develop into one of us"), the other the woman who carried it (she whom the law forced "to serve as an incubator for months and then as an ostensibly willing mother"). There were other supporting briefs too, fifteen opinions submitted to the Court by a mix of doctors and lawyers and clergy.

For all that, Blackmun wished to know more. There was the history of abortion—medical, legal and otherwise. And there was the continuing matter of its constitutionality. And so, when John Rich completed his clerkship in July, the justice turned to another clerk.

His name was George Frampton. Like Rich, he was twenty-eight and left-leaning and from the Great Lakes, like Rich the son of a professor who had come to the Court with degrees from Harvard and Yale and interests that extended beyond the law. Having gotten his BA in physics and philosophy, and an MA in economic theory, Frampton had spent the two years since his JD far from the law—volunteering with Vista in inner-city New York, driving a cab, joining a peace initiative in the Middle East where he had lived with wife, Betsy, on a kibbutz in the Galilee amidst mushrooms and apples.

A law school classmate clerking for Blackmun had mentioned his fascinating friend. And when Frampton met the justice over tea, he overcame his hesitation to work for a judge he viewed as conservative. "Blackmun," says Frampton, "was such a nice, modest, sweet, down-to-earth man."

Frampton had been clerking for ten months when the justice turned to him for help on *Roe*. "'You write the legal part and I'll write the facts,'" Frampton recalls Blackmun telling him. With that, the justice drove to Minnesota.

Blackmun was off to the Mayo Clinic, the medical research center he had served as counsel. There, over a fortnight of reading in late July, he found answers, filling notepads with facts and citations that convinced him, among much else, that early-term abortions were safer than childbirth and that, as the journalist Linda Greenhouse summarized, "the criminalization of abortion was a relatively recent phenomenon."

Back at the Court, Frampton was typing away on his IBM Selectric. Blackmun was still in Minnesota when the clerk finished his draft. He asked the justice's secretary to lock it in a desk drawer out of reach of the incoming clerks. Says Frampton: "I didn't want them to get their hands on it."

Blackmun read the draft, ready to pencil in comments between the triple-spaced type. The draft made two fundamental claims: that the right to privacy did indeed encompass abortion, and that that right could be extended through the second trimester of pregnancy. Impressed, Blackmun put his pencil down. Says Frampton: "he took that with very few edits and sent it to be printed."

Still, Blackmun continued his research, reading in late August of a Gallup poll about abortion and public opinion. The numbers were striking. Significant majorities of Republicans, Democrats and even Catholics agreed that "the decision to have an abortion should be made solely by a woman and her physician." The judge filed away the article and readied for *Roe*. The case was to be reargued in six weeks.

———

ON OCTOBER 11, 1972, two years after appealing *Roe* to the Supreme Court, Coffee returned there.

Roe had not much changed her life. Having packed away the quill pens given her by the Court, she still worked in bankruptcy. She was still single, too, telling United Press International back in February that she dated "intelligent, educated men." And while Coffee delighted in the prospect of seeing abortion legalized, her co-counsel delighted no less in being the one to argue for its legalization. Ten months after Weddington did so, her life had been upended. She had quit her job as a city attorney in Fort Worth after her boss objected to her returning to the Court to argue *Roe* a second time. "I could not bear the thought," wrote

Weddington, "of not being involved in the Supreme Court action." But after opening a firm in Austin with her husband and running for state representative, her marriage had begun to falter. The election was upcoming as Weddington rose to argue *Roe* a second time.

As before, Weddington argued for the right of women to privacy. As before, the state argued that it had a compelling interest in preserving fetal life.

Both lawyers had studied the judicial inclinations of the nine men now seated before them, of the two Williams, Douglas and Brennan, for example, who had, respectively, authored *Griswold* and *Eisenstadt v. Baird*, a recent case about contraception that extended the right of privacy from married couples to individuals. But of the experiences that might have informed those inclinations, the lawyers knew nothing. The fight for abortion was grounded in privacy for good reason. Simply put, even though abortion touched millions of lives, it was bound up in sex and in shame. And on this Wednesday morning, those millions included not only Weddington, who'd had an abortion, but Justice Lewis Powell.

Powell was a lawyer in Virginia when a young messenger at his firm took his girlfriend to get an illegal abortion. The abortion killed her. The messenger had been charged with manslaughter, and went to Powell for help.

Powell had said nothing publicly of that experience—just as Weddington had said nothing of her abortion, and Blackmun had said nothing of the unwanted pregnancy in his family. And yet those experiences undoubtedly informed their thinking on abortion; the two Nixon appointees, like the minister's daughter, were pro-choice. Personal experience opened eyes. As Oliver Wendell Holmes wrote in 1881: "The life of the law has not been logic: it has been experience."

═══

TWO DAYS AFTER LISTENING to *Roe* argued a second time, only Byron White and William Rehnquist were sided with Texas. Granted a 7–2 majority, Blackmun returned to the opinion that would shape the rest of his life.

It had been eleven months since Burger assigned him *Roe*. Blackmun had still not settled on when exactly in the course of a pregnancy abortion ought to tip from legal to illegal—on when, in other words, the interest of the state in the fetus would supersede the interests of the woman. He had settled temporarily on the end of the first trimester. But Justice Powell now suggested to him the end of the second trimester— the point at which a fetus could survive outside the womb. That point was known as viability.

It was Frampton who'd introduced the concept of viability to Blackmun. The clerk had read of it the previous year, he says, in at least two articles, one written by retired Supreme Court Justice Tom Clark, the other by a lawyer named Cyril Means. It had struck him as wise. "Viability seemed like the obvious mix of science and religion, or science and ethics," says Frampton. He adds: "This court [was] not going to say that until the baby pops out and is given a name and is put in a bassinet, that baby has no rights."

Frampton had left the Court in August. A month later, in September 1972, a district judge in Connecticut named Jon O. Newman had become the first to attach constitutional significance to viability. Blackmun became the second. "With respect to the State's important and legitimate interest in potential life," he wrote into his third and final draft of Roe, "the 'compelling' point is at viability."

A watershed opinion had been written. Upon its release the next month, tens of millions of American women would have a constitutional right to end their pregnancies.

Blackmun situated that right within the right to privacy. He situated the right to privacy within the Fourteenth Amendment (not the Ninth, as the Texas court had thirty months before). And he situated his decision—Roe v. Wade, 410 U.S. 113—within millennia of jurisprudence, his opinion referencing sources from Plato to Parliament. Blackmun circulated the opinion to his fellow justices four days before Christmas. They were impressed, complimentary even in dissent.

Blackmun was mindful, however, that others might not be; his opinion would negate statutes in forty-six states and the District of Columbia. As he had jotted on a notepad two months before: "It will be an unsettled period for a while."

Chapter 11

Mildred Jefferson arrived in impeccable dress at the WGBH-TV studio in Boston. Her fellow Harvard alum, Justice Blackmun, was due to deliver his *Roe* opinion any day. In anticipation of it, the doctor readied, in December 1972, to speak to the camera of the evils of abortion.

Mildred had first taken to the airwaves back in July 1970, decrying abortion in a debate aired on Boston's Channel 2. She had only just awakened to the procedure, roused by the decision of the American Medical Association to suddenly accept what for so long it had not. She'd marshaled medicine and science in her arguments, speaking of fetal development and hysterotomy abortion—the removal of a fetus through an incision in the abdomen.

That same year of 1970, the pro-life community had also begun to turn toward science, after a Benedictine priest and professor in Minnesota named Paul Marx showed his Catholic students a medical film of an abortion. The students had recoiled, and the movement was thus transformed. "Instead of simply rehashing the philosophical and constitutional arguments against abortion legalization," observed professor Daniel Williams, "the pro-life movement would use the power of fetal photography to convince the public that every abortion killed a human baby." Indeed, by the close of 1972, such photographs (magnified and in color) would help to sell 1.5 million copies of "Handbook on Abortion," a tidy grouping of questions and answers written by a pro-life Cincinnati obstetrician and his wife.

Barbara Rockett saw in Mildred the same potential to transform. Rockett had enlisted Mildred to the cause after hearing her decry abortion at a medical meeting. And after watching her on TV, she spoke of Mildred to a priest named Paul Harrington, who then wrote to the doctor. Identifying himself as a representative of "the Catholic Bishops of Massachusetts on the abortion issue," the monsignor praised Mildred's presentation and hoped she might thenceforth provide "helpful assistance."

Mildred thanked the priest. She was open to collaborating. But she also wished to elucidate her position. She was, she wrote, "not so much 'against abortion' as . . . 'for the sanctity of life.'" She added that what upset her even more than abortion was that doctors were performing them.

To stand for life was, suddenly, to stand against the medical establishment, that which Mildred still hoped to join. And, in the fall of 1970, she founded, with Dr. Rockett and others, the Value of Life Committee, an organization dedicated to saving the unborn from "their destruction."

VOLCOM's opposition to abortion was not absolute; it opposed those abortions "sought for economic, sociologic or eugenic reasons, or for reasons of convenience." But Mildred had little sympathy for the woman carrying an unwanted fetus. Such a woman could have chosen (as she had) to abstain from sex or to practice birth control. (Mildred approved of diaphragms, condoms and "educated rhythm.") And unlike others in the pro-life movement who presented women as victims of male doctors, Mildred did not. Hers was a philosophy of self-determination; pity was pitiful, abortion too. "The woman who arranges her life haphazardly, relying on abortion to remove complications," wrote Mildred, "is unworthy of being called woman." Of those "complications" come of rape or incest, she simply wrote, "Society's efforts should be turned to ameliorating the circumstances that result in unwanted pregnancy."

Mildred feared a change in the law; her eye was on *Roe*. In 1972, she was among the signatories of a brief filed to the Court that she later described as "scientific evidence of the humanity of the unborn." Mildred sought to advance this idea not only with medical slides and arresting language but with her self-described "20-tooth smile."

Mildred's crusade left little time for her husband. If Shane wished to be at her side, he says, he had to accompany her to VOLCOM meetings. Abortion left Mildred little time for medicine, too.

⸻

MEDICINE HAD ONCE CONSUMED MILDRED. Back in 1951, she had been a new MD and aspiring surgeon when she told a reporter that what most defined her was "singleness of purpose." That purpose had gone unfulfilled. Twenty years after medical school, her board certification had still not come.

But in 1971, she completed her stint as chief resident in surgery. And the following spring, at long last, the American Board of Surgery certified Dr. Mildred Fay Jefferson.

The moment was bittersweet. A lifelong goal had finally been realized. It had, however, been so long deferred that the dream had withered. More, it had given way to another career. Still, she who at age seven had snipped the frenum of her tongue-tied cousin and dreamed of becoming a surgeon now resolved at forty-five to find time for medicine, opening a medical practice on Harrison Avenue at the Boston University Medical Center.

The university quickly made Mildred an assistant clinical professor of surgery. But board certification did not change her lot. Mildred remained, as the director of surgical services at Boston City Hospital put it, "a black female . . . competing in a man's world." Though she needed desperately to build her practice, and more than once asked the chairman of surgery at her hospital to refer patients to her, he "refused to do so," he acknowledged, even as he attested to knowing "nothing of a derogatory nature concerning her."

Mildred would not speak publicly of her ordeal. She rebuffed the overtures of a Boston caucus devoted to black students and faculty. "I have found the whole emphasis on ethnicity and separatism self-defeating," she wrote in reply. "There is no way to say 'black is beautiful' without provoking a response of 'white is right.' I prefer to let my life speak for itself."

Of course, that life had been shaped by the realities of race and gender. And two decades after her graduation from Harvard had turned her
into a celebrity—the first black woman to do this and that—Mildred
had grown disillusioned. She was apt to speak in private not of the
determinative power of her will but of an existential unfairness that
her thwarted career had only confirmed. And she had thus chosen not
to conceive a child with her white husband, never mind that childlessness was at odds with everything she publicly stood for: the power of
self-determination, the insistence that every conception culminate in a
birth, the assertion that propagation was the very purpose of woman—
"the essence and reasons we exist as female human beings," she later
said. In perhaps the only public comment she would ever make on her
childlessness, Jefferson alluded both to the inequity of life, and to her
midlife conversion from nurture to nature. Said Jefferson: "I believe
that biology is destiny."

Mildred stood, in 1972, at a road forking between medicine and
activism. She knew which direction she would travel. The same facts
of her birth that were obstacles to overcome in medicine were, in the
pro-life movement, assets, her race and gender and religion of great
benefit to a community desperate to expand beyond white Catholic
men. Indeed, the doctor—a black Methodist woman—embodied the
movement's aspirations.

There was something else about Mildred that foretold the future
of the movement: she saw great opportunity in politics. As she would
soon tell the Senate: "right-to-life organizations will become a permanent part of the political scene."

———

IF EITHER POLITICAL PARTY could be seen, in the run-up to _Roe_, as puta-
tively pro-life, it was the Democratic; Catholics had long tended to be
Democrats, and flag-bearing politically liberal Catholics like Edward
Kennedy denounced abortion without pause. But pro-life efforts to for-
mally ally themselves with the left had gained little traction in the sixties, and family planning remained resolutely nonpartisan. Republican
Dwight Eisenhower and Democrat Harry Truman—former presidents
bound by a fear of overpopulation—came together in 1965 to co-chair

a Planned Parenthood committee. And in 1967, twelve Democratic and nine Republican senators supported the Therapeutic Abortion Act in California, which made abortion legal through twenty weeks so as to protect the mental or physical health of the pregnant woman.

Two years later, prominent Republicans weighed in. "We need to make population and family planning household words," Representative George H. W. Bush told Congress in February 1969. Added President Nixon in July: "No American woman should be denied access to family planning assistance because of her economic condition."

Nixon would soon sign a bill subsidizing contraception and abortion, too, the latter at military hospitals. But then he about-faced. For, as the professors Linda Greenhouse and Reva Siegel would observe four decades later, Republican strategists had come to identify Catholics and, more specifically, abortion, as rich in political opportunity. In March 1971, the president (prompted by a memo from advisor Pat Buchanan) revoked the permissive abortion policy he had only just instituted and disavowed a report on population growth that advocated the nullification of "unwanted fertility." "Abortion on demand," announced Nixon, "I cannot square with my personal belief in the sanctity of human life— including the life of the yet unborn."

Nixon's support buoyed the pro-life movement. Having watched in dismay as sixteen states legalized abortion in various circumstances from 1967 through 1970, the movement now helped to defeat all twenty-five legalization initiatives proposed in 1971. But in 1972, the pro-choice found in courts, both state and federal, the victories denied them by legislatures; judicial rulings legalized or liberalized abortion laws in seven states.

If the American legal battle over abortion was in its infancy, its political battle had only just been conceived. And in the months leading up to the *Roe* ruling, the fight for public opinion took to the air like the seeds of a dandelion. In October, one month before a referendum on abortion in Michigan, the Catholic church funded ads throughout the state which suggested to priests that they correlate the question of whether to have an abortion with the question of whether to shoot one's neighbor. In November, upwards of 65 million people watched a two-part episode of *Maude*, a new TV sitcom on CBS, whose protagonist found herself pregnant at forty-seven. (She chose to have an abortion.) And in December, a woman named Jimmye Kimmey homed in on the word "choice" as the most effective rejoinder to "life." "Right to life is short, catchy, composed of monosyllabic words—an important consideration in English," wrote Kimmey, the director of an organization advocating the repeal of abortion law. "We need something comparable. Right to choose would seem to do the job."

————

MILDRED JEFFERSON APPRECIATED the power of words. She could use them to bludgeon or inspire, and she rewrote her favorite sentences until they were just right. Between 1972 and 1973, for example, she changed her declaration that it was not yet time "to legislate that only the wanted, the perfect and the privileged have the right to be born" to "the perfect, the privileged and the planned"—an alliteration the movement would come to summon without cease.

Mildred's name was carrying. And yet, few knew who she was. Her desire for privacy was becoming almost pathological, the doctor inviting no one to her home, letting slip, as Daniel Williams put it, "no snippets of autobiography."

Mildred was guarded for good reason. Not only was her husband white and her father estranged and her title as surgeon misleading, but her hoarding had forced her husband from her home.

Shane still saw Mildred daily, if only to drive her about—to her ailing mother in Roxbury, to yet another pro-life function. The *Roe* ruling was imminent when, in December 1972, he drove her to the WGBH-TV studio in Boston.

The station was a member of PBS. It had invited Mildred and three others to debate abortion on a national TV show called *The Advocates*. Asked on air to define abortion, Mildred was mindful, as always, to humanize the fetus. An abortion, she said, was any method "to get rid of the boy or girl before it can be born."

Mildred then described those methods, speaking in her clear contralto of suction and D & C and saline and hysterotomy, narrating a carousel of graphic slides with plain and unhurried language: "This makes a mush of the developing baby. . . . Arms, legs and ribs may not break down so easily. . . . This one had the outer layer of its skin scalded off." The audience sat silent, agape. When a young lawyer from the ACLU named Brenda Fasteau asked Mildred if illegal abortion did not lead to horrors worse than those she had just described, Shane listened as Mildred parried the question. What mattered, she said, was what could be done to prevent those horrors. "The alternative to illegal abortion is not legal abortion," she said. "It's not being pregnant at the time when one should not be."

Fasteau tried again. What of the mother of four who finds herself pregnant at thirty-nine and "feels she simply cannot raise another child?"

The doctor did not answer. To be a mother at thirty-nine, said Mildred, is to be thought attractive at thirty-nine. "Having a baby is one of the guarantees—absolute proof—that you are sexy." The room burst into applause, the lawyer unable to respond before time ran out.

Lawrence Lader watched in dismay. PBS had broadcast the segment on stations around the country, and the airing of fetal slides, he felt, presented by the doctor, had been horribly effective. As he told the board at NARAL, the advocacy group he had helped to found: "Their impact was overwhelming."

Philip Moran agreed. Moran was a local lawyer who'd met Mildred months before through the pro-life advocate Joseph Stanton. The three were among the organizers of Massachusetts Citizens for Life, a lay-led organization that would incorporate in one month and soon after join the National Right to Life Committee, a pro-life umbrella group that would become the most powerful in the nation. Seeing Mildred on television, he was in awe. "I remember watching that show and thinking, this woman is the greatest," says Moran. He adds: "That's what propelled her onto the national stage."

All at once, Mildred was a pro-life celebrity.

Off in Sacramento, the governor of California had tuned in. Ronald Reagan had supported legal abortion, signing into law the 1967 Therapeutic Abortion Act. The bill had made abortion legal when pregnancy threatened the physical or mental health of a woman, and Reagan had expressed confidence that Californians would support its "humanitarian goals." Still, Reagan had not thought the bill perfect; he lamented, for example, that it did not require the women getting abortions to live in-state or the facilities providing them to be of a certain size. He'd also insisted that the bill drop a provision allowing abortion in cases of fetal deformity. Now, more than five years later, a doctor on television had convinced Reagan to oppose *all* abortion except to save the life of a woman. The governor sat down to write her a letter.

"I had to tell you how truly great you were in your testimony on the 'Advocates,'" Reagan wrote to Mildred on January 17, 1973. "I wish I could have heard your views before our legislation was passed. You made it irrefutably clear that an abortion is the taking of human life."

Five days later, the Supreme Court would make clear that the law disagreed.

Chapter 12

At ten o'clock on the winter morning of January 22, 1973, nine men robed in black sat down on chairs of mahogany, eight of them quiet as the author of their forthcoming opinion in *Roe v. Wade* began to read a statement about the case.

"The abortion issue, of course, is a most sensitive, emotional and controversial one," Harry Blackmun said, after describing the statutes that had brought *Roe* and *Doe* to the Court. "We are aware of this, and we are fully aware that, however the Court decides these cases, the controversy will continue."

Blackmun had long recognized the challenge of adjudicating abortion. He noted in the second paragraph of his opinion "the deep and seemingly absolute convictions that the subject inspires." Indeed, even those justices who concurred with his opinion weighed in, three of them penning opinions of their own. Two more wrote in dissent—six opinions in all.

The courtroom was full, Sally Blackmun among the throng. Pregnant and unmarried six years before as a sophomore in college, she had worried that to have an abortion, as she later wrote, was to risk not only physical harm but "embarrassment to my family and [my father's] career." Now, newly divorced, she waited to hear if he had ruled on the side of choice.

Blackmun continued. He noted the legal history of abortion, that the question of when life begins was an open one, that the Court believed that a right to privacy was implicit in the Constitution, that there were two state interests the Court had had to protect: "the health of the pregnant woman" and "the potentiality of human life."

"We thus have, in tension," Blackmun continued, "the pregnant woman's right of privacy, on one hand, and these two distinct state interests, on the other."

The justice then spoke his ruling: agency over the fetus would transfer incrementally—trimester by trimester—from woman to state. "Viewed under this analysis," he concluded, "the Texas statute must fall."

The statutes of forty-five other states and the District of Columbia would fall too (among them statutes invalidated by *Roe*'s companion case, *Doe v. Bolton*). And though in time Blackmun would, at this same mahogany bench, participate in 3,874 rulings, he would henceforth be known for just one.

A team of printers had turned that singular ruling into linotype, typesetting hot lead in the basement of the Court. And a group of reporters and editors now turned their newly printed copies of *Roe*, fifty-one warm pages, into news and editorials. *Roe*, wrote the *New York Times*, was "a major contribution to the preservation of individual liberties and of free decision-making." The *Washington Post* called it "wise and sound . . . balanced and graduated." The *Wall Street Journal* felt it had "struck a reasonable balance on an exceedingly difficult question."

The *Journal* did, however, express reservation over "whether the court stepped too far into the legislative arena." It was a question that had been asked about the Supreme Court before.

Policy-making is primarily the function of legislators, not judges. But sometimes, a case invalidates a law. *Lochner v. New York*, for example, overturned a New York law that capped the number of hours in a workday. Justice Oliver Wendell Holmes dissented in that 1905 ruling, writing of "the right of a [public] majority to embody their opinions in law." That the will of the majority (and its elected representatives) could be invalidated by a mere nonet of unelected judges would come to be called, in the words of a law professor, "the counter-majoritarian difficulty." The difficulty often arises in cases centering on issues not specifically addressed in the Constitution. One such issue is sex. The 1965 case upon which *Roe* rested, *Griswold v. Connecticut*, had also begotten accusations of overstepping; Justice Hugo Black had accused his fellow justices of usurping "from Congress and States the power to make laws based on their own judgment of fairness and wisdom."

Eight years later, Byron White wrote much the same. He and William Rehnquist alone on the Court opposed *Roe*, and White argued in his dissent that the ruling was "an exercise of raw judicial power." White made clear that he also found distasteful *Roe*'s assertion that, as he wrote, the Constitution "values the convenience, whim, or caprice of the putative mother more than the life or potential life of the fetus."

Blackmun left the capital two days after the ruling, flying to Iowa to give a speech in the hometown of one of his clerks. His presence sparked protest. "Picketed!—" noted Blackmun in his planner, "police protection."

The protection was necessary. Among various conservatives and Christians, *Roe* was anathema. J. P. McFadden, on staff at the *National Review*, described it as "morally indistinguishable from Hitler's genocide." William Buckley, who founded that magazine, likened it to the case of Dred Scott, the notorious Supreme Court ruling that in 1857 denied freedom to a black man. The evangelical magazine *Christianity Today* called it a victory "for paganism," while the National Conference of Catholic Bishops described it as "erroneous, unjust and immoral."

Blackmun had expected backlash. But the righteous anger was nonetheless jarring. He was a sensitive man, prone to melancholy; his favorite piece of music was "Liebesleid," ("Love's Sorrow)," a plaintive Viennese melody. And as he began to read his way through the first of some eighty thousand letters that he would receive about *Roe*, he held onto their wrath, recalling decades later the letters that likened him to Pontius Pilate and Hitler, his death prayed for, his birth mourned.

That it was Blackmun who was assailed was ironic; it was at the suggestion of others that his opinion had moved the legal threshold for abortion forward by a trimester. More, the justice had sought initially to void the Texas law on the simple grounds of vagueness, without holding that there was any constitutional right to abortion.

Still, for every curse cast at Blackmun there was a blessing, for every pro-life wail a pro-choice exhalation. The president of Planned

Parenthood called *Roe* "wise and courageous." Added M*s*. magazine: "this ruling will mean much less suffering."

———

ON THE JANUARY morning *Roe* was announced, Curtis Boyd was, as every Monday, in his New Mexico clinic performing abortions in defiance of the law. The radio was tuned to NPR in the hope of news on *Roe*.

Boyd was not optimistic. That a court laden with four Nixon appointees would rule for *Roe* he could not fathom. And so, it was a shock to hear that, suddenly, his work was legal. *Roe* had, in fact, affirmed the rights of doctors even more explicitly than the autonomy of women.

"It's all over. It's all over. The issue has been won," a dumbstruck Boyd stood thinking. Recalls his aide, Eva Cox: "we walked around almost in disbelief."

Roe took effect at once; this same day, a doctor in Texas named Fred Hansen performed a legal abortion on a nurse who'd planned to end her pregnancy out of state. The clergy who worked with Boyd wished him to reopen his Dallas clinic immediately, arranging for a line of credit to help him do so. Within the month, Boyd hired two doctors and bought a small wooden building, opening the first legal clinic in all of Texas, Louisiana, Arkansas, and Oklahoma.

Boyd commuted weekly between his two clinics, closing one when he traveled to the other. It was surreal to practice in plain view. But the doctor had been wrong; his work, post-*Roe*, was no less fraught, his battle not ended. In fact, it quickly intensified. For the change in law antagonized those opposed to it—among them the residents of Athens, Texas, dismayed by their native son. "Preachers were preaching about [Boyd] from the pulpit," his wife, LaMerle, recalled decades later. Boyd, though, was undeterred. And his wife suddenly understood that he would, ever more, hold fast to abortion to the exclusion of all else—even her. The couple spoke.

"My commitment was to the cause, to a fair and just society," Boyd recalls telling LaMerle. "She thought 'fair and just' didn't involve her and the children. And all I could say was, 'You're right.'" The divorce was quick, the doctor offering up money, not time. "He would not agree to any child visitation schedule because he was too busy," recalls

LaMerle. Boyd was free now to devote himself wholly to abortion, and he soon had both his clinics running simultaneously.

═══════

IT HAD BEEN more than a century since abortion was legal throughout the United States. But the country quickly adjusted to *Roe*. The IRS made abortions tax-deductible. A majority of insurance companies included abortion in their maternity benefits. Clinics opened in thirty-four states. And by the end of 1973, at least 745,000 women had ended pregnancies in compliance with the law.

Mildred Jefferson was horrified. *Roe*, she wrote, had enabled the American woman "to put a contract on her unborn child."

Roe also inspired the pro-life movement to identify a new core objective—undoing *Roe*. As its machinery hummed to life with protests and amendments and "photo-postcards of aborted babies" mailed to legislators, Mildred gave voice to it all, the silver-tongued doctor speaking at age forty-five not only for VOLCOM, which she had helped to found, but for Massachusetts Citizens for Life, Americans United for Life, the National Right to Life Committee and, thirteen days after *Roe*, the Community Church of Boston. The church rented a town hall on Clarendon Street where Mildred read some five thousand words that moved from fetus to philosophy. *Roe*, she concluded, was emblematic of a society with "an extermination complex."

Many agreed. And many defied the law. The National Conference of Catholic Bishops instructed hospital workers to refuse "to provide abortion on request." State legislatures did the same; come April, pro-choice activist Lawrence Lader noted that across the South, "almost no public hospitals are complying with the Court decision." Just eight days after *Roe*, a Maryland congressman proposed the first of many "human life amendments," or HLAs, to the U.S. Constitution.

The amendments stated that personhood began at conception. American law did not agree; Weddington's *Roe* brief had made clear that a fetus was not a person in the eyes of the Constitution, noting "there are no cases which hold that fetuses are protected by the Fourteenth Amendment."

Nonetheless, tantalized by the prospect of negating *Roe*, the

National Right to Life Committee, a polity of pro-lifers incorporated just after the ruling, threw its growing weight behind the amendments; by April, it had induced sixteen state legislatures to call for their passage in Congress. The NRLC, wrote Daniel Williams, "effectively redefined the movement."

Mildred was part of that redefinition. The NRLC board carried representatives of each state, and come June, the transplanted Texan represented hers. Soon after, the NRLC elected Mildred vice chair of the board.

Still, the doctor angled for more, making known at every turn her pedigree, that of a minister's daughter turned surgeon. She caught the eye of President Richard Nixon, who wished to appoint her to a medical board. In March 1973, just six weeks after *Roe*, Nixon's deputy assistant, Alexander Butterfield, requested that the FBI vet her, and the bureau quickly interviewed thirty-six of her acquaintances. L. Patrick Gray III, the bureau's acting director, reported back to the White House that "all . . . comment favorably concerning her character, associates, loyalty and reputation."

Still, some of those interviewed expressed concerns. Dr. Sidney Farber, who'd known Mildred both at Harvard and at his clinic, raved about the doctor: "a superior woman whose potential has yet to be tapped." But the renowned researcher also feared that the misogyny that had railroaded her career had left her with a "possible resentment" that might infect her work.

Mildred was still awaiting her presidential appointment when, months later, on a Sunday in October, she stood before a crowd of thirty thousand people assembled to call for passage of an HLA.

The crowd stood outside the Missouri state courthouse. There, seven white judges had once ruled that a black man named Dred Scott was not legally a person. The great-granddaughter of slaves now argued that a fetus was.

Mildred issued a warning to pro-choice politicians. "We will consider they are bargaining in blood," she said, "and will not vote for them." The doctor also took aim at doctors. Said Mildred: "I am not willing that my profession should exchange the role of healer for that of social executioner."

Mildred could afford to decry the medical community. She was less and less a part of it. An article she wrote that year on bile ducts was the second and last she would ever publish in a medical journal. And save the occasional consultation, she practiced no medicine. Opposing abortion was now both her life and her living.

———

LINDA COFFEE HAD NEVER imagined that of all the abortion cases, it would be *Roe* that secured a federal right to abortion. Back when she first appealed the federal panel's ruling, abortion cases were pending in eleven other states. But on this Monday, a car radio told her that *Roe* had made abortion legal throughout the land. She phoned Weddington.

President Johnson had died that same day; Coffee spoke first of LBJ and then of *Roe*. Weddington had already heard the news. Back in November, she had won election to the Texas House of Representatives. And at the State Capitol, first thing that morning, well-wishers and reporters had flooded her office with flowers and calls for comment—the *New York Times*, the *Today* show, the Associated Press.

The wire service identified Weddington as the lawyer "who submitted the class action suit that led to Monday's ruling." Neither she nor Coffee would ever correct the record—Weddington happy to absorb the recognition of two, Coffee to go unrecognized. Says Coffee: "I don't particularly care."

Her mother, however, did. Days later, inside the Dallas headquarters of the Baptist General Convention of Texas, where Mary Coffee worked as a secretary, a reporter for the Baptist Press overheard her speaking of her daughter. Recalls Robert O'Brien: "She was proud."

The mother could afford to be. For although evangelicals were shifting on the matter of abortion, the Southern Baptist Convention had resolved in 1971 to protect "the emotional, mental and physical health of the mother." Sitting down with Linda Coffee in her law office, O'Brien found a woman of two minds. On the one hand, Coffee was confident in the rightness of *Roe*. Indeed, her chief complaint with it, as she would soon tell a student at Baylor writing a thesis on *Roe*, was that she felt the law ought not to restrict abortion until the third trimester. And yet, as she now told O'Brien, she "would have little personal sympathy for a woman who used abortion at any stage as contraception or to avoid personal responsibility." She added: "From my personal Christian perspective, it would tear me up to have to make such a decision, unless an abortion took place in the very early stages." Coffee then clarified the point. "I don't think there's a moral responsibility," she said, "to continue a pregnancy which is only at the point where life will eventually result."

Coffee would assert years later that to believe in personhood at conception "is essentially a matter of faith." Coffee did not have that faith, did not believe in God. She did, though, put stock in the Bible; back in high school, her knowledge of it had won her a pin from a local jeweler. And she enjoyed religion. She was no less a member of the Park Cities Baptist Church than she was a feminist who months before had supported Shirley Chisholm, the New York legislator turned congresswoman, for president. The O'Brien piece—a meditation on the difficulty of reconciling sex and religion—was thus true to Coffee.

The reporter hoped to speak to Jane Roe next. Three days after winning her case, Coffee contacted Norma to see if she wished to remain anonymous.

NORMA HAD NOT heard from Coffee in the nearly three years since Coffee arrived at her home on San Jacinto Street with an affidavit to sign. Norma had obliged but moved on, telling no one that she was Roe—not her mother in a trailer on a riverbank in Louisiana or her father fixing TVs in an electronics shop in Old East Dallas or the women she drank with in gay bars in midtown or even Consuela Gonzales, her partner of two-plus years.

The women had met when Norma applied for a job at a market off Fort Worth Avenue, and Gonzales, the manager, drove her home. The women were almost seventeen years apart. But they were soon a couple, and Norma took to calling Gonzales "my little boy."

Gonzales had been born in Dallas in 1931 to Spanish and Mexican parents. She was their fifth surviving child; two had died. The family was poor, with high cheekbones and brown eyes and little else. They ate beans and tortillas, hammered coffee can lids underfoot to keep mice from filling the frame house they rented on Pearl Street. Father Antonio, a tailor's assistant, was not around and mother Clementia ironed clothes at a laundromat in downtown Dallas, returning home exhausted.

Jesus offered ballast. And the mother passed to her kids a love of both the Catholic church and manual labor—the young Consuela, who went by "Connie," committing herself to both, to a lifetime of holy cards and hard work.

The girl was strong. She could lift and carry as much as most boys. And she was not long out of elementary school at Cumberland Hill when she began to hammer and paint and caulk, to build things and repair junk. One had to hustle. One had to get by. After she miscarried as a young teen, Gonzales never got pregnant again; better to have no child, she felt, than one not cared for. Besides, men were not for her.

Gonzales did not tell her mother that she was gay. But others did. "She was seen in public," says her niece, Mary Helen Sandoval. "Gossip." Connie soon left home.

Decades later, Gonzales had had few relationships when in 1971, she met Norma. They got along well, one liberated at twenty-three, one responsible at forty. Gonzales suggested that Norma have her tubes tied. Norma did so. "I told her," recalls Gonzales, "you could have a better life."

Norma was not in a good place. She was getting by in Old East Dallas, selling an underground newspaper devoted to the narcotics, the amphetamines and barbiturates, coursing through Texas. Norma herself took "mostly downers," she said. They left her depressed. Only months before, having just given up a third child, she had been high and drunk on Wild Turkey when she tried to kill herself a second time, cutting her wrists with a safety pin. "I passed out," said Norma. "My dad discovered me."

A band of thin parallel scars was still forming on her wrists when Norma met Connie, moving weeks later into the house on Cactus Lane that Connie had bought with money earned spackling and painting. There, in northeast Dallas, Norma now had what she had not had before—a home. "It was clean," she said. "It was orderly."

Norma got a cat and hung a photo of her young self—a girl looking through cat's-eye glasses at a German shepherd on a dirt road. Soon after, she asked Connie to take down her pictures of Jesus. Said Norma: "I always felt like He was watching me, you know, doing my cocaine, drinking my booze."

Norma had not gone to work with Connie at that market off Fort Worth Avenue. Instead, she had, together with Connie, begun to paint and clean apartments in a pair of buildings on Dixon Street in segregated South Dallas. The buildings had a combined six hundred units. When a tenant moved out, a manager alerted Norma and Connie. The women, in sneakers and industrial clothes, drove off to Northwest Parkway to pick up keys from the office of realtor Dan Matise. Norma never told him that she was Jane Roe. Matise knew only that she was gay and hardworking and "rough as a cob," he says. Together with Connie, she earned twenty dollars per cleaning, sixty per paint job—enough to have the paper delivered and buy cheesecake and get high and host what Norma called "poison parties," weekend bashes that spilled over with beer, wine and vodka, pot, pills and cocaine.

Women also flowed through the home. But not men. Three times men had gotten Norma pregnant, and she was resolved to let them go—not only Woody and Pete and Bill but the pregnancies, the daughters and *Roe*, too, which, much like men, had left her to carry a child she did not want.

In the winter of 1973, Norma was wallpapering her kitchen with Connie when the radio announced the *Roe* ruling. Norma told Connie that she was the plaintiff Jane Roe.

It felt good to let go of a secret. And when Coffee called Norma, days later, with the name of a reporter at the Baptist Press, Norma phoned him at once. "It's great to know that other women will not have to go through what I did," she told O'Brien, her name in newsprint a first time on January 27, 1973.

Norma had been in her second trimester when she met her lawyers and sought an abortion. She told O'Brien that she would not do so again. "It's hard to determine when human life begins," she said. "I wouldn't want to wait over three months for any abortion, because I might be ending a human life after that time."

The Associated Press picked up O'Brien's scoop—the plaintiff anonymous no more. But the *Dallas Morning News* ran the story on page 30, and no more press found her. Jane Roe was left alone to live and work with the woman she loved.

It was no surprise that Norma was disregarded. In the eyes of the law, Jane Roe was little more than an unwanted pregnancy. The Blackmun opinion had had to affirm that she even existed.

If the public did wonder who Jane Roe was, it had been left to assume that the plaintiff who'd won the right to get an abortion had gotten one. But amidst the reams written about *Roe*, there was one clip that carried news of a baby, the AP reporting that Jane Roe had delivered and relinquished her child for adoption.

The piece was tiny, 138 words long. But it contained a big mistake. Jane Roe had not, as Weddington told the reporter, carried her baby to term so as "to avert the possibility that the Supreme Court would declare her case moot." She had, rather, delivered her baby because she had not been able to abort it, her pregnancy too far along.

The narrative of Norma had begun. And a few months later, a reporter from *Good Housekeeping* named Joseph Bell called her.

Norma wondered why. Her own lawyers had not much cared to know her. She, in turn, had not much cared about their case; when, months later, Norma listed in her red plastic datebook the important events of 1973, she included the Yom Kippur War, the Texas State Fair and the closing of a local theater, but not the lawsuit that bore her assumed name.

Bell wished to profile Norma. And, asked to look back at a quarter century of pain and missteps, Norma lied. She turned girlfriends into roommates. She turned an adoption into a kidnapping. She pinned the loss of a marriage on a beating rather than an affair. She did away with her second pregnancy. And asked of her third, of the conception that had led her to court, she did not speak of her hazy if consensual affair with a hustler named Bill. She spoke of a rape.

Three years before, Norma and her lawyers had said nothing of her impregnation or her pregnancy. (Only one justice had asked to know more, Rehnquist wondering how many months pregnant the plaintiff had been when she filed suit.) Norma's affidavit had simply stated that she was pregnant with an "illegitimate" child. But now, with novelistic detail, Norma rid herself of the sin of wanton sex, telling the reporter Bell of footsteps heard on a stretch of unlit blacktop in rural Georgia, of ripped clothing and gravel burns, of her rape by a man "who looked ten feet tall."

Norma did, however, speak one bit of truth. Asked about her child, she confessed that she had no idea who or where it was.

Just one person, in fact, did know who that child was: the lawyer who had found her a home.

Three years had passed since Henry McCluskey brokered the baby's adoption. He had not told the adoptive family of the baby's tie to *Roe*. And he had told no one—not Norma and not Coffee—the name of the family that adopted her.

———

THE *ROE* RULING was six months old when Coffee picked up a copy of *Good Housekeeping*. It was hard to know what to think. As Weddington would later write: "Neither Linda nor I knew what was and what wasn't true about Jane Roe."

Coffee didn't much care. She had put *Roe* behind her. And, having turned thirty on Christmas day, she decided to leave town, signing up for a trip to Israel with other Baptist singles. They would fly to Athens, then boat to the Holy Land.

Her trip was upon her when, in late June 1973, her friend McCluskey went missing. Coffee was worried. She was in Israel when, weeks later, two fishermen found him dead in a ditch beside a Dallas dam, his body bound, two bullet holes beneath his right shoulder.

Coffee returned home to a parade of articles in the Dallas papers she would remember as "salacious." For beneath the horrible facts— McCluskey robbed and drugged and shot by a man named William David Hovila—were intimations of a physical relationship, the lawyer identified by the *Dallas Morning News* as "a bachelor," his killer "an admitted homosexual." (Hovila would assert from prison that the men had been lovers.)

Family and friends would eulogize McCluskey in the Baptist church on Gaston Avenue where he and Coffee had met as kids. His father, a lawyer, would tend to the 149 clients his son left behind. But in all the paper remains of his practice, there was no mention of the *Roe* baby, of she who had been born in the spring of 1970 after birthing a suit.

The only person who had ever known her identity was now dead.

PART IV

"The Raw Edges of Human Existence"

Chapter 13

When Norma became pregnant with her third child, her adoption lawyer turned to the mother and father raising her second. "We already had adopted one of her children," says Donna Kebabjian. "We decided we did not want another."

And so the girl born on June 2, 1970, did not join her older half-sister. She became instead the beloved only child of a woman in Dallas named Ruth Schmidt. Ruth named her Shelley Lynn.

Ruth had grown up in a Lutheran home in Minnesota, one of nine kids. That she would marry young was a matter of course, and at seventeen, she did, wedding a military man from her hometown. The couple moved to an air force base in Texas, where they learned that Ruth could not conceive.

In 1960, Ruth met the brother of another wife on the base. His name was Billy Thornton. He was of a different world, a lapsed Baptist from small-town Texas who pumped gas and smoked and drank. He was striking—tall and slim with tar-black hair and a "deadbeat, thin, narrow moustache," he says, that had helped him to buy alcohol since he was fifteen. It had helped him to woo women, too. Billy had fathered—he was pretty sure—six kids with four women. ("In that neighborhood," he says.)

Billy liked Ruth, so young and blonde. Seven years his junior, Ruth liked Billy. Never mind his children or her husband, the two of them ran off.

The couple was still together a decade later when Billy's brother Gene adopted a baby girl. Ruth wanted one, too, and Gene introduced the couple to his adoption lawyer. A few months later, on a spring morning in 1970, Henry McCluskey phoned to say that their baby girl had been born. She was three days old when Billy drove her home. Ruth was ecstatic. Says Billy: "You ain't never seen a happier woman."

Ruth cleaved to her daughter. Twenty-seven years old, she was at last a mother, and did not care to whom Shelley had been born. Nor did she know. The lawyer McCluskey had divulged only that Shelley had two half-sisters.

McCluskey, of course, had not spoken of *Roe*. Ruth and Billy were oblivious to the fact that their daughter's conception had begotten a lawsuit. When on January 22, 1973, the Supreme Court granted her birth mother the right to have ended her pregnancy, her parents knew only that their Shelley Lynn was two and a half, a toddler partial to spaghetti and pork chops and Cheez Whiz casserole.

Ruth and Billy did not hide from their daughter that she was adopted. Ruth, in particular, says Shelley, "felt it was important I know that I was *chosen*." But even the chosen wonder about their roots. Shelley was five when she decided that her birth parents were most likely Elvis and the actress Ann-Margret. She took to warning her mother, she says, that if ever she wasn't good to her, the stars would take her away.

Ruth enjoyed motherhood—playing the tooth fairy, dressing Shelley in dresses and pigtails. And Billy, a maintenance man for the apartment complex outside Dallas where they lived, was present for Shelley as he hadn't been for his other kids. He kissed her before bed, and when she woke, sat her on his lap to watch cartoons. Whenever a tenant in their complex moved out, he took Shelley with him to rummage through all they had left behind there off Highway 30 in Mesquite— "dolls and books and things like that," says Shelley.

Shelley was seven when her father found work as a mechanic in Houston. The family moved, and then moved again and again, off always to where Billy found work, the little girl happy at every stop to make friends and take in excitements—ballet with cousins, horseback riding with a neighbor, a run of bedrooms all her own.

But each stop was also one step further from her start in the world. Mindful of her adoption, Shelley wished to know who had brought her into being—her heart-shaped face and blue eyes, her shyness and penchant for pink, the anxiety that seized her when now her father began to drink, Billy losing himself in cans of beer until he would yell and be gone. "You could never see it coming," says Shelley. "It was just like, boom!"

Shelley had her safe spaces. "I had tea parties with my stuffed animals," she says. When she was seven, she also began to imagine herself stealing away to a beautiful field of bluebonnets with an oak tree and a swing on it. There, says Shelley, she was safe.

In the fall of 1978, Billy and Ruth married eighteen years after they met, so that their daughter, says Billy, would finally inherit at age eight an undisputed last name.

Shelley Thornton was thankful for her parents, for their love and occasional treats: Daiquiri Ice at Baskin-Robbins, Gloria Vanderbilt jeans. But as Ruth doted on her daughter, her husband felt neglected. Says Billy: "Everything was Shelley."

Billy began to drink more. He drove drunk. He fought with Ruth. Doors slammed. Says Shelley: "They would split up, and then he'd come back."

The only child watched her mother issue second chances, watched her father squander them. Billy was home less and less. Then, one day in 1980, says Shelley, "it was just that he was no longer there." Shelley was ten. A week passed before Ruth explained that he would not return.

Shelley wondered about her father. She wondered about her birth parents. And she began to wonder most of all about the two older sisters her mother told her she had. She wished to know them, to speak with them, to talk about her father or how much she hated science and gym. She began to look hard and long at every girl in every park. Before long, she was phoning city halls, looking for her sisters' birth records, asking her mother to adopt another child so that her own record might be dusted off.

"I would go, 'Somebody has to know!'" says Shelley. "Someone! Somewhere!"

A FEW MILES AWAY, in the heart of Houston, one of the sisters Shelley so desperately sought had arrived a few months before, in the summer of 1980. Jennifer was twelve. Her parents wished her to have a new start and had sent her to her sister Cindy, who was twice her age.

About the time the Kebabjians had declined to adopt Shelley, Jennifer had begun to feel hemmed in. She would crawl out of her crib, upturn the kitchen, head down the hall. Her parents took to locking her door at bedtime. But then Jennifer climbed out her bedroom window, a girl of three or four spotted by neighbors running through the front yard in red pajamas. "So then," says Cindy, "we had to lock her windows too."

Jennifer was allowed in time to venture outside her yellow room and explore the rolling lawns that surrounded her brick house. Still, she remained restless, impulsive. At school, she would rise from her chair mid-lesson to do cartwheels or walk to the window. Her first-grade teacher suggested that Jennifer be tested. At age six, she was diagnosed as hyperactive.

Sports were a healthy outlet for Jennifer; she took to tennis, volleyball, basketball, track, soccer, Jennifer the goalie and right wing on an undefeated fourth-grade team. Mother Donna cheered her every zig and zag, a perennial "team mom."

But off the field, that same mother insisted on structure—the manners and chores, thank-yous and cleanings, that she and her nine siblings had grown up with in Utah. Cindy followed suit; she even joined the drill team. But Jennifer marched to no beat, apt to plug a sink and turn on the faucet. Says Jennifer: "It was always mass destruction in my pathway."

Jennifer was not simply difficult; she was riven by fear. Fireworks scared her. So did policemen and clowns and most men. She was not yet ten when her parents, exasperated, started her on Ritalin.

Still, most days were good. Jennifer was happy playing with the friends who swam in her pool, the relatives who came by on holidays, the exchange students from Chile who lived for a time upstairs. And she was thankful to her parents, to her mother who cooked every meal and drove her about, and to her father who was always there for his baby no matter how many others he had helped deliver overnight. "I was the favorite," says Jennifer. "I was the spoiled brat."

Indeed, no one made the soft-spoken doctor quite so happy as his Jenny, whose dark brown hair fell below her waist. She loved him back. Though her favorite TV shows were *Happy Days* and *Laverne and Shirley*, she was happiest when the news came on so that her dad would sit back in his recliner and she could lie on top of him.

Setrag was just about the only man who didn't scare Jennifer. Her parents wondered if she had been abused and sent her to therapy. No repressed memories came forth.

Jennifer herself wondered about her past, about unknowns that might explain who she was: her tan skin, her oval face, her restlessness. She knew she was adopted; her parents had told her so from the start. But when Jennifer asked to know more, they did not volunteer what they knew—that she was the second of three girls born to a woman named Norma.

The youngest of those girls had imagined their mother to be a movie star. But to Jennifer, she was "a ho." Jennifer judged herself unkindly, too, as not only different but less than, a view that persisted even after Cindy went off to college and the younger sister had her parents to herself, her mother and father driving her weekends in the Lincoln to a lake house in the town of Mabank where they bought her a boat, a Sunfish all her own.

Jennifer, meantime, had been coming to realize, she says, that she "looked at females." She kissed a girl on a sleepover in sixth grade. The kiss felt right. Soon after, her fear of men dissipated.

But seventh grade brought new anxieties, Northwood Junior High beset with peer pressure and schoolwork and competition and drugs. Jennifer was on edge. Ritalin was no more help than the tutoring and counseling her parents now got her.

Jennifer was twelve, the age at which her biological mother had unraveled. Jennifer began to smoke pot and do speed. She stopped playing ball. Her body began to change, Jennifer skinny with big feet. She tried not to notice that it was girls she found alluring. She fell behind in her classes and began to sleep with boys, an adolescent ever more lost in drugs and sex.

Donna was a conscientious mother. She'd saved baby teeth and track ribbons and homework, tucking away that A+ paper about earthquakes that she herself had typed. But, she now wondered, to what end? Her daughter was a dervish. Forty-seven years old, the mother was tired. She suggested shock therapy and a local psychiatrist agreed. But Jennifer refused. "I was like, fuck you," she says. "Fuck you, mom. I'm not getting it done. I thought they were going to electrocute me."

Jennifer was still in seventh grade when she found herself talking to a boy at a party in a crowd by a pool. They walked off and ended up in an alley. And, says Jennifer, "I think he tried to rape me." Jennifer pushed the boy away. But she grew despondent. "I was hating life," she says. "I hated myself." Finally, in 1980, her parents drove her to her sister in Houston so that she might start life anew.

―――――

SOME THREE HUNDRED MILES EAST, on a muddy riverbank in Louisiana, the first of the three girls born to Norma was not quite certain that the younger two existed. Melissa was, in fact, in the dark about much of her family, unsure of who exactly was whom. She had been handed off from her mother, Norma, to her grandmother, Mary, to her aunt, Velma. And if the little girl was content, she was increasingly confused. For if her mother was Mary, as the family said, why did Mary live across the river? Why was her supposed sister, Norma, so much older and detached? That rainy night in 1969 when Norma finally came to visit, she had left the girl of four locked in a car.

Still, as Melissa turned five and six and seven, those questions could wait. She found herself in a good home, in a good family, raised by her aunt Velma like one of her own, Melissa sharing a bedroom with GG, Chris and baby Kim—cousins turned friends. They called her Missy. Says Melissa: "we played under a big pecan tree, playing house, sweeping the dirt with our brooms, having babies."

Melissa was with Mary just over the Atchafalaya when, in 1973, the river flooded. She watched it breach the levee beside their trailer and then cascade down it, rising up their steps, sweeping away their dog.

The Mississippi also flooded. It was clear that controlling its flow into the Atchafalaya would require vigilance, require ongoing maintenance and money. Still, the floodgates held, the waters receded. And after Melissa rejoined her cousins, the Atchafalaya, with its crawfish and mud, beckoned to her. Every night, she waited for quiet Bob and sweet Velma to fill the metal pail outside their wooden home with water warmed by the same logs of pecan and ash that cooked their potatoes and fowl, their grits and jambalaya. Says Melissa: "I always wanted the first bath."

Melissa cleaned up nice. She wore her long brown hair in a ponytail, wore pants or skirts to school and dresses to church, where a Baptist preacher sang out against sin and warned of hell. The service scared her. For little Missy recognized her family in its admonitions—the old and the young who drank, the trio of uncles who cheated on her aunts.

Still, Melissa loved that family, the nine Gautreaux brothers and sisters, Mary on down, who'd settled within seventy miles of the Louisiana house where they'd grown up.

Velma was thought to be a tenth. But she had in fact been born to Mary, the eldest. And when, from time to time, Velma brought Melissa to see her grandmother across the river, the girl got upset. Says Velma: "Melissa was a happy, contented child—as long as she was at my house."

The child, though, was in the legal custody of her grandmother. And when, months after the 1973 flood, Mary readied to move back to Texas along with her husband, the life Melissa had known for five years was over. The girl of eight said her goodbyes. Recalls Velma: "We both cried."

Melissa and Mary settled into a trailer seven hundred miles northwest, in the Texas town of Pampa. There the girl got a pixie cut and returned to school. But an hour northeast of Amarillo, few could understand the clipped Cajun English she had learned in the woods of Yellow Bayou, and so the girl was a second-grader a second time.

Melissa was nine years old when she heard whispers that changed her life. Mary was not her mother; Norma was. Mary acknowledged the truth and the girl was indignant. Recalls Melissa: "I would say, 'That

ain't my mama!'" But Norma was her mama. And she remained unfit to
mother, instructing Melissa, with every visit the girl now paid her in Dallas, to roll into cigarettes the marijuana—Acapulco Gold, sinsemilla—
that she grew and baked and sold from her small brick house.

Back in Pampa, the peddling of drugs was but one more sin for
Melissa to account for. Here, too, she took in the weekly reproofs of a
Baptist preacher, Melissa and the rest of his flock warned of makeup
and dance and swiveling hips. The girl put away her fake nails and
stayed up nights with worry. "I felt filthy," she says. She adds: "I thought
I was evil."

Melissa began to wonder if she might be gay, too. Having learned
that Norma was her mother and that her mother had a girlfriend, her
classmates, she says, began to taunt her: "You have the genes!"

Melissa wondered about genes, about inheritance, about her brown
eyes and curly hair, about the two other children she now heard that
Norma had birthed. She wondered if they existed. But she found it hard
to muse upon two phantom siblings in the face of two real mothers.
After Mary got divorced in 1975, she returned Melissa to Norma, along
with an old Plymouth and hundreds of dollars a month.

Norma did not care for children; she cared for redheaded women
and beer and Bob Marley. Nor did she know *how* to care for them. She
fed Melissa fast food, and sat her on an ice chest in the back of a cargo
van as it careened along. She left her alone to take in the lovers and
stoners and prostitutes and strippers and plumes of pot that passed
through 11343 Cactus Lane. And when Melissa had to write a report
on drugs, Norma sent her to school with capsules taped to cardboard—
barbiturates, amphetamines, black mollies, yellow Quaaludes—a
fourth-grader left to inform her classmates of the properties of each.
She might have added that alcohol was a curse; too much of it and her
mother would get angry and leave her for days.

Connie never left. She was stable, conscientious. And she now told
Melissa that her mother was an important person, a plaintiff named
Jane Roe who would one day "be in the history books."

The girl did not understand. Soon after, she was left to make sense
of another revelation when a short man named Woody arrived at the
door. He wore leather sandals, ripped jeans, a white tee. "He looked

just like Sonny Bono," says Melissa. "He wasn't ugly." Melissa never saw her father again. Meeting him, though, convinced her that Norma really was her mother, and that her siblings were real. She wished to know more. But Norma had no answers. When Melissa asked her why she had given them up, Norma went red with rage.

Norma scared her daughter. She was volatile. After a year in her home, Melissa phoned her grandmother, begging her to take her away. When Mary and Raymond arrived unannounced, Norma was drinking.

Melissa had witnessed violence. She had seen Mary burn Raymond with a skillet of hot beans, had seen her, drunk at the wheel, drag him along a stretch of gravel. And she now watched Norma go at Mary with a crochet hook. "Stabbed her in the back," says Melissa.

Connie wanted Melissa to stay put, and she grabbed a loaded rifle from the bedroom and pointed it at Raymond. The trucker was unfazed and put his arms around the girl and his wife. Says Melissa: "He got us out." They drove the hundreds of miles home, Norma and Connie following in their van, honking and screaming, says Melissa, "like fucking dogs."

Melissa was happy to be gone from her mother. But Mary, her wound healed, waitressed days and bartended nights. Raymond was gone, too, off hauling furniture. Melissa was all but alone. At age eleven she went to live with a waitress Mary knew, at twelve to sleep on the couch of a classmate. Says Melissa: "I was with everybody but my family."

Melissa returned to Mary's trailer. She was twelve, the age Norma had been when she slipped into alcohol and drugs, and Mary encouraged her to have a drink. Melissa declined. She would stick with Coca-Cola. She would be stable and secure. She would forge a family that was different in every way from her own.

That same year, Melissa met a boy at school. His name was Randall. He was the offspring of a rape, half-black and half-white. That his mother was gay besides bound the pre-teens further, a boy and girl on the outside looking in. They went to movies and rode bikes and played ball and shared a first kiss. All the while, Melissa ran her home—washed the clothes and wrote the checks and did the errands, a schoolgirl in polyester driving at age thirteen the old family Plymouth even before the state granted her a "hardship license."

It was then that Melissa fell in love. David was a year older, a loner with blond hair and big muscles. His trailer was just two blocks from hers but of another world. His parents lived at home and cooked dinner and drove the kids to school. More nights than not, Melissa ate with David at his table, slept under his aluminum roof.

It was enthralling to be part of a household unbroken. But to muse upon someday starting her own family was to confront sex. And sex, fraught as it was with repercussion—in this world and the next— terrified Melissa.

There was, however, something that scared Melissa even more than sex and God—the prospect that she might yet grow into her mother. Says Melissa: "Everything Norma stood for, I didn't want to be." That included being gay. She hoped to determine that she was not. And so, in the spring of 1980—after her grandmother reassured her that she would not be damned—the girl of fifteen lay down with her boyfriend in a trailer off a dirt road in the grassy plains of north Texas.

Chapter 14

I n 1977, one year after a crochet hook and a rifle had failed to stop the seizure of her daughter, Norma mailed her a sleeping bag stuffed with all Melissa had left behind—toys and bedding and clothing outgrown.

Norma had had nothing to do with her eldest child since their parting. And nothing but stretch marks remained of her second and third. Her children were gone from her, and she told herself that she had done right by them. "I gave them a chance at life by giving them away," she said. But giving them away had caused her pain. As she would soon tell *Parade* magazine: "Almost every day, when I drive to the job and see kids in a playground or walking to school, I can't help wondering if maybe one of them isn't the one I gave away."

In this, Norma was typical of women who placed children for adoption. A study of more than six hundred such women would conclude that they are "at risk for long-term physical, psychologic, and social repercussions." The study added that such women "have more grief symptoms than women who have lost a child to death." The difference was a matter no doubt of open-endedness, adoption the surrendering of a child who continued to live. As the novelist David Mitchell observed: "Grief is an amputation, but hope is incurable hemophilia: You bleed and bleed and bleed."

Norma blamed her predicament on Mary. "My mother never taught me how to be a mother," said Norma. "I didn't know what a family should be like."

Her brother Jimmy was equally at a loss. Having retreated from his family as a boy, he had fled it at eighteen, joining the navy. Now, decades after the infidelities of his mother had unraveled her family, the son remained undone, unemployed, unmarried, a thirty-something inter-acting with people less and less, given to fits of violence and jags of porn. Some in the family wondered if Jimmy was schizophrenic. But Norma again pinned the blame on her mother, speculating (with no cause) that Mary had molested Jimmy, a succubus ruining her son. Said Norma: "That's just the feeling I get."

Norma seldom saw Jimmy, or the rest of her family. Her life was with Connie. Still, Norma strayed from her partner over and over, sleeping with women amidst the rosaries and Stations of the Cross that Connie set about their home on Cactus Lane. "I loved having an affair," said Norma. "It kind of like puts the frosting on everything."

Norma had never been one for monogamy. She no more wished to be faithful than to wear a bra. Sex was best unrestrained. "That's all we had back then," recalls her friend Andi Taylor. "It ran our lives."

Sex, though, was no simple pleasure. It was profane; so Norma had heard tell in a hundred Kingdom Halls. Because Norma was gay, it was illicit, too. Most of all, it was powerful—of consequence. Sex precipi-tated and ended marriages, begat children then let go. Sex was, in fact, at the heart of near all Norma had known—from the straying of her hus-band and mother and the conversion of her father to her delinquency as a girl and her plaintiffship as Roe.

That plaintiffship had moved past Norma. When, in 1973, she'd vis-ited an abortion clinic to see what her suit had made legal, the Planned Family Clinic of downtown Dallas greeted her less as a pioneer than a curiosity. ("She's a lesbian who was raped on gravel," an employee whispered to a young counselor named Judith Hower.) In the seven years since *Good Housekeeping* first reported that rape, the media had shown little interest in Norma, until an author named Barbara Milbauer approached her in 1980.

Norma lied again. She told Milbauer that three men had raped her, not one, and she recalled their words and shades of skin. Her tale would fill the first seven pages of a book called *The Law Giveth*. That book was not yet complete when, in 1981, the *Dallas Times Herald* did a story on

Norma, and the press began to turn to her every January on the anniversary of *Roe*. She was a good interview—open, forthcoming. Still, Norma had never much contemplated abortion. She had simply wanted one. But the press wished to know her thoughts, and her thoughts were a jumble.

On the one hand, *Roe* was about abortion and abortion was of sex and sex was of sin. Abortion was of death, too, and there were times when Norma felt guilty; while full playgrounds brought to mind the children she had birthed, empty ones brought to mind the children others had not.

On the other hand, *Roe* was about her. Blackmun himself had described Norma's predicament; the suit, he wrote, had been meant to resolve "the problem of bringing a child into a family already unable, psychologically or otherwise, to care for it." Norma began to call *Roe* "my law." She chose "Freedom Lady" as her CB radio handle, and went for the first time to a meeting of the National Organization for Women.

NOW rented an office from an abortion clinic on Routh Street in uptown Dallas. Norma began to volunteer for NOW, stenciling signs for an upcoming convention. She also began to tell people who she was, among them the director of the clinic, Charlotte Taft.

Taft had come south from Connecticut, a blue-eyed baby boomer with a calico cat and a red VW and two degrees in feminist studies. She had founded her clinic in 1978 after working a year under Curtis Boyd, and it was soon performing some five thousand abortions a year, a tally that might have been higher still had Taft and her staff not cautioned every woman come to Routh Street that all three of her options—abortion, adoption and motherhood—could lead not only to happiness but sadness. The aim was to prevent misgivings; Taft says that clinic counselors also raised with patients topics "connected with regrets" such as God and religion, killing and murder.

Norma introduced herself. It did not take Taft long to see in Norma the regret Taft sought to spare others. For as Norma continued to reach out—at an open house, over the phone—she was often drunk and told Taft not only of her struggles with love and money and life, but of her ambivalences about abortion and adoption and motherhood and being gay. Taft, who was gay but as yet closeted, saw in Norma the self-loathing come of an upbringing rooted in shame—even as she pinned her lot on others. Says Taft: "She needed to find someone to blame."

Norma continued to craft a life story that was both exculpatory and untrue. It included things she might have done but did not; she told one journalist that she'd searched through a hospital for her third daughter after a nurse took the baby away. It included things that might have been done to her but were not, such as her abuse at the hand of her ex-husband Woody. Above all, it included ever more tales of sexual violence that by all accounts Norma did not suffer: her rape by Sister Veronica, her rape by a maternal cousin, her rape by a stranger in a Dallas alleyway, her rape and impregnation by a trio of men in Georgia. As Norma remarked late in life: "I like my version a lot better."

A decade after *Roe*, the only rape Norma had yet conjured was the last. She told Taft that she wished to confess publicly that it had not happened. Taft was shocked. She was on the board at NARAL. And, she says, "what I recall was begging Norma to inform the national [pro-choice] organizations before she told the media."

Taft had also beseeched Norma to go to therapy. Norma had agreed, and had begun to see a man she met through Taft's clinic named Herbert Croner.

———

CRONER FIT THE PART of the psychotherapist. He'd been born seventy years before in Germany, and had a thick accent to go with his goatee and glasses. He had come to America in 1946. And he'd told all, from his daughter Jennie to the *Dallas Morning News*, of the life he had left behind: his middle-class home, his medical studies, his work in the German resistance, his translating at Nuremberg, his internment in concentration camps.

Save the last, none of it was true.

Croner had been born in September 1913, the second of six children in a poor Jewish family in Hamburg. His father, Walter, was a waiter who struggled with employment after serving in the First World War. Croner was fifteen when he left school for the workforce, apprenticing with a grocer in 1929. One year later, he left home after his parents cut him off for his far-left political views. He moved into an orphanage.

Croner was a wisp of a man, five feet four and skinny with blue-gray eyes. And he was in poor health. He suffered from bad headaches and epilepsy, and soon from psychopathy, too, admitted to a state hospital in 1931 while working in a smoked fish restaurant. Two years later, one month shy of twenty, he tried to commit suicide by drowning.

Over the next five years, Croner worked a number of jobs— doorman, porter, distributor of leaflets—until his arrest in 1938 for being an unemployed Jew. Over the seven years after that, he "had not one free day," as the historians Christiane Jungblut and Gunhild Ohl-Hinz noted in a book about Hamburg's Holocaust victims. Croner was a prisoner in the concentration camps at Fuhlsbüttel, Auschwitz and Dachau.

Croner was liberated in 1945, the number 84973 tattooed on his left forearm. He weighed fifty-five pounds. But unlike his parents and four of his siblings, he was alive. Upon arriving in the U.S. a year later, at the age of thirty-three, he began to fashion for himself a new life story, telling the *Pittsburgh Press* that he'd been studying medicine when he was expelled from Hamburg University.

Decades later, living in Dallas with a wife and daughter, Croner had reinvented himself completely. He was not a Jew, he said; the Nazis had imprisoned him because of his work in the resistance. He had a doctorate in philosophy, he said; he pointed to a degree he had bought from a diploma mill that called itself the Minnesota Institute of Philosophy. And after he went to work in 1972 for the Salvation Army as a night watchman on Browder Street, he began to tell people that he was a counselor employed by the church; he had cards printed up. Soon after, he had patients, too, Croner seeing them at his home, often free of charge. "He didn't have the actual training," says his daughter Jennie. "But he could give some good advice." She adds: "It was someone he liked being."

Croner was temperamental. He was often depressed or enraged or "just elsewhere," says Jennie, lost most often in thoughts of the war. His marriage collapsed. But in 1981, Croner, his eyes bright, his thin brown-gray hair long in the back, married a woman he was counseling. Sixty-eight years old, he had a new wife and patients and a community, fellow liberals he had known since the sixties when, for a time, he wrote for a black newspaper called the *Dallas Post Tribune*. Among the causes Croner championed was legal abortion.

Back in 1937, Croner's younger sister Anna was a single mother in Hamburg struggling to support her daughter and her sick mother when, as the historians Jungblut and Ohl-Hinz wrote, she had two abortions. She was hospitalized after the second with a high fever, only to be sent to prison for six weeks for having broken the law.

Forty-four years later, Croner was a member of the Choice Foundation, a Dallas nonprofit devoted to reproductive rights. The foundation was connected to Charlotte Taft's abortion clinic, and Croner and his wife met Norma and Connie. The two couples became friends, had each other over for dinner. Norma and Connie painted the Croners' home, and Croner began to look after Norma; he sent a journalist a letter in her name asking that she keep Norma's private life private, that she take "into account my feelings as a human being."

Croner was soon exploring those feelings, speaking with Norma in regular sessions at his home beside White Rock Lake in Dallas, and at all hours over the phone. "She'd call him in the middle of the night when drunk, when she'd had a fight with Connie," recalls Taft. Connie would also alert Croner when Norma was depressed.

Croner soon died, killed by a stroke in 1984 at age seventy. He had been caring and charismatic, and Molly Ivins eulogized him as one of Dallas's "strongest champions of social justice." Of course, he had been a fraud, too. And perhaps it was less than a coincidence that Norma landed on the couch of someone who had fashioned for himself a life story every bit as fantastical as hers. Says his daughter Jennie: "Broken people find one another."

———

NORMA HAD NOT YET publicly confessed to lying about being raped when, in 1983, she walked into another Dallas clinic and asked for a job. "She said she was Norma McCorvey—*Roe v. Wade*, pro-choice and all that stuff," recalls Patricia Pinkusiewicz, owner of the Aaron's Women's Health Center. Pinkusiewicz hired her.

Norma had worked many jobs. She had been a waitress and drug dealer, prostitute and painter, respiratory therapist and bond-runner—

paid five dollars an hour to retrieve prisoners whose bail was posted. She now wished to be a counselor, too, and would later say that she was. But Pinkusiewicz saw that Norma was less equipped to give help than receive it; she smelled of alcohol and asked patients for money and only periodically showed up for work. The abortion provider thus kept Norma from her clients, having her file papers for a few months until she let her go.

Norma soon got a job at another Dallas clinic, scheduling appointments and answering phones: "Abortion Providers of America!" But she lost that job just as quickly. Recalls Pinkusiewicz: "She had a name. But that's about all she had."

That name, however, was growing. A veteran of print, Jane Roe now appeared from time to time on air, too, interviewed in 1982 on KXAS-TV in Fort Worth. Still, in-person interviews made Norma nervous. To calm herself, she drank before them, favoring vodka because it had no smell, she said. When a former CBS executive named Fred Friendly, at work on a book about the Constitution, flew her to New York, Norma was literally shaking, recalls his wife Ruth, when the women met at the airport.

Norma worried about appearing like a rube. But the week she spent in the Friendly home just north of the city lifted her. The TV pioneer, she wrote, treated her "as an important person with something valuable to say." Yet she remained wary. For as she jotted on a spare sheet of paper, there were people "who were out to use me for sure profit." That *Roe* might profit her, too, she had not yet imagined.

───────

NORMA WAS HOME with Connie when a man telephoned from Los Angeles. His name was Michael Manheim. He was a television producer and hoped, he said, to make a film about *Roe*. When he flew to meet Norma, he told her that he had written his honors thesis at Harvard on the politics of birth control in El Salvador. She asked if he had met movie stars. He said he had. Norma was aboard and got a lawyer named John Alan Goren to negotiate a deal.

Goren had left the SEC to work in entertainment law, and now repped a pack of jingle writers. *Roe* offered something new, and in June 1985, he sent releases to Norma's former attorneys asking Coffee and

Weddington to cooperate with the film. The producer, wrote Goren, "wishes to make a sensitive portrayal of her life."

Norma had long since come to know that a life story could be modified. And now again, she presented herself as a victim, told the press that to be Jane Roe was to have her trash picked through and her house egged and her phone number deluged with so many ugly calls that she'd changed it sixteen times. Little of it was true. But the larger point was: the illegality of abortion had caused Norma to suffer. She was done in by the simple sight of a playground.

Champions of *Roe* were unsure what to make of its plaintiff. She was neither reliable nor educated. She was, in short, no Mary Doe—the married abortion advocate Marsha King, who might have been the pro-choice flag-bearer had the courts granted her standing.

Norma, though, wished to belong, to take company with her pseudonym. She wanted a seat at the table. And in the summer of 1987, pro-choice leaders finally gave her one. NOW invited Norma to speak at a Dallas protest against Robert Bork, the circuit judge (and foe of *Roe*) whom Ronald Reagan had nominated to the Supreme Court.

A sticker on the bumper of her 1984 Olds Omega told of her opposition to the judge. And, putting black pen to paper, she contrasted abortion with the killing of children by all means including *oven*. "That's what I call murder," she wrote. "So we, the women of America, should unite together to keep Robert H. Bork out of the Supreme Court."

It was Weddington who rewrote the speech that Norma ultimately delivered. "The nomination of Robert Bork to the Supreme Court represents a threat to our personal privacy," Norma told the crowd of more than three hundred. "I never want to know that another woman has gone through the fear and sadness that I went through."

One month shy of forty—and two months before the Senate would reject Bork—Norma was still getting to know *Roe*, its language and legatees. Supporters of *Roe* were, in turn, still getting to know Norma. That same summer, she confessed on television that she had not been raped. She had, she told the journalist Carl Rowan, become pregnant "through what I thought was love."

Pro-choice leaders were horrified. "A little bit of hell broke loose," recalls Charlotte Taft, the abortion provider Norma had confided in years before. "Everybody had to pick up the pieces. Okay, now what are we supposed to say about this woman?"

What they said was that Norma's admission had no bearing on *Roe*. For as Weddington told the UPI, she and Coffee had excluded from the suit any mention of rape. "No fact was ever presented to the Court unless I was certain we could prove it," she said.

The press had long reported the same. The author Milbauer wrote that Norma's lawyers had been sure not to predicate *Roe* on a rape lest it limit its scope. But the reason that *Roe* made no mention of the alleged rape had nothing to do with legal foresight. It owed, rather, to the simple fact that Norma had not mentioned it to her lawyers. (Coffee recalls that she first became aware of the alleged rape while reading that *Good Housekeeping* article months after the ruling.) Norma, though, told Milbauer that she had told her lawyers that she'd been raped. And pro-life advocates were suddenly abuzz with the suggestion that *Roe* hinged on a falsehood. "As a result of McCorvey's lie," a preacher in Ridgeway, Virginia, wrote to his local paper, "more than 20 million babies have been aborted." Added an aide at the Congressional Pro-Life Caucus: "This false information was all part of a very faulty case."

Norma heard the talk. But she was neither apologetic nor perturbed; she was relieved. "I was getting tired of carrying that thing around with me," she told the press. The plaintiff was incredulous, too, amazed that her words mattered, that newspapers nationwide had reported them in 18-point type.

A decade and a half after winning her suit, Norma was coming to grasp what it meant to be Jane Roe.

Chapter 15

For all the blowback, the heated headlines and protests, that followed *Roe* in 1973, the new ruling had taken immediate hold. The matter of abortion was legally closed. The Supreme Court dissolved at once the dozen other abortion cases awaiting its consideration. And in December 1975, when the Senate gathered to vet a potential justice for the first time since *Roe*, no one so much as asked the judge his opinion of it. The Senate confirmed John Paul Stevens without opposition. *Roe* appeared as secure as any other ruling.

Still, among the minority of Americans who opposed *Roe* was a minority that did not surrender to it. As *Roe* took root, so did their dissent, seeded here and there in the noncompliance of hospitals, the insubordination of clergy, the proposals of human life amendments to the Constitution.

Mildred Jefferson championed the last. The doctor had come to see politics as the most likely path to overturning *Roe*. And in the summer of 1974, having been appointed chair of the National Right to Life Committee, she testified to the Senate in support of the idea of an HLA, of the legal protection of life from the point of conception.

It had once mattered to Mildred how a child was conceived; at VOL-COM, she had not opposed ending pregnancies resulting from rape or incest or those that imperiled a mother. But the doctor now testified that to abort the product of incest or rape was no less a crime than to abort any other. The pregnant woman, health permitting, bore a moral responsibility to carry her child. "I do not look upon pregnancy as quite the burden as some other people may," she said.

At the time Mildred testified, HLAs had been introduced by members of Congress from Maryland, Virginia and Massachusetts. All three had stalled. Congress found them too extreme. And growing numbers of pro-lifers began to try to *restrict* abortion even as they still hoped to criminalize it.

Law and politics offered a variety of means to do so. That same spring, an assistant district attorney in Boston charged a local obstetrician with manslaughter, alleging that an abortion he had done via hysterotomy had killed a fetus that might otherwise have lived outside the womb. The suit—*Commonwealth v. Kenneth Edelin*—hinged on the question of viability. To assert that the aborted fetus had been viable, the prosecution called upon Mildred Jefferson.

Jefferson was hardly qualified to testify. As the defense noted, she had no expertise in obstetrics, embryology or perinatology, had not delivered a baby since 1951, and had never performed an abortion. But the prosecution said that she would merely provide "definition of terms and basic anatomy." Allowed to proceed, Jefferson told the jury that an abortion was the termination of a pregnancy until its twentieth week, at which point the fetus—the "baby," she called it—was viable.

Jefferson had redefined abortion. She had also fixed the point of viability earlier than had *Roe*; the ruling put it at between twenty-four and twenty-eight weeks. Though the Supreme Court justice Sandra Day O'Connor would later posit that technology would one day enable fetuses to survive birth ever earlier, it would become clear that fetal lungs struggled to function before twenty-four weeks; a study published in the *Journal of the American Medical Association* in 2015 reported that just 11 percent of babies born earlier survived "without major morbidity."

In the Edelin case, the gestational age of the aborted fetus could only be guessed at; estimates ranged from twenty to twenty-four weeks. Still, Jefferson asserted that the fetus Edelin had killed had not only been viable but *born*. For although it was dead when Edelin removed it, C-section-like, through an incision in the abdomen, he had, prior to its removal, detached the placenta from the uterine wall. This was standard procedure in a hysterotomy, but Jefferson said that it amounted to manslaughter. "Once the placenta is completely separated," she said, "and the offspring is no longer attached to the mother, even if it has not been removed from the uterus, it has been born."

Jefferson was contesting the very definition of birth. Still, she swayed the jury; it convicted Edelin of manslaughter. Though the Massachusetts Supreme Judicial Court would later reverse the jury's verdict, the case not only put abortion providers on notice but restarted a national conversation on fetal rights, broaching the question of what constituted life.

The NRLC was overjoyed, not least with its medical witness. A recent committee report had noted that Jefferson "can exhort for an hour without notes." She was, it added, "at once tender and unyielding." Of course, she was black, too, and as such had been of particular use in a case in which an all-white jury was deliberating the fate of a black man—Edelin the first black ob-gyn chief resident at Boston City Hospital. As Edelin himself later noted, with Jefferson on the stand, the prosecuting attorney could "inoculate himself against the charge of racism which was always swirling around my indictment and my case."

Only months after the trial, in July 1975, the NRLC elected Jefferson its president. She had reached the summit; forty-eight years old, there was perhaps no pro-life advocate more powerful than she.

———

THIRTY MONTHS HAD PASSED since Jefferson swayed Ronald Reagan. His conversion to pro-life had likely been genuine; the governor subsequently wrote to her pledging to help the cause "in any way." But becoming pro-life was expedient, too. The governor hoped to be president. And as Republican strategist Pat Buchanan had noted to Nixon, there were votes to be won opposing abortion, not only among Catholics but among "social conservatives distressed about loss of respect for tradition."

Reagan had not yet announced his candidacy when, in October 1975, he announced that he supported the "aims" of a human life amendment. "The interrupting of pregnancy," he said, "is the taking of a human life."

Reagan would soon lose the Republican nomination to Gerald Ford. But he had secured the pro-life vote. In so doing, he had "changed the partisan equation on abortion," as the author Daniel Williams observed, the governor binding opposition to abortion to Republicanism.

Abortion was no longer merely political. It was becoming *partisan*. But if Reagan had brought home that fact, it was Jefferson who'd prompted him to do so. For her committee, as the *New York Times* wrote, was "turning abortion into one of the major issues of the 1976 Presidential campaign." In particular, it was challenging candidates to address the question of an HLA. The GOP responded, endorsing at its national convention—six years after a Republican president about-faced on abortion—the "enactment of a constitutional amendment to restore protection of the right to life for unborn children."

Never before had either political party mentioned abortion in its platform. Never again would they not; Democrats declared this same bicentennial summer that any attempt to undo *Roe* was "undesirable."

Politicians conform. And in time, like Richard Nixon and Ronald Reagan before them, a raft of Democratic pols, mindful of their new party line, would flip, too: Ted Kennedy and Dick Gephardt and Al Gore.

Mildred was delighted by the Republican support. She'd made clear that opposition to abortion forgave all sins. (She'd been open even to the candidacy of Alabama governor and segregationist George Wallace, noting that he had never "supported abortion on demand.") More, as historian Jennifer Donnally would note, she'd "helped to polarize the American party system." Indeed, save for the occasional pro-life Democratic candidate (such as Ellen McCormack, who ran for president in 1976), pro-lifers could increasingly focus their support on one political party: the GOP. Mildred christened it the "party of life," the lifelong Independent ensuring that the NRLC back Gerald Ford for president.

It was a meaningful endorsement. The NRLC had grown enormous: it had a million members and 2,800 chapters. The election was but a few months off when the committee converged on the Hynes Auditorium in Boston for its annual convention.

———

MILDRED COULD WRITE AND SPEAK, foretell and inspire; this election season, she had her army of middle-income Americans disrupt the rallies of pro-choice candidates with trumpets playing Taps. But nuts and bolts came loose in her hands. The vendors servicing the NRLC convention went unpaid.

Shane Cunningham might have known better than to entrust logistics to his wife. Mildred struggled not only with money but with space and time; she had let their home clot with clothing and paper, and would set out for engagements, he says, after she was scheduled to have arrived. More difficult still, says Shane, Mildred maintained an "absolute refusal to bend."

That absolutism was helpful in the fight against abortion. But it was incompatible with both management and marriage. Mildred and Shane were separated not only by the rising tide that had swept him from their home but by a complete absence of mutuality. Says Shane: "I was unable to do anything because I devoted myself completely to her."

Mildred in turn made little time for Shane. "He'd call into the office to talk to her and she was always too busy," recalls pro-life activist Judie Brown. "'I'll get to you when I get to you.'"

Shane was not alone in accommodating Mildred and her demands. Everybody did; while the NRLC board slept at the Washingtonian on trips to DC, Mildred stayed at the L'Enfant Plaza, a limousine driving her to and from meetings. Mildred was worth it. As Henry Hyde, a Republican congressman, would later tell a pro-life lobbyist: "You know what the best strategy for the pro-life movement would be? Someone ought to pay Dr. Mildred Jefferson just to travel around the country and speak out on behalf of the unborn."

The impact of Hyde on the movement was equally great. For in 1976, he proposed banning the use of Medicaid to help poor women pay for abortions.

The previous spring, as the Senate debated whether federal dollars ought to be used for abortion, Mildred, the newly elected NRLC president, had charged her committee to put in "the long, tiring work necessary to support" pro-life politicians. She'd then asked leaders of the New Right, including Paul Weyrich, for advice, and in 1976, she hired a lobbyist named Thea Rossi Barron.

Barron was a lawyer who'd moved from Michigan to DC with her three kids after her husband had an affair and filed for divorce. She was freethinking, a Catholic Democrat who approved of contraception and viewed abortion—the termination of lives—as a matter of civil rights, not religion.

Jefferson wished Barron to concentrate on the Democrats—"the people we risked losing," says Barron. So Barron made weekly trips to the Hill, handing her powder-blue card to the aides of senators and representatives she felt it best for her and Mildred to meet. "We kept tabs on every vote," says Barron. That June, she was thrilled when the Hyde amendment (attached as a rider to a congressional appropriations bill) passed a vote in the House and headed to the Senate.

That same day, the NRLC gathered in Boston for its annual convention. Henry Hyde gave the keynote address. "I stand before you as a 634-month-old fetus," he said. The congressman took Mildred's hand, their arms raised to great applause.

Days later, the Senate rejected his amendment. But the NRLC was ready. The committee boasted a national army of volunteers whom Barron could call upon to contact members of Congress, de facto lobbyists who, wrote Barron, were "informed, articulate and respectfully persistent." Now, just four months before a congressional election, they took to their phones, notifying senators who'd opposed the Hyde amendment that if they did not reconsider it, they would not be reelected.

Come September, the amendment passed.

The particulars of the Hyde amendment would take years to settle. And at first, its longevity was not assured. But the following September, Barron secured endorsements from the president, Jimmy Carter, and from Jesse Jackson, too—the reverend attesting in a letter to Congress that "as a matter of conscience I must oppose the use of federal funds for a policy of killing infants." Congress voted to renew the amendment. And in time, owing to the amendment, an estimated one in four women who would have had abortions funded by Medicaid gave birth instead.

The Hyde amendment was a great pro-life victory. Buoyed by Mildred and the NRLC, a conservative congressman had made the first chink in the armor of *Roe*.

The success of Hyde enforced Mildred's belief that the great task of the pro-life movement was, as she said, "to wring more political effectiveness" from its growing numbers. To do so, conservative strategists began, in 1977, to form political action committees centered on abortion. Among them was a PAC that Mildred and her NRLC colleague Carolyn Gerster founded that fall, devoted solely to the passage of an HLA.

To support pro-life candidates, however—to funnel donor dollars directly to them—one must define pro-life. The NRLC now had to decide whether to back politicians who (in keeping with the Hyde amendment) did not oppose abortion absolutely but rather condoned it in cases of rape and incest and when pregnancy imperiled the mother.

In the years since *Roe*, Mildred had come to tolerate fewer such exceptions. And she now concluded that to be pro-life meant to oppose even those abortions that saved the mother's life. As Mildred told *Ebony* magazine in 1978: "You can't give the individual the private right to kill, no matter what kind of justification they can come up with."

On paper, her organization agreed. *Ebony* noted that the NRLC policy was "no abortions, ever, no matter what the circumstances." But in truth, just three of Mildred's fifty-plus fellow NRLC board members shared her absolute opposition to abortion.

Mildred found herself more and more at odds with her peers. Beginning her third year as president, she was mired in disputes over her opposition to sit-ins, her continued lobbying of Congress in pursuit of an HLA, and her mismanagement of committee funds. The NRLC debt had risen to $200,000, and John Willke, the Cincinnati obstetrician who'd written "Handbook on Abortion," the bestselling pro-life booklet of questions and answers, blamed Mildred.

Mildred was aghast. "No abortion-advocate's attacks," she wrote, "can measure up to the aggravated assaults I have had to endure from some of the people who are supposed to be on our side."

Willke wielded great influence in the committee. Political and ambitious, he headed a faction that turned on the president. "They had a concerted plan to get rid of her," says Judie Brown, whom Mildred hired to run PR for the NRLC. Indeed, by 1978, just one of her eight fellow executive committee members voted with her on issues ranging from publicity to fundraising.

Policy alone did not account for the Willke–Jefferson divide. Envy did, too. Says Brown: "She got far too much national media and he wanted that media for himself."

Mildred was indeed a fixture on television. She spoke to Barbara Walters, David Frost, Phil Donahue, Ted Koppel, Tom Snyder. Always, she was on point, pithy. Asked about pro-life aggression against abortion providers, she told Jim Lehrer that the NRLC "opposes violence not just against the unborn but those who are born as well."

Mildred was not merely the public face of her committee. Over the five years since *Roe*, she'd become the lifeblood of the pro-life fight. She flayed abortion with arguments keen and precise. She expanded the pro-life base beyond the confines of Catholicism. She helped to transform abortion into political capital, and political capital into legislation and votes. And as much as anyone, it was Mildred who delivered those votes to the Republican Party, a party that would soon elect as U.S. president someone she herself had talked into the pro-life fold. But for all that, in 1978, the NRLC voted her out of office; Mildred lost her bid for reelection to a fourth term. She lost her cool, too. Recalls former NRLC board member Philip Moran: "She went into a fifteen-minute tirade."

Mildred was not simply out as president; having lost her position on the board to Moran, she was cut completely from its leadership. Wrote Mildred: "In the heat of battle, I have been unhorsed."

Mildred continued on—like a Texas mustang, she later said, "unbridled and unbossed." If she had lost her platform, the power of the NRLC, she had not lost her zeal. Her name—Mildred Fay Jefferson, M.D.—was soon on a half dozen mastheads, the doctor, an apostle of the unborn, become a trustee and advisor and expert witness and consultant and speaker.

Mildred soon desired a pro-life outfit all her own, "a platform to accept speaking engagements," says Brown. She turned for help to a direct mail developer in Tulsa.

His name was James Bothell. Bothell had fundraised for the NRLC, developing software that generated lists of people the committee then beseeched for (tax-deductible) help. His mailings had a 12 percent response rate, far above the norm. He'd raised more than $250,000 in 1976, more the year after that. "It's not me," he said. "It's the issue."

Bothell had left the NRLC along with Mildred, claiming it failed to pay him what remained on his contract. He sued. An initial ruling went his way and he got a court order to stop the NRLC from using his donor list. He then dismissed his suit and teamed up with Mildred to form the Right to Life Crusade. It was little more than a P.O. box in Tulsa and a nonprofit ID. But Bothell and his mailings kept Mildred afloat. For $500 an appearance—at graduations and debates and seminars and rallies and conferences and dinners—the doctor spoke in her strong, flat contralto of the evils of abortion and the goodness of family.

On the matter of family, however, Mildred had little experience. She had no siblings, no children. Her father was estranged. And on the same day, May 19, in the spring of 1978, she lost both her mother, Gurthie, and husband, Shane. (Shane had long ago decided to leave Mildred once he no longer had to drive her to visit Gurthie.)

Mildred disdained divorce. It shamed the divorcee and harmed the children, she said. She told a reporter that her parents had been "very selfish" to divorce, and told Shane that filing for divorce "violated the rights of the children we might have had."

Shane moved on. Eight years had passed since he and Mildred had lived together. And two years prior (just after the 1976 NRLC convention), he had begun an affair with a woman in his building whom he would later marry. Mildred fought the divorce. She later told a New Hampshire pastor named Robert Mears that it was "a blow both personally and politically." She added: "The divorce is my only vulnerability."

Mildred had been careful to cover up her other vulnerabilities. Having chosen, for example, not to bring a child into the world—even as she insisted that every other woman, once she'd conceived, do so—she told friends that she'd been unable to conceive. And to erase the blot of divorce, she ceased entirely to speak Shane's name, retreating into the absolutism of her work.

Mildred had once been in a car that had spun but left her uninjured. She had thus realized, she told that New Hampshire pastor, "that Christ was with me and had intervened to save my life." More, it followed that her words on abortion came from on high. "The things I'm saying are not really what I am saying," she would tell Pastor Mears. "I am a conduit through which they are revealed." "Are you saying," asked the pastor, "that God is speaking through you?" Mildred answered yes.

Mildred had never discussed God with Shane and did not attend church. But she had come to see herself as a prophet. And like a prophet, she began to warn of cataclysms, of the hell to come if abortion were to remain legal, of the "genocide" of blacks followed by the "extinction" of all.

UNDER *ROE*, the number of legal abortions in the U.S. was steadily growing. Six years after the 1973 ruling, the annual total had doubled to 1.5 million, or roughly three abortions for every seven live births. But if that fact signified victory for the pro-choice, it galvanized the pro-life. By 1979, according to the work of a political scientist named Greg Adams, congressional voting records on abortion made clear that a decade after Republican strategists first sought to politicize abortion, the pro-life movement and its PACs had begun influencing politicians— Republicans increasingly pro-life, Democrats pro-choice.

It would take another decade for the public to mirror that divide. To hasten that shift in public opinion—and continue to grow their base beyond Catholics—a trio of conservative strategists began to court evangelicals, turning to the televangelist Jerry Falwell for help.

Falwell had enormous reach. The pastor of a Virginia megachurch, he had that same year founded the Moral Majority, a national lobbying group with an agenda (and a PAC) whose beating heart was opposition to abortion.

If abortion was a matter of life and death to Catholics, it was largely a matter of sex to evangelicals. The evangelical Baptist theologian Carl F. H. Henry told the press back in 1971 that "the connection between easy abortion and sexual promiscuity is obvious." And one day after the *Roe* ruling, Chuck Colson, the Nixon advisor and soon-to-be evangelical, told the president that abortion "encourages permissiveness." Nixon agreed. "A girl doesn't have to worry about taking the pill anymore," he said. "She can go down to the doctor and have an abortion for five dollars."

Falwell decried abortion at rallies and in newsletters and on prime-time TV. As hoped, the ranks of the pro-life began to swell with evangelicals. But abortion was merely a gateway. As the conservative strategist Richard Viguerie would soon observe: "The abortion issue is the door through which many people come into conservative politics."

Among those people was Mildred Jefferson. Having long publicly opposed abortion, she now also opposed welfare and school busing and affirmative action. Most off-putting, she said, was the proposed Equal Rights Amendment, which sought to ratify legal equality for women and which, a few years before, she had told the Senate she agreed with in principle.

Reagan also opposed the ERA. And as he ran for reelection, Mildred minded the president, phoning his physician, for example, when in the midst of a televised debate he appeared to her confused and dehydrated. Reagan was appreciative. He had remained in touch with the doctor since writing to her in 1973. Two days after his inauguration in 1981, Mildred sat beside the president in the Oval Office, dressed in navy wool crêpe.

Mildred had met previous presidents. Ford had invited her to a gathering of pro-lifers, while Nixon (weeks before his resignation) had appointed her to a board dedicated to world population. But Mildred had skipped the meeting with Ford, and admonished the Nixon staff (in red type) to "NOT EVER" address her as "Ms." With the election of Reagan, she had, for the first time, a friend in the White House. Recalls the pro-life firebrand Judie Brown: "There was an electricity between those two people. He absolutely loved her."

The presidency of a man unreservedly pro-life was not just a coronation of the cause but of Mildred, too. It was the doctor, as much as anyone, who in just one decade—"from 1970 through Reagan," says her fellow advocate, Anne Fox—had elevated the movement from fringe special interest to political power. Added Judie Brown: "She was the architect of the anti-abortion movement."

That movement, however, no longer needed Mildred. It belonged to the lawyers now. And whereas they fought abortion with state restrictions patterned, as a young pro-life law professor soon argued, on the incremental fight for civil rights, Mildred saw herself in the all-or-nothing abolitionists. It was time for her to move on. Having left medicine for the pro-life fight, she decided to leave abortion for politics, announcing outside Faneuil Hall in early 1982 that she would run for the Senate against Ted Kennedy, declaring him "an aging Ken doll without a mind of his own."

Mildred had filed the requisite papers, registered as a Republican. But despite her efforts—wearing red, white and blue, keeping a photo of herself and Reagan at the ready, speaking of gun rights and capitalism as much as of abortion—she failed to win the support of enough delegates to get on the primary ballot. A second run two years later was no more successful.

Mildred claimed foul play. She alleged that election officials kept her off the ballot because she was "the symbol of the [pro-life] movement." She said that owing to "influential adversaries," it was unsafe for her to travel alone.

It was true that Mildred had adversaries. But the majority of her run-ins had nothing to do with abortion. They concerned unpaid rent and credit card bills, and the would-be senator found herself fighting a slew of lawsuits. She got evicted from her medical office.

Mildred said nothing publicly of her legal and financial problems, much less her age and divorce and her hoarding. She had a persona to maintain. She offered journalists little more than a list of six acceptable ways to print her name and honorific. "IT SHOULD NEVER APPEAR AS 'Mildred Jefferson,'" she added.

The doctor still had her sinecure at BU and did occasional consultations. But a decade after *Roe*, Mildred couldn't practice medicine. Abortion was all she knew. She returned to it now, speaking to groups like Californians for Biblical Morality and counseling Reagan on those occasions when he invited her to the White House to discuss abortion.

Mildred had just spoken with the president and others about abortion and unwed mothers when, in 1984, a Christian publisher in Nashville printed an essay under Reagan's name titled "Abortion and the Conscience of the Nation." Written by his staffers, the essay cursed *Roe* and valorized the president, stating that, as governor, he had not wanted to sign that 1967 bill on abortion. Reagan, it said—"with jaw set and eyes aflame"—was "a champion of all that is right and true and just."

The president, however, was no longer a champion of HLAs. He had come to see the amendments as political non-starters. And having determined that the road to toppling *Roe* ran not through the legislature but the judiciary, he'd appointed more than one hundred federal judges when, halfway through his presidency, a legal advocacy group called Americans United for Life held a press conference titled "Reversing *Roe v. Wade* through the Courts."

The AUL was among those advocating incremental change; it believed that *Roe* would most likely be undone through "a series of steps which would completely empty it of content," as their chief staff counsel, Thomas Marzen, put it. In the years since *Roe*, the Supreme Court had indeed taken steps regarding abortion, issuing a quartet of opinions that, like the Hyde amendment, restricted federal funding for it. But other opinions had leaned pro-choice, the Court asserting for example that minor girls did not, for the most part, need parental consent to get an abortion, and that fetal remains need not be buried.

Mildred read all the opinions. When they upset her, she appealed to Congress to investigate the offending justices for "dancing to the tune of the population control advocates."

Mildred was not alone in viewing the Court through the prism of abortion. In the years since the Senate had confirmed the pro-choice Justice Stevens without mention of *Roe*, the confirmation hearings of each subsequent justice had spotlighted it. The word "Roe" was spoken, for example, forty-nine times during the hearings of Sandra Day O'Connor, whose stance on abortion was debated. Antonin Scalia, ardently pro-life, was put through similar paces. And in 1987, when Reagan nominated Robert Bork to the Court, abortion was one of several issues—including contraception and civil rights—that torpedoed his nomination. Bork had previously called *Roe* a "wholly unjustifiable judicial usurpation of state legislative authority." Senator Ted Kennedy put that assessment to ruthless use. "Robert Bork's America," wrote Kennedy on the day of his nomination, "is a land in which women would be forced into back-alley abortions."

A decade had passed since congressional voting records on abortion began to divide along party lines. Abortion was now, in the late 1980s, a steadfast indicator of political affiliation. Congressmen voted their party line on abortion 80 percent of the time. The public was similarly divided. Indeed, *Roe* had come to be the tip of an iceberg that separated people's worldviews—"both the marker and the symbol of their different interests," wrote the sociologist Kristin Luker.

Luker noted that the great majority of activists on both sides were women. On one side, in general terms, was the churchgoing housewife who was a mother of at least three children and viewed abortion as anathema to her being. On the other was a woman both secular and educated. She too was a mother, albeit of one or two children. But she was also employed and saw the availability of abortion as a necessary corrective to the impediments that an unwanted pregnancy might impose. The two sides, concluded Luker, were unbridgeable. "Since the core issue is motherhood," she wrote, "a gain to one side is matched by a loss to the other."

Of course, it was the pro-lifer who was most aggrieved by national policy; in the years since *Roe*, a woman wanting an abortion had only to look in a phone book. And having failed to overturn *Roe* with money and votes and amendments, the pro-life movement had turned to bodies, shifting its front lines from organizations like the NRLC to upstarts like Operation Rescue, from legislative and judicial battles to physical ones with sit-ins and marches and the blockading of clinics—tens of thousands of middle-aged and middle-income Americans arrested for carrying out the disruptive vision of a former monk in Ohio named Joseph Scheidler. (Scheidler laid out that vision in a 1985 book titled *Closed: 99 Ways to Stop Abortion*.) Violence followed. In the five years preceding the Senate rejection of Bork in 1987, opponents of *Roe* had bombed and set fire to fifty-four clinics.

The battle over *Roe* had thus become, wrote the historian David Garrow, "a domestic war." That war divided the nation. When Senator Kennedy warned of the dystopia that would come of a Supreme Court one-ninth Bork, half of America nodded.

The Senate rejected Bork, 58–42, and then quickly confirmed his replacement, Anthony Kennedy. But if vilifying Bork, and his arguably extreme views, had worked—Kennedy would help to preserve *Roe* for decades to come—the Democrats had set a destructive precedent. "Their fight legitimized scorched-earth ideological wars over nominations at the Supreme Court," Tom Goldstein, a scholar of the court, told NPR. Added Joe Nocera in the *New York Times*: "The Bork fight, in some ways, was the beginning of the end of civil discourse in politics."

Chapter 16

Norma had told *Parade* magazine that she "never wanted to make a career out of being Jane Roe." But in 1988, her long-ago affair suddenly bore unimaginable fruit when Holly Hunter signed on to play her in the film that Michael Manheim was producing. The film, to air on NBC, would pay Norma $60,000.

Off in San Angelo, Texas, a lawyer named Tom Goff wondered whether Norma's pseudonym might continue to provide. He recalled that the plaintiff Ernesto Miranda had earned money signing printed copies of those rights his arresting officers had not read him. Norma, Goff imagined, could do the same with copies of *Roe*, and he had an advertising executive design a framed print of its syllabus for her to sign. Goff then asked a friend in San Angelo to win her over. Says Sarah McCallister: "My part was to make her feel safe."

McCallister was right for the part. Though she worked on an air force base, overseeing payroll, she was a free spirit, a single mom and former hippie still getting high at forty-four. McCallister got Norma on the phone and was soon off to Cactus Lane.

The women spent weekends together, sharing cocaine and conversation. From time to time, their talk turned to reproduction. Both women had had hysterectomies. And both had experienced anguish resulting from pregnancy, McCallister confiding that while she had raised two kids, there had also been a miscarriage, a death at birth, an adoption, an abortion. She thanked Norma for helping to legalize the last. Though the prospect of money had led her to Norma, her appreciation for the plaintiff was genuine; she was angry that—despite Norma's recent invitation from NOW to protest Bork—the sisterhood of *Roe* had excluded its protagonist. Says McCallister: "We believed Norma had been wronged."

Norma liked McCallister, her dancing and auburn hair. She also liked that she and Goff gave her money and clothing and jewelry and had her photographed. But come the fall of 1988, the plaintiff had yet to sign copies of their document. Says Gus Clemens, the adman who designed it: "I think it's accurate to say that [we] were manipulating Norma, and that Norma was manipulating us."

Their collaboration was still stalled when, in February, Holly Hunter visited Norma. Norma was not the same woman Hunter was to portray. After nineteen rewrites, a television script had conventionalized Norma, rid her of her drug use and homosexuality and her many resentments, too. Norma understood that one could play with truth. Two months later, on April 4, 1989, she did so herself when three bullets pierced her home and car.

Norma was pretty sure of the shooter. A furious woman had recently accused her, Norma said, of shortchanging her on a sale of pot. But the police made no arrests, and it occurred to Norma that she could pin the shooting on *Roe*. The public would believe it. Indeed, a few years before, after a bullet entered the Virginia home of Justice Blackmun, it didn't matter that the FBI concluded the shot had been fired randomly. Wrote his daughter Sally: "Someone was out to kill Dad."

Norma now let it be assumed that abortion had motivated another shooting, the plaintiff once again turning a lie into breaking news. Wrote the Associated Press: "the incident was symbolic of a dangerously intensifying battle over abortion."

Norma told the Dallas police that she wished to speak to the FBI. But when the FBI got in touch, she never responded. She was, she said, in hiding, never mind that days later she appeared in the nation's capital to march with Connie and 300,000 others in support of *Roe*.

The march was days away when Norma gave a talk that Goff had arranged at Georgetown Law School. The students were transfixed, and Goff had another idea: what if Norma were Jane Roe full time? What if she were the face of a foundation that helped poor Texas women get abortions?

Norma liked the idea. Hoping to plug it, she readied a speech, practicing it beside Connie the night before the march. "Hello," she said, cigarette in hand. "The courts call me Jane Roe."

Jane Roe, however, had just confessed to lying about being raped. And officials at the march did not invite her to speak alongside Bella Abzug and Gloria Steinem. "We don't know anything about her," explained Sheri O'Dell of the National Organization for Women. "If she wants to be a leader that's fine, but she should go out fighting in the trenches and become a leader."

In the meantime, the movement sought to leverage Norma. NARAL, for example, was readying talking points to share, in a few weeks, upon the airing of the NBC film. "The movie is essentially irrelevant to our comments," read the memo. "We should look at this as an opportunity to get our message out."

The DC march ended, and Norma and Connie and Goff and McCallister found their way onto a podium in a VIP area beside the Capitol. Famous attendees greeted the plaintiff with hugs and hellos: Morgan Fairchild, Betty Friedan, the former pro-lifer convert Jesse Jackson. A plan was coming together. But then, suddenly, a woman wearing shoulder pads and eyeliner appeared beside Norma. Recalls McCallister: "she just came right up on the podium and took her literally out of our hands."

Her name was Gloria Allred. Allred knew firsthand what *Roe* meant; she had been raped in 1966, and an illegal abortion had left her in an ICU. She had gone on to become a lawyer representing women abused or harassed. She preferred her clients boldfaced.

Norma did not need a lawyer. But Holly Hunter would soon thank her at the Emmys, and Allred took her on as a client, telling Norma of book contracts and speaking tours, introducing her, right there at the march, to more celebrities: Cybill Shepherd, Gloria Steinem, Marlo Thomas, Glenn Close, Jane Fonda. The lawyer then flew Norma to Los Angeles, "trotting her out," noted a reporter, "for the television cameras."

Norma had been working on her soundbites. "Women's freedom will not be abridged," she had told the *New York Times* weeks before.

But she remained uncomfortable at a mic, and Allred got her lessons with a media-training firm that typed up for her a list of pointers: "Say Versus rather than 'V.' 'Abortion' instead of 'It.' If you're asked a three-part question, answer the one you like best."

Goff and McCallister followed Norma to LA. They had incorporated the Jane Roe Foundation, and were thrilled when Allred convened a brunch to support it. The brunch, at the restaurant Baci, would benefit Norma as well as "the Jane Roe Foundation which is located in Dallas, Texas," Allred told the press. The roomful of pro-choice activists, including Leonard Nimoy and Valerie Harper, paid $100 a plate. But months later, Allred had sent the foundation no money. "How can somebody get by with raising money and saying they're going to give it to a foundation," McCallister asked a reporter, "and then not do it and not even account for it?"

Allred told the paper that all proceeds from the fundraiser had gone to Norma; she disputed having earmarked money for the foundation. Goff and McCallister let the matter go. Their foundation would never get off the ground.

Years later, Allred asserted that she "wouldn't raise money for an organization . . . and allow it to be siphoned off to an individual." But she had, without question, siphoned off *Norma* from Goff and McCallister. Back in Texas, the two never saw Norma again.

Norma did not say goodbye. It mattered little to her who was at her side. People came and people went. Besides, Allred had put her up in a Holiday Inn on an LA pier, and Norma now called room service. "I never thought in my wildest dreams," said Norma, "that I'd be able to pick up a phone and speak to a desk and say, 'Bring me a steak.'"

It was, in a sense, *Roe* that paid for that steak. Days later, it paid for her flight back to DC; Allred had arranged for Norma a seat in the Supreme Court where, on April 26, 1989, abortion was again on trial. The case, *Webster v. Reproductive Health Services*, concerned a Missouri ban against the use of public resources for abortion.

Norma stood between the Court building and a pack of press, her white heels on the white marble plaza. She wore plum lipstick, gold earrings, a dress of black and white, and Allred gave instruction: photograph now, question later. A battery of lenses rose.

Allred had given Norma the week of a lifetime—movie stars in LA, the *Today* show in New York, and now the high court in DC—and she stepped beside her client with a sign that read "Keep Abortion Legal." The women held it aloft and then, video rolling, ascended the staircase as a couple might, locking arms and then holding hands, clasping a shoulder and then a waist. They entered the Court. It was the first courtroom Norma had ever seen and she noted in her datebook that "it was beautiful." They sat, and oral arguments began.

Sarah Weddington was in the audience, too. This courtroom had changed her life, her argument on behalf of an anonymous plaintiff catapulting her to the Capitol even before *Roe* was won. The lawyer had gone on to serve three terms as a state representative, and other high posts had followed—at NARAL, in the White House, at the University of Texas. *Roe*, though, had remained the summit of her life, "her career a long study in anticlimax," wrote *Vanity Fair*. To have peaked in her twenties was no easy thing. "I did have some real psychological problems for a while," Weddington reflected years later. "We expect our lives to be a progression."

Through the years, Weddington had endured other hurts. She had divorced, and also been made to resign her post as the chief lobbyist in Washington for Texas, accused of excessive comp-time and travel. But to the pro-choice movement, she remained the youthful victor in *Roe*. Over and again, they paid her to tell of the time when there were no women on the Court and no ladies' room in the lawyers' lounge. *Roe* was the meat of a lecture that would soon earn Weddington the title of best college speaker, *Roe* the drumroll to her every public word. As she would soon introduce herself to the Senate Judiciary Committee: "My name is Sarah Weddington. I am the attorney who litigated and won *Roe v. Wade*."

Roe, though, had been won by two lawyers, not one. And, like Mary Coffee, who had kvelled to the Baptist Press about her daughter Linda, there were some who tried to make that fact known.

Rick Johnston, for example, a Coffee client who was on the State Democratic Executive Committee in North Dallas, told any and all that Weddington had had a co-counsel. Virginia Whitehill, a former board member of Planned Parenthood in Dallas who'd worked with both *Roe*

lawyers, had recently told an author writing of *Roe* that the quiet counsel had contributed every bit as much as the charming one, a point she
wished to sharpen nearly thirty years later. "Sarah's the frosting on the
cake," says Whitehill, "but Linda's the cake." Her daughter would raise
the issue directly to Weddington. Says Margaret Whitehill: "I mentioned to her that she was switching 'we' to 'I.'"

Coffee, though, said nothing. And in April, 1989, she did not travel
to DC to hear the *Webster* arguments. She was occupied with a legal matter in Dallas that would soon cast her even further from the public eye.

———

COFFEE HAD NOT found a partner among the Baptist singles she'd traveled to Israel with in the summer of 1973. Back home in Texas, she had
devoted herself to her work. There was community in law; though Coffee was "not a people person," says Peggy Clewis, the firm secretary,
she had been a member of the Texas Bar for five years. But on August 1,
seven months after *Roe*, she neglected to pay her fifty-dollar membership fee. She finally did so on the last day of October, but not before the
back of her registration card was stamped "Delinquent Notice."

Delinquencies happen, of course. But Coffee was soon delinquent twice more, waiting until October, in both 1975 and 1976,
to pay fees due in August. She was nonetheless made a partner in
1975, a shareholder in what was now Palmer, Palmer & Coffee. And
having publicly mused about becoming a judge, she was continuing
her quiet rise despite the misogyny that still gripped the law. Coffee
told stories of clients who threw fits upon learning their lawyer was
a woman, and of juries who were extra "attentive" because it was a
woman addressing them, and of opposing lawyers who were timid
because, explained Coffee, "they feel to some extent they're picking
on a cripple."

Coffee understood gender politics; though she favored pantsuits,
she wore dresses to court for important cases. But, having filed *Roe*, she
continued the feminist fight. She spoke on a panel on sex discrimination
moderated by her mentor, Judge Hughes. And, between bankruptcies,
she took on a raft of pro-bono clients that included a young girl who

wished to be a Cub Scout and a supermarket employee passed over because of her sex.

All the while, Coffee worried about *Roe*—that it was only benefiting the well-to-do, that abortion clinics were as impersonal as assembly lines, that state legislatures were eroding the right to choose. Regarding the last, *Roe* was just months old when Coffee confided to a student at Baylor her disagreement with Weddington, the lawyer turned state representative who now wished to require a young girl wanting an abortion to get the consent of a parent.

Coffee had never doubted her work on *Roe*. She was lucky; her family was pro-choice, her church too. Abortion, the former Southern Baptist Convention president Wayne Dehoney said in 1976, posed "no moral or theological problem." It did, however, pose an ideological problem, as evangelicals were increasingly becoming pro-life. Come 1980, the SBC joined them, opposing all abortions save those to protect the life of the mother.

The church changed its terminology, too. The unborn now grew, in the words of its resolutions, from "fetal life" to "a developing human being" to "a living individual human being."

All at once, Coffee was at odds with her church. And not simply on the matter of abortion. It had recently seen fit to denounce homosexuality, too, labeling it "deviant moral behavior."

Coffee was heartbroken. A lifelong sanctuary had now repudiated not only what she did but who she was. Says Coffee: "I thought it was just terrible."

Still, Coffee had the law. Single through her thirties, she cleaved to it. "For a long time, I thought there was something wrong with me for being so interested in wanting a career," Coffee reflected in 1980. But then, she said, she had begun "to talk to other women, and found out that many of them thought the way I did."

If Coffee confided in them her indifference to marriage, she said nothing of being gay. She had never come out. She had dated men. She had kept quiet her role in the suit her friend McCluskey had brought against the sodomy laws.

It is one thing, however, to be discreet, to bow to convention, another to suppress one's orientation. Marooned by her church, Coffee was forty when, in 1983, she responded to a personal ad that began with the capital-lettered words: "LESBIAN SEEKS."

The ad sought a woman of "intelligence" and "modesty." Coffee possessed both, and she sent off a letter describing herself as a work in progress. She signed her letter "Lee." Soon after, on a cold night in December in East Dallas, she met Rebecca Hartt.

Hartt was a decade younger than Coffee, the youngest child of a Presbyterian family in nearby Richardson. She was thin and pert and chatty and sold pest control for Orkin. Though her father, a county judge, was Republican, Hartt leaned left.

Over Mexican food, the conversation flowed, Coffee telling Hartt that she'd met Hartt's father while clerking for Judge Hughes. When Hartt mentioned having heard Weddington speak, Coffee volunteered that she'd worked with Weddington on *Roe*; her name was Linda, not Lee. Hartt had Coffee over for a nightcap, the women, in slacks and blouses, drinking brandy and Benedictine.

Soon, after a subsequent date, Coffee stayed the night. For her next visit, she packed gourmet beans and a grinder and a pot to make good coffee in the morning. Her girlfriend, meantime, had all she wanted. Says Hartt: "My idea of happiness was a woman, a dog, and books." Coffee had recently bought a Spanish home beside a Dallas reservoir. Hartt moved in, her Rhodesian ridgebacks and Bible in tow.

Coffee was suddenly living a life she wanted. She not only had a good job and a nice home but a better half with blue-gray eyes. She even had a spot on a semi-pro women's football team called the Shamrocks, Coffee their helmeted center, the name Lea appliquéd in yellow felt across the padded chest of her green jersey. "I did not use my real name," says Coffee. "My mother would have died."

Mary Coffee did not learn of her daughter's ball-playing. She did, though, learn of Hartt. And despite the anti-gay turn of her church, Mary Coffee was good to her. The years that followed were thus happy ones for the couple—of family Christmases and dog christenings and Bastille Day celebrations, the last in honor of the Huguenots, who had helped develop the ridgebacks Hartt so loved.

Hartt kept busy. "I got people registered to vote," she says. "I got slums torn down." She kept house, too. (The one time Coffee used a vacuum cleaner, its belt came off.) Coffee was the breadwinner, billing clients $125 an hour. In 1986, she began supplementing her work at the firm with work of her own, a solo practitioner litigating bankruptcies from a suite on Elm Street.

Coffee updated her résumé. But, as before, it included no mention of *Roe*; Coffee had left the case behind. So it was a surprise when a representative of NBC brought her and Weddington and Norma together to discuss their participation in the upcoming film.

Much had changed since their last meeting. Back in 1973, Weddington had envied Coffee. ("I remember feeling jealous," she wrote years later, noting that, unlike Coffee, she had not been on law review or clerked for a judge.) But now, Weddington peered down at her. "She said," recalls Coffee, "'*I* did the case.'" Coffee said nothing.

Weddington was no more generous with Norma. "Sarah came on real strong, saying that she and I get paid for the, quote unquote, 'consulting work,'" recalls Coffee. "She said right in front of Norma: 'Well, we should get paid more than someone like *her*.' Everyone gasped. I was embarrassed."

In the end, it was agreed that the lawyers would each be paid $20,000, a third of what Norma was paid. Coffee was content. She had all she needed, above all a good name. But then, in the spring of 1989, she was indicted on charges of fraud for allegedly concealing documents and forging a signature. She faced five years in prison.

The indictment was big news; the *Dallas Times Herald* ran it on the front page of its second section—just below word that someone had fired shots at Jane Roe. Coffee was shell-shocked. "I spent about two weeks where I could barely get out of bed," she says.

The lawyer needed a lawyer. She hired one fresh from the U.S. Attorney's Office in Dallas. His name was Kim Wade and he wanted exposure on a big case, says Coffee. He also knew that Coffee would help in her representation. He agreed to represent her for $15,000, less than a third of what others were asking. Besides, he says, his father had told him that Coffee was "brilliant and very forthright." His father was one to know. He was Henry Wade—the DA whom Coffee had bound to *Roe*.

Coffee told Wade that she was innocent. She explained that she had signed the name of a client because he was out of reach in Hawaii, and had disclosed doing so in his bankruptcy filing. "She felt she'd not done anything wrong," says Wade, "and the facts bore her out."

Coffee helped assemble those facts. She noted that in a federal criminal case, there is nationwide service of process. The records of the client in Hawaii could thus be subpoenaed. Coffee drafted the subpoenas herself.

The trial was a few months off when the movie on Norma aired in May 1989. A beauty named Annabella Price portrayed Coffee on television sets across the country. The fictional Coffee had few lines; the script belonged to Weddington and Norma.

Sixteen years after *Roe*, it still did. As Coffee prepared for a trial that had nothing to do with abortion, Weddington and Norma arrived at the Supreme Court in the hope that the *Webster* ruling would preserve their legacy.

Off in Dallas, the abortion provider Curtis Boyd prayed for *Roe*. Having sacrificed so much of his past for abortion, he was waiting to learn if it would overtake his future, too.

Chapter 17

The issuance of *Roe* in 1973 had been a great comfort to Curtis Boyd; the same police car that had once quickened his heart now protected him and the clinics he ran in Texas and New Mexico. But abortion had also separated the doctor from his friends and family, his practice and home. And 1974 found Boyd, thirty-seven and single, living alone in a Dallas hotel.

Work was just a few blocks away, a small wooden building on Fairmount Street that had previously housed an architecture firm. Boyd's clinic had four procedure rooms. They were always filled. Post-*Roe*, in 1973, the number of legal abortions in America had jumped 27 percent, to 744,600. Boyd had performed roughly 1 percent of them.

As the number of legal abortions rose, the number of illegal ones fell, from an estimated 130,000 in 1972 to 17,000 in 1975. The number of deaths resulting from illegal abortions fell, too, over that same period, from thirty-nine to four. It was, noted the author Leslie Reagan, "an improvement in maternal mortality that ranks with the invention of antisepsis and antibiotics."

Boyd was amazed. As he later told the press, *Roe* had "disappeared" the fevers and bleedings and perforations he had witnessed during his medical training. But the stigma of abortion remained even after its legalization. Indeed, Boyd saw that many of his patients did not submit his bill to insurance for fear of suffering the scrutiny of a parent or spouse. He saw that a trickle of protestors began to block the entrance to his clinic, sitting and singing Christian songs until the police carried them away. And he saw that the state board of medical examiners was monitoring him, trying to trip him up on details, insisting, for example, that he add "M.D." to the plastic lettering of his name outside his clinic.

Compliance, though, did nothing to ingratiate Boyd to the medical community. He tried desperately to destigmatize his work, turning his clinic into a nonprofit, complete with a board of local clergy and doctors. But the Dallas doctors kept away. "They thought, oh—he's an abortionist," says Boyd. "They didn't want to associate with me."

The pro-choice, however, embraced him. Boyd had made abortion obtainable even before the law had. Now that his work was legal, the doctor was invited here and there to help plumb the implications of *Roe*, of not only millions of abortions but the consequences of those abortions—the marriages they preserved or made avoidable, the genetic abnormalities such as Down syndrome that they reduced in disproportionate number. Among the activists and lawyers Boyd met were Weddington and Coffee, who joined him one evening at the Dallas home of abortion reformer Virginia Whitehill.

At every stop, Boyd was clear: abortion, as he saw it, was not the mere termination of pregnancy. It was a means to self-determination, fulfillment. He had never forgotten his high school crush, Virginia, who had been made to deliver an unwanted child and shamed for conceiving it. The experience, says Boyd, had changed Virginia; he had seen her once with her child, and she was "hard and closed." It had changed Boyd, too. And he offered his patients counseling, each woman encouraged to discuss her feelings and thoughts so as to find, says Boyd, "a greater serenity."

Boyd's assistant, Reggie Cox, helped him instill that serenity. At his clinic in Santa Fe, she spoke, she says, "in low gentle tones," offering patients instruction and explanation and massage, too, careful to rub a hand, a forehead. Patients were helped, and in 1974, Boyd hired a woman named Glenna Halvorson to do the same at his clinic in Dallas.

Halvorson was ten years his junior, an eldest child born in 1947 to an atheist and an agnostic in Modesto, California. "My friends and their mothers," recalls Halvorson, "always wanted to save my soul."

Free of religion, Halvorson had found sustenance in school: she earned a BA in literature and was pursuing a doctorate in developmental psychology. She was drawn to complex issues. (She'd worked as a counselor for both schizophrenics and the subjects of a Dallas desegregation project.) She took now to abortion, devising a regimen of questions to help guide a patient toward clarity and a plan of action. Was the pregnancy a secret? Did the patient wish to start a family? Might an abortion rupture her relationship with God?

Boyd was pleased. Halvorson was a very good counselor. She was also recently divorced and beautiful, lithe and fair with green eyes and long blond hair. The doctor asked Halvorson to assist him with the home birth of a friend in a house in the woods. The two were soon a couple, bound by their work.

That work, however, continued to isolate Boyd from other doctors, abortion a scarlet letter A. When he sought to join the board of a Catholic hospital in Santa Fe, it hesitated to approve him. And though *Roe* had relieved him of the great fear that a dead patient might lead to the loss of his license and to prison, carrying that fear for years had left him, he says, "emotionally exhausted."

Boyd needed a change. Having trained doctors to run both his clinics, he left Texas for New Mexico in late 1974, retreating with Halvorson to Santa Fe and then to an adobe cottage in the hippie commune of Truchas. There, on a wooded ridge high in the Sangre de Cristo Mountains, the couple raised vegetables and Arabian horses. The doctor delivered babies, too, presiding over the home births of new friends. Says Boyd: "I was trying to get centered again."

The ranks of abortion providers, meantime, were growing; four years after *Roe*, the number of hospitals and clinics and private doctors performing abortions had increased by a thousand, to 2,526. And in 1977, a new organization of providers, the National Abortion Federation, invited Boyd to join its board. He accepted.

Boyd was overjoyed. Here at last was legitimacy, validation, community. And in 1978, after Boyd and Halvorson married on a mesa in Truchas, they said goodbye to their twenty acres of vegetables and horses and moved into a high-rise in Dallas. They were ready to return to work.

Boyd was delighted to be back in the procedure room. Restored by his exile, he remained at age forty expert at his craft—patient through dilation, skilled with a curette, able to evacuate a fetus through ever smaller cavities.

Still, Boyd knew his limits. The instruments needed to abort a fetus change as the fetus grows. And though *Roe* permitted abortions through twenty-four weeks, Boyd performed none past sixteen. "Just because it's legal," says Boyd, "doesn't mean there's a doctor who knows how to do it."

Still, five years after *Roe*, Boyd now wished to go further.

Boyd knew that to move past sixteen weeks would increase the risk of complications. But he now had hospital admitting privileges in both Texas and New Mexico. They enabled Boyd, he says, to "take a little more risk." Slowly, he pushed deeper into pregnancy, aborting larger and larger fetuses with larger and larger forceps and dilators. "It was just a matter of skill development," says Boyd. By 1980, he had reached twenty weeks. He wished to go further still.

More than a century before, doctors in Scotland had used a genus of seaweed called laminaria as a dilating agent. The seaweed expanded as it absorbed water, and the doctors found that if they inserted into the vagina dried sticks of it packed in wet sponge, the sticks expanded and the cervix dilated.

Boyd was initially skeptical of laminaria's usefulness. But medical professionals in Japan had used it in recent years to great effect. And after a gynecologist he knew named Mildred Hanson returned from Japan with sticks of it and instructed Boyd on technique, he marveled. The seaweed, a brown algae, opened a cervix more safely and easily than any manual dilator. Within a year, Boyd was using it to abort fetuses up to twenty-four weeks. He had reached viability.

Boyd worked ten hours a day, five days a week. With repetition came refinement, the lessening of pain and time. Boyd shaved minutes off the procedure that had come to be called "dilation and evacuation"— second-trimester abortions dropping from thirty minutes to fifteen, first-trimesters to ten.

Boyd had long taught the procedure to the doctors who worked for him, instructing them on how to use forceps "to disarticulate the fetus," he says, "to take it out in parts" before a curette and vacuum then emptied the uterus of any fetal remains. Now, he began to teach it through the National Abortion Federation, running NAF workshops that drew hundreds. At every turn, Boyd also communicated the radical notion that abortion was something positive, an assertion of self. And yet, having finally reached viability, his thoughts turned from the pregnant woman to the unborn. "I began to identify more with the fetus," says Boyd. "It's a living human organism from conception and it has the potential to become a person."

Boyd was unsure when that potential was realized. Still, he remained certain that if ever a woman—in the thirty or so years during which she could conceive—found herself carrying a fetus she did not wish to birth, it would be his duty, his *privilege*, to abort that pregnancy.

His wife, Glenna, was no less committed to providing abortions. She worked beside her husband, their days crowded with patients, their clinics performing some thirty abortions per day, some eight thousand per year. Nearly all were routine. Just one in five were second-trimester, one in one thousand beset by complications.

In 1980, that one in one thousand was named Vanessa Preston. Preston was twenty-two, a minister's wife who had a young child and was not ready for another. She was in her second trimester and came to Boyd for a dilation and extraction, the procedure the pro-life would rebrand "partial-birth abortion." Boyd had begun the abortion when amniotic fluid entered Preston's bloodstream and lungs. She had a seizure and went into cardiac arrest. Boyd resuscitated her. But her heart stopped again. And the doctor, having safely seen through more than fifty thousand abortions, had to tell a husband that his wife was dead. "It was a horrible experience," recalls Boyd. "I kept thinking, I have these magic hands. Magic only takes you so far."

A medical examiner exonerated Boyd. But pro-lifers didn't, heckling him daily, calling him "murderer" as he walked to and from his clinic.

═══════

LATER THAT YEAR, Ronald Reagan was elected president. He quickly let down the pro-life movement when a human life amendment died in the Senate and he said little. Still, throughout his presidency, Reagan remained vigorously pro-life—nominating William Rehnquist, who had dissented in *Roe*, to be chief justice of the Supreme Court, and withholding federal funds from family planning concerns, both at home and abroad, that performed or espoused abortion.

Boyd worried that such policies would raise the cost of abortion; the Hyde amendment already banned Medicaid dollars from offsetting it. Wanting to remain affordable, the doctor kept his fee low—$150 per procedure. Demand was great; Reagan was still in his first term when Boyd opened a third clinic, three procedure rooms in Albuquerque. Boyd was earning some $150,000 a year.

Back in the seventies, Boyd had begun to use his dollars to influence elected officials—a thousand dollars here or there getting him face time with senators and attorneys general. He would then share with them polls indicating that their constituencies were pro-choice.

Now, a decade after *Roe*, Boyd was among the larger private abortion providers in the country, and he increased his lobbying, meeting annually with a hundred or so politicians sympathetic to his cause. His pitch, he says, was simple: "I'll campaign for you or I'll campaign against you. Whatever does you the most good."

Boyd, however, kept his politics out of his clinics, and instructed his fifty-plus employees to do the same. Says Boyd: "The service has to speak for itself."

That service was the legal and affordable termination of unwanted pregnancy. Boyd and his wife wished it to be comfortable, too, and sought new ways to relieve their patients of pain: visualization, hypnosis, nitrous oxide. The pro-life were unmoved. Glenna wrote in her dissertation of the harassment she and Boyd endured. They were called killers, said to be poor practitioners motivated by money. She titled her dissertation "Surviving a Holy War."

The front lines of that war were abortion clinics. The election of Reagan had inspired the foot soldiers who stood in protest outside them, and a growing number now gathered daily on Fairmount Street to yell into bullhorns and hand out leaflets and block Boyd's door and sometimes burst through it.

There was little to deter such protests; obstructing clinics was a misdemeanor, not a felony. Reagan looked the other way, even sending a letter of blessing to the Florida church of a woman whose daughter participated in an attack on several clinics. In his second term, such attacks increased in number and violence—windows broken, fires set, bombs thrown.

Doctors were chastened; a 1985 poll revealed that while eight of ten obstetricians and gynecologists were pro-choice, just one in three performed abortions. And so, even as the number of abortions in America did not diminish under Reagan, the annual total steady at 1.58 million, the number of abortion providers did. The sum total of hospitals, clinics and private doctors providing abortions fell by 11 percent, to 2,582. The decline would continue well past Reagan's presidency.

Boyd was a target. He received a handwritten death threat, a protestor asked if an accident had befallen his son Kyle, and a Molotov cocktail filled the lab of his Dallas clinic with smoke. But the doctor was undeterred and protected his staff, outfitting his clinics with cameras and motion detectors and automatic locks and bulletproof glass and buzzers and intercoms and police-alert buttons. He hired security guards, too. Even so, on Christmas Eve in 1988, an arsonist torched his Dallas clinic. The damage totaled $100,000.

———

OVER THE COURSE OF FIFTEEN YEARS, Boyd had come to recognize many of his protestors. Some of them came to him for abortions, which he provided.

That a woman would protest abortion and yet seek one herself was no surprise to Boyd. Men had secretly brought their girlfriends, daughters and wives to him for as long as he'd been in practice. A predicament could take hold of anyone. Abortion was far too commonplace to be had only by those who supported it; by 1989, nearly 24 million abortions had been performed in the U.S. since *Roe*. Two Canadian studies would report that 34 percent of women who had one favored "abortion restrictions," while 43 percent "voiced anti-choice attitudes." And analysis of data from a Guttmacher Institute survey of patients would find that 4.1% of women who had abortions believed abortion should be illegal "in all or most cases."

Boyd understood that contradiction. The doctor did not shy away from the unalterable fact that abortion was the intentional killing of prenatal life. And he saw clearly that, a generation after *Roe*, the stigma enveloping abortion had grown so strong that even those who devoted their lives to providing it were not immune; his aide Reggie Cox retired now, in 1989, having never told her family of the nineteen years she had worked alongside him.

———

AMERICAN LAW IS mindful of the degree to which abortion and, more generally, sex, is stigmatized. Though the law stipulates that a defendant (and the public) have a right to know who has filed suit, a 1961 case involving sex prompted the Supreme Court, for the first time, to grant a plaintiff pseudonymity. A decade later, it was sex again that prompted the Court to allow Norma to be called Jane Roe.

It was thus little surprise that even Roe's lawyer had not revealed that she herself had had an abortion. Asked in 1986 if she'd had one, Weddington had responded that the question was "irrelevant."

In a sense, she was right. The lawyer no more owed an explanation as to why she had fought to legalize abortion than any woman owed an explanation as to why she had one. And yet, of course, the question of whether Weddington had had an abortion was entirely relevant. For experience forms conviction; Weddington would later confide that in the momentary hush before she argued *Roe* in the Supreme Court, she had thought back to her abortion. And when, in a few years, she would finally write of her abortion publicly, she did so, she said, "to explain . . . why I had spent this much time on this issue."

And therein lies the paradox of legal abortion. It rests upon a right to privacy. And so, though it is common—at 1992 abortion rates, one in every 2.3 women in America would at some point have one—nearly all of the women who do keep it secret, which enables half of the country to castigate the procedure as something cruel and unfamiliar.

If there is an antidote to secrecy, it is revelation. As Justice Blackmun noted in his preamble to *Roe*, exposure— to a story, a person, "the raw edges of human existence"—can change a mind. The psychologist Gordon Allport demonstrated this with his "contact theory," which argues that interaction with a minority group diminishes prejudice. As Herman Melville wrote: "see how elastic our stiff prejudices grow when love once comes to bend them."

The pro-choice had thus pursued a strategy of exposure; dating back to pre-*Roe* "speak-outs" and the 1972 debut issue of *Ms.* magazine, there were women who went public with their abortions. And when abortion returned now to the Supreme Court in the case of *Webster v. Reproductive Health Services*, 2,887 women recalled their abortions in an enormous amicus brief, each stepping forward, as poet Adrienne Rich once beseeched, "to take responsibility for the voicing of her experience."

In the months preceding *Webster*, no woman had voiced her experience as loudly as Norma McCorvey. The former plaintiff was everywhere—on podiums and TV. Norma wished the world to know that she was Jane Roe. And, having carried a pregnancy that helped others to end theirs, she went looking, this same spring of 1989, for the child she had birthed—a baby turned teenager who was oblivious to who she was.

PART V

Undue Burden

Chapter 18

Decades after her father left home, it would occur to Shelley that the genesis of her unease preceded his disappearance. In fact, it preceded her birth. "When someone's pregnant with a baby," she reflected decades later, "and they don't want that baby, that person develops knowing they're not wanted."

As a girl of ten, however, Shelley had yet to consider her fetal self, or even the alcoholism that in 1980 had cast her father, Bill, from her Houston home. She did, though, have a pair of realizations. She wished one day to find a partner who would *stay*. And she would be a secretary. A secretary lived a steady life. And Shelley desired to live as steadily as possible.

Shelley sought out surrogates for her missing father—an old neighbor named J. C., whom she called Papa, and an uncle named Johnny, a fireman and Sunday school teacher who, alongside his wife, Carol, was as steady and reliable as his brother Billy was not. Johnny and Carol instructed Shelley on the ways of a good Baptist. Says Shelley: "Everything I learned about God and church and Jesus, I learned from them."

Scripture was everything for Shelley's aunt and uncle, above all John 3:16, which promised eternal life to all who believed in Jesus. Shelley believed. She believed in her uncle, too. But some cavities cannot be filled. And all through eighth grade, Shelley wondered about her biological family—her birth mother and older sisters.

Mother Ruth offered no answers. She knew nothing of Norma or her daughters. And she told Shelley little of her past with Billy. Only when Shelley happened at age fourteen upon a hidden marriage certificate did Ruth confess that she'd deserted one husband for another. Secrets abounded.

That same year, in 1984, Billy got back in touch with Ruth and asked to see their daughter. Ruth demurred. She believed her ex an irredeemable drunk. To be certain that he never came calling, she quickly moved with their daughter almost two thousand miles northwest, to the third floor of a concrete building in Burien, a town outside Seattle where Ruth's sister lived with her husband.

The town "was so not Texas," says Shelley; its rains and people left her cold. After a lonely summer, the new girl at Highline High was unhappy, teased for her Texas accent, hard-pressed to find a subject she liked outside of French.

Shelley had blue eyes and a heart-shaped face. She was shy and slight; she would graduate high school at 98 pounds. Still, she weathered ninth grade, shedding her accent and taking on friends. The next year, she had a boyfriend, a muscled classmate named Seth who was popular and blond and liked to wear camouflage. He was also adopted.

Shelley had had her first kiss at twelve with a boy named Kevin, who told her she needed practice. Shelley practiced with Seth a lot—at home, at the movies, in the bus station parking lot where she watched him skateboard. The boy gave her a necklace.

Shelley was happy. No longer shy, she liked attention and got it. "I could rock a pair of Jordache," she says. She had her crushes, too, John Stamos among them, Shelley hurrying home daily from school to take in episodes of *General Hospital*. But then, life changed.

Shelley was fifteen when she noticed that her hands had begun to shake. She could make them still by eating. But the tremor would return. She shook when she felt anxious, and she felt anxious, she says, around "everything." More, she was soon depressed, too— "sleepy and sad," she says. But she confided in no one, not her boyfriend and not her mother. She simply continued on, steady, content to watch her soap and her skateboarding beau, to eat when her hands shook, to seek out secretaries on vocation day at school, to just say no to drugs and alcohol and cigarettes and hooky and sex, save the last with Seth.

That relationship was subject to bouts of jealousy. Come her senior year, Shelley was single, left to look again for a man who would never leave, someone like her friend Todd.

Todd lived in Shelley's apartment complex, with his father and step-mom and one of his sisters. He was a beanpole—six-plus feet and 140 pounds. He ran track and would soon run far from Burien, traveling the world as a marine. But beside Shelley, he lingered, walking with her to Pizza Hut or the library, happy to pass the time with his friend, to talk of their relationships and of their fathers who drank.

Billy remained in touch; he phoned Shelley every so often to tell the youngest of his seven children that he missed her. But such hellos were brief and rare. And when Shelley thought back to Texas, to the blue-bonnets that sprouted in spring, it was less her father she missed than her Papa J. C., the neighbor turned grandfather who phoned and wrote and footed the down payment on her Datsun when she and her mother moved to the nearby town of Kent. Family was commitment, not blood.

In 1988, Shelley graduated from Highline High. She was about to start secretarial school when her cousins told her another family secret: Ruth had been unable to conceive. The daughter she'd adopted told her mother that she wished to know, once and for all, the full truth of her life. Only then, said Shelley, would she not be "blindsided."

That October, Shelley's friend Todd returned home from boot camp. Between his exertions—and the double portions he was made to eat—he had found himself thinking of Shelley. "She was the one I was always missing," he says. "She was kind of my safe space." Now, before flying off to military police school in San Antonio, he phoned her. "I told her that I was going to marry her," he says. It was less a proposal than a prognostication; he had no ring. Shelley said okay.

———

IN THE SUMMER OF 1980, Norma's middle child, Jennifer, spent six weeks in Houston. Her parents had dispatched her to her older sister in the desperate hope that a move might do what Ritalin and tutoring and counseling had not—help her survive those pre-teen riptides that had nearly drowned her earlier that spring. But back home in Richardson, Jennifer turned thirteen and junior high again dragged her under. "I started drinking," recalls Jennifer, "hiding from my parents."

Jennifer remained uncertain about her sexuality. Questioning who she was, she wondered more and more about the birth and adoption records her father had told her he'd filed away. Still, Jennifer told her father that she wished to wait seven years to read them. At twenty-one, she said, she'd be "mature enough to deal with whoever my mother and father were."

In 1983, Jennifer started tenth grade at a private school with classes and teams that suited her; she took oceanography and ran track. But she knew no one who identified as gay. And when, at sixteen, she had sex with a girl at school, it was "scary," she says. Soon after, Jennifer erupted, brawling with girls and sleeping with boys. She got suspended and her mother, Donna, cried. "My mom," says Jennifer, "thought I totally lost my mind."

Jennifer began to wonder anew about her birth mother. She asked her parents to see her adoption records. But she reconsidered, and retreated into church and work, the salad bar at a nearby Albertson's that she now managed. Work offered up a measure of self-worth, and she switched to a high school where students could hold jobs in the afternoon. She began helping a respiratory therapist tend to her equipment and treatments. Life improved.

Jennifer soon had a boyfriend, a blue-eyed blue-collar weightlifter one grade above named Ricky. His mother worked at a telephone company, his father at a cardboard factory. Ricky worked at an auto body shop, and Jennifer admired that he had restored by hand his own car, a 1971 Caprice Classic. The couple had been together two years when Jennifer painted her first name under its hood. Soon after, Ricky offered her his last.

Jennifer had her concerns. Ricky had gotten angry when once she thought she was pregnant. She had never felt safe enough to confide in him her feelings for women. Still, Jennifer had begun to mend beside Ricky. She had stopped using drugs and sleeping around. And in the spring of 1987, one year after graduating high school, she put on a wedding dress, pink lace offsetting her tan skin.

Nineteen years old, Jennifer was happy to be a wife, and happy cleaning cars at an auto body shop. But home with Ricky in their wooden ranch house in the town of Oak Cliff, the couple was coming apart. They had begun to drink together a few nights a week, and fights followed, Jennifer angry that Ricky spent less time with her than with his mother and his car. Ricky retreated further; he ate his meals at his parents' house and drove off in his Chevy at all hours. He and Jennifer were both drunk the night she left him; she drove the thirty minutes from Oak Cliff to Bedford and moved in, as years before, with her sister.

Jennifer began tending bar at a pool hall south of Dallas called Speeds. She learned on the job and earned more than a thousand dollars a week in tips. The bar also offered her a tap with no bottom, and half her nights, Jennifer drove home drunk. "I was nothing but a lush," she says.

Jennifer was at the bar when she met a man named James, a military veteran out of work. They began to sleep together. Ricky got word of their relationship and quickly reconciled with Jennifer. But Jennifer continued to sleep with James even after she moved back in with Ricky. Ricky then came upon the couple speaking in his living room, and he punched his wife—"cold-cocked me in the jaw," says Jennifer. She phoned the police and returned to her sister.

The couple was not yet divorced when, in 1988, Jennifer began dating another James, a hotheaded policeman from Wilmer, just south of Dallas. The couple drank together, and a woozy James would tell of his family, of an absent father and a mother gone crazy after causing a car crash that killed her daughter—a sister James had barely known.

Jennifer, meantime, learned from her sister that her birth mother had had two other children. Jennifer, said Cindy, was the middle of three. Jennifer was stunned; she had two more siblings! But Cindy said they had no idea who they were.

In the fall of 1988, Jennifer turned twenty-one, and at last asked her father for her adoption records. She hoped they might lead not only to her birth mother but to her sisters, too. Her father, though, had no records; he did not say why he'd led her to believe he did. Jennifer said nothing.

A DECADE BEFORE, in 1979, Jennifer's unknown older sister Melissa told herself that she would be different. Unlike her mother, Norma, and grandmother, Mary, she wouldn't drink or sleep around. She would have a family. It would be calm and intact. She would spend nights at home talking over dinner with a husband and children.

Melissa was fifteen. Sex with her boyfriend had just assured her that, unlike her mother, she was not gay. And so, she remained with David, the blond boy who lived two blocks down the dirt road from the trailer she shared with her grandmother.

Melissa was often alone in that trailer. Mary had divorced Raymond and taken up with a man named Tex, the owner of a bar called the Yellow Rose. The couple liked to drink. Mary was drunk when one night she fell off a porch and broke her ankle, drunk when another night she got into a fight with a pool cue. Melissa had to pick her grandmother up from jail in the big brown family Plymouth.

In 1980, Norma's brother Jimmy moved in with Melissa and Mary. He was thirty-five. And he was tormented. The schizophrenic impulses that had flared in him since adolescence now convulsed his every day. Jimmy was apt to shout aloud racial slurs, says Melissa, or leave the house naked or steal some little thing. Melissa would then find her uncle and pay for whatever magazine or candy he had taken and coax him into the Plymouth for a ride back to the trailer. But sometimes, Jimmy was less pitiable than dangerous; he lit fires in the kitchen and set knives under his bed and forced open closed doors. Melissa needed to escape. And so, fifteen years old, she went down the road to live with David. Says Melissa: "There was a mom and a dad there."

David's mother and stepfather were raising their three kids with love. And having long been passed among the members of a broken family, Melissa took refuge in one that was whole. She ate meat and potatoes at their table, and cut through the plains on a motorized bike with their son, and talked life through with their daughter Tammy, her best friend. But as the months passed, Melissa longed for her missing sisters—the two phantoms younger than she. Every girl on every street was a possible relation. Melissa began to approach strangers. "Where are you from?" she would ask. "Wisconsin? Oh." She ached to be one of three, and she looked wistfully at every large family she would happen upon at a local water park or cafeteria.

Melissa was self-sufficient; at age eleven, she'd fashioned dolls out of yarn and thread and zippers and buttons after Norma had withheld her belongings. Now sixteen, she ended her relationship with David when he began to drink and smoke. "Reminded me of Norma," she says.

But Melissa could not return home, and remained beside her ex two more years until she moved into an apartment of her own, working between classes at a bank and a skating rink to pay the rent. She was eager to be gone from Pampa. And in 1984, one month after graduating from Pampa High, she packed up her bed and her 45s and her pool cue and moved an hour southwest, starting college in Amarillo that same summer.

Melissa was busy. She had four classes, three jobs, two roommates and a boyfriend named Rick. She had little time to study, but it was all good; she was nineteen and free. When she withdrew from a class and got two C's and a D, that was okay too. She dropped out of college and enrolled in beauty school.

Beauty had long drawn Melissa. She took note of hair and nails and skin the way Mary and Norma minded breasts. And she prettied her own with purple dye and red polish and a fake tan. Men liked her—her considerateness and her laugh and her tight Levi's, too. She liked them back.

Melissa, though, was guarded. She'd seen her mother and grandmother run through dozens of partners. "Watching all the sex stuff," she says, "I should have been a slut." But she wasn't. Twenty years old, she had had sex with just three men—her boyfriends David, Rick and Dee. She remained in search not of mere love but faithfulness, that which she had seen most in Norma's unshakeable partner. Says Melissa: "I always wanted a man like Connie."

Melissa was out with her boyfriend when a well-built man with feathered hair, she says, called out to her: "Why don't you leave that little pipsqueak and go out with me?" Outmatched, boyfriend Rick was quiet. Flush with liqueur punch, Melissa was charmed. She and the man went to a movie.

His name was Kerry. He worked in concrete but was midway through a degree in social work. He was brash, disarming. By the time Melissa got her cosmetology license and a job at a mall cutting hair and waxing eyebrows, he was her boyfriend. At the end of every long day, Kerry drew her a bath.

Melissa was in love. But she had her doubts. Kerry had many female friends. "He was always at someone's house," she says. A few months into their relationship, Melissa caught him cheating. Still, she did not leave—not even when Kerry began to yell and hit her, too.

Melissa told herself that her boyfriend was only violent when drunk. He would apologize when sober. It comforted Melissa further that Kerry, who was learning to tend to families scarred by neglect and abuse, knew that what he did was wrong. Besides, Melissa fought back with her teeth and nails; the combat left her bruised but excited. Says Melissa: "It raised my endorphins."

Six months after they met, Kerry lowered to one knee and presented her a ring inside a box inside a box inside a box. The couple married in March, Melissa Sandefur become Melissa Mills, a bride in a white sequined dress with train and veil.

Among the guests at their small Amarillo church was the mother of the bride. Norma had barely seen Melissa in years, and would "freak out," says Melissa, if she met one of her boyfriends. (Upon meeting Kerry, Norma had locked herself in a bathroom.) It was thus no surprise when Norma got high and drunk at the wedding, and had a coughing fit, too, one hack breaking a rib, sending her to a hospital and disrupting the ceremony. Melissa seethed. "Everything Norma stood for," she says, "I didn't want to be."

Most upsetting to Melissa was Norma's rejection of motherhood. And yet, she took pride in her mother's plaintiffship. Melissa believed in *Roe*.

Melissa, however, could not imagine ending a pregnancy. Even *preventing* a pregnancy made her uncomfortable; it seemed to her scarcely different than relinquishing a child. "Norma gave everybody up," says Melissa. "I didn't want to be that way." Melissa told Kerry that they would therefore rely on rhythm. Jordan was born the following fall, mother and father welcoming her into the old trailer Mary had gifted them.

Melissa had long feared that she might resemble Norma in motherhood. But she loved being a mother and loved her little girl, introducing her to dolls and ducks and Clifford the Big Red Dog. She also loved her husband.

Kerry had been faithful since the wedding, and was no longer violent. He'd begun working with children at a Christian halfway house. And he let Melissa know that he himself had been abused, raped and beaten as a boy by a man seeing his mother. He had then been sent at age ten to a Christian school for at-risk boys. Four years later, he'd had sex with one of his teachers.

It was hard not to wonder what life at that Christian school had done to Kerry. Still, Melissa believed more in the determinative power of genes than experience. She had always feared becoming Norma, and she now saw a piece of Norma in her growing daughter; Jordan was just a wee girl when she began to make clear that she wished to dress like a boy. Melissa didn't mind. She had the intact family she'd craved all her life.

Still, Melissa thought often of who was missing from it. When she saw Norma, she would ask her about her sisters. But, recalls Melissa, Norma would say, "I don't know nothing." And she didn't.

In the spring of 1989, however, it occurred to Norma that there might be advantage in finding the teenager she had come to call the *Roe* baby. Her celebrity ascendant, Norma partnered with an investigator to find her.

Chapter 19

Norma had told the press that she was Jane Roe way back in 1973. But not until 1987—when she recanted the lie that she had been raped—did the press take much notice of her. And it was two more years before Norma was famous, lifted from the veil of a pseudonym by five weeks of press in the spring of 1989.

The shooting at her ranch house, on April 4, had summoned the press. They had followed Norma from her Dallas home to that DC march to that LA fundraiser to that Supreme Court hearing and on back to Dallas, where *People* magazine had watched her watch Holly Hunter portray her on TV, Norma gleeful that Hunter was wearing her necklace and headband.

An old friend in Northern California named Judith Hower was one of many who tuned in. Hower had been chopping wood outside the small cabin she shared with eleven cats and a friend when her roommate said that Norma was on TV talking about a shooting. Hower hurried inside, then mailed Norma a letter. She invited her to come west.

Hower had met Norma sixteen years before when, months after *Roe*, Norma arrived at the Dallas abortion clinic where Hower was a counselor and blood technician. Norma's chaperone had whispered to Hower that Jane Roe was "a lesbian who was raped on gravel." The words had rung in her ears, for she herself was closeted. Hower phoned Norma with a simple message: "I'm gay. I need a friend."

Norma invited Hower to her home and soon after, in 1974, to move in with her and Connie and their poodle, Julio. Hower loaded up her orange Subaru. "Without a blink of an eye," she says, "they took me in."

Hower was twenty-three, with long hair and wire-rimmed glasses. She got high on marijuana and acid and held the belief, she says, that "there was more to this world than meets the eye." Norma and Connie called her their "little hippie."

Hower was a good roommate. She would step between Norma and Connie when alcohol turned Norma mean. And she was up for sponta-neous fun—a nighttime drive to Mexico for days of drinking, an unan-nounced visit to little Melissa in Louisiana where, it turned out, the girl of nine had just run away and left her grandmother a note. Norma took her home, then brought her back. Says Hower, using the nickname Andi Taylor had given Norma: "Pixie could not handle being a mother."

Hower was of a different world than Norma and Connie. Raised in Oklahoma, Episcopalian and well-educated, she had studied chemistry at Oklahoma State and then worked at Halliburton alongside her father. But if Hower was successful, her GPA in college 3.93, she struggled with depression and being closeted. Marijuana would lift her mood, but only briefly.

Hower began dating a woman at her clinic. When the relationship ended, she left the clinic and began painting apartments alongside her roommates and a woman named Debbie, who was soon her girlfriend. Hower earned just four dollars an hour. But she felt a deep sense of belonging, and had Norma and Connie to thank for it. Says Hower: "They saved my life."

It was thus bewildering when, soon after Hower moved in with Debbie, Norma arrived drunk at her doorstep and proclaimed her love. Hower sent Norma home; she had seen her trysts and felt for Connie. Besides, she had a girlfriend.

Two years later, Hower was single. Debbie had met and married the leader of an evangelical Christian cult. Hower started drinking and then joined the cult, letting go all her possessions save a Bible, a sleep-ing bag and some clothes. But the cult demanded that she renounce her homosexuality. And in the fall of 1976, Hower broke down, scream-ing outside her boarding house until police arrived. She left town that night, moving west to a trailer in Santa Rosa.

Hower had been in California a few hours when she joined a silent retreat run by nuns. She began to reconsider her faith. Soon after, she let her Christianity go and moved with an ex-nun to a bohemian town called Forestville. It was there, years later, in May 1989, that Hower—single, unemployed and months shy of forty—saw her old roommate on television and invited her west. Norma accepted, telling her over the phone that she had split from Connie.

Hower met Norma at the airport. Hower was nervous; she had pot on her person and there were detection dogs about. But none approached, and she drove her old friend home, catching up with Pixie in her blue pickup and then her redwood cabin. Norma phoned Connie to tell of the California evergreens that touched the sky. When she returned to Dallas days later, she told Connie that she and Hower had had sex.

Connie did not kick her out; she never did. She simply said, "See you whenever," and Norma returned to LA, parting indefinitely from her partner of nineteen years and her green-eyed Siamese cat. Norma was en route to Hower when she stopped to see her lawyer Allred at a pro-choice rally.

Norma's newfound feminism delighted Hower. Hower was in love. But living with her girlfriend was difficult. Norma was often drunk on beer and vodka. She was soon bulimic, too, and shared her pride in having discovered a way to not gain weight. "She was not happy to hear it was a disease," says Hower. There was also between the women "a vast educational difference," says Hower, as well as an "issue of vocabulary" that made it difficult at times for Norma to understand her. And then there was the matter of money; they had little of it. Hower was getting by on unemployment insurance.

The women were certain that Norma would soon be earning a good living. NBC had paid her to tell her story, and her lawyer was intent on wringing more from it; this spring of 1989, Allred arranged a run of talks and fundraisers, interviews and statements, made newsworthy by *Webster*, the impending Supreme Court decision. There would be a book on Norma, too—once Allred found someone to write it. And there was something else in the works, something potentially more explosive than all the rest. Says Hower: "We were trying to find the *Roe* baby."

THE COUNTRY WAS CONSUMED by *Roe*. But few questioned whether its plaintiff had given birth. "It wouldn't have occurred to me to wonder," says John Rich, the Blackmun clerk who helped research *Roe*. "I was obsessed with law." But some did wonder, wonder about the boy or girl who, as the author Barbara Milbauer wrote, had been born to an "unwilling mother."

That that child might learn of her parentage was a discomforting thought. To do so would be to learn that her birth mother had gone to great lengths to abort her. It would be to learn of *Roe*, and of the millions who would thus make claims on her. Still, as Milbauer wrote a decade after the ruling, that child was no doubt ignorant "of its singular place in American history."

Norma had never looked for the child. And she'd never reconsidered her desire to abort it. "I would much rather have had an abortion," she told the press in 1985. "I knew I couldn't take care of it. I knew I couldn't love it." She repeated the thought in 1989. Had she had an abortion, she told the press that spring, she would have been spared the pain of "wondering is my son or daughter in kindergarten."

But she now said that she was looking for her child. And in a television studio in Manhattan, Jane Pauley asked her why.

Norma: "I'd like to meet her."
Pauley: "And say what to her?"
Norma: "I love you."
Pauley: "This strikes me as a contradiction."

Norma was speaking very, very quietly. She appeared stoned, and Allred took the question. No, there was no contradiction, the lawyer told the national audience. "What this is all about is choice."

But it was, in fact, about publicity. It had been twenty years since Norma conceived her third child, and yet she had begun searching for her the very month she'd retained a celebrity lawyer. And she wasn't looking for her middle child, only her unknown youngest, who'd led to her booking on the *Today* show.

Weeks later, that child was feeling good. Shelley had almost finished secretarial school and was off to a tanning bed. As she walked, on
a sunny Sunday in mid-May, through the parking lot of her Washington
apartment complex, a woman approached.

=====

TOBY HANFT HAD grown up in a broken Jewish home in Brooklyn. Born in
1949, the middle of three, her mother died in 1957 of leukemia. Three
years later, Toby lost her father as well, to suicide. He had remarried.
And after his widow then remarried, the couple mistreated their step-
daughter Toby and her younger sister, forcing upon them constant
housework and spending on them little to no money. Says her older
brother Jeffrey: "They had torn underwear."

Hanft got pregnant her junior year at Lafayette High. Abortion was
illegal and, according to Jeffrey, her stepparents pressured her to carry
the child. Hanft gave birth and placed her daughter for adoption.

Hanft graduated high school and moved at nineteen to San Francisco. She became a secretary and a seamstress, and then a follower of
Reverend Sun Myung Moon. She left the Moonies after two years, and
between 1972 and 1977 had three sons with three men.

It was then, says Jeffrey, that his sister set out to find her missing fourth child. Her husband, the father of her youngest, was a cop
and helped her do so. Mother and daughter had "a cold reunion," says
Hanft's son Jonah. But a hole in her life had been filled. And she began
working to connect women with the children they had given up. "Her
big thing," says Jonah, "was not just finding but reuniting."

Hanft relied upon information not legally available—Social Security numbers, birth certificates. "It was almost underworld," says Jonah.
"You had to know cops." Her sons helped, Hanft paying them to scan
microfiche birth records for the asterisks that might denote an adoption.

Finding people paid well. Hanft charged $1500 for a typical search,
twice that if there was little information to go on. She delivered. By
1989—when Norma made public her hope to find the Roe baby—Hanft
had found more than six hundred adoptees and misidentified none.

The missing child of a celebrity sold papers. And the National
Enquirer—which only weeks before had found the daughter comedi-

enne Roseanne Barr had given up as a teen—offered Norma help, and turned to Hanft to provide it.

Hanft was thrilled. She opposed abortion. And a commission to search for the *Roe* baby would provide not only exposure but the means to indict *Roe* in the most visceral of ways. She set everything else aside and worked in secrecy. Recalls Jonah: "This was the one thing we were not allowed to help with."

It was not an easy job; the adoption lawyer who'd placed Shelley was dead. Still, Norma gave Hanft her child's place and date of birth, its gender too, and Hanft homed in: on June 2, 1970, there had been thirty-seven girls born in Dallas County. One was adopted. Jonah recalls the moment of her discovery. "Oh my God!" his mother called out. "Oh my God! I found her!"

Hanft normally telephoned the adoptees she found. But this was *Roe*. So she flew north, resolved for the first time to present herself in person. She was waiting in a maroon van in a parking lot in Washington when Shelley walked by. Hanft stepped out and introduced herself.

Hanft told Shelley that she was an adoption investigator sent by her birth mother to find her. Shelley felt a rush of joy. The woman who had let her go now wished to know her. Shelley began to cry. Wow, she recalls thinking. Wow! Hanft hugged Shelley. Then she told her, Hanft recalled, that "her mother was famous—but not a movie star or a rich person." Rather, said Hanft, she was "connected to a national case that had changed law." There was more to tell, and Hanft asked Shelley if she would meet with her and her business partner, the man in the van beside them.

Shelley told Hanft that she would phone her, and took her card and hurried home.

Shelley would have liked to speak to her high school friend Todd, to tell of the blond woman in jeans and leather jacket who had stepped from a van and changed her life. But in the seven months since he had called to say that he would marry her, he hadn't phoned. Two days later, Shelley and her mother drove downtown to dine atop the Space Needle with Hanft and a mustachioed man named Reggie Fitz.

Fitz had been born into medicine. His great-grandfather Reginald and his grandfather Reginald and his father Reginald had all gone to

Harvard and become eminent doctors. (The first was a pioneering pathologist who coined the term appendicitis.) Fitz, the eldest of four, was expected to wear the white coat too.

But Reggie wanted to write. He studied American literature at Middlebury and American society at Brown. And in 1980—having dropped out of Brown and written for a medical journal—he took a job at the *National Enquirer*. His family disapproved. "Even at his funeral," his third wife, Joan Marie Hart, recalled decades later, "his own son was saying, 'It's just a rag.'"

Fitz loved his work; he wrote of wonder drugs and weight gains. And on this spring night in Seattle, he readied to land a major scoop.

Shelley was sky high; six hundred feet aloft, the answers she had sought all her life were suddenly at hand. She listened as Hanft began to tell what little she knew of her mother: that she lived in Texas, that she was in touch with the eldest of her three daughters, that her name was Norma McCorvey.

Ruth read the tabloids, the glossy gossipy sheets on sale at every checkout counter. Only weeks before, Norma had appeared in *Star*: "Mom In Abortion Case Still Longs For Child She Tried To Get Rid Of." Norma had told *People* magazine the same just days before. "I want to find out what he or she looks like," she said—never mind that she knew its gender. "I wonder whether they'd like me and what I stand for." Despite the press, Norma's name was not familiar to Ruth or Shelley. Neither was her connection to *Roe*. When Hanft began to circle about *Roe*, speaking of unwanted pregnancies and abortion, Ruth interjected. "We don't believe in abortion," she said.

Hanft turned to Shelley. "Unfortunately," she said, recalling her words days later, "your birth mother is Jane Roe."

Shelley recognized that name. Only days before, she had happened upon Holly Hunter playing her on television. The bit of the film she'd watched had left her with the thought that Jane Roe was indecent. Shelley had wished that Hunter—whom she loved—had not portrayed her. "I was very upset," says Shelley. "The only thing I knew about being pro-life or pro-choice or even *Roe v. Wade*, was that this person had made it okay for people to go out and be promiscuous."

Still, it was hard to grasp what exactly Hanft was saying. The investigator handed Shelley the recent article about Norma in *People*. "She looked at it, and it sunk in," Hanft recalled. "She threw it down and ran out of the room." When Shelley returned to the table, she was, recalled Hanft, "shaking all over and crying."

All her life, Shelley had wished to know the facts of her birth. But having mused as a girl that her birth mother was a beautiful actress, she now knew otherwise. Her mother was synonymous with abortion. That fact began to splinter in her mind. More even than Norma's fight to legalize abortion, it was Norma's want to abort *her* that pierced her thinking.

Ruth beheld her daughter. Having been gifted Shelley, having chosen to mother and raise and love her, she now spoke. "My mom," says Shelley, "wanted proof that Norma was my birth mother."

Hanft and Fitz said that a DNA test could be taken. But first, this man and woman Shelley did not know had a question for her: was she pro-choice or pro-life? Says Shelley: "They kept asking me what side I was on."

Two days before, Shelley had been off to get a tan, a teenager on the brink of another summer. "All I wanted to do," she says, "was hang out with my friends, date cute boys, and go shopping for shoes." But now, suddenly, ten days before her nineteenth birthday, she was the *Roe* baby. The question hung in the air.

Shelley was afraid to answer. She suddenly wondered, she says, why she had to choose a side, why anyone did. She finally offered, she says, that she couldn't see herself having an abortion.

Hanft would recall something different—that Shelley, like her mother, had stated that she was "pro-life." And Hanft and Fitz told her of the recent story in the *Enquirer* about Roseanne Barr's baby. Fitz said he was writing a similar story on Norma and Shelley. He was on deadline, besides.

Shelley and Ruth were aghast. They hadn't even ordered dinner yet. But they hurried out. "We left the restaurant saying, 'We don't want any part of this,'" says Shelley. "'Leave us alone.'"

Shelley began to cry. "Here's my chance at finding out who my birth mother was," she says, "and I wasn't even going to be able to have control over it because I was being thrown into the *Enquirer.*"

Control was crucial to Shelley; not for nothing had she never been drunk. Back home, she wondered if perhaps she might speak to Norma and make the tabloid go away. Hanft arranged a phone call. Nineteen years after Norma had let her daughter go, she picked up the phone.

The news that Norma was seeking her child had appalled the pro-life camp. "What is she going to say to that child when she finds him?" an NRLC spokesman had mused to the press. "I want to hold you now and give you my love but I'm still upset about the fact that I couldn't abort you?"

Speaking to her daughter for the first time, Norma did not mention abortion. She said hello. She said that she'd given Shelley up because, Shelley recalls, "I knew I couldn't take care of you." She told Shelley that she wondered about her "always."

Shelley listened—to her words and her smoker's voice. She asked Norma about her father. Norma said little but his first name and what he looked like. And when Shelley asked about her two sisters, Norma referred to the elder as Cheryl and refused to say if she knew the second. Norma wished to speak only of them, the protagonists of *Roe*. She told Shelley that they could meet in person—like Roseanne and her daughter, she said. The *Enquirer* could help.

The conversation left Shelley distraught. Norma wanted the very thing she did not—a public outing. And she now saw plainly that she carried within her a great secret, the secret of a lifetime. To speak it, to tell that she was the *Roe* baby, was to risk an unmasking. She confided in a friend from secretarial school named Christie Chavez, who called Hanft and Fitz and took careful notes on what they said.

The news was not all bad; the tabloid would agree to withhold Shelley's name. But it would not kill its story. And Hanft and Fitz said that a mole at the paper might sell her out. After all, they told Christie, the pro-life movement "would love to show Shelley off as a healthy, happy and productive [person] in the world." They added that were Shelley to become known, she would lose all privacy and be in "grave danger too." They recommended that she change her Social Security number, her date of birth, her name.

Ruth was appalled. Her daughter would have little need to hide if the *Enquirer* backed off. The mother "begged and pleaded," she says, for them to kill the story. But the *Enquirer* did not budge, and Ruth turned to a lawyer who was a friend of a friend. That Thursday morning, she and Shelley visited his office high above Pioneer Square.

The lawyer suggested that the investigator had recorded Shelley, that her leather jacket had been zipped to hide a device. Shelley, he said, should trust no one. He instructed the *Enquirer* to publish no identifying information about his client and to cease contact with her.

The tabloid agreed, as before, to protect Shelley's identity. But it cautioned her not to push them aside. If Shelley did not participate in their story, Fitz said, the odds were greater that one of his co-workers would sell her out.

Shelley was stuck. To come out as the *Roe* baby would be to lose the life, steady and unremarkable, that she craved. But to remain anonymous would be to ensure, as her lawyer put it, that "the race was on for whoever could get to Shelley first." Her mother was distraught. "What a life," Ruth jotted on a note to no one, "always looking over your shoulder."

Norma had speculated that the life of her youngest would be fraught. "I'd look down at my belly, and I'd think, God, you poor little guy," Norma had reflected a few years before. "I don't love you. I'll feed you. And I'm going to take care of you and make sure you're going to come out healthy. But my God, what you—the cross that you're going to have to bear."

Norma herself had now placed that burden upon her child. And Shelley wrote a list of all she might do to confront it, resolving to meet with Norma, to get a copy of the *Roe* ruling, to take a DNA test.

The prospect of the last, however, unsettled Shelley. For her conversation with Norma had been unpleasant. She had the thought that she might not wish to confirm their relation; better, she thought, "to tuck her away as background noise."

Norma was upset. Her plan was coming apart. On June 2, nineteen years to the day after she had birthed and let Shelley go, she asked the lawyers for proof that Shelley had been born to her in Dallas Osteopathic. Hanft, though, had made no mistake, and Norma soon wished to make things right. "My darling," she began a letter to Shelley, "be re-assured that Ms. Gloria Allred . . . has sent a letter to the Nat. Enquirer stating that we have no intensions of [exploiting] you or your family." Allred followed suit, phoning Shelley's lawyer to say that the *Enquirer* had sought out his client without consent from hers. But as Hanft made clear, she had searched for Shelley "in conjunction [with] and with permission from Ms. McCorvey." She had faxed Norma a photo of Shelley. And the tabloid that paid Hanft had Norma's gratitude on record. "Thanks to the *National Enquirer*," read a prepared statement, "I know who my child is."

On June 20, 1989, in bold sanserif type—and just below a photo of Elvis—the *National Enquirer* presented its scoop on its cover: "Roe vs. Wade Abortion Shocker—Enquirer Finds Jane Roe's Baby." The "explosive story" unspooled on page 17, offering details of said child— her approximate date of birth, her birth weight, the name of her adoption lawyer. The child was unnamed but said to be pro-life and living in Washington.

"I want her to know," the *Enquirer* quoted Norma, "I'll never force myself upon her. I can wait until she's ready to contact me—even if it takes years. And when she's ready, I'm ready to take her in my arms and give her my love and be her friend."

Shelley made clear that that day might never come. "I'm glad to know that my birth mother is alive," she said, "and that she loves me— but I'm really not ready to see her. And I don't know when I'll ever be ready—if ever." She added: "In some ways, I can't forgive her. . . . I know now that she tried to have me aborted."

Shelley struggled to digest that last indigestible fact. But to opponents of *Roe*, it was exhilarating. Here was the pro-life case incarnate, the would-be abortus who had lived. Days after the *Enquirer* piece ran, the National Right to Life Committee seized upon her existence. "This nineteen-year-old woman's life was saved by that Texas law," said a spokesman. Were *Roe* overturned, he said, countless others would be saved too.

The NRLC was careful to stop there. For Norma and her lawyer now disavowed the *Enquirer* story, telling a reporter that the alleged *Roe* baby had not tested her DNA. The story thus went all but unread, picked up by none save a few Gannett papers and the *Washington Times*, a conservative daily founded by Sun Myung Moon, the messiah claim-ant whose church had for a brief time included Hanft.

Shelley had read the story, however, and been deeply pained by it. Having gone to work as a secretary at a law firm, she worried about the day when some hack would knock on her door and tell the world that the *Roe* baby was she.

Chapter 20

On July 3, 1989, the Supreme Court ruled on *Webster*. *Roe* had survived. But it was diminished.

The case concerned a Missouri law which banned the use of public resources for abortion—be they funds or facilities or employees. The Court found that the law was legal.

The ruling empowered states to regulate abortion more than *Roe* ever had. What's more, *Roe* now rested on a single vote. Among the 5–4 *Webster* majority, only Justice O'Connor stopped short of calling for *Roe*'s abolition. Wrote Justice Blackmun in his dissent: "a chill wind blows."

The ruling lifted Mildred Jefferson. She'd had a difficult year. Her father, Millard, had died in November. Ronald Reagan had departed the White House. And Jefferson was less and less the voice of a movement than of her two-person Tulsa nonprofit, the Right to Life Crusade. Still, home in Boston, the doctor declared *Webster* "a triumph of the democratic process."

IN THE DAYS leading up to *Webster*, Norma had sweated over *Roe*. Recalls her girlfriend Hower: "it was a legacy she had left and she didn't want to see it destroyed." When the ruling came down, her lawyer had her tear up a copy of it before a phalanx of cameras.

If Norma had transformed herself from cleaning woman to profes-

sional plaintiff, Allred had turned her from plaintiff to pioneer, chris-
tening her client of three months "the Rosa Parks of the abortion rights
movement." But it was happenstance more than conviction that had
turned Norma into Jane Roe. And speaking in her blue high-tops to
audience after audience this summer of 1989, she made faux pas her
California girlfriend still recalled thirty years later.

Norma, says Hower, told one group that young women wanting
abortions ought to be required to get a parent's consent. She told another
that she considered a fetus viable once a heartbeat was heard. The audiences gasped. "I thought, wow, this is Jane Roe," says Hower. "She needs
to be able to speak to the issues without sounding like an idiot."

It was not merely pro-choice protocol that eluded Norma. She knew
little of the history she herself had altered. And so, Hower bought a
book about feminism and read to her about Margaret Sanger, Bella
Abzug, Gloria Steinem. "I would say, 'Look, Pixie, look!'" recalls
Hower. "'You're part of this crowd!'"

Norma saw herself in these women; she copied out a poem in which
the Australian activist Joyce Stevens listed indignities that necessitated
the feminist fight. She wrote words of her own, too, statements and
speeches lamenting *Webster* and declaring that "all women today have
become Jane Roe."

Still, Norma was as yet capable of little more than clichés. She offered
to pay Hower to write her a speech. Hower did so, and drove Norma
in her blue pickup to waves of women wanting to hear it—audiences
at Sonoma State University, the California Nursing Association, the
East Bay Democratic Club. Allred, meantime, booked Norma at events
that were more high-profile and lucrative, Norma riding in a Rolls in a
gay pride parade in San Francisco, eating chocolate and raspberries at
Spago. But the events were tiring. Despite the movie stars—Ali Mac-
Graw, Richard Dreyfuss—Norma began to sit them out, skipping a
march in Sacramento even after Allred had a senator phone to urge her
to come. Says Hower: "Gloria was asking a lot of Pixie, and Pixie wasn't
getting anything in return."

Actually, she was. Like that benefit at Baci, many of the events
Norma now headlined brought in cash; a tour of universities in California, Pennsylvania and New York paid her a few thousand dollars a

speech. "I feel we were a bit deceptive," says Hower. "I think the people thought [their money] was going to the pro-choice movement—not to keep her alive."

Norma made no apologies. The movement did not look after her; she remained, as that NARAL memo on her TV movie had put it, "an opportunity to get our message out." Indeed, Gloria Steinem soon asked a writer named Angela Bonavoglia to include the story of Jane Roe in a book of profiles related to abortion.

Bonavoglia sat down with Norma and a tape recorder in a quiet room at 66 San Fernando Way, a San Francisco home hosting, on this September night, a fundraiser for the city DA. It was Norma's forty-second birthday.

Allred had okayed the interview; Bonavoglia's book would feature such luminaries as Grace Paley, Ursula K. Le Guin, Whoopi Goldberg. Still, Allred had her sights on something more for her client—a proper biography (with a proper contract). To that end, she had introduced Norma to a young journalist named Alyssa Lenhoff.

Lenhoff had just resigned her job at a local paper after her publisher took issue with a positive article she'd written about gay fathers. Allred instructed her on what to write about Norma. Recalls Lenhoff: "There was pressure to imply a certain kind of story—[that of] a staunchly pro-choice victimized person."

The *New Yorker* magazine would later call Allred's career "a decades-long project to expand the boundaries of legitimate victimhood." Victimhood had long guided Norma, too. When speaking of Norma, Allred sounded that note over and again, telling reporters, for example, that the reason her client had struggled to recount for them the oral arguments she'd heard in the Supreme Court in the case of *Webster* was that the shotgun blasts outside her home had damaged her hearing. But Norma's hearing was fine.

Lenhoff got to work interviewing Norma. When one day Norma arrived at her brownstone in the Haight with a duffel, Lenhoff let her stay for weeks, lending her clothes.

In return, the biographer asked only for facts. Norma struggled to provide them, lost in "circular conversations," says Lenhoff. "She would go back and the facts would change." Still, Lenhoff had outlined eight chapters when, in late fall, Allred introduced her and Norma to two literary agents, a husband and wife, in San Francisco. Norma was put off by the woman's age and astrological sign. Lenhoff had had enough and told Norma she was done.

Norma didn't mind. Lenhoff's insistence on facts had seemed an unnecessary strain. After all, Holly Hunter had just won an Emmy for portraying a version of her that was at best sanitized. Besides, Norma had just begun another project—the Jane Roe Women's Center.

It was her former lawyer, Goff, who'd planted in Norma the idea of forming a foundation. Norma had big plans for the JRWC; it would fund abortions for poor women and register them to vote and create a bureau of pro-choice speakers, beginning with her. It wasn't long before the center boasted a board that included Susan Kennedy, who headed the California Abortion Rights Action League, and Del Martin, a feminist powerhouse who'd fought for decades for the rights of women, gay women above all. A prominent lesbian lawyer named Donna Hitchens helped incorporate the center, three strong gay women in the service of another.

NOVEMBER DREW TO A CLOSE. Norma and Hower had been together six months, a half-year crowded with cats and all things *Roe*—a long-lost daughter, a Supreme Court ruling, talks and a book, a foundation and an Emmy. Watching Hunter accept her award, Norma had leapt with joy, the real Jane Roe alone with her girlfriend in a cabin in a California forest.

Norma had grown beside Hower. Her girlfriend had helped her to find her voice, to understand feminism and her place in it. Still, Norma remained volatile. Drunk on screwdrivers on the last night of November, she became enraged when Hower asked for the money Norma had promised in exchange for writing her speech. Says Hower: "I couldn't believe the monster I was facing."

The couple had planned to fly the next day to Oklahoma to visit Hower's father and sister. Norma refused to make the trip. A week or so later, Hower returned from Oklahoma to find Norma gone. Says Hower: "There was no note."

Hower soon realized that Norma was next door; she had begun an affair with a neighbor nine years her junior named Sharon Bragg. Hower was distraught. Norma was not. She changed lovers as she had lawyers—without fuss. There was no need for regret. Only yesterday she'd been a delinquent and a dropout, a prostitute and a drug dealer. Now she was Jane Roe—a commodity, a draw, an American hero; half of the country was in her debt. New doors would always open. Norma refused to speak to Hower and drove off with Bragg to the foothills of Oakland, leaving Hower behind with thirteen cats and a photo Norma had inscribed to her with everlasting love.

Norma liked her new girlfriend. Bragg was tall and thin, a student of marine biology who loved to fish. In early January, she accompanied Norma to a party in San Francisco where Norma's board member Kennedy introduced Norma to a California Abortion Rights Action League colleague named Barbara Ellis.

Ellis asked what Norma was doing for the anniversary of *Roe*. Norma had no plans, and Ellis, appalled, invited her to speak at Laney College, a local community college where her chapter of CARAL was hosting an event. They agreed on a fee, $1000, and Norma invited Ellis over to her place, the women talking over beer and classic rock.

Norma liked Ellis at once. She was a California native with blue eyes, a fast walker who carried in a backpack the gear she needed to register voters: a clipboard and pens, a collapsible table and stool. She was as warm at forty-eight as she'd been at eighteen cheerleading at Willow Glen High. And she was no snob. Her parents, a dental assistant and a firefighter, had skipped college, and so had she, eloping after her senior prom.

Ellis was living in Berkeley with her second husband and two kids when, in 1968, footage of police beatings at the Democratic National Convention "radicalized" her, she says. A year later, she was happily pregnant when she began to gather signatures in support of legalized abortion. She had long since joined CARAL when, a generation later, in early 1990, she sat with Norma in her home off High Street and listened to her story.

It was a shock to Ellis to hear that the movement had sidelined Norma at that women's march in DC. But if the leaders at NOW and

NARAL did not care to know Norma, the feminist rank and file did. Ellis confided in her new friend that she and four carloads of colleagues would, in protest of the recent *Webster* decision, be postering over Webster Street signs in downtown San Francisco. Norma was in. And on the eve of another *Roe* anniversary, it was her car stopped by the cops. Norma smiled all through her night at the station. "It was hilarious," says Ellis. "The women police officers were having their pictures taken with Norma."

Earlier that same January day, Norma had given her talk at Laney. Though Hower had helped Norma make sense of *Roe*, and Allred had gotten her public speaking lessons, the plaintiff remained unpolished at a podium, still veering into platitudes. "I do not promote abortion," she said to applause in the Laney gym. "I promote personal choice."

Ellis had the idea that she and Norma could speak in tandem, Norma telling of her life and Ellis contextualizing it with a primer on reproductive rights. The talks would be unpaid, but Norma was aboard. After more speaking lessons, Ellis drove Norma in her blue Honda to gigs all through the Bay area, Norma filling the ashtray with smoked Marlboros. Says Ellis of their collaboration: "It was phenomenal."

Norma agreed. Before meeting Ellis, she'd been lonely in Oakland, her girlfriend Bragg busy at work. But now, week after week, she stood before a crowd—a law school in San Francisco granting her an honorary degree, a college in Santa Rosa inviting her to speak at its commencement, a queue of candidates for assemblyman, attorney general and governor seeking her endorsement. Life was surreal. Indeed, peering down at an open history textbook before a talk at Las Positas College, Norma saw her own face.

Norma had begun a second year alongside Ellis when Oprah Winfrey flew the women to Chicago, greeting them in the green room along with Rita Moreno and Polly Bergen. Moreno and Bergen had contributed to Gloria Steinem's book *The Choices We Made*, just as Norma had. After it came out in 1991, Norma got more gigs, she and Ellis continuing their drives about California.

Norma had been out west a year and a half. It had been a period of unrest in world affairs: the Tiananmen Square protests, the fall of the Berlin Wall, the coming collapse of the Soviet Union. But Norma was oblivious to all that. She had assumed the well-worn look of a hippie, a forty-something in sneakers and jeans and floppy collars, her hair a burnt orange, a dyed nest that covered her ears and forehead and teal eyebrows, too. She felt good beside Ellis. Ellis put her on a pedestal, content to listen and defer, to ask nothing of Norma but her company. If ever Ellis needed time away from Norma, she simply told her that she had to be at work; she'd taken a job making lattes in Berkeley for that very purpose. Ellis was also forgiving—even after Norma propositioned her daughter, an undergrad in Colorado.

NORMA WAS NOT meant for constancy; only Connie had managed to remain beside her much more than a year. And come spring, her relationship with Bragg ended much as it came into being—with a furious fight, Norma so vicious that Bragg returned to their home in the company of police and moved out, leaving nothing behind but a folding patio chair.

Norma would have to leave, too; their lease, paid for by Bragg, was due to expire. When Ellis came by, she found both Norma and her home a mess—pizza boxes in the oven, trash on the floor, Norma drunk on beer. *Roe*, however, beckoned. The women drove north in early May 1991, to a conference in Oregon where Norma was to share a stage with Kate Michelman, director of NARAL.

Two years had passed since feminist leaders had rebuffed Norma at that DC rally, and she was beginning to speak openly of her distaste for them—or, more accurately, of their distaste for her. Norma told a reporter that upon seeing Weddington, the lawyer had "barely acknowledged" her. She told another that other movement leaders "became complacent and took me for granted." Neither Steinem nor Bonavoglia invited Norma to their book parties back east.

Ellis had seen for herself how NOW and NARAL marginalized Norma. "They seriously shunned her," she says. "I think it's called elitism." There was, she says, just one "high status" woman among them who did not: Gloria Allred.

The lawyer, in fact, continued to go to great lengths to stand beside Norma, to have her close while speaking into the camera of every threat to *Roe*: an abortion bill in Louisiana, the nomination of Clarence

Mildred Jefferson, shown here in 1947, was nineteen years old when, that January, she became the first black woman admitted to Harvard Medical School. The acceptance was national news.
(SCHLESINGER LIBRARY, RADCLIFFE INSTITUTE, HARVARD UNIVERSITY)

Mildred's career as a surgeon was thwarted by racism and misogyny. Her dream dashed, she joined the pro-life movement in 1970, and quickly became a star. After Ronald Reagan, who had supported legal abortion as governor of California, heard Mildred in debate, he wrote to her, days before *Roe*, that she had "made it irrefutably clear that an abortion is the taking of human life."
(RONALD REAGAN PRESIDENTIAL LIBRARY, PHOTOGRAPHER JACK KIGHTLINGER)

HIGHEST-RANKING STUDENT

Curtis Boyd was born in 1937 into a fundamentalist Christian family on an East Texas farm. His grandmother encouraged him to preach, and he was ordained a minister at sixteen. He is shown here two years later, in 1955, upon his graduation from high school.
(THE ATHENIAN, ATHENS HIGH SCHOOL. COURTESY OF CURTIS BOYD)

Abortion was not yet legal when Boyd left family medicine to perform abortions full-time. After *Roe*, he became one of the leading abortion providers in the country. He helped to pioneer the standard method of second-trimester abortion, and—after the 2009 murder of his fellow abortion provider George Tiller—became the largest provider of third-trimester abortions in the country. (ANDY LYMAN/NM POLITICAL REPORT)

Linda Coffee was a bankruptcy lawyer in Dallas when in 1970, she filed *Roe v. Wade*, contesting the Texas law against abortion. Her co-counsel, Sarah Weddington, hesitated to attach her name to the suit. "I think she was just cautious," says Coffee. Coffee is shown here in 1972, eleven months before the Supreme Court ruling. (BETTMAN/CONTRIBUTOR)

After Weddington argued *Roe* in the Supreme Court, Coffee was forgotten. Coffee had not seen he[r] co-counsel in twenty-seven years when in 2019, the Texas branch of the National Women's Politic[al] Caucus brought them together on an Austin dais, pictured here. (Rodolfo Gonzalez)

On March 3, 1970, Coffee paid fifteen dollars to file *Roe v. Wade* at the federal courthouse on North Ervay Street in Dallas. The lawyer saved her receipt, shown here. (Courtesy of Linda Coffee)

IN THE UNITED STATES DISTRICT COURT
FOR THE NORTHERN DISTRICT OF TEXAS
DALLAS DIVISION

JANE ROE, PLAINTIFF	X	CIVIL ACTION
	X	
VS.	X	
	X	NO. CA⊖3-3690
HENRY WADE, DEFENDANT	X	CA-3-3691

AFFIDAVIT OF JANE ROE IN SUPPORT
OF MOTION FOR SUMMARY JUDGMENT

STATE OF TEXAS   (
                 (
COUNTY OF DALLAS (

BEFORE ME, the undersigned authority, on this day personally appeared NORMA McCORVEY, to me well known, who after being by me first duly sworn, did depose and say as follows:

(1) My name is NORMA McCORVEY, I am over the age of twenty-one and am fully competent to testify. I presently reside at 4706 San Jacinto in Dallas, Texas.

(2) On March 3, 1970 I filed a lawsuit in the United States District Court for the Northern District of Texas, Dallas Division, which cause is presently pending under cause no. CA 3-3690. I filed this suit under the fictitious name of Jane Roe for the following reasons:

(a) I am not married at the present time and have not been at any time in the past six years.

(b) Because of my pregnancy I have experienced extreme difficulty in securing employment of any kind. I feared the notoriety occasioned by the lawsuit would make it impossible for me to secure any employment in the near future and would severely limit my advancement in any employment which I might secure at some later date.

(c) I consider the decision of whether to bear a child a highly personal one and feel that the notoriety occasioned by the lawsuit would result in a gross invasion of my personal privacy.

Norma was about to give birth when, on May 21, 1970, her lawyers filed an affidavit on her behalf, laying out the reasons for her suit. Among them was that the abortion providers Norma could afford were both illegal and dangerous, and that she considered "the decision of whether to bear a child a highly personal one." Coffee kept the affidavit, the first page of which is shown here. A copy submitted to the court did not have Norma's name. (COURTESY OF LINDA COFFEE)

Thomas to the Supreme Court, the harassments of Operation Rescue. It did not matter to Allred that Norma was untruthful, uneducated, unstable, unscripted too, or that Norma blew off events or spoke out of turn or drank. And it did not matter to Norma that she, Jane Roe, was so transparently beneficial to Allred's career, or that the lawyer had promised to recast her, to "polish that old diamond up," as Norma told a reporter. What mattered to Norma was that Allred treated her with respect. The day that Allred rode in a Rolls beside her in that gay pride parade, Norma wrote of her in her datebook: "I LIKE / LOVE HER."

Two years later, however, there were signs that the plaintiff was readying to leave California, and Allred, behind. Norma had just told a reporter that the southern branch of CARAL had refused to share with her its list of donors, donors she hoped might fund her proposed women's center. But she was still out west when she arrived in Oregon for that conference. Cigarette in hand, coat-hanger pin on her left breast, she spoke of being shot at. She had no more wished to die at the hand of a pro-lifer, Norma told the local paper, than "on a butcher table from an illegal abortion."

The next day, May 5, the Eugene paper, the *Register–Guard*, centered its story on Norma, noting that Kate Michelman "also was at the conference." Norma delighted in that "also," giddy that this once, she—not Michelman or Weddington or Steinem—had come first.

Norma told the paper that it had been "hard to go from being a house painter to a feminist leader." Her past was on her mind. And just before driving north, she had telephoned Connie to come get her. When Norma arrived back in Oakland, she found her partner, still lovesick at sixty, ready to take her back, no questions asked.

"It was sudden," says Ellis. "I wasn't even there when she left. I was pretty crushed."

———

NORMA HAD BEEN gone from Cactus Lane for two years. But the house was unchanged, the cats out back, the Oldsmobile in the drive. Connie was happy to have Norma home, to have their ranch house fill again with Marlboros and Marley, horoscopes and polished stones—lapis to ground Norma, bloodstone for focus.

Norma, though, had changed. *Roe*, Connie saw, now defined her. Norma asked most every person she met, in every market or salon, if she was for or against her law. "The fact is," she told a Dallas reporter, "I just don't want someone who's anti-choice doing my nails."

It went without saying that Norma would no longer clean homes. *Roe* would provide. Indeed, her honoraria and royalty payments covered her Beefaroni and beer, her cat litter and occasional cocaine. *Roe* provided direction, too. It wasn't long before Norma was volunteering for a doctor who performed abortions, offering up counsel to women in his recovery room.

That doctor believed in Norma. His name was Lamar Robinson and he hired a marketer named Arthur Young to promote the Jane Roe Women's Center; it soon had a 900 number and a newsletter, patrons paying $9.95 per call and thirty dollars per subscription for updates on all things *Roe*.

Norma was thrilled. Dr. Robinson paid her bills and rented her an office. But Norma missed her audience. And so as to devote herself to it, she left Connie again, moving into her new office, an apartment on the upper floor of a condo in North Dallas. "I'm really not ready for a personal relationship right now," she told a reporter. "Don't really have the time."

Arthur Young encouraged Norma to speak her mind about *Roe*. "She doesn't need to be translated," he explained. "She's painfully honest and very real." Indeed, Norma implored women "to get off their complacent asses and hit the streets." But the JRWC struggled for money; it wasn't able even to pay the $1100 it owed its lawyer, Donna Hitchens. It had funded no abortions and registered no women to vote when, in 1992, Dr. Robinson withdrew his support and it closed. Norma returned to Connie.

Norma had long since found in trauma and sex the means to explain away her failures. Asked, some twenty years later, about the collapse of her center, she returned to those same realms, saying that her patron Robinson had stopped paying her bills when "he found out he couldn't sleep in my bed."

ROE GAVE NORMA STATUS that housecleaning did not. And when the JRWC closed, she began to volunteer for the Choice Foundation, a Dallas non-profit devoted to reproductive rights. She was soon under the eye of its director, a woman named Janie Bush.

Bush had spent her first years in the east Texas town of Tyler, born there in 1948 to a family of Methodists. Tiny and chatty, the third of six children, what marked her most was a want, she says, to correct the "unfairness in the world." When a friend in middle school told her that her stepfather "was messing with her," Bush took her to the juvie officer at the local police station.

Bush was studying journalism at Texas Women's University when, in 1967, she got pregnant. She knew of a doctor outside Dallas who performed abortions. But she was still pondering whether to have one when her first trimester passed. Beset by guilt and shame, she dropped out of college, moved to Dallas, and gave birth to a girl she placed for adoption. Twelve years later, Bush had married and divorced when a state employee she knew let her know that her daughter, who had spina bifida, was again in need of a home. Bush took custody, thrilled to be able to choose to be a mother. And she had begun working at the Choice Foundation when, almost two decades after _Roe_, Norma joined the office.

Bush trained the Choice volunteers to be clinic escorts. Norma, though, had neither "the temperament nor the capacity," she says, to escort women through thickets of protestors. Instead, Bush had her cut out newspaper articles related to reproductive rights. "Norma wanted to be involved," says Bush, "but I think, more than anything, she wanted friendship."

Friendship with Norma was no simple thing; a pleasant dinner was apt to give way, says Bush, to "hateful" phone messages left after too many drinks. Even after Bush had Choice honor Norma at its annual dinner—for "her accidental place in history," Bush says—Norma felt that she had been patronized. Norma wished to be taken seriously.

That same year, 1992, literary agents on the California coast let Norma know that they wished to sell her story. Their names were Eric and Maureen Lasher. They'd left New York for the palms and celebrities of Pacific Palisades, and flew Norma west, introducing her to Malibu and Tony Curtis and a magazine writer they represented named Andy Meisler.

Meisler was a gentle man with no pretensions; he favored jeans and would later author three guides to the TV show *The X-Files*. Norma liked him at once. Back home in Dallas, she readied for his bimonthly visits with lines of cocaine and capsules of Valium, she said, sharing with Meisler, in talks on her bedroom floor, the stories of a life that the Lashers then sold to HarperCollins for $65,000. Norma got half.

Norma's previous attempt at a book had collapsed when her biographer insisted on the truth. But Meisler did not press Norma on her facts. "It all sounded plausible," he says. Norma lied even about her recent history, telling Meisler, for example, that the whereabouts of her youngest child were unknown to her. "Of my many sorrows," Meisler wrote in her voice, "this is without a doubt the worst."

———

SIX MONTHS AFTER the *Enquirer* trumpeted word of "Jane Roe's Baby," Shelley had suffered no new intrusions. No more press had found her, and the two friends she'd told of *Roe* had said nothing of it. But even a kept secret is a great weight. As the calendar turned to 1990, Shelley never stopped wondering about the day when it might spill.

Shelley remained angry that the *Enquirer* had dispatched an investigator to find her. But her upset at Norma had receded. It was helpful to know one's birth mother, no matter who she was. It was of further comfort to know, as Shelley had told the *Enquirer*, "that she loves me." And so, Shelley was once again left to live the steady life she desired, a secretary content to touch-type and file and spend her free hours with her new man.

His name was Doug. He worked at IBM, offering technical help to clients. He had asked a woman in the office named Ruth about the pretty girl in the photograph on her desk. Ruth had told him that she was her daughter and that she was single. But Shelley was then eighteen, nine years his junior, and he waited a year to call. They met at Taco Bell, and Shelley knew that she'd found a man who would stay. "As long as I had that one person who would never leave me," says Shelley, "I would be fine."

Doug was a gentleman. He'd been raised in Albuquerque on cars and courtesy, and was mindful to ask Shelley what she wanted on her burger, to fill up her Honda CRX lest her hands smell of gas. He spoke in a soft voice, and told Shelley that he'd left his Catholicism because, she recalls, "he didn't like what he saw as the hypocrisy of confession."

Shelley could be open with Doug. And when she told him of *Roe*, he set her at ease. "He was just like, 'Oh, cool. Or is it not cool? You tell me. I'll go with whatever you tell me.'"

Shelley had confided her secret. But she wished to be rid of it, to be a normal teenager again, less mindful of abortion than of boyfriends and shoes. Come January, she resolved to never be aware of another anniversary of *Roe*, so that if ever someone asked about it, she could say, "I have no feelings on it," and her words would be true.

The anniversary passed. But weeks later, on a Sunday night in February, Shelley was home with her mother in Kent when there was a knock at the door. Shelley opened it to find a young woman, thin and blond and pretty.

Her name was Audrey Lavin. She was a producer for the tabloid TV show *A Current Affair* and had worked the eight months since the *Enquirer* story to find Shelley. She was kind and told Shelley that she would do nothing without her consent, but Shelley felt herself flush, her hands still trembling when, the next day, flowers arrived with a note.

Lavin wrote that Shelley was "of American history"—both a "part of a great decision for women" and "the truest example of what the 'right to life' can mean." Her desire to tell Shelley's story owed, she wrote, to "an obligation to our gender." She signed off with an invitation to phone her at the Stouffer Madison Hotel. Ruth phoned their lawyer.

Roe had resurfaced, had pulled Shelley under a second time. "It was like, oh God!" she says. "I am never going to be able to get away from this!" Shelley felt paranoid, suspicious. Her lawyer again instructed her to trust no one. Says Shelley: he "had us freaking scared."

Shelley took stock. The steady life she desired would not be hers, and all because Norma had led a tabloid to her doorstep.

It was then, in early 1991, that Shelley found herself pregnant. She was due to deliver two months after she had planned to marry.

Shelley did not know of the unplanned pregnancies in 1922, 1940

and 1964 that had redirected three generations of women in her biological family. She knew only that if she was excited to be a wife, she was,
she says, "not at all" eager to be a mother. Doug, she says, suggested she
have an abortion.

Shelley had long considered abortion wrong, had thought *Roe* a
means only to promiscuity. But her connection to it had led her to think
it through. It now seemed to her that abortion law ought to be free of the
influences of religion and politics. Religious certitude left her uncomfortable. And, she later reflected, "I guess I don't understand why it's a
government concern."

It had upset her that the *Enquirer* had described her as pro-life, a
term that connoted for her, she says, "a bunch of religious fanatics going
around and doing protests." But neither did she embrace the term pro-
choice. For Norma was pro-choice, and to abort her future child would
thus render Shelley no different than Norma. She determined to give
birth. "There wasn't any choice," says Shelley. Abortion was "not part
of who I was."

Two weeks later, on March 19, Shelley and Doug married, standing
before a justice of the peace in a chapel in Seattle.

Doug asked Shelley to give up her career and stay at home, there
in the Washington town of Maple Valley. That was fine by her. The
more people she knew, the more people she worried might learn of
Roe. Indeed, at the start of her every friendship, says Shelley, she found
herself thinking: "Yeah, we're really great friends but you don't have a
clue who I am."

In October 1991, Shelley gave birth to a boy. She loved her baby
and took him with her every Sunday morning to church. But her fellow
Baptists asked why her husband was not with them, and she stopped
going. She would focus her energy on her family—her son and husband
and mother and father, Billy phoning every so often from Texas to say
that he loved her.

Shelley thought of her sisters, too. And in 1993, three quiet years
after *Roe* had again knocked at her door, one of them came calling.

Chapter 21

Melissa had been married two years when, in 1989, she and Kerry sold their trailer for the down payment on a starter home, a small brick house with three bedrooms in Amarillo.

Kerry had been faithful since the wedding. And he had not been violent. He was again the man Melissa had fallen for, a happy ham who had Melissa perm the back of his mullet. In 1992, he began counseling boys at the same residential Christian school where years before he'd been both cared for and abused. Says Melissa: "He was like a god when he went back."

Social work, however, barely covered the mortgage. "We were penny-poor," says Melissa. And so, she left haircutting for nursing, taking a loan of $15,000 to enroll in a course that taught her to immunize, to catheterize, to prepare a patient for surgery. A year later, she was a licensed vocational nurse, and she started in on a second degree to become a full-fledged RN.

The white coat suited Melissa. For so many years, she had tended to her family—her drinking grandmother, her schizophrenic uncle. To act as Norma had not: this remained for Melissa the great imperative of her life.

MELISSA DID NOT KNOW SHELLEY. But she knew of her. She'd read in the *Enquirer* that her youngest half-sister had been found. Filled with excitement, she'd asked Norma to connect them. Norma had refused. But now, four years later in 1993, Melissa reached out to Shelley through Norma's lawyer, sending along her address: 5203 Royce Drive, Amarillo.

Shelley was shocked and thrilled, hopeful and sentimental. On the first of September, she put pen to paper.

"Dear Cheryl," Shelley began, addressing her sister with the name Norma had told her instead of Melissa. "I am so so so happy that you want me in your life and you want us to be sisters. . . . Please God, let it be true." Shelley wrote that she had dreamed of finding her sister even before she knew her to exist, adding, "There was never a single day that I haven't thought of you."

Melissa exulted. Here, at last, was a sibling! She was real, with favorite colors and foods and animals and TV soaps that she listed in a swirly script. She'd pined for Melissa as Melissa had for her, and had signed off with love and a phone number.

Melissa set the letter in her bedside drawer and telephoned her sister. All at once, neither was an only child. In the months that followed, the sisters gave each other a hundred answers to a hundred questions, twenty-somethings aching to make up for lost years. "I want to be with you so bad and get in your way and mess up your room and bother you on dates," Shelley wrote to Melissa. "Maybe Kerry will pretend he's not married to you and just taking you out to a movie and I can sneak in the back seat and then (of course, you're going to the drive in) when he tries to kiss you I can jump up and yell, 'I'm thirsty! I'm hungry! I can't see! I have to go to the bathroom!'" She added: "I love you, Melissa!"

Melissa told Shelley that she loved her too. The sisters made a plan to fly Melissa to Washington with money they would earn stuffing mailings into envelopes.

Melissa marveled that her younger sister seemed so at ease. While her own marriage was volatile, and money short, Shelley had written to Melissa of her quilting and strong marriage. Says Melissa: "She had the love of her life."

But Shelley was not at ease. Her hands were still prone to tremble, her mood to darken. She feared being outed as the *Roe* baby. And, as she told Melissa, she worried about their mother—that Norma might be angry that Melissa had found her, that Norma might reject her again.

Shelley wrote to Norma asking her to confirm their relation. Norma did so. "She's admitting that I am her daughter," Shelley wrote to Melissa. Shelley added that Norma wished to meet her.

Shelley was unprepared to meet her mother. She wished to meet Melissa only. And she was right to worry about Norma. Though Norma confirmed her parentage, she was jealous of the relationship her daughters were forming, and phoned Shelley to say that she and Connie wished to join her and Melissa when they met. Shelley demurred. Norma grew angry, angrier still that Shelley and Melissa wished to find the sister between them. Norma could have helped them do so; it was her old doctor, Richard Lane, who had led the Kebabjians to Jennifer. But Norma had never shown interest in her middle child and told Shelley that she had no desire to have her found.

Shelley was not only overwhelmed by Norma; she felt hurt by Melissa. Though Melissa was counting down the days to their meeting, she was cutting hair on weekends at a truck stop in Amarillo to earn extra money, and had less time for Shelley. Shelley pushed off their meeting to the following spring.

———

ALL HER LIFE, Melissa had craved family. And she was now in particular need of it. Her husband was increasingly aloof, quick to fight. Melissa wondered why. Couples therapy had offered no answers when Kerry confessed to a one-night stand.

Melissa was crushed. But Kerry said that the woman meant nothing, that she was a stranger in Dallas. He said he felt guilty. Melissa forgave him but then found panties under the floor mat of his car. Kerry said they'd fallen from the laundry bag of his secretary and told Melissa, she recalls, that the cheating she suspected "was all in my head, my hormones."

Melissa then learned that she was pregnant. She told Kerry but, she says, "he looked disappointed." Days later, she saw him pushing his secretary on a swing in a park. She left, taking their daughter to live for a week with Mary. Kerry moved out.

Melissa was devastated. She feared, she says, that all was lost—"a marriage, a family, civility." More, she was shaken by the thought that she was becoming Norma. She'd had sex at fifteen to confirm that she was not gay, like Norma, and had forsworn birth control, she says, so as not to prevent, as Norma had tried to, the birth of a future child. She thus decided now to do what Norma had not, and remain with her husband.

Kerry moved back in. But Melissa was on edge. She began to take Lorazepam and returned with Kerry to therapy.

The counselor whom Melissa and Kerry saw at their local church in Amarillo told Melissa that it was her Christian duty to abide her husband's indiscretions and make herself available for sex. "You need to submit yourself to him," the therapist told her. "If he wants it in the morning, you submit yourself. If he wants it in the afternoon, you submit yourself."

Melissa confided in her sister. But Shelley struggled to relate. She said, recalls Melissa, that were Doug to cheat on her, she would leave him at once. Melissa took no comfort in her words.

Shelley had meant well. And the next time Norma phoned, Shelley told her that she wished that she, Shelley, could be there for her sister. Norma, says Shelley, responded that Melissa had "other family" and didn't need her.

———

IT IS A DAMAGING THING to be forced to carry a pregnancy one does not want. According to a watershed study begun in 2008, a woman denied an abortion is more likely, among much else, to live in poverty and suffer anxiety. Her unwanted child suffers too, at "increased risk," one study noted, "for negative psychosocial development and mental well-being." Shelley was not alone in being born unwanted. There were, alas, millions of such children. But only *her* conception had precipitated the legal right to abort those millions.

Shelley had not let go of the hope that Norma might yet seek to forge a relationship with her. Still, the daughter remained wary of her birth mother, mindful that it was the prospect of money and press that had led Norma to seek her out.

Somewhere inside, Norma understood Shelley's caution, her bitterness. She'd spoken to one reporter of the cross her youngest child no doubt bore. To another, she wondered: "How could you possibly talk to someone who wanted to abort you?" Neither of those interviews, however, was published. And when, in the spring of 1994, Norma phoned Shelley to say that she and Connie wished to come visit her, the mother and daughter were quickly at odds after Shelley responded, she recalls, that she hoped Norma and Connie would be "discreet" in front of her child. "How am I going to explain to a three-year-old," Shelley told Norma, "that not only is this person your grandmother but she is kissing another woman?" Norma yelled at her, and then said that Shelley should thank her. Shelley asked why. For not aborting her, answered Norma. Shelley was appalled. "I was like, what?! . . . I'm supposed to thank you for getting knocked up by some john in a bar and then giving me away?" Says Shelley: "I told her I would never ever thank her for not aborting me."

It had been twenty-four years since Norma had first let Shelley go, five years since the *Enquirer* had tried but failed to bring them together. As mother and daughter now hung up their phones in anger, they seemed to be parting for good. "Norma gave me up again, a third time," says Shelley. She adds: "This is when Norma and I called it quits."

———

LIFE WAS DIFFICULT for Melissa. She was pregnant with the child of a cheating husband. And because money was tight, she left nursing school to get a job. She wanted to work at Planned Parenthood but, as the daughter of Jane Roe, feared the press it might generate. She went to work at a mental health clinic instead.

Still, Melissa was excited. Her sister was at last coming to visit in May.

Shelley, though, was having second thoughts. She wished to have nothing to do with Norma and it pained her that Melissa did. "I told Melissa, 'I can't do this,'" recalls Shelley. "'She is still in your life.'" Countered Melissa: "She's still my mom whether I like it or not."

Shelley needed more time and again postponed her trip. "I was shocked," says Melissa. "I was just fucking disappointed."

Shelley apologized. "The more we talk (and fight) the more I realize we are family and sisters through and through," she wrote to Melissa.

"I love you and I should tell you that more often." Shelley rescheduled her trip for July. But Melissa could not reschedule the days off she had taken. And when Shelley flew to Texas in July to see her old neighbor, she didn't visit her big sister six hours west on Route 287. She didn't phone. A relationship had unraveled.

Melissa laid Shelley's letters in her bedside drawer. It was soon hard for her to recall what had troubled Shelley. All she could remember was that her sister had been trying to decide whether to spend money on a sewing machine or on having another child or on returning to school. She wondered which Shelley chose. As the months passed, she wondered too about the sister between them, the one she and Shelley had resolved to find.

———

JENNIFER THOUGHT OFTEN OF FAMILY, of its frailties and fractures. Her marriage to Ricky had ended with a punch to the jaw. Her boyfriend James, unstable and prone to drink, offered little hope of a more stable home. And she had lost all hope of discovering her past when, in 1988, her father told her that he did not have any records of her adoption.

A year later, divorced and drinking ever more, Jennifer moved in with James. The couple settled into an old brick house just south of Dallas, empty save for a shag carpet.

James volunteered at a fire station. Jennifer was not working. She'd broken her foot at the auto body shop and was still collecting workers' comp. Home in her empty house, she steeped her nights in alcohol, drinking with James and alone too, quietly wondering, at age twenty-two, if she was gay.

Jennifer also wondered all the more about the unknown genes she had inherited when, in the summer of 1990, she found herself pregnant. Jennifer did not consider abortion. "I wanted the baby," she says. As her March due date approached, she swelled, gaining sixty-six pounds. She married James and took his name, the new Mrs. Jennifer Ferguson determined to live healthily for their child. She quit drinking and smoking and drugs. Says Jennifer: "I followed everything to the tee."

James, though, remained depressed. He still drank, and was prone to sorrow and anger; he suspected his pregnant wife of cheating. One night, he slapped her while they were playing cards. Jennifer found herself in a second bad marriage, caring not only for a baby with a cleft palate but a volatile husband.

Their son was just a few months old when, one day, James jerryrigged the exhaust pipe of his old Ford to the hose of a vacuum cleaner. Jennifer found him inside the house, she says, "throwing up and acting all irrational." She called 911. James went to an ICU. Jennifer returned to work.

The Texas Workforce Commission had just pointed Jennifer toward a course in a flower shop some sixty miles south of her duplex in Garland. She got a job fashioning bouquets. She had never enjoyed anything so much, and was good at it, too, setting lemongrass among bundles of long-stemmed liatris and lilies. Stargazers were her favorite, white and magenta and fragrant.

Jennifer worked alone and tirelessly, arranging and selling flowers. The shop, in the Texas town of Italy, was one room. But it felt boundless, an escape, and Jennifer quickly fell for the woman who delivered her bouquets, a teenager with spiky hair named Tamala. She was the first person Jennifer had ever met who identified as gay. The question of whether Jennifer was, too, burned inside her. Wishing to make her crush clear, Jennifer cut down her mullet to short spikes. Soon after, she cornered Tamala in the bathroom and kissed her.

Jennifer knew they could not be; Tamala was in love with another woman. And of course, there was James and her kids; Jennifer had given birth to a second child that fall of 1993. But the kiss, her first with a girl since high school, told Jennifer at last that she was gay. She began to speak over the phone to a friend of Tamala's named Misty.

Misty lived ninety minutes north, not far from the JC Penney where she worked. She was also gay and married to a man, a tugboat captain who cheated on her. After a few months, she drove south to meet Jennifer, and a night together at Tamala's confirmed what they had both sensed on the phone. "I'm a lesbian," Jennifer recalls telling friends. "I'm with a girl."

To come out in small-town Texas in 1994 held much the same peril for Jennifer as it had for her birth mother a generation before. Cops in paddy wagons no longer raided gay bars. But sex between men was still illegal, and she remembers the gasps: "You're what?!" Says Jennifer: "I lost a lot of friends."

Jennifer drove with her kids to Misty every weekend, when Misty's husband was off on his boat. Misty was pregnant, and Jennifer told James that she was helping a pregnant friend. James was suspicious and showed up one weekend unannounced. Misty's parents told him their daughter was gay. He wondered if Jennifer was, too.

Jennifer had always been up-front and blunt; her friend Crystal's mom had nicknamed her "bitch." And it was vivifying to be out as a lesbian. But confronted by her husband, Jennifer lied. She feared the truth might take her kids from her.

Jennifer also said nothing to her parents. She was certain that her homosexuality would only deepen her mother's disappointment in her. "I was always the bad," says Jennifer, "the black sheep." Worse still, she says, her parents would no doubt wonder what *she* had been wondering ever since junior high—if her genes were to blame, "if there was anybody else in my family I didn't know who was gay."

———

THE FIGHTS FOR the legal rights of women and gay people had long overlapped. Just as Coffee had helped McCluskey fight the Texas sodomy laws, Jane Roe had begun to publicly denounce homophobia, responding in the spring of 1994, for example, to a "Dear Abby" letter in which a woman worried that a gay babysitter might harm her granddaughter. "Homosexuals, in my opinion, are caring, nurturing loving people," Norma wrote, adding, "we love children and have other things to do when we're alone with children, like find the right kind of ice cream."

Norma was comfortable speaking about homosexuality in a way she'd never been about abortion; she'd known she was gay long before *Roe*. She had been beaten for it by her mother. And, working on her memoir with Meisler, she saw anew that amidst the rubble of her life, Connie was her lone constant. The book was due out this summer when Norma wrote her a note expressing pride in their having come back together.

I Am Roe got excellent reviews. The book was brave and urgent, said *Kirkus*, "a compelling exploration of how one woman negotiates being a symbol and being herself." The *New York Times* named it a Notable Book of the Year, Norma honored alongside Ken Kesey, Doris Lessing and the late Bertolt Brecht. Wrote the *Times*: "Norma McCorvey's powerful account of her difficult journey from private woman to public symbol underscores the gulf between myth and reality in American politics."

Roe was indeed awash in myth. But the "reality" that Norma presented was anything but real, her book twenty chapters of traumas imagined. Those who knew Norma were bewildered. Says her former girlfriend Hower: "It was a pack of crap."

The lies were purposeful; they rid Norma of sin. Sex enjoyed with a female student became rape by a nun. The relinquishment of her child became a kidnapping. And she who'd fought to abort her third pregnancy asserted that her mother had sought to abort *her*. The claim was baseless. But Norma, who remained ambivalent about abortion, was essentially stating that she was not to blame; she'd only sought to do what her mother had sought to do to her. As she wrote now on a piece of yellow paper: "Why didn't my mother ever teach me how to be a mother?"

Chapter 22

Norma had only just begun, in the spring of 1989, to fully immerse herself in *Roe* when she spoke to Linda Coffee for the last time. Norma asked her former counsel to help her get out of paying a lawyer who'd negotiated her fee for the NBC movie. Coffee told her she could not do so. Ethics aside, she was busy readying for a trial—her own.

Coffee's indictment for alleged fraud had been issued that same spring, and she and her lawyer Kim Wade met repeatedly in his office over Mexican takeout. "I wanted to make sure that she was prepared to testify under direct examination," says Wade. He adds: "It was terrifying for her to go before a jury."

The trial began in August, and Coffee testified that she had neither concealed documents nor forged a signature. "Some of the jurors really reacted negatively when the prosecutor was screaming at me," she says. "One of the men covered his ears."

Back in law school, Coffee had taken no classes in Evidence because she never thought she would try a case. But the records she'd subpoenaed corroborated her testimony. At the close of her seven-day trial, judge Joe Fish acquitted her, preventing the case from being ruled on by the jury because, he determined, the prosecution's evidence was "insufficient to sustain a conviction."

Seated in the courtroom, Coffee's parents and partner exulted. The case, says Coffee, "was just gone." But despite her exoneration, her humiliation remained and she struggled to enjoy all the good in her life: her partner and dogs and home. "It was a travesty," recalls her partner, Rebecca Hartt. "The damage was already done to her psyche."

Her old co-counsel tried to lift her up. Over dinner, Sarah Weddington told her that she, too, had endured bad press. But unlike Weddington, Coffee was sensitive and shy. Forty-six years old, she retreated further into herself. "She became less and less talkative," says Peggy Clewis, a secretary at her firm. "She kind of withdrew." Adds Virginia Whitehill, the Texas feminist who'd worked with both her and Weddington, and who hosted them for dinner after the trial: "She didn't want to see anyone anymore."

Coffee was depleted, distracted. And for the fourth time since joining the Texas Bar in 1968, she failed to pay her membership fee when it was due, the lawyer delinquent again just two weeks after her acquittal.

Coffee quickly paid the $120 she owed. She was back in good standing. But "she looked tore-up," recalls Kent Frank Brooks, a lawyer who partnered with Coffee on a bankruptcy case the next year. "She was troubled." Brooks had been excited to work with Coffee. But he wound up not only doing their oral argument but writing the briefs as well. All the while, he says, "she was muttering a little bit about money problems."

Those problems persisted; in September 1991, the Texas bar again suspended Coffee after she failed to pay what she owed. She paid up and was reinstated in November. But she had fallen behind in her mortgage, a bankruptcy lawyer suddenly facing bankruptcy. Coffee had, in fact, little more to her name than *Roe*. But as her legal legacy neared its twentieth anniversary in 1992, it, too, was suddenly in peril.

———

WHEN COURTS RECOGNIZE a new constitutional right, or liberalize in some way the social order, the public usually acclimates. The constitutional scholar Geoffrey Stone noted, for example, that when, in the decade before *Roe*, the courts rid public schools of prayer and made interracial marriage legal, 79 and 72 percent respectively of the American public disapproved, rates that dropped over time. But abortion was different. Opposition to *Roe* became more hostile after its issuance. Some blamed *Roe* itself for that hostility.

Ruth Bader Ginsburg, then a federal judge on the DC Circuit Court of Appeals, had famously written that the ruling "appears to have provoked, not resolved conflict." It had, she would soon add, "halted a political process that was moving in a reform direction." Her argument would carry. As the columnist David Brooks later wrote: *Roe* "set off a cycle of political viciousness and counterviciousness that has poisoned public life ever since." But for *Roe*, he added, "we would have seen a series of statebystate compromises reflecting the views of the centrist majority that's always existed on this issue."

Not so, said John Rich. The former Blackmun clerk who had helped to craft the *Roe* ruling believed that had *Roe* not legalized abortion, the abortion statutes in many states would likely have remained "extremely strict." Professors Linda Greenhouse and Reva Siegel agreed. They noted that "liberalization efforts seem to have stalled after 1970," and that the Republicanizing of opposition to abortion preceded *Roe*. "Political realignment," they wrote, "better explains the timing and shape of political polarization around abortion than does a courtcentered story of backlash."

What is without doubt is that *Roe* galvanized those opposed to it. Only weeks after the ruling, a Catholic weekly observed that *Roe* had "nationalized the antiabortion movement." That movement had achieved great legislative and judicial successes: the Hyde amendment, the Supreme Court ruling in *Webster*. And yet, almost two decades after *Roe*, its overarching goal remained. As Kenneth Starr, then the Solicitor General under George H. W. Bush, wrote in a 1989 brief: "*Roe* was wrongly decided and should be overruled."

Two and a half years later, in April 1992, that overruling seemed at hand. Abortion had returned to the Court. And with the recent appointment of Clarence Thomas, the quartet of justices who'd made clear their intention to overturn *Roe* seemingly had their fifth vote.

The case was *Planned Parenthood v. Casey*. At issue were five Pennsylvania abortion regulations which mandated, for example, that women or girls wanting an abortion had to first notify their spouse or get consent from a parent. Five local clinics and a doctor had filed suit against Robert Casey, the prolife Democratic governor of Pennsylvania, and a district court had declared the regulations unconstitutional. But an appeals court had upheld all but one of them. The Supreme Court would now decide whether they were in conflict with *Roe* and whether *Roe* itself would remain good law.

=======

ABORTION IS GIVEN TO ABSOLUTES. "It is," wrote the bioethicist O. Carter Snead, "the pristine exemplar of a 'vital conflict.'" And Roe, in just one generation, had come to pit America against itself, choice and life engaged in a war: "a domestic war," "a holy war," "an emotional and intellectual civil war."

Some Americans, however, were unsure on which side they stood. Like the writer Anna Quindlen, they were left "hating the idea of abortions, hating the idea of having them outlawed."

The journalist Roger Rosenblatt postulated that most Americans were similarly conflicted. How else, he wrote, to make sense of a 1990 poll that showed that 70-plus percent of Americans considered abortion a form of murder and yet wished to preserve the right of a woman to have one? He suggested a policy of "permit but discourage."

The Democratic Party was not by rights opposed to that. In 1992, its platform sought to make abortion "less necessary." But pro-life leaders wanted to outlaw it entirely; having long pledged to protect the unborn, the Republican Party now asserted that the "right to life . . . cannot be infringed."

It was thus no surprise that the few attempts at compromise failed. The Common Ground Network for Life and Choice, a tiny organization promoting dialogue through workshops and papers, folded. And a 1979 meeting between pro-choice and pro-life leaders at a hotel in DC ended when a young woman pulled back a blanket in her arms to reveal an aborted female fetus.

Mildred Jefferson had been present at that meeting, and expressed sympathy for the saboteur. The doctor was not one to acknowledge the other side. The writer Katha Pollitt would observe that abortion was "one of those subjects about which people have not only their own opinions but their own facts," and Jefferson would, for example, dismiss as "all wrong" verifiable studies on the harmful effects of teen pregnancy. That Jefferson herself recalled hearing of pregnant teens back in Texas who had died "with no real good explanation" had no discernible effect on her. The impermissibility of abortion was both her start and endpoint.

In this, Jefferson was not alone. Regarding abortion, the tail wagged the dog not only in politics but in constitutional theory. "A great number of Americans have decided what kind of constitution they want by asking what kind would benefit their side of the abortion argument," wrote the legal scholar Ronald Dworkin. And, of course, conservatives wanted the government to intervene when it came to abortion, liberals for it to butt out. As a new NARAL slogan put it, shifting its focus from personal autonomy to government intrusion: "Who decides? You or them?"

In the spring of 1992, the Supreme Court prepared again to answer that question in the case of *Casey.*

OVER THE THOUSAND WEEKS that had passed since *Roe,* Harry Blackmun had absorbed the damnations of the half of America that opposed it. Even at eighty-three, the justice continued to read his way through bags of hate mail.

Roe precipitated other attacks, too. The *Yale Law Journal* ran a withering assessment of it just three months after the decision. *Roe* was "bad," wrote professor John Hart Ely, "because it is bad constitutional law, or rather because it is not constitutional law and gives almost no sense of an obligation to try to be." Robert Bork concurred. "In the entire opinion there is not one line of explanation," he wrote, "not one sentence that qualifies as a legal argument."

Roe was indeed short on constitutional analysis. Blackmun devoted just two paragraphs to his argument that the Constitution guaranteed a right to privacy and with it abortion. (He did, though, cite within them fourteen cases from which he intuited that right.) And as the years passed, legal critics offered up so many alternate legal analyses of abortion, rooted the right to abortion in so many amendments, that Richard Posner dubbed it "the Wandering Jew of constitutional law."

Of course, legal scholars praised *Roe,* too. A group of nearly nine hundred American law professors had filed a brief in *Webster* affirming the legal right to abortion "as delineated . . . in *Roe v. Wade.*" Rooting that right in privacy, contested as it was, also proved a valuable precedent for numerous cases having little to do with abortion, including the right to sexual intimacy and the right to die.

Blackmun observed it all. The justice was a champion of women; while on the Court, he would hire female clerks at a greater rate than any other male justice. And his jurisprudence had caught up with him. Having largely pinned the legality of abortion to the rights of doctors, not women, it was women—and their "fundamental constitutional right . . . to terminate a pregnancy"—that he invoked in the first sentence of his dissent in *Webster*. Blackmun had evolved.

The justice was the last member of the seven-vote *Roe* majority still on the bench. And as arguments began in *Casey*, in April 1992, he listened with his two hearing aids, his singular achievement in the hands of his fellow justices. David Souter was among them.

―――――

SOUTER WAS DEEPLY GROUNDED; the writer Janet Malcolm would note that he possessed a "moving absence of self-regard." The justice had grown up in a farmhouse in the New Hampshire town of Weare, and had returned to Weare after his schooling at Harvard and Oxford, there to live until the Supreme Court took him from it, in October 1990, as an unmarried man of fifty-one. Resettled in the capital, he did his best to live without fuss, to jog, to eat his apples core and all, to write longhand by natural light; no electric lamp lit his chambers until dusk.

Souter had spoken of Weare at his Senate confirmation hearing. But he'd said little of *Roe*, telling the Senate committee that it would be "inappropriate" for him to comment on it. Pro-choice leaders were sure that the Bush appointee was a foe. "I tremble for this country if you confirm David Souter," warned Molly Yard, president of NOW, at his confirmation hearing. "He will be the fifth vote to overthrow *Roe v. Wade*."

To know the judge, however, was to know that he "thought and cared more deeply about the Constitution than he did about politics," as Dahlia Lithwick wrote. It was also to know that his judicial hero was John Marshall Harlan II, a justice who believed deeply in the power of precedent. Asked again and again about *Roe*—the ruling so dominated his hearings that one senator labeled them "a mockery"—Souter had made clear to the Senate committee his respect for what he termed "extremely significant issues of precedent." That *Roe* had been law for a generation, he intimated, might be every bit as important as the question of its rightness.

Souter knew that abortion was likely to return to the Court. His first term on the Court was ending when, in June 1991, he asked his four outgoing clerks to write down their thoughts on the matter. Just one argued in favor of *Roe*, that clerk handing Souter thirty-two crystalline pages that centered on stare decisis—the doctrine that held, as Souter did, that legal precedents should ordinarily not be overruled. On the matter of abortion, wrote the clerk, that doctrine was particularly compelling. "*Roe*," he wrote, "implicates uniquely powerful stare decisis concerns."

Prominent among those concerns, wrote the clerk, was that the influence of *Roe* on the selection of justices posed a particular danger. "If *Roe* is overruled," he argued, "the public will understand that the Court's reversal is explainable solely by reason of changes in the composition of the Court." Thus, he concluded: "The damage to the public understanding of the Court's decisions as neutral expositions of the law . . . would be incalculable." The memo added that all of the proposed legal rationales for overturning *Roe* would threaten *Griswold*, the landmark decision recognizing a right to contraception. And it was relevant to the goals of stare decisis, wrote the clerk, that a generation of women had acclimated to *Roe*, had "shaped their lives around that right."

The memo further argued that *Roe*, while not beyond criticism, had a grounding in constitutional law "stronger than it currently seems fashionable to recognize." Still, the clerk allowed that if Souter felt it prudent, concerns over stare decisis would be less severe with "a relatively minor adjustment of *Roe*," namely, replacing the trimester framework with the "undue burden" standard of regulation that Justice O'Connor had endorsed a decade before; any law that unduly burdened a woman's right to obtain an abortion would be invalid.

All of this Souter read. And he had just concluded that the Court ought to reaffirm *Roe* when, in conference two days after oral arguments in Casey, a majority of his fellow justices concluded the opposite.

Souter was dismayed. And as Rehnquist, the Chief Justice, prepared to write a majority opinion in support of Pennsylvania and its abortion regulations, Souter set out to rescue *Roe*, reaching out to Justice O'Connor, and then, with her, to Justice Kennedy.

O'Connor and Kennedy were unlikely allies of *Roe*. The first had told a Senate committee of her "abhorrence of abortion as a remedy." The second, in ruling on *Webster*, had stated his desire to overturn *Roe*.

But O'Connor—who was married—was troubled by the requirement of spousal notice. And Kennedy now wanted to find "some stable, defensible middle ground on *Roe*," as the former Blackmun clerk Edward Lazarus later wrote, "an endeavor Kennedy could sell to himself as truly judicious and advancing the country's welfare." And so, the trio of justices, working in stealth apart and together, wrote an opinion that upheld *Roe* at its core. "Rehnquist and Scalia were stunned," observed the *Los Angeles Times*. "So, too, was Blackmun."

The ruling was a compromise. Half of it, which Blackmun and Stevens now joined, upheld the "essential holding of *Roe*," namely, the right to an abortion through viability. The other half adopted a new subjective standard of abortion regulation, O'Connor's "undue burden." The three justices concluded that four of the five Pennsylvania regulations cleared that standard, and that became the decision of the Court: Blackmun and Stevens joined the troika in striking down the spousal notification requirement, and the remaining four justices voted with them to uphold the other regulations.

The "undue burden" standard, which was now effectively the law, did away with the trimester framework of *Roe*; henceforth, states could impose certain abortion regulations from conception on. "Even in the earliest stages of pregnancy," the ruling explained, "the State may enact rules and regulations designed to encourage her to know that there are philosophic and social arguments of great weight that can be brought to bear in favor of continuing the pregnancy to full term . . ."

Still, the great upshot of *Casey* was that it preserved *Roe*. And on June 29, 1992, O'Connor, Kennedy and Souter each read aloud portions of their joint opinion, the first time in forty-four years that an opinion of the Court carried the name of more than one justice. It was Souter who spoke the meat of it. "The ability of women to participate equally in the economic and social life of the Nation," he said, "has been facilitated by their ability to control their reproductive lives."

It was a remarkable sentence. For it spoke of equality, not privacy, the legal grounds which Ginsburg and others had famously asserted ought to undergird *Roe*.

The justice, in black robe and graying hair, then turned to the legal underpinning of *Casey*—the reliance on precedent that, he said, now called upon both sides of the abortion debate "to end their national division by accepting a common mandate rooted in the Constitution." He continued, reading aloud a paragraph that would stand, in the words of historian David Garrow, "among the most memorable lines ever authored by an American jurist":

> The Court is not asked to do this very often, having thus addressed the Nation only twice in our lifetime, in the decisions of *Brown* and *Roe*. But when the Court does act in this way, its decision requires an equally rare precedential force to counter the inevitable efforts to overturn it and to thwart its implementation. Some of those efforts may be mere unprincipled emotional reactions; others may proceed from principles worthy of profound respect. But whatever the premises of opposition may be, only the most convincing justification under accepted standards of precedent could suffice to demonstrate that a later decision overruling the first was anything but a surrender to political pressure, and an unjustified repudiation of the principle on which the Court staked its authority in the first instance. So to overrule under fire in the absence of the most compelling reason to re-examine a watershed decision would subvert the Court's legitimacy beyond any serious question.

Souter finished speaking. He had been true to himself and also to the example of his hero, Justice Harlan. Having engineered a remarkable rescue of *Roe*, the justice, his second term on the Court now complete, drove his Volkswagen home to New Hampshire.

A Supreme Court laden with eight Republican appointees had affirmed *Roe* and, with it, its aging author Blackmun. His legacy was intact. So, too, was that of its plaintiff. Two years later, having just retired from the Court, Blackmun recalled hearing that Norma McCorvey wished to shake his hand.

PART VI

Born Again

Chapter 23

Norma's memoir and its engagements had run their course when, in mid-1994, she took a job answering phones at an abortion clinic in north Dallas called A to Z.

Norma had been Jane Roe half of her forty-seven years. But she had spent just a few months among abortion providers—filing papers at a clinic in 1983, answering phones at another in 1984, and offering counsel, years later, to the pregnant patients of a Dallas doctor. And when word of her new job reached Charlotte Taft in her clinic on Routh Street, Taft worried. A decade prior, Norma, drunk and hurting, had confided in Taft her discomfort with abortion. She was beset, Norma told her, by thoughts of childless playgrounds. "I did not imagine that Norma had changed and so I was dismayed," says Taft of hearing the news that Norma was back at a clinic. "Norma would not engender calm or confidence in a patient." She adds: "I think she was ambivalent about abortion."

Back in 1969, Norma had found an unlicensed doctor who, for $500, would perform an abortion. But years later, she began to tell another story, that while pregnant with the *Roe* baby she'd gone to an illegal clinic to get an abortion only to find that it had just been shuttered, dried blood still on the floor. As she later recalled to the radio host Terry Gross: "It smelled like death."

That abortion clinics were abattoirs was an axiom of the pro-life.

And as Norma passed her days in the clinic, more and more aware of what her lawsuit had made legal—the killing of embryos and fetuses—that idea began to root in her.

Norma was increasingly upset, on edge. She grew surly with patients, and was fired. Her coworkers had a doctor examine her. She was forty-eight but looked sixty, recalled the doctor, Jasbir Ahluwalia. "Run-down, depressed, crying, suicidal."

Of course, Norma's depression had preceded *Roe*. Before the ruling, she had tried to kill herself, twice. And she had been taking Valium for years when now Dr. Ahluwalia injected her with hormones. Norma, in turn, asked him for a job, and the doctor paid her six-plus dollars an hour to answer phones at an abortion clinic he owned in north Dallas.

Months later, *Texas Monthly* arrived at A Choice for Women to watch her work. "How far along into the pregnancy are you, dear?" Norma asked a caller. "Six weeks? It'll be $295 and a one-day visit." A second call from a woman in Amarillo was more complicated; her husband was in prison and she had slept with his friend and she was injecting cocaine and wondered if she should have an abortion. "Well, I can't really make that decision for you," Norma answered. "I can give you fees. I can give you alternatives. We'll work with you however we can." Norma asked if she had a pastor to turn to. "How about your mom? Your dad?"

Such conversations reinforced for Norma the necessity of *Roe*. By 1995, despite her ambivalence, she knew where she stood: if abortion was fraught, it needed to remain legal. "This issue," she told the Associated Press, "is the only thing I live for."

━━━

IN DECEMBER 1994, days before *Texas Monthly* contacted Norma, two abortion clinic workers in Massachusetts were murdered.

That opponents of abortion had killed grown humans in the name of fetal ones could not be called a surprise. Pro-life protest had been escalating ever since *Roe*, sit-ins and marches giving way to the blockading and bombing of clinics. Pro-life rhetoric all but demanded bloodshed. As Professor Daniel Williams wrote: "If abortion killed human beings, and if it really was a 'holocaust,' as opponents of abortion had been saying for decades, violence that saved unborn lives and prevented God's judgment on a disobedient nation was justified."

Or, as Randall Terry, the founder of Operation Rescue, said of abortion: people had best begin "acting like it's murder."

The issue was personal for Terry. As he told the journalist Susan Faludi: "I was conceived out of wedlock. I could've been aborted."

Terry had instead been "raised at the knee of feminists," as one of his aunts, a Planned Parenthood communications director, told Faludi. She and her three sisters had all been pregnant pre-*Roe* as unwed teens, and three of them had gone on to fight for reproductive rights. But in 1976, Terry, a dope-smoking high school dropout, had found God while hitchhiking about the country. And he was back home, selling ice cream in upstate New York, when a customer spotted his Bible and asked if he was a Christian. Days later, Terry became one—the intense boy with glasses and a great big halo of hair born again at the age of seventeen.

Terry soon found a mentor, a Pentecostal preacher given to glossolalia. Terry began street preaching. He then enrolled at a fundamentalist (if unaccredited) Bible college where the books and films of Francis Schaeffer, an evangelical philosopher, opened his eyes to abortion. As Terry later recalled to journalists James Risen and Judy Thomas, he had "sobbed convulsively" while watching a Schaeffer film about abortion. "I sat there and prayed: God use me to fight this evil."

Terry graduated from Bible college in 1981, reconnected with his mentor and founded a church. But the church ousted Terry, upset that, among much else, he suggested that bombing an abortion clinic was justifiable.

In 1984, Terry, twenty-five, began to protest an abortion clinic in Binghamton, New York, patrolling its parking lot together with the woman he had married three years before. The couple had been unable to conceive. After months outside the clinic, the Terrys convinced a woman to forgo an abortion and then raised the baby girl she birthed, along with the baby's older brother. The Terrys, though, stopped few other abortions.

A local Charismatic church began to back Terry. He soon had enough financial support to quit his job selling tires. And in 1986, Terry and six others barged into that same clinic and chained themselves to it.

"It's for Jesus and for the least of his brethren," Terry said as he awaited the police. "Hallelujah!" It was his first arrest and it was vivifying. He received a misdemeanor.

The standard-bearers of the pro-life movement, organizations like the National Right to Life Committee, made a point of separating their protest from religion. But many of the smaller groups did not. (Back in 1982, a Christian group calling itself the Army of God kidnapped an Illinois provider, holding him and his wife hostage.) That the Bible did not mention abortion did not matter; they intuited its proscription in books from Jeremiah to Luke. Bullhorn in hand, Terry now fought his crusade in the name of Jesus. "We must obey God rather than men," he instructed his disciples, quoting the Apostle Peter. His militia of otherwise docile Christians blockaded clinics about the country. By 1990, their arrests numbered in the tens of thousands.

On the matter of violence, Terry toed the line. He never outright called for it. But he stated in an Operation Rescue training tape that "violence" and "force" were "the logical response to murder. [And] abortion is murder." As the years passed and pro-life activists vandalized hundreds of clinics, Terry was pleased. Doing so, he later said, was as "ethically legitimate" as it would have been to destroy the crematoria of Auschwitz.

The Holocaust was a regular reference point for Terry. He was certain that, just as history had come to judge the genocide of the Jews, so too would it one day judge abortion. It followed, then, that history would judge him as it did Dietrich Bonhoeffer, that clearheaded German pastor who decried the genocide. It was not lost on Terry that Bonhoeffer had wished Hitler assassinated. "Tyrannicide is legitimate," said Terry years later, adding, "I believe that abortionists should be tried in a court of law and executed under Nuremberg principles."

Terry would soon go further. "When I, or people like me, are running the country," he told a gathering of the radical right U.S. Taxpayers Alliance, "you'd better flee, because we will find you, we will try you, and we'll execute you." Though Terry would never call for the *extrajudicial* murder of abortion providers, the effect of his words was clear.

"We have bullets being delivered to clinics with staffers' names on them almost daily," a Planned Parenthood spokeswoman told the press. Operation Rescue went so far as to print leaflets with the names and addresses of "Wanted" abortion providers, among them a doctor in Florida named David Gunn. In the winter of 1993, a Christian fundamentalist shot Dr. Gunn in the back just outside his clinic.

The murder, two decades after *Roe*, triggered a pro-life shooting spree; over the twenty-one months that followed it, activists shot eleven more people, four of them dead. "You sow blood, you reap blood," says Terry. He adds: "Operation Rescue had zero culpability."

OPERATION RESCUE LABELED Curtis Boyd a "Wanted" man, too. It had had the doctor in its sights for years. Back in 1990, not long after an unidentified arsonist set Boyd's Dallas clinic on fire, members of Operation Rescue had burst into his clinic and chained themselves to its furniture and equipment. More attacks followed: tires slashed in Boyd's parking lot, obscenities painted on the homes of his staff.

Boyd had testified to a House subcommittee about the toxic backdrop to such attacks: the condemnations of abortion by the president and pope, the pressures exerted on abortion providers by district attorneys and medical examiners. Such stresses, he said, had prevented the mainstreaming of abortion medicine. "What we end up getting," he later noted, "are some of the best doctors and some of the worst."

It stood to reason that with the ruling in *Roe*, medical residents in obstetrics and gynecology would be required to learn to perform abortions. But by 1992, just 12 percent of ob-gyn residency programs included abortion training, and the medical accreditation body found itself forced to mandate such training. Still, that same body allowed for the exception of medical residents "with moral or religious objections"— exceptions that mirrored the "conscience clause" legislation that Congress had passed immediately after *Roe* for similarly conflicted doctors.

For other doctors, religion was precisely the reason that they *did* perform abortions. Curtis Boyd was one. "It was my Christian values that brought me to this work," he told the press. Decades after *Roe*, the doctor remained religious. Many of his patients were religious, too, among them dozens of Catholic women who asked him to baptize their aborted fetuses.

The day after the murder of Dr. Gunn, Boyd spoke out against Operation Rescue on NPR. So did others. Linked now in the public imagination with murder, Operation Rescue was soon bankrupted by lawsuits and denuded by Congress. In May 1994, President Clinton signed the Freedom of Access to Clinic Entrances Act. FACE made it a federal crime to "injure, intimidate or interfere with" anyone providing an abortion or getting one. Blocking the entrance to a clinic was now punishable by months, not days, in jail. The number of protesters plummeted. Operation Rescue had been laid low.

That same year, the organization selected a new director, a minister in Dallas named Philip "Flip" Benham. Benham would guide Operation Rescue, in the words of professor Carol Mason, "toward symbolic action." And the living symbol of *Roe*, Norma McCorvey, was right there in town. Says Benham: "We knew where she was."

———

BACK IN 1973, Benham had welcomed *Roe*. He had finished his army service that same year as a clerk in Germany. And home in upstate New York, he was, he says, in favor of "anything to overcome the problems we guys got girls into."

Benham moved the next year to Florida, where his father bought him a bar in Kissimmee. Suddenly, Benham had, at age twenty-six, not only a college degree and a wife and a daughter but a bottomless tap. Most nights he drank. Benham became an alcoholic, he says. The next spring, he suggested to his pregnant wife that she have an abortion. She had twins instead.

Benham had been a saloonkeeper three years when, in 1976, a customer who sold coffee urns invited him to an evangelical church. Benham went. Come 1980, he had closed his bar, graduated as a lay minister from a seminary in Kentucky, and opened a Free Methodist church in Dallas.

It was in Dallas, two years later, that Benham heard a minister named Bill Gothard posit that God first became flesh not when Jesus was born but when He was conceived. "I said, 'Oh my gosh!'" recalls Benham. "Children in the womb!" Benham had found his calling: the abolition of that which might have killed his twin boys. In 1988, he joined Operation Rescue, cofounding a chapter in Dallas and preaching at his church that abortion was murder.

Benham began to protest outside clinics. He was arrested for the first time that October. He had been arrested dozens of times more when, in 1992, the local Free Methodist superintendent told him, says Benham, that their "church would be a lot better served if I was left without appointment." All but defrocked, Benham turned full-time to fighting abortion.

Benham was no Randall Terry. He was less apt to rebuke than embrace. Handsome in his fifth decade, he beckoned would-be sinners with bright blue eyes and blow-dried hair and holy words that he read from his leatherbound Bible—a book "fat and soft as a baby," one journalist noted. The preacher liked to sniff it and hold it aloft and quote from it, too. A favorite passage was Deuteronomy 30:19: "Now choose life, so that you and your children may live."

To choose death was to risk the wrath of God. After Benham was arrested and sentenced to jail in Houston during the 1992 Republican National Convention, Norman Mailer observed that the "preacher started praying for the judge to repent or she would 'be stricken from the face of the earth.'" (Benham says he merely prayed for her to be stricken from office.)

Behind bars, Benham worried that he and his wife, a nurse expecting their fourth child, might not survive without his pulpit. Abortion earned Benham very little money, just a few hundred dollars that supporters offered him, he says, to "keep doing what you're doing." But then, says Benham, the Lord provided. A pastor let him know that a kindred Christian wished to pay him a thousand dollars for every day he spent in Harris County jail. Twenty-eight days later, Benham exhaled. "When that check came in," he says, "we realized we could make it through the year."

Benham continued his fight. And he soon noticed that many of the women who countered him at abortion clinics were gay. He wondered why.

It was true that among advocates of reproductive rights, lesbians were overrepresented. "I think it comes from a place of feeling passionately about sexual self-determination," notes the history professor

Johanna Schoen. But Benham soon determined, he says, that gay women and what he termed "abortive women" were bound instead by a disregard for God's law. "It was just a different colored glove covering the same fist," says Benham. "The fist of the devil."

In 1980, Jerry Falwell wrote that after abortion, homosexuality was the greatest crisis facing "moral Americans." Benham began in 1993 to preach the same, telling that homosexuality was an evil born of the Sodomites. But if Benham decried sin, he spoke above all of Christian love. He seemed an antidote to the perceptions of violence that still clung to Operation Rescue. And he had just been named its national director when, months later, at a pro-life conference in Chicago in 1994, he argued that the Bible did not sanction the murder of abortion providers—an opinion, he said, that left him in the minority among his peers. Said Benham: "It's sin. It's murder."

Benham said the same, of course, of abortion. And that June, at a book signing in a Dallas café, he called out to the author—Norma McCorvey. "You ought to be ashamed of yourself!" he said. "You are responsible for the deaths of 35 million babies!"

Benham kept Norma in sight. She was, after all, right there in Dallas. And in early 1995, when the lease of his Dallas office was due to expire, Benham had his secretary, Ronda Mackey, go look for a new one—right next to an abortion clinic.

―――――

FOR TWO DECADES, the pro-life movement had established what it called "crisis pregnancy centers," small, nonprofit Christian outposts that offered free pregnancy tests and other shiny lures that obscured a hook: the dissuasion of women from abortion. The CPCs set that hook with fear—with graphic images, with threats of damnation, with claims that abortion caused cancer or depression. Lawsuits followed. In 1991, a congressional committee laid the offending practices bare. "In essence, the issue is misleading advertising," wrote Senator Ron Wyden, who chaired the committee. The committee noted that the centers were guilty of occasional abuse, too, including the "attempted physical restraint" of women seeking abortions and "personal recriminations from clinic staff." Centers were even accused of strong-arming clients into relinquishing their children for adoption.

In response, two Christian umbrella organizations refashioned CPCs as healthcare providers of sorts, centers offering up not only pregnancy tests but counseling and, sometimes, ultrasounds. "These woman-centered strategies renewed the movement's credibility," a sociologist named Kimberly Kelly later observed in a paper about the movement. Though the centers continued to spread untruths about the medical dangers of abortion, the Supreme Court would defend their right to do so. In time, the centers would receive federal funding (much of it for promoting abstinence); and by 1991, there were two thousand or so about the country. That number would only grow, CPCs far outnumbering abortion clinics.

CPCs often opened just beside clinics. Doing so was a way to skirt the forbiddances of the federal FACE law, a way to ensure, says Benham, that "we could talk to moms going into the abortion mill." (The activist Joseph Scheidler had included the tactic in his book *Closed: 99 Ways to Stop Abortion*.)

Benham's secretary Mackey first tried to rent an office beside the clinic on Routh Street. But she found no available space and turned next to Markville Drive. An office was available. And it was perfect—literally next door to an abortion clinic and Jane Roe, too.

Norma had been at her desk the better part of a year when, on the last day of March 1995, Operation Rescue moved in. Benham called his office Life Choices. A sign in the window offered free pregnancy tests.

A mere wall now separated life from choice—9222 Markville from 9224—and Norma told the press that that she was "horrified." She noted that one month earlier, Operation Rescue protests had helped to shutter A to Z, another Dallas clinic where she had worked. Violence would follow, she said.

Benham beamed. "At the killing center, at the gates of hell," he said, "is where the church of Jesus Christ needs to be." And Thursday through Saturday—those days that A Choice for Women performed abortions—Benham led protests that left Norma red with anger. They left her with chest pains, too. After spitting in the face of a protestor, Norma stopped working weekends.

Norma remained on edge. Exiting the clinic in distress one May day, she told the first person in her path, a young man with a rosary in his pocket, that she needed a margarita. "She was really upset," recalls Rene Nevarez. "She said: 'Do you want to go with me?'"

Nevarez was twenty-one. He had been a young teen in El Paso, a Catholic of Mexican descent, when he saw *The Silent Scream*, that most famous of pro-life films made with the ultrasound images of an abortion. His niece had been born unplanned around that same time, and Nevarez became a middle-school activist, standing in quiet prayer outside clinics. Four years later, he joined a clinic blockade. He had been arrested three times when he took leave from the University of Texas at Austin to protest abortion full-time, first in New Mexico and then outside the clinic in Dallas where he now stood in khakis and a buttoned shirt. He was used to being cut down or looked past by the women he spoke to entering the clinic. But Jane Roe, their great enabler, had now invited him for a drink. Staggered, he ducked into the Operation Rescue office to tell Mackey that he was off with Norma. Norma then drove him in her red truck to Five Compadres, a Mexican restaurant nearby on Greenville Avenue. "By the time we got there," says Nevarez, "she was kind of curious about why I chose my path."

In the fifteen years since Norma had volunteered at NOW, her reentry into the pro-choice movement, she had only confronted those opposed to *Roe*. Now, seated on a Dallas patio with a young and soft-spoken man devoted to its undoing, she did not scream or spit; she asked why he did what he did. Nevarez, in turn, did not preach. He simply answered Norma, telling her over a glass of Shiner Bock that his opposition to abortion stemmed from his Catholic faith and that it somehow felt all the more personal given his birth some nine months after *Roe*. Norma listened. She told her story, too. Says Nevarez: "She wanted to make sure that I knew she'd never had an abortion."

Nevarez had long thought of the plaintiff seated before him as someone who'd brought about "a great evil," he says. But suddenly, she was "no longer Roe," says Nevarez. "She was just another person with concerns." When, hours later, Benham phoned his young volunteer to ask, says Nevarez, "if I gave her the gospel," Nevarez felt himself changed. "I remember thinking Flip's approach is all wrong," he says. He told

Benham that he and Norma had "just talked." Looking back on it, this felt right. Says Nevarez: "Opening up a conversation seems exactly what Jesus would do."

It was not, however, what Benham would do. "He yelled at me that I shouldn't have taken an alcoholic for a drink," says Nevarez. "I said, 'Look, I'm a Catholic and I don't have a problem with a beer.'"

———

IF BENHAM WAS DISPLEASED, he took note nonetheless. He was getting a bead on Jane Roe; she left him angry voice messages. One recent morning, he had approached her to apologize for having heckled her at her book signing.

Norma was thankful. She began to seek Benham out, speaking with him as she smoked in the parking lot on those days the lot did not convulse in protest.

The plaintiff and the preacher were not dissimilar. Each had lived forty-seven years divided neatly between the holy and profane; while Benham had left the saloon for Jesus, Norma had left Jehovah for the saloon. Sharing a bench outside their opposing command centers, they spoke of their pasts, of sins and alcohol. Norma told Benham that he reminded her of one of the Beach Boys, and offered to divine his future with rune stones. Benham told Norma that she reminded him of himself, and that he was praying for her. "She was looking for something," he says—time and attention and love. Benham called her "Miss Norma" and laid an arm across her shoulder and gave her a Bible and shared with her favorite passages, like that verse in Deuteronomy about choosing life.

Many pro-life activists know people who were almost aborted—people like Benham, the father of two boys he had not wanted but now loved, and Mackey, whose mother had told her many times that she'd wished to abort her. Pregnant at sixteen with a second child, Mackey's mother had simply not had the money to travel the four hundred miles from her Texas home in Waxahachie to Mexico. When then Mackey herself got pregnant at twenty, her fiancé's parents wanted *her* to have an abortion. She gave birth instead to a preemie named Emily.

Seven years later, Mackey had divorced and remarried. Emily worked beside her, a little girl helping to change minds on a patch of parking lot in north Dallas. "I wasn't afraid to say anything," recalls Emily. She took to calling out: "My mommy almost killed me."

Outside the clinic, Norma took note of Emily, her precocity and ponytail. Emily took note of Norma, her cigarettes and girlfriend. Her mother told her to keep clear of the clinic workers. But Emily, recalls her mother, replied that they "need Jesus too." She began to chat with Norma. When Norma invited Emily inside, her mother allowed her to go, she told her, "as long as they're not killing babies." The girl would disappear into the clinic, cartwheeling and backbending and softening hearts. Norma began calling her Em, and she and Connie drove her around in their old red truck.

Emily often asked Norma to come to church. Norma said no but appreciated the invitation. The girl simply wished to save her soul. "I wanted her to go to heaven," says Emily, "and spend eternity with Jesus."

It had been twenty-five years since Norma relinquished her youngest child. The prospect of motherhood had left her cold. "I had viewed their conceptions with alarm," she would soon write of her daughters, "and their births with dread." In the years since, she had been no more maternal. Still, getting to know Emily, Norma saw what might have been—"a child, not a problem," as she soon wrote.

A part of Norma ached for her role in *Roe*. Says Benham: "She began to see me as someone who could help her work things out."

———

BEFORE *ROE*, Norma could not have imagined that the law might do right by her. She had skirted it all her life. In fact, the Supreme Court was readying to hear her case in the fall of 1971, when Norma was arrested and charged with "operating open saloon."

A generation later, Norma remained a symbol. But a symbol of what exactly was unclear. She was different things to different people: a martyr, an opportunist, an everywoman. To at least one reporter, she was Mayella Ewell. Says Jamie Bennetts, who interviewed Norma in 1989: "She kind of reminded me of the fake rape victim in *To Kill a Mockingbird*."

The comparison was remarkably apt—and not simply because Norma, like Mayella, had lied about being raped. Both women were poor and aspired to more, both were wracked with self-hatred and the dread of a parent, both were willing to blame others for their lack. Also, both wanted something that society condemned. And, summoned by the law, both had been used and made to play a role. Norma was an archetype come to life.

In Harper Lee's novel, however, the trial ended and society lost interest in Mayella. But, as Norma saw, fascination with *Roe* would be unending.

———

NORMA ENJOYED WORKING at the clinic, and she got Connie a job beside her. Still, she was hungry for more attention. Her memoir had just come out when a young woman named Meghan O'Hara cold-called her while in Texas for a wedding.

O'Hara had been born into a Catholic family of nine in central New York, raised in that same "Burned-over District" that had grown both Benham and Randall Terry. Her family was religious but not dogmatic. After college at Holy Cross, O'Hara had landed an internship eleven stories up in midtown Manhattan at the feminist flagship, *Ms.* The magazine, however, soon seemed to O'Hara just another hierarchy. She left, and then read *I Am Roe*.

As O'Hara saw it, the book was a tale of a damaged hero unembraced by feminist groupthink. She wished at once to make a film about Norma. O'Hara was just twenty-five and had no experience in film beyond a part-time job as a production assistant at HBO. But she had idealism to spare. She also had a day-old tattoo of a sun on her lower back, and she showed it to Norma. "I literally dropped my pants in the restaurant," she says. Norma was aboard.

In the year afterward, O'Hara returned to Norma several times with two young partners and a borrowed camera, filming her recounting her life. But the beginning of her film was generating little interest. As O'Hara recalls: "Nobody wanted to hear the story of fucked-up Jane Roe who's a lesbian and works in an abortion clinic."

But then a reporter got word that Jane Roe and the director of Operation Rescue were chatting on a bench off Markville Drive. After his piece on the unlikely duo ran on the front page of the *Fort Worth Star–*

Telegram, the Associated Press picked it up and the *Today* show invited them north. Soon after, Cinemax bought O'Hara's film.

The confusion that a preacher and a little girl had sowed in Norma was real. So was the warmth she felt in their midst. But it was the spotlight they put on her that brought a radical thought to mind: what if she joined them? What if she switched sides? "I was lonely for some excitement," Norma reflected years later. "I needed to do something that would cause media attention. Isn't that awful?"

It wouldn't be hard to do. The seed had been planted. As for her feelings on abortion, well, she knew how to pledge allegiance to ideologies not quite her own; though she believed in the right of a woman to choose, she'd never fully shaken the thought that abortion was a sin. Besides, what offended her most about the pro-life was not their fight for the fetus but their disregard for it once it was born. As she told a reporter: "I still haven't met an anti-choice person who's adopted an unwanted child."

On June 17, on a couch off Sixth Avenue in midtown New York, Norma sat with Benham on the set of the *Today* show. She wore a black dress and white pearls, and told the reporter Jack Ford that she was "looking for a spiritual path." Ford asked Benham if he hoped to convert Norma, and Benham answered that Miss Norma did as Miss Norma wanted. He was, he said, "simply lifting up a gospel and a Jesus that I think she's looking for." The preacher smiled even as he spoke, white teeth bright against skin tan as leather.

Back in Dallas, Norma felt good—flush with a love the pro-choice camp did not give her. Twenty-five years after unprotected sex had cast her into the role of a lifetime, she readied to write her second act.

———

SIX YEARS HAD PASSED since the National Organization of Women had denied Norma the opportunity to speak at that large DC rally. Norma was not yet "a leader," a spokeswoman had said. Despite having dedicated the years since to their cause, to their idioms and orthodoxies, Norma was no dearer to the pro-choice. In 1993, she was not among those invited to witness President Clinton sign several orders protecting *Roe*. And this spring of 1995, NOW had rebuffed Norma yet again, at another rally. Even on those rare occasions when pro-choice leaders sat Norma beside them—say, at the confirmation hearing of Justice Souter—she was little more than a prop, Eleanor Smeal and Molly Yard and Helen Neuborne and Elizabeth Holtzman and Gloria Allred speaking for her much as Coffee and Weddington had once spoken for her pseudonym.

Back when Norma first met her lawyers, she had made clear that she wanted to end her pregnancy, wanted, as she later wrote, to "be the first girl in Texas to get a legal abortion." Her lawyers had made clear, in turn, that this was unlikely. But if she was to become their plaintiff, it was not unlikely; it was impossible. For Norma was then roughly at the midpoint of her pregnancy and her suit had not yet been filed.

Over the two decades that followed, Norma had not blamed her lawyers for their expediency. ("They didn't really lead me to think they could get me an abortion," she recalled in 1991. "I was just hoping so much.") She had described Weddington in particular as "a wonderful person." But through those years, Norma had not known that Weddington had worked with an abortion referral network in Austin. When now the lawyer wrote in a memoir not only of her work in that network but of the abortion she herself had had three years before Norma had sought one, Norma was furious, left to wonder a first time if Weddington might have helped her to have one, too.

That Weddington had not helped her would-be plaintiff explore the possibility, however remote, of ending her pregnancy, was hardly surprising. Norma had been more valuable to her and Coffee pregnant than not. But it was discomforting just the same. And from the very day the Court had ruled on *Roe*, Weddington had offered up a version of events that explained away that discomfort, telling the Associated Press that Norma had carried her pregnancy to ensure she'd have standing in the eyes of the law. Three years later, the lawyer repeated the lie.

"A decision had to be made about whether Jane would continue her pregnancy or whether we would seek funds to send her out-of-state for an abortion," Weddington told a roomful of banqueters at a 1976 conference on abortion in Colorado. "As her lawyers, Linda and I explained to her that, although we could not say for sure, the case might be declared moot and later thrown out if she had an abortion. She decided to carry the pregnancy to term to save the case."

In truth, Norma had shown no such valor. And her lawyers had shown no such sympathy, ushering Norma into a pro-choice world that would always care more for her pseudonym than for her.

Norma knew this. She had concluded that her lack of pedigree was the underlying reason why. "I think they're embarrassed," Norma told the press in 1993. "They would like for me to be college-educated, with poise and little white gloves." She repeated the point the next year, quipping, "I don't have a Vassar education." Flip Benham couldn't have agreed more. "The Vassar girls," he would soon write of Norma's pro-*Roe* crowd, "always had their snoots so high in the air."

It was, of course, poverty that had led Norma to *Roe*; she had no money to fly to where abortion was legal. In the decades since, legal abortion had remained very much a matter of money; even as the Hyde amendment prevented the poor from using Medicaid to pay for it, the growing body of abortion regulations made it ever more expensive. Women were forced, for example, to make extra trips to their abortion provider in order to get one, made to pay for extra travel and child care and time off.

Pro-choice leaders evoked the tragic endpoint of all that legislation; they spoke of Rosaura Jimenez, a single mother in southern Texas who'd had two legal abortions paid for by Medicaid and then died from an illegal one in 1977, one year after the Hyde amendment had made legal abortion too expensive for her. And yet, those same leaders, so concerned with politics and influence, could be indifferent to the needs of the rural abortion providers on the front lines. As the head of a clinic in Tuscaloosa, Alabama, would reflect years later: "With the national organizations, we seem to be left out."

A decade before, the sociologist Kristin Luker had noted that life and choice divided along class lines. Class now divided the pro-choice, and Jane Roe was of a feather with the other side—those bound less by career and education than family and God.

EVERY MORNING, little Emily asked God to care for two wayward souls: her biological father and Miss Norma. Whenever she saw Norma, she continued to ask her to join her family in church, not stopping until mid-July when Norma went to her mother and said she would.

Mackey had begun spending time with Norma, teaching her, she says, "to be a woman"—to watch her language and her anger, to wear pantyhose and bras. Norma was happy beside her. The secretary was pretty company, lithe with a long neck and bright blue eyes.

It seemed to Mackey that Norma was ready to accept Christ. She alerted Benham and also the pastor Morris Sheats. Days later, on a Saturday night, Norma took her seat beside Mackey toward the rear of Sheats's church on Willow Lane.

Sheats had been preaching since 1956, when, at age sixteen, he says, he'd been filled with the Holy Spirit and spoken in tongues at the close of a church service in Lubbock, where his father was pastor. Almost four decades later, he held a doctorate in ministry and was in the process of growing his second megachurch. Sheats was excited that Jane Roe was coming to Jesus. But he made no use of the fact that she was coming to him. He had seen the born again presented as trophies, and, he says, "it bothered me."

And so, even as Jane Roe sat before him, the pastor made no mention of abortion. As was his practice, he simply departed mid-sermon from John 3:16 with its promise of eternality to ask if anyone present was "tired of living a sinner's life." He invited any person who wished to know Jesus to approach the altar.

Earlier that same day, Norma and her colleagues at the clinic had signed a memo which stated that contact with Operation Rescue staff was forbidden during work and "immoral" after it. But here she was with Mackey. Norma hit her on the leg. "I want to go up there," Norma told her. The women rose. Hands clasped, they walked forward along the concrete aisle of Hillcrest Church.

Sheats was not one for rigid liturgies. His was a nondenominational church and he simply asked Norma if she had come forth to receive Christ into her heart. Norma felt "all warm inside," she would recall.

She answered yes. Moved, he says, by the plainness of her dress, the pastor led her in a homespun prayer of acceptance and repentance, asking Christ to cleanse her heart. Norma then sat a few minutes with a counselor who explained what it was to live a Christian life.

Two years shy of fifty, Norma was born again.

———

NORMA QUIT THE CLINIC at once, leaving behind her phone and halogen lamp and silk flowers, and headed one door over to answer calls beside Mackey at Operation Rescue. The women had grown close, hugging their hellos, exchanging "I love you"s. And weeks later, on August 8, she whom Norma called Miss Ronda reminded her to put on a bra beneath her white tee and overalls. She would soon be in water.

Benham had made plans to baptize Norma in the backyard pool of a family in Garland that attended his church. To share his great triumph with the world—the baptism of Jane Roe—he had reached out to an evangelical Christian reporter who covered religion for ABC.

Her name was Peggy Wehmeyer. She had become a Christian in college after a woman from a campus ministry spoke to her sorority about the messianism of Jesus. And she had remained a Christian even after she'd learned that her mother was Jewish, a refugee from Nazi Germany. Benham saw Wehmeyer as "a lady I can trust," he says, a reporter free of the secular bias of the national media; she had reported, for example, on Catholic women who lifted aborted fetuses from a dumpster so as to bless and bury them. Forty and blond and pretty in a punch-pink dress, Wehmeyer sat down with Norma hours before her baptism, eager to tell Norma's story on ABC *World News Tonight*.

Norma had long devoted herself to *Roe* for reasons less ideological than practical; her plaintiffship got her money and praise, too. But she had also been possessive of what she had called "her law" and there had been a genuineness to her advocacy, a desire to see millions of women have access to what she had been denied. Now, seventeen days after her Christian rebirth, Norma forgot herself and the golden crucifix about her neck, and told Wehmeyer that she still supported abortion through the eleventh week of pregnancy. More, she spoke with envy of the many women she had met whose education and careers owed to *Roe*. She added: "I honestly have to say that I resent the fact that I never could have an abortion."

Wehmeyer would honestly report that Jane Roe, no matter her rebirth, remained pro-choice. But she had prepared on this day to tell of a Christian rebirth and steered Norma back to Jesus. Asked Wehmeyer: "Can we talk a little bit about that you came into the Lord and you had this wonderful feeling of peace when you went forward and you were surrounded by people you loved?"

Norma complied, telling of her friends at Operation Rescue. "They genuinely love me," she said. "And they care about my salvation. I care about my salvation. My girlfriend cares about my salvation."

Norma had misstepped again. An ABC staffer spoke up. "I just wonder about your lesbianism," she said gently. "That's something that is actually not tolerated in the Christian community." Norma replied that her sexuality had nothing to do with her Christianity, and Wehmeyer responded with a question: "What if your new church that you love says to you, 'We accept you but you can't be a lesbian and be here?'"

Benham had not intimated to Norma that to accept Jesus would be to let go of Connie. And Norma now said that were he or another to do so, she would tell him in turn not "to lay with [his] wife." The interview ended. Norma walked outside to the preacher, ready to be cleansed of her sins in the chlorinated waters of a Texas pool.

A PASTOR STRUMMED a guitar, and some forty Christians began to sing "Amazing Grace." They had gathered to witness the baptism of Miss Norma, and she joined them now in song, seated on a wooden beam between Miss Ronda and Connie.

Connie did not sing. Benham's courtship of her partner had angered her deeply. She had warned Norma—even today, on the twenty-mile drive over from Dallas—to avoid him. "She kept saying," Norma later recalled, "'It's not too late. We can turn around. We can go back.'" But Norma did not want to go back. And Connie, dressed in white slacks and a black button-down shirt, sat quiet as Benham lifted his soft black Bible.

Benham spoke of Psalms and Ephesians and Exodus. The words

cascaded from his mouth in practiced diminuendos, Miss Norma not
merely a born again Christian but "God's poem" and "a living epistle"
and "an oak of righteousness."

Connie knew better. The woman she had loved for twenty-five years
was anything but righteous. Connie loved her just the same, her love for
Norma fixed, independent of deservedness. But if Connie had looked
past infidelity and neglect, she now saw clearly through her large square
lenses that her lover was in the thrall of an evangelicalism that damned
not only abortion but homosexuality. When Benham asked Norma if
she would renounce "the sinful desires of the flesh," she said only yes,
accompanying the preacher into water, her body, grown thick in recent
years, soon submerged to the breast.

Benham wore shirt and tie, his blue eyes alight in a pool of aqua-
marine. The high-water mark of a career was upon him—Jane Roe "the
ultimate convert," as the conservative columnist Ross Douthat later
put it. Four months after moving next door to Jane Roe, Benham spoke
her name. "Norma Lea McCorvey," he said, placing a small pink towel
over her face, "I baptize you in the name of the Father and of the Son
and of the Holy Spirit." The preacher dipped Norma backward, her face
submerged, and then returned her to her feet. "Hallelujah!" he shouted.
"Here she is! New Creation! Hallelujah!"

Norma rose from the pool, her feet bare. She was rid of sin. The
flock of Christians about her began to sing "I Pledge Allegiance to the
Lamb," and one by one they hugged her, Miss Ronda, beautiful in a
form-fitting pantsuit, taking her into her long bare arms.

A pastor named Daniel Vinzant would soon tell those gathered that
they would need to form a "hedge of protection" about Norma. But
for now, Connie was free to walk to her lover unimpeded. The women
embraced, stroking the hair and cheeks and forehead of the other. Benham stood inches away, smiling.

Said the preacher: "Oh, praise the Lord."

Chapter 24

"There is an extraordinary development today in the politics of abortion," the anchor of ABC World News Tonight began. "It involves the woman at the very center of the legal battle over abortion, the name synonymous with the right to choose." A clip of Benham dipping Norma backward in a swimming pool followed, and Ted Koppel welcomed her to Nightline.

Norma wore a silver cross over a black blouse, the crucifix refashioned by Benham from the melted metal of a pro-choice charm. Just two days had passed since her baptism. And on this night, August 10, 1995, Norma told Koppel that she now volunteered for Operation Rescue and thought abortion wrong. She added, however, that she felt it ought to be legal through the first trimester. Koppel asked if those two thoughts were not incompatible, and Norma answered that her friends at O.R. were praying that she would "come full circle."

That Jane Roe had, at least in part, denounced abortion was big news. "'I'M PRO-LIFE,'" read the cover of the New York Post. Added President Clinton: "The rule of Roe vs. Wade is it permits everybody in America to make that same decision."

The pro-life were less restrained. Here was a miracle. Said Benham: "God has given Norma to us."

Norma attributed her about-face to a discomfort with abortion that had grown unignorable. Her fellow Christians welcomed her with all from a billboard in north Dallas to a televised prayer of thanks on The

700 Club. A reporter at *World*, a Christian magazine, wrote that "Jesus won," and the head of Texans United for Life quipped that "The poster child has jumped off the poster."

The pro-choice were left trying to understand why. Linda Coffee told a local reporter that Norma was "a person who has a great need for attention, and obviously Flip Benham has filled that need." The abortion provider Charlotte Taft felt that it was the claim on truth that had drawn Norma to religion. Said Taft: "She got to be right." Her old lawyer Gloria Allred saw in her conversion something less exalted: money. "It's a career choice as well," she reflected years later.

Indeed, it was. Just as Allred had helped Norma to wring money and press from the pro-choice, Norma expected the other half of the country to offer up as much—books and movies, salaries and speeches.

Still, Norma would likely have remained pro-choice had pro-choice leaders embraced her. "All they ever wanted me to say was, 'Keep abortion safe and legal,'" Norma recalled in her home to the filmmaker Meghan O'Hara. But, she continued, "I had other things that I wanted to say. And I think that's why I became pro-life and that's why I had Flip Benham baptize me. 'Cause it, to me, that was just like a big slap in the face, like hey, fuck you!" Her conversion was, in other words, a way to demonstrate that the pro-choice had sold her short. Added Norma: "It's like, look what I did, you know? And I didn't need your help!"

Norma was angry, above all, at Weddington, who had not told her that she'd had an abortion and had made no effort to help Norma have one, too. As Norma now told Koppel: "She lied to me."

Asked for comment, Weddington belittled Norma. "What she does," she said, "isn't going to affect one vote, one opinion-maker, one lawyer, one Supreme Court judge." She added: "All Jane Roe did was sign a one-page affidavit. She was pregnant and didn't want to be."

Such comments reinforced the notion that Weddington—and all the pro-choice movement—had used Norma. Some on the left took her rebirth as a sign to look within. "There is a moral responsibility to treat the principals in these cases as complete human beings," said a spokesman for People for the American Way, a liberal advocacy group. He charged that Norma was a plaintiff betrayed. The feminist author

Naomi Wolf agreed. "Norma McCorvey should be seen as an object lesson for the pro-choice movement," she wrote. She asserted that the movement needed to better listen to women.

The movement had no choice but to listen to Norma now. Koppel suggested to her that the pro-life might use her, too. "What if," he asked, "they try to turn you into some kind of a symbol?" Norma responded that Benham had assured her that "there will not be any exploitation of my political status."

Benham had, in fact, *already* sought to make political use of Norma, inviting her to appear outside Dallas City Hall the next day with pro-life political folk including Bay Buchanan and Alan Keyes and Bob Dornan. Congressman Dornan, his red hair parted to the left, brought to the rally copies of three speeches he'd given over the years on the House floor. Each had mentioned Norma and was meant, he said, to alert the public that she had never had an abortion. He added that Norma's three girls were no doubt "dying to reconcile with her" but wanted her to publicly state "that she's glad that she never aborted them."

Norma's daughters were perhaps not immaterial to her conversion. Setting aside her other motivations—her discomfort with abortion and her resentment of pro-choice leaders and her desire for more headlines and paychecks—her fight for others not yet born could be seen as a desire to make things right. Still, Norma would not be speaking with Dornan. She had declined Benham's invitation and recorded a new greeting on her answering machine stating that she would be making no more public comments or appearances. She would be minding only herself. "I'm not pro-choice, I'm not pro-life," she now told the *New York Daily News*. "I'm pro-Norma." She added that Benham would not come between her and Connie. "I wouldn't leave Connie," she said, "if God himself came and offered me salvation."

Pro-life leaders had made a public point of embracing Norma as she was—blunt and blue-collar. But they could not abide her homosexuality. Still, Benham was unconcerned. The born again need time, he said; he noted to the press that he himself had owned a saloon for the first six months after accepting Christ. He added: "Norma will be set free from it."

Connie fumed. "He's the devil," she told the Associated Press. She added that she would see to it that Norma not fall further under his influence. "I will talk to her day and night if I have to," she said.

Norma told Connie not to worry; Benham would not come between them. Indeed, she was holding tight to her partner, driving with her each morning in their red truck to Markville Drive before one stepped right and the other left, Norma into the Operation Rescue office to fight abortion, Connie—having risen from janitor to patient aide—into the clinic to provide it.

NORMA HAD OBSERVED the emotional power her presence had on others; upon hearing her speak, many women wished to *touch* her. Still, she needed now to appeal to a very different population. She had been a Christian just one month when she penned a poem about a playground—that which had come to evoke for her not only the open-ended pain of adoption but the finality of abortion, every empty swing a legacy of *Roe*.

"Dear Lord," she began, writing on a paper newsletter of Hillcrest Church. "I sit across from a playground that I visited this eve with a small child. I know of such places where children play and know that I'm the cause of them not being full."

The words were a fair approximation of scripture. After Benham pruned their more graphic verses ("she was talking about body parts," he says), the poem, titled "Empty Playgrounds," began what would come to comprise a sort of Book of Norma, a gospel of sacrifice and faith, of loss and love, that Benham and a growing number of apostles readied to communicate to the masses.

The first of these was a producer of Christian films named Dan Donehey. Donehey had been a lapsed Catholic from a suburb of Boston when the Supreme Court ruled on *Roe*; he didn't give it much thought. Five years later, though, he was born again, when he argued against abortion in a college class on persuasive speech. He got a poor grade and vowed, he recalls, to "be as articulate as possible on that subject." So he had been in the years since—producing pro-life films and representing the National Right to Life Committee to the media.

Donehey was home in Fredericksburg, Virginia, when he heard that Jane Roe had become a Christian. He wished at once to make a film about her conversion and flew to Texas within the month, speaking with Norma and also to the trinity that had led her to Christ: Benham, Mackey and little Emily. The result was *Reversing Roe*, thirty minutes of interviews, B-roll footage and voiceovers.

The film told of the spiritual awakening that had saved Norma from the self-interest of the pro-choice camp. It closed with her gazing at empty swings as a musical rendition of her poem played. "Obvious to everyone now," Donehey wrote upon its release months later, in January 1996, "God used the child Emily to become friends with and touch the heart of 'Jane Roe.'" He added that as Norma grew as a Christian, her "position on abortion came into accord with God's word."

Indeed, Norma declared herself among the one in six Americans who believed abortion was impermissible even to save a woman's life. As the Operation Rescue newsletter reported, she now opposed abortion without "compromise," "exception" or "apology."

Norma did not, however, oppose homosexuality. She did not consider it a sin, and she remained with Connie. But after Benham told her that a passage in Corinthians made clear that homosexuality could be vanquished, Norma made him a vow. "The couple assured me," Benham later recalled, "they were not having sex."

Connie was sixty-four. Having made peace with Norma's appetite for sex, she did her best to make peace with her abstinence. "The love is still there, it's just that the sex is not," she told the filmmaker O'Hara. "Norma chooses to be that way and I go along with it."

It was a horrible concession. But it enabled Connie to hold onto Norma. "I still have my friend," Connie told O'Hara. So that she would not lose her, Connie made another concession: she quit her job at the clinic and went to work with Norma at Operation Rescue.

Connie had been comfortably Catholic all her sixty-four years, setting rosaries and Stations of the Cross about her home. She did not put her faith in the evangelical Benham. "He never could get me to believe his way because he's not God," she told O'Hara. But Norma did believe in him. And so, months later, Connie too waded into water, baptized by Benham in an inflatable pool in his backyard.

The largest religious denomination in the country had grown by one more. But Benham was not satisfied. Norma remained gay and out.

Benham had long worked with Exodus International, a ministry founded to curb the sinful desires of gay Christians. Its president, Alan Chambers, claimed a "success rate" of 33 percent. The nonprofit would later close, Chambers left to apologize for promoting "sexual orientation change efforts" that drove many Christians from religion and some to commit suicide. But in 1995, the organization was in full swing, and Benham invited a counselor to speak with Norma in the Operation Rescue office. The conversation upset her. "I could just tell that Norma was unsettled," says Sheree Havlik, an O.R. volunteer. "She didn't feel that she needed whatever the lady was [offering]." Havlik spoke up. "I said, 'Norma, you don't need to be cured. There's nothing wrong with you. It's not like you act on any of this.'"

That last was not true. Norma was indeed denying herself, in the name of Christ, her partner of twenty-five years. But she did not deny herself an occasional night with a stranger.

Sex had long been at the core of who Norma was. "She was a sexual being," says O'Hara. The filmmaker remembered Norma telling her that she would lie half-naked in her backyard to sun herself below the waist. Sex and sexual organs were for Norma things to esteem and behold. Indeed, the act itself mattered to Norma. Her partners, female and male, would long recall her prowess. Norma enjoyed sex with both genders, but it was women she most desired. As she'd reflected years before: "I never have found a tenderness with a man that I have found with a woman."

But a woman was now forbidden. This Norma had known from her youth, from the preaching of her father and the beatings of her mother and the declaration of the juvenile court of Dallas that she was, after running off with that girl at age thirteen, "a delinquent child."

Norma had disregarded the court, her parents and, while a Witness, Jehovah too. And though she and Connie would no longer share a bed, Norma would not debase their relationship by denouncing her homosexuality.

Benham tried to manage the problem. He told the press that God was "healing Norma of her homosexuality." And with his every reference to Miss Norma, he feminized her, "rearticulated her," as a master's thesis on Norma put it, "as an obedient Christian woman." Norma, in turn, the thesis noted, spoke of Benham in words that "coded herself as straight," not only referencing his good looks but saying, as she did to O'Hara, that he and she were mindful to "never get too close to each other."

For all that, however, the most prominent member of Operation Rescue remained stubbornly gay. Benham felt something had to be done. Homosexuality was simply incompatible with opposition to abortion. "[If] I know where you stand on abortion," he once said, "I know where you stand on everything else."

Benham told Norma that it was not enough that she and Connie abstain from sex. They also had to abstain, in the words of Thessalonians, from "all appearances of evil." Norma, he said, had to move out.

Norma had left Connie before. But always, there was the understanding that she would return, and the couple had continued on, sharing their home, their bed, their pickup, the women side by side for 200,000 miles. But when Norma now told Connie that Operation Rescue wished her to move into a separate home that O.R. would buy, both women were undone. "I couldn't finish my dinner," Connie recalled, wiping away tears. Added Norma: "I wept. . . . Connie's always been there. Connie will always be there. And I know that. And I love her. And she loves me."

Norma had been in thrall to Benham ever since sitting down with him on that bench on Markville Drive six months before. She told O'Hara that he was "like a prophet." But he had now guided her to a terrifying precipice. Wanting counsel, she turned to the pastor at whose altar she had been reborn.

Morris Sheats had welcomed Norma to Christ by asking her to let go of her sins. In the months since, he had also urged her to let go of her hatred of her mother, and had helped her to mourn her father when she'd brought home his ashes in a blue glass urn. Asked by Norma if it was her Christian duty to leave Connie, the pastor said no. If she and Connie "could stand before God with a pure heart," Norma recalled Sheats telling her, "he would encourage us to stay living together."

The words were a balm to Norma. And for the first time, she defied

Benham. She would not leave Connie, she told him, would not leave their ranch house on Cactus Lane. "This is my home," she said. "Just because my heart has turned to Jesus and has turned to God, doesn't mean that I'm going to love God or Jesus any more if I live someplace else."

Benham was furious. "Flip had a fit over the whole thing," Norma later told the Associated Press. "He said he was my leader." She added: "I don't like for people to try to control me."

That Benham and Norma had clashed was no surprise. The minister could be as volatile as she. His temper was fierce and he often yelled in the O.R. office. A volunteer named Jessie Anne Nobles would recall that he regularly fired her and others, only to rehire them weeks later. Adds Mackey: "It was his way or the highway . . . I was like, wow—what a way to start your day in the ministry."

Benham had to tread carefully with Norma. The new year, 1996, was just weeks away. Much was planned for the January anniversary of *Roe*, the first since Norma, as Benham wrote, had waded "in the fountain of life." Needing Norma to publicly represent Operation Rescue, the minister set aside his desire to separate her from Connie and simply declared her straight.

"Norma has repented of her lesbian relationship," he told O'Hara. "And Norma is not a lesbian. She is a born again Christian."

———

PRO-LIFE LEADERS WERE still agog over the rebirth of Jane Roe when, in January, they gathered to meet her at Georgetown University, convened by an evangelical clergyman named Rob Schenck.

Schenck had moved to DC sixteen months before, leaving his home in western New York to minister to (and informally lobby) government officials. His ministry, Faith and Action, was rapidly gaining recognition and donors. Norma had only just been baptized when Schenck decided to bring her to the capital. "I was thinking principally," he says, "that we needed to showcase the biggest prize we had yet won in the abortion wars."

Schenck had fought on the front lines of those wars; he was one of six core members of Operation Rescue when, in 1992, he held a fetus in his arms outside a clinic in Buffalo. Now, on the eve of another *Roe* anniversary, he gathered the extreme flank of the pro-life army to publicly embrace their former foe, not only Benham but Pat Mahoney of the Christian Defense Coalition, Frank Pavone of Priests for Life, and Operation Rescue founder Randall Terry.

"Everybody wanted a piece of Norma," says Schenck. "Everybody was looking for their photo."

Only months before, Terry had declared in this same city that he wanted to see abortion providers executed. Now, as the cameras clicked, he gave Jane Roe a choreographed kiss on the left cheek. "We forgive you in Jesus's name," he said. He repeated the words.

Norma wore a red rose and a silver crucifix. Stepping to the podium, she proclaimed Jane Roe dead. The crowd of three hundred cheered. "Glory!" they shouted. "Hallelujah! Amen!" The next day, Norma stood with Connie outside Dallas City Hall before hundreds more pro-lifers.

Norma was one of them, of their same culture and caste; the journalist Debbie Nathan would note that "her bargain clothes"—her hiking boots and checkered leggings—"matched those of most of the audience." Benham introduced her as she had introduced herself the day before, saying that Jane Roe was dead but that "Miss Norma McCorvey is alive in Jesus Christ."

Six years prior, Norma had needed to learn the language of the pro-choice when she entered in earnest the public conversation about abortion. Becoming pro-life required no such work. Aside from those weighted words like "abortionist" and "mill" and "partial-birth abortion" (the last coined one year before as a terrifying term for dilation and extraction), its language was familiar to her; it came from the same Good Book that had filled her youth with the admonitions and ecstasies of Jehovah. Standing beside Connie on the twenty-third anniversary of *Roe*, she asked the crowd before her for forgiveness and then suggested that she was not merely alive in Christ but wished to sacrifice herself as He had. "Lord," she said, "use my body to make your precious children whole again."

Benham did not often call upon Miss Norma to speak. She was apt to get herself in trouble. (In March, after telling a clinic worker "to find Jesus," she'd pushed her and ended up with a Class C misdemeanor.) It was best, says Benham, to keep Norma "under wraps." And so, that spring, when the minister stood outside the Supreme Court and screamed for the justices within to heal the land in the name of Jesus, Norma simply knelt at the foot of a marble step, closed her eyes and held an open palm to the wet sky. And when Benham placed a fetus, blue-brown and inches long, in an open casket outside a clinic in Chicago and called upon the gathered press to meet the plaintiff who'd been "bought by the blood of Jesus Christ," Norma said only "Amen" and began to cry.

Benham had given Norma a Bible and a crucifix and a business card that read "Miss Norma, Slave for Christ." He gave her about $200 a week, too. But he had also denied her many things, beginning with sex with Connie. Forced to drink and smoke far from the office, Norma began to tire of both Benham and Operation Rescue.

One year after Benham moved O.R. to Markville Drive, the land-lord sued for nonpayment of rent. Benham said that the landlord had agreed not to charge them rent as long as the abortion clinic remained next door; the landlord wanted the clinic to leave. But the clinic did not leave. After appearing before a judge, O.R. agreed to leave in exchange for two more rent-free months. Benham packed up his fetal growth charts and posters proclaiming Jesus "the Standard" and set-tled into a building a few miles down Interstate 635. Norma split her time between the new O.R. office and her garage, where a chair and a desk shared space with a growing pile of her papers. In August, one year after her baptism, she added to the pile a photo inscribed to her by Pat Buchanan.

Decades before, Buchanan had been one of the first to politicize abortion. He had noted to Nixon that there were votes to be won oppos-ing it. Norma had met him this summer of 1996 at a pro-life convention in Anaheim, which she'd attended without Benham. "I wrote my own ticket," said Norma. "When Flip said no, I said, 'What did you say?' I didn't recognize that word."

Norma was free to spend time with whomever she wished. And among the attendees at that Anaheim convention was a priest from New York named Frank Pavone.

===

FATHER PAVONE WAS a little man with eyes and hair as black as his Roman collar. He was thirty-seven years old, and had decided upon the priesthood exactly twenty years before as a teen growing up in the working-class New York town of Port Chester.

It was mathematics that had led Pavone to God. "You start dealing with concepts like infinity," he says, "and infinity is not too far from eternity." The high-schooler began attending Mass every day. That same year of 1976, after bussing with a contingent from his hometown to the annual March for Life in Washington, DC, he attuned to *Roe*.

Pavone planned to minister to the young, enrolling in a New Jersey college run by the Salesians of Don Bosco, a religious order devoted to Christian youth. But after graduating, he stepped from his studies— first to work at an information desk at the Department of Motor Vehicles, and then to evangelize to the poor through a Catholic ministry in the Bronx. Soon after, he decided to become a parish priest. He was a seminary student in Yonkers studying theology when he came to believe, he says, that abortion was "the most important moral issue that society was facing." Bookish and ambitious, he wished to preach to all humanity that abortion ought never be allowed. He taped to his wall a map of the world above a quote by the English minister John Wesley: "All the world is my parish."

Pavone graduated in 1988 atop his class. After John O'Connor ordained him a priest in midtown Manhattan, the Cardinal assigned him to a parish on the eastern shore of Staten Island.

Months shy of thirty, Pavone remained focused on abortion. "I was being called to a bigger ministry," he says. The priest spoke of it from ever larger platforms: at his and other parish churches, on local TV, and, come 1991, through Priests for Life, a national clerical organization founded the year before. Pavone wished to relinquish his diocesan duties so as to focus solely on abortion, and Cardinal O'Connor permitted him to do so, Pavone appointed PFL director in the fall of 1993.

Pavone did not rely merely on bumper stickers and faith to communicate the evils of abortion. He marshaled law and medicine, reading countless books from *Abortion and the Constitution* to *Abortion Practice*, which he shared with pro-life leaders on trips about the country. Among them was Flip Benham. He had known Benham nearly two years when, in 1995, an acquaintance faxed Pavone that Benham was to baptize Norma that same day.

Back in seminary, Pavone had met Bernard Nathanson, a co-founder of NARAL who had turned pro-life. His defection had shaken the pro-choice base like no other prior to Norma's. Nathanson had taught Pavone a lesson he now recalled: "Never discount anyone. People can change on this subject." The priest telephoned Norma that same day. "I said," he recalls, "I'd love to be able to meet you and give you a blessing."

That Pavone had approached Jane Roe was no surprise; he was, the evangelical Schenck said, "the de facto chaplain of the movement," and he made it his business to keep company with all from Mother Teresa to Terri Schiavo. He soon traveled to Cactus Lane to bless Norma, tracing the sign of the cross on her forehead. He blessed her home, too, with holy water, leaving behind a jar of it that Norma and Connie then mistakenly drank.

The priest believed homosexuality profane. But, he says, "it was not a focus of my ministry." Besides, recalls Pavone, Norma referred only "to a past relationship with Connie." The plaintiff and priest fell into a friendship, seeing each other often when Pavone stopped in Dallas along his travels.

Benham liked Pavone. The priest treated abortion as "a gospel issue," says Benham, "a battle over who is Lord and whose law reigns." But he did not much like Catholicism. He viewed it as a sort of Christianity-lite, all love-thy-neighbor and confession. Says Benham: "You go to confession on Saturday and live the way you want the rest of the week."

Norma was mindful of her mixed company, mindful that Christianity had different branches. Her maternal grandparents had been Catholics turned Pentecostal, while her parents had embraced Jehovah. Norma, meantime, had renounced God at fifteen in that state school for girls. When, thirty-three years later, she returned to Him, she was evangelical.

Norma knew little of Catholicism despite her stint in Catholic school. Father Pavone reacquainted her with its Masses and saints. She had been born again just a few months when she asked the priest, he recalls, if there was "such a thing as a born again Catholic." He assured her there was.

Pavone says that he did not suggest to Norma that she become one. Always, after they met, she returned to the world of Benham and Operation Rescue. So she did at the conclusion of that Anaheim convention, flying in August 1996 to meet Benham in San Diego, there to protest abortion (and presidential nominee Bob Dole) under the media glare of the Republican National Convention.

———

PROTESTS TAKE PREPARATION. And for about a year, a man named Troy Newman had readied Operation Rescue for the convention.

Newman had lived in San Diego all his thirty years, moving there with his parents after his adoption at birth in Alaska. His parents had divorced when he was seven, and his father, a sergeant in the army, was often overseas. His mother had remarried and divorced three more times, a fact, she often told her son, that "excommunicated" her from their Catholic faith.

Newman, though, went weekly to Mass, and was an altar boy until hair metal and motorcycles seized his attention in high school. But he felt adrift in his college years and, at age twenty-two, walked into an evangelical church. Wishing to repent, says Newman, for years of promiscuity and drugs, he answered a call to the altar and recited the "Sinner's Prayer." He pledged himself to Christ.

Newman got a degree in computer science and took a job maintaining flight simulators. But his heart was in the Bible. In 1991, months after he married, he and his wife were on a beach in San Felipe when a man saw the "Jesus" bumper sticker on their pickup and told them about Operation Rescue. The man was an O.R. volunteer named Peter French and, back in Orange County, he took Newman to a protest.

Newman had never pondered abortion. (Earlier that year, he'd gone to Planned Parenthood when he needed a blood test for his marriage license.) But seeing a photo of an aborted fetus was a shock. It brought to mind his adoption. "I look at these children," he said years later, "as people that might have been me."

Newman began to volunteer for O.R. He had charisma and beach-boy looks, and it wasn't long before he was running a local office out of his home, protesting and preaching that abortion was murder. He began to picket not only clinics but the doctors who worked in them, putting their addresses on fliers that urged passersby, he says, "to tell them to stop killing." Newman opposed killing the doctors themselves, he says, but found himself pondering if doing so was "permissible theologically."

Newman was readying to convert to Presbyterianism when, in 1995, he left his job in aerospace to fight abortion full-time. He would live on donations. With the RNC coming to town—and with it a cluster of pro-life leaders—Newman saw a chance to make his name. He spoke with pro-life leaders by phone, and secured every church and venue and permit that their protests and prayer would need. He secured a fetus, too, male and nineteen weeks old, for Benham to display at a memorial for the unborn. "The mom put the baby in formaldehyde and donated it to us," says Newman. "A very pro-life lady." He adds: "Flip lied and said it was an abortion. But it was a stillborn." Benham says he didn't know it was a stillborn, though he recalls the memorial leaving him "very uneasy."

The convention began on August 12, 1996, and Newman welcomed Benham and hundreds of O.R. members to town. Benham frustrated Newman; he veered from the script, creating a schedule all his own. Still, Newman admired the hold that Benham had on his flock. "There was crying," says Newman. "He would whip them into a frenzy." Helping Benham at nearly every protest and vigil and rally and fundraiser was Jane Roe. Says Newman: "He would trot Norma out."

The long days took a toll on Norma. And every night, out of view of Benham, she accepted an invitation from Newman to join him and others at a Mexican café in central San Diego for beer and margaritas.

The protests had lasted nine days when Norma returned home depleted and unsure, she later recalled, if she was "cut out" not only for Operation Rescue but for Benham. As she wrote to Mackey: "He's too tough for even me and I'm pretty tough."

NORMA KNEW THAT money followed media. But years had passed since HarperCollins and NBC had paid her for her memoir and her TV movie. She was still hoping for a big pro-life check when, in late 1996, an editor at the Christian imprint of HarperCollins phoned Benham.

Her name was Janet Thoma. Raised an Episcopalian in Pennsylvania, she had become an evangelical in New York, born again at twenty-six in a Schenectady church. "I wanted a closer walk," she says. "And I'm very Bible-based."

Thoma was powerful. Months shy of sixty, she was in charge of acquisitions for Thomas Nelson, a publisher grown rich selling Billy Graham and the New King James Version translation of the bible.

Thoma wished to use that power to fight *Roe*. Having brought to market a book by Jerry Falwell about a rape victim who regretted having an abortion, she saw opportunity in Norma. Benham put her through.

Norma had been here before; three years prior, she'd sat down with a biographer on her bedroom floor. But the story she now told was refracted through a Christian lens, and it thrilled Thoma—that of a life in full compliance with evangelical ideals after profane beginnings. Indeed, having been born again, Norma was now, she said, appalled not only by abortion but homosexuality.

That Norma had finally come into line was no surprise. Her conversion aside, her book deal depended on it. So she spoke to a raft of Christian journalists about her lesbianism, telling one that it was a sin, another that Connie was now straight and Christian, a third that she herself had never really been gay. "I chose to be a lesbian," she said, "because every time I became involved with a man, it seemed I would become pregnant and I didn't want to be pregnant anymore."

Ready to proceed, Thoma constructed, chapter by chapter, an outline of Norma's life. "You have to have enough in your proposal to convince the publishing company it's worth taking," she says. "I took . . . the McCorvey book and pushed it through." The publisher agreed to pay Norma $80,000.

Benham suggested, he says, that Norma use the money to pay off her mortgage. Norma did not, although she fixed up the house a bit:

paint and furniture, a walk-in closet. Thoma turned her over to a writer named Gary Thomas, a young Baptist from Washington state with degrees in English and theology.

Thomas earned little for his work; his most recent book, a memoir by Evander Holyfield, had paid him $3,000. And he had little time to write; after flying to meet Norma in February, he had one week to extract from her—a woman prone to anger, fatigue and unreliability— the story of a life.

Still, Thomas had read both the book proposal and *I Am Roe*, and had worked in a pro-life ministry. Besides, his job was not to plumb the soul of a subject, he says, but simply to get down on paper the stories she told.

As before, the stories Norma told were less true than conjured. She told Thomas, for example, of having helped to perform unhygienic abortions on Markville Drive, though (as contemporaneous accounts in both *Texas Monthly* and the *Los Angeles Times* confirm) she had only worked the phones. Norma depicted Benham as a man of God whose mere voice made her weak in the knees. She added that Benham had made clear to her, wrote Thomas, "that he would not baptize someone who intended to live the homosexual lifestyle."

Benham, though, had failed to convince Norma to leave Connie. And in the spring of 1997, Norma decided to leave Benham.

Chapter 25

The three Christians who had led Norma from choice to life had been well situated to win her over. Little Emily had pulled at the heart of a woman injured by the surrender of three daughters. As for Flip Benham and Ronda Mackey, as the filmmaker O'Hara put it, "he was a father figure and she was this sexy woman."

Norma did not disguise her feelings for Mackey. "I started loving you the day you let your first born go with me alone," she wrote to Mackey on her birthday. She called her Rondadita and added in a subsequent note: "You are not only beautiful on the outside but also on the inside."

Such effusions did not make Mackey uncomfortable; she thought of Norma as a child, she says, a child nineteen years her senior whom God and her daughter and her boss had helped to enlist in the fight against abortion. Still, Mackey spoke to her Operation Rescue colleagues, and Norma wrote to them in turn. "I just couldn't believe [Mackey] thought I would want anything other than her friendship," wrote Norma. "Too much gossip."

Mackey, meantime, had had it with Benham. "If I didn't show up on time, Flip would call and yell at me," she says. "I was like, whoa, whoa, whoa. This is supposed to be volunteer." In early 1997, Mackey decided to leave O.R. to volunteer instead at a crisis pregnancy center in Garland, a few miles east. Norma was bereft. "I'm sad, very sad," she wrote to Mackey.

Norma had also contemplated leaving. Benham had come between her and Connie. But only now that he had driven Mackey away did Norma decide to join her.

Norma's upset aside, it made financial sense for her to leave Benham. She was in great demand as a speaker. (Her words—among them a promise to "strive in the name of Jesus to end this holocaust"—had just been cast in bronze at a memorial for the unborn in Chattanooga.) Benham, who was not himself driven by money, had been indifferent to the money he knew Norma could command. "It's an industry," he acknowledges of the pro-life movement. "We'll go ahead and get speakers and compete with each other for a piece of the pie."

The pro-life pie had many different pieces, from its crisis pregnancy centers to those organizations that fought abortion with law or politics or direct action. That Norma had, for thirty months, resided in the last—alongside not only advocates of civil protest but those who fostered violence—had kept the more mainstream at bay. The National Right to Life Committee, for example, did not promote Norma's film *Reversing Roe* for fear of aligning itself with Operation Rescue.

But Norma would now be leaving O.R. She would be open to all, and just in time for the twenty-fifth anniversary of *Roe*.

―――――

MUCH HAD CHANGED in that quarter-century. *Roe* was no longer a mere ruling. It was an orientation, a north star guiding all from judicial appointments to religious resolutions to political platforms. There was no surer gauge of political ideology in America than *Roe*, no surer prompt of legislation; thirty-nine states now required minors wanting abortions to get the consent of a judge or parent.

Roe, of course, had also become a business; there was always more to wring from it. And Norma was about to leave Benham when, that summer of 1997, she asked Mackey if she would help her start a ministry. "What hurt the most," says Benham, "was that Miss Ronda went with her."

Only two years before, Norma had told Ted Koppel that she believed in first-trimester abortions. Mackey had thus not thought Norma ready to share her story. "Her theology isn't straight yet," she told the press.

"She's like a new infant; a new baby doesn't understand about the world around it." But Norma's theology was now in line, and Mackey got going on the newsletters and press releases that would be the meat of the ministry. Norma had her checks decorated with images of fetuses, and chose as her logo a smiling and ponytailed girl on a swing. Norma's ghostwriter wove a mention of the ministry into her book's last chapter. And Mackey then enlisted a born-again accountant she knew from church, a happy man named Ron Allen who, thirteen years after his rebirth, now did the books, pro bono, for Benham and a hundred or so Christian nonprofits. Roe No More Ministry was nearly incorporated when, on the last day of summer, its namesake turned fifty.

Middle age suited Norma. Her face was prettier than before, rounder and rouged and set off by a feathered cut that softened the permanent arch of her brows. Eager to promote a ministry in advance of a book, Norma hit the road again, off to a conference in Tampa to join Benham for a session on the gospel of Jesus Christ.

Privately, Norma did not speak kindly of Benham. She would soon write to a friend of her joy that he had been imprisoned for trespassing at a Virginia high school. (Benham was handing out fliers to students.) But publicly, Norma told of their split in only the Christian terms he himself had taught her. ("A still, small voice told me God was calling me to something else," she wrote.) Back beside Benham in Tampa, Norma cordially knelt so that he and a roomful of Christians could lay their hands upon her.

Norma, though, knew nothing of the Christian circuit. And days later, in Alabama, the Eternal Word Television Network turned her away at the door for wearing shorts. But Mackey was at her side, and Norma put on a skirt and knocked again. She was soon on air with Pavone while an on-screen real-time tally of abortions in America counted seventy-five performed during their twenty-three minutes together.

The circuit forbade more than mere immodesty—smoking and drinking and cursing, too. Norma was guilty of all three, not to mention homosexuality, and some worried about her. "You've got to be compassionate about change," says her ghostwriter Thomas. "Let her grow, let her develop, let her be in a safe place. Don't put her in front of a banquet." But banquets raised money. They sold books. And Norma continued to peddle hers, a guest, that January of 1998, not only at countless crisis pregnancy centers but on *Larry King Live* and at the Senate, where John Ashcroft brandished, in pro-life solidarity, the sonogram pictures of a grandchild not yet born.

Seated before a Senate subcommittee, Norma was meant to speak only against abortion. But she chose to recall that she had been forced to carry a child she had not wanted. She spoke also of Sarah Weddington—the lawyer who had had an abortion but left uninvestigated whether her client might have one too. "She lied to me," said Norma, repeating what she had told Ted Koppel.

It was clear that two-plus years after Norma's conversion, the anger that had in part precipitated it remained. Still, Weddington offered up to the press no regrets but one. "I wish," she said, "I had picked somebody else." There had, however, been no one else for Weddington and Coffee to pick. Their other potential plaintiff, Marsha King, had been found not to have legal standing.

Norma was everywhere this silver anniversary of *Roe*; both the book and the film about her were released that month. They told very different stories. *Won by Love* told of a holy little girl who had helped Norma to know and love Jesus, whereas *Roe vs. Roe* rested on the forbidden love between two women. Still, the two stories were connected. For Norma's rebirth had been contingent upon the renunciation of her homosexuality.

That renunciation fit snugly into the evangelical view that homosexuality is, at heart, a choice. "The lesbian nurse can be converted," wrote the professor Carol Mason. "This is the moral of the story of *Won by Love*." She adds: "We get the lesbian love of Connie Gonzales replaced by Christian love."

Norma had not foreseen that exchange. She had, just after her baptism, told a Christian reporter that she would sleep with whomever she wished. But renouncing and then denying her homosexuality had proved to be the price of her conversion. Even so, she continued to pick up women in bars until, one night in Austin, an old and discomforting thought that she'd first confided to a friend in California a decade before overwhelmed her—the possibility, that is, that she might unknowingly buy a drink for the middle child she had given up. Said Norma: "Wouldn't it be horrible to think that I slept with one of my daughters?"

Norma stopped going to gay bars. She contented herself with Connie, though to hear Norma tell it, Connie was everything but her partner—her mother, her godmother, her cousin, her "sister in Christ."

Connie did not protest. She still rode beside Norma in their pickup, still shared a home with her if no longer a bed. This was enough. It had to be. "I don't care what she does," Connie had told O'Hara, beginning to cry on camera, "as long as she's happy." And sometimes she was. "YOUR THE REASON THAT I'M OK," Norma wrote to Connie in January while off with Mackey on a book tour that took them through twelve states in fifteen days. "TAKE CARE MY SWEETIE . . . YOU'LL NEED TO TAKE CARE OF ME WHEN I DO GET BACK."

Norma was in need of care. She had begun again to drink before interviews, favoring vodka, as she had years before, so as not to smell of alcohol. The interviews often ended badly. "She would throw the pen down and start cursing and walk off," says Mackey. Other times, she would simply not show.

It was on Mackey, keeper of the ministry, to pick up the pieces. But the pieces could not easily be picked up; when Norma stood up Moody Radio, the Christian network was so angry that it considered barring all Thomas Nelson authors from its hundreds of affiliate stations. The publisher was angry, too, faxing Mackey that it still had eight thousand copies of *Won by Love* in its warehouse.

Mackey could handle a ministry, and also the chaperoning and upkeep of Norma: shots of B12 in the rear, pats on the back to feel for a bra. But the struggle to keep Norma to her word—and to mollify angry Christians when Norma went off script—was too much. "I started having panic attacks for the first time in my life," says Mackey. Thirty-one years old, she found herself crying, short of breath, unable to eat. She alerted Thomas Nelson. The publisher stopped the tour.

Mackey and her husband believed in Norma, in the providence of her rebirth. "I know God wants to use you in a mighty way to reach millions of people," Ron Mackey wrote to her. Mackey, who worked in information technology, had done his best to help Norma, joining the board of her ministry, minding his kids while his wife minded Norma. But Norma was sabotaging their efforts. Back in Dallas, the Mackeys turned to their pastor and Jesus, too, stopping by their chapel, wrote Ron, "to seek God."

Sheats suggested more earthly help; Mackey was soon on meds and in therapy. After six years of battling *Roe*—"of going full blast against abortion," as Ron wrote to Norma—Mackey needed to mend.

Norma was unchanged. She faxed and phoned Mackey at all hours, canceling interviews, arguing fees. And though Mackey had helped her for seven months at no cost, Norma emailed her in March that she'd have nothing more to do with her. Wrote Norma: "I'M LOOKING FOR ANOTHER FAMILY THAT I CAN LOVE IN SICKNESS IN LIFE, AND IN DEATH." Norma grew angrier still when Mackey shared her note with a friend. "If I see Ronda again," Norma told the woman, "it will take three or four people to pull me off her."

Mackey had endured such outbursts from Norma for three years. She was at peace when, now, she cut Norma loose. She wrote back to say that she and her girls would miss her.

"I Love You," she wrote to Norma. "Your Sister in Christ, Ronda."

———

IN THE DECADE since Gloria Allred had led Norma away from the Texans who brought her to that DC march, Norma had come to know that there was always another someone ready to take her hand—to take a cut, too. She was Jane Roe. She soon had another agent and another gig, off to Indiana in March 1998 to join her ghostwriter Thomas at a prolife banquet in Tippecanoe County. Still, the "insatiable yearning" that one journalist noted in her—for publicity, for love—remained. Norma wanted more.

Father Pavone understood that yearning. The rewards of ministering to a local parish had never been enough for him, and his holy war on abortion had lifted him nearly as high as *Roe* had Norma. The priest was now stationed in Rome, an official of the Pontifical Council for the Family. He hoped that Norma might lift him higher still, and he mailed her books and had her introduced to Catholics back in Dallas. "I recall hearing Norma likes hanging out with the Catholics," says Fonda Lash, who coordinated sidewalk counseling for the local Catholic Pro-Life Committee. "It was going around."

Still, despite Pavone's influence on Norma, it was, as much as anyone, a Baptist pastor who was now leading her to the Catholic church.

———

DANIEL VINZANT HAD first seen Norma from across a sidewalk. He believed less in protest than in prayer; starting in 1994, he had driven north to Dallas once a week from his home in Waco to stand outside Norma's clinic on Markville Drive with a psalter and rosary beads. When Norma became a Christian, Benham asked Vinzant to recite a prayer at her baptism, and it was Vinzant who invited those gathered to form a "hedge of protection" about her. Months later, Vinzant invited Norma to speak to his congregation at Trinity Church of Waco.

Vinzant had been born in Waco in 1956. His parents were blue-collar Baptists, and they had raised their four kids with "laughter and scripture," says Vinzant. Jesus was a presence in his life. His beloved grandmother Alice Luceil read the Bible aloud to him; by age nine, Vinzant himself had read through it twice. Vinzant was not yet thirty when he was a pastor to some thirty families, a father of three children besides.

The only blight on those years was the loss of a fourth child seven months after her conception. Ten years after that miscarriage, in 1992, Vinzant awoke in a sweat with the life-altering thought, he says, that what had died within his wife was a baby, worse still, that he had never mourned her. He resolved to fight for the unborn and began, on summer days, to set up wading pools outside the local Planned Parenthood for kids to play in, "to show," he says, "the contrast—here's living, happy children."

Trinity Church loved its sandy-haired pastor, his malapropisms and generosity; he was apt to say "spear" when he meant "sphere," and collected his salary only after the church settled its other weekly debts. But Vinzant had a secret: though he was Baptist by birth and had gone to Baptist college and Baptist university and Baptist seminary, he increasingly wished to be Catholic. Even as Vinzant ministered to his own evangelical flock, he went to Mass every week of his pastorship, stealing away on Sunday mornings to a church across town, where he sat out of view in the choir loft.

Vinzant had first glimpsed Catholicism at eighteen, when a boy he'd mentored at church converted to Catholicism and invited him to his confirmation. The stained glass and incense and candles of that Catholic church in north Waco had entranced Vinzant, and he began to return to it for Mass, "picking up the liturgy," he says, "picking up the movements." Eighteen years later, his love for Catholicism deepened when he took up the pro-life fight. Four years after that, in 1996, he began a master's program in Catholic theology at the University of Dallas, staying at its Dominican priory one weekend a month.

Vinzant had only just met Norma. But in the year since her baptism, they had come together at Operation Rescue meetings at that same priory, privately confiding, says Vinzant, their unease with both the harshness of O.R. and the abstemiousness of Benham. The death of Norma's father, in late 1995, drew them closer; when Norma asked Vinzant where the souls of the dead go, he comforted her with Catholic dogma, telling her, he says, that her father had had the choice in his last hour to join God for eternity.

Vinzant let Norma know that he was now in town every month. She and Connie began to visit him at the priory, three friends drinking orange juice and watching squirrels jump amidst the mesquites and cedars. The following September, Norma and Connie began to join him monthly for Mass, too.

———

NORMA KNEW THAT another conversion would bring upon her another wave of press. But it was more than the prospect of publicity that drew her to Catholicism. Catholicism spoke to her. For if Norma wished of religion one thing it was absolution, the assurance that she could be forgiven not only *Roe* but all her trespasses, the drink and drugs and sex and relinquishment of children. She was comforted by confession. "She got to feel the forgiveness," says Pavone. He adds, "Catholicism uses the senses much more than the Protestants." This pleased Norma, the ash and wafer and incense and beads. In early 1998, she emailed Pavone to ask how to pray the rosary.

Norma was ready for a second religious rebirth. In May, one month after attending a Mass Pavone led in Houston, Norma emailed the priest. "The decision is in from the Big Guy," she wrote. "I have it on good aurthory that I should become Catholic." Pavone responded one minute later: "Praise the Lord!!!" He wrote that he would be informing the pope, and Norma requested that Pavone "tell him I love him and will look forward to hopefully just touching the hem of his garment." Days later, Pavone emailed Norma that she was a vessel of God. "The work He wants to accomplish through you has only just begun," he wrote.

The same was true of the work Pavone hoped to accomplish through Norma. He was contemplating when to make public her intentions when, off in Waco, on June 8, Norma did so herself. She told her friend Vinzant, along with his Protestant congregation, that she was ready to complete her spiritual journey "by coming home to my Mother Church, the Roman Catholic Church."

Here was news. But it was not Vinzant who alerted the press. It was Pavone who immediately went to work on a press release—writing in the name of Norma, who then okayed "every word," he says. "He would do that," recalls his former personal assistant Jenn Morson. "'This is what she *would* have said.'"

It was important to Pavone that the rendering of a second conversion, of a Catholic rebirth, be of the same supernatural stuff as an evangelical one. For Norma had attested that accepting Christ, and the holy words of her pastor, had pounded her heart and doused her in sweat and flooded her with tears and turned her "extremely hot" and "unbearably chilled" and so light she could "almost float." Standing there at the altar of her church, Norma had, she wrote, seen in the eyes of her pastor Jesus Himself.

And so, one week after Norma's new proclamation, the release Pavone sent to the world also invoked God. "I clearly heard the Heavenly Father say to me that I was to be with Him soon," it quoted Norma. "I was very scared of this, thinking that it meant I was to die. I consulted my dear friend, Fr. Frank Pavone, head of Priests for Life, who has been the catalyst to bring me into the Catholic Church. I told him of my concerns, and his advice to me was to continue to pray and to ponder this message. I listened to him and came to realize that what

God was actually saying to me was to 'come ALL the way home to Him' in his Church—the Church Jesus Christ Himself founded, the Mother church."

Thus was a Catholic conversion presented, in the words of Pavone, as the "full flowering" of an evangelical one. The release made no mention of Vinzant, but noted that a priest in Dallas named Edward Robinson would ready Norma for her confirmation.

———

FATHER ROBINSON HAD joined the Dominican order in 1935 in his native Minnesota. Having come to Dallas in 1966, he had begun serving its diocese as a pro-life coordinator the year after the *Roe* ruling. That he would ready Jane Roe for the Catholic faith seemed the culmination of his eighty-four years, and he began meeting Monday nights with Norma and Connie in the same priory where they had attended Mass with Vinzant.

Norma asked Robinson many questions—about the catacombs in Rome, the upside-down crucifixion of St. Peter. The priest gave Norma answers and, on August 10, he took her confession, reading *I Am Roe* in preparation. As Norma told the Catholic News Service: "Father said he was going to use my book as my confession, so I was brief."

One week later, Norma sat before Fathers Robinson and Pavone at her parish in Dallas. She wore a long blue shift with white flowers and a shawl of light blue lace, the latter a gift from a pro-life advocate named Lynn Mills. Norma had met Mills in Chicago at a trial of the pro-life activist Joseph Scheidler. Mills had become her "sponsor" and sat now beside her rubbing her back. Connie sat rows behind.

The two priests, one with black hair, one white, wore matching vestments and divided the service between them, one placing his fingers wet with chrism upon Norma's forehead, the other placing a wafer in her mouth. The wafer signified the body of Christ, and Pavone told Norma that it contained all of humanity, among it "all the babies that were lost . . . the babies that didn't get a chance to play in the playgrounds. He has given them back to you now in His flesh."

As Pavone spoke, Norma cried. But she was not thinking of the 37 million legal abortions in America in the quarter-century since *Roe*.

She was moved by the thought of connecting with children lost to adoption, not abortion, the three girls she herself had let go. "It was," she soon recounted, "like having my own children come back to me all at one time. It was like seeing all their faces, even though I've never known them."

Norma did, of course, know her eldest. Owing to the mistake of a nurse, she had momentarily held her second child, too. But the absence of her third child, she whose conception had most changed her life, had taken a particular toll on Norma; way back in 1981, she had told a journalist that "abandoning" her had filled her with guilt, and that she wondered about her "all the time." Added Norma: "I don't think I could handle loving this child."

PART VII

Repercussion

Chapter 26

The last thing Shelley had told Norma, back in the spring of 1994, was that she would never thank her for not aborting her. Hanging up the phone, Shelley had then resolved to leave her birth mother permanently behind. To do so, Shelley had cut off their one known common link, her sister Melissa, canceling the trip the sisters had planned. When Shelley returned to Texas that summer to visit her old neighbor, she did not tell Melissa.

One year later, that neighbor, J. C. Shelby, died. Back in Texas for his memorial, Shelley again did not contact Melissa. She was, she says, "terrified" that doing so would lead her back to Norma.

In running from her birth mother, Shelley was coming to resemble her. Norma had long cut herself off from family. Shelley had, too. Taken as a girl from her father and his drinking, her instinct had remained, she says, "to run and hide." And just as she ran from her sister, she now cut off her father after they fought over the seating at J. C. Shelby's memorial. She would not speak to Billy for eighteen more years.

Shelley returned to her steady life in Washington, to her mother and child and her husband, Doug, who still put gas in her car and was unruffled by *Roe*. "He has his opinions of Norma," Shelley reflected years letter. "But he doesn't try to cloud my feelings about her."

Shelley had struggled to be at peace with her parentage even before learning of Norma. "To hear that someone . . . gave you away is difficult to reconcile, even on the most basic level," she says. That the person who gave her away was Norma McCorvey had been no less difficult to accept. Shelley struggled to see where her birth mother ended and she began. Many times, says Shelley, she asked herself: "How can I come from such a despicable person?"

Shelley told herself, she says, that "knowing who you are biologically is not knowing who you are as a person." She told herself that she had many influences. Her mother, for example, had taught her to mind her language and her marriage, too. (Ruth had looked after her baby son so that Shelley and Doug could celebrate their first anniversary on the Washington coast.) And Shelley told herself that, unlike Norma, she was rearing her child. "I knew what I didn't want to do," says Shelley. "I didn't want to ever make him feel that he was a burden or unloved."

Shelley held her little son close. Together, they watched *Aladdin*, and scissored through reams of construction paper, and ate Campbell's chicken soup with noodle stars that Shelley cooled with two ice cubes in every bowl. She would protect her son. That was why, though she told him she was adopted, she never told him from whom. When Shelley gave birth to girls in 1999 and 2000, she kept her secret from them, too.

Shelley, in fact, told almost no one about Norma. To speak of her birth mother would be to lose herself, to no longer be Shelley, she says, but the *Roe* baby—someone to befriend or betray because of *Roe*. But to not speak of it, says Shelley, was to keep "this big huge secret about this part of who I am." As her twenties passed, Shelley felt increasingly isolated, unable, she says, to "be complete friends" with anyone she met.

Between the births of her girls, Shelley had moved with Doug into a four-bedroom rambler in Tucson, where he had gotten a job. She was unhappy. The depression that had first come upon her at age fifteen was suddenly, at age thirty, unremitting, heightened by the rapid births of two children. She felt she could not breathe and sought help. A doctor told her to buy a pair of shoes. A second doctor prescribed antidepressants. Shelley then got her tubes tied. "I am done," she told Doug.

The kids were growing. They were coming to resemble her and Doug, and Shelley found herself ever more mindful of whom she resembled, of where her anxiety and sadness and temper had come from. "You know how she can be mean and nasty and totally go off on people? I can do that too. Well." Adds Shelley: "I hate that I am like this." Indeed, that Shelley saw Norma in her every peremptory snap was painful. She did her best to tuck Norma away, she says, "in a dark little metal box, wrapped in chains and locked."

But Shelley was not able to lock her birth mother away. In the decade since Norma had been thrust upon her, even as Shelley threw out her letters from Melissa, and was careful to not note a legal anniversary, and changed the channel whenever the godforsaken thing came on TV, Norma and *Roe* were nonetheless "always there," says Shelley. Unknowing friends on both sides of the abortion issue would invite Shelley to rallies. Always, she declined.

And yet, all through the 1990s, Shelley had slowly become almost possessive of *Roe*. It was *her* conception that had begotten *Roe*, *her* gestation and prenatal viability that had ignited the brushfire. Just as Norma had come to call *Roe* "my law," so too—in the first years of the new millennium—did her daughter begin to lay claim to it, to not change the channel and instead listen in and correct the talking heads, if only to herself. Says Shelley: "I would be like, you guys don't even know what the story is there, so you really need to shut up." She wondered about Norma. And she began—in the privacy of her home, when the kids were asleep and Doug was out working on the used cars he bought on Craigslist—to google Norma too. "I don't like not knowing what she's doing," says Shelley. Shelley then began to google herself, a thirty-something in Tucson searching for the *Roe* baby.

———

ROE V. WADE: the name is misleading. The case does not at heart pit Roe against Wade, a pregnant woman against a district attorney. It pits that woman against the fetus she carried. Yet nowhere does the ruling mention Norma by name or refer explicitly to the fetus that became Shelley.

The ruling, though, alludes to both. "For purposes of her case," wrote Blackmun of the anonymous plaintiff, "we accept as true, and as established, her existence; her pregnant state . . . and her inability to obtain a legal abortion in Texas." As for her child, Blackmun noted just a few paragraphs later that "the normal 266-day human gestation period is so short that the pregnancy will come to term before the usual appellate process is complete."

The latter was a bit of judicial housekeeping. Blackmun simply wished to make clear that, in legal terms, the suit was not moot just because the anonymous plaintiff was no longer pregnant when her case reached the Supreme Court. But implicit in that observation was that a baby had been born.

In the three decades since *Roe*, few had wondered publicly about that baby. It was logical to assume that having won the legal right to abortion, its plaintiff had had one, and even historians of reproductive rights did so; one professor would write that Norma, along with the born again plaintiff of *Doe v. Bolton*, "claimed to regret their abortions." But some wondered about the *Roe* baby. "Does he know his birth mother fought and won in the United States court system for the right to slaughter him?" a Tennessean named Holly Hampton wrote her local paper. "Does he know that he is alive due to the grace of God and judicial lag time?" Pro-life leaders were hungry to find the child. In 1994—one year before Norma joined Operation Rescue—O.R. decided to confront her at a Dallas book signing. The first question they prepared was: what happened "to the baby that you were trying to abort?"

In the spring of 2010, that baby turned forty. Shelley had her midlife frustrations. Her husband slept in a separate bed due to his snoring. Her teenage son showed little initiative and smoked pot. And after a teacher told her younger daughter, then six, that she was bound for hell if she didn't accept Jesus as her savior, Shelley stopped sending her kids to Bible school.

Not that Shelley was religious. She and Doug no longer went to church and didn't speak to their girls of Jesus and preferred their holidays "secular," says Shelley, Christmas and Easter little more than presents and ham. It was enough to live and let live. And Shelley was living as she wished to; save for the bright colors she'd begun to dye her hair, her days, she says, were "very dull"—consisting of television and knitting and her secretarial work at a photo studio. Her anxieties over *Roe* and Norma were worry enough.

Still, twenty years after learning the identity of her mother in a restaurant high above Seattle, Shelley thought less about Norma than about her sisters. Her daughters brought them to mind every day. "It could be something as simple as [them] yelling at each other in the morning," says Shelley. "And I'll be like, I never got to do that with my sisters."

===

SHELLEY'S SISTER JENNIFER had known for some time that her second marriage would end. Her husband, James, struggled with drink and moodiness, and had slapped her, too. She had resolved, after the birth of their second child in 1993, to have no more children, and had gotten her tubes tied. James aside, Jennifer was in love with Misty, the woman she had met that year through her crush at the flower shop and had been visiting on weekends.

Jennifer felt alive with Misty as she never had with a man. And in February 1995, Jennifer arrived at a crossroads.

Jennifer had been out drinking and dancing with men from the fire department when she came home drunk. James was suspicious. The couple began to yell. Someone had called the police when, says Jennifer, James "cold-cocked me and I flew over the hood of the car." Two officers arrived to see Jennifer punch James in the jaw. They cuffed her and took her to the precinct. When the police chief escorted her home, they found the kids in the house and James saying goodbye into a video camera, his car running inside the garage.

James survived. But Jennifer thought of Misty. She knew that to go to her would be to leave her husband for good. She lifted the phone and put it down, then lifted it again. She called Misty, and her marriage was over. Says Jennifer: "I just couldn't do it anymore."

Neither could Misty. Her husband was cheating on her, and she was due in days with her first child. Her husband moved out a week after her daughter was born, and Jennifer drove ninety miles north, her Toyota filled with kids and garbage bags of clothes.

For the first time in her twenty-seven years, Jennifer was partnered with a woman. When her divorce was complete, her custody of the kids secure, she came out to her ex. Says Jennifer: "I was like, 'Yup, I'm gay.'"

It was no small thing to be out in rural Texas. Best Jennifer and Misty could tell, they were the only gay couple among the six hundred residents of Trenton. Misty's family tried to break them up. Her mother, a Sunday school teacher, ranted in the name of God against their homosexuality, while her siblings outed Jennifer to her father. But Misty and Jennifer simply stopped going to church. And Jennifer was happy that her father, who didn't tell her mother, now knew who she was. One year later, he heard Jennifer calling out for Misty after surgery for a hernia and understood that the love she felt for her partner was the same that he felt for his.

Jennifer and Misty were indeed in love. Rid of their men, they resettled in nearby Bonham. Theirs was a stable home, three children and two mothers roosting in an old wooden house just south of Oklahoma. Misty handled homework and discipline, Jennifer the cleaning and cooking, mindful every day to set out snacks for school. The family was close; they went together to softball games and soccer practice, museums and zoos, on trips to California and Florida.

Jennifer was more mindful of her blessings for having not had them. And reminders of her chaotic past were frequent, as when, in 1996, her ex went to prison after the youngest child of his new girlfriend died in his custody.

Jennifer clung to her kids, to Misty, to the flowers she arranged. She had a new home, too, a double-wide mobile she bought in Trenton. Misty bought the adjoining land and, in 2003, started in on a nursing degree. Jennifer was proud of her. But their relationship began to fray. "She would be gone all day," says Jennifer, "and then she would want to study."

Jennifer was twelve when an instability she presumed she had inherited from her biological parents overtook her. And her daughter was twelve when, in 2006, she started drinking and skipping school and sneaking boys into her bedroom in the hope, she told Jennifer, of having a baby. Her son began to slip away, too, smoking pot and then meth. Jennifer tried to take care of her kids as she had been cared for—getting her daughter tutoring and smashing her son's pipe. But her kids were coming apart, and so was she. Jennifer had just turned forty when, in 2007, she began to have panic attacks.

Soon after, a miserable two years began when Misty and her daughter left. Jennifer was distraught. She needed family and called home. Her mother, Donna, asked why she was upset, and Jennifer told her that she was gay, and that Misty had been her partner and had left. Donna said almost nothing. "She was like, 'Oh,'" says Jennifer. Months later, Jennifer's father died.

Jennifer was still adjusting to life without her partner and her father when, in 2009, her son went off to the army. The home felt empty, and soon afterward it burned to the ground with everything Jennifer had in it—photographs and furniture and clothing—after one of the cats knocked over candles her daughter had lit beside the bath.

Jennifer and her daughter spent two months in motels paid for by the Red Cross and her mother. After some time with Misty, they rented an apartment in Austin but got evicted after Jennifer's son, back from basic training, urinated off their balcony. They moved again.

Jennifer felt numb. She was empty-handed, unemployed; a bum shoulder had forced her from the flower shop, and she had nothing left of the minimum wage she earned in the office of an engine repair company. It was summer in Texas and she wanted a drink.

Jennifer had been sober twenty years. But there was a gay bar close by, on Highway 35. There she succumbed to Southern Comfort and drugs, a daily haze of hydrocodone, pot and cocaine that she bought from a woman at the bar who was soon her girlfriend, an obese drug dealer everybody called GZ. Jennifer got arrested for driving drunk and GZ began to abuse her. "She choked me," says Jennifer. "She hit me. She scratched me. She bit me."

Jennifer was again enveloped in chaos and hurt. She was desperate to escape it, to be healthy above all for her kids. She found herself drawn to a regular at the bar named Lisa, who took a job in the parking lot after arriving one night with a motorcycle group called the L. O. W. Riders.

Lisa was large, with a blond ponytail and a big smile. She was relaxed and quiet. Jennifer would stare at her at the bar, and wander out to the lot where Lisa would giggle about her mullet and where, on Halloween, Jennifer leaned in to kiss her. Lisa pulled away. She liked Jennifer. But she had overcome a cocaine habit and was only interested in someone sober, and single besides.

Soon after, Jennifer was single after GZ got arrested for beating her and for drug possession. After nine months of abuse, a third relationship had come to a violent end. Jennifer felt empty. "I didn't have shit," she says. "Something had to change."

The sun rose, and Jennifer went to Lisa—tranquil, healthy Lisa. She vowed to rid herself of drink and drugs. Lisa, though, was not convinced. Jennifer pleaded. She had been close to sober for a month, consecrating her new self with a buzz cut, when, she says, she gave Lisa an ultimatum: "Either we get together or I'm leaving." The women were a couple when they moved with two cocker spaniels and a cat into an apartment in the Austin suburbs. There Jennifer found a job, stocking the garden department of a Walmart in Hutto. Come 2011, she felt reborn.

Her son and daughter, however, were not sober. And their struggles brought back to Jennifer the question of her roots. "It was always a curiosity for her," says Lisa. "Who am I? Where did I come from?"

———

JENNIFER'S OLDER SISTER, Melissa, knew her origins all too well; she'd been a girl of nine when she learned the distressing fact that Norma was her mother, not her sister. And the ambivalence of inheritance was again in her thoughts when, twenty years later, in the fall of 1994, Melissa gave birth to a second child, a daughter, Chloe, whose round chin and large eyes were unquestionably of her father.

Melissa felt estranged from her husband. In the year since she had come upon Kerry pushing his secretary on a swing, her anxieties had bled into anger. Since Chloe's birth, she'd been depressed, too, unaided by her daily exercise and Lorazepam. Melissa started on Prozac, which helped with her tears. But, she says, "it kept me so flat." She was perpetually tired and rarely smiled and lost thirty-five pounds.

Kerry had moved back home when, in March, Melissa found herself in an interminable line in a Walmart, waiting, waiting, to exchange baby clothes that did not fit. An hour had passed when the line closed, and Melissa did the swap herself, heading for the door with new clothes after laying down the old. A policeman grabbed her arm. "I felt like such a loser," she says.

Melissa told the cop that she needed to phone her husband "but that he might not come because of his bitch-ass girlfriend." The cop did not cuff Melissa; he felt for her. But he did fine and arrest her. After Kerry drove her home, Melissa was left to contend not only with a job and kids and a derelict husband, but the indelible stain of a misdemeanor.

Two months shy of thirty years old, Melissa had hit bottom. "I had no crying in me," she says. "That's how I knew I was messed up. Even Coke didn't taste right." Things got worse still when Kerry began to beat her again, as he'd done before their marriage seven years before. "He'd grab me by the neck," says Melissa, "or push me up against the wall."

It had once been alcohol that turned Kerry violent. Now it was only anger. "He knew he'd done wrong," says Melissa. Melissa would eject Kerry from their Amarillo home. Upon returning to it, he would hit her again.

Melissa and Kerry returned to therapy. But they spoke less of his abuse than his affairs, and the sessions led nowhere—the husband insisting he was no longer cheating, the wife suspecting he was. "I thought I was crazy," says Melissa. "Like my mom."

In 1998, Kerry confessed that for years he'd been sleeping with a pair of secretaries. Melissa was shattered. But she would not leave Kerry. She would not do what Norma had done. She still yearned for the intact family that remained out of reach—her husband unfaithful, her sisters phantoms, her mother absent, her father missing. Melissa did not know that her father, Woody, had died a few years before, in Reno.

———

MELISSA WAS NOT merely heartbroken. She was humiliated. "Everybody knew" about Kerry, she says. The girls were five and ten, able to understand some of what was being said. And so, after a decade in Amarillo, the family drove off in their Dodge, settling in San Antonio where Kerry left social work for sales, a stocker at Walmart.

Change did the couple good. They rented a big old wooden home with a porch and took pleasure in fixing it up—new paint, new furniture. They no longer went to church, but found friends through Walmart. Melissa got a good job with a local obstetrician. But in 2000, the browser on the family computer alerted Melissa that Kerry was frequenting a chat room to romance big-breasted women. Soon after, Jordan came upon her father video-chatting with one.

Melissa had long been told by her grandmother Mary that, when it came to men, you took the bad with the good. Melissa tried to live by that. But in 2002, she accused Kerry of having an affair with a colleague. She shoved him and he grabbed her neck, choking her so hard that their daughters ran to the neighbors to call the cops. "I wanted him to go to jail," says Melissa, her eyes welling with tears. But she didn't press charges. She would keep her family together.

One week later, Kerry got promoted. He would be an assistant manager at a Walmart outside Houston. The family moved again, Melissa telling herself that they would at last find peace in a suburb called Katy.

It was in Katy that Jordan came out to her parents in the backseat of the family van at a burger drive-through. She was in high school, and she confided that a youth leader at their local church had said that gay people go to hell. Melissa responded that God would accept her. Kerry did not. "He wanted to beat her straight," she says. Instead, he wept and blamed Melissa for passing on gay genes. Melissa responded that his horribleness was the reason their daughter did not want to be with men. Soon after, in early 2004, Melissa discovered through a phone bill that Kerry had rekindled an old flame in Amarillo.

A decade had passed since Melissa first discovered Kerry's philandering. She could take no more, and kicked Kerry out. Wanting at last to prune her husband from the family tree, she phoned Norma for the name of a lawyer.

It so happened that Norma and Connie were set to fly to Ireland, that Catholic country where a reformed Jane Roe could pack a hall. She invited Melissa along.

Of all her missing relations, Melissa craved her sisters most; the letters she still kept in her bedside drawer attested to how close she had come to meeting Shelley. But a mother's rejection is primordial. Though Mary had stepped forward to help raise her granddaughter and had become for her a surrogate mother, Melissa had never stopped hoping that Norma might reclaim her.

Melissa had thus been devastated when, a few years before, Norma had appeared on the cover of her second book holding a little girl, and written of Emily as she'd never spoken of her—of her "purity of soul that makes it all worth living." Even years later, the mention of Emily made Melissa cry; she wondered why Norma could not love her the same way. Norma had a sense of why. "I love children," she emailed a friend, "(as long as their someone else's and they don't stay long)."

Neglect and combustibility had marked Norma's forty years as a mother. And it crushed Melissa now to think that she, like Norma, was the matriarch of a broken family.

Melissa had never been farther than California. And though Norma drank her way through their week abroad, slipping away for countless pints and a tattoo—a sacred heart of Jesus inked into her left shoulder—Melissa understood that Norma had wished to help her. Kerry then pleaded with Melissa for another chance, and she granted him one on the condition that he go weekly to a Christian counselor whom Norma recommended. The marriage continued.

Months later, in 2005, Kerry got promoted again, asked to manage a Walmart in Galveston. It was a very good job with a very good salary. So Melissa quit her job and the family moved into a big brick home they bought in Katy. Melissa found herself happy to tend to their girls and to be with Kerry, too, the couple taking walks and cleaning their yard, weekending with friends and vacationing with the kids in Hawaii and Florida and Mexico.

Years passed and they were good. But Melissa still yearned for her sisters and went looking again for Shelley, searching the internet and calling information. "I was looking in Washington," she says. "She wasn't in Washington."

There were signs, meantime, that Kerry was cheating again. And in the fall of 2008, Walmart fired him for fraternizing with a subordinate. "He was a dog," says Melissa. "He was making $250,000 and lost his job for a piece of ass. All that sacrifice. All the years up and down." Soon after, Chloe saw her dad buying fireworks for the children of a woman he knew. A phone bill confirmed that the woman was yet another lover. Melissa kicked Kerry out of the house. After twenty-one years, a marriage was finally over.

All her life, nothing had so mattered to Melissa as the preservation of family. But she now worried that her refusal to leave Kerry had bled her kids more than it had sustained them. She dropped them off with friends, and then checked herself into the nearest hospital. "I couldn't think," says Melissa. "I couldn't breathe."

There was an empty bed in the cardiac unit, and Melissa lay there for three days until the obstetrician she had worked for came by and told her that she could live without Kerry but that her kids couldn't live without her. Melissa got out of bed and drove her station wagon home, and a friend loaded half of everything she owned onto a flatbed truck and drove it to Kerry.

Kerry fought the divorce, and then the settlement. He sold their home for a loss and left Melissa nothing more than insurance and alimony. After Melissa moved with her daughters into a Katy apartment, she was determined more than ever to find her sister.

Melissa went online. But in the fall of 2009, it was not Shelley she found but Edgewater2112, a man on Match.com six years her junior who lived in Louisiana and worked with his hands. His name was Eric. Says Melissa: "I wanted to meet someone away from anyone I knew. I wanted to start over."

Eric was tall and rail-thin with bright eyes, hollow cheeks, and a prominent nose. Melissa liked his looks. She liked that he had four siblings but no kids and no ex-wife. She liked that he loved art and also his job with tile and paint and cabinetry. Most of all, Melissa liked that Eric was not Kerry. He was peaceful and honest and unpretentious and capable of restraint.

In February, Melissa drove east to a hotel in Lafayette, where Eric greeted her with purple and yellow flowers and a card. The couple shared a few exotic beers and then, back at his place, filet mignon.

Melissa was soon seeing Eric every other week. He cooked country meals like shrimp creole and jambalaya that recalled for Melissa those happy early years she had lived in Louisiana. She was falling in love and told Eric of her family and of *Roe*. He was surprised that she had a famous mother. But he didn't really care. What moved him were Melissa's genuineness and good intentions. In the spring of 2011, she invited him to move into the apartment she shared with Chloe and two cats. Eric packed his belongings and three joints, too. He smoked them, but none more. For Melissa asked him not to.

If Melissa finally had a better half, the whole of her small family was growing smaller still. Norma was rarely in touch, Mary rarely lucid.

And Raymond, the old trucker Melissa had called dad, had wasted to 103 pounds when, on Christmas Eve, he died.

Melissa was desperate to replenish her family. She thought about having another child. But it felt too late; she was forty-six. And so, in 2012, it was just Chloe and the cats who joined her and Eric in the Katy home they bought and decorated with African art. Melissa feared the future.

"I've tried to fill in the hole but it's still empty," she said. "I don't want to be old and alone. I don't want to be old and alone."

Chapter 27

"Emily's invitation to church."
"Babies in the freezer."
"100% Pro life."

Norma wrote out her talking points on orange index cards, her journey from choice to life distilled to a dozen or so steps. The cards had helped Norma on her lecture tours. But they stopped short of her conversion to Catholicism. And having just given her the sacrament of confirmation, Father Pavone set out to help her sell the addendum to her story, Priests for Life quickly publishing a booklet titled "My Journey into the Catholic Church."

To narrativize Norma's conversion was, of course, to lay claim to it. And every photo of Norma in the booklet included Pavone. It Catholicized Norma's roots, too; whereas the priest had recently acknowledged that Norma was "unsure of the details of her religious background," the booklet asserted that her mother was Catholic and had often dropped the young Norma off at Mass. "I liked it so much and was often moved to tears," Norma attested. "I felt the presence of God."

The narrative of Norma thus continued to evolve, and she began to criticize the evangelicals' tactics. "The Catholics are nonviolent," she told a reporter, this fall of 1998. "There is no storming into an abortion mill or chaining people to staircases. You accomplish nothing, and some say Operation Rescue set the movement back twenty years."

Evangelicals took note. There was a sense among them, says Rob Schenck, the reverend whose ministry had brought Norma to DC, "that we had lost a prize and she was now on somebody else's mantel." He adds: "We all knew that we were competing for basically the same donor pool. And one way you did was grabbing people like Norma and saying, she's with me—and not with you anymore."

Norma had helped Schenck's bottom line; inserting photos of her into his ministry newsletter had roughly doubled donations, he says. But Pavone's booklet, eleven glossy pages, was a fundraising tool of a different order. "It would be extremely valuable as a premium," says Schenck. "If somebody made a contribution they would get that booklet . . . along with a second ask."

Of course, the new Norma also lost a few speaking gigs. (One Baptist pastor wrote that Norma was now "condemned before God.") Catholics and Protestants had sparred for centuries over everything from sacraments to saints, and their antipathies sometimes still simmered. The president of the Southern Baptist Theological Seminary, for example, would soon tell Larry King that "as an evangelical, I believe that the Roman church is a false church and it teaches a false gospel." But Catholics and evangelicals were united on abortion. The pro-life movement was "as close to an ecumenical movement as American history has seen," one history put it. Norma remained in demand in both communities, and departed in September on a two-month speaking tour of fourteen states. She was preparing for a dinner at a crisis pregnancy center in South Carolina when her agent spelled out the twofold purpose of their every event: "Glorify God in all we do. Raise lots of money."

Norma was paid about $800 per talk, money she divided with her ministry. And, having long cashed her checks at 7-Eleven, Norma struggled to hold onto what little she earned. "She was destitute financially," says her accountant, Ron Allen. "She made $20,000 or $30,000 a year. As far as I know she lived hand-to-mouth."

The Catholicization of Jane Roe had, however, done wonders for Pavone. Since confirming Norma, he had seen donations to Priests for Life jump. Within two years, they would more than quadruple, from $1.3 million to $5.3 million.

NORMA CRAVED PUBLICITY, but had little appreciation for those who helped her get it. As she emailed her new speaking agent in July: "NO ONE WILL 'CONTROL' ME."

Anything could set Norma off—a check not yet received, a letter opened on her behalf. Her speaking agent, Bill Hampton, was soon exasperated. "We never know when you are going to get upset with us," he wrote to her. That Norma would move on was inevitable and, in 1999, she did, entrusting her travel and booking to a speaking firm in Nashville.

Still, Priests for Life remained Norma's bullhorn. Despite her volatility (and her Coronas and Marlboros), PFL did its best to spread her gospel. Pavone himself helped Norma to write her talks, and moderated some conversations with her. The conversion of Jane Roe remained a great testimony not only to the evil of abortion but to PFL. Her rebirth was a sacrament of sorts, an atonement, as her teacher Father Robinson told the press, "for any complicity she had in this abortion business." He added: "She is perfectly at peace."

Norma, however, was not at peace. Fifty-one years old, she had bound her life to an endless discussion of genocide and God. The anniversary of *Roe* had become a sort of macabre pro-life holiday—a day of prayer and fundraising and mourning and marching that every January drew many tens of thousands of Christians to the capital and left Norma, sure as her annual turn at the podium, depressed.

Her depression was clinical, said her doctor. And though it had preceded *Roe*, *Roe* played a part, the feeling that every year "another million deaths," as a lawyer she met at the march put it, were on her head. So did the demands of the anniversary. "They were overscheduling her," says Sheree Havlik, a friend from Operation Rescue. "She was not as strong as people thought." Adds Havlik: "Every January, I was really pulling her out of the trenches."

And yet, every January, Norma took to the podium alongside the pols and quarterbacks and clergy. Abortion was her living. After she gave a talk at the 1999 march that she titled "National Day of Death," she flew around the country to give it again and again. By year's end, she had been paid $25,000 and been mailed, at her Dallas P.O. box, hundreds of letters—invitations and rosaries and poems and forgiveness, Christians letting Norma know that *Roe* was not her fault, that God had chosen her because He knew that she would return to Him.

Norma read every note, tucking them away in her garage. They were kind but wearyingly earnest; a woman Norma had just met wrote that God had granted her a glimpse of Norma's beauty. Norma found herself tiring of her fellow pro-lifers, those lily-white believers who spoke, said Norma, as she did not—"Lord Jesus Christ this, and Lord Jesus Christ that." She called them the "little Christians."

Norma remained her salty self. Sex in particular, the hint of it, still clung to her. She was often braless and bawdy, happy to present herself as a would-be Jezebel; she told the Reverend Schenck that were she looking for a man, "I'd put my hands on you." The next January in DC, she stood beside her friend Karen Garnett, due in four months with her fifth child, and told any and all: "We're pregnant."

Norma's homosexuality, however, was no joke. In the five years since Schenck had brought her to Georgetown, donors and pastors, mindful that he had her ear, had phoned him, he says, with their concern that Connie remained a "shadow lesbian presence in her life." Their worry was unsurprising. Opposition to homosexuality was as intense in their circle as opposition to abortion. Indeed, Benham had recently confessed to a professor of politics that he would support abortion to prevent the birth of a gay child. "Instead of building bridges to homosexuality," he wrote that winter, "we need to be storming the gates of hell."

His fellow pro-life advocates said much the same. Randall Terry decried the desire of "homosexuals and lesbians . . . to glorify their perversions." Troy Newman feared the wrath that "abortion and homosexuality and other sins" would bring upon America. Frank Pavone lamented Norma's previous "spell of lesbianism and bitterness." And Schenck would both liken homosexuality to polygamy and call for a constitutional amendment to bar gay marriage.

Norma knew of their damnations. It was Benham and company who had led her to renounce her homosexuality as the profane folly of a woman desperate to avoid another pregnancy. And yet, these same men clamored for her company. "Nobody was going to cut her off, because she was too valuable," says Schenck. "She was kind of a trophy."

Back in the capital in 2000, at a Mass on the eve of the march, that trophy, recalls her pregnant friend Garnett, was feeling "anxious and claustrophobic."

Norma was in the care of Pavone on this trip. The priest joined her on discussion panels and at breakfasts at the Hyatt. But Norma was tiring of him. Pavone was on the board of her ministry—and occasionally had Priests for Life donate a few hundred dollars to it. But Norma did more for him and his coffers than he did for her. "I was hoping that you would be more helpful and a friend," she'd faxed Pavone only weeks before. "King Herods I have."

Norma was thus open to finding herself a new keeper when, at a banquet hours after the march, a lawyer from Texas approached.

"I said," recalls Allan Parker, "'Miss Norma, I think you're going to be involved in overturning *Roe v. Wade* someday.'"

———

ALLAN EDWARD PARKER JR. was born in Houston on the last day of summer in 1952. Four younger siblings had arrived when, in 1962, the family moved to the plains of Oklahoma. There, in the city of Duncan, Allan Sr. went to work for Halliburton, helping the oil giant ship sand and mud for the drilling of wells.

The Parkers were practicing Catholics, the children baptized, the sons altar boys at Assumption Catholic Church. Allan was spiritual; he loved the Latin Mass. He was physical, too—hiking and fishing, playing football and tennis and wrestling. But he was small. By ninth grade, he had left sports behind (save his job managing the wrestling team), turning instead to debate and books and a Catholic youth group.

Parker started college in 1970. He was an underclassman at the University of Oklahoma when his number for the Vietnam draft lottery came up: sixteen. He got the news while in Wyoming on a summer job cutting wheat, and thought of moving farther north to Canada. "I was kind of a hippie," he says. "I had long hair." But he had a girlfriend back home, and enjoyed school besides. So he returned to Oklahoma and enrolled in ROTC, committing to spend a few years with the army post-college in the hope that the war would then be over.

Parker majored in economics. But it was a course on the history of science that molded him, the knowledge in particular that "major scientific theories," he says—from the phlogiston theory to spontaneous generation—"often turn out to be wrong." Henceforth, he would be skeptical of science.

Parker was still in college when, in 1973, he married his girlfriend of two years, a Presbyterian named Susan. A daughter soon followed. In 1976, Parker finished up his stint on an army base in North Carolina and began law school.

Parker had taken the LSAT on a whim. The practical promise of law appealed to him, and he graduated from the University of Texas with high honors. But he studied at the expense of his marriage, he says, and Susan retreated into the Bible, becoming born again.

Parker was no more available to his wife when he became a corporate lawyer in Corpus Christi. Despite her pleadings, he refused marriage counseling. But in 1981, he consented to join her on a Catholic retreat devoted to marriage renewal. Parker was writing his thoughts about life and marriage during a session on communication when he found himself "alone with God," he says, and submitted to Him, born again at the age of twenty-nine.

Parker and his wife left their Presbyterian church for what he termed "an evangelistic" Baptist one. Parker left his job, too, to teach education law and civil procedure at a Catholic university in San Antonio. In 1989, his university sent him to Strasbourg for a course on international human rights law.

Parker had never given abortion much thought. Back when *Roe* was decided, a few months before his marriage, his reaction to it had been "So what?" But now, in France with his wife and three daughters, he was assigned the pro-life position in a classroom debate. By the time he returned to Texas, his research had won him over, the lawyer swayed in particular by two facts—that various international pacts (including the International Covenant on Civil and Political Rights) prohibited the execution of a pregnant woman, and that the American Convention on Human Rights—a union of Central and Southern American (and largely Catholic) countries—declared that life began at conception.

Parker became an evangelist, he says, wanting above all "to tell people about Jesus." Back home, he took steps to activize his Christianity. He founded a branch of the Christian Coalition. He founded a local organization to mediate disputes between Christians. And in 1998, having left teaching to work full-time at the Texas Justice Foundation, a nonprofit he founded to legally defend school choice and school vouchers, he turned to abortion, helping a pair of young lawyers take aim at local clinics. The lawyers collected affidavits from eleven women who said that abortions had injured their uterus or colon. The case had not yet been settled (in their favor) when, in 1999, those same two lawyers connected Parker with a man named Harold Cassidy, a pro-life lawyer in New Jersey who was focused not on the physical toll of abortion but the emotional one.

Cassidy had litigated the famous Baby M adoption case, arguing a decade before that a would-be surrogate mother could only make an informed decision to surrender her child once she had delivered it. The New Jersey Supreme Court had agreed. Cassidy was readying now to file a suit that would enable him to argue against abortion on similar grounds.

That a woman is less likely to surrender a child after birth than before it is little surprise. The most vivid sonogram, the strongest fetal heartbeat, is no match for the wallop of an actual baby, let alone a baby one has birthed. So antithetical is adoption to most women that, as one study revealed, more than nine in ten who seek abortions too late in their pregnancies to get them go on to raise the child they had wanted to abort. Birth changes things. And Cassidy argued that in preventing birth, abortion denied a woman her right to a relationship with her child.

Cassidy was now representing a plaintiff who was a minor, and who claimed that she had been coerced by her parents into having an abortion.

The right to choose, of course, enables one to choose motherhood. And there had been, alas, great multitudes of women forced or coerced into having abortions—millions in China alone over the previous three decades. Those women had suffered. Cassidy's client had too, she said.

Cassidy hoped to support his case with amicus briefs filed by the born again plaintiffs Jane Roe and Mary Doe. (The latter, a woman named Sandra Cano who was the plaintiff of *Doe v. Bolton*, had become pro-life like Norma.) Norma, of course, could not speak to the emotional consequences of abortion; she'd not had one. But she had been exploited by her lawyers, she said. Needing a lawyer to help Norma submit a brief, Cassidy asked Parker if he would represent her. Parker said he would, and Cassidy told Parker that he could meet Norma at the upcoming March for Life in January 2000.

Parker had read Norma's second memoir, *Won by Love*, when he approached her at that DC banquet. He was prepared to help her submit that brief for Cassidy. But, as he now told Norma, he imagined that she might do something far more consequential—tackle *Roe* itself.

"He was talking about his whole vision," says Norma's friend Karen Garnett, who spoke to Parker the morning after he approached Norma. He wanted, she recalls, "to get a whole bunch of affidavits together to overturn *Roe*."

The affidavits Parker intended to collect would be from women testifying that abortion had caused them emotional harm. Once he had collected them, he would introduce them to a court, thereby exposing, he later explained, "the lie that abortion is good for women."

———

PRO-LIFE ADVOCATES HAD long maintained that abortion not only killed the fetus but did harm to those around it. It harmed the would-be fathers, "post-abortion men" guilt-ridden yet powerless. Most of all, it harmed the would-be mothers, women beset, they said, by breast cancer and a psychological condition that they named post-abortion syndrome.

In time, these diagnoses were widely dismissed, debunked. The conservative *Weekly Standard*, for example, labeled post-abortion survivor syndrome "crankery," while the National Cancer Institute reported "no association between induced and spontaneous abortions and breast cancer risk." But post-abortion syndrome—the idea, as Mother Teresa wrote, that every abortion killed not only a baby but a mother's "conscience"—persisted in the public consciousness. Though the scientific community scoffed, Parker had learned in college just how often that community was wrong. He believed in PAS. Hitching himself to Norma, he would turn it into a legal weapon in the war on *Roe*.

———

A MARRIAGE COUNSELOR named Vincent Rue was the first to label and clinically define PAS.

Rue had been born in 1948 into a Catholic family in Los Angeles that soon numbered ten. His father was a marriage counselor who also taught at a local women's college. "Psychologically and biologically, a woman is destined to be the chalice of life, by nature dependent on man," James Rue told a gathering of Catholic psychologists in 1964. He added that educating women to become professionals put a strain on their marriages; they ought to be taught instead, he said, to be wives and mothers—"the true identity of womanhood."

The son decided to become a marriage counselor, too, and began his master's degree at Saint Louis University. There, in 1972, he presented a paper proposing that the federal government do something his father had advocated on a state level: create a Department of Marriage and the Family. "The DMF would coordinate existing but fragmented family services," a subsequent article explained, "provide premarital, sexual, child-development and family-life education and counseling." The department would also guard against "practices that are detrimental to marriage and the family."

Rue's proposal made no mention of abortion. But one of his advisers at the university was a pro-life activist named William Brennan, who was writing a book titled *The Abortion Holocaust: Today's Final Solution*. Another mentor, a priest named Paul Marx, was also active in the fight against abortion. He had just written a book titled *The Death Peddlers: War on the Unborn*, and had spearheaded the use of fetal photography as a pro-life tool. Two years earlier, while a senior at Saint John's University in Minnesota, Rue had helped Marx research the growing push to legalize abortion. The two had concluded, says Rue, that proponents of legal abortion were exaggerating the number of women killed by illegal abortion. Says Rue: "There was a lot of so-called science that wasn't scientific."

Abortion was legal when Rue, by then a doctoral student in family relations at the School of Home Economics at the University of North Carolina at Greensboro, began to help a professor assess its impact on women. Focusing on a local problem-pregnancy counseling service, they determined, says Rue, that "abortion counseling was a kind of myth." Rue returned to California in 1975 to practice alongside his father, and began to ask every female client if she'd ever been pregnant. "If they brought up abortion," says Rue, "they'd burst into tears."

Rue had been a therapist for six years when an acquaintance from graduate school arranged for him to testify to Congress about the psychological toll of abortion. Rue decided to give it a name: post-abortion syndrome. In November 1981, he listed for Congress twenty-four of its effects, from depression and anger to infertility and psychosis. Rue described PAS in much the same terms that psychiatrists described post-traumatic stress. Says Rue: "It's a type of PTSD."

The next year, Rue spoke at a convention of the National Right to Life Committee. In his audience was a woman named Olivia Gans, who went on to help found an organization called Women Exploited by Abortion. Its members began to share stories of PAS. And in 1987, an engineer turned activist named David Reardon published *Aborted Women, Silent No More*. The book resonated with the pro-life movement, and the year it was published, leaders of the National Right to Life Committee spoke of PAS to President Reagan.

Gary Bauer, a senior Reagan advisor, suggested to the president that his Surgeon General write up a report on the purported syndrome; if morality had not succeeded in outlawing abortion, perhaps public health could. Reagan authorized the inquiry, and Dr. Koop reviewed the literature. In time, however, the doctor declined to write a report, explaining in a 1989 letter to Reagan that the 250-odd studies he had reviewed on abortion and mental health were "flawed methodologically." He concluded that "the data do not support the premise that abortion does nor does not cause or contribute to psychological problems."

Pro-life advocates were angry; they felt that the pro-life Dr. Koop had betrayed the cause. "He's afraid to apply his own views and values," the chairman of the Conservative Caucus, a lobbying group, told the press. The doctor responded on *Good Morning, America* that he had "always been able to separate my personal beliefs from my responsibilities as Surgeon General."

The American Psychological Association entered the fray, appointing a panel to glean what it could about PAS from the existing literature. In 1990, the panel reported that instances of psychological distress following abortion were "relatively rare." One study, for example, revealed that women were four and a half times more likely to express relief than guilt over an abortion performed in the first trimester (when more than 90 percent of abortions are performed).

Subsequent studies would indicate much the same. The Turnaway Study, a longitudinal study of a thousand women who sought to end their pregnancies, would find, in the words of its principal investigator, "no link between receiving an abortion and subsequent adverse mental health outcomes." Added the future president of the American Psychiatric Association in a 1992 article: "There is no evidence of an Abortion-Trauma syndrome."

That wasn't to say that abortion wasn't something fundamentally grave. "Abortion is a right that ends in sorrow, not celebration," wrote Sarah Blustain, a proponent of choice. It wasn't to say that there weren't women harmed by abortion. This abortion providers knew. The conscientious among them, people like Curtis Boyd and Charlotte Taft, used screening and counseling to flag uncertainty and prevent regret. Still, one cannot fully predict the aftershocks of any decision. Sorrowful stories of abortion were a staple of the annual March for Life, jeremiads the poet Gwendolyn Brooks had evoked years before in a midcentury poem. Wrote Brooks: "Abortions will not let you forget."

The question, then, was not whether an abortion could cause a woman grief. It was, rather, one of prevalence, of scope, a point Dr. Koop had stressed while testifying to Congress in 1989. Yes, he said, he had seen abortion take an "overwhelming" psychological toll on an individual. But from a public health perspective, that toll was "minuscule." Indeed, a 1992 study cited in the *American Psychologist* would show that abortion has no greater impact on mental health than other, ordinary stresses, such as pregnancy or birth—let alone the birth of an unwanted child.

That same year, the Supreme Court ruled in *Casey* that restrictions on abortion that did not unduly burden women were legal. Among the restrictions it upheld was a Pennsylvania law that—contrary to medical consensus—required doctors to warn women of the "possible detrimental psychological effects of abortion." By 1999, "informed consent" laws were on the books in thirteen states.

If the medical community had discredited PAS, its very diagnosis was for some women a comfort. There is relief in pinpointing the source of any problem. "You can't repent depressive symptoms," a psychology professor named Brenda Major told the journalist Emily Bazelon. "But you can repent an action." A cluster of religious organizations began to fund retreats for "post-abortive women" that fingered PAS as the root cause of their emotional hurt. Priests for Life was among them, and Father Pavone soon had Norma attend one. "I am so scared but, hopefully I will live," she emailed a friend. "I do not consider myself post abortive."

Allan Parker, however, did. And as he prepared, in early 2000, to use Norma to challenge *Roe*, he wished for her to put in writing the ways in which abortion had harmed her.

On February 14, just weeks after meeting Norma in DC, Parker arrived at her Dallas home.

NORMA WAS HAPPY for the visit. She had begun to look past Pavone. And in her four-plus years with the pro-life movement, she had had little to do with its legal flank, working instead with entities rooted in direct action and counseling and politics. Alongside Parker, Norma would now be able to fight *Roe* with the law.

Parker arrived on Cactus Lane with a tape recorder and three lawyers. The group hoped to interview Norma so as to prepare her affidavit for the abortion case in New Jersey. After introductions and readings from the Bible and small talk—how great it would be to convert Oprah, someone said—Norma told a life story that had little truth in it, from her claim that she had lived as a young hippie beside an oak tree in Lee

Park to her familiar lie that she had helped doctors to perform abortions. "The women," said Norma, "were digging their nails into me in an effort to endure the pain."

Talk turned to the affidavit Norma had signed thirty years before. "I am particularly interested in the lies," Kathleen Cassidy Goodman told her. She asked Norma if she had any evidence or memories "to support calling Sarah Weddington a liar."

Norma did not, and Goodman moved on in search of something incriminating. "Did you ever do drugs with Weddington?" Norma answered that she wished she had. "Me too," allowed Goodman.

Norma, though, came through; she told the lawyers that Weddington and Coffee had drunk with her "a couple of pitchers of beer" when first they met. She said that when her lawyers had her sign her affidavit, she had not known the meaning of the word "abortion." She said that they had not explained that abortion ended a fetal life.

None of this was true, not the implication that the lawyers had unsteadied Norma with alcohol nor the assertion that she had not known the intent of her lawsuit. Norma had been unequivocal about wanting an abortion, and had known the meaning of the word. If the lawyers had misled Norma at all, it was in not extinguishing her hope that she might be able to both file suit and end her pregnancy.

Parker had gotten what he wanted. The affidavit Norma would sign a month and a day later would assert not only that *Roe* was "built upon false assumptions" but that its plaintiff had been "exploited by two self-interested attorneys."

Parker also was an attorney with interests. But he asserted that those interests came from on high. "God is going to overturn *Roe v. Wade*," he told Norma. "God is going to anoint us. God is going to work for us, through us, to do His work."

One month later, Norma stood with Parker at the National Press Club in DC to announce the submission of her affidavit on behalf of Donna Santa Marie, the pseudonymous plaintiff in New Jersey represented by Cassidy.

Norma knew the drill. She had stood by as Allred and Benham and Pavone spoke to the press in her name. And she was quiet as Parker did the same, trumpeting her affidavit, untruths signed and notarized. The lawyer then released a second document which declared in her name that "the most important relationship that a woman can ever have" is the relationship with her child.

It was, at best, an ironic statement coming from Norma. It continued, asserting that, unlike abortion, adoption "at least gives the mother the hope that her child is alive and able to pursue happiness."

That very hope, however, torments many women. As Virginia Whitehill, a board member of Planned Parenthood in Texas, observed, adoption was "even more painful than an illegal abortion" because whereas the angst of abortion "healed eventually, the suffering over having given up a child went on forever." Indeed, only months before, a study of six hundred women who'd relinquished children to adoption had found them "at risk for long-term physical, psychologic, and social repercussions." This Norma understood. "We're not animals," she told the journalist Monika Maeckle back in 1981. "We can't just have a litter and walk away." Yet Norma had walked away three times.

After the press conference, Parker submitted Norma's brief to a New Jersey court. He also issued a public call to women to submit their abortion stories to his website for his affidavit-collecting project, disseminating an instruction sheet with suggestions of what those women might have endured, from coercion to physical pain.

Parker then formed a branch of his foundation to find those women. He called it Operation Outcry. "The plan," Parker's colleague Goodman said, "is to present one million names." Norma McCorvey was the first.

Of course, Norma had not had an abortion. But Parker had her speak of PAS everywhere from Florida to London. Her appearances raised money and helped produce nearly four hundred affidavits, which the lawyer then submitted to the court in the case that Cassidy had brought, *Marie v. Whitman*.

The affidavits testified that abortion had caused the women lifelong trauma. "For a long time inability to hold or be near babies," wrote a woman named Shirley, who had had two abortions. "Severe depression," wrote another named Wendy, "especially in January, knowing my child would be another year older." They were searing testimonies, testimonies intended to change the law.

═══════

PARKER SPOKE OFTEN of God. If the law was his métier, God was his master. And the lawyer told of the catastrophes God would bring if *Roe*
remained law: natural disaster, terror attack, financial collapse. As
Parker later wrote: "It is my duty as a watchman on the wall (Ezekiel
33:6) to warn you and others of the coming judgment upon America."

Like Benham and Pavone before him, Parker also testified that God
Himself had directed him to work with Norma. Having found a scriptural basis for the collection of his affidavits—verses from Isaiah about
the sweeping away of lies—the lawyer told that he had been in the Dallas
airport, on his way home from meeting Norma, when God planted in
him that passage along with the idea to work with her.

The first sentence of Parker's bio now attested that Norma was
in his legal care. And though Pavone maintained his ties to Norma—
introducing her at a 2001 benefit at the Waldorf, having his organization
book her travel and talks at the start of 2002—Norma was with Parker
now. In June 2002, she was the keynote speaker at a Justice Foundation
dinner that attracted sponsors from Regal Cinemas to Taco Bell and
raised money for the continued collection of affidavits.

The submission of affidavits, however, did nothing to help the
plaintiff known as Donna Santa Marie. A New Jersey district court
dismissed her case, and the Third Circuit Court of Appeals upheld the
dismissal on Christmas Eve. Parker was undeterred. The centerpiece
of his work remained Norma. And courts of law were capable of mir-
acles; the Supreme Court had only just ruled that his fellow evangelical George W. Bush would become president. And so, in 2003, Parker
reintroduced Norma—and *Roe*—to the courts.

═══════

ROE WAS JUST WEEKS OLD WHEN, in February 1973, John Hill, the newly
elected attorney general of Texas, and others, requested that the Supreme
Court rehear it. The Court denied their requests. But now, thirty years
later, Parker hoped it might reconsider.

Deep within the Federal Rules of Civil Procedure lie the precon-
ditions of a do-over, an opportunity for a litigant to have the federal

courts "relieve" a prior decision. The court may do so, states Rule 60(b)
(5), when "applying [the decision] prospectively is no longer equitable."
As Parker, a former professor of civil procedure, later explained: "You
have to show that changes in legal and factual conditions make it no
longer just . . . to give the decision future application."

Parker wished to apply Rule 60 to *Roe*. Specifically, he wished to
argue that, three decades after its passage, three changed conditions
now rendered *Roe* unjust.

The first was a change in law. Only months before, Texas had signed
a bill which made it legal to surrender to the state a baby at birth. As
Parker put it: "A woman now has a feminist right to be separated from
her child." Similar "Baby Moses" laws were beginning to pass around
the country, and Parker reasoned that they represented a humane alternative to abortion, and thus argued for its legal end.

Parker contended that two additional factual changes argued for
vacating the decision in *Roe*. One was that, in the decades since the
ruling, science had come to definitively prove that human life begins at
fertilization. The other was that his pool of affidavits demonstrated that
abortion was a source of trauma for women, not relief.

Of course, neither of these alleged changes could be called fact.
They were the contentions of a pro-life advocate. But Rule 60 offered
Parker a way forward. On June 17, 2003, he and Norma announced to
a group of reporters in Dallas that they were filing a motion to have
Roe reheard.

The name of their case was *McCorvey v. Hill*—William Hill was the
Dallas County DA—and it argued that Norma's affidavit in *Roe* was
fraudulent. Pro-lifers were titillated. As Pat Buchanan wrote: "What if
Roe v. Wade was based on fraud, deceit and lies?"

It wasn't. (The only lie in Norma's 1970 affidavit was the claim that
she'd wanted an abortion for reasons other than simply not wanting a
child.) Indeed, as Norma later made clear, if there was a dubious affidavit, it was her new one, signed and notarized six days before.

Some of the affidavit's untruths were trifles: that Norma's second
child had been raised by its father, that Norma's childhood imaginary
friend Janie had inspired her pseudonym. Others were not. Norma
asserted falsely that she had helped to take patients' blood pressure,

and then held their hands as they endured painful abortions, in fetid and filthy clinics. (Both Benham and Pavone later acknowledged they knew this to be untrue. Parker insists that Norma's declarations about her role in the clinics was true, despite contemporaneous accounts to the contrary.) Then there was the lie at the heart of the affidavit, that Norma had not known the meaning of abortion when a pair of unscrupulous lawyers had turned her into Jane Roe.

Truth, however, was beside the point. (Parker's press release declared that "the link between abortion and breast cancer is now known.") What mattered to Parker was reopening Roe. Toward that end, he now submitted, along with Norma's brief, a thousand or so affidavits from women attesting that they had been hurt by abortion.

══

PARKER WAS NOT the first to try and sway a panel of judges with personal stories of abortion. Back in 1989, for example, in an amicus brief filed to the Supreme Court in Webster, nearly three thousand women had written of their abortions in the service of choice. The pro-choice used private disclosures to try and sway public opinion, too—from the 1972 debut issue of Ms. magazine, which included the names of fifty-three women who had had abortions, to the 2003 website "I'm Not Sorry," created coincidentally as Parker readied his case.

Research indicates that personal testimonies do influence opinion. Just one in four people, a study would show, react negatively when a woman confides she has had an abortion; a sizeable majority "respond with support and sympathy."

And yet, only the tiniest percentage of the 42 million legal abortions performed in the three decades since Roe had been talked about publicly. Fewer still had been seen; years later, a journalist would reflect that the only photo of an abortion she had ever seen was in the 1976 book Our Bodies, Ourselves. The stigma of abortion had only grown, a stigma so intense that in January 2003, NARAL, an organization devoted to its defense, dropped the word from its name.

Months later, Parker filed his suit. The pro-choice all but ignored it. NARAL president Kate Michelman called it a "sad anti-choice publicity stunt." The movement filed not a single brief defending *Roe*—a "stunning non-response," wrote Lynn Paltrow, a leading advocate for reproductive rights. Added Paltrow: "The pro-choice movement failed to appreciate how serious and strategic anti-choice activists are when they bring cases unlikely to win in the short term."

The court dismissed Parker's suit after just two days, on grounds that too much time had passed for *Roe* to be reopened. The Supreme Court decision, wrote judge David Godbey, "was certainly final in this litigation."

Parker appealed. Yes, years had passed since *Roe*. But, as one Harvard law professor noted, "the implication was that the period of delay corresponded to a period of traumatic repression." While waiting for the federal appeals court in New Orleans to rule, Parker sent his client abroad—to England and Ireland and Canada and Uruguay—to talk up both her case and his affidavits. The narrative of Norma now climaxed not, as before, in a plaintiffship or a baptism or a confirmation, but in the consecrated vision of a lawyer.

Not that Norma was at peace with Parker. Her case had made the lawyer someone of note in the pro-life world; Pat Buchanan compared him to Thurgood Marshall, a Christian TV network hired him to host a program called *Faces of Abortion*, and conservative power brokers from Dick and Betsy DeVos to the Covenant Foundation funded him. As with so many of her previous collaborators, Norma felt that Parker got more than he gave. She emailed him angry notes that he was a "user" who would no longer be her "mouth-peace." But always, after her outbursts, Norma cooled and the lawyer spoke for her again, asserting that his client was a vessel of God who wished only to overturn *Roe*.

THE PRO-LIFE HAD welcomed Norma with the promise that they cared for Norma, not just Jane Roe. As Robert Cooley, a pro-life activist in Connecticut, wrote to Benham two days after her baptism, it was "vital to be more jealous for her spiritual well being than for her public relations value to the movement." Nearly a decade later, there were indeed those who wanted nothing but her well-being. Karen Garnett, who'd accompanied Norma to DC while pregnant with her fifth child, saw to it that a Catholic pro-life group gave her a stipend of $500 a month. Father Robinson (who'd recommended that Garnett do so), buffered Norma with weekly Masses and daily notes, offering up to her unceasing prayer and pardon.

Norma was thankful. She sent the old priest poinsettias and bird food, updates on her ministry and health. Still, Robinson and Garnett were less friends than exemplars. When Norma needed to talk, she often turned, if not to Connie, then to Daniel Vinzant, the former Baptist pastor who'd helped bring her into the Catholic church.

Vinzant had become Catholic two days before Norma. His conversion had exacted a price; he soon lost his pulpit and then his wife. The shame of impending divorce forced Vinzant from his beloved Waco. He had moved to Dallas, in January 2000, with his two teenage sons, when back home, on October 14, a car crash killed his daughter.

Jesus was a comfort to Vinzant in his grief. So was Norma. She set in his daughter's casket, he recalls, "a little clutch purse filled with a rosary and a lipstick." She, alone among his friends, left unchallenged his contention that while he would soon be civilly divorced, he remained religiously married. And she and Connie invited Vinzant and his sons for Thanksgiving—and most of the holidays after that, too. "She was alone. We were alone," says Vinzant. "I was always comfortable with Norma and Connie because I was never judged."

In turn, Vinzant didn't judge Norma. "I just loved," he says. He had come to see that life could be lived in more than one way. In the coming years, he and Norma would share a hundred or more Sundays, passing them at Mass and at an Olive Garden and in his used Nissan singing along with Creedence and Chicago and the Eagles. They talked too. Says Vinzant: "pure gossip."

———

IN SEPTEMBER 2004, the federal appeals court in New Orleans affirmed the dismissal of McCorvey v. Hill. Its three judges agreed that too much time had passed to reopen Roe. But one of them, a Reagan appointee named Edith Jones, lamented that fact, writing of Roe's "perverse result" and of her hope that the Supreme Court would revisit it. "Although McCorvey has no 'live' legal controversy," she wrote, "the serious and substantial evidence she offered could have generated an important debate over factual premises that underlay *Roe*."

Foremost among that evidence, wrote Jones, were Parker's affidavits, testimony to the potential long-lasting psychological toll of abortion. Parker was desperate to introduce those affidavits to the Supreme Court. And in January 2005, he and Norma stood on the dais at yet another March for Life with news to share. Nellie Gray, who had founded the march in 1974, on the first anniversary of *Roe*, walked to the lectern to introduce them.

Gray was eighty, a little woman with a large pouf of dyed brown hair over her forehead. She had been born in Texas in 1924, and become a committed Catholic at eighteen. She had first learned of abortion in the pages of *The Cardinal*, a 1950 novel in which a doctor decides to let a woman die in delivery rather than abort her child with a craniotomy. In Gray's memory, however, the baby died, and she soon opposed abortion absolutely; "No exceptions, no compromise," she said. After *Roe* became law, Gray, who was single and had no children, left her job as a lawyer in the Department of Labor to fight abortion full-time. Thirty-two years later, her annual march anchored the fight on *Roe*. She turned to Norma and her lawyer.

"They are trying to overturn [*Roe*]," said Gray, wrapped in a blood-red scarf and shearling. "This is Ms. Norma! Ms. Norma McCorvey of *Roe v. Wade*!"

Norma stepped to the microphone and told her audience that only one week before, her lawyer had petitioned the Court to hear her case. Standing to her right, Parker clapped wildly.

One month later, however, the Supreme Court denied certiorari; *Roe* would remain the law.

Parker was undeterred. The feminist poet Muriel Rukeyser famously wrote that "if one woman told the truth about her life . . . the world would split open." And Parker saw what few others did—that his affidavits could yet provide the legal means, as the activist David Reardon wrote, to "change the abortion debate so that we are arguing with our opponents on their own turf, on the issue of defending the interests of women."

Months later, Congress cited Parker's affidavits as evidence about PAS in a report on House Bill 1233, a proposed ban on abortions in South Dakota. When abortion returned to the Supreme Court with the 2007 case of *Gonzales v. Carhart*, a case concerning a federal ban against a method of late-term abortion, the justice at its center cited PAS in his decision.

"While we find no reliable data to measure the phenomenon," Justice Anthony Kennedy wrote in explaining why the Court had upheld that abortion ban by a 5–4 vote, "it seems unexceptionable to conclude that some women come to regret their choice to abort. . . . Severe depression and loss of self-esteem can follow."

It was a remarkable opinion. Ever since *Roe*, the pro-life argument against abortion had focused on the fetus. It had now shifted to the woman. Parker had helped to bring that shift about, and Justice Kennedy cited a Parker amicus brief in his opinion. In so doing, the justice legitimated both Parker and PAS as never before.

The court's new rationale for banning abortion, wrote Linda Greenhouse in the *New York Times*, "was a development that stunned abortion rights advocates and that represents a major departure from how the court has framed the abortion issue for the past 34 years." Added the Yale law professor Reva Siegel: "The [Operation] Outcry affidavits express the new rallying cry of the antiabortion movement."

It was Norma whom Parker had designated the lead plaintiff of that operation, Norma he had ridden to the high court. Though her lingering torment owed not to abortion but to its unavailability, Norma now stood—for the second time—at the vanguard of a legal movement.

As the law professor Mary Ziegler later wrote: "Norma McCorvey is patient zero in this narrative—the first victim of abortion rights."

Chapter 28

onzales v. Carhart made clear, in 2007, that institutional opposition to abortion would henceforth center not only on the fetus
but on the ostensible harm abortion did women. It was also evidence of the renewed pro-life focus on third-trimester abortion.

Late-term abortion had rallied the movement before. Back in 1991,
a six-week protest of Dr. George Tiller—the most prominent provider
of third-trimester abortion in the country—had revitalized Operation
Rescue. Before that, the 1975 trial of Kenneth Edelin, the medical resident who'd aborted a fetus in its sixth month, had made real the questions of life and viability that *Roe* had only considered. The indictment
of Edelin had pointed a way forward for the pro-life movement, suggesting that public discomfort with third-trimester abortion might one
day be harnessed to great effect. So, now, it was—*Gonzales v. Carhart*,
as history professor Johanna Schoen wrote, "the logical culmination"
of *Edelin*. Where *Edelin* had marked the first indictment of a doctor for
performing a legal abortion, *Carhart* marked the first approved ban of
an abortion procedure. And like so much that was important in the
pro-life movement, that culmination owed a debt to Mildred Jefferson,
whom *Edelin*'s prosecutors had designated their first witness.

MILDRED WAS A PRO-LIFE star back then, elected president of the National
Right to Life Committee only months after the 1975 trial. But three

years later, she was ousted as president and lost her place on the board
as well. A decade after that, in the fall of 1989, when the NRLC's former
lobbyist Thea Rossi Barron passed along the suggestion of Congressman Henry Hyde that the committee pay Mildred $75,000 annually to
be a roving pro-life emissary, its executive director did not even respond.
And with Reagan gone from the White House, Mildred's chief connection to the pro-life movement was the tiny outfit in Tulsa that she and
a direct mail developer had run for a decade.

The nonprofit kept busy. There were robocalls, Jefferson telling
listeners that in the course of the call "ten babies will die" but that (for
twenty-five dollars a month) "you as a committed Christian" can do
something about it. There were TV commercials, a closeup of a thumb-
sucking fetus giving way (as the thump of a heartbeat slowed) to a 900
number and a run of rhetorical questions: "If he is not a child, why is he
growing?" "If he is not a human being, what kind of being is he?" "If he
is a living, human child, why is it legal to kill him?" There was a booklet, "Abortion: Have We the Right?," which Jefferson had donors buy
from the nonprofit for high school libraries. And there were mailings,
cards printed with questions and answers on issues from viability and
adoption to rape and incest. "Only rarely does pregnancy result from
rape or incest," Jefferson wrote, citing a ten-year study conducted by the
Presbyterian Journal. "Rape and incest as reasons for legalizing abortion
are nothing more than emotional arguments to which some people are
unfortunately sensitive."

THE CALENDAR TURNED TO 1990. Twenty years had passed since Jefferson first volunteered her thoughts on abortion, lamenting at that
medical society meeting that the AMA had turned pro-choice. Now
sixty-three years old, she still made herself heard—issuing statements and running for office, a fourth go at Ted Kennedy, a fourth
opportunity to expound in newsprint on her future plans (two
Senate terms, she said) and the ways in which legal abortion had
gutted the black community.

There were many among the pro-life who decried the particular
effects of abortion on African Americans. Mildred, in the words of one

observer, was their "matriarch." The great-granddaughter of slaves, she cast *Roe*, as a fellow activist had put it years before, as just another tool of the white man "to limit our population by inducing us to abort our unborn children."

Such arguments were controversial. (Blackmun himself had written in *Roe* that "racial overtones tend to complicate and not to simplify the problem.") But they were understandable, too, because the birth control movement bore the indelible stain of eugenics.

━━━━

THE AIM OF BIRTH CONTROL is to separate sex from procreation. In that separation, the founder of the birth control movement saw the emancipation of women. Wrote Margaret Sanger in 1914: "Enforced motherhood is the most complete denial of a woman's right to life and liberty."

Feminism alone, however, did not fuel the fight for legal contraception. Fears of overpopulation, and of the propagation of the poor and the unsound, did too. The feminist Sanger was thus also a eugenicist, part of a movement that desired to better the human gene pool by increasing or decreasing certain populations.

The British polymath Francis Galton coined the term eugenics in 1883 from the Greek for "well-born." His belief in selective breeding led others—among them captains of industry, academics and politicians—to call for selective sterilization. "Society," the former president Theodore Roosevelt wrote in 1913, "has no business to permit degenerates to reproduce their kind."

Six years before Roosevelt weighed in, Indiana became the first state in the country to make sterilization law, mandating the sterilization of "criminals, idiots, imbeciles and rapists." Two dozen states followed over the next twenty years. In 1927, the Supreme Court, by an 8–1 vote, declared sterilization constitutional in the case of *Buck v. Bell*. "It is better for all the world if, instead of waiting to execute degenerate offspring for crime or to let them starve for their imbecility, society can prevent those who are manifestly unfit from continuing their kind," wrote Justice Oliver Wendell Holmes. "The principle that sustains compulsory vaccination is broad enough to cover cutting the Fallopian tubes."

The Nazis would help to curb the U.S. appetite for sterilization. It didn't matter that before the war, American eugenicists had aided their German counterparts (so much so that, in 1936, Heidelberg University granted the U.S. eugenicist Harry Laughlin an honorary degree). Or that after the war, as Professor Paul Lombardo notes, American doctors would continue to forcibly sterilize women "in the silence of mental hospitals." (By 1963, upwards of sixty-five thousand American women would be robbed of the ability to bear children.) Germany had put sterilization to ghastly use and thus stigmatized it. In his defense at Nuremberg, Karl Brandt, the Nazi chief medical officer, cited the Holmes opinion in *Buck v. Bell*.

The Nazi party, however, had not yet been formed when, in 1919, Sanger proudly noted that eugenics was in step with birth control, both movements, she wrote, "seeking to assist the race toward the elimination of the unfit."

Sanger identified groups that she felt ought to be sterilized: "the feeble-minded, the insane and syphilitic." She did not speak of race. As the author Dorothy Roberts observed: "Sanger did not tie fitness for reproduction to any particular ethnic group." Still, she traded in a theory that did; eugenics was, Roberts noted, "fed, nurtured, and sustained by racism." Indeed, there were many black women who went to a doctor for one medical procedure only to receive a hysterectomy, among them the future civil rights activist Fannie Lou Hamer who, in 1961, went to North Sunflower County Hospital in Ruleville, Mississippi, to have a small uterine tumor removed. "I would say," recalled Hamer, "about six out of the ten Negro women that go to the hospital are sterilized with the tubes tied."

Of course, medical mistreatment of black Americans extended back at least a century, from the experimental surgeries of Dr. James Marion Sims on enslaved women to the appropriation of black bodies for use in medical training. And in 1932, five years after *Buck v. Bell*, the Public Health Service began its notorious study of syphilis in Tuskegee, Alabama, knowingly withholding treatment from black men for decades until they died. Mindful that the black community had reason to distrust the white medical establishment—and not long after a federal court ruled, in 1936, that doctors could provide contraception for medical purposes—Sanger formed what she called the Negro Project, enlisting black ministers to speak well of her clinics.

"We do not want word to go out that we want to exterminate the Negro population," Sanger wrote in 1939, "and the minister is the man who can straighten out that idea if it ever occurs to any of their more rebellious members."

Sanger also enlisted to her cause black intellectual leaders, among them W. E. B. DuBois, founder of the National Association for the Advancement of Colored People. Like Sanger, he believed in eugenics (if not sterilization). "The mass of ignorant Negroes still breed carelessly and disastrously," wrote DuBois, "so that the increase among Negroes, even more than the increase among whites, is from that portion of the population least intelligent and fit."

Birth control could thus be used to cull as much as to empower. And as the clinics that Sanger planted in black neighborhoods took root—and her American Birth Control League became in 1942 Planned Parenthood—the black community came to distrust not only birth control but its white purveyors. Come 1954, a black pathologist in Chicago named Julian Lewis wrote that birth control, and Planned Parenthood in particular, was leading the black community toward "race suicide."

The charge took, echoed by all from Langston Hughes to Dick Gregory to a group of black nationalist organizations that in 1967 passed a resolution calling birth control "black genocide." Five years later, a social worker in Minneapolis named Erma Craven asserted in a much-cited essay "that the unborn Black baby is the real object of many abortionists." She added: "The whole mess adds up to blatant genocide." Much of the black community agreed; a poll conducted in 1973 by two black professors in Massachusetts found that 39 percent of black Americans believed that "birth control programs are a plot to eliminate blacks."

The Brooklyn-based congresswoman Shirley Chisholm dismissed such talk as "male rhetoric, for male ears." The great majority of black women approved of birth control—80 percent of black women in Chicago, for example, in 1970. Still, a conspiracy had entered the zeitgeist. And for good reason. "Negroes don't want children they can't take care of," explained a black social worker in upstate New York named

Urelia Brown, "but we are afraid to trust you when your offered help has so often turned out to be exploitation."

———

IF THE PREVENTION of pregnancy had begotten talk of genocide, it was no surprise that the termination of pregnancy would, too. Black distrust of *Roe* was fanned by the alarming fact that women of color remained far more likely than white women to die from illegal abortions—twelve times more likely in the span that bookended *Roe*, from 1972 to 1974.

Still, black women continued to have abortions. They did so at an increasing rate that by 1975 was almost triple that of white women, a discrepancy that Mildred Jefferson, the beaming black face of the pro-life movement, regularly pointed to as evidence of an ongoing genocide. "The people who are fewer," she told the press, "will disappear faster."

The melding of *Roe* and race was of increasing political importance. In the 1980s, the National Organization of Women created a "Women of Color Program," the NRLC "Black Americans for Life." Long after she lost her job atop the NRLC, Mildred continued to speak about race and abortion, at a 1985 symposium, for example, during Black History Month in Boston.

Mildred had never made an issue of her own ethnicity. ("I refuse to represent any kind of differentiation," she would later say.) She said that race, like all accidents of birth, was in no way determinative; one simply achieved what one deserved.

But Mildred had not achieved what she'd deserved. The life in surgery she'd worked toward had run aground on racism and misogyny so overt that its perpetrators spoke freely of it to the FBI. Still, as her friend Ruth Marin recalled to the bureau, the only "bitterness" Mildred expressed was aimed at black groups that expressed bitterness, Mildred "feeling that in the United States, anything can be attained through the Democratic process."

But where had that process gotten her? Despite her talk of self-determination, Mildred was powerless against the prejudices of the medical establishment. The pro-life establishment, meantime, had left her behind. Her attempt at a third career had failed when she'd been unable yet again, in her fourth bid for the Senate, to even get on the ballot. In February 1990, Mildred could remain quiet no longer, telling the *Boston Globe* that her candidacy had been done in by a prejudiced press, by "a political apartheid based on race, sex and bank account."

Mildred had snapped. Never before had she publicly said such things. She would not do so again; she quickly resumed her attacks on the very policies and movements that might have helped her as a poor black woman. "Social programs are killing more people than they help," she wrote in the *Chicago Tribune* months later. As for feminism, she added, "it gives the insecure woman the idea that to establish confidence and power, she has to be willing to destroy her nurturing and caring instincts."

———————

MILDRED HAD LONG resisted efforts to level the playing field between the sexes. A former Harvard classmate recalled that, decades after their graduation, Mildred had dismissed as "self-indulgent" efforts to lift restrictions on the women's dorms at Harvard. Mildred remained staunchly traditional about gender roles in marriage, too. "I like someone else to carry my luggage in airports and take care of the checkbook," she told a reporter. "I like being protected. I consider it a step down to equality."

Still, when in 1974 equality seemed on the verge of becoming law—the Equal Rights Amendment awaiting ratification after its passage by Congress—Mildred told the Senate that she supported "the principle" of the ERA.

Months later, the conservative crusader Phyllis Schlafly declared on the front page of her newsletter that "ERA means abortion." It did not matter that many first-wave feminists had strongly opposed abortion, among them the suffragettes Susan B. Anthony and Victoria Woodhull. Schlafly ignited a movement that defeated the proposed amendment. In so doing, she "unearthed the political gold of misogyny," as former Republican strategist Tanya Melich put it, politicizing women's rights as others had abortion. As the historian Jill Lepore later observed: "These two issues would together produce the greatest cleavage in American politics since the debate over slavery."

Mildred came quickly to denounce feminism almost as fervently as she did abortion. She wrote in 1977 that feminists lived in "a gray world, without love, romance, courtesy and charm." The next year, she labeled them "terrorists." It was no wonder. Feminism wished to open up worlds to women beyond motherhood. And like the dictatorship Margaret Atwood imagined in *The Handmaid's Tale*, Mildred had come to see childbearing, as she later told the historian Jennifer Donnally, as "the essence and reasons we exist as female human beings."

That Mildred had not borne children was thus an embarrassment; unlike 84 percent of U.S. women, she had not, as she saw it, fulfilled her reason for being. Friends wondered why. "I wanted to ask her so many times," recalls Russell Gary Heikkila, an actor turned pastor. The rumor, says Anne Fox, a friend from Massachusetts Citizens for Life, was that Mildred had felt that children would impede her work. A decade after her divorce, Mildred did not tell that she'd *chosen* not to have children. She said, recalls the pro-life leader Judie Brown, that she'd been unable to. To speak otherwise, says Brown, "would have contradicted everything she said in her speeches."

Thus did Mildred continue to present herself as someone she was not. And in 1993, Dr. Joseph Stanton, a pro-life leader in Massachusetts, wrote to Mildred that one particular untruth—that she was a doctor on faculty at Boston University Medical Center—threatened to bring shame upon all the movement. He suggested that she put the word "formerly" before those medical positions she alleged she held.

It was Stanton who—at that 1967 medical society meeting—had first spoken to Mildred about the threat of legalized abortion. He had rejoiced when she'd joined his fight. But divisions over strategy in the years since had turned personal. "It is all too obvious," he wrote to Mildred unkindly, "that you have problems, that the world-beater image of the glory days of the NRLC presidency have faded."

Mildred was not one to accept a rebuke. The next fall, at a conference in Houston of black conservatives, she identified herself, as always, as a working surgeon. She was not delusional. She knew that she was neither a practicing surgeon nor on staff at BU. But reality was not her guide. "I do what I do for a sense of principle," she once said, "like Don Quixote."

It had long been objectionable to Mildred that she, a woman of principle, should be subject to the responsibilities of everyday life. She had never quite seen fit, for example, to pay monies she owed—whether rent on Beacon Street or a mortgage on Harrison Avenue or taxes in Roxbury. She had thus lost her apartment and her office and her family home. Other attempts at renting had ended in arrears. Having moved from Roxbury to Cambridge in 1988, she was, by 1995, in debt—down $9,071 in rent and maintenance.

Back in 1978, Mildred had inherited from her mother some seven acres of her native Panola County, and with it the modest proceeds of its drilling for oil and gas. The money had been enough to cover some of her rent. But the payments had dwindled, and Mildred, sixty-eight years old, turned for help to James Bothell, her partner in Tulsa. The local paper had recently written of his success in parsing public data with computers, and he quickly raised what Mildred needed. The doctor wrote her landlord a check for the full amount she owed, money payable from the "Right to Life Crusade Operating Account."

———

MILDRED TOLD ALMOST NO ONE where she lived. Instead, she instructed her fleet of pro-life drivers to drop her off a block or two away from the small brick building off Inman Square where, on the second floor at 1264 Cambridge Street, paper rubble filled the four rooms of her home.

Mildred walked a lot, too—to the handful of P.O. boxes she rented, to the health food store, to her hair salon in Roxbury. Always, she carried an umbrella and a whistle—for protection, she said. Always, she walked on the shady side of the street, a scarf and a hat on her head, weights around her ankles; she was 109 pounds and wished to stay fit.

The doctor did not go for medical checkups. She'd come to believe in holistic medicine, and ate daily rations of vitamins and almonds. She'd sworn off hospitals, too. A speech to the John Birch Society offered a clue as to why. "I don't like," she said, "being so much under someone else's control."

That same woman sanctioned no abortion ever. She was thus outside the pro-life mainstream; in 1996, Mildred was not among the signatories of a much-discussed statement on abortion and sexual mores. Still, her friend Judie Brown, who shared her extreme views, invited Mildred the next year to a convention in Tampa along with other pro-life leaders: Jerry Fallwell, Flip Benham, Norma McCorvey.

The pro-life movement could celebrate real progress. The annual number of legal abortions performed in the U.S. was steadily dropping, from a high of roughly 1.6 million in 1988 to roughly 1.3 million a decade later. Still, legal abortion was no closer to extinction. The writer Molly Ivins had written in 1973 that abortion was "somewhat more serious than getting your ears pierced." A quarter-century later, it was even safer, the number of deaths per 100,000 legal abortions having dropped from 2.1 in the five years after *Roe* to 0.5. It was easier to have one, too; by 2000, pregnancies up to ten weeks along could be ended with just a few pills.

Mildred carried on with her routines—the daily roundup of her mail, the weekly hair appointments, the monthly meetings of Massachusetts Citizens for Life. She slept just three hours out of twenty-four and kept the TV news on, the better to flag bias and issue the statements on abortion that she linked to nearly every major current event. (*Roe*, she declared, was "more devastating to the U.S. future" than 9/11.) The work was all-consuming. One day, she paused to reflect upon its costs. "THINGS THAT I HAVE TO DO THAT I DO NOT LIKE TO DO TO FIGHT FOR LIFE," she wrote in a spiral notebook. The list that followed was long: "ASK FOR MONEY, LIVE IN EXILE FROM MY USUAL LIFE, ABANDON THE ARTS, SCRATCH SKIING, FORGO FASHION, RESTRICT MY PERSONAL FREEDOM . . ."

Control and freedom. These were what Mildred craved for herself but crusaded to deny others. Having chosen not to have a child, she desired to obligate every potential birth.

Mildred lamented the personal cost of her crusade. But at one time, it had made her a star—the third most admired conservative woman in America in 1981, according to *Conservative Digest*. Twenty-eight colleges had granted her honorary degrees. And in 2002, President George W. Bush nominated her for a position on a new committee aiming to protect human subjects (fetuses included) from medical research.

But if Mildred was celebrated, she remained hidden. When, now, she appeared in *African American Lives*, a reference book edited by the Harvard professors Henry Louis Gates, Jr., and Evelyn Brooks Higginbotham, her bio conceded that she remained out of reach. "Many aspects of her life," it noted, "including her mother's name and her early history, are difficult to determine, as she vigorously guards her privacy."

———

MILDRED TRIED to make sense of her hoarding. Much of the paper that clotted her home concerned abortion, and she began telling people that she was amassing an archive. "She wanted to keep everything ever written about *Roe v. Wade*," recalls Kathleen Bothell, whose husband ran her Tulsa nonprofit. She wished to write about it, too, and in 2003 she told a pro-life organization in DC that she had taken leave from medicine to write a book. Soon after, she faxed another organization that she was "on self-assigned sabbatical to finish four books."

Mildred was not on sabbatical. And she was not writing one book, let alone four. She wrote, in fact, little more than comments on her own bio. Beside the mention on her CV, for example, that she was "the first Negro woman" to graduate from Harvard Medical School, Mildred inserted mention of her fierce opposition to affirmative action, which fated its recipients, she wrote, "to unending intellectual bondage."

There was no evidence that Mildred had been so enslaved. If she had been helped through medical school by a scholarship established to promote "American ideals," the medical establishment had stonewalled her career precisely because she was a black woman. Mildred did not address that fact in her bio—the eternity she'd been made to wait for her board certification. (Her CV noted only that she'd "served the equivalent of three complete general surgical residencies.") Now that her fight against abortion was all but behind her, she was still looking for something else to do.

Mildred had aspired not only to elected office, but also, she told the press, to own a chain of newspapers or be the dean of a medical school. Such heights, however, were no more within reach than the books she claimed to be writing. So, in 2003, Mildred, seventy-six years old, made it known that she wished to host the weekly cable TV show that her chapter of Massachusetts Citizens for Life was starting. Recalls the MCFL chapter chair, Brendan O'Connell: "She was very eager."

Mildred was unyielding in debate; a Harvard professor named

Malkah Notman had observed that she didn't so much listen to her opponents as repeat her own opinion over and over again. Mildred had a knack for leveling the outrageous charge; she would soon insinuate that Sarah Weddington—"a very impressive looking gal"—had seduced the members of the *Roe* majority. ("Those seven men who signed the majority opinion would have given her anything she asked for," said Mildred.) The MCFL television show, however, would have pro-life guests and a pro-life audience. And that October, Mildred and O'Connell, a warm Boston native of forty-nine, became co-hosts of *Life Matters*.

———

MILDRED'S LANDLORD WAS CONCERNED. A plumber who had fixed a broken pipe in her apartment had alerted him to her hoarding. She had refused to allow his management company to enter her apartment. And that same autumn of 2003, the landlord wrote to Mildred that there were city officials who needed to assess whether her apartment was safe.

It wasn't; not only was there was no egress, but the floor might collapse under all that weight. That much was clear when a housing inspector from the Cambridge Inspectional Services Department knocked on her door. "The newspapers were piled up to my chest," recalls Dusty Maguire. "There were pathways between them."

Maguire told Mildred that she needed to discard the papers. But, recalls Maguire, "she said, 'This is my research. I can't get rid of it.'" In 2004, a lawyer representing Cambridge filed a complaint alleging that Mildred was in violation of the State Sanitary Code. Mildred refused to clean her apartment, and her trial was set for October 2005.

Mildred got a lawyer, a friend she knew from MCFL named Thomas Harvey. He told the court that she needed time, and the judge postponed her trial until December—and then again, at Harvey's request, until February and September and November and February and May and June and July and September, when, late in the summer of 2007, Harvey left the law for a seminary and handed his client off to another MCFL lawyer, Mildred's old acquaintance Philip Moran.

Moran accompanied Mildred to Cambridge District Court, conferring in the lobby with the judge, the building inspector and the opposing attorney. "We all came to the conclusion," says Moran, "that she was a wonderful woman who needed help." She also needed to clean her apartment. When still she refused, an exasperated Moran handed her off in November to another lawyer named Larry Washburn, who asked the judge for yet more time. The judge complied.

Mildred's Tulsa crusade continued to pay her rent, a monthly bill that now rose by $350 to just shy of $2,000. Friends footed smaller bills for her, too—her medical society dues, tanks of gas, the salads she ate at the S & S Deli, where an older waitress named Patsy always sent Mildred home with a day-old bagel and any mail she had had sent to the deli. Says the owner, Amy Baum: "We thought she was homeless."

Mildred lived just down the block. But her home was less her apartment than the local MCFL office where, in a former candy factory in Boston, she still met monthly with her friends. Abortion was their bond. But abortion was not why they sent her home from meetings with dinner, or helped her fend off eviction, or showed up in their sedans those hundreds of times Mildred called from the airport or the state-house or the funeral of some fellow pro-lifer to say she needed a ride. They did so because they loved her. Still, they never elected her president of their chapter—though she ran every year—until 2007, when she ran unopposed. The board groaned. "The only consolation I have with her election to the Presidency," wrote Moran, "is that there is so little money for her to squander."

Mildred wasn't up to the job. She was eighty and fell asleep during the meetings she was supposed to run. In 2008, her friend Anne Fox unseated her. Mildred was gracious. She still had her TV show—those twenty-five minutes of every week when the Boston Neighborhood Network beamed her out into a Catholic city.

Life Matters was the peak of her week. Prim and patriotic in her navy suits and white hats, a scarf of red, white and blue around her neck, Mildred spoke of informed consent, abortifacients, stem-cell research, Supreme Court nominees. But she also exasperated her co-host. "She wasn't interviewing the guests," says O'Connell. "It was all about Mildred."

In early 2008, O'Connell told the MCFL board that he no longer wanted to work with Mildred. After a shouting match, the board reached a compromise: O'Connell would keep the name and the rights to the show, and they would help Mildred start a new one. So they did, *Vital Concerns* debuting one year later, a theme of drum and trumpet introducing the doctor.

Mildred smiled widely that first broadcast, her brown skin, rubbed for years with lanolin, radiant in the studio light. She was, on that February afternoon in 2009, where she wished to be. After twenty-five minutes with her guest, a mother of nine who chaired the state chapter of Democrats for Life, Mildred signed off, declaring into her lavalier mic, as she would after every show, that to fight for life was to care for "the whole family of man." Mildred was still aglow when a friend from MCFL drove her home.

His name was John Curry. He was a post office custodian and former paratrooper who had come north from West Virginia in 1978. He'd been driving Mildred ever since, and she was comfortable beside him, letting him call her "Doc," singing with him the music they both loved: Conway Twitty, Merle Haggard, Elvis. His girlfriend, Marie O'Donnell, had also been driving Mildred for decades, and often joined her and John on their drives to the studio. Always, Mildred watched from her window for their Lincoln before heading down to meet them in the lot behind the S & S Deli.

———

MILDRED NO LONGER walked much. Her balance was off and her eyesight was failing and she had dental issues. Still, her ankle weights and almonds—along with her friends and her Tulsa crusade—had gotten her this far. So had God. Mildred belonged to no church, but was sustained by absolute belief; "no nuances," says Anne Fox. Everything was ordained—even the piles of paper that had led to her standoff with the city of Cambridge.

On May 13, 2009, after nearly four years of continuances, the court finally ruled in the case of *Commonwealth v. Mildred Jefferson.* Judge Michele Hogan ordered the city of Cambridge to move Mildred's stuff into a storage unit at her expense.

Mildred was bereft. She would have to part from her papers. But then something unforeseen happened: the city of Cambridge balked.

"I went to Public Works," recalls the housing inspector Dusty Maguire. "They said, 'Beat it. It's not our job.'" The papers stayed put.

Mildred still wanted to use her papers to author a narrative of the pro-life fight. But she was eighty-three and had not yet begun to write. In 2010, she welcomed the chance instead to speak of her impact on the movement, sitting down with a doctoral student in a diner in Porter Square. "I don't think anyone else could have done what I did," she told Jennifer Donnally.

If Mildred was proud, she was tired, too; sipping from a glass of hot water, she strained to speak over the chatter and clatter of diners and dishes. Still, she remained vigilant, fending off unwanted topics as always she had, telling Donnally on this late September day that her ex-husband—seventy-four and spry—was dead. She added that she would be, too, were it not for those in the grassroots who had kept her alive—"literally, literally, literally."

———

EIGHTEEN DAYS LATER, on October 7, Curry and O'Donnell drove Mildred to the television studio. She looked ill. Her eyes were puffy, her face and legs swollen. Her voice was throaty. She was cold.

Curry parked and the three friends walked to the set. Mildred kept her coat on and skipped her usual powders and creams. She was uncomfortable and did not sit. But as she leaned back onto the edge of her chair, and her theme of drum and trumpet introduced her along with a pro-life friend and a former Texas congressman, Mildred was at peace, a dying woman speaking into a camera in defense of the unborn. She chose, on this day, to speak of the past, of the influence she'd been able to exert on the pro-life movement, having come north, she said, with her "genes from the plains."

Mildred was in the car heading back to Cambridge when her friends said that they wished to drive her to Mount Auburn Hospital. Mildred refused. "There is nothing dignified, there is nothing kind," she'd said on air only months before, "about dying neglected behind a hospital door—or any other door." Mildred wanted to go home—or as close to home as she would allow them. Curry and O'Donnell obeyed. They would, they said, call her over the coming days, and they did—on Friday and Saturday and Sunday. They called on Monday, too, and Mildred told them that she'd fallen on the street but had been helped home. She said that she might soon need them to take her to a dentist. But then, she didn't call. When Curry and O'Donnell returned the following Thursday to pick her up in the S & S lot and drive her to her show, she wasn't there.

A few years before, Curry had learned where Mildred lived, when she asked him to examine the pipes in her cellar. He now rang her door-bell at 1264 Cambridge. There was no answer. The neighbors hadn't seen her. So Curry and O'Donnell called her landlord, who said that the building inspector had seen her the previous day. But Curry and O'Donnell were skeptical and called the police, who said they had to wait a few days before entering her home.

Two days later, Curry and O'Donnell returned to Mildred's build-ing with a couple of police officers and firemen. They rang the door-bell, but there was no answer. The firemen jimmied the door open and brought Mildred down on a stretcher, her tiny body in a bag beneath a sheet. Hours later, it fell to Anne Fox to identify her friend. Mildred, she says, was dry and withered—"like a leaf."

———

IN THE END, the legacy of Dr. Mildred Fay Jefferson was both the political might of the pro-life movement and the political divide in the country that that movement helped to deepen. Mildred was also, of course, the first black woman to graduate Harvard Medical School. All of her obitu-aries trumpeted that fact, but none noted that it was prejudice that had redirected her from surgery to abortion.

Mildred had found salvation in the pro-life fight. It had landed her atop a movement that prized not only her gifts but her biography. (Mich-igan senator Robert Griffin commented that the movement could not have fashioned a more perfect spokesperson: "a beautiful, articulate, educated, black woman, a surgeon, and not even a Catholic, but a Meth-odist.") More, her fight had given her the penitential opportunity to counter her decision not to have a child, Mildred pillorying those who would, as she famously put it, winnow the population to "the perfect, the privileged and the planned."

Mildred left behind no heir, and no will. Three of her MCFL friends settled her affairs. They had her cremated and flew her ashes home to a cousin in Texas. The great swells of her paper remains they traded to Harvard in exchange for the payment of a few months of overdue rent.

It took months to process those remains, to convert into 10.09 linear feet in the Schlesinger Library the "books, papers, periodicals, newspapers, treatises, and personal memorabilia" that had, in the words of her divorce, made her home all but uninhabitable. Here was a life.

It could not be known exactly how Mildred died. The medical examiner labeled heart disease the probable cause, arrhythmia following a hardening of her arteries. But the police surmised that she'd fallen trying to leave; she had been found at the cluttered foot of her door. And thus did Mildred come to an end as sad as it was apt, enveloped by the written record of her forty-year fight for the unborn.

Chapter 29

Curtis Boyd stood in a chandeliered conference room before some four hundred people. It was the spring of 1990, and the crowd of doctors and clinic workers and administrators had gathered at an Atlanta hotel for the annual conference of the National Abortion Federation. Having discussed dilators and bulletproof glass, the crowd readied to grant Boyd its highest award.

The doctor was worthy of it. Neither the risk of jail before *Roe*, nor the rise of physical threats after it, had stopped him from performing abortions; when, a few months hence, protestors would burst into his clinic and chain themselves to furniture, Boyd simply rescheduled his appointments for the next day. Abortion was his all. Since performing his very first in 1967, blindly moving a curette about a uterus to end a pregnancy not more than ten weeks along, he had devoted himself to bettering his technique even as he forged ever later into pregnancy, moving from curettes to forceps, from ten weeks to twenty-four, from the first trimester to the cusp of viability.

Skilled as Boyd was, it was neither his technique nor his having performed abortion when it was illegal that most defined him as a provider. Nor was it his contributions regarding pain management, or counseling, or the establishment of clinic standards. It was, rather, his complete impenitence about his work. As Boyd saw it, abortion was not a necessary evil; it was, as he'd testified to a House panel only months before, "a good and moral choice." He would soon repeat those words verbatim three times in a law review article. The thought was central to his being.

It was also radical, out of step with much of the pro-choice movement, out of step even with many of his fellow providers. "I don't like doing abortions any more than women like having them," Henry Eisenberg, a doctor in Syracuse, wrote two years before. "I am, I know, presiding over a tragic moment in my patient's life."

Most abortion providers fell somewhere between Eisenberg and Boyd, between abortion as tragedy and unmitigated good. They felt, as President Clinton would soon put it, that abortion ought not only to be safe and legal but "rare." Among that majority was Mildred Hanson, the trailblazing gynecologist who'd taught Boyd how to use laminaria to dilate a cervix and who sat now in his audience at the Atlanta hotel. "I have often paused and thought about what I'm doing," she reflected years later. "Is this the right thing to do? Is this ethical?" She added: "I think that all of us who do abortions go through that same ethical soul-searching process."

Boyd had gone through it too. In the mid-1980s, he had found himself thinking about the fetus—mindful as never before, he says, that it had "the potential to become a person."

Dilation and evacuation—the procedure Boyd had helped to pioneer—had led him to crisis. For D & E was as grim as it was safe. "There is no possibility of denying an act of destruction," said Dr. Warren Hern of the procedure at a 1978 meeting of Planned Parenthood physicians. "It is before one's eyes. The sensations of dismemberment flow through the forceps like an electric current." The doctor, one of the fathers of the field, noted that "significant emotional reactions of medical and counseling staff tend to accompany this procedure." Michael Freiman, for example, a doctor in St. Louis, had only to observe the procedure once to know that he would never perform it; upon seeing "a small arm with a hand" fall into a surgical pan, Freiman told a journalist, he felt ill.

Few in the pro-choice movement would ever publicly confront the loss of fetal life that defined their work, an unwillingness that the feminist Naomi Wolf charged was a shameful "blind spot." But some pro-choice thinkers did. Christopher Hitchens noted that "in order to terminate a pregnancy, you have to still a heartbeat." Judith Wilt wrote that the "freedom to abort a fetus is a monstrous, a tyrannous, but a necessary freedom in a fallen world." Andrew Sullivan wrote that "abortion is always and everywhere a moral tragedy." And Camille Paglia went further. "I have always frankly admitted that abortion is murder, the extermination of the powerless by the powerful," she wrote. Still, she added, "the state in my view has no authority whatever to intervene in the biological processes of any woman's body."

Boyd continued to perform second-trimester abortions even as he grappled with the ethical questions they posed, thinking the matter through on long walks over Texas fields and New Mexico mountains. "Intellectually, I thought this is the right thing to do," says Boyd. "But I had this emotional reaction." It was two full years before he overcame that reaction, concluding that until viability, the interest of the fetus was secondary to the desires and needs of its mother. Says Boyd: "She has the ultimate right to decide what is best for her and her family."

Often, D & E was best. For it was often right at the edge of viability that fetal abnormalities presented themselves through amniocentesis or sonography, and D & E enabled women to abort deeper into pregnancy without the emotional burden of delivery. (Other second-trimester methods, including prostaglandin and saline amniocentesis, not only induced labor but carried the additional horrible risk, tiny as it was, that the attempted abortion would result in a live birth.) D & E had thus emerged as the preferred procedure for second-trimester abortions. And on this May day in 1990, one of its pioneers stood before a roomful of abortion providers. "I love my work," said Boyd. The room rose in applause and Boyd, fifty-three and overcome, began to cry.

———————

TWO DECADES HAD PASSED since *Roe*. Having presided in his clinics over more than 100,000 abortions and just one maternal death, Boyd considered himself, at last, a master. Says Boyd: "I really had arrived."

Boyd was not simply skilled at performing abortions. He was an excellent teacher, conveying how best to use a tenaculum and curette— tearing no cervix, puncturing no uterus. "You have to always know where is the end of that instrument," says Boyd. "Are there any ridges in there? Pockets to the side?" Throughout the 1990s, Boyd taught at NAF workshops and at his clinics in Texas and New Mexico, where doctors traveled several times a year to watch him work.

The respect of his fellow providers was, however, the only respect Boyd got from the medical community. He recalled to the sociologist Carole Joffe the many insults hurled by his fellow doctors at abortion providers. "You were either a drug addict, an alcoholic, a ne'er-do-well, you couldn't maintain a practice or you were owned by the Mafia," he said. The legalization of abortion had done nothing to lessen the stigma of his work. (Boyd had Joffe give him a pseudonym.) *Roe*, in fact, had breathed new life into old tropes, chief among them that abortionists like Boyd were in it for the money.

It was true that legalization had expanded the opportunity for profit. Two companies on Wall Street had, in the run-up to *Roe*, pushed stocks based on estimated abortion revenues. In states where it was legal, some doctors upped by a third the amount they charged for an abortion. But organizations like Planned Parenthood threatened to not refer patients to a doctor unless the doctor capped the cost at $350. And *Roe* ultimately made abortion not only safer but less expensive. Boyd, for one (mindful that many of his patients were of moderate means and paid out of pocket), charged just $150 for a vacuum aspiration, the typical first-trimester abortion. (A D & E cost three or four times that.)

Still, Boyd made a good living. He was earning then, he says, about $200,000 annually, more than he would have earned as the family doctor he'd once hoped to be. It was enough to cover the costs of his three children, two houses and alimony. His income, though, was anything but stable, dropping in the 1980s as more clinics opened, rising in the 1990s as clinics closed. In 1993, Boyd closed his clinic in Santa Fe, which was losing money. Still, his larger clinics in Albuquerque and Dallas were profitable, together ending some fifty pregnancies daily.

Boyd performed no abortions past viability. *Roe* (and *Doe*) did, however, allow for third-trimester abortions—and not only when pregnancy threatened the physical health of a woman; a threat to her mental health was justification enough. Two decades after the ruling, seven states—including New Mexico, where Boyd operated—had enacted no gestational-age limits on abortion. Still, mindful of the fetus, Boyd put down his instruments at viability.

But then something made Boyd reconsider. A doctor in Kansas began telling him stories about his patients.

———

GEORGE TILLER was a young doctor, a U.S. Navy flight surgeon in California, when, in 1970, he readied to start a residency in dermatology. But then his parents, sister and brother-in-law died in a plane crash. And when Tiller returned home to Wichita to close down the family practice of his late father, Dr. Jack Tiller, he decided instead to take it over. It wasn't long before several of his new patients confided that his father had ended their pregnancies, in violation of the law.

Tiller had never been one to break the law. He was a straight arrow—a crew-cut Republican, a Christian son of Kansas who went to church with his wife and four children (the youngest of whom, born to his late sister, he had adopted). He was aghast to learn that his father had performed abortions. "The only [thing] worse than a woman that would request an abortion," Tiller later recalled thinking, "was the physician that would do the abortion." But his thinking changed. His patients explained that their decisions to abort had had less to do with any future babies than with the futures they hoped for themselves. Tiller saw, he said, that they had desired to be rid of their pregnancies no less than his cancer patients desired to be rid of their tumors, their desperation "equal in magnitude."

It was a desperation Tiller recognized. He had been midway through college when an unintended pregnancy threatened his future. "I can remember the terror and the anxiety associated with thinking that I was going to be a dad," he said, telling the story publicly for the first time at the age of sixty. "Medical school was gone." (The situation Tiller feared did not come to be; whether the woman was not in fact pregnant or miscarried, Tiller did not say.)

———

ABORTION WAS NOT YET LEGAL when Tiller performed his first. It was a near disaster; what began with dilation and curettage ended with pulmonary edema and blood transfusions. The doctor vowed to be better prepared in the event he performed another. With the passage of *Roe* in 1973, he began performing abortions at the local hospital and then at his office.

Tiller did not enjoy the work; it was, he later reflected, neither intellectually stimulating nor technically challenging. As a medical field, abortion lacked prestige, too. But performing abortions deepened his connections to his patients. "It is that invitation into the innermost resources, into the inner sanctums of a woman," he later explained, "that is the addicting part of this particular field."

Tiller had found his life's work. He was an abortion provider. He was a feminist, too. The local Planned Parenthood office started referring patients to him. Soon after, in 1976, Tiller opened a women's clinic, advertising it in the Yellow Pages. "My practice just went absolutely nuts," he recalled. Tiller was thirty-five, and abortion was soon the great bulk of his work. He joined the National Abortion Federation.

Tiller did not perform abortions past the first trimester. (So as to gauge the approximate gestational age of the fetus, his nurse, Cathy Reavis, used a baseball and a softball during pelvic exams.) But around 1980, he reconsidered. A patient in his family practice had a son who had Down syndrome and was low-functioning. She came to Tiller sobbing, telling him that caring for her son made her a prisoner in her home. Tiller was moved. "He did say," recalls Reavis, "'you know, she's right. Nobody understands what a woman, what a mother, goes through.'" Tiller began performing abortions into the second trimester, "particularly with fetal abnormality," he recalled. Says Reavis: "He started ordering larger instruments."

Like Boyd, Tiller was working with forceps and laminaria. And in the early 1980s, after hearing Boyd speak on D & E, Tiller flew to Dallas to watch him work, spending several days at his clinic. Tiller worried that he didn't have the skills to abort late in the second trimester, that he might harm a woman while removing a fragment of her fetus. "He said," recalls Boyd, "'I can't do it the way you do it. You have magic hands.'"

Tiller, though, had other options. A handful of doctors had recently begun using drugs to end pregnancies in the second trimester, injecting into the fetal heart or body either a heart medicine called digoxin or a derivative of ammonia called urea. Once the fetus died of cardiac arrest, the doctors induced labor so that the woman gave birth to a stillborn. "The concept that you could end the fetal life before you did the induction did not [previously] exist," says the abortion provider Charlotte Taft. She adds that abortion via injection rather than dismemberment was often less upsetting to the pregnant woman—"even if it's ironic that you don't want to hurt something you're going to be killing."

Tiller took to this new procedure. It was, he felt, more humane and safer, too, says the longtime manager of his clinic, JoAn Armentrout; Tiller did not have to dismember the fetus and risk injuring the woman unless he failed to induce labor. He began performing the procedure at around twenty-one weeks, says Reavis, using an ultrasound machine to see exactly where to inject the digoxin. Comfortable with his technique, he pushed further into pregnancy. "The patient wasn't maimed," he recalled. "The patient wasn't killed. So, we went to the next gestational level. And we went to the next gestational level."

In 1985, Tiller crossed over the threshold of viability.

That threshold is not a fixed point. The percentage of fetuses that survive birth in any given week of gestation varies, as do the scars those fetuses may bear if born. The lines demarcating trimesters are similarly fluid. Some chart pregnancy over the roughly thirty-eight weeks that follow conception, others over the forty weeks that follow the first day of the last menstrual period. Furthermore, the trimesters are not of equal length. (Using the forty-week model, they are twelve, twelve and sixteen weeks long.) Then there is the matter of technology. In 1983, Justice O'Connor asserted that advances in science would inevitably lower the point of viability that *Roe* had fixed at twenty-four weeks. "The *Roe* framework," she wrote, "is clearly on a collision course with itself."

═══

IN ONE SENSE, third-trimester abortions are less controversial than late second-trimester abortions; whereas the great majority of second-trimester abortions are elective, nearly all third-trimester abortions end pregnancies that were "initially desired," as the *Washington Post* reported. Still, if second-trimester abortions are fraught, the notion of third-trimester abortions is explosive. Even the National Abortion Federation was uncomfortable with them. In March 1985, at a meeting

in Dallas, NAF's Medical Advisory and Education Committee resolved
to sanction the renegade Tiller.

"Dr. George Tiller, formerly a NAF member, is advertising nation-
ally that he will perform abortions at 26 weeks," read the minutes of
the meeting. "Our staff must deal with inquiries about referrals to
Dr. Tiller."

Six NAF members were present at the meeting, including its president, Boyd's wife Glenna. They resolved, with one dissent, not only to
stop referring patients to Tiller but to refer complaints about him to the
Kansas State Board of Medical Examiners. Glenna and the other surviving members of the meeting say that they do not recall sidelining Tiller.
But Charlotte Taft, then an NAF member, recalls the fear of "public perception" that surrounded third-trimester abortions. Tiller was unfazed.
"He just felt," recalls his clinic manager Armentrout, "if they don't want
to take care of the woman, I will."

Third-trimester abortion was an altogether new field of medicine.
And like Boyd and Warren Hern, Tiller was proud to stand in defiance
of the medical profession. The doctors were mavericks, alpha males
who spoke freely of their contributions, Boyd of his brilliance as provider and teacher, Hern of his writings (which included the standard
textbook on abortion). Tiller, too, knew where he stood. "If I'm not on
the front line," he liked to say, "there is no front line."

An American flag marked Tiller's clinic on South Bleckley Drive in
East Wichita. The building was an oblong slab of beige stone, window-
less and flat-roofed save for the little metal chimney of a crematorium. In
time, the clinic would stand as secure as a nuclear bunker, equipped by
Tiller with fencing and floodlights, cameras and alarms, metal detectors
and off-duty police to ward off even the most determined foe.

Tiller believed in formality, order. He had lived by it in the military.
He had been saved by it in Alcoholics Anonymous, the doctor joining
the movement in 1984 after an arrest for driving drunk. Tiller wore a
suit and tie to work, and insisted that even his most tenured employees
call him "Doctor." The process he had developed for performing third-
trimester abortions was precise and regimented, four days that passed
from digoxin to dilation to delivery.

Tiller was certain of the rightness of his work. He saw it as a "ministry," he said, and ran his practice complete with counseling and group therapy. Meantime, he had his own gestational limit—twenty-six weeks and four days in cases of elective abortion. It was at that point, he said, that the second trimester actually ended. Beyond it, he would only abort when, as *Roe* allowed, pregnancy threatened the physical or mental health of a woman, or in cases of fetal abnormalities such as hydrocephalus or spina bifida. "Nature makes mistakes," he said.

The pro-life were unmoved. Two in five abortions Tiller performed were third-trimester. The reasons for many of them were hard to question. But Tiller's opponents charged that many of the alleged maternal mental health disorders that prompted the abortions were in fact "readily treatable." And the *New York Times* would report that of the 2,800 viable fetuses Tiller would abort from 1998 into 2009, "many were perfectly healthy."

Tiller was unrepentant. That a woman would seek to abort a healthy fetus only attested to the degree to which her pregnancy threatened her health. Besides, per Kansas law, a second doctor unaffiliated with the provider had to attest to the need for any abortion after twenty-two weeks. "Babies and families are to be blessings and gifts," Tiller told a reporter in late summer of 1991, "not condemnation and punishment."

Tiller spoke to the press, that September, having just endured forty-six days of protest. The demonstrations, held by Operation Rescue, had roiled Wichita; police made 2,657 arrests. They marked a new approach for O.R., the organization having decided to protest a single Middle American doctor rather than a string of big-city clinics, as it had in Atlanta and New York. Doing so was a way to "personalize the struggle," the reporters James Risen and Judy Thomas wrote. More, in targeting Tiller, O.R. had, for the first time, focused that struggle on third-trimester abortion.

Protesting Tiller invigorated O.R.'s fundamentalist base. But it also turned Tiller—unbowed at fifty—into a pro-choice hero. The *New York Times* would later call him "the nation's pre-eminent abortion practitioner." Tiller became a symbol of unflinching resolve. His renown only grew when, in 1993, he returned to work one day after a would-be assassin shot him in both arms.

"Dr. Tiller was a rock star," says his employee Armentrout. "We couldn't go to any convention without everybody asking, 'Where's Dr. Tiller?'" Indeed, those who had once shunned him now celebrated him. In 1994, NAF honored Tiller with the same lifetime award it had granted Boyd.

Tiller was now the father of a sub-specialty; both Dr. Hern in Colorado and Dr. James McMahon in California had followed Tiller into the third trimester. Though the number of third-trimester abortions performed in America would never account for much more than one in one thousand abortions, that one would invite more scrutiny, more questions, than the other 999. For if most Americans (including Randall Terry of Operation Rescue) agreed that a woman had a right to end even a third-trimester pregnancy that would otherwise kill her, what of the pregnancy that would only debilitate her? And if half the country agreed that a woman could abort a non-viable fetus, what of the fetus that would live but be deformed? What of the fetus only *somewhat* deformed? Dr. McMahon would soon testify that of the 1,358 viable fetuses he had aborted, nine had had nothing wrong but a cleft lip.

Tiller understood the questions. He noted that when couples looked at the third-trimester fetuses they aborted, they were often divided—mothers noticing "everything that was right," fathers "what was wrong." Still, Tiller brushed the questions aside. He said that his patient was the woman, not the fetus, and that at any stage of pregnancy, women "simply want non-judgmental help." In this respect, he added, women wanting to abort had much in common with the alcoholic wanting to become sober.

Of course, performing abortions was also Tiller's living. (One third-trimester abortion earned him several thousand dollars.) Mindful that Drs. Hern and McMahon were not simply peers but competitors, Tiller spoke little of his work. Too much transparency could hurt the bottom line. It could also provide fodder for the pro-life—as McMahon was about to learn.

McMahon performed third-trimester abortions differently than did Hern or Tiller. Rather than euthanizing the fetus with digoxin and inducing labor, he used forceps to pull the fetus out of the vagina feet first until only its head remained in the uterus. He then punctured the base of the head and suctioned the spinal fluid from it so that the skull could be collapsed and the fetus more easily delivered.

McMahon called his procedure "intact dilation and evacuation." Unlike the abortions Hern and Tiller performed, it spared the woman the burden of labor. But it was also a ghastly way to kill a viable fetus. After an Ohio doctor presented a paper on the procedure at a 1992 NAF seminar, an anonymous source mailed it to the National Right to Life Committee, which then distributed it widely (along with drawings) in the pro-life community. Reaction was swift; within a year, Florida congressman Charles Canady introduced an amendment to a bill on abortion, banning the procedure. Though the ban failed, politicians in both parties decried the procedure; it was, said Democratic senator Daniel Patrick Moynihan, "as close to infanticide as anything I have come upon in our judiciary."

McMahon defended the procedure. He testified that owing to the anesthesia administered to the woman, the fetus fell into a coma and thus did not suffer. But the president of the American Society of Anesthesiologists testified that, at most, the anesthesia provided the fetus minor relief of pain. In 1995, Canady and others branded the procedure "partial-birth abortion" and passed a ban. Twelve years later, in *Gonzales v. Carhart*, the Supreme Court upheld the law that declared the procedure illegal.

Tiller thus rarely described his procedure. Not until the late 1980s did he even allow doctors to observe him at work. Among them was Boyd, watching Tiller as Tiller had watched him.

The two doctors had much in common. Over the following years, they discussed their shared feminism and Christianity, the rewards and dangers of their work. And as Tiller told of the trials that brought women to him late in pregnancy, the gulf of viability that separated him from Boyd began to recede.

"That's what changed me," says Boyd. "The women's stories."

———

BOYD HAD ALWAYS been motivated by a concern for women. Born to Primitive Baptists in east Texas, he had seen women forced to bear a man's child.

The notion of "woman as womb," as the poet Adrienne Rich termed it, lingered long after *Roe*. In 1976, the Supreme Court Justice Byron White lamented that the Court assigned "a greater value" to the right of a mother to end fetal life "than to a father's decision to let it mature into a live child." Two years later, the pro-life leader John Willke spoke of "the right of a husband to protect the life of the child he has fathered in his wife's womb." As the sign of a protester held outside Boyd's clinic put it: "What Man Would Allow His Baby to be Aborted?"

Some men tried to prevent such abortions. One robbed Boyd at gunpoint, another tried to blackmail him, a third set his Albuquerque clinic ablaze, causing nearly a million dollars in damage. Boyd carried on, mindful that the woman was his patient, not the man. Pre-*Roe*, those women never once leveled charges that could have landed Boyd in jail, and always, in the years since, they offered their gratitude, telling him, as he later recounted, "I don't know what I would've done if you hadn't been here."

After performing his first abortion, that of a fetus ten weeks old, Boyd had advanced later into pregnancy by fourteen weeks over fourteen years. There, at viability—at twenty-four weeks—he had stayed some fourteen years more. But challenged by Tiller—and after many talks with his staff—he was now, around 1995, open to moving past viability. He was coming to see it as an "arbitrary" cutoff, he says, an "artificial barrier" that could occur at any point over several weeks. He asks: "Last week it was okay [to abort], this week it's not?"

By the close of the millennium, Boyd had come to believe that the interest of even a viable fetus was secondary to the interest of the woman carrying it. He had come to believe that it was moral to abort a fetus past twenty-four weeks.

Still, Boyd had never done so. He found himself torn. "I felt philosophically, this is all well and good and I support it," recalls Boyd. And yet, he says, "I felt uncomfortable being the one doing it."

Boyd groped for the root of his discomfort. He found it in a hypothetical: What if a woman came to him on the eve of her delivery to abort her child? What if she came to him just before that? Boyd knew that he would never help such a woman. And so, he feared crossing over into viability. Says Boyd, "I thought I'd be confronted with an impossible [situation]."

Boyd set that thought aside. He told himself that the fetus was not truly viable, could not be assumed to live, until week twenty-seven. He thus resolved to perform abortions into week twenty-six—some two weeks further than he had before.

Unlike Texas, New Mexico law imposed no gestational limit on abortion. And Boyd was in his Albuquerque clinic when, in the early aughts, he performed his first third-trimester abortion.

A larger fetus cannot be extracted with laminaria and forceps alone. So Boyd began, as he had learned from Tiller, to give his patients large doses of a drug called Misoprostol to elicit contractions. Nearing seventy, his beard flecked with white and gray, Boyd was soon comfortable in the third trimester, his hands and heart catching up to what his mind had determined was okay.

Still, the doctor resolved to go no further. Any woman wanting an abortion past twenty-six weeks he would refer to George Tiller.

———

THIRTY YEARS HAD PASSED since *Roe*. James McMahon had died, and there were now just two doctors aborting fetuses past twenty-six weeks. "Dr. Warren Hern and myself are the only late-term abortion providers in the Western Hemisphere, Europe and Australia," Tiller said. "That's amazing."

As such, Tiller was busy. Together with a few doctors he'd begun to train, he aborted, on average, some 250 viable fetuses each year. He charged, on average, $6,000 for each such abortion. In 2003, the procedures grossed him $1.5 million. Tiller later testified that his profit margin was 38 percent, and his opponents focused on what that profit had bought him—a mansion, nice cars, membership at a country club. Of course, Tiller also had great expenses, from security to insurance. Then there was politics; Tiller would donate almost $1 million to pro-choice candidates through a PAC he founded. If he was wealthy and renowned—"The most famous person in Wichita," wrote GQ—he was also despised, likened by the pro-life leader Troy Newman to such sadists as Saddam Hussein and the Nazi doctor Josef Mengele.

Newman headed a spinoff of Operation Rescue that would soon legally assume that famous name. He'd relocated it from California to Kansas with the sole intent of shutting Tiller down.

Newman had long pondered whether the murder of abortion providers was permitted theologically. In 2003, a decade after a would-be assassin shot Tiller in both arms, Newman concluded that it was not merely permitted by God but commanded. He wrote that the government had a responsibility to "execut[e] convicted murderers, including abortionists, for their crimes in order to expunge bloodguilt from the land and people." When, that same year, a man named Paul Hill was set to be executed for the double murder of an abortion provider and his bodyguard, Newman wrote that Hill ought to have been allowed to argue in court "that his conduct was justifiable defensive action."

Few noted his words; profiles of Newman the next year in *Rolling Stone* and the *Los Angeles Times* made no mention of them. Newman told the *Times* instead that "violence will never, never, never be the solution." The solution, he said, was harassment.

It had been done before. Back in 1985, the activist Joseph Scheidler had encouraged his followers to visit "pain and unpleasantness" upon abortion providers. A raft of providers testified the next month to a House subcommittee that activists had threatened them and their families at work and at home. Now, two decades later, in 2004, Newman and his volunteers set out to harass Tiller and his staff, following them to the mall, a restaurant, sifting through their garbage in the hope of unearthing some incriminating crumb, threatening to boycott anyone who did business with them—"from the guy who mows the clinic's lawn to the cafe that sells Tiller his morning latte," as one reporter put it. Newman disseminated their addresses and phone numbers.

"I want these employees to realize that their lives have changed," Newman told the press. "As long as they're embedded in the abortion industry receiving blood money, they can't live a normal life. They just can't." Tiller thus remained a living target. "If I could get my hands on Tiller . . ." the right-wing television host Bill O'Reilly told his millions of viewers in 2006. He stopped himself. "Can't be vigilantes."

Tiller had not been the same since his 1993 shooting; he intimated in a speech in 2008 that he suffered post-traumatic stress. "What I found out," he told the Feminist Majority Foundation, "was I wasn't nearly as tough as I—as I thought I was." Still, Tiller was not one to retreat. He continued to go to work, to his country club, to his church. He told himself (and others) that anger was not his friend, that attitude transcended circumstance. If an unanswerable question came to mind, he wrote it down and put it in a "God Box" that he kept in his drawer.

Tiller was thus not only at war but at peace. And he was at his church on the last May morning of 2009, ushering at Reformation Lutheran, when a man approached, raised a pistol to his forehead and shot him dead.

———

THE NAME OF THE MAN was Scott Roeder. He had grown up not far off, in Topeka, and lived there with a wife and son until 1992 when he was born again while watching the evangelical TV program *The 700 Club*. Roeder was soon not only Christian but anti-government, consumed at age thirty-four with two perceived evils: abortion and the IRS. When, the next year, a woman named Shelley Shannon shot and wounded Tiller outside his clinic, Roeder began visiting her in prison.

Roeder would soon divorce his wife and leave his job at an electric company. But he stayed in touch with abortion activists. A decade later, in 2002, he later recalled, he had lunch with Troy Newman.

Newman had just moved to Wichita in the hope of closing Tiller's clinic. As Roeder later told the journalist Amanda Robb, he asked Newman a question: "Something like if an abortionist—I don't even know if it was specifically Tiller . . . was shot, would it be justified?" Newman answered, Roeder recalled, "If it were, it wouldn't upset me."

Newman would come to influence Roeder. Like Newman, Roeder would liken Tiller to the Nazi Mengele. Like Newman, he would begin to shadow Tiller—not only outside his clinic but in his church and a Wichita courtroom where, in 2009, a jury acquitted Tiller of charges brought against him at the behest of Operation Rescue.

Roeder was exasperated. He told a fellow activist that "justice had not been served."

The assassination of the most prominent abortion provider in America elicited outrage from the pro-choice, beginning with the newly elected president, Barack Obama. The extreme wing of the pro-life movement spoke up, too. "George Tiller was a mass-murderer," wrote Randall Terry in a statement. "We grieve for him that he did not have time to properly prepare his soul to face God." Father Pavone wrote that while the murder left him "saddened," he wished to remind America that the person who committed it might yet prove to be "an angry post-abortive man or woman, or a misguided activist, or an enemy within the abortion industry, or a political enemy frustrated with the way Tiller has escaped prosecution."

Roeder was none of those people: he was a pro-life activist with ties to Operation Rescue. Hours after he shot Tiller, the police pulled him over in his Taurus, an ichthys on its bumper, and found a piece of paper on his dash that read "Op Rescue" and "Cheryl."

Cheryl Sullenger was Newman's deputy. She had served two years in prison for attempting to blow up a clinic, and, along with Newman, had classified the murder of an abortion provider as a "justifiable defensive action." But now, together with Newman, she released a statement decrying Tiller's murder. Operation Rescue, they wrote, was dedicated to "peaceful and legal" protest.

It was in the obvious interest of both Newman and the greater pro-life movement to distance themselves from Roeder. Newman would soon tell a reporter that he didn't recall having ever met the gunman.

To rid Wichita of Tiller had been Newman's sole purpose and daily bread for seven years. Now that Tiller was dead—and his clinic closed for good—Newman was at a loss for what to do. He remained in bed for two days, and told people that he had "abortion fatigue."

So did all of Wichita. Eighteen years after O.R. had first descended upon it, the city was exhausted. Without delay, Tiller's church replaced a strip of bloodied carpet, his widow sang a prayer at his memorial, and the paper remains of his practice were moved to a vault hundreds of feet below ground, in an old Kansas salt mine.

There was now just one clinic in the nation aborting viable fetuses. Wanting to recruit another, the president of NAF phoned Boyd. "She said," he recalls, "'What are we going to do about this?'"

Boyd was unsure. That Tiller aborted viable fetuses had meant that Boyd didn't have to. Still, there had been women pregnant with viable

fetuses whom Boyd regretted turning away, the last an Orthodox Jewish woman whose fetus had Tay-Sachs disease, a genetic disorder that
kills babies within a few years of birth. Boyd had decided then that,
henceforth, he would go past viability; he told himself that owing to the
"miscalculation" of gestational age, he already had.

In 2008, a woman from New York who was twenty-seven weeks
pregnant—but thought she was twenty-four—came to Boyd "pleading"
for an abortion, he says. He set down his forceps (which were effective
only until week twenty-six) and got some digoxin from his pharmacy.

The procedure went well. Still, first experiences "induced anxiety,"
says Boyd. (Back in medical school, he'd fainted the first time he saw a
belly cut open during a bowel resection.) Never before had he injected
a drug into the beating heart of a viable fetus. "You're thinking," says
Boyd, "do I want to be doing this? Do I want to be the one providing
this service?" The gratitude of his patient reinforced for Boyd that the
answer was yes.

Without telling his staff, Boyd used digoxin a handful more times in
2008 to end pregnancies twenty-seven weeks along. Now, after the 2009
murder of Tiller, NAF asked Boyd if he would enter the third trimester
in a more regular way.

Boyd wanted to. He had gotten past the emotional hurdle of using
digoxin. And, he says, "you got to twenty-seven weeks, you realize, I can
keep going." Nevertheless, he remained tormented by that hypothetical
woman who would come to him for an abortion on the eve of birth.
Knowing that he would turn her away "represented an inconsistency in
my philosophy," says Boyd. Going past twenty-seven weeks would also
require assembling a new staff, finding people at peace not only with
third-trimester abortion but with the dangers it would bring.

Of course, Boyd and his wife were already in the crosshairs; only
two years had passed since a fire set in their Albuquerque clinic had
forced them to relocate. The couple said yes: they would continue the
work of Tiller.

The Boyds invited to their clinic Susan Robinson and Shelley Sella,
doctors Tiller had trained to help handle his third-trimester workload.
Like the Boyds, the two doctors saw their work as a sort of ministry.
They too wished to provide patients not only abortions but counseling

and ceremony, the opportunity to view or bless or bury the aborted fetus. They too felt that if third-trimester abortions were sometimes necessary, they were always wrenching. "I think the reason I've struggled," Sella later reflected, "is because I think of them as babies."

The Boyds had their doctors and staff in place. In January of 2010, seven months after Tiller's assassination, they stepped into the breach, offering abortions through at least the twenty-eighth week of pregnancy. Read their website: "Appointments for late abortions are now available."

———

TROY NEWMAN ACTED QUICKLY. He labeled Albuquerque the new "late-term abortion capital of the world," wrote about Boyd, and dispatched a pair of Operation Rescue volunteers to stand outside his clinic, a rectangle of stucco and pastel. But New Mexico is temperate and pro-choice; the O.R. volunteers often stood alone. And Newman soon turned his focus to another doctor trained by Tiller who'd begun to perform third-trimester abortions in Nebraska.

The Boyds grew their practice. Between their two clinics, they were soon providing some 15,000 abortions annually, a total that placed them, they say, among the four largest private abortion providers in the country. They were the largest provider of third-trimester abortions, aborting by 2012 between two and three hundred viable fetuses per year—roughly the same number as had Tiller.

Like Tiller, the Boyds were mindful to donate to sympathetic organizations and politicians. But despite their lobbying, a law passed in Texas the very next year suddenly threatened their Dallas clinic.

———

ROE WAS ONE DAY OLD WHEN, in 1973, Bella Abzug, a House representative from New York and leading feminist, urged Congress to codify it. She foresaw the potential of legislation to erode *Roe*, and had just introduced the Abortion Rights Act—H.R. 254—to bar states from creating new laws on abortion. Congress, however, ignored her bill. *Roe* itself allowed for future legislation, granting states the right to impose regulations from the second trimester onward ("to the extent," wrote

Blackmun, "that the regulation reasonably relates to the preservation and protection of maternal health"). Just weeks after the ruling, "there were rumors," the journalist Molly Ivins noted, that a fleet of new laws on abortion would soon be proposed.

Those rumors proved true; within two years of *Roe*, state legislatures had passed fifty-eight bills targeting abortion, restrictions that ranged from limits on post-viability abortion to allowing hospitals to refuse to provide abortion. But as the years passed, the large-scale erosion of *Roe* that Abzug feared did not come to be—not even after the 1989 *Webster* ruling, which was in essence, as Roger Rosenblatt wrote, "an open invitation to state legislatures to test how far they could regulate abortion." State legislatures were largely divided, and a scant few of the proposed regulations became law. Over one nineteen-year stretch in Texas, for example, just two of eighty-four proposed bills on abortion passed.

Years went by. The Supreme Court again invited states to issue new regulations, most notably in the cases of *Casey* and *Gonzales*. And in 2011, one year after Republicans took control of twenty-six state legislatures and twenty-nine governorships, states enacted ninety-two abortion regulations—nearly triple the number of regulations in any other year since *Roe*.

The laws had many parents. But they owed as much to Americans United for Life as to anyone.

AUL was founded in 1971 as an educational organization. It published *Abortion and Social Justice*, a book of essays arguing against abortion, it explained, "in terms acceptable to humanists and theists alike." A brief it filed in *Roe*, asserting the personhood of the fetus in legal terms, endeavored to do the same. But after the passage of *Roe*, the AUL turned to law and policy, drafting model legislation for pro-life lawmakers. Success came with the Illinois Abortion Law of 1975 which declared, using the language of a model AUL bill, "that the unborn child is a human being from the time of conception." Thirty-five years later, the organization deployed its model bills to remarkable effect. "There's a spectrum of involvement," says AUL senior counsel Clarke Forsythe. He adds: "Maybe we've influenced 75 percent of the legislation passed."

The new laws were a welter of mandated consent and counseling, of waiting periods and warnings. They were intrusive—literally, in the case of a 2012 Texas sonogram bill. (Texas state representative Carol Alvarado brought to the House floor a transvaginal probe for all to see.) Intrusion, of course, was the point. Abortion was already safe—more than a power of ten safer than childbirth. (There were 0.6 deaths per 100,000 legal and induced abortions versus 8.8 deaths per 100,000 live births.) Abortion regulation was intended not to protect women but to deter them from ending their pregnancies—to make abortion, as professor Carol Sanger wrote, difficult to get "legally, financially, emotionally, practically."

The new laws intended also to make abortion difficult to *provide*. They regulated clinics by passing what the pro-choice termed TRAP laws—the Targeted Regulation of Abortion Providers. These were the bane of Boyd. Among much else, Texas law now required the doctor to tell patients of a nonexistent link between abortion and breast cancer and to ask if they wished to see the ultrasound image of the fetus they intended to abort.

The Boyds did their best to survive the TRAPs. After Texas Republicans, for example, mandated in 2003 that only hospitals or ambulatory surgery centers be allowed to abort fetuses at least sixteen weeks old, the Boyds moved to a clinic on Greenville Avenue that met every benchmark.

In 2013, however, those same Republicans mandated that doctors performing abortions in Texas must have admitting privileges at a nearby hospital. Boyd worried that the bill, House Bill 2, would close his clinic. His worry was well-founded: to get admitting privileges, doctors often must admit a certain number of patients to a particular hospital. But owing to the safety of abortion, abortion providers admit so few patients that they rarely meet that number. It was a point of pride for Boyd, for example, that four decades after *Roe*, just one in five thousand of his patients required hospitalization.

Boyd, meantime, was also working less, content at age seventy-six to train others. But with the passage of HB2, he suddenly couldn't work at all in Texas. He hadn't had admitting privileges since his years on staff at St. Vincent hospital in New Mexico. When, a month after HB2 went into effect, his medical director went on maternity leave, only one doctor on his staff had admitting privileges—a local ob-gyn who helped the Boyds treat a few patients each month.

The Boyds made a plan. They hired a new doctor due to get admitting privileges in spring. They waited on their medical director to return from maternity leave. And they had their part-time ob-gyn work extra hours. Still, the months that passed in wait were miserable. The Boyds were forced to turn away patients while continuing to pay their staff for work not done. In time, HB2 would shutter more than half of the clinics in Texas, the number dropping in fifteen months from forty-one to nineteen.

The Boyds' Dallas clinic was one of the nineteen that survived. By May 2014, it was back at full tilt, poised to perform another thousand abortions per month in full compliance with Texas law.

———

THE SUPREME COURT had fixed the cutoff for abortion at viability. But there were philosophical arguments that could be made to abort or preserve a pregnancy at every point along the forty weeks from conception to birth. Some asserted, for example, that the Court should have fixed the cutoff a few weeks before viability or a few weeks after—when the fetus, they said, could begin to feel pain or to think.

Such arguments hinged on questions of life and justness. The philosopher Judith Jarvis Thomson famously argued in support of choice that "the right to life consists not in the right not to be killed, but rather in the right not to be killed unjustly." Boyd agreed. Having moved past viability, the question for him now was not whether a fetus could survive outside the womb but whether, he says, given its condition and gestational age, it could "have an acceptable quality of life."

It was left to Boyd and his staff to address that question. Unlike in Kansas, the law in New Mexico did not require doctors performing third-trimester abortion to get approval from a doctor unaffiliated with their clinic; in New Mexico, the abortion provider alone could determine the validity of the abortion. And the doctors Sella and Robinson did turn some women away. (A folder in a desk drawer in Boyd's clinic read "LATE-TERM: REFUSE.")

Still, says Boyd, the doctors performed nearly every abortion that did not pose a physical threat to the mother. And that hypothetical woman—she who would decide at week thirty-nine to abort—continued to haunt Boyd. As the years passed, he says, he continued "trying to reconcile my philosophical belief with reality."

───────

BOYD HAD BEEN providing third-trimester abortions for five years when, sitting down to write a speech in 2014, his thinking on the matter reached its natural end.

Boyd now saw, he says, that no matter how many women came to his clinics, the hypothetical one he feared was never among them. It thus followed that she did not exist. And if she did not exist, Boyd thought, there was always a legitimate reason a woman sought an abortion. And if there was always a legitimate reason a woman sought an abortion, she must always be allowed to have one—from conception to birth, menarche to menopause. It was, for Boyd, a liberating thought. So was its converse—that so long as a fetus remained in utero, it had no personhood and thus no right to life. "With breath, it transforms from a fetus into a baby," says Boyd. He adds: "If it doesn't take that breath, it was never alive."

Boyd had come to a radical conclusion. ("I am in the extreme minority," he acknowledges.) He was not, however, the first to reach it; the third-century Greek philosopher Porphyry, for example, had written the same. That Boyd had, too, seemed almost inevitable. Abortion had always been for Boyd an assertion of women's autonomy. Forty-seven years after performing his first, he had concluded that that autonomy must be absolute.

Boyd finished writing his speech. He delivered it, in the fall of 2014, at a conference in Bogotá, Colombia. "The pregnancy," Boyd told his audience, "if we are to respect individual autonomy, must remain under the ultimate control of the pregnant woman until the time of birth."

Chapter 30

More than anyone, Linda Coffee had set *Roe* on its legal way. But twenty years after the case she filed made legal abortion constitutional law, the lawyer was, in the words of her hometown paper, a "historical footnote." She was not on hand when, in 1993, President Clinton signed five executive orders to safeguard *Roe*—the great achievement of her life.

That was fine by Coffee. The reporter Joseph Bell had recently tracked her down only to find, he noted, that she was "hostile" to his questions.

Coffee had always preferred to have her work speak for itself. "She hid her brilliance beautifully," recalled a lawyer named Molly Bartholow, who occasionally opposed Coffee in the Dallas bankruptcy court on Commerce Street. Bartholow had represented creditors in disputes with debtors represented by Coffee. She'd observed just how smart Coffee was. Owing to *Roe*, she admired her, too. Says Bartholow: "Linda and Sarah Weddington are my heroes."

It had thus upset Bartholow to hear of Coffee's indictment on fraud charges. Though she was exonerated, that ordeal had landed Coffee in bed, and, two weeks later, she'd failed again to pay her Texas Bar dues.

Those dues were rising. The annual fees, including membership and a new occupational tax, now topped $400. Coffee had been delinquent twice previously, in 1991 and 1992. Because her second delinquency had passed ninety days, her license was suspended. Worse, she continued to practice, a violation of rule 8.04 a (11) of the Texas Disciplinary Rules of Professional Conduct.

The Bar could have disciplined Coffee, but did not do so. (A spokesperson for the Bar declined to comment on her case.) Coffee paid her bills and carried on, back in good standing in the summer of 1993, when she found a note of foreclosure on her front door.

Rebecca Hartt had not known, she says, that her partner had fallen behind on their mortgage. But she might have guessed. In the wake of her public shaming four years prior, Coffee had withdrawn. Her work had sputtered. Having fallen into debt, Coffee needed now to declare bankruptcy, to do for herself what she had done for countless others.

On August 12, Hartt filed for Chapter 13. Coffee then issued a report on what Hartt owed her lender. The court refused to discharge their debt.

The ruling was no surprise. Fifty and forty years old, Coffee and Hartt had little income. That same September, Coffee was again late in paying what she owed the Texas Bar. And her license was again suspended the following summer when she lost her home. "They came in with a moving truck," says Hartt, "and took out every stick of furniture."

Hartt would look back on the foreclosure as the turning point of her life. Her childhood had been one of choir practice and homemade strawberry ice cream, her first decade with Coffee marked by dog christenings and Bastille Day celebrations. But the good days were over.

The couple moved downtown, into an apartment on Main Street. Coffee fought insolvency, representing Hartt in suits against their mortgage lender and a collection agency. But the suits changed nothing. Hartt was unemployed. Even after Coffee paid the fees necessary to get her license reinstated in November, she had few clients, and less and less of the restraint and tact needed to speak with them. "I would just be very frank about things," she acknowledged. "I didn't want to change that.'"

It had never bothered Coffee that bankruptcy law was fickle. Though she sometimes went without pay for six months, work remained her anchor. But her firm had begun to wither after its founding partner Phil Palmer developed lung cancer. Coffee was soon the last of the ten lawyers on staff, and she spent her days alone in her office. Recalls the firm secretary, Peggy Clewis: "She talked to herself a lot."

Coffee was in good standing less than a year; her license was suspended again in December 1995 for failing to pay those same four hundred-plus dollars. The suspension continued for years, Coffee nonetheless taking on new clients: opposing a bank in 1996, a biotech company in 1997, an employee screening company in 1998, an insurance company in 1999.

Still, the Texas Bar received no complaints about Coffee and imposed no punishments. In early 2000, she was again in good standing. But late that year, her license was again suspended after she failed to pay her fees and to take the required continuing education courses. After a dying Palmer closed his firm in 2001, a delinquent Coffee was left to rely on her mother to pay her bills.

To look at Coffee was to see a fallen star. "She was almost in the fetal position when she walked down the hall," recalled the lawyer Bartholow, who knew Coffee from court and who happened to be the trustee assigned to her bankruptcy case. "She always had her hand in her face or her hair." *Roe* had forgotten Coffee even as it remembered her former co-counsel anew with every anniversary. In 2003, Planned Parenthood of North Texas named Weddington its Humanitarian of the Year.

Weeks later, Coffee lost her mother. Sixty years old, Coffee moved with Hartt into the East Dallas home Mary left behind.

═══════

THIRTY YEARS BEFORE, days after *Roe* became law, Mary Coffee had proudly connected her daughter with the official news service of the Southern Baptist Convention. The Baptist Press had blessed the lawyer's work.

But there was no longer any room for Coffee in her church. Sixteen million strong, the SBC had come to repudiate not only abortion but homosexuality and gender equality. The church now asserted that "a wife is to submit herself graciously to the servant leadership of her husband." Same-sex attraction was "pathological, abnormal, and mostly if not entirely a matter of external influence, learned behavior, acquired taste, and personal choice." Regarding abortion, the SBC now put the interests of the zygote—"a human being, created in God's image"—ahead of the mother.

It was a source of some pain to Hartt that her partner did not believe in God. "I have always considered her a virtuous pagan," says Hartt. Still, Coffee had believed in her church. Rejected by it, she had been left to lean on other supports: her family, the law. But her parents were now dead, and her career was dying. In the spring of 2005, after taking on a new client, a couple in Dallas at odds with a car dealer over the return of a leased Toyota, Coffee lost her license for the last time.

Thirty-five years before, Coffee had stood in a Dallas courthouse and spoken of a lawsuit that concerned nothing less, she said, than "fundamental human freedom." *Roe* had gone on to safeguard that freedom for millions of women. Not one of those millions had come to her aid through her years of struggle. Money was a source of growing stress for her and Hartt. More and more, they fought.

Coffee felt that Hartt drank too much. Hartt could also be bossy; the secretary Peggy Clewis recalled a dinner with the couple at their inherited home when Hartt "harassed Linda a lot." Coffee shrank from conflict and described herself as "slow to anger." But physical exercise now relieved little more than her insomnia. And Coffee came to see that she could no longer afford to lawyer; "economics," she says. She came unmoored. In April 2006, the police arrived at her home on Wabash Circle Drive to find that she had "assaulted" Hartt. She would soon assault her partner twice more, punching Hartt in the mouth and hitting her with a purse, its brass buckle cutting the back of her head.

Hartt was bleeding onto her shirt when she crossed the street that July afternoon to seek help from a neighbor. "She was kind of introducing herself and said, very apologetically, 'I'm a lesbian,'" recalls Mary Carter. Hartt told Carter that her partner had struck her and they called the police, who arrested Coffee and noted that the precipitating argument had involved money. Hartt and Coffee, they wrote, had "no food, no electricity, and no phone." Coffee's sister, whom she rarely saw, posted her $500 bail.

Years before, as Hartt had stood by Coffee through her trial for fraud, her mother had likened her love for Coffee to the love of Jesus for mankind. But Hartt now prepared to testify against Coffee. She let the charges drop after Coffee agreed to take a course on battering intervention and prevention, and also to submit to a psychiatric evaluation. Coffee had nearly completed her six-month course on domestic violence when, in September 2007, she met with a psychiatrist in Dallas. The doctor flagged "possible underlying psychopathology." Coffee did not see her again; she had met the terms of dismissal.

Coffee and Hartt and their dogs had been getting by on gifted groceries and providence—an oil painting they found in the attic fetched $850—when, that same summer of 2007, they received a citation for back taxes.

Coffee and her sister owed more than $23,000 on their mother's home. The sisters paid their bill with a reverse mortgage, says Hartt. But they needed money, and Coffee answered an ad in the *Dallas Morning News* from a pharmaceutical company that wanted blood—pints and pints of it—to test treatments for a range of medical problems.

Coffee had a fear of needles, was "a hard stick" besides, she says. And donors had to submit to ten or fifteen withdrawals in a day. But the company, Covance, paid between three and six thousand dollars a study. Over the next few years, Coffee, sixty-something and broke, rolled up her sleeves seven or eight times, paying her bills in blood.

Coffee took another job, too, as a surrogate juror; a pair of lawyers were paying forty dollars to help them test out arguments before going to trial. Legal professionals were told not to apply. But Coffee did so and enjoyed the work; seated behind a two-way mirror with a plate of cookies, she assessed damages in a pair of cases, answering questions about a construction worker who had lost an arm, and a patent infringement case involving a computer program. Hartt marveled. "Here is the *Roe* attorney being a professional juror," she says. "They don't know who she is."

Coffee wanted it that way. There were few things she so disliked, she says, as "braggadocio," and secrecy had come to feel for her a form of modesty.

Nonetheless, Coffee was proud of *Roe*. "With very little resources," she says, "we put together something that's still standing." In 2008, she told a reporter from South Dakota who managed to reach her that she was glad a proposed state ban on abortion had failed. Said Coffee:

"I think it would have raised some constitutional questions." It was her lone public comment in years.

Coffee was disinclined to profit from *Roe* as so many others had. Come 2010—having earned little more from *Roe* than a few royalty checks from NBC (the last, in 1995, for $86)—she was again broke. She would have to sell her mother's house, and she turned to a realtor named Scott Jackson.

Jackson was a fifth-generation Dallasite. He and his mother, Glenda, had sold the home of Henry Wade a few blocks over, on Velasco Avenue, where a chaw-speckled wall recalled the DA and his spittoon. Now, a decade later, Jackson set out to sell the cream-brick ranch of the woman who'd bound Wade to Roe. It would be a difficult sell. Coffee and Hartt had no money to run the air conditioning during showings. And they had to sell before their next property tax bill was due. The sale closed in early 2011 with twenty days to spare. Coffee accepted $281,000 from a developer, $88,000 less than she'd asked.

Coffee and Hartt drove east, off to a railroad town in east Texas where they bought a little white house. The town of Mineola had changed little in the sixty years the house had stood. Then, as now, it was dotted with pines and azaleas and Baptist churches. Since 1950, the population had risen by just 20 percent, to 4,500. There was plenty of room in its ten square miles for two more, and Coffee and Hartt furnished their house with a $500 bed from Sears and whatever could be found secondhand.

Coffee had always been frugal; back in 1960, she was seventeen when her fellow exchange students in New Zealand dubbed her "banker." She and Hartt got by, with Medicare and Medicaid, Social Security and food stamps; every month, the couple drove off to a food bank in Quitman for $100 of non-refrigerated foodstuffs: rice and pasta and peas and dried cereal and powdered milk and canned fish. They shared the last with their beloved ridgebacks.

New difficulties arose. Hartt was diagnosed with breast cancer, and the women were out walking the dogs when a car struck Coffee and broke her hip. Home in their little house with no heat or air conditioning, the women struggled to care for each other—Coffee uncommunicative and compulsive, chewing toothbrushes till the bristles went flat,

Hartt nervous and perhaps even paranoid. Says Hartt: "The sister and Linda were against me."

Hartt had not let go that six years before, Coffee had hit her; she'd even kept her bloodied shirt. There remained between the women "little love," says Hartt. Still, she admired her partner, and likened her to Cordelia and Minerva—Coffee both exiled and wise. And for all that the women had suffered, they shared occasional joys, too—a long hike to a picnic on the Sabine River, a feast on Bastille Day, the one day each year when the women ate as once they had, Hartt preparing eggplant and lamb and sorbet.

Home in conservative Mineola, Coffee and Hartt invited no one into their house. And they confided in no one their two great secrets: that Coffee had helped to legalize abortion, and that they were gay. There was reason to keep quiet. Hartt would soon find in her mailbox an absentee ballot sent from the Conservative Republicans of Texas, a piece of political mail that cautioned that a vote for "liberals" was a vote for "abortion on demand" and "teaching homosexuality as an acceptable alternative lifestyle."

EVERY DECADE OR SO, Coffee was recognized alongside Weddington for her part in Roe: her face in a mural at Vanderbilt Law School, her name in a Good Housekeeping ranking of world-changing women. And so, as the fortieth anniversary of Roe approached in late 2012, and Coffee turned seventy, it would be best, she thought, if at least one person in Mineola knew of her past in case a camera crew came looking.

Coffee turned to the instructor of an exercise class she took at a nearby church, a former teacher named Christine. Coffee knew that Christine liked to read, and she handed her a book from the library with instruction to look up her name. Christine soon returned the book to Coffee with a question about the fetus that Jane Roe had wished to abort. "She asked me if I would've killed it," recalls Coffee, laughing. "That sounds pretty pro-life to me."

Coffee need not have bothered. January 2013, the ruby anniversary of Roe, came and went without so much as a phone call.

ANOTHER YEAR HAD PASSED, the thirtieth that Coffee and Hartt had spent together, when, on a February morning in 2014, Hartt stood in her home, a skinny woman with salt-and-pepper hair, mussed and short. She wore nylon pants over flannel, a jacket over a hoodie over a shirt. But her layers and her space heaters were no match for the winter air. It was twenty-three degrees outside and not much warmer in her home— forty degrees in the living room, fifty-six in the hall, sixty in the bedroom off the porch where she and Coffee ate their breakfasts on a small desk. Hartt was cold. She thought of the olive shrub that she'd planted just outside. "Though the fig tree may not blossom," she said, reciting a passage from Habakkuk that she kept in her wallet, "yet, I will rejoice in the Lord."

The temperature outside had risen to thirty when, the next morning, Coffee, in black sweats and a zippered green sweatshirt, walked the few blocks to her exercise class at First Baptist Church. She was seventy-one—the age her father had been when he was diagnosed with Alzheimer's. Fearing his fate, she'd undertaken to get in shape and had dropped thirty-five pounds.

At a quarter past eight, Coffee and five other seniors began to lift their heels and bend their knees and circle their arms, a half dozen Texans moving to the light strains of Christian music that emanated from a speaker in the ceiling above: "Praise Him for what He has done." It was Christine leading the class—the one person in Mineola who knew that among them was a women's rights pioneer. But Coffee was safe; *Roe* would not find her here. And after a square dance and a stationary march, Coffee still had energy to burn and began to jog in place and then to run, her gray hair falling over her eyes.

Coffee smiled as she ran. She was happy. At nine o'clock, she and the others retired to a small room where Christine read from the Bible: John, Romans, Psalms. A man named Charles spoke of visiting the sick. A woman named Pam said that they had best remember those who had no heat. Coffee said nothing, and then walked out into the cold.

Chapter 31

Ever since meeting Norma in 1971, Connie had been her Giving Tree, happy to stand beside her despite her regular maltreatment and neglect. A friend who was witness to their relationship thought Connie "masochistic." Connie said simply that she held Norma in the same mental space she held her mother, Clementia. Connie had thus carried on for three decades, tending to Norma and, now, to her ministry too, helping her to fight *Roe* as assiduously as she'd helped her to defend it.

Connie answered the mail and the phones at Roe No More. She even made the occasional public appearance for Norma when Norma was out of town. Connie, though, was slowing. She turned seventy in 2001 and had poor hearing, troublesome sinuses and feet. She found it harder to travel, and backed out of a trip with Norma to a Catholic conference in New Zealand. But she could still fix a faucet or mend a fence for her neighbors on Cactus Lane. And she continued to make Norma smoothies and help her through her insomnia and depression and worsening cough, never mind that Norma, ever since her Christian rebirth, refused to share her bed.

Norma continued to damn homosexuality; she wrote to a gay advocacy group in Dallas that homosexuals "are very unstable people who want to 'prey' on innocent children, men [and] women who are walking with God." Yet Norma would later reflect that, of all her sacrifices for *Roe*, it was the abnegation of her homosexuality that she had found "the hardest thing." Having been unable to consecrate her union with Connie with anything more than silver rings, Norma still avoided weddings—those Christian celebrations of heterosexual love.

———

IF THERE WAS ANYONE in the pro-life world Norma might have spoken to about her lesbianism, it was Sheree Havlik. Havlik would come to call Connie a close friend. And only Havlik had tried to comfort Norma after Flip Benham enlisted a therapist to "cure" her homosexuality.

Havlik had joined Operation Rescue back in 1995, after a teacher told her twelve-year-old daughter that abortion was a necessary corrective to the turpitude of men. Benham had then asked Havlik to balance the O.R. books, which she did on Friday afternoons on her way home from her management job at Raytheon.

Havlik was a decade younger than Norma. The youngest of six from a Catholic home in Cedar Rapids, Iowa, she had married at eighteen, become a mother at twenty and graduated college at twenty-two with a degree in physics. She smiled a lot, and had green eyes and big blond hair.

Havlik took in strays; in addition to her three children, she was raising a fourth, a friend of her youngest who was escaping a broken home. More and more, she began to look after Norma, too, lending her a winter coat and appraising a poem she wrote and greeting her at the office and at pro-life events—at christenings for babies who had been "saved," at memorials for those who had not. Havlik was soon visiting Norma every Friday on her way home from O.R.

Norma lamented to Havlik that people only cared to know her, not Connie. So Havlik began to spend more time with Connie, who in turn asked Havlik to look after Norma during those spells when Norma was depressed. Summoned by Connie one bleak day, Havlik found Norma in her bedroom seated with a book. The blinds were drawn, the lights off save one lamp. Norma told Havlik that she was in a "deep, deep depression" and had no control over her thoughts. Havlik sat and took her hand, and Norma returned to her book. She was reading of Dymphna, the patron saint of the mentally ill. Tradition said that Dymphna had rebuffed the advances of her mentally ill father only to be decapitated by him. Norma finished her reading, and then showed Havlik the razor blades she kept hidden in a crack between her bathroom sink and the wall.

Norma spoke to Havlik openly of her depression. But it was harder to speak of her lesbianism. Being gay was in conflict with the "Christian principles" that her own ministry espoused in its articles of incorporation. So Norma only repeated to Havlik what others told her—that she "acted gay" because men had hurt her, that her decades with Connie were the result not of desire but "dependency."

Norma was indeed dependent on Connie. And as Connie stopped accompanying her on her travels in the first years of the new millennium, Havlik took her place, looking after Norma on trips to New Orleans, San Juan, London. Always, she returned her without incident to Connie.

CONNIE WAS SEVENTEEN YEARS older than Norma. She was growing tired. It took her longer to maintain the house with hammer and paint. She drove less. And in the summer of 2004, Norma was at the wheel on a drive to Houston when Connie suddenly went limp beside her. Connie revived but, days later, began to slur her words. Norma drove her to Baylor University Medical Center and then phoned Havlik, who arrived to find Connie paralyzed by a stroke.

Connie left the hospital a month later, signed out by her "goddaughter" Norma. Her speech was comprehensible only to some, her right side impaired. Still, she committed herself to rehab. She rose quickly from wheelchair to walker to cane, and once again put on her own jeans and plaid shirts. But if Connie could take care of herself, she no longer could care for Norma. Their neighbor Utah Foster was out mowing his yard when Norma told him, he recalls, that Connie "needs to hurry up and get better so that she can take care of her."

But Connie wasn't getting better. She returned in August to the hospital, while Norma flew off to Ohio and South Dakota and Winnipeg and San Juan. Even when Norma was home, she was away. Says Havlik: "She started drinking really heavily."

Money was a second stress. Connie's Social Security and Medicare went only so far. And Roe No More had earned Norma just $62,000 in three years. Rebranding it Crossing Over Ministry gave her income only a temporary bump. Norma blamed those who booked her talks, whether Pavone or Parker or Eberle Associates, a conservative outfit in Virginia. And in 2004, Norma turned over the business of being Jane Roe to a makeup artist in New Jersey named Hector Ferrer.

Ferrer had come to the States as a baby in 1965, moving from Puerto Rico to Philadelphia with his parents, a homemaker and a handyman. He got his GED. After years of fun with women in Miami, Ferrer moved to New York City in 1991 to become an actor. He had just enrolled in acting school, spritzing perfume in department stores to pay tuition and rent, when his girlfriend got pregnant. Ferrer left school for a second job doing makeup and moved with his girlfriend from Queens to the suburbs of Jersey.

Fatherhood did not domesticate Ferrer; he was unfaithful and left his girlfriend when their daughter was three. She was almost five when, in 1997, during an Easter service at a local theater where Ferrer managed the ushers and bar staff, Ferrer found himself overcome by guilt over his promiscuity. He answered an altar call. "The Lord came upon me and I was weeping," says Ferrer. Thirty-two years old, he was born again.

Ferrer contacted the many women he was sleeping with. "I'm hanging it up," he recalls telling them. "I'm serving the Lord." He continued, however, to see one woman. She was soon pregnant. In 2001, tests revealed that their son, who was now three, had a rare genetic disorder called Dubowitz syndrome.

Upon his rebirth, Ferrer had pledged to refrain from sex until marriage. But it was only now, one month after learning that his son would be stunted physically and intellectually, that Ferrer was true to his chastity ring, serving the Lord "one hundred percent," he says. He was soon raising his son by himself.

In 2004, Ferrer had the idea to produce skits for churches about secular ills, from pornography to abortion. On a whim, he sought out Jane Roe to see if she might participate. She declined; she was busy with her lawsuit, *McCorvey v. Hill*. But she spoke to Ferrer for two hours. He blessed Norma and her suit. After hanging up the phone, Ferrer told himself that he'd found a new calling: fighting abortion. Months later,

Norma called to ask if he would work with her. Ferrer was in the middle of a makeup job in Jersey City. "I lost it," he says. "It changed my life."

Norma began to phone Ferrer weekly. They talked and prayed, and she called him *mijo*, "my son." He began booking her talks, and she sent him bits of money and business cards that read "Evangelist–Creative Director." The two then met at the 2005 March for Life, and they got on well—two working-class Christians who were children of divorce and had divorced themselves. Ferrer remained star-struck by Norma, which suited her. Still, the ministry would earn Norma just $15,000 all year. Connie applied for food stamps, and Norma turned to Troy Newman for help.

———

A DECADE HAD PASSED since Norma had met Newman in San Diego, the two going out for drinks after long days of protest during the Republican National Convention. Newman had since moved from California to Kansas, the better to protest Dr. Tiller. When Norma emailed Newman that she was in need of money, he forwarded her plea around the country. Within days, word that Jane Roe was destitute had landed on the front page of the *Dallas Morning News*.

"We've got a little bread left and some more potatoes," Norma told the paper. "We're just trying to keep our faith together and hope up." The paper noted that Norma was caring for her "friend" Connie Gonzales, who had been incapacitated by a stroke.

It was no truer that Norma was caring for Connie than that she and Connie were hungry; seeing the article, Connie's family was aghast. But it occurred to Sheree Havlik, who knew the couple best, that Norma *believed* they were hungry. ("Whether I was right or wrong," Norma once said, "I was always right in my mind.") Regardless, Norma was happy to be back in the papers, happy too when food began to arrive at her door. Havlik was among those dropping off groceries and money, until Connie showed her with a smirk their stocked pantry. Says Havlik: "I just started laughing."

Norma had wrung from *Roe* another gift. But Connie was still declining. She'd had surgery to unclog an artery in her neck, she needed supplemental oxygen and she had begun to lose her memory.

Some six months before, Norma had driven Connie and Havlik and a social worker they knew to a nursing home in south Dallas, where Norma intended to commit Connie. Norma had not told Connie where they were going, and Connie refused to leave the car. In the months since, as Connie played solitaire and watched her Cowboys, Norma had come to see that it was she who must leave. In the summer of 2006, she accepted an invitation from her old friend Flip Benham to fly off to Mississippi to protest an abortion clinic, the last in the state.

The protest drew a counterprotest. As hundreds faced off in Jackson, Benham readied, in a church parking lot off North State Street, to burn not only copies of *Roe* but a rainbow flag and a Koran.

Abortion and homosexuality were standard fare; Islam was new. Radical pro-lifers had long blamed the Jews for abortion. (Robert Cooley, an activist in Connecticut, had stated that "the majority of abortionists are Jewish.") But they were slowly extending their disdain to Muslims, Randall Terry, for one, arguing that Islamic terrorism followed from "the words and deeds of Muhammad."

New provocations got Benham press. Papers covered his blaspheming of Islam just as they had his call for a boycott of Disney (in response to a gay-friendly insurance policy). Though Cooley had long ago cautioned Benham not to use Norma, Benham now asked her, outside that Mississippi clinic, to strike the first match.

Norma was not in simple terms a racist; her own partner was not Anglo. But nor did she mind bigotry. She'd been happy to accept the speaking invitation of a white supremacist newspaper called the *Jubilee*, happy to use in her second memoir what one professor termed "overtly anti-Semitic, white supremacist language." She set the holy book on fire.

Still, Norma did have her red lines. This same July week in Jackson, another old friend, Father Pavone, crossed one of them.

———

PAVONE CERTAINLY HAD NERVE. Back in 2000, he'd attempted to found his own religious order devoted to countering abortion. "Is it not likely," he asked, "that God would set aside for Himself and His Church a group of men who would dedicate themselves to fighting for the sanctity of life?"

Pavone quickly secured fifteen men to join his order, and a half-million dollars in pledged support. What he did not have, however, was the blessing of the Catholic church. Cardinal Edward Egan had told Pavone to leave Priests for Life and go back to a parish. Furious, Pavone had released a statement through PFL: "We are shocked at what has happened and frankly can't make heads or tails of it." Still, he was careful to note that he was "continuing to negotiate with the Cardinal through all the proper channels and in accordance with the demands of Canon Law."

Pavone was unafraid to clash with the church. (He chose, for example, to back the Iraq war, which the Vatican opposed.) And the church caved; it decided to allow Pavone not only to remain with PFL but to create his religious order—if he found a bishop willing to back him. This he did, in 2005, when Bishop John Yanta welcomed Pavone (and his plans for a $130 million seminary) to Amarillo, where forty-nine parishes dotted the dry plains of the Texas Panhandle.

The Catholic community was wary. One Catholic scholar called Priests for Life a "guerrilla group." Norma took note. Said Norma of Pavone: "He's naïve like a fox."

Norma rarely saw Pavone anymore. "She walked away," he says. She'd not only cut ties with the priest but had cut him from her story; she now said that God Himself—not Pavone—had instructed her to become Catholic. Pavone, however, still touted the testimony he'd written in her name calling him "the catalyst that brought me into the Catholic Church."

In the summer of 2006, Pavone arrived in Mississippi, where Norma had just ignited a Koran. Benham had invited Pavone to Jackson to lead a memorial procession for a fetus in a city park. Norma disapproved.

A decade had passed since Norma had found herself at her first fetus memorial, where, outside a clinic in Chicago, Benham had set a fetus in an open casket. Norma had been too upset to join the procession that passed by it.

Years later, in 2004, Benham had embarked on a walk across America with an aborted fetus, when Norma emailed a friend that God Himself had told her that aborted fetuses were meant only to be buried—"not to be seen by man, put on display, not to be carried around in jars." Added

Norma: "HOW WOULD YOU OR MEMBERS OF YOUR FAMILY
FEEL IF YOUR BODY WAS CARTED AROUND THE WORLD SO
OTHERS COULD SEE YOU IN DEATH . . . [?]" Norma had phoned
Benham (and Pavone) that same month, beseeching them to bury the
fetus. But it remained in its jar, continuing on with Benham across the
country for six months.

The Catholic church deplored such exhibitions; Pavone's own diocese would state that "no one who is pro-life can exploit a human body
for any reason, especially the body of a fetus." But Pavone said that it
was no less important for the pro-choice to face the realities of Roe than
it had once been for white people to face the realities of Jim Crow.

Pavone had come to Mississippi to officiate at the memorial of
another fetus. And he and Benham had asked a woman named Patricia
McEwen to get it there.

NOT MANY YEARS BEFORE, McEwen had been an academic, a liberal lapsed
Catholic teaching creativity and innovation at SUNY Buffalo. She was
pro-choice and had remained so even after becoming born again in
1991, one year shy of fifty.

It was a miscarriage that changed her thinking on abortion—though
not one of her own. (Two lost pregnancies had left McEwen childless
before a divorce in 1987.) It was, rather, the miscarriage of a horse, a foal
born seven months before it was due.

McEwen had bred horses for some twenty-five years. One morning
in 1993, on her farm outside Buffalo, she came upon that fetal foal at the
feet of its mother. It had been conceived just four months before. But
already discernible was the predominant marking of its father—a wide
blaze on the forehead that narrowed to a tiny strip on the nose. All at
once, it struck McEwen, she says, that what lay before her was a horse.
It followed that what humans miscarried and aborted were babies. One
year later, McEwen left academia for Operation Rescue, moving to Florida where she took an O.R. course on the Bible and abortion.

McEwen had been with O.R. for about two years, she says, when
in 1996, she began to work remotely with Benham, helping with
everything from press to newsletters to the chaperoning of Norma.

What set her apart, though, was one task in particular: transporting aborted fetuses.

———

IT WAS THE RESPONSIBILITY of abortion providers to dispose of the embryos and fetuses they aborted. They did so, in the words of the consent form Charlotte Taft used at her Dallas clinic, "in a matter we deem appropriate." In the years following *Roe*, that usually meant putting the fetal remains in a garbage disposal or dumpster.

It was not a cumbersome job. The typical abortus is tiny; nearly 90 percent of abortions are performed by the twelfth week of pregnancy, when the fetus weighs an ounce and is two-plus inches long. Though, by 1980, clinics were aborting fetuses through the twentieth week of pregnancy, fetuses of flesh and bone, these too could be set out in sealed plastic containers for a garbage truck to pick up.

Still, throwing out embryos and fetuses is not simple. Doing so, says Taft, often left her and other providers feeling uneasy; ethics aside, it smelled of concealment, and they wished to be transparent in their work. Also, refuse could be stolen. And so, clinics began farming out the task of disposal to waste management companies and pathology labs, which picked up the tissue and had it incinerated or put in landfill.

With more than one million annual abortions in the U.S., there were many tons of tissue to dispose of. Oversight and negligence were inevitable. And it was the gross negligence of a pathology lab in California that thrust the question of fetus memorials onto the political stage.

The lab was owned by a man named Malvin Weisberg. He had fallen behind in his payments, and in 1982, authorities repossessed a shipping container on his property. Inside it were sixteen thousand embryos and fetuses. It fell to the state of California to determine what to do with them—whether to incinerate them as medical waste or bury them as human beings.

The dilemma generated headlines, and the president weighed in. Wrote Reagan: "To hold a memorial for these children is most fitting and proper." Lawsuits followed, and the ACLU argued that a burial would be religious and thus conflate church and state. The California Court of Appeals agreed. After the Supreme Court let the ruling stand, pro-life forces held a memorial for the embryos and fetuses still in county storage. Pat Boone sang a song he wrote titled "16,000 Faces."

Soon after, a Los Angeles County board, following the ruling of a local judge, ordered that the embryos and fetuses be buried in a nonreligious ceremony. On October 7, 1985, they were laid to rest in six pine caskets. But the ceremony, in an east Los Angeles cemetery, was religious and political, too—with clergy and hymns, flags and politicians. Reagan again weighed in. "Just as the terrible toll of Gettysburg can be traced to a tragic decision of a divided Supreme Court," he wrote, "so also can these deaths we mourn."

The California case was a cause célèbre. A growing number of pro-lifers now desired not only to bury fetuses, but to memorialize them. Among them was a group of activists who, in 1988, stole the dismembered remains of several thousand aborted fetuses from a pathology lab in Chicago. The group then reassembled the bodies and staged funerals for them around the country, placing the four best-preserved fetuses in an open casket. Operation Rescue followed suit the next spring, Randall Terry presenting a blackened fetal body to a phalanx of press in Los Angeles. In 1993, Benham got involved, holding a memorial outside Dallas City Hall for a dismembered fetus he and Ronda Mackey had stolen earlier that year from a freezer in a clinic off Highway 75. A Dallas obstetrician had pieced it back together.

The handling of fetuses was "bizarre and fetishistic," as one journalist wrote. But the aim was clear. Memorials weaponized the fetus—"transformed remains into dead babies," wrote the history professor Johanna Schoen, and "medical procedures into murder." They were soon a staple of the pro-life fight. Benham, for one, began to stage them annually, each ceremony complete with casket and flowers, a priest and "Amazing Grace." Of course, each memorial required a fetus, too. And in 1996, Benham asked his new volunteer McEwen to procure one. She did so, from a pastor outside Washington DC who'd let her know, she says, that he had an aborted male fetus in a jar of formaldehyde.

McEwen stowed the fetus under a towel in her closet. As the months passed and its memorial approached, the fetus triggered thoughts in McEwen of her miscarriages, "reminded me that my children were dead," she says. McEwen was greatly relieved when Benham told her that, henceforth, Pavone would provide (and store) all fetuses. Says McEwen: "He had a source." McEwen, though, would still need to "figure out," she says, "how to get the baby from Father Frank to where the memorial was."

Pavone was based, along with PFL, in a brick building in Staten Island. The building contained a chapel. There, down the hall from an enormous photograph of the priest with eleven toddlers in pastel onesies, Pavone stored a few fetuses in jars of formaldehyde. Whenever it was time for a memorial, McEwen would fly north to pick one up. "They'd welcome me into the building and pass me the baby," she says. McEwen would then head to the airport, ready to tell security that she, Dr. Patricia McEwen, was carrying "a medical specimen." It didn't matter that her doctorate was in organizational communications. "They didn't know I wasn't a medical doctor," she says. Flying with a fetus in her carry-on, she would find herself wondering about its past. "Who was this baby?" she says. "Who was her mother? Who was her father? Why didn't they want this baby?" These trips, couriering the dead, were stressful. Still, they felt right. "Very often a baby who's gone through an abortion has never had any love," says McEwen. "This way, they have love."

Security measures after 9/11 grounded McEwen; liquid could no longer be carried onto a plane. Henceforth, she found volunteers to drive every jarred fetus to its memorial. Once it arrived, McEwen determined with a mortician exactly how many minutes, given the air temperature, the fetus could be out of its jar.

Pavone usually officiated at the memorials. And more often than not, says McEwen, the same female fetus lay in the casket before him. The fetus had been killed by saline amniocentesis; though it had been aborted at roughly twenty weeks, it was intact. To hold it, says McEwen, "was like holding a newborn baby." Pavone had the fetus returned to him in Staten Island after each memorial. "Father Frank had charge of her," says McEwen. "He just didn't want to bury her." Pavone disputes that he ever unlawfully sourced or neglected to bury the fetuses he displayed.

On July 20, 2006, Pavone stood over a fetus in a Mississippi park. It was ninety-three degrees in Jackson. The fetus had been resubmerged in fresh formaldehyde when the priest told the Mississippi press that he would not bury it in Mississippi as planned but would bury it, months later, in Alabama.

Norma was disgusted. She found herself out of step with the men who had guided her in the eleven years since her baptism. She did not attend the memorial at which Pavone officiated. After leaving Mississippi, she never saw Benham again.

━━━

JANE ROE BETTERED every résumé; Weddington regularly noted her plaintiffship, Allred her patronage, Benham her baptism, Pavone her confirmation, Parker the Supreme Court citation that had come of their partnership. Her books and films and nonprofits had lifted scores more. And as Norma approached sixty, in 2007, she continued to partner with ever more Christians—with senators and advertisers who paid her to speak their words, with societies and documentarians who had her weepily rue *Roe* in films they titled *I Was Wrong* and *Whatever Happened to Jane Roe?*

That last question had occupied Frank Di Bugnara for three years.

Di Bugnara worked at a production studio in Phoenix overseeing hundreds of shoots a year: music videos, short films, documentaries. But none of those projects were his own. And when, in 2004, while driving his Toyota Tercel on Interstate 10, he came upon Norma telling the conservative commentator Sean Hannity her story, he wondered all at once, he says, if he'd finally found at age twenty-eight "the one thing I want to give birth to."

Di Bugnara's interest was unsurprising. He was Catholic and had been prone as a child to worry "about adult things," he says, abortion among them. His distress had lifted when, at age fifteen, he'd approached the altar in a church in Arizona, where one of its members had been said to be receiving messages from Jesus and Mary. He'd not yet left the altar when that woman, a pharmacist named Gianna Talone, approached and prophesied, he recalls, that he would one day do a great and positive thing.

Di Bugnara returned home, a high-schooler wondering earnestly, he says, how he might be "an instrument of positiveness in the world."

Now, more than a decade later, hearing Jane Roe speak on KFYI, he thought that perhaps, at last, he had his answer.

Months later, Di Bugnara pitched the idea of a film to Norma over a steak lunch in Dallas. She told him that another movie producer had bought her story. But two years later, over an O'Doul's in Phoenix, she told him that things had soured with that other producer and that if he was still interested, so was she.

Di Bugnara was not rich. He rented his home, drove a used car. But he had founded his own production company. After a run of successful years, he had enough cash on hand to buy out that producer and pay Norma, too.

Norma needed money. Beyond the $500 that those Texas Catholics gave her monthly, her ministry would earn her just $11,000 this year. She was still looking for another big check.

———

ON SEPTEMBER 22, Norma turned sixty and celebrated her birthday with Connie and their friend Daniel Vinzant. Over lunch, Vinzant gave her a CD by Bobbie Gentry.

Forty years had passed since Gentry had topped the charts with "Ode to Billie Joe." The country song was haunting and spare, and listening to it now, Norma was "enraptured," says Vinzant.

Gentry sang of a family discussing the suicide of a Mississippi teenager who'd jumped off a bridge. The family was unaware that one among them had, that same day, stood beside that teen and thrown something into the water. Gentry said that the song was about "unconscious cruelty." But millions of listeners focused instead on the unnamed object the couple had thrown. Like many of them, Norma was sure it was a baby. She was certain, too, that the song was about abortion, and she wished to go to the Tallahatchie Bridge.

By chance, Norma was due back in Mississippi twelve days later, invited by a woman named Margie Casey to speak in support of a new crisis pregnancy center in the small city of Senatobia.

Casey was a native Mississippian who, twelve years before, had chosen to carry her child to term despite its spina bifida. Her daughter was alive and well when Norma arrived to help Casey raise money for the new CPC. That same day, Casey took Norma to a memorial for victims of abortion. There, on Highway 6, Casey told her the story of a woman named Judy Wiggins, who'd accompanied them and was sitting on a bench close by.

Wiggins was just shy of thirty-six and had six children. Between her second and third, she'd had also four abortions—the consequence, she says, of three destructive years of abuse and depression. Wiggins had been a victim of sexual abuse as a child. But she had come to determine, she says, "that the source of my shame and a lot of my depression have their roots in my abortion experience." When she got pregnant again, Wiggins had changed course; she chose to have her baby and marry its father and join a church and be born again. Wiggins and her husband, Tim, were baptized in a river in Austin.

Norma listened and walked over to Wiggins and looked her in the eye. She said, recalls Wiggins, "I want to apologize for the role I played in your abortions." Norma asked for forgiveness. "Nobody had ever really acknowledged any part they may have played in my abortion experiences," says Wiggins. "That really netted my heart to Norma."

The women hugged and cried. Later that night, as Norma drank a spritzer she herself mixed from two bottles of wine and a Sprite, she spoke to her new friends about the Tallahatchie Bridge. The truss bridge had long since collapsed, replaced where it stood by another just like it. Norma went to the unincorporated town of Money to commune with the spirit of a song. She'd just left the bridge when she phoned Vinzant to share her certainty that what had been thrown from it was a baby.

NORMA RETURNED TO CONNIE only to leave her again days later, flying to New Jersey on October 12, 2007. She was off to see her handler and friend, Hector Ferrer.

Ferrer was in high spirits. A month before, at his local New Jersey church, he had finally realized his dream, producing theater in the service of God—skits on domestic violence, pornography, abortion. He was readying to stage more skits at his church that weekend, and Norma had flown north to headline the event.

Ferrer had been helping Norma to share her testimony since 2004.

But he had only just begun to share his own, and would soon make it his practice, at the end of every telling, to call his son David on stage. It was a climax that moved every audience. And it absolved Ferrer, turning sin—a second child born out of wedlock—into something heroic, the choice to raise a damaged son whom he (and his ex) might have aborted.

Abortion was the center of Ferrer's life. Bringing Norma to his church was a highlight of his forty-two years, and word of the event spread on Christian Newswire. But on Saturday, the night before the event, Ferrer was at his home in Teaneck when the church called him, "frantic," he says, because Norma was outside on the church steps smoking cigarettes and drinking beer. She had refused to return to her guest quarters. The beer was nonalcoholic, she'd said.

Ferrer understood the stresses of working with Norma. But he could not abide her disrespecting his church. He pleaded with her to return inside. Norma refused, and soon taxied to the airport, never to see Ferrer again.

———

NORMA MISSED CONNIE when she was away. She had signed a note to her, that summer of 2007, "Much Love Your baby Girl, Norm." But they fought often. Their friend Havlik began to worry that Norma might harm Connie. "I did get a couple of phone calls," says Havlik, "when Norma would say, 'You better tell Connie to leave me alone or else I'm going to stab her with these scissors.'" Soon after Norma returned from her trip to Ferrer, the police came to the house to quell a fight between her and Connie. After the police left, so did Norma, driving to Waco with a carful of clothes and her cat.

In the decade since Daniel Vinzant had introduced Norma to Waco, she had found sanctuary in the city, fleeing from time to time to a motel at the corner of Highways 6 and 84 before returning home. "She would always say," says Vinzant, "'Waco was my Bethlehem.'" But now, after a few days in Waco, she didn't feel like returning to Connie, and she phoned Mississippi, telling Margie Casey that she had liked Senatobia and wished to return. Casey told her that she was welcome in her home, and Norma drove northeast, a hitchhiker helping her to pass the nine hours en route.

Casey put two of her kids into one room so that Norma could have a room of her own. A few days later, Casey called a realtor, a Presbyterian from Memphis named Debbi Caldwell who had a duplex to rent. Meeting Norma gave Caldwell pause. Norma's hair was dyed a bright red, her car was stuffed, and she was smoking. "She looked like a homeless person," says Caldwell. Still, Caldwell trusted Casey. And Casey told her, she says, that Norma was a famous woman who had come to Mississippi "to witness to all the churches in the area." Caldwell hadn't heard of Norma; she scarcely knew of *Roe*. But after Casey's church footed the security deposit, Norma signed a year lease and moved in.

The apartment was lovely, three bedrooms and two baths on Robinson Street. Casey and Wiggins soon supplied it with dishes and food, blinds and furniture; Casey gave Norma her brother's love seat and her grandmother's bed. Norma, though, was difficult. She asked to paint her bedroom black. She smoked in violation of the lease. And she didn't pay her rent. Caldwell was down $650 at the end of the month.

Norma was earning a little bit of money; her move had roused a few local churches to reach out. There remained a trickle of larger engagements, too, out-of-state jobs that paid Norma three or four thousand dollars. Norma had Judy Wiggins do the bookings and come along with her. The trips were difficult for Wiggins; she had four kids at home. Norma, meantime, broke commitments and needed minding when she kept them. But Wiggins felt called upon to spread the message that no one was beyond the reach of Christ. Though she took no money for her help (and received no thanks from Norma), she found her work with Norma redemptive. In the privacy of their travels, some half-dozen trips over the next eighteen months, Norma made clear to Wiggins her view that abortion was complex, that there were times it ought to be legal.

"Most people downplayed that," says Wiggins. "[Norma] was very much manipulated into using other people's rhetoric. In her alone time, she could be more forthcoming about her true beliefs. One-on-one in a hotel room is where she could tell you that she definitely believed in exceptions." Adds Wiggins: "She personified the abortion debate . . . complicated and conflicted about her own beliefs as many of us are."

———

SENATOBIA WAS A DRY CITY, and Norma contented herself with O'Doul's. But she was dyspeptic even when sober. And she was soon at odds with the locals—no longer welcome at the post office and said, at the beauty salon, to be fleecing small churches. She was fleecing Caldwell, too. After three months of unpaid rent, the realtor served Norma papers in December. A judge ordered Norma to pay up or go to jail. Norma paid.

Norma had to leave her apartment at once. She was unsure where to go. She didn't want to return to Connie, and her family couldn't put her up—her mother Mary withering, her daughter Melissa at loose ends, her brother Jimmy in a Texas nursing home where he would die in just weeks. So she turned back to *Roe*, calling the pro-life firebrand in Kansas who'd recently circulated her plea for money and food.

"She said, 'I have to get out of here,'" recalls Troy Newman. "I sent a van down—one of our truth-trucks."

Eight years had passed since Newman had had the idea to turn trucks into mobile billboards. He now operated a fleet of ten Isuzu diesels pasted with huge photographs of tiny bodies. Days after Christmas, a young couple dispatched by Newman drove one of them onto Robinson Street. All of Senatobia held its breath. "It had the fetus—it had the baby on the side," says Wiggins. "It was a lot."

Norma climbed in. Then, together with her cat, she was gone, driven six hundred miles through Tennessee and Arkansas and Oklahoma and Kansas in a truck plastered with gruesome images of aborted fetuses.

Chapter 32

It excited Norma to be where Dorothy had found Oz. Norma arrived in Kansas in the last week of 2007, and settled into the cottage of plywood and tin that Troy Newman had built in his backyard.

Newman had moved to Kansas in 2002 to harass George Tiller. He was still in that fight, living with his wife and five kids on acres of pastureland and hedge apple in the town of Towanda. They were twenty-five miles from Tiller's Wichita clinic. And twenty-five yards from Newman's front door, Norma had all she needed: a bathroom, a bed, a mini-fridge, a hotplate. Still, within days, she was depressed— "because it's January," she told Newman. She had to return to DC for another *Roe* anniversary. And back in the capital, she endorsed Ron Paul for president, appeared in a documentary titled *American Holocaust* and marched once again in protest of *Roe*, this time on the arm of Wiggins, her Mississippi friend.

It was a thrill for Wiggins to see up close the leaders of a movement she venerated. Here were Pavone and Parker, Terry and Schenck. But Wiggins soon wished to be back in her local crisis pregnancy center. "Seeing the famous folks was a bit disillusioning," she says. To know these men was to be subject to their egos and agendas. Watching Pavone try to get Norma to attend a PFL retreat for former providers of abortion, it struck Wiggins that the movement was using Norma. "Norma was never given time to mature in her faith before she was paraded around like a prize," she says. "She was never just allowed to be Norma McCorvey, saved by grace."

There were those who had never wanted anything more for Norma than grace: pro-lifers like Wiggins and Sheree Havlik and Daniel Vinzant, pro-choicers like Herbert Croner and Barbara Ellis and Charlotte Taft. Still, Norma remained drawn to the movement leaders. Says Wiggins: "She really wanted that paycheck and she wanted the notoriety." Norma returned to Newman.

Newman had made good use of Norma. He'd flown her to Wichita for a vigil outside Tiller's clinic, and put her on the back of his book. ("The former Jane Roe" called *Their Blood Cries Out*, "an excellent exposition of justice and mercy.") But now that Norma was in his backyard, Newman asked little more of her than to sign a letter to South Dakota politicians in advance of a proposed state ban on abortion.

Norma whiled the winter away—on a barstool in the Newman kitchen, in her cottage with her cat, at a local pub, at the wheel of her rented compact in south-central Kansas. "I was just trying to keep her together," says Newman. "Fed, housed." He tried to get her money, too; he sent out a solicitation letter with instruction to mail Norma checks at a Kansas P.O. box. Still, Norma wanted more. "She was very jealous that Troy had other obligations—such as his wife," recalls Wiggins. Three months after Norma's arrival in Kansas, that upset turned to anger when her cat darted from her cottage and wound up dead.

Norma wished to leave, and Newman resettled her in an apartment his extended family owned in Wichita. There, on a ground floor off Main Street, Norma had only to pay for electricity. All through spring, she was content. But Newman had not heard from her in several weeks when, one summer day, he went to the apartment to find that she had returned to Texas. The air was stale and Newman opened a window. Someone then stole Norma's TV and Norma cut Newman off, another friend let go. Says Wiggins: "She just went through people."

———

TO BE WITH NORMA WAS, inevitably, to be in her crosshairs. She possessed little empathy and less guilt. She could be cruel to those who sustained her. Only Connie, imperturbable and submissive, had managed to remain at her side, her partner for thirty-seven years. But when, that summer of 2008, Norma returned to her, even Connie was exasperated. "If you brought [Norma] up," says Havlik, "she would get kind of angry."

In the months since Norma had driven off to Waco, Connie had cared for herself. But she could no longer care for Norma. Now that the women were back together, that fact continued to pull them apart. Utah Foster, seated on his porch one house over, would never forget when Norma kicked over a grill, furious that Connie had not made her steak big enough. "Even after she had her stroke," says Foster, "she still tried to cook for Norma." Connie began to cry and Norma drove off.

Norma drove off a lot over the coming months—to events in Kentucky, DC, Louisiana. She was happier away. The money helped, too. And in November, the big check she was hoping for arrived, the filmmaker Di Bugnara wiring $50,000 from a Bank of America in downtown Phoenix. "It was reckless," he says. "I closed my eyes and I jumped." Norma bought a new Honda Fit.

Di Bugnara, meantime, had bought himself five years in which to make his film. He hired a researcher and then a screenwriter. Together, they worked all through spring to write and rewrite his script.

Norma was impatient to see it. Di Bugnara placated his subject with phone calls and a Christmas basket and hundreds of dollars, payments the lawyer Allan Parker negotiated against the check Di Bugnara was to write when his film actually started shooting. The payments left him uncomfortable. But to Norma, it was just business.

That same spring, in May 2009, Norma received an invitation from Randall Terry, the pro-life provocateur who had told her, he says, to "make money while you can."

TERRY HAD ONCE been the face of the war on abortion. Operation Rescue was his baby. But after government regulation crippled O.R. in 1994, he was no longer able to mobilize thousands to blockade abortion clinics. Terry turned instead to Christian radio, preaching against abortion and of the coming Christian America, which would subject women to men with "righteous testosterone flowing through their veins."

Terry himself had been all but neutered. Legal judgments against Operation Rescue had left him bankrupt, a run for Congress badly defeated. He had also lost his claim on righteousness; having written of those "pathetic males" who abandon their wives for younger women, Terry was censured by his church in 1999 for having left his wife, Cindy, after "repeated sinful relationships and conversations with both single and married women." (Terry responded that he had "only had sex with his wife.")

In 2001, Terry was forty-two when he married a woman sixteen years his junior. "Now you see the unfortunate demise of one who was used so powerfully by God and is now on a back burner," Benham told the *New York Times*. (There was additional snickering when one of Terry's children declared himself gay, another Muslim.)

Terry moved to Nashville in a failed attempt to write gospel and country songs. He was back in upstate New York selling cars when, a month after his marriage, he alerted former supporters that he had "resumed ministry." A move in 2008 to a DC suburb did little to reestablish his political bona fides. "The movement has gone by him," Pat Mahoney of the Christian Defense Coalition told the *Washington Post*. And so, in 2009, Terry reached out to the surest bet there was in the pro-life world: Norma McCorvey.

Terry knew Norma. Back in 1997, he'd paid her a few thousand dollars and flown her north to Binghamton to stump for him in his bid for Congress. He brought her back the next year to sign two thousand bookplates to slip into copies of Norma's book *Won by Love*; he signed them too and sold more than five hundred at $100 apiece.

Money aside, Norma liked Terry. He was coarse and anti-establishment. He was also an antidote to Benham—someone to sin with. After almost every March for Life, the two would meet up at the Dubliner bar in DC, Norma complaining over Guinness, says Terry, "about the pro-life leaders who took advantage of her."

A decade later, in May 2009, Terry had fallen out with those same men. Wanting to protest an upcoming speech by President Obama, he turned back to Norma, paying her $1,000 to walk with him (and some blood-splattered dolls) across the campus of Notre Dame.

Terry had a good thing in Norma. Like the fake blood he bought by the gallon, Jane Roe demanded attention; the Indiana press covered their arrests. Norma, in turn, had no beef with Terry. He paid her. She was thankful for the escape from Connie, too, and told Terry about Connie's stroke and the stress it had caused. After Norma returned home, Terry invited her to stay with him in the brick colonial his few remaining supporters were renting him and his family in Virginia. That July, Norma flew northeast.

Terry asked Norma to join a few protests he was staging in DC. Norma obliged, heckling the judge Sonia Sotomayor during her Senate confirmation hearing, and dumping pink plastic fetuses onto the desk of House Speaker Nancy Pelosi in advance of a vote in Congress on healthcare reform. After a week of rest, Norma flew on August 6 to Arizona, where a movie script awaited her input.

Many had come to know the futility of trying to extract from Norma her story. Asked by Di Bugnara to recount the sixty-two years that had led her to a screenwriter's couch in Phoenix, Norma cut their sessions short, overcome by traumas she'd only imagined: the abuse of a husband, the physical wresting away of the *Roe* baby. Di Bugnara felt responsible for her pain. When Norma flew home, he wondered, he says, if it was wise to work with someone "so unstable."

Norma touched down in Dallas. She had phoned Connie to tell her to leave the screen door open. But she arrived home on Cactus Lane to find it locked.

Connie was approaching eighty. She had known Norma exactly half her life. In those forty years, she had endured much, above all her abandonment, Norma having left her for long stretches in California, Mississippi and Kansas. Still, Norma had always returned. But, unable now to open her door, Norma grew furious. She had explicitly told Connie to leave it open.

Norma did not ring the bell. She did not knock. She loaded her bags into her Honda. Then, on that hot summer night, she drove off, leaving Connie forever.

PART VIII

The Family Roe

Chapter 33

In early 2010, I was reading a magazine article unrelated to *Roe* when a passing mention of its plaintiff, Norma McCorvey, stopped me short. "She never had the abortion she'd been seeking—her case was decided too late—and she gave the baby up for adoption," wrote Margaret Talbot.

I thought of the baby. It would now be forty, and it seemed to me likely that it had come to know of its difficult start in the world. *Roe* would be a heavy load to carry. I wondered if he or she might wish to speak of it.

I sent Norma a note. She wrote back that she didn't want to talk about her youngest child, so I turned to Connie, arranging to visit her on Cactus Lane.

CONNIE SAT OUTSIDE her Dallas home in an aluminum folding chair, smoking a Marlboro Light. Her short hair was a dark gray, and she wore white sneakers, blue jeans and a teal shirt that was loose about her thinning arms and neck. She had aged in the ten months since Norma had left, her memory and muscles slipping away. On this June morning, her caretaker, a niece named Linda, stood beside her, helping her to find elusive words.

Connie had not spoken to Norma since she'd driven off, not even when Norma had returned home to get some things. Connie had sat at the dining room table, quiet as Norma stuffed armloads of clothing into plastic bags and tried to pull free a rosary from behind a cabinet. It was stuck. Norma had left it behind with nearly all she possessed—the ashes of her father, her papers, the silver ring that Connie had given her to mark their commitment.

Connie now wore that ring. She was heartbroken. She was angry, too, and wished me to know that the stories Norma told were not true. Norma had not been shoplifting when they met. They had not been shot at over *Roe*. As for the deep concern Norma professed in her memoirs for her children, Connie was clear. "Please!" she said. "She's a phony."

Connie did not know where those children were. She did not even recall the name of the eldest, whom she had known years before.

Seven months later—after I'd searched in vain for Norma's two younger children in the records of the murdered lawyer who had brokered their adoptions—I returned to Connie in January 2011. She and her niece told me that her home would soon be foreclosed.

———

CONNIE HAD BOUGHT her house back in 1967, 1,300 square feet for under $15,000. The home had risen in value to more than $80,000, a nest egg in northeast Dallas, when, in 2004, Connie had her stroke.

In the months that followed, Norma had tried to move Connie out of the house. When Connie stayed put, Norma tried to transfer ownership of the house to her nonprofit, Crossing Over Ministry. A lawyer named Peter Parenti explained that Connie had to agree to the transfer. Connie did not do so. So, in 2005, Norma took out a large loan against the property, borrowing $92,000 that she and Connie were to repay over thirty years. The money went quickly, and, in 2009, Norma left Connie and their debt behind. Connie was soon in default, owing more money monthly (in mortgage and escrow) than she received from Social Security. By March 2010, she owed $4,000.

One friend tried to help; Sheree Havlik applied on behalf of Norma and Connie for a hardship loan that would lower their monthly $900 payment. But both women needed to sign the application, and Norma refused. Come April, a Dallas law firm sent a note to 11343 Cactus Lane on behalf of a mortgage company. One sentence stood out: "ORDER

FOR FORECLOSURE CONCERNING NORMA MCCORVEY, CONNIE GONZALES."

Nine months later, when I returned to Connie, she was resigned to losing her home just as she had lost Norma. She and her niece alerted me to the mass of papers Norma had left in the garage.

The papers were in bags and boxes and baskets and a filing cabinet, a jumble Connie and Linda planned to throw out along with the rest of the mess—broken furniture and old clothes and a stained box spring. I asked if they would give me the papers instead. They agreed, and Linda dumped them into garbage bags that I put into the trunk of my car.

The papers were an account of the life of Jane Roe—of her books and films and nonprofits, her speeches and taxes and letters. They contained traces of Norma, too—of her medical ailments, her children. In a 1998 interview with the *National Catholic Register*, I found the birthdate of her youngest: June 2, 1970.

That child, I learned online, was one of thirty-seven girls born that day in Dallas County. Another article in Norma's papers told me that her daughter had later lived in Washington state. That fact helped me winnow my list of thirty-seven down to one. The Dallas County records department then confirmed for me that that child, number thirty-two on my list, had been adopted.

I didn't call Shelley. In the event that she didn't already know that Norma was her birth mother, such a call would upend her life. Instead, I phoned her mother, Ruth, and identified myself and asked if she had known the adoption attorney Henry McCluskey. She said that she had. She said that she knew about Norma, too, and I promised her that I would not write about Shelley without Shelley's consent. Ruth thanked me for calling her first and agreed to tell Shelley I'd called. Shelley would tell me if she wished to talk. Until then, I would look for her sisters.

Fifteen months later, in June 2012, the doctor who had delivered Jennifer forty-five years before told me her surname. Five months after that, on a Friday in November, a manager at the Walmart where Jennifer worked helped me reach her by phone. Jennifer was amazed. Only weeks before, her partner Lisa had resolved to hire a private investigator to help Jennifer find her birth mother. Forty minutes after I called, the couple met me at a McDonald's off Texas State Highway 79.

Jennifer wore flip-flops, shorts, a T-shirt, many rings on many fingers. Her black hair was short and spiky. She introduced her partner
and sat opposite me in a booth as I told her who her birth mother was.
Jennifer had not heard of Norma McCorvey—or of *Roe v. Wade*. But to
look at Jennifer is to see Norma. Gazing at a photograph of Norma set
atop a gray fiberglass table, Jennifer took in their many resemblances.
She was seized by one in particular. "I think it's interesting to know,"
she said, fingering three silver rings in her right ear, "that my mother
is a lesbian." Hours later, Jennifer shared her joy in a post on Facebook: "happiest moment in life," she wrote, "just found out who my
bio mother and sister are."

———

AT NOON THE NEXT DAY, two hours southeast in the town of Katy, I sat
opposite that sister in another food court abutting another highway.
Melissa was coiffed and composed, with a tanning bed glow and a diamond necklace that dipped into the V of her sweater. She ordered salad
and an iced tea.

Melissa was overcome to learn that she had a second sister right
there in Texas. "I always wondered if the other one was real," she
said. "I can't believe she's so close." She began to cry. "I'd like so
much to have . . ." She stopped, unable to speak the word. A family?
Melissa nodded.

Melissa still kept at her bedside the letters Shelley wrote to her back
in 1993. She had been waiting nineteen years to meet her. But she would
have to wait just one day to meet Jennifer. The next morning, her middle
sister drove with Lisa the 120 miles to Katy. Melissa opened her front
door with a gasp: "You do look like Norma!"

The sisters hugged. Both wore jeans and a halter top. Settling into
a leather couch with their better halves, they spoke of childhoods and
children, parents and homes, marriages and divorces, jobs and hopes.
They spoke of *Roe* and Norma, too.

Talk of the last continued over salad and spaghetti. "She's just a
very difficult person," Melissa offered. "She's got a lot of anger in her."
Lisa noted that Jennifer did, too. The conversation quickly turned to

the inevitable question of nature and nurture; while Melissa speculated that it was "giving up her babies" that had impaired Norma, Jennifer felt that it was Norma who had impaired her. "It's answered a lot of questions in my mind about why I am the way I am," she said, "why I did the things I did."

After lunch, the sisters drove off beneath a kettle of vultures past hayfields and ballfields and churches to the bedside of their progenitor, Mary. Norma's mother lay supine in Room 103 of an old-age home on George Bush Drive. Melissa introduced Jennifer, along with Lisa, to her grandmother, and Mary asked a question: "Y'all like the gay life?" "It's different," answered Jennifer. Minutes later, Mary, her mind clouded, asked the question again and then again, a family getting to know itself between peals of laughter.

Still, Melissa noted that their family remained incomplete; fathers aside, a mother and a sister were missing. As Melissa and Jennifer hugged goodbye, they expressed the hope that they would come together with Norma and Shelley.

Days later, I phoned Shelley's mother. I let her know that I had met with Melissa and Jennifer, and passed along their numbers. A week later, Shelley called me back. She now wished to talk. She told me that coming together with her sisters was bound to end unhappily because "it's always going to be about that other thing." Still, she now wished to try; she'd already left Melissa a message. Jennifer then sent her an email, a thousand capital-lettered words of introduction that ended with her joy in knowing, she wrote, "THAT I REALLY DO HAVE TRUE BLOOD OUT THERE." Shelley responded and was soon in regular touch, delighting in Jennifer's bluntness. Jennifer nicknamed her "Princess."

The sisters were a trinity now. Shelley had the thought, she told me, that they could present a united front against their birth mother. Suddenly, she felt able to confront Norma herself, too. And so, twenty-three years after learning of Norma, she opened *I Am Roe* for the first time, and looked back at her 1989 to-do list with its resolutions to take a DNA test and to meet Norma. Then she confided her great secret in a friend.

I HAD LONG WRITTEN of people whom historical circumstance burdened with secrets. They included Jahangir Razmi, an Iranian photographer whose photo of a firing squad upset his government and made him the only anonymous winner of a Pulitzer Prize. People like Razmi have a difficult lot. As the critic Dwight Garner observed: "Anonymity combined with extreme events: never a happy combination."

It thus did not surprise me when, weeks after I connected her with her sisters, Shelley spoke of how great a burden her secret was. "Secrets and lies are like the two worst things in the whole world," she told me. "I'm keeping a secret but I hate it."

It was a gray winter morning in Tucson. But Shelley was awash in color, from her deep purple hair to pink fingerless gloves she'd knitted, gauntlets that extended over her forearms. Shelley had suggested that we meet in a bagel shop. There, over soup, she spoke to me for hours not only of Norma and *Roe* but of her daily life, of her job in a call center doing data entry for mail-in prescriptions. Her fingers shook with a tremor long caused by her anxiety, and, with a swig of Dr. Pepper, she swallowed a pill for a migraine. How good it would be, she said, to be rid of the mistrust of people she had carried since 1989 when that stranger in a leather coat approached her in a Washington parking lot. Said Shelley: "It's exhausting."

Shelley told me that our meeting provided hope. "It's helping me not be so paranoid about everything," she confided weeks later. She began to take to the prospect of having her and her sisters tell their story. "I would like at some point for the three of us to get it out there," she told me. "This is who we are. We have nothing to do with [Norma]. We are ourselves."

Shelley and her sisters soon made plans to meet, to come together in Texas in March. As their summit approached, they continued to speak, talk turning inevitably to Norma, to the mother who had relinquished all three women to adoption.

Only one of them truly knew Norma. And Melissa, forty-seven, would in time tell her sisters of their mother's combustibility and caprice and callousness, of her devastating propensity to scorn her own while giving what little love she had to others. It brought Melissa to tears to recall that the same woman who told her granddaughter Jordan that she'd burn in hell for being a lesbian told a packed ballroom that little Emily, the girl who'd brought her to Jesus, had a "purity of soul." Still, Melissa loved Norma. On those rare occasions that Norma was tender with her, Melissa was at a loss. "I get mixed up," Melissa told me after Norma texted her, on the first day of 2013, that she loved and missed her. "It's just really hard for me."

It was no less hard for Shelley that Melissa was in touch with Norma. Back when Norma demanded that Shelley thank her for having not aborted her, Shelley had hung up the phone wanting never to hear from Norma again. She now feared that Melissa would, inevitably, lead her back to their birth mother. It occurred to Shelley that, among the sisters, only Jennifer had been spared Norma. Said Shelley: "Jennifer kind of got the better end of the deal being the secret one."

Jennifer did not disagree. And yet, even as learning of Norma had helped her to make sense of herself and her children, it was a source of pain for Jennifer that Norma had not looked for her as she had for Shelley.

Norma had, in fact, rarely spoken of her second child, saying if asked that the child was being raised by its biological father, a doctor. Jennifer wondered who that man was. But for now, she was counting down the days to March when she and her sisters would finally come together.

———

THROUGHOUT HISTORY, society has offered up different solutions for the unwanted child—from the mountaintop in Sparta to the foundling wheel in medieval Rome to adoption. American law began to regulate the last in 1851. But with the advance of abortion technology over the century that followed, women carrying unwanted children increasingly sought to address their problem *before* birth, not after it. That Jennifer and Shelley existed at all was almost unusual. Leading up to *Roe*, the unwanted pregnancy in the U.S. was roughly four times more likely to end in abortion than adoption.

Together with Melissa, Jennifer and Shelley were the legacy of a family, of generations of women, whom pregnancy had stripped of choice—Bertha made to marry in 1922, Mary made to give up a child in 1940, Norma made to carry a child in 1969. Norma's daughters, mean-time, knew from their own lives the great consequences of pregnancy. All were pro-choice, each saying that although the idea of abortion as birth control left them cold, a woman should not be forced to have a child. "I've always been pro-choice," says Melissa. "Not that I want to kill anybody."

On March 14, 2013, Shelley approached the open door of a house on a dead end in the brick-manufacturing Texas town of Elgin. Jennifer saw Shelley from her living room and walked toward her. The sisters hugged, then hugged again. They had not yet sat when Shelley laughed. "My boobs are bigger than yours," she said.

The sisters sized each other up. They noted their differences: their brown and blue eyes, their faces oval and heart-shaped. They noted their similarities: their spring allergies, their penchants for pink and Dr. Pepper. The conversation continued for many hours—carrying over the burble of a fish tank, over the strumming of a guitar in a Mexican res-taurant, over the hum of a highway that led eastward the next morning toward Melissa. The sisters compared lives, looking at each other for clues, returning always to the mother who had let them go.

"This is where the egg donor lived," said Jennifer of Norma, as we drove through the town where Norma had moved after leaving Connie. "She calls her the egg donor," said Shelley. "I call her the skanky ho slut." Seated behind me, the sisters laughed, and on we drove along State Highway 71 past herds of cattle and rectangular puffs of bluebonnets.

It was half past noon when the sisters stood at Melissa's door, kin come at last. Melissa was teary as she hugged Shelley, then Jennifer, and Eric handed each a potted rosebush, the blooms red as blood.

The three sisters sat on a couch, Melissa in the middle. They were similarly sized—pink, blue and black T-shirts covering medium torsos, their six feet not quite reaching the floor. Yet, side by side, their differ-ences emerged—the chins round and receded and cleft, for example, that recalled Woody, Pete and Bill. Melissa had readied photo albums. As the sisters turned the pages—pointing and laughing at relatives unknown yet familiar—their discussion again flowed from physical bodies to experiences: the tubes Jennifer and Shelley had tied, the abuse and infidelities Melissa and Jennifer had endured, the desperate hopes that each of them had had of finding one another. An hour had passed when Melissa set on her granite countertop a stack of old letters, the sisters beginning to read aloud what the youngest of them had written the oldest twenty years before. Jennifer came upon mention of her sisters looking for her—the middle sister they had named Sarah—and began to cry.

Eric and Melissa were preparing a feast: pork ribs, macaroni and cheese, baked beans, potato salad, salad, rice with pork liver and green onions, frosted carrot cake. But dinner was not quite ready, and the sisters walked outside. Shelley joked that she would move into the lot next door. Then, together with Jennifer and Melissa, she crossed the street to a playground.

The sisters did not know that playgrounds had long tormented their birth mother, that they reminded her of *Roe* when empty and of her lost daughters—them—when full. They did not know, as they settled into the rubber seats of a swing set, that the logo Norma had chosen for her ministry was a girl on a swing. They knew only that they were at last together. And on this warm and breezy Texas afternoon, Melissa, Jennifer and Shelley—faces to the sun—began to sway, to bend their knees and pump their legs, their feet brushing wood chips, their hands gripping warm metal ropes, the sisters—women become girls—smiling and laughing and rising to the sky.

Chapter 34

On the summer night in 2009 when Norma returned home from Phoenix to find her screen door locked, she drove one hundred miles south to Waco. The two nights she spent in the town she called her Bethlehem did not reawaken in her a desire to be with Connie. So she drove on farther south—sixty miles to the town of Bartlett, fifty miles to the town of Bastrop, and then a few miles more to a country town where, on Main Street, she entered the chamber of commerce and heard her name.

"I said," recalls Adena Lewis, who ran the chamber, "'Norma McCorvey—what are you doing in Smithville, Texas?'" Norma did not quite answer. "I'm tired," she said. "I'm just tired.'"

Norma had had an exhausting month—removed from a Senate hearing room for heckling a future Supreme Court justice, lying and crying to a filmmaker in Phoenix, fleeing in fury her partner and home. But it was the general turmoil of her life that bled her. On this Thursday morning, August 13, the stranger who recognized Norma told her that she'd landed, recalls Lewis, in "'the perfect place to rest.'"

Smithville *was* tranquil, 3.7 square miles that were home to 3,800 people (and one giant gingerbread man). The town lies some forty miles southeast of Austin, and two miles south of a state park. It was to that park—a thousand acres bursting with loblobby pine—that Lewis now sent Norma, highlighting the route on a map and writing her cell number on it. "The state park just captivated her," recalls her friend Daniel Vinzant. "That drive on that day made her ecstatic."

Norma was still on a high when, two days later, she phoned Lewis from a local eatery. She was moving to Smithville, she said, and wanted help finding a home. Lewis connected her with a woman named Lauren Nailen, who welcomed Norma to her bed-and-breakfast at no charge. The women became fast friends, fellow Christians happy to sit beside the pool, recalls Nailen, and "talk about what we used to do before we were born again."

Norma stayed at the Auberge LaGrange near a month, eating bowls of tinola, a Filipino soup Nailen made for her of chicken and spinach and ginger. In September, days before turning sixty-two, Norma moved into a house a few miles east of town. By year's end, she had settled into a cottage on Burleson Street, pecan trees all about. When 2010 brought another *Roe* anniversary, Norma was happy to be in Smithville, skipping the March for Life for the first time since her conversion.

Roe found her, however. Her lawyer Allan Parker happened to meet a Catholic filmmaker named Peter Mackenzie at a pro-life event in San Antonio. Mackenzie had written a pro-life film script called *Doonby* and was set to shoot it in Smithville. Parker told him that Jane Roe happened to live there and suggested that Mackenzie put her in his film.

═══

MACKENZIE HAD WANTED to help the pro-life cause ever since his native England legalized abortion in 1967. "It wasn't a religious thing," he says, in a voice made croaky by throat cancer. "It was a moral issue." Decades later, he wrote *Doonby*. The film recounts the spiritual awakening of a sleepy town, a rebirth brought about by a man revealed, in a Hitchcockian twist, to have never been born but aborted.

Abortion, of course, lends itself to dramatization. It figures in plotlines in Eugene O'Neill and Edith Wharton, in *The Godfather Part II* and *Fame*. Back in 1964, the screenwriter William Goldman wrote of a producer warning a playwright that "there better not be a big abortion scene—I'm bored with them already."

Still, representations of abortion are anything but static. The author

Katha Pollitt, for example, observed that while women writers give it a "bloody realism"—the poet Sharon Olds writing of soaked slippers in "The End"—men use it most often as "a symbol—of modern alienation, of a larger sterility." To hear men tell it, abortion is something a man might talk a woman in or out of; Hemingway wrote of a man telling his lover that "it's really an awfully simple operation," while Richard Yates wrote of another telling his wife that "the very thought of it makes my stomach turn." The women do as prompted; one has an abortion, one does not. (When Yates's antihero about-faces and tells his wife "I wish to God you'd done it," she gives herself an abortion and dies.)

Roe had since empowered women. But in 2010, as Mackenzie readied to shoot his film, rare was the script that depicted abortion in America as it usually was—something done in safety and without regret. Instead, films and TV shows elevated mortality rates and soft-pedaled state restrictions. A pair of recent films, Juno and Knocked Up, presented women who were hard to find off-screen—women happily carrying to term desperately unwanted pregnancies.

———

THE IDEA OF having Jane Roe in his film excited Mackenzie. He set aside a small part for her, that of a woman who seeks to dissuade her young neighbor from having an abortion. Mackenzie then met with Norma for lunch, and she was aboard.

Norma liked the script. She also liked that Mackenzie would pay her some $25,000; she had little income beyond the $500 those Texas Catholics still sent her monthly. In late May, Norma moved back into the Auberge LaGrange, where Mackenzie was housing his cast, a plaintiff among actors.

Norma made an impression. John Schneider, the former Dukes of Hazzard star and the film's leading man, told the press that he had expected Jane Roe to be "complicated, protective and cerebral," but had found her instead to be "down to earth, open and unaffected." She was, of course, also prone to anger and drink, and thirsty for attention. It struck Mackenzie that she resembled a type common among actors—someone poor and uneducated, he says, "pitchforked into fame and limelight."

Norma loved the stage. She hadn't acted since Catholic school, when she played a peasant girl in *South Pacific*. But she could still recite the lines from *Macbeth* she'd memorized as a girl about the brevity and meaninglessness of life. And she'd been playing Jane Roe for forty years. Cast now as Nancy Thirber, she recited her lines with emotion. "You don't have to do this," she pleaded, slowly looking up at a young beauty named Erin Way. "Children are a miracle—a gift from God!"

Norma and her fellow actress sat down a day later at a local diner. Over a plate of fried zucchini, Norma told Way that she'd never had an abortion. "She said," recalls Way, "'I think people forget that I'm a mother.'"

DOONBY FINISHED SHOOTING IN JULY, and Norma set off to look for a new home, visiting a handful of century-old cottages with a realtor. "She just liked to look at the houses," recalls Jeannie Ralph. "And then she would say, 'Well, I better rent something before I buy.'" Norma settled on a small wooden house a half mile away, two rooms with a kitchen and bath.

It was Norma's fourth home in the year she had lived in Smithville. But she resided above all at the local bars, chief among them Huebel's, which had been serving up beer since 1945. Norma had been drinking almost as long; she'd struggled with alcohol since her first drink at age twelve in 1959. Now, several days a week, Norma set down dollar bills for dollar beers at first call, drinking ten or so Bud Lights until a friend drove her home.

Norma tended to tell her story when drunk. She gave her new friends copies of whichever of her two books suited them. To a bartender named Susan DeVine—who remained thankful at forty-two that she'd been able to terminate a pregnancy at seventeen—Norma gave *I Am Roe*. To Henry Lee Taylor, she gave *Won by Love*.

Taylor had met Norma that summer of 2010 after buying a round at Huebel's. The two were soon drinking buddies, meeting at the bar every few weeks over cigarettes and large quantities of beer.

Taylor's opposition to abortion was personal: "I could have been wasted," he says. Instead, he'd been born and put into foster care and adopted at age two. Forty-one years later, he had, much like Norma, lived a life marked by poverty and alcohol and familial estrangement. Says Taylor: "Having similar bruises helped connect us." Like Norma, though, Taylor had been saved. He was now, in fact, a Baptist pastor. And if he turned to vodka to help him sleep, and was in infrequent touch with his children, he had a strong third marriage and a good job directing funeral services at a tony home in Austin where he was, he notes, the first black hire.

Norma still spoke of abortion from time to time. But those conversations were private. Since skipping the March for Life months before, she had continued to step back from *Roe*—letting her ministry dissolve, and cutting off, once again, her strongest remaining tether to *Roe*, the lawyer Parker. Norma had now been depleted by both sides of the abortion debate—"scorned, rejected, snubbed, discredited and excluded" before her conversion, in the words of a pro-choice activist, and exploited after it by a group that included Benham, Parker, Newman, Terry, Schenck and Pavone. "Which is it Fr. Frank," Norma emailed Pavone one year before. "Just for show or DO YOU REALLY Care as you claim?"

"She feels at the end of the day a little bit like she doesn't have a side to belong to," says the actor Way. "She's a little bit of an orphan."

Norma was, of course, partly to blame for her alienation. She was disagreeable and opportunistic. Still, she had never felt quite at home in either camp. "On the pro-choice side, she could be who she wanted to be but they didn't respect her," says Melissa. "On the pro-life side, they respected her but she couldn't be who she wanted to be."

Who Norma wanted to be was gay and pro-choice—but only *moderately* pro-choice. Norma no more absolutely opposed *Roe* than she'd ever absolutely supported it; she'd long since decided that abortion ought to be legal for precisely three months. In this, Norma had remained consistent, publicly stating her position decades apart, days after both *Roe* and her Christian rebirth.

It was exposure, a youth lived among both the religious and the bohemian, that had tempered Norma. That exposure only grew after *Roe*. Countless women—on both sides of the ruling—had confided in her the abortion stories they kept from others. Norma related to both sides, and confided her ambivalence about abortion to friends pro-choice and pro-life alike—the abortion provider Charlotte Taft, the abortion opponent Judy Wiggins.

If Norma was uncomfortable with the increasing surety and absolutism of both movements, she was hardly alone. Like her, a majority of Americans resided in what Norma termed, after her conversion, "the mushy middle." Indeed, a poll would soon reveal that whereas 1 percent of Americans felt that abortion ought to never be legal and 28 percent felt that it should always be legal, 52 percent felt that it should be legal sometimes, their support dropping by trimester from 61 to 27 to 14 percent.

Norma thus reflected the majoritarian middle ground. She embodied the national ambivalence, the desire for legal yet limited abortion, as no Schlafly or Steinem could. That stood to reason. The two conflicting forces that had most shaped abortion in the U.S. had also shaped her—sex and religion the helical strands of her DNA. As her lawyer Parker once noted: Norma was "a microcosm of America."

———

NORMA HAD BEEN in Smithville a year when, on the first fall night of 2010, the bartender DeVine threw her a birthday party. There was alcohol and cake and flowers and presents. DeVine gave Norma a brown lap blanket to keep her warm. Norma was soon drunk and pole dancing. "I like my life now," Norma would tell a reporter. "I keep a simple routine. No complications."

Life in Smithville was indeed uncomplicated for Norma. There was beer and billiards and a black cat she named Mr. Baby. But if the town was good to Norma—DeVine at her door every morning to talk over coffee—it was an escape.

There was a couple in town who reminded Norma that she'd run not only from Connie but her homosexuality, too. Rosie Lopez and Teri Costlow had met in 2005, a client and a counselor at an outpatient rehab facility in Long Island. They became a couple and, in 2009, opened a facility of their own, a residential recovery program in Smithville complete with twelve steps, therapy, meditation and yoga. Beside it, they opened a weekend-only restaurant staffed by their residents.

There at the Comfort Café—where the prices were merely suggested—
they came to know Norma.

Costlow felt indebted to Norma, to the plaintiff whose suit had
enabled her to have a legal abortion at eighteen. But it was Lopez, a
fellow free spirit who'd struggled with addiction and religion and her
sexuality, who felt a kinship with Norma. She had let go of religion but
not belief, and was free now to love whom she wished. Her God was not
only accepting but capable of wonders—like bringing to her Jane Roe.

Lopez wished for Norma to heal as she had. Over endless hours
with her on the café patio, she came to believe that what Norma admired
above all was authenticity, living a life unapologetic. But shame and guilt
were preventing her from doing so. "Religion wounded her more than
Roe wounded her," says Lopez. "She lost her identity."

Indeed, having lived for fifteen years in a world that damned her
homosexuality, Norma began in 2011 to present herself to pro-life
friends as straight—or at least as someone trying to be—first texting
her friend Henry Taylor that she was praying for a husband, then telling
her old friend Ronda Mackey that she was looking for one. "I'm dating
men now," she told her over the phone. "I'm having sex with them."

Mackey had seen Norma just once in the thirteen years since her
work on Norma's ministry had left her on meds and in therapy. When
Mackey responded that it would be better if Norma married before
having sex, Norma screamed at her, "I thought you'd be proud of me!"
Norma never spoke to Mackey again. But she took her words to heart.
For she then told her Mississippi friend Judy Wiggins not that she was
looking for a husband but that she'd *found* one, and was married. Wiggins responded with the hope that he treated her well. Upset with her
response, Norma cut her off, too. And here, the fantasy of her hetero-
sexuality reached its inevitable end. Norma told her friend Daniel Vinzant that she'd been married but that the marriage had been annulled by
the mother of the man she had wed—Frank Di Bugnara.

In the six years since Di Bugnara had heard Norma on his car radio
outside Phoenix, he had come to reconceive the film he had titled *Roe v.
Norma* as less about Norma than *Roe*. Still, his fascination with Norma
had only grown. "I was in deep," he says. Thirty-five and single, he gave
her story nearly all his time, strengthened by the thought that his film

was the contribution to humanity that that holy pharmacist in Scottsdale had foreseen back in his boyhood.

Di Bugnara had brought Norma back to Phoenix for a fundraiser
the year before. And as he flew about the country to network and raise
money, he remained in touch with his protagonist, sending her occasional texts and emails (and, when asked, money too). That Norma had
imagined them marrying, Di Bugnara was wholly unaware.

But for the law, Norma would likely have married Connie. They
had exchanged silver rings. But Norma had left her behind, and friends
now helped Connie get by. Sheree Havlik tended to her after a fall. Her
neighbor Utah Foster took her to the bank. But her body, her speech
and memory were deteriorating. Dementia was encroaching. Her debt
was growing. In August 2011, sixteen months after that first notice of
foreclosure, her niece Linda picked up the phone. "They gave us thirty
days," she says. Connie and her niece moved in with another niece, her
house of forty-four years put up for public auction.

———

NORMA WAS USED TO MOVING. In the two years before her arrival in Smithville, she had lived in Mississippi and Kansas and Virginia and Texas.
In the two years since, she had lived in an inn and three houses. In late
2011, she moved into a subsidized apartment in a public housing complex called Smithville Gardens.

Norma now qualified for Section 8 housing; she gave few talks and,
since *Doonby*, her income had dropped below the federal poverty level.

Few might have imagined that Jane Roe was living in the projects on
MLK Boulevard. The affidavit she signed in 1970 had opened worlds to
her, from Manhattan to Hollywood to London, Norma feted and mon-
etized and profiled and portrayed by a movie star who called her Pixie.

Decades before, Norma had told her girlfriend Diane that she would
be famous. But once she was, she sometimes wondered to what end.
Back at the abortion clinic on Markville Drive, she'd even lain on an
examining table, her feet in stirrups, so as to better picture the life she
might have lived had she gotten the abortion she sought. Would she
have been happier? Come to Smithville, it had done Norma good to
leave *Roe* behind. And when she briefly returned to it—joining a pro-life

march in Dallas weeks into 2012—she was undone when a stranger asked how she lived with the blood of millions on her head. Hours later, in the middle of an on-air conversation about *Doonby* with a talk show host, Norma hung up and then posted on Facebook that the film was terrible.

The filmmaker Mackenzie was exasperated. Still, he says, he felt for Norma. She'd been leeched for as long as she'd been Roe. Plus, she'd already helped him, telling the *Hollywood Reporter*, for example, that it was God who had led her to Smithville and thus to *Doonby*. "I obeyed," she had said. "I had no family there, no friends. I just obeyed."

———

NORMA WAS IN POOR HEALTH, beset by depression and insomnia and a bad hip that slowed her walk. When one day she grew short of breath and landed in the hospital, she learned that she also had COPD, chronic obstructive pulmonary disease. Her chest began to tighten more often, and she took to calling Melissa, who would alert the Smithville police.

Norma thought often of her daughters. She texted her friend, the pastor Taylor, that her "heart has been low for my youngins." And when a reporter came to her in Smithville, she had the accompanying photographer shoot her on a playground swing—that which evoked for her not only the millions lost to *Roe* but the three girls she herself had lost to adoption.

There were other women like Norma who'd placed for adoption children they'd wished to abort. A ten-year study would later show that 85 percent of them, even five years after those adoptions, had come to be thankful that they'd not had an abortion. It was, it seemed, the human condition to feel for any child once it was birthed.

Still, whenever Norma expressed regret at having let her children go, she did so without emotion. Says DeVine: "There was a disconnect." Nor was Norma there for the one child still in her life. When on Christmas Eve, Mary's husband Raymond died, and Melissa mourned the man she had come to love as a father, Norma offered her no comfort.

It had always been this way for Norma; she demanded a great deal but gave little. And so, in February 2012, Mackenzie did not bother inviting her to attend the screenings of his film in Mississippi and Texas. Norma remained at home with Mr. Baby and a second cat she named Cuddles.

———

DOONBY WAS UNAPOLOGETICALLY PRO-LIFE. The film was also gritty—much of it took place in a bar—and the evangelical community did not support it, says Mackenzie. But the Catholic community did; the daily paper of the Vatican called it "moving and thought-provoking," and true to the "painful regrets [of abortion] epitomized" by the person and performance of one Norma McCorvey.

Father Pavone had introduced the film to the Holy See, arranging a screening at Castel Gandolfo, a town near Rome where the pope vacationed. The priest, though, was increasingly at odds with his superiors in the U.S. After an audit revealed mismanagement of funds at Priests for Life and Pavone refused to open the books, a bishop in Texas had ordered Pavone to move to Amarillo. But nine months later, in the spring of 2012, the Vatican released Pavone, and he returned to New York in "good standing."

Norma, meantime, remained in Texas. And when, that summer, the manager of the housing project told her that her cats had to go, she instead moved with them into the home of a nurse who for twenty-three years had felt in her debt.

Heidi Erwin had been a senior in high school when she got pregnant. She loved her boyfriend and they would later marry. But she was desperate to go to college and did not hesitate to have an abortion. Years later, in 2010, she'd happened upon Jane Roe at Huebel's and done her best to thank her. Says Erwin: "I had a lot of respect for Norma. Maybe I was in awe of her." She bought Norma a beer. Two years later, in July 2012, Erwin had bought her many more when she and her husband put Norma up in the bedroom they kept in their garage.

The great majority of women who have abortions have children, too. Erwin was among them, and her son and daughter, eight and four, darted about the yard outside Norma's door. Norma showed little interest in them. She stayed inside most days with her cats and cigarettes. And when she did speak with Erwin and her husband, Democrats who believed in choice, she was apt to turn surly. She seemed agitated. Her mood was not improved when, in August, she gave up alcohol, contenting herself with O'Doul's.

Smithville had provided Norma a refuge from *Roe*, a three-year slatch between waves. The town had not used her in any way. Still, Norma wished to be gone. "She was withdrawing," says Erwin. Norma asked the filmmaker she'd imagined to be her husband to take her away, and Di Bugnara flew her to Phoenix in September, happy for the opportunity to introduce her to a group of investors. But a French dip sandwich got her sick and then angry, and she returned to Texas at once.

Di Bugnara still had another year on his contract with Norma. But over four years, their collaboration had produced five minutes of film and cost him hundreds of thousands of dollars—a loss, he says, that "had a permanent and massive impact on the trajectory of my life." He abandoned the project and never saw Norma again.

Norma moved right along. That same September, she flew to Randall Terry in West Virginia for $1,000 and one last strop of his razor. "Do not vote for Barack Obama," she said in an ad endorsing another Terry bid for Congress. "He murders babies."

NORMA STILL TOLD LIES. She told the innkeeper Nailen that—like the biblical Esau selling his birthright for a bowl of lentils—she'd taken on her plaintiffship for "a piece of pizza and a beer." She told a British reporter that on the day *Roe* became law, she had felt like a "mass murderer" and slit her wrists. She told the *Doonby* director that an abortion provider had instructed her to reassemble an aborted fetus. And wishing now to leave Smithville for good, she began, as so many times before, to invent another peril, telling her friend Vinzant, he recalls, that she was "in a dangerous place," that the man putting her up in his garage made her feel uncomfortable.

Finding Norma a new home would not be easy; she smoked and had cats and struggled with stairs and had no money for rent. But Vinzant wrote to Catholic friends in Dallas. In early November, a woman just northwest of the city volunteered to take her in to the little gray stucco home that she shared with one of her seven children.

Her name was Angie Heiter. She was sixty-four, a year younger than Norma. She had brown hair and brown eyes and almost always wore green. Having lost her husband to cancer a few years prior, and laid him to rest beneath a tombstone that read "ETERNALLY PROLIFE," she'd moved to Irving and taken a job answering phones at an Indian holding company. Church, though, was her lifeblood, a traditional Catholic church called Mater Dei where she taught rosary-making and headed pro-life activities. Heiter had just been named pro-life person of the year by the same Catholic organization that sent Norma monthly checks when, one Sunday in November 2012, volunteers drove Norma to her. Norma departed Smithville as abruptly as she'd arrived.

Chapter 35

Norma tried to do as Angie Heiter asked. Arriving at her home, northwest of Dallas, in late 2012, she didn't touch her iron skillets and went outside to smoke and kept the litter box in her own room. She kept her distance, too—asleep when Heiter went to work, in her room when she returned home, Norma watching TV from her twin bed as Heiter listened to the Guadalupe Radio Network or made her rosaries.

Heiter had been making rosaries for thirty-five years, using string and wire and beads to help her fellow Catholics keep count of their Hail Marys. The Virgin Mary had promised to provide "necessities" to those who prayed the rosary. And as Heiter told her church, the greatest necessity was "to save our souls!"

Norma agreed; she was desperate to be saved. And she began to make rosaries too, hanging them by the score on a horizontal wooden pole opposite the kitchen. "I was cranking these out like a machine," she said. "Twenty, twenty-one a day."

Norma loved rosaries. Like the patron saints, their beads and crucifixes brought her comfort. But, like figures of Christ, they could make her feel guilty, too, and she tried to avoid the plastic Jesus on the lawn, the copper one on the living room wall. Less comfortable still were Heiter's many reminders of *Roe*, from the bumper stickers on her Honda to the "PRAY TO END ABORTION" placards piled in the living room. That another *Roe* anniversary was approaching had Norma more and more on edge. She stopped driving, stopped taking her meds. "This whole roe anniversary has her so very upset," noted a concerned neighbor in an email. "It is at a crisis point." *Roe* was a week shy of forty years old when, in January 2013, its plaintiff fell into a panic and called 911.

Norma sent the ambulance away. But she remained in crisis until that neighbor, a retired doctor turned patient advocate named Nancy Hokamp, helped to stabilize her, organizing her medicines and setting up her computer.

Norma told Hokamp that she was lonely. So the doctor wrote a note to her Catholic helpers, urging them to spend time with Norma, to share with her a coffee or a walk or a song or anything—as long as it had nothing to do with *Roe* or rosaries. Added Hokamp: "What she desperately needs is FRIENDS."

The Catholics listened. They saw Norma and her torments in a different light than did the doctor. ("She offers her sufferings for others," wrote Heiter.) But they did as advised, creating a "care calendar" and alerting each scheduled visitor to her medicines and vitamins and inhalers and favorite foods: chicken soup and burgers, pastrami and pizza, deviled eggs and toast. They saw to it that she got Medicare and Social Security. By February, Norma had improved, stable and uplifted.

It was then, in March, just a few hundred miles to the south, that, unbeknownst to Norma, her daughters met for the first time.

Norma thought often of her girls, beginning with Melissa—"the one I want to love me," she reflected. She hoped to one day know her second child, too. But she worried about her third. "There's something about that girl," said Norma, "that tells me to stay away."

———

SHELLEY WAS no less wary of Norma. In the nineteen years since their last phone call, she had vowed to never speak with her birth mother again. But one day after soaring high and secure with her sisters on those swings, she changed her mind. She wanted to show Norma, said Shelley, that "you have no impact on me, you have no impact on how I raise my children, you have no impact on how I turned out as a person."

Shelley had spent much of her two days with her sisters sussing out her inheritance. It was startling to see her grandmother Mary look back at her with blue eyes that recalled her own. But mostly, the sisters just got to know one another. Over lunch at a barbecue pit on Highway 71, they found that they agreed about both the necessity of legal abortion and the hypocrisy of the church. They took comfort in their agreements and their individuation, too: Shelley funny, Melissa nostalgic, Jennifer blunt.

Jennifer had written to Shelley that she had long been "COLD AND NONCHALANT" but was learning "TO LOVE, AND CARE AND FEEL FOR OTHERS." She'd credited her growth to her partner of three years. And Jennifer now drove her sisters to Lisa, who was home, east of Austin, making them fajitas of beef and chicken, onions and peppers. Dinner was almost ready when Melissa gave Shelley an impromptu haircut in the kitchen. Shelley beamed in her bob, two rhinestone barrettes pinned just so. "I always wanted my big sister to do my hair," she said. Melissa settled into a recliner in the living room. Crouching beside her, Shelley rested her head on her chest. Melissa patted Shelley's back, and began to cry.

———

THE SISTERS DIDN'T SLEEP MUCH, rising early after a late-night run to Walmart. They discussed, on this March morning, spending another weekend together. Then they hugged goodbye and Shelley flew home.

The joy of their time together lingered. "I was totally being treated like the baby sister all weekend," reflected Shelley. "I loved it. I loved it!" Jennifer took comfort in the revelation that her sisters had once looked for her, Melissa that they had at last been found.

Still, coming together had been complicated. Shelley regretted that she had pulled away from Melissa those many years before and had never apologized. Melissa, who had idealized Shelley, found it difficult, she says, to take in what she saw as her limitations. Jennifer was also taken aback by Shelley, she said, by how little she worked and how much she slept.

Still, the older sisters felt for Shelley and each other, too. As the months passed, they kept in touch with texts and calls, Melissa reporting that she had lost one job but found another, Jennifer that her son had slugged a cop, Shelley that she had reconnected by phone with her estranged father who forty-three years before had adopted her from Norma.

Norma, meantime, was doing okay. She was still vulnerable to panic attacks but took her meds most days, ingesting them with Sprite and cigarettes and TV dinners. Lifted by her Catholic callers, she felt good enough to drive, off in her Honda to the Waffle House and the mall. She no longer made rosaries but filled her days with joke books and word searches and lots of TV: game shows and M*A*S*H and *Letterman*.

Angie had hoped that Norma might join her at Mater Dei. But her famous boarder had reduced her Catholicism to the saints she called out to in traffic, and the sacramentals she set about her room: crucifixes nailed up alongside butterflies, holy cards spilling from a hatbox, rosaries on her night table beside her pills and perfume.

As for *Roe*, Norma had nothing in her room but a tin of pro-life buttons. She had left her advocacy behind, had lent her name to no one since that bilious ad for Randall Terry. *Roe* took too much. Still, Norma, a borderline personality with a tenth-grade education, had recognized her value to both sides of an American monument. "I now see a certain genius in her migration among the different pools," the Reverend Schenck, no less a political operator than a clergyman, would soon reflect. "She had a business plan in her mind. In moving, she was endearing herself to larger constituencies."

Norma had been mindful to keep moving. But she rarely planned ahead. She lived in the moment. Driving west for some peach cobbler in Oak Cliff, a song came on the radio from back when Norma was pregnant with the *Roe* baby, and she began to wave an e-cigarette to the beat of Badfinger. "If you want it, here it is, come and get it," Norma sang from behind the wheel of a car paid for by *Roe*. "Will you walk away from a fool and his money?"

Norma had made a career from *Roe*. But that career was over. Within a year, Norma would attend her very last function, speaking over brownies to Catholic medical students in the home of her doctor.

———

IF NORMA HAD come finally to leave *Roe* behind, the child connected to it had just resolved to meet her birth mother.

Still, back home, a thousand miles from her sisters, Shelley was losing her nerve. It made her uncomfortable that both of her sisters were in touch with Norma. She began to pull away from Jennifer and Melissa, returning fewer and fewer of their texts.

On October 13, 2013, their grandmother Mary died. She had lived ninety years, just long enough to meet all three daughters Norma had given away. But when Melissa informed her sisters of Mary's death, one of them chose not to come to her funeral, lest Norma come too. Said Shelley: "I'm not ready to deal with that."

Shelley was not alone in her wariness. Norma had injured nearly all who knew her, and even those closest to her kept away. Melissa had seen her just twice in four years, Melissa's daughters Chloe and Jordan not once since their grandmother had, five years before, called one a "nigger lover" and the other a "fornicating homosexual." Norma had disparaged her mother most of all; among much else, she'd publicly accused Mary of kidnapping her child. Mary wondered how the Lord Jehovah could possibly forgive Norma her sins. "You can't trust her," Mary had said two years before, smiling to reveal a solitary tooth rooted in silver in her upper gum. "She's like an eel."

———

IT WAS MELISSA who readied Mary for her wake, dressing her in a gray dress and a black sweater and a teardrop diamond necklace that suited her hair, a pouf of white that Melissa curled and styled in a shag. Four days after her death, as her body lay in a casket open to the waist in a funeral home in Katy, Melissa sat with Eric on a dimpled leather couch down the hall, doing her best to tell a priest how her grandmother had lived.

The priest was young, a ruddy Indianan named after Daniel Boone. He was trying his best to glean a few kernels to serve in his eulogy the next morning. "Kind of a traditional mom?" he asked. "When you came home, she was there and stuff?" "No," said Melissa. She noted to the priest that she had done Mary's hair, and the priest asked if Mary had done her hair. "No," said Melissa.

Outside the funeral home, Norma stepped from her car. She had driven from Irving, passing the four hours with the help of James Taylor and a few pills for anxiety. It was almost seven when, beneath a full, chalky moon, she walked to where Mary lay.

Norma wore pink and orange shoes, black leggings and a black tee with the face of a cat on the breast pocket. Enormous blue glasses hung from the neck of her shirt, and a yellow clip fastened a shawl to her short golden hair. She set down her aqua purse. Crossing herself, she laid a rosary beside her mother and pressed down on a vial of rose water. A mist settled over Mary.

Norma remained where she stood, looking down, chewing gum. Her granddaughters, and then Melissa, approached, and the women began to share memories of their matriarch, of her temper and salty tongue. They laughed and cried, and continued to reminisce back at the house until Melissa found herself alone with Norma and calmly told her that her second child had been located. She lived in Elgin.

Norma gasped—she had long gone drinking in Elgin, she said—and Melissa said that her sister would be coming the next day with her girl-friend. "She's gay?" asked Norma. "All right!"

Norma asked, on this October night, if she should be nervous; would Jennifer be friend or foe? She wondered, too, if Jennifer was okay. Melissa told her that Jennifer had had problems with alcohol and drugs, much as she had. But Melissa said there was no reason to worry, and then introduced Norma to me, the writer in the room. "He's brought me to people that I'm going to need," she said. By this, Melissa meant her sisters, who would be emotional reinforcements now that Mary and Raymond had died. Norma understood that she was being asked to behave. One year after telling me that she wouldn't speak to me unless I paid her a thousand dollars, she simply said, "Thank you."

Melissa had tears in her eyes. Norma took her hand and said that only weeks before, a solitary wish had seized her in the hospital: "to meet all my daughters before I die."

Melissa told Norma that seeing Jennifer would be a shock. "Just like me?" asked Norma. "Yes." Melissa added that Jennifer hoped to

learn who her father was, and Norma asked if she had light or dark
skin. Melissa said dark, and Norma answered that her father was "the
little registered nurse I had the affair with." She did not recall his name.

―――――

AT EIGHT the next morning, Melissa and Norma stepped outside as
Jennifer and Lisa pulled into the driveway. Jennifer hugged her sister
and then her mother, and Norma called her "sweetheart." Mother
and daughter shared a smoke and Melissa's daughter Jordan appeared,
three generations of gay women come together. All went inside for
coffee and then drove to Houston National Cemetery, where Mary
would be buried because the man she had married twice had served
in Korea.

Jennifer had long "built up hatred" for her biological mother, she
says, for the ghost who had given her up and never come to find her.
She had decided that if ever she met her, she would tell her, "I fucking
hate you."

But forty-six years after their umbilical parting, Jennifer felt joy. As
she neared the cemetery, Lisa was laughing. "You and mommy dearest,"
she said, "can go for a walk."

The priest was late and the family stepped from their cars. Jennifer
smoked another Marlboro with the mother she so strikingly resembled,
and Norma joked about needing to be somewhere else. "I do have a
10:30," she said. Everyone laughed and Norma asked Jennifer if she'd
been born in August. No. Norma tried again. "I think I had a spinal
block for you," she said.

The priest arrived and all drove to Committal Service Shelter B,
where a casket lay covered in roses and lilies and delphiniums. Melissa
said that Mary had been a good person, and Jennifer said that she was
thankful to have met her. Norma then spoke of a mother she'd decidedly
not had—one "always willing to love people I loved," she said. Then
the family returned home and looked at photos and compared tattoos
and ate a Cajun feast in honor of their departed Louisianan: sirloin tip
roast with jalapeños, green beans with pork, dirty rice, raw scallions,
pumpkin and pecan pies.

JENNIFER RETURNED HOME and went to work. Walmart had promoted her to assistant manager, and she was busy studying for a pair of exams on management and food handling. Her mind, though, was on Norma. Jennifer had told Jordan after the memorial that knowing Norma was her mother "explains my life." Norma now sent her amiable texts by the dozen. Said Jennifer: "It's been mind-fucking."

Jennifer phoned Shelley. She told her that meeting Norma had been liberating. But Shelley was unmoved. "She's blocked by everything that happened to her when she was eighteen," says Jennifer, speaking of when the *National Enquirer* confronted Shelley. "There's so much she can do and be a part of if she would allow it." Still, Jennifer understood the uniqueness of her burden, understood, she says, that if ever Shelley were to meet Norma, she would "look at her and go, 'Why the fuck did you want to kill me?'"

Melissa understood that, too. That same October, after Mary died, she spoke to Norma about Shelley. "I said to her," she recalls, "'How would you feel if someone tried to abort you?' She says, 'But I didn't do it!' I said, 'Yeah, but the intent was there! . . . And everybody knows it!'"

Shelley wanted relationships with her sisters. "The whole kit and caboodle," she says. And when she had surgery to fuse vertebrae in her neck and her sisters phoned to see how she was, she felt loved and cried. But it still pained Shelley that her sisters had relationships with Norma. After warning Jennifer that those maternal ties would surely come to burn, she again pulled away.

It was not simply the specter of Norma that kept Shelley from her sisters. "I didn't know *how* to go to them," she says, noting that she grew up without siblings. She also feared that her sisters might hurt her or that she might hurt them. "If I say no, I don't want to be a part of this anymore," she reflected, "then I won't hurt anyone anymore, won't disappoint anyone."

But in retreating from her sisters, she was disappointing them terribly. "I can't get close to the girl!" lamented Melissa, who'd already found and lost Shelley twenty years before. "Let's do this! Let's not fuck around!" Added Jennifer: "You don't get a break in sisterhood."

NORMA HAD BEEN HAPPY to meet Jennifer, and excited to hear that she was gay. But her daughter's lesbianism led Norma to grapple anew with the sad fact that having long been out and proud, a lesbian tying a bandanna around her left thigh to signal her availability, she had since repudiated her sexuality. "I let politics run my life, I let religion run my life," she reflected weeks later over toast and grape jelly at a Waffle House. "I shouldn't be that way."

Hours later, it occurred to Norma that she had, at least, stood her middle ground on abortion. "I can understand a woman making a mistake and going to have an abortion," she said at a Starbucks. "There's sanctuary, there's peace." But, she added, if a woman wanted multiple abortions, or just one too late in a pregnancy, "that's when a state should have a compelling interest in a woman's uterus."

Forty years after *Roe*, its plaintiff spoke with a command she had not had at the time of its filing. And yet, Norma remained at sixty-six her impolitic self. On this November afternoon, a Christian woman named Donna phoned to say that through Norma she'd found grace following an abortion. Norma reflected after hanging up that it was more difficult to be pro-life than pro-choice. "It's really a lot harder on this side because you gotta act like you care," she said. "But I don't really give a shit."

MONTHS LATER, in early 2014, Shelley found herself considering a return to therapy. "Because," she said, "I'm scared of being Norma."

That Shelley resembled Norma was clear. It had been apparent to the very first person who'd met them both in adulthood. "She's very, very fragile," the private investigator Toby Hanft had noted of Shelley. "She's very much like her birth mother."

Shelley did not disagree. "The emotional similarities—that would be the linchpin," she reflected. Shelley, though, had chosen not to *confirm* their relation, because to confirm that she'd been born to Norma would be to lose the possibility that she hadn't. "I wasn't going to have a choice in the matter," she explained.

But the prospect of confirming the truth appealed to her mother and two sisters. In February 2014, the women spit into vials, each pleased when a genomics company confirmed they were kin.

Norma wanted proof that she'd birthed her youngest, too; the public assumption that she'd had an abortion continued to upset her. But Norma's attempts to meet Shelley had failed, and she blamed her daughter. "Shelley thinks she's got everyone over a barrel because she's, quote unquote, the *Roe* baby," said Norma. Norma added that she no longer wished for them to meet. The thought, she said, seemed "very taboo."

Off in Arizona, that spring, Shelley found a therapist in the Yellow Pages. She began seeing her three times a week.

Shelley devoted little of her therapy to *Roe*. "We skirted around the edges of it," she says. Rarely, even, did she speak of Norma. She looked back instead at the years before she had heard of *Roe* or Norma, back to her adoption and childhood when she had begun to retreat from an alcoholic father. "My first instinct is to run and hide," she says. "Let's pretend this is not happening."

Shelley still did run and hide, escaping to the safety of that imagined swing in a Texas field, a vision strangely similar to Norma's imagined playground. And though her sisters reached out to Shelley all through spring—to say happy birthday and invite her to a baby shower and, says Melissa, "just to let her know I'm still here"—Shelley did not respond.

On December 15, 2014, Shelley flew north to a Seattle hospital where her mother was on life support. Ruth could not speak but could understand. Shelley asked if she was in pain; she told her mother to blink once for yes and twice for no. Ruth blinked once and Shelley asked her mother if she was "ready to go see Grandma." Ruth again blinked once. Shelley spoke to the nurse about removing her mother from life support and told her mother not to worry. Her mother was still alive when, fifteen minutes later, Shelley walked out of the room.

Shelley did not tell her sisters that her mother had died. "I couldn't talk to anybody," she says. "I could barely breathe." But she posted the news on Facebook. Jennifer alerted Melissa, and the sisters texted their condolences and love. Shelley did not respond and

Melissa texted again. "Please let me know you are doing okay," she wrote. "I really do worry about you girly." Shelley again was silent, and Melissa found herself fighting the recurring thought that Shelley, she says, was "just like Norma."

———

NORMA CONTINUED TO distance herself from *Roe*. In early 2014, when another anniversary came upon her, she did nothing but a short interview with Priests for Life, passing the day stripping and sanding a pair of wooden end tables on her porch. She was feeling good and got a peace sign tattooed on her right shoulder. She was all the happier when confirmation came that Melissa and Jennifer were indeed of her haplogroup, of her same maternal line. But with the arrival of spring, she stopped taking her antidepressants and her mood darkened. She pinned her sadness on her local church, its priest and parishioners. "I'm tired of bleeding for everyone," said Norma from the hospital on the last day of May. "I can't do it anymore."

Norma had been admitted with a bad cough, air hunger too. Puffs on her nebulizer provided only temporary relief. Her anxiety was high, and she did not return home until after a voluntary one-night stay in a psychiatric clinic. Said Norma: "I raised hell in that behavior center for a good seven straight hours."

Back home, Norma was cared for by a health worker, a kind woman named Christy who took her vitals over talk of animals. Norma found herself thinking of Connie, and pondered calling her. Instead, she texted Melissa in late June to ask if she could move in. But Melissa had recently hosted her for Christmas and Easter, and the memory of those holidays—Norma shoplifting makeup at the mall, throwing up cantaloupe with no effort to get to a bathroom—left Melissa little choice. "My family can't take it," she says. "I'll lose Chloe. I'll lose Eric. I'll lose myself."

That same spring, Eric proposed. He and Melissa had been together three years. Melissa was overjoyed, and touched that Eric had put a diamond that had belonged to Mary into her engagement ring. But the next day, at a barbecue celebration, Eric drank four beers. Watching her fiancé slur his speech, Melissa sank. "It just really hurt my soul," she says.

Eric was six feet and 130 pounds. He had little tolerance for alcohol. But Melissa had none. She waited for her daughters to leave before telling Eric that until he curtailed his drinking, the wedding was off. "I've seen it too often," she said, ticking off a list of names: Mary, Norma, Kerry. "I hate a drunk."

NORMA WAS NOW hospitalized almost monthly—for bronchitis or pneumonia or anxiety. It seemed that when she moved next, it ought to be into a nursing home. Melissa hoped that Father Pavone might cover the cost.

The priest had, in fact, just spoken to Norma about the possibility of her moving into a nursing home, and had asked his staff, he said, to find one that would accommodate her cat. He planned to find a donor to cover the cost; he would reach out first, he said, to Marjorie Dannenfelser, president of the Susan B. Anthony Foundation. But as the months passed, the only word from Pavone was to ask Norma if she would speak over the phone to a pro-life group in Spain. Norma said no.

Over the last ten days of 2014, Norma was between hospitalizations when she went to Melissa for another Christmas, and asked through tears to stay. The daughter was forced again to turn her away. "I can't live with you," she told Norma. "I doubt if we'd make it a month."

JENNIFER FELT BAD that the weight of Norma fell upon Melissa. Then again, that was Melissa's choice. "She's too fucking nice," said Jennifer. "I would've washed my hands of that shit a long time ago—parent or no parent."

Jennifer had the relationship with Norma that she wanted; a year after their meeting, they shared little more than holiday texts. The joy she had felt upon finding her mother had receded into contentment. Having also found her sisters, there remained for Jennifer just one great unknown: the identity of her father.

Norma could not remember his name. And those papers she had left behind held no clue. But Norma welcomed my interest in her life and did her best to help me piece it together. She authorized a letter, for example, that I sent in 2015 to the Dallas Independent School District. The district sent me her old file. There, in a handwritten note from 1966, was word that Norma (having returned briefly at age eighteen to high school) had lived with a woman named Glenda Diane Hyman. I looked for Hyman, and found her days later in a mobile home in the horse country of north Texas. Hyman told me not only of her girl-friend Norma but of the man she had found naked in bed beside her, a vocational nurse named Pete Aguilar she had tried to stab with a butcher knife.

Six days later, on the last of March, Aguilar welcomed me into his Dallas home, a tidy ranch decorated with Buddhas and candles, pillows and plants: a cactus, an ivy, a jasmine. Aguilar was seventy but looked much younger. He had bright brown skin, thick silver hair, and a little body that he kept fit with yoga and biking and jogging and weights and lots of sex; at present, he said, he had a half-dozen partners, men and women he preferred to sleep with in pairs.

Forty-eight years had passed since Aguilar had last slept with Norma, forty-seven since she had called to tell him that he was the father of a girl. He had hoped it was true. But in all the years since, he had told just two people that he might be a father: his brother Joseph, who had grown upset with him at the news, and a married man named Rey who had been his lover for a quarter-century. "We were having a threesome," says Aguilar. "It was Father's Day. And he said, 'You've got to call.'" Aguilar never did call Norma. He was afraid to know for certain if he really had fathered a child, afraid to know if Norma really had placed her for adoption. He pushed the thought aside, retreating into his relationships, his work and the miniature schnauzers he raised for show.

Over time, though, it became harder to push thoughts of Norma aside. For she began popping up on his television.

Aguilar was unsure exactly what *Roe* was. He always changed the channel when its plaintiff came on. But he wondered about the daughter who might be his. And one day, in 2005, while at work at the hospital, Aguilar saw Norma. He was in shock. He had just turned sixty and hadn't seen Norma in the nearly forty years since he'd run from her, naked and drunk, at knifepoint. Norma didn't recognize him. Aguilar composed himself and said nothing and escorted her to the patient room. Then he opened her chart and wrote down her number and slipped it into a kitchen drawer where, in the decade since, it had remained.

Aguilar was happily retired, at peace but for one great unknown. Told now that Norma had indeed given birth to a daughter who'd been adopted and wished to find her father, he was overcome. "When you have something that's been lifted off your . . ." Aguilar stopped. He began to cry.

Aguilar wished at once to confirm his paternity. "I feel bad," he said. "Like I've missed out on forty-seven years." He sent a vial of his saliva to a lab in North Carolina, hoping at age seventy to meet the child he had fathered at twenty-two.

JENNIFER GASPED WHEN I told her that her father had been found, gasped again at word of his bisexuality; neither of her parents was straight. Three months later, on the last day of June, she and Lisa drove their pickup to meet Pete at a bistro called Mimi's in Round Rock.

As Pete drove south through a downpour on I-35, he found himself contemplating his bisexuality. He had never confided it to his family. And he had come to see, he now said, that had he been better able to accept himself, he might have lived a more domestic life, might have been a dad.

At a quarter after six, Pete rose from a booth in his shorts and short sleeves to hug Jennifer. "You look so much like your mother," he said. Father and daughter sat, their elbows on the table between them. Their faces were some three feet apart, and their resemblances popped into focus—the high cheekbones and round chins and coloring that had once led kids to call Jennifer "half-breed." The two looked quietly at their menus. "I've never acquired a taste for fish," said Pete. Jennifer hadn't either. They ordered parmesans and asked each other about their work, Pete saying that he loved Walmart, Jennifer speaking of her respect for the medical field.

Talk turned to Norma. Jennifer listened, rapt, as Pete told her that he'd proposed to marry Norma upon learning that she was pregnant, and had sent her a dozen yellow roses upon Jennifer's delivery. Pete had tried to do right. "I always dreamed," he said, "that you were going to come knocking on the door."

Pete and Jennifer stepped from the restaurant and snapped a photo and made plans for a next meeting. As Pete drove north, he was quiet, taking in the remarkable fact that he was not merely a father but a grandfather and a great-grandfather, too. "I don't know if it's the right word," he said, "but I feel complete." To his left, a sun was setting, to his right, a full moon rising. Pete was aglow. The next morning, Jennifer texted that she was happy they had met. They began to speak once or twice a week. Jennifer was soon calling him Pops.

———

IT HAD BEEN a difficult half-year for Shelley. After the death of her mother, she had quit her job and separated from Doug. He was too controlling, she said. Encouraged by her therapist, Shelley withdrew money from their account and moved out after twenty-four years of marriage, settling in August 2015 into an apartment of her own before filing for divorce.

If Shelley was no longer a wife, she remained a mother. And, she says, her daughters "were vulnerable enough to say, 'We still need you. We need you to get out of bed.'" Months passed, and Shelley got a chihuahua named Molly and a boyfriend named Mike. But she stayed away from her sisters. "For me, family is *difficult*," says Shelley. "I have so many trust issues." She adds: "It just didn't seem real. It just didn't seem genuine."

Shelley wanted to be close to her sisters, she said. It was a matter of process and time, and of coming to see both Melissa and Jennifer as distinct from Norma.

———

NORMA WAS FRAIL. She walked with a cane, a patterned aluminum stick she bought at Kroger's. The ten or so cigarettes she smoked daily left her with an almost perpetual bronchitis that returned her to the hospital again and again. She worried about the end. "I will die a terrible death," she'd written a friend a few years before, "a nurse finding me in a bed dirty and all alone." In March 2015, Norma was at Baylor when she told Melissa that, should it come to it, she did not wish to be resuscitated.

Soon after Norma returned to her room in the home of Angie Heiter, she had a drink of Baileys Irish Cream. Angie expressed disapproval. Norma, who had taken to calling her "mother," screamed at her that what she needed was "a good hard prick and a drink."

Norma had long tired of reproach. Guilt, she said, came of the incompatibility of sex and religion—the fact that "one makes you feel good and the other one makes you feel bad." Having been made to give up what made her feel good, she had all but let go of what made her feel bad. Still, Norma hoped that religion might help her in death. That June, she accepted from Angie a small brown scapular to wear about her neck so that she might be spared "eternal fire."

Just east of Norma, in a little Dallas home, her partner of forty years was facing a death more imminent. Connie was rail-thin and her heart was weak. She slept away most days. But she was ready; she'd spent her last dollars to cover her own cremation, and had given away the silver ring that Norma had left behind. On June 26, the day the Supreme Court legalized gay marriage, Connie died.

Three days later, seated on her back porch on a peeling rocker, Norma looked out at her yard of crabgrass with glassy eyes. Norma, though, was not one to mourn. With a deep draw on her cigarette that glowed the ash between her fingers the orange-red she had dyed her hair, she said only that Connie had had a "rough life," and then drove off to the mall to commemorate it with a meal of Chinese food and cheesecake.

———

NORMA REMAINED a burden for Melissa, a body to keep fed and clothed and breathing. And yet, the daughter was desperate not to lose her. Having lost Mary and Raymond, she struggled to hold close those few people still in her family—not only her mother, ever disagreeable, but a daughter who was aloof and a sister who was apart, and a fiancé she loved but whom therapy and AA and Al-Anon had brought no closer to becoming her husband. Even Jennifer, so busy with work, was rarely free. Fifty years old, Melissa wanted more. It was thus a thrill when, on a September Saturday, a sibling she had only just discovered pulled into her driveway.

Melissa had always wondered if her father had had other children. A few years before, she'd reached out to a McCorvey in Houston, a cousin whom Eric had found online. But the inquiry had led nowhere, and Melissa remained unaware that Elwood John McCorvey had indeed fathered a son.

His name was also Elwood, though he went by Ray. He was fourteen months younger than Melissa, born in the summer of 1966. Like his older half-sister, he had grown up in a poor and broken Texas home, his father "absent and unfaithful," he says. Ray was six when he and his mother left.

The father had had no more contact with his son when, in 1996, he died. But the son still ran from his example. A decade later, Ray had a stable life, settled in Utah with a wife and two sons and a job as a fireman. Still, Ray wondered about his father—about his medical history, and about the family rumor that he'd married Jane Roe. In June 2015, I found Ray and told him it was true. Ray flew to Melissa, who took her brother in with a hug. "He's short like me!" she laughed.

The siblings did not look much alike; Ray had the square jaw and strong features of his mother. But he and Melissa were driven by the same desire to be, respectively, the father and mother they had not had. Over dinner with Eric and Jordan and Chloe, Melissa and Ray spoke of their families and their father. Ray shared what little he knew of the man—his fondness for speedboats and women. Melissa recalled that the one time she'd met him, he had called her "kid" and given her ten dollars to go buy a slushie.

Melissa had now met the whole of her immediate family. She had, at last, a relative who was not only stable but would make time, too, Ray texting and calling and visiting, driving his family to Melissa for a Thanksgiving meal while on a cross-country trip. Still, Melissa found herself less invested in her brother than in her sisters. For only they were of Norma.

NORMA HAD LIVED in Smithville three years when she left for Irving. She had lived in Irving another three when, days before Christmas, it was clear that she would have to move again. She was at constant risk of falling and of pneumonia, too. Her host Angie told Melissa that it was time to move Norma into a home.

On the last day of 2015, Melissa and Eric packed Norma up—her oxygen tanks and coloring books and clothes—and drove her to their home. Norma sat beside Melissa, Eric behind them in Norma's Honda with her cat, an Eiffel Tower of rhinestones dangling from the ignition.

The next day, Melissa's ex, Kerry, had a heart attack. A week later he died, and Melissa turned from her mother to her daughters, bringing her girls to his body and kissing his face so that they might better grieve for their father. After his funeral, Melissa turned back to Norma, finding her a bed in a facility in Houston. Frustrated that Norma was not getting her meds, Melissa moved her into the nursing home where Mary and Raymond had lived and died. There, at Heritage Park in Katy, Jennifer and her granddaughter Jenessa came, in late January, to visit.

Norma beamed at her great-granddaughter and told Jennifer how proud she was of her rise at Walmart. Jennifer thus knew a different Norma than the one whose maelstroms left her sister physically ill. "My stomach is in knots whenever I speak to her," allowed Melissa. "My throat tightens, my neck tightens, my head hurts, my heart palpitates."

Still, Melissa would not wash her hands of her mother. She would pay her bills—for her phone and her car and her trips to Walmart. She would tend to her, would stock her mini-fridge and replenish her coloring pencils and cut her hair and mind her health—her anxiety and COPD and weakening heart. Melissa drove her to the hospital three times in February. When then in March, Norma phoned to say she had a bloody nose, Melissa and Eric drove right to her.

Eric had put together a dresser for Norma the day before, three wooden drawers Melissa filled with tops and bottoms from Sears and Goodwill. Melissa now got Norma dressed, mindful of the oxygen tubing that ran over her ears and under her nose. She put a blue pin in her white hair, and told Norma that she loved her. Norma told her the same, and Melissa laid her down, turning a metal crank at her foot to raise Norma's head. Eric smiled. "This," he said, "is a Medicaid bed."

He and Melissa had only just applied for Medicaid for Norma. They were careful to reduce her assets, to set aside the bulk of her money, $6,500, for her death—her ceremony and coffin and cremation and urn. "You have to be poverty-level," explained Melissa. "Then you get a bed and they feed you. And you get sixty dollars a month."

That Jane Roe was in need of such help was a sad reflection upon the multi-million-dollar movements to which she had first given her body and then her soul. "The movement doesn't take care of you," attested Kass McMahon, a pro-choice activist who'd met Norma a quarter-century before. The same was true of the pro-life. When now Melissa reached out to Father Pavone for financial help, she got none. "They didn't do nothing," she said of Priests for Life. "Not a damn thing."

Pavone's PFL had an annual budget in the millions. He did as he pleased with it, never mind the continued calls for oversight. (New York Cardinal Timothy Dolan had cut ties with the group after Pavone refused in 2014 to submit to an audit.) But the priest's ties to Norma had withered along with her commitment to his cause. Norma grew animated when, on this March afternoon, the talk in Room 306 turned to the Texas case about abortion regulation that was currently before the Supreme Court. "Women have been doing abortions for thousands of years and they're always going to do them," she said over the hum of bubbling saline. "So you might as well make it the hell legal and stop trying to criminalize the woman."

One month later, Medicaid approved Norma. Melissa was in high spirits. So was Norma. She told Melissa that a filmmaker had come to her from Brooklyn and paid her $3,000 for her story.

His name was Nick Sweeney. He was a thirty-something from Sydney, Australia, a gay man who had an interest in sex and sexuality. His previous two films were about transgender youth and men who dress up as female dolls, and he was mid-production on a film about a sex robot. Jane Roe would be his next subject.

Norma McCorvey was born in 1947 in Simmesport, Louisiana, at the head of the Atch-afalaya River. Before moving to Texas in 1950, she lived in the little house pictured here. It was up on piers to guard against flooding. (COURTESY OF NORMA MCCORVEY)

Norma became the plaintiff Jane Roe in 1970. But she did not join the pro-choice community until 1981, when she went to a meeting of the National Organization for Women. Here she is, a decade later, at a conference in Oregon for reproductive rights. (JOE WILKINS III)

Months after Norma gave birth, in 1970, to her third child, the *Roe* baby, she met her lifelong part-ner, Connie Gonzalez. The women are pictured here in 1994 at their Dallas home. (TAMMYE NASH)

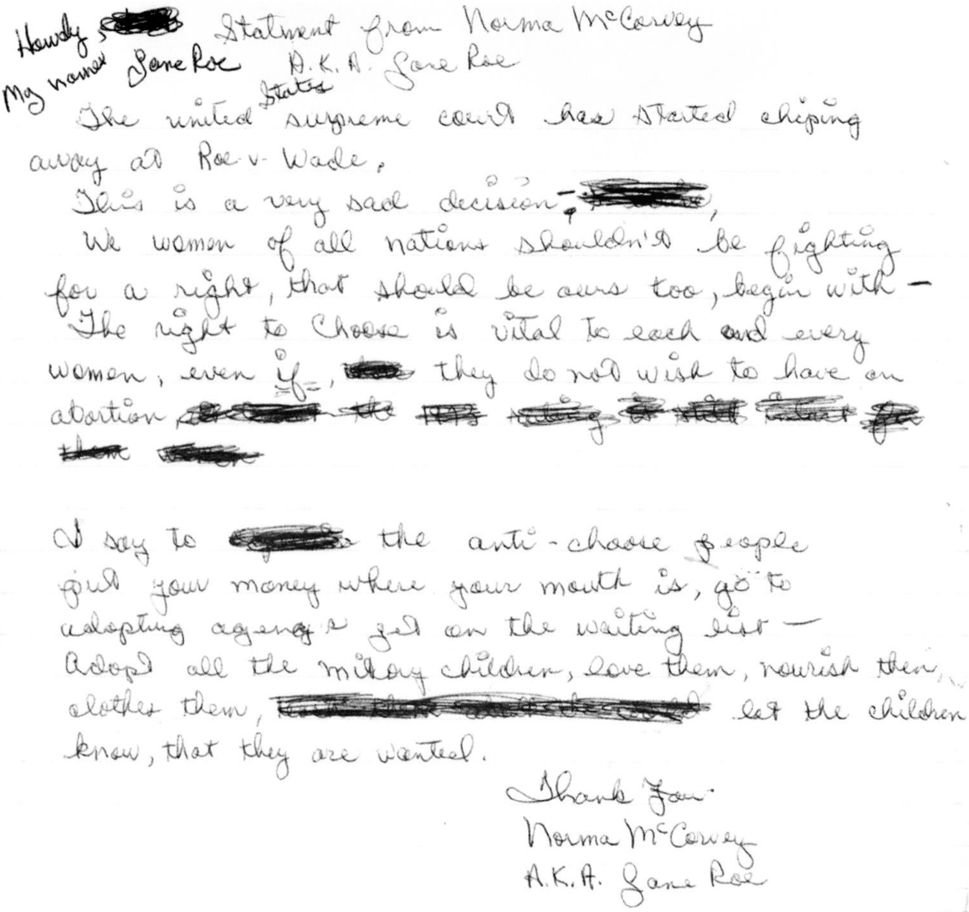

Howdy, ~~xxx~~ Statement from Norma McCorvey

My name Jane Roe A.K.A. Jane Roe

The united States supreme court has Started chiping away at Roe v. Wade,

This is a very sad decision ~~xxx~~,

We women of all nations shouldn't be fighting for a right, that should be ours too, begin with —

The right to Choose is vital to each and every women, even if ~~xxx~~ they do not wish to have an abortion ~~xxxxxxxxxxxxxxxxxxxxx~~

I say to ~~xxx~~ the anti-choice people put your money where your mouth is, go to adopting agency's get on the waiting list — Adopt all the mikory children, love them, nourish them, clothes them, ~~xxxxxxxxxxxx~~ let the children know, that they are wanted.

Thank You,
Norma McCorvey
A.K.A. Jane Roe

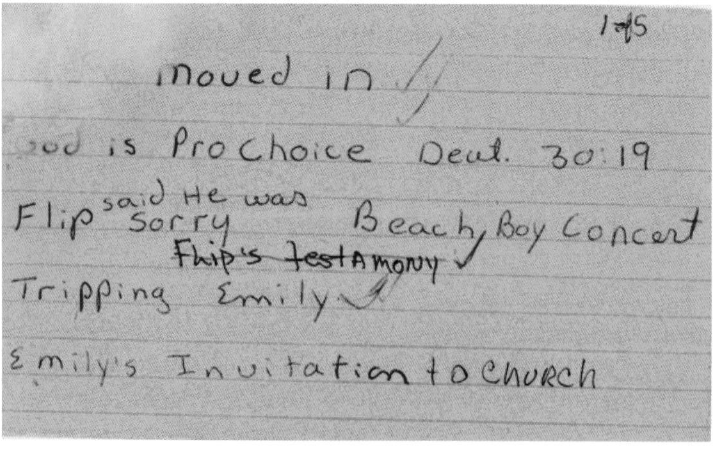

---

1 of 5

moved in ✓

God is Pro Choice Deut. 30:19

Flip said He was sorry   Beach Boy Concert
Flip's ~~Testamony~~ ✓
Tripping Emily ✓

Emily's Invitation to Church

Norma had begun to turn her plaintiffship into a career when in 1989, the lawyer Gloria Allred met her at a rally in Washington, DC, and took her to Los Angeles. Pictured here are the handwritten drafts of speeches she gave before and after she became an evangelical Christian in 1995. (SCHLESINGER LIBRARY, RADCLIFFE INSTITUTE, HARVARD UNIVERSITY)

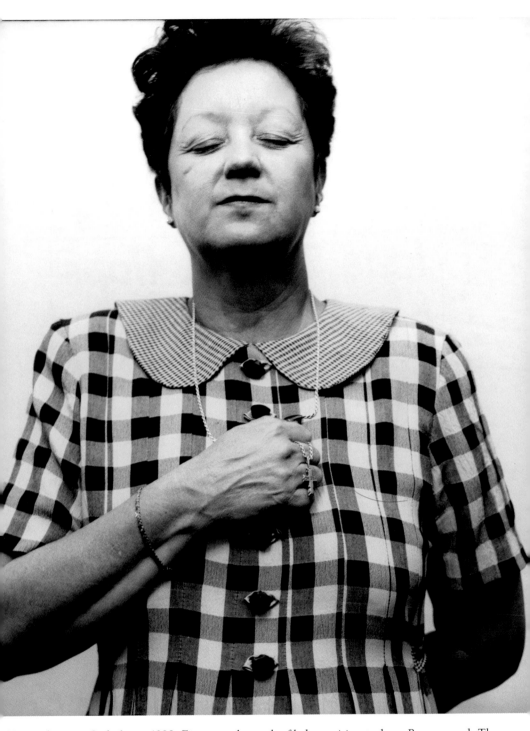

Norma became Catholic in 1998. Five years later, she filed a petition to have *Roe* reversed. The 2003 case, *McCorvey v. Hill*, was dismissed. But one of its arguments—that abortion caused women psychological harm—helped to shift the pro-life focus from the fetus to the pregnant woman. To that end, Norma's lawyer, Allan Parker, had begun collecting affidavits from women asserting that abortion harmed them. Norma provided the first. Though she'd not had an abortion, Norma thus became, as Professor Mary Ziegler later wrote, "patient zero in this narrative—the first victim of abortion rights." Here she is, photographed by Annie Leibovitz in 1998, crucifix in hand. (ANNIE LEIBOVITZ/TRUNK ARCHIVE)

NEW YORK POST

LATE CITY FINAL

FRIDAY, AUGUST 11, 1995 / Hot and hazy today, upper 80s; warm and humid tonight, 72 / Details, Page 22 ★★

50¢

Jane Roe flip-flops on abortion

'I'M PRO-LIFE'

Norma McCorvey, better known as Jane Roe when she won a landmark Supreme Court case in Roe vs. Wade, stunned the nation yesterday when she turned her back on freedom of choice on abortion and vowed "to save babies."

Full story: Pages 4 & 5

DOMINICK DUNNE'S MISSING SON FOUND SAFE Page 3

Over and over again, Norma lied to the press, telling them, for example, that she had been raped, that she had been shot at because she was Jane Roe, that she had no money for food. She also declared herself uncompromisingly pro-life though, in truth, her views were not absolute. When she became a Christian in 1995, the *New York Post* put her on its front page. (NEW YORK POST)

Norma had three daughters with three different men, and gave each child up for adoption. The sisters looked for one another and finally came together in Katy, Texas, on March 14, 2013. Melissa is seen here hugging Shelley the very moment they met. Hours later, the three sisters walked outside and crossed the street to a playground. (JAHANGIR RAZMI)

Norma is seen here in Smithville, Texas, where she moved in 2009. Over the last years of her life, she increasingly detached herself from the pro-life movement and *Roe* too. She spoke openly of the toll her plaintiffship had taken, and reiterated what she had first stated publicly in 1973: that abortion ought to be legal through the first trimester of pregnancy.
(Bob Daemmrich/Bob Daemmrich Photography, Inc.)

For as long as *Roe* had been law, Norma had been telling her story—
that she had been raped by a nun and beaten by her husband and had
her daughter kidnapped by her mother, and been shot at because of
Roe. Her story was part of the culture, presented that very summer in a
play in Oregon titled *Roe*. That Norma would now be the subject of yet
another production delighted her. But Melissa feared that those extra
dollars might deny Norma Medicaid, and with it her place at Heritage
Park. Weeks later, on May 2, the facility kicked Norma out anyway,
after she returned from a few hours with Sweeney with cigarettes on
her person. Melissa was furious at the filmmaker.

Norma, meantime, was furious that Melissa had spent her remaining money on her funeral. A week later, after being transferred to a
smoking facility in nearby Richmond, Norma texted Melissa a miserable message, likening her daughter to her mother. "I should had abort
you," she wrote. "your just a damn trouble maker and a whore like Mary
sandefur." Said Melissa: "She's vindictive, mean, hateful."

———

MELISSA AND ERIC had just returned from a rare escape, a few days in New
Orleans with Jennifer and Lisa that summer of 2016, when they readied
to see Shelley for the first time in three years. Shelley was in Texas to see
her uncle and aunt. But hours before she was to visit Melissa, she texted
that she had a migraine and wouldn't be able to make it.

It was hard to know whom to pity more, the sister who had tempered
her expectations and was still disappointed or the sister wracked with
anxiety by the mere prospect of dinner. But the migraine lifted. Shelley
texted that she could visit after all. She arrived just past eight with her
two teenage daughters. "She's probably mad at me," she said to Eric.
But Melissa only hugged her. By the time Shelley left with her girls, talk
had turned from the weather and credit card interest rates to *Star Wars*
and first concerts. The next evening, Jennifer joined them, the sisters
together for just the second time. Shelley spoke of her divorce and the
death of her mother. "I went through a really hard time after I saw you
guys," she said. But, she added, her therapist had told her that her sisters
would "be there when you get through this." And here, now, they were.

―――――

WEEKS LATER, in late July, Norma got booted from another facility for refusing to do her therapy. Melissa found her a bed in a home not far off in Brookshire, where residents were allowed six cigarettes a day.

A life among alcoholics had bled Melissa of her tolerance for addiction, and it pained her that Norma smoked. More, Norma's lungs were profusely damaged. She was back in a Katy hospital with pneumonia when, in September, she turned sixty-nine, and celebrated her birthday with Melissa and the family over Chinese food and chocolate cake.

The filmmaker Sweeney was with them. That he stood by as Norma smoked cigarettes and drank coffee upset Melissa. But one October day, as Norma cursed up a storm on camera, it struck Melissa, she says, that Norma was "performing." The realization helped Melissa. For as Norma continued to bounce among nursing homes, she continued to perform: refusing therapy, refusing X-rays, fighting with roommates. Melissa understood that Norma was living the last months of her life. And she had her for the holidays, and bought her DVDs of westerns and whodunits, and took her to get her nails done, oxygen tanks in tow. In February, when Norma felt hot, Melissa gave her a pixie cut. Norma thus had short hair when, a week later, she returned to the hospital with another pneumonia. She was soon unresponsive.

Two years had passed since Norma had told Melissa that she would rather die than be resuscitated. But Melissa was unprepared to let go. Valentine's Day found Norma breathing through a tube in a Katy ICU, a stuffed brown cat rising and falling on her abdomen.

Two days later, Norma was breathing on her own. As a respiratory therapist named Jesus removed the tube from her throat, Melissa knew that she would not have Norma intubated again. She set out to find her a place to die, settling on a new facility called Sterling Oaks. It was there, two miles from Melissa's home, at 2:30 in the afternoon of February 16, that Norma lay down in Room 204.

―――――

MELISSA HAD TEXTED her sisters that Norma was breathing through a tube. Jennifer did not respond; she had not yet come, she says, "to learn to love her." Shelley inquired where Norma was. She wondered if Norma might yet reach out, might yet apologize. Were she to do so, were she now, said Shelley, to call and say, "I'm dying, I want to say hi," Shelley would fly right to her. She had long had the private desire for Norma to "feel something for another human being," she says, "especially for one she brought into this world." Told that Norma would soon die, she felt that desire acutely. "I want her to experience this joy—the good that it brings," Shelley reflected. "I have wished that for her forever, and have never told anyone. . . . She doesn't understand that even though she doesn't deserve it, people care about her."

On this winter day in Tucson, Shelley was still contemplating whether she would fly to her birth mother. "I'm sitting here going back and forth and back and forth and back and forth and then it's going to be too late," she said. Shelley was certain of just one thing. "I don't owe her a final visit," she said. "I don't have to be the bigger person because I'm not the person who screwed up."

NORMA HAD BEEN at Sterling Oaks two days when Melissa arrived to spend the night. It occurred to her that she had not slept in the same room as her mother since she was a girl of eleven visiting her on Cactus Lane. As Melissa shifted and propped Norma just so, laying her on her left side, blankets between her knees, Norma also retreated to her past, muttering a Cajun remnant of the Louisiana she had left in 1950 as a toddler: "*Fils de putain.*"

Melissa fed Norma spoonfuls of ice chips from a Styrofoam cup. A nurse practitioner with a purple afro then gave Norma morphine and a hug. After a few minutes of breathing in a medicinal mist, Norma fell asleep, a rosary over the corner of her pillow, on her wrist a purple plastic bracelet that read in white letters "DNR."

Norma was hazy. In the middle of the night, she called out to Melissa to ask if she was "going the right way." Melissa responded that she ought to "just keep going," and then told her that she was proud that she was her mother.

Word was circulating in the pro-life community that Norma was at the end, and a priest from a local high school arrived to give her the

last rites. Others stopped by with rosaries and good wishes, and Father
Pavone called from Rome with word that he had led a prayer service for
Norma at St. Peter's. After a hailstorm this Friday morning gave way to
warm air and sun, Eric and then Chloe arrived.

Chloe was twenty-two and dressed in black. But even now, she
greeted her grandmother with the same good cheer that had long lifted
her family: "Hey, sweet lady!" She gave Norma a kiss. After Melissa
slowly fed Norma a lemon tart, she drove off with her daughter to the
Katy nursing home where Norma had last lived and packed up her stuff:
a wooden crucifix, a dead poinsettia, a lamp, coloring pencils, purses,
a cane, a brush, slippers, clothes. When they returned to Norma, they
found her weak but clear-headed. "Jell-O," she said. So they fed her
Jell-O and a bite of white bread with butter, and she drank water with
thickener in it. "You're in God's hands," Melissa told her. Said Norma:
"I've got angel eyes."

Those eyes had opened only somewhat the next morning, hazel
half-moons, when, at ten minutes past nine on February 18, I entered
her room.

Melissa had asked me to go to Norma so that she might go home
for a shower. Norma was agitated and breathing quickly. I phoned
Melissa and told her to come right away. She did. "I'm here now," she
told Norma. "I love you."

Melissa was crying. She kissed Norma's cheek. "You've been a good
mother," she said. "I love you, Mama."

Minutes before ten, Melissa borrowed a stethoscope from a nurse.
She pressed its chestpiece to Norma and listened. Norma was calming,
relaxed by a dose of morphine just before my arrival. Melissa laid an
iPhone on her chest. As Paul Simon sang of diamonds on shoes, she
knelt at Norma's shoulder. Eric looked at Melissa with tears in his eyes.
"It breaks my heart to see her sad," he said.

Norma's breathing was slowing and a hospice nurse arrived.
There was no need for her now. She left, and Melissa combed
Norma's hair, and the music played on, some Christian songs that
Norma's friend Karen had readied: "Lord, I Need You," "10,000
Reasons." Chloe then recalled that Norma loved Bob Marley. His

paean to unity, "One Love," was playing when, at 11:07 that winter morning, Norma died.

Melissa removed the flow of oxygen from beneath Norma's nose, and said that she wished to cut her hair. Chloe suggested that they put it in a wet perm. Melissa thought that a good idea and instructed the funeral home not to come for a few hours; Jordan and Jennifer were en route, and she wished for them to have time with Norma. Melissa then spoke of her mother. "She made me strong," she said. Eric kissed Melissa and said that, in caring for Norma, she had set a beautiful example for her kids. It had in fact been heroic, and Melissa bent down and kissed her mother on the forehead.

Chapter 36

In 2015, the Supreme Court legalized gay marriage. Some felt that the Court had overstepped and they pointed as a warning to *Roe*—another sweeping ruling that forty-two years before had also hinged on privacy. As a federal judge wrote during a trial over a California constitutional amendment banning gay marriage: "The Supreme Court has constitutionalized something that touches upon highly-sensitive social issues," and its ruling has "plagued our politics for 30 years."

But gay marriage was not abortion. Within a few years, few even recalled the name of the ruling that made it legal. Indeed, Americans who could name a Supreme Court ruling were twelve times less likely to cite *Obergefell v. Hodges* than *Roe*.

———

ABORTION IS FREIGHTED with points of universal contention: religion and sex, gender and autonomy, life and death. Yet, it had uniquely cleaved the United States. As the journalist Michael Kinsley observed: "No other nation obsesses about abortion the way we do."

At the time of *Obergefell*, the U.S. was one of fifty-eight countries to allow abortion for any reason (until varying points in pregnancy). Many of those countries had eased their restrictions in the decades after *Roe*. In most cases, the *Economist* observed, doing so "was enough to settle the debate. Not in America."

Many reasons were put forth. The *Economist* noted that unlike the U.S., European nations "justify abortion on the basis of health rather than rights." It noted, too, that the U.S. had established its abortion policy not through legislation or referenda, as had Europe, but through its courts. The law professor Mary Ann Glendon also cited the courts, as well as the American traditions of "individualism and libertarianism." The essayist Christopher Hitchens agreed that the courts and American individualism were factors, and pointed to others too, including American feminism and hedonism, while the author Roger Rosenblatt added to the list America's optimism and "preoccupation with evil." All but Glendon asserted that the crisis owed as well to America's religiosity and conservatizing of sex. America was the most puritanical of developed countries; Rosenblatt quipped that Americans would "reproduce themselves by fission" if they could. Abortion was perfectly suited to divide the country.

The abortion divide politicized and absolutized all manner of American institutions. The public fell in line. By the time Republican senator Arlen Specter stated in 1995 that he wished to "take abortion out of politics," doing so was no longer possible. Abortion stayed put; Specter left his party.

Specter's fellow Republicans had come to argue that because a fertilized egg will become a person, it already is one (at least in a moral sense). Though a zygote was but a single cell, that cell carried the moral weight of, say, a homunculus—that miniature yet fully-formed person once believed to have dwelled within every spermatozoon. It could no sooner be killed than a baby. As the Republican platform put it: "The unborn child has a fundamental right to life which cannot be infringed."

The GOP did little to help the woman it demanded bear that child, opposing policies designed to ease the burdens of motherhood. (The United States, for example, is the only developed country in the world without guaranteed paid maternity leave.) This was a "weakness of the Republican Party," acknowledged the conservative columnist Ross Douthat. Still, there was no indication that political pressure would force the party to change. As professor Daniel Williams noted: "The pro-life cause remained the one moral issue that was capable of attracting a younger generation to the Republican Party." The cauldron of abortion in America would thus simmer on, brought to an annual boil by the March for Life in Washington.

The march was but one front in the pro-life war on *Roe*. The movement fought with law and language, protest and politics, therapy and technology. It was nimble, too; having failed to add a personhood amendment to the Constitution, it had pledged itself to incremental change. And having humanized the unborn with all from "precious feet" pins to ultrasound—imaging put to use at crisis pregnancy centers about the country—it had shifted its focus from the fetus to the woman carrying it. The strategy was so effective that, in a remarkable inversion of *Roe*, the Supreme Court had come to muse about the "psychological harm" to women come not of "maternity or additional offspring," as Blackmun had written, but of abortion.

At the time of *Roe*, the pro-choice had not foreseen a war. NARAL's executive director told her board after the ruling that "the Court has spoken, and the case is closed." Forty-four years later, another NARAL director would lament that mistake. The movement, she said, had "started to lose ground the moment we decided that *Roe* was the end point and not the beginning point."

The pro-choice had been playing catch-up ever since. In the wake of the 2010 election, they not only faced numerous laws restricting access to abortion but also the notion that those laws existed to protect women—in essence—from themselves.

Abortion was among the most common of medical procedures, on a par with circumcision and cesarean birth. It was among the safest too, and no more a risk to the psychological health of a woman than pregnancy or birth. And the new laws (which required, for example, that women getting abortions first have ultrasounds) provided women no medical benefit. But these truths did not matter. The pro-life had taken hold of the abortion narrative. The pro-choice were desperate to take it back.

———

JUSTICE BLACKMUN HAD noted in his preamble to *Roe* that personal experience was likely to influence one's position on abortion. It could influence what others thought of abortion, too. As the writer Ursula K. Le Guin reflected in 1986 to a graduating class of college women: "When we women offer our experience as our truth, as human truth, all the maps change."

The pro-choice had long tried to change the American map with stories of abortion: in a 1978 book called *The Ambivalence of Abortion*, in a 1989 amicus brief filed in *Webster*, in a series of events and publications begun in 2000 called the Abortion Conversation Project. Still, only a tiny percentage of the millions of American women who'd had abortions told their stories. More, as the history professor Johanna Schoen noted, those few who did were more likely to speak of abortions they'd had before *Roe* than after. There was somehow less shame in having had to break the law to have an abortion than in having had one legally. Whereas Ali MacGraw and Whoopi Goldberg, for example, wrote years before of the risks they'd taken to end their pregnancies pre-*Roe*—one alone with a man in a locked room on the seventeenth floor of a filthy New York City building, the other alone with a coat hanger—the journalist Susan Dominus noted in 2005 that "no celebrity in recent memory has admitted to ending a pregnancy."

That same year, however, two documentaries told the stories of women who'd had abortions, most of them after *Roe*. The women wished to be rid of their secrecy and shame. "I was just kind of angry that no one had ever talked about [abortion]," one of the filmmakers, Penny Lane, who'd had an abortion, said on camera. "It just seemed like I would've been able to handle it a lot better had I had those stories to access."

The documentaries presaged a new era of disclosure, unrestrained and unapologetic. Forty years after Lawrence Lader had called abortion "the dread secret of our society," a co-producer of one of the two films, Jennifer Baumgardner, began selling T-shirts that read "I had an abortion." In 2010, an activist named Angie Jackson went to a clinic in Tampa for a medical abortion and tweeted in real time its effects: "cramps are getting a bit more persistent . . . definitely bleeding now." Women began to share their abortion stories in greater number than ever before, often via a crop of initiatives that began to spring up online: 1 in 3, The Abortion Diary, #ShoutYourAbortion, We Testify, #YouKnowMe. "There is," wrote the professor Elizabeth Kissling, "a bold new movement of feminist activists challenging and resisting abortion stigma."

Curtis Boyd had been challenging that stigma for decades. A generation before the feminist Katha Pollitt exhorted the public in 2014 "to
start thinking of abortion as a positive social good," Boyd had declared
abortion "a good and moral choice." He knew that nearly all women
who had abortions were glad they did; the heralded Turnaway Study put
that number at 95 percent. How much better it would be, thought Boyd,
if women learned of abortion from women who'd had them instead of
from some pro-life billboard like the huge pink one across the street
from his clinic in Albuquerque.

Still, that billboard was of little deterrence. Boyd's Albuquerque
clinic performed some three thousand abortions annually, his clinic in
Dallas twelve thousand more. And though Medicaid covered abortion
in New Mexico, and the Boyds accepted it—content to be paid below
cost so as to treat every patient—they were well paid for their work, and
drove about Dallas and Albuquerque in a pair of Mercedes.

———

BACK IN 2013, the Texas House bill that had nearly closed Boyd down had
succeeded in closing more than half of the clinics in Texas. Several of
them sued the state. In 2016, their suit, *Whole Woman's Health v. Hellerstedt*, returned abortion to the Supreme Court.

Much was at stake. The bill required that abortion clinics meet the
standards of ambulatory surgical centers, and that doctors performing
abortions have admitting privileges at a nearby hospital. Similar restrictions had shuttered clinics all around the country.

The number of abortion providers had been falling, besides; within
another year, they would number just 1,587, down by nearly half from
their 1982 high, and almost exactly the total in 1973. Five states, meantime, had just one clinic, and two states, New York and California,
accounted for nearly one in three of the total number of legal abortions
in the country.

That number was falling in lockstep with the number of clinics,
down by nearly half from its high of 1.6 million in 1988. And the rate
of abortion in the U.S.—the number of abortions for every thousand
women of reproductive age—was at its lowest in the forty-four years
since *Roe*, down from a high of 29.3 in 1981 to 13.5 in 2017. The remark-

able decline owed to efforts on both sides of *Roe*. While better contraception (and increased access to it) helped to prevent pregnancies,
regulations helped to prevent abortions.

And yet, the number of women wanting abortions remained enormous. Unwanted pregnancy is an inevitable consequence of heterosexual sex. (The professor Katie Watson estimates that a woman who is
sexually active through her fertile years and wishes to have two children
must prevent between sixteen and twenty-nine pregnancies.) Though
there were fewer clinics and more regulations, women continued to
exercise their legal right to terminate pregnancies; in 2016, they ended
roughly one in five of them.

In late 2015, as the Supreme Court readied for *Whole Woman's
Health*, Boyd attested in an amicus brief that the forced closure of
so many Texas clinics had overrun his own—even as he doubled his
administrative staff and increased hours by 50 percent. The women
he'd turned away had either left the state for care (Boyd noted that his
New Mexico clinic, though a four-hour drive from the Texas border,
had "been inundated" with women from Texas) or stayed put to wait
weeks for an appointment. Texas HB2 had thus pushed women deeper
into pregnancy, wrote Boyd, changing "both their procedure options
and the amount of time they must stay at the facility."

This was crucial testimony. Opponents of abortion in the U.S.
claimed that the abortion laws of even liberal nations in Western
Europe were more stringent than those in the U.S. And indeed, abortion was only legal through twelve weeks (counting from the last menstrual period) in Switzerland, and fourteen in France and Germany. But
the comparison was faulty. Whereas the U.S. erected barriers to abortion, created regulations that pushed women into the second trimester,
as Boyd now attested, those European nations *removed* most barriers to
access during whatever period of pregnancy abortion was legal. Switzerland and Germany, for example, did require a woman to consult with a
doctor prior to her abortion. But, as in France, the procedure was covered in both countries by health insurance. And none of the countries
required girls or women wanting an abortion to get parental or spousal consent, have ultrasounds or be issued unscientific warnings about
the procedure's effects. As the feminist journalist Michelle Goldberg

wrote: "We would happily trade the situation in which abortion is free, widely available and uncontested in the first trimester in exchange for these sorts of restrictions."

On March 2, 2016, the Supreme Court sat for oral arguments. The case hinged on a simple question: did the Texas restrictions benefit the health of women seeking abortions? That June, the Court said no. (Texas could not provide a single instance when its requirement of admitting privileges had benefited the health of a woman.) The regulations were simply obstructions designed to prevent abortions.

The Court's 5–3 ruling was a huge victory for the pro-choice. (Justice Scalia died before the case was argued.) Boyd was ecstatic. No longer would it be difficult to employ doctors. The ruling was also "great for the women of Texas," he said. "It's going to roll through the whole country. It's going to be like gay marriage."

———

THE COURT HAD not yet delivered its ruling when, in May, Donald Trump secured the Republican nomination for president. The real estate developer had long supported legal abortion. Back in 1999, he had said that he was "very pro-choice . . . pro-choice in every respect" (though he added that he hated "the concept of abortion"). But in 2011, he told conservative commentator Laura Ingraham that he was pro-life. Four years after that, he told the press that he supported a ban on abortion past twenty weeks. A month later, he declared that his opposition to abortion was complete save for the exceptions of rape, incest and the life of the mother.

Trump, though, was unversed in pro-life doctrine. In 2016, two months before securing the nomination, he told the pundit Chris Matthews at a town hall meeting in Wisconsin that women who have abortions ought to be subject to "some form of punishment."

There was logic to what Trump said. If a fetus is a person and abortion the taking of a human life, how can one not prosecute those who are party to it? As the pro-life activist Troy Newman once put it: "The woman is the same as a contract killer, hiring out the murder of her defenseless child." More, it followed that a woman ought to be punished for merely endangering the fetus, say, by smoking or drinking. Indeed, women had been already.

Back in 1969, a man in California had killed the viable fetus his ex-wife was carrying when he kneed her in the abdomen. He was tried for murder and found not guilty. In response, California had enacted a fetal homicide law. Dozens of states followed, enacting feticide laws that treated fetuses as separate victims of crimes. But what was meant to protect pregnant women (and the fetuses they carried) came to target them. By 2005, according to a report by the nonprofit National Advocates for Pregnant Women, 413 women had been prosecuted in the years since *Roe* for harming the fetus they carried.

"These laws," wrote the *New York Times* in 2018, "have meant that pregnant women who were addicted to drugs, were suicidal, were in car accidents, fell down stairs, delivered at home, refused C-sections or went about their lives in ways that were perceived to harm their pregnancies have been detained and jailed for a variety of crimes, including murder, manslaughter, neglect, criminal recklessness and chemical endangerment."

That list of alleged crimes did not include abortion. Abortion was legal. But eight states decreed that self-induced abortion was not. And in the years since *Roe*, nineteen women (in those states and others) had been arrested for ending their pregnancies, charged with a variety of offenses including self-abortion, concealing a birth, abuse of a corpse and murder.

The GOP, however, no longer wished to prosecute women for abortion; it didn't even want to blame them. As Katha Pollitt observed: "Today, abortion opponents blame everybody but the woman." It was a paradoxical shift; the pro-life now deemed women having abortions both perpetrator and victim. And so, at once, the Republican establishment renounced Trump's gaffe. He recanted it. "The woman is a victim in this case," he said, "as is the life in her womb."

———

TRUMP NEEDED the evangelical vote. He asked the president of the Southern Evangelical Seminary in North Carolina how to get it. Richard Land responded by suggesting a running mate. "I said," recalls Land, "'pick Mike Pence.'"

Pence was the governor of Indiana. More, he was, as Land explained, "the 24-karat-gold model of what evangelicals believe an evangelical politician should be." That model began with opposition to abortion. And Pence was vigorously pro-life. He had introduced the first bill in Congress to defund Planned Parenthood, signed into law multiple bills restricting abortion, and announced on the House floor that he longed to see *Roe* "sent to the ash heap of history." After adding Pence to the ticket, Trump explained how he intended to dispose of *Roe*. "That'll happen automatically, in my opinion," he promised in a debate with Hillary Clinton, "because I am putting pro-life justices on the court."

ONCE UPON A TIME, one could not assume how a new justice on the Court would rule on abortion. Pro-choice leaders, for example, had been certain in 1992 that Justice Souter would vote to overturn *Roe* right up until he engineered its rescue. But presidents left less and less to chance when selecting justices, relying on organizations like the Federalist Society, a group of conservative lawyers, to vet potential picks. What mattered above all was *Roe*. "These Supreme Court nominations always come down to the same thing," Republican senator Orrin Hatch told the *New Yorker*. "It's one case: *Roe, Roe, Roe*."

The confirmation of nominees was no different; the journalist David Kaplan called them "proxies on *Roe*." They were thus purely political; during the confirmations of the four justices nominated to the Court by presidents George W. Bush and Barack Obama, just two of the votes against them went against party lines. After Justice Scalia died in early 2016, the politicization of the confirmation process reached its inevitable climax when the Republican-controlled Senate refused to even consider the nominee put forward by President Obama.

Election day would thus determine not only the president, but a seat on the Court. And Trump made public the list of judges that the Federalist Society and others had assured him would toe the GOP line. It was kritarchy: government by judges. As David Kaplan wrote: "Constitutional law had become the continuation of politics by other means."

BETWEEN HIS PICK of Pence and his pledge to overturn *Roe*, Trump secured the pro-life vote. But he went further, meeting with groups of evangelicals that included Troy Newman and Flip Benham, and enlisting Frank Pavone too, appointing the priest to two advisory groups—one Catholic, one pro-life.

Two days before the election, Pavone stood over a fetus, discolored and prone on an altar between two lit candles. "Here before me lies a baby killed by abortion in the second trimester of pregnancy," said the priest, looking into the camera of a live Facebook feed. "We are going to let this baby's body bear witness to our nation as we begin the process to elect our next president."

Pavone wore his traditional black and white. As he preached, a note on the screen distilled his message. Whereas Trump would protect the unborn, wrote Pavone, "Hillary Clinton and the Democratic platform says yes, let the child-killing continue."

The Catholic community was quick to register its disgust. "Everyone who respects the dignity of every human person should reject and disavow this atrocity," wrote the director of public policy for the archdiocese of New York. He noted that Pavone had "desecrated" the altar; canon law stipulated that it "be reserved for divine worship alone."

Pavone's own diocese in Amarillo was no less appalled. It declared that "no one who is pro-life can exploit a human body for any reason, especially the body of a fetus." And despite Pavone's claims to the contrary, the diocese would later assert that he was no longer a priest in good standing. Nonetheless, his video generated press and, by election day, had been viewed 707,000 times.

OFF IN EAST TEXAS, Linda Coffee found herself deep in Trump country. Only a few months before, her town of Mineola had made the national papers when a local candidate for a seat on a state board declared that Obama had been a gay prostitute. Coffee was not among the 84 percent of Wood County that voted for Trump.

She was, however, among the 69 percent of Americans who didn't want Trump to make good on his pledge to overturn *Roe*. As election day passed, no political issue was googled more; the search "Trump on abortion" rose more than 4,000 percent as the polls began to close.

The election brought Coffee back to the winter of 1970 when, all of twenty-seven, she had filed *Roe*. The choices she had made then still echoed in ways small and large. It was because she had filed *Roe* in Dallas that now, as every January, thousands gathered in protest outside a Dallas courthouse. And just as she had rooted *Roe* in *Griswold*, the legal right to abortion in America was rooted in a right to privacy.

Coffee was seventy-four. Her life was in Mineola, where she walked her ridgebacks and read the paper in the library and did her best to get by. Seven days before Trump took office, she and her partner Rebecca Hartt drove to the food bank just north in Quitman to pick up their usual cardboard box of food dried and powdered and canned that would help them through another Texas winter.

———

TRUMP HAD BEEN president eleven days when he selected a Colorado judge named Neil Gorsuch as his nominee for the Supreme Court. Gorsuch had much in common with the man he would replace. Like Scalia, he was a constitutional originalist. He believed that the political left had involved the courts in matters better left to lawmakers. ("American liberals," he wrote, "have become addicted to the courtroom, relying on judges and lawyers rather than elected leaders and the ballot box, as the primary means of effecting their social agenda.") And a book he'd written on euthanasia suggested that he was opposed to *Roe*. Citing his assertion "that all human beings are intrinsically valuable and the intentional taking of life by private persons is always wrong," *National Review* quipped: "Gee, might that principle have any application to abortion?"

Gorsuch sailed through his confirmation hearing, offering up "pablum posing as humility," as journalist David Kaplan put it. After Senate Republicans eliminated the Supreme Court filibuster (which required sixty votes for nominee approval), fifty-one Republicans and three Democrats voted him onto the Court.

The pro-life were emboldened. Scalia had been replaced by a fellow conservative, and Trump was in the White House. Yes, the Supreme

Court had only just invalidated unnecessary abortion regulations. But by the close of 2017, Republican statehouses—helped again by Americans United for Life, that legal advocacy group whose model bills had driven the surge in pro-life legislation—had passed sixty-three more, among them seven types of abortion bans that concerned, for example, gestational age, gender, race and disability.

And yet, *Roe* still stood—"the Great White Whale," wrote Kaplan, of the GOP. So long as it did, it would remain a shape-shifting leviathan, blamed and credited for everything from a rise in breast cancer to a drop in crime. *Roe* would remain a call to arms, too, used by both political parties to sell policies having little to do even with "women or unborn children," as the author William Saletan noted, but with "husbands, parents, businesses, and taxpayers."

But then, in the summer of 2018, the end of *Roe* was suddenly in sight.

———

ANTHONY KENNEDY had been a justice on the Supreme Court for thirty years. For the last twelve, he had (with the retirement of Justice O'Connor) found himself smack in its ideological middle. Whether Kennedy sided with the flank to his left or right had often determined law; he was the all-important fifth vote. Empowered to interpret the Constitution for all 330 million Americans, he had tipped the Court in both directions—legalizing gay marriage and Trump's "Muslim ban," too.

In late June 2018, the justice informed the president that he was retiring; Trump would have occasion to replace him on the Court. The news roiled the nation. Kennedy's retirement, wrote the Harvard law professor Jack Goldsmith, "is the most consequential event in American jurisprudence . . . probably since *Roe v. Wade*."

Those consequences began with *Roe*. It was Kennedy who in 1992 (along with Justices O'Connor and Souter) had preserved *Roe* via *Casey*, upholding the legality of abortion through viability. He was, in the words of law professor Mary Ziegler, "the firewall for abortion rights." With his retirement, the bloc of justices assumed to oppose those rights—Gorsuch, Clarence Thomas, Samuel Alito and John Roberts—was poised to grow by one.

Trump quickly selected their fifth. Brett Kavanaugh was of the Beltway—raised in Bethesda, groomed in the junior Bush's White House, steeled on the DC Circuit Court of Appeals. His writings were classically conservative—friendly to business and gun rights and executive power, wary of affirmative action and immigration and abortion. Regarding the last, the judge had stepped into the mire only months before.

The case concerned a Mexican teenager detained by the U.S. after crossing illegally into Texas. She was pregnant and wished to have an abortion. The Trump administration would not allow her to leave her shelter to have one. After a federal district judge said that U.S. law entitled her to one, the administration appealed. An appeals court granted the administration time to find the woman a legal custodian so that she would not be in government custody when she had the abortion. But finding her a custodian was proving difficult. After she appealed, the appeals court ruled in her favor. Kavanaugh dissented. The ruling, he wrote, created "a new right for unlawful immigrant minors in U.S. government detention to obtain immediate abortion on demand."

Those last three words were significant. The pro-life had appropriated the phrase from feminists to signify extremism—the demand for abortion at any cost. Yet, it was not abortion that dominated Kavanaugh's confirmation hearings but allegations of sexual assault, a college professor named Christine Blasey Ford testifying that Kavanaugh, young and drunk, had forced himself upon her and tried to remove her clothing. Kavanaugh was confirmed to the Court by the slimmest of margins, 50–48, and forgotten for just a moment was abortion—the conclusion about the fate of *Roe* that much of the nation had reached upon word that Justice Kennedy was retiring. As Mark Joseph Stern put it in *Slate* that same day: "The constitutional right to abortion access in America is living on borrowed time."

—————

NOVELISTS HAVE LONG IMAGINED the toppling of *Roe*. It is a useful plot point, an almost plausible judicial turn that, in novels such as *When She Woke* by Hillary Jordan, quickly lead past the recriminalizing of abortion to the wholesale loss of women's autonomy. With the retirement of Kennedy, that fiction was suddenly fathomable. That same year, another novel grew from the same dystopian premise, Leni Zumas's *Red Clocks* telling of a Christianized America in which its states ratify to the Constitution a personhood amendment.

There is no more direct way to illegalize abortion. The Fourteenth Amendment mandates that no state may "deny to any person within its jurisdiction the equal protection of the laws." As *Roe* itself acknowledged, were the word "person" to include the unborn, then "the appellant's case, of course, collapses, for the fetus' right to life would then be guaranteed specifically by the Amendment." Almost fifty years after *Roe*, some still argued for a personhood amendment, among them a Notre Dame professor named John Finnis who would soon write an essay titled "Abortion Is Unconstitutional." Still, even Scalia and Thomas, the lone justices to have called outright for the overturning of *Roe*, rejected the notion of a personhood amendment. What they wanted instead was what Trump advocated on *60 Minutes* a week after his election—to see the matter of abortion returned to the states.

Even before *Roe*, a woman's residence had mattered a great deal if she wanted an abortion. When, in 1971, *Roe* was being argued in the Supreme Court and the lawyer representing Texas suggested that the unhappily pregnant woman in Texas had only herself to blame—"she makes her choice prior to the time she becomes pregnant," he said—Justice Potter Stewart responded, "Or maybe she makes her choice when she decides to live in Texas." Decades later, geography still mattered. Were the Court to overturn *Roe*, it would matter even more.

How each state might legislate abortion post-*Roe* could not yet be known. The Center for Reproductive Rights, a global legal advocacy organization, estimated that in a post-*Roe* America, abortion would be illegal in at least twenty-four states, legal in twenty-one. Clarke Forsythe, of Americans United for Life, estimated the numbers at sixteen illegal, thirty-four legal.

The question was a matter of degree, as well as of politics and God. Democratic and secular states would facilitate abortion, Republican and religious ones would restrict it. The divide also corresponded to the general welfare of women. Half of the women in America who have abortions live below the federal poverty level. And a report by the Cen-

ter for American Progress, a nonpartisan policy institute, showed that
where abortion (and contraception) is more readily available, women
are not only in better health but "have higher earnings and face less
occupational segregation."

To return control over abortion to the states would thus not simply
invite a red and blue state divide but increase, in particular, the burden
on the poor, forcing them to secure the money and child care and time
off needed to travel to where abortion was legal.

And yet, it is also likely that criminalizing abortion in the U.S.
would neither significantly lower the number of abortions nor raise the
number of maternal deaths. Rather, as Michelle Oberman, a professor
of law who has studied the effects of abortion bans in Latin America,
wrote, it would occasion a sharp rise in medical abortions, those pregnancies terminated by abortifacient drugs like mifepristone and misoprostol which end pregnancies up to ten weeks along (and which can be
obtained online through a slew of feminist organizations). It would also
lead inevitably to the prosecution of those women, whose doctors would
face pressure to report them. And, wrote Oberman, "Law enforcement
will wind up targeting the poorest, most marginalized women."

IN 1972, only months before *Roe*, the essayist Susan Sontag reflected that
gender-based reforms, including legal abortion, "actually reinforce the
power of men." Such reforms placated women and thus, she wrote,
helped "to conserve the present system of marriage and the family."
Only when reforms were politicized did they mobilize the majority of
women, wrote Sontag, "who have not yet begun to think consciously
about their oppression."

A half-century later, abortion in America was nothing if not politicized. Were the fall of *Roe* to trigger the regular arrest and prosecution
of women for exercising what had been for decades their legal right, their
anger and unrest would likely be seismic.

"I don't think you can put all those different genies back in the
bottle," the medical historian Andrea Tone told the Associated Press.
"I don't think women will put up with the absence of privacy and dis-
cretion that birth control and abortion provide." Added the journalist

Michael Kinsley: "If abortion becomes a legislative issue again, all those pro-choice women and men who have been voting Republican because abortion was safe would have to reconsider, and many would bolt."

Just as *Roe* had galvanized the pro-life, its overturning would thus likely galvanize the pro-choice. And just as Republicans had warned of the political cost of turning too often to the courts—"litigation addiction," wrote Neil Gorsuch in 2005, "invites permanent minority status for the Democratic party"—so too might the GOP be subject to the consequences of its judicial activism.

But even some on the left believed that overturning *Roe* might calm political divisions. Yes, at first, wrote the law professor Jeffrey Rosen, doing so "would probably ignite one of the most explosive political battles since the civil-rights movement, if not the Civil War." But that battle, he argued, might ultimately leave America less riven, a place where elected officials, so long beholden to their activist bases, could come to "reflect the popular will"—the majority view, that is, that abortion be legal and unfettered through the first trimester only.

Norma was of that majority, though she agreed with Rosen as to the battle that overturning *Roe* would ignite. She had imagined that battle thirty years before, in a piece of fiction she wrote in California. Over ten handwritten pages, Norma had set Jane Roe onto the San Francisco streets with a throng of women armed with scissors and bats. After her protagonist threw a manhole cover through a storefront window, she looked up at a TV screen in a bar at Market and Powell to catch a press conference at the Supreme Court. "I wanted it louder," wrote Norma. "I wanted to hear every word they said."

⸺

FOR ALL THE SPECULATION about the Court overturning *Roe*, there is reason to think it won't want to do so. As Justice Robert Jackson noted in a 1944 speech: "To overrule an important precedent is serious business."

Indeed, in law, precedent is sacrosanct. It protects the integrity of the Court, enables society, as the Court reflected in 1986, "to presume that bedrock principles are founded in the law rather than in the proclivities of individuals." As such, even when the Court believes that a prior ruling is wrong, if society has come to rely upon it, and it is workable, and its central facts haven't changed, respect for precedent— the legal doctrine of stare decisis—holds that ordinarily it shouldn't be overturned. Just thirteen times, in fact, according to the *Washington Post*, has the Court overturned "major precedents" concerning constitutional rights that had stood for ten or more years.

The new rulings were often landmark decisions, from *Brown v. Board of Education*, which outlawed segregation (and overturned *Plessy v. Ferguson*), to *Lawrence v. Texas*, which legalized gay sex (and overturned *Bowers v. Hardwick*). But it wasn't always clear why the Court chose to overturn one ruling and let another stand. Kavanaugh, the newest justice, would soon assess its reasoning, writing that the Court was apt to let stand a prior decision if overturning it would "unduly upset" those who relied upon it, and apt to overturn it if it was "grievously or egregiously wrong" or had "caused significant negative jurisprudential or real-world consequences."

Roe survived in large part because it was established precedent. (The famed lawyer Archibald Cox, for example, defended *Roe* as established law even as he criticized both its legal reasoning and its failure to consider, he wrote, "the most compelling interest of the State in prohibiting abortion: the interest in maintaining that respect for the paramount sanctity of human life.") And when *Roe* next returned to the Court, Kavanaugh would likely apply what he had now written.

Chief Justice John Roberts, however, cared as deeply about the reputation of the Court as he did about precedent. It concerned him that, were *Roe* overruled, the public would understand, as the Souter clerk cautioned back in 1991, "that the Court's reversal is explainable solely by reason of changes in the composition of the Court." And so, though Roberts had once helped to write a brief which declared that "*Roe* was wrongly decided and should be overruled," many believed that he might prefer to see the ruling *dismantled*.

There were many paths to do so. The Court could endorse an interpretation of "undue burden" that could accommodate ever greater restrictions on clinics and women. Or it could invalidate the right (as guaranteed by *Doe*) to end those pregnancies after viability that threatened a woman's health, physical or otherwise. The Court could even do away with viability as a legal threshold altogether, deciding instead that the interest of the state overtook that of the woman at some earlier point in pregnancy.

Of course, the only way to know what the Court would do was to have another abortion case come before it. Lifted by the retirement of Kennedy, pro-life activists got to work.

FOR DECADES, the pro-life movement had committed itself to incremental change—to disassembling *Roe* "doorjamb by doorjamb," as Scalia once put it. But with the appointment of Kavanaugh, overturning *Roe* seemed possible, and many pro-life leaders changed course. In 2019, legislators in six states passed so-called "heartbeat" bills that banned abortion from the moment (at six weeks' gestation) when the fetal heartbeat is generally detectable. The bills were a clear violation of *Roe*. That was the point—to force the Court to address them.

It had long been said that people supported abortion for three reasons: "rape, incest, and me." (Regarding the last, the press had recently reported that two pro-life Republican congressmen, Tim Murphy and Scott DesJarlais, had been found to have pressured various partners to have abortions.) But five of the six new six-week abortion bans made no exceptions for rape and incest. And Alabama's bill outlawed all abortion (except to save the life of the pregnant woman) from the moment of conception. Months later, a man sued a clinic in Huntsville on behalf of an embryo aborted at six weeks by his ex-girlfriend. (The suit, dismissed by a county circuit judge, identified the embryo as "Baby Roe.")

If the pro-life were daring the Court to act on *Roe*, the pro-choice were readying for its overturning; by the close of 2019, twelve states had introduced legislation to safeguard abortion until at least viability. (Oregon and Vermont protected that right through the whole of pregnancy.) Democratic politicians, meantime, reintroduced a 2013 bill called the Women's Health Protection Act, which would protect abortion until viability under federal law. In the run-up to the 2020 election, the Democratic field had left behind the old party line that abortion should be safe, legal, rare. For why should it be rare? The candidates, observed

NARAL president Ilyse Hogue, are "setting the tone that [legal abortion] is something we should own proudly."

With *Roe* threatened, its opposing sides pulled further apart. Their leaders, the critic Caitlin Flanagan wrote, were blind to "the truth that the best argument on each side is a damn good one"—on the one hand, the humanity of a fetus, and on the other, the untold reasons a woman might wish to abort it. To defend or defeat *Roe* was all; with the recent establishment of pro-life research organizations like the Charlotte Lozier Institute, even science was up for grabs. The damage to America was existential. Wrote the *Atlantic* in a piece on abortion: "A deliberative democracy where even basic facts aren't shared isn't much of a democracy at all."

IN THE SPRING OF 2019, as Republican lawmakers waged an ever more intense war on *Roe*, its two initial architects came together in Texas, Coffee and Weddington seated on a dais in Austin set with glasses of water and potted succulents.

The women were headlining a fundraiser for the Texas branch of the National Women's Political Caucus. The organization had reached out to Weddington. And, two years after I noted in an article that she'd all but cut Coffee from the story of *Roe*, she suggested that Coffee join her. As the former Caucus head, Donna Blevins, put it to their audience: "We realized that nobody had heard from Linda in a while."

Twenty-seven years, in fact, had passed since Weddington had seen her former co-counsel. Weddington and other pro-choice leaders had preferred to look away, never once addressing the alarming fact that the lawyer who had first brought *Roe* into being was living in poverty.

Coffee remained, at age seventy-six, uncomfortable before an audience, unsure even how to hold a mic. ("Hold it like a lollipop," offered Weddington.) But she was animated and clear, and spoke of the 1969 *Belous* abortion case that had first sent her mind racing, and of the people who had led her to *Roe*: Sarah Hughes and Henry McCluskey and Norma McCorvey. The roomful of Texas women listened. They were, in a sense, the "et al." in the case caption Coffee and Weddington had revised when they made *Roe* a class action suit. And they gave Coffee what for so long she had gone without: applause.

———

ONCE UPON A TIME in America, there was a middle ground on abortion. Coffee herself had expressed the hope that abortion would become "sort of obsolete," while her church, the Southern Baptist Convention, had both affirmed "the sanctity of . . . fetal life" and endorsed abortion in all manner of cases including whenever pregnancy threatened "the emotional, mental and physical health of the mother." Even activists like Curtis Boyd and Mildred Jefferson, devoted to opposing ends, had initially agreed that choice and life had their limits; until 1978, Boyd would perform no abortion beyond sixteen weeks, while Jefferson, and the Value of Life Committee she helped to found in 1970, sanctioned abortion to protect the health of the pregnant woman, as well as in cases of rape and incest.

But as those two Texas doctors had gone—one who believed that the unborn attained personhood at birth, the other at conception—so had their respective movements.

The doctors' contributions had come at a cost. The tiny Texas town of Carthage had set a bronze bust of Mildred, complete with stethoscope and cap, under an oak in a local park. But in 2020, a decade after her death, few could say they'd known Mildred well other than her ex-husband in Chile, some friends in Boston, and a cousin in Carthage who kept her ashes and remembered her in prayer. Abortion had been her all. So it was for Curtis Boyd, an old man on the front lines both venerated and scorned.

Boyd had once been a crew-cutted country doctor in east Texas, delivering babies, not aborting them. But when, in 1967, a destitute woman told him that she couldn't feed the three kids she had, let alone a fourth, the doctor had ended her pregnancy and become aware of the great demand to end more. "You either had to not do it at all," he told himself, "or you'd end up doing nothing else." Fifty years later, Boyd had performed some 250,000 abortions.

In 2017, months after Boyd turned eighty, a second woman died from an abortion in his clinic, thirty-seven years after the first. Her name was Keisha Atkins. She was twenty-three. Readying to deliver a fetus already euthanized, she became short of breath and went into cardiac arrest. An autopsy revealed blood clots in her lungs; Boyd and his clinic were not held liable. But, he says, "It doesn't make it any less painful."

The pro-life were livid. Everything about Boyd galled them—his success, his pride, his Christianity; he was, they said, a backslidden minister. Above all, there was his work in the third trimester. There was no greater GOP rallying cry than late-term abortion; Trump spoke again and again of Democrats ripping babies from wombs.

The pro-life establishment tried to stop Boyd. A new congressional committee—formed the year before, to investigate, in the words of its Republican chairwoman, the procurement and sale of "baby body parts"—subpoenaed Boyd, demanding that he provide documents about his provision of fetal tissue to a New Mexico academic center. The Texas governor, meantime, signed into law a state senate bill that banned dilation and evacuation, the very procedure that Boyd had helped to pioneer and that forty years later was the standard method of second-trimester abortion. But the New Mexico attorney general exonerated Boyd after he provided those subpoenaed documents. And a district judge in Texas declared the state abortion ban unconstitutional after Boyd and his fellow providers filed suit.

Texas appealed the ruling; Boyd faced the possibility that his case could rise all the way to the Supreme Court. Come March 2020, he was mired in more litigation, after the Texas attorney general banned, in the name of a pandemic, all abortions except to save the life of a pregnant woman.

The Texas governor had ordered an end to non-essential medical procedures so as to preserve medical resources for the fight against the coronavirus. But nearly all abortions were performed in clinics, not hospitals, and thus had no bearing on that fight.

It was hard to square the Republican safeguarding of prenatal life with its disregard for policies that safeguarded postnatal lives—say, increasing aid to nations where pneumonia and malaria and diarrhea killed millions of young children each year. The virus brought that dissonance into focus. Even as Texas officials fought to protect the unborn, they fought no less arduously to un-protect the elderly and others by quickly opening up the economy, a risk the Texas lieutenant governor shrugged off. "There are more important things than living," he explained on Fox.

In late April, Texas lifted its abortion ban. Boyd reopened his clinic. Says Boyd: "We made it through."

Boyd was used to working through obstacles. He was used to worse; he had been on an FBI list of potential terrorism targets for years. As he continued now at eighty-three to work a few days a week, a graybeard in colored scrubs, he knew that few would have chosen, as he had, to live for half a century on the front lines of an American war. "It's not your normal rational behavior," he reflected. "Something's got to be going on. Something has to be driving you."

Best Boyd could tell, that something was the memory of his young crush, Virginia, done in, nearly seventy years before, by a pregnancy. "It never left me," he says. "And I knew there were millions like her."

———

BACK IN 1980, *Christianity Today*, the magazine founded by Billy Graham, warned of the danger of single-issue politics. "Too narrow a front in battling for a moral crusade, or for a truly biblical involvement in politics, could be disastrous," it wrote. "It could lead to the election of a moron who holds the right view on abortion."

Forty years later—and four years after he got 81 percent of the white evangelical vote—Trump was running for reelection. *Christianity Today* wrote an editorial calling for his removal from office. "Can we say with a straight face," it read, "that abortion is a great evil that cannot be tolerated and, with the same straight face, say that the bent and broken character of our nation's leader doesn't really matter in the end?"

Father Pavone could indeed say just that: the right view on abortion overrode any flaw in character. Six weeks before the election, he tweeted of "this goddamn loser Biden and his morally corrupt, America-hating, God hating Democrat party." The priest added that he would not grant absolution to any Catholic who voted for a Democrat. The diocese of Amarillo condemned his words and asked people to "pray for Father Pavone."

The evangelical community, meantime, was praying for Trump. Days into 2020, Trump joined its leaders at a megachurch in Miami. "We ask you Father that he can be the Cyrus to bring reformation, to bring change into this nation," said the pastor of the church, Guillermo Maldonado. "Release his power."

Nine months later, the Supreme Court justice Ruth Bader Ginsburg died, and Trump nominated a federal appeals court judge in Indiana named Amy Coney Barrett to succeed her.

In the half-century since Ginsburg had co-founded a law journal devoted to women's rights, she had done as much as anyone in America to advance feminist ideals. But her decision, in her eighties, not to leave the bench during the Obama presidency now threatened those ideals and with them legal abortion—that which she had voiced support for at her 1993 confirmation hearing despite her criticisms of *Roe*. "This is something central to a woman's life, to her dignity," she had told the Senate Judiciary Committee. "It's a decision that she must make for herself."

Barrett was no less clear about her opposition to abortion. A Charismatic Christian and a mother of seven, she had signed ads (as a member of both a pro-life group in Indiana and a faculty group at Notre Dame) vilifying *Roe*. Read the first: "It's time to put an end to the barbaric legacy of *Roe v. Wade* and restore laws that protect the lives of unborn children." Barrett had ruled on abortion, too. In 2018, she was a member of the U.S. Court of Appeals for the Seventh Circuit when she joined a dissent arguing that two Indiana abortion regulations ought to be legal: one requiring fetal remains to be cremated or buried, the other banning any abortion decided upon because of the race or sex of the fetus or because the fetus had a disability.

A quarter-century before Barrett's confirmation hearing, the future Supreme Court justice Elena Kagan had lamented that hearings had become "a vapid and hollow charade, in which repetition of platitudes has replaced discussion of viewpoints." Still, Barrett confirmed at her hearing that she did not consider *Roe* a "superprecedent"—that is, as the judge explained in a 2013 law review article, a case "that no justice would overrule, even if she disagrees with the interpretive premises from which the precedent proceeds." Barrett believed, in other words, that *Roe* could be overturned.

Days before her death at age eighty-seven, Ginsburg had dictated a statement: "My most fervent wish is that I will not be replaced until a new president is installed." That wish was not granted; in late October, eight days before the 2020 presidential election, the Senate confirmed Barrett without a single Democratic vote.

Roe had survived its predicted end before. But the ruling was now in genuine peril. Six of the nine justices on the Supreme Court were conservatives. Though Trump lost his bid for reelection, he had appointed a third of them. Weeks into 2021, in the Court's first abortion case since Barrett's appointment, the trio of Trump justices joined their fellow conservatives to uphold a regulation requiring women wanting abortifacient drugs to pick them up in person. (The requirement had been suspended because of the coronavirus.)

The first two of Trump's appointments, Gorsuch and Kavanaugh, had also ruled as expected in the one previous abortion case come before them. That 2020 case, *June Medical Services LLC v. Russo*, had gone the pro-choice way: by a 5–4 vote, the Court had struck down a Louisiana law that required abortion providers to have hospital admitting privileges. It did so only because Roberts, who sanctified precedent, had honored a ruling, only four years old, in a nearly identical case.

Two hundred and seven members of Congress (all but two of whom were Republican) had signed a brief urging the Court to consider overturning *Roe*. It was only a matter of time before the Court's conservative majority accepted a case better suited to doing so. In the spring of 2021, it added *Dobbs v. Jackson Women's Health Organization* to the coming fall docket. The case centered on a Mississippi law that banned abortion after fifteen weeks. The law was in direct conflict with the viability threshold, and was thus, in the words of conservative analyst Ed Whelan, "an excellent vehicle for overturning *Roe*."

Jane Roe had foreseen that day. Indeed, two weeks after Trump was inaugurated and two weeks before she died, Norma had shared with Melissa her belief that Trump, through his appointments to the Court, would succeed in overturning *Roe*. Said Norma: "That little Richie Rich is going to get his way."

Chapter 37

Norma had been dead some two hours when her daughter Jennifer arrived and bent down to kiss her forehead. She asked Melissa if Norma had had any final wishes.

Norma had often made light of death. She'd texted a drinking buddy in Smithville that she wished, upon dying, to be drawn in a white carriage to her resting place by three white virgin horses. But, as Melissa now told Jennifer, Norma had worried about what awaited her in death. "She had so many demons," said Melissa. Melissa began to cry and told Jennifer that, in the end, Norma's final wishes were modest: to have a funeral of bright colors and flowers.

Jennifer comforted Melissa. She told her that Norma looked peaceful. She kissed Norma again and stroked her hair and gave Melissa a hug. "I love you," she said.

Two men in suits arrived to take Norma to the funeral home. Melissa told them to keep her mother's whereabouts private. And she asked me to alert the press. The *Washington Post* obituary was online within minutes. Front pages around the country reported the death of Jane Roe.

Melissa and the family returned home. She and Jennifer sat on the couch and talk turned to their sister. Melissa hoped, she said, that Shelley could now move forward. She added that Shelley was not the only child Norma hadn't wanted. "She didn't want you," she told Jennifer. "She didn't want me either." Melissa then phoned Shelley. The conversation was brief. Says Shelley, "I was like, 'Okay. Thank you for letting me know.'" The death was a relief, she says—"like now you can start putting things in perspective, now you can start putting this behind you." Shelley felt sadness for Melissa and, for Jennifer, the worry, she says, that despite being new to the family, she might now land "in the middle of a storm."

Melissa was wary of that coming storm, too, of the public reaction to Norma's death. She had decided, along with me and her sisters, to have her name withheld from the press. The obituaries would refer to them as I had referred to them in a profile I'd written of Norma before any of us had met—Melissa by her first name, and her sisters not named at all, alluded to only as having been placed for adoption.

That an article might upend their lives was no mere hypothetical to Shelley. Her life was still divided by that May day twenty-eight years before when a tabloid reporter approached her in a parking lot. Fear of another intrusion terrified Shelley; only weeks before, she'd worried to her sisters that the focus of candidate Trump on *Roe* might spur more journalists to look for her. With the death of Jane Roe, that fear had now come to pass; a London tabloid, the *Daily Mail*, had assigned a reporter to find her, while a Christian adoption agency created an ad noting that "Roe's baby was never aborted." And when Father Pavone began to plan a memorial for Norma and asked Frank Di Bugnara if he would help foot the bill, the filmmaker suggested in turn, he says, that Pavone get a DNA sample from Norma—the root of a hair, the swab of a cheek—in the hope that the *Roe* baby might one day be found.

———

THE *WASHINGTON POST* obituary was true to Norma, to her contradictions and schisms. In life, she'd been "bickered over like a prize heifer," as a local paper once put it. Now, in death, she was again pulled in different directions, celebrated, in the words of a master's thesis, as both "feminist icon" and paragon of the "conversion narrative."

Still, even now, Sarah Weddington disparaged Norma. "It would have been nice," she told the press as she had before, "if I'd picked somebody else."

It is true that a different plaintiff would have better represented the notion of choice. As Kaki King, the daughter of the plaintiff Mary Doe, reflected decades later: "My mom just wasn't ready to have a family."

If supporters of *Roe* still kept their distance from Norma, those who opposed abortion held her close, presenting her as a testament to the transformative power of faith, a symbol as black and white as the portrait Annie Leibovitz had taken of Norma a dozen years before—eyes closed, crucifix held to her heart.

Norma would have appreciated the testimonials. She'd never felt bound by the truth. The televangelists and advocates who now eulogized her didn't either, endlessly promoting the lie that the *Roe* ruling had been predicated on her allegation of rape. They even went so far as to report that "when she died . . . her pro-life friends were at her bedside, praying the rosary and the Divine Mercy Chaplet." Death was not an end but an opportunity. None tried to seize it more than Frank Pavone.

The priest was in Rome when Norma died. He had led a prayer service for her at St. Peter's Basilica the day before. Thirty-six minutes after she died, he offered up prayer to Melissa over the phone. Nineteen minutes after that, he called (via Facebook video) for the public to pray for Norma. And it was not yet evening when the priest sent out a mass email and a press release, too. One day later, he posted on his website the many articles and interviews that Priests for Life had devoted to Norma over the years. He then phoned Melissa about the upcoming memorial.

Melissa told Pavone that the memorial would be held in Katy the following Saturday. The priest had already announced that he would be holding memorial services for Norma around the country. But he wished to organize her private memorial, too, and told Melissa that he wanted the speakers to include Flip Benham and Rob Schenck and Allan Parker. Melissa was clear. "It was like, no!" she recalled the next day. The priest forged ahead. "They're wanting to make it a circus and it's starting to get out of hand," said Melissa. She added: "I don't know how Norma did it all these years."

Melissa asked Father Pavone to help pay for the memorial. He was noncommittal, she says. So Norma's Catholic friend Karen Garnett had her new organization, a nonprofit in Dallas called Culture of Life Network, pay for police, catering and flowers.

Norma had been dead five days when, on a Thursday morning,

Melissa drove to the funeral home with a curling iron and makeup. Preparing Norma for her wake felt good. But Melissa was on edge, not only because of the pro-life caravan en route to Katy but because Shelley had called her a few days before, angry about Norma. Melissa told Shelley to let her go. "I'm thinking," she says, "'Fuck, she's gone!'" The next day, Melissa wrote both her sisters a note, sending love and the hope that they might now together "start a new chapter."

Norma was due to be cremated the following afternoon, after the wake. Driving to the funeral home, both Melissa and Eric were contemplative. Eric noted that the foxtail ferns and hibiscus out front had survived a recent frost, while Melissa spoke suddenly of Connie, whose example she had always admired. "It doesn't matter who gives birth to you," she said. "It's who loves you and who cares for you."

Melissa and Eric stood over Norma's poplar casket and looked down at her body, supine in a bed of cream crepe. Melissa was pleased. "She came out good," she said.

It was true. Norma looked elegant. She wore lace and satin, a blue evening dress Eric had spotted at Dillard's. Her thin lips, a deep red, were curled in a slight smile, and the blues and grays about her eyes and cheeks were as subtle as twilight. Beyond a simple silver necklace and bracelet, her lone adornments were religious—a rosary in her left hand and, in her right, a pouch adorned with a likeness of St. Christopher in which Norma had long carried a bar of soap.

Melissa wished to give Norma's hair more curl. So she plugged in her iron and added volume. After a spritz of hairspray, she returned home with Eric, where an email from Shelley lifted her up; Shelley had done a lot of thinking, she wrote, and would be in touch. Melissa sat down for a sandwich, and noted that she could understand the pro-life position a bit better. Had abortion been legal decades before, she said, "I wouldn't have had my sisters."

HOURS LATER, Melissa was back beside Norma in a private room when Jennifer arrived. She'd dressed in a bright color, as Norma had wished, and the likeness between mother and daughter was all the more striking for their matching blues. Wanting for the moment to remain unknown—

the anonymous second child Jane Roe had birthed and let go—Jennifer did not join her sister when, at five o'clock, Melissa stepped out in her dress of red satin to take in a growing crowd.

Of all the people gathered in the Schmidt Funeral Home on Route 99, just two had, like Melissa, known Norma before she became famous—a cousin from Louisiana and the woman Norma had loved and lived with after giving birth to Melissa.

Diane Hyman had hoped to adopt Melissa. It had pained her to see her girlfriend neglect her baby girl. But Mary had adopted Melissa first. Now, fifty years later, Hyman had driven five hours from her mobile home in Whitesboro to say goodbye. Looking down at Norma, she saw the scar on her right cheek covered in makeup and recalled the day in 1965 when Norma drove her Rambler into a tree.

Others took their turns at her side. Here was Rene Nevarez, the young Operation Rescue volunteer whose drink with Norma preceded her evangelical turn, and Daniel Vinzant, whose love had drawn her to Catholicism, and Hector Ferrer, the makeup artist from Puerto Rico who'd run her ministry, and Sheree Havlik, who'd minded not only Norma but also Connie, and Henry Taylor, the pastor who'd drunk with Norma in Smithville. Taylor left her side with teary eyes. "In my fifty years," he said, "I've never met a more exploited person."

Taylor did not name names. But those whose careers Jane Roe had lifted were now passing by her casket: Benham, Pavone, Parker, Terry, Schenck.

The last of them had a secret. Having fought abortion for twenty-five years, the reverend was now pro-choice. "I no longer believe," Schenck would soon confess, "you're excluded [from God's grace] if you're homosexual, or if you've had an abortion, or if you perform them."

Schenck had come to Texas awash in the regret that he had exploited Norma. It struck him that the movement leaders there with him were exploiting her still. Randall Terry, for one, had turned her memorial into a film shoot. "People were exasperated by that," says Schenck. "He set up a production area at a nearby hotel."

Pavone, meantime, had tried to open the memorial to the press. Melissa had said no. His audience was limited to the eighty or so mourners before him when, solemn in cassock and stole, he knelt beside Norma's casket and recited the rosary.

———

THE NEXT MORNING at ten, Melissa and Jordan stood over Norma and laid beside her body a few items to be cremated with her: a metal peace sign, a pirate eyepatch, a photo of Melissa as a baby. Thirty minutes later, her memorial began, the family walking into the sanctuary to "Amazing Grace."

That the memorial would serve Norma's eulogists was clear; after an opening prayer from Pavone, Allan Parker read the passage from Isaiah that he had designated the scriptural basis for his collecting of affidavits. The lawyer then turned to *Roe*. "Open wide, oh grave," he said. "Here come fifty million children." After a Psalm came Benham. He who had baptized Norma read of baptism from his Bible, the black book aloft in his right palm, its soft white pages, heavy with marginalia, falling from both sides of its worn leather spine. The preacher, in jeans and a vest, smiled as he spoke, his teeth bright white. And between each verse of Romans, he addressed the family Norma had left behind with the same penetrating attention that had won Norma to him. "Jesus saved her," he said. "Melissa, he saved her. Eric, he saved her." Melissa nodded and dabbed her eyes, and Benham continued. "Jesus stands on the other side of that grave." "Jordan and Chloe—he stands on the other side of that grave."

Benham sat and Pavone rose, the priest, in black suit and white collar, reading from John of eternal life. He told Melissa and Jordan and Chloe that the pro-life movement was with them. And he delivered a homily that told of a Norma who had never been afraid to cross over into an unknown. "Norma," he concluded, "you do not belong to death. You belong to Christ."

Norma, of course, had complained bitterly about each of the men now remembering her, sometimes with good cause. And after they finished, her friend Karen Garnett offered up to Melissa what the leaders on both sides of *Roe* had never offered Norma: an apology. "It has been said that she has been used, exploited," said Garnett. "I, on behalf of

everyone in her life, I ask for her forgiveness and your forgiveness." She
then thanked Melissa for the care she had given her mother. Said Garnett: "I was able to witness personally the love of this family."

More helpful words could not have been spoken. With teary eyes,
Melissa stepped to the lectern and thanked those who had been there
for her and her mother. After a few reflections from Jordan and the
Reverend Schenck, the ceremony closed with the Lord's Prayer and a
hymn: "How Great Thou Art."

—————

NORMA WAS DUE now to be cremated. The room had cleared out when
Melissa slid a pair of blue sunglasses up the bridge of her nose. She
kissed Norma's forehead, and Eric did the same. They had joined the
crowd eating sandwiches and dessert in another room when Randall
Terry approached.

Terry wore a pinstriped suit and cowboy boots. He had converted
to Catholicism, and said that Norma could not be buried in a Catholic
cemetery if she were cremated. Catholicism required that the body be
buried whole. He added that he would cover the cost.

The pro-life had long wanted what the pro-choice did not: to claim
Norma as their own. Now that Norma had died, Terry desired to claim
her body, too. Melissa told Terry that she would speak to her family.

Melissa retreated with Eric and her girls to an empty room. She
noted that they hadn't been able to afford a burial. But Jordan pointed
out that Norma had wanted to be cremated, and Melissa said that she
too had wanted that; she wished not only to hold onto Norma's remains
but to prevent the desecration of her grave. "I didn't want anyone to hate
on her," she said. Chloe said that regardless, she was wary of entrusting Norma to someone as incendiary as Terry. "We'd have to face the
backlash," she said. Melissa had just decided that they would proceed
with Norma's cremation when the general manager of the funeral home
told her that Catholics were cremated all the time.

Three days later, Melissa set a blue ceramic urn on her bedroom
dresser and told her mother that she missed her and loved her and
would draw from her strength.

Soon after, Allan Parker phoned Melissa. He wanted to talk, she says, "about me being the face of *Roe* and stepping in where mom left off." Melissa wasn't interested. "I don't know how Norma did it all these years," she says, "being picked apart by all those people."

———

THE PRESS CONTINUED to reflect upon the life of Jane Roe. But the stories they reflected upon were the stories that Norma herself had told, the *New York Times* reporting on its daily podcast that she had been abused in school and by her husband, and had gone to a bloody and abandoned clinic for an abortion, and had lived "a childhood of almost unrelenting woe." Little of it was true.

The documentary *AKA Jane Roe* would also take Norma at her word, transmitting on FX those same stubborn lies: the abuse and the bloody clinic and the shooting she pinned on *Roe*. The film would produce one more, a big one that made national news. As a *Times* headline put it: "Roe v. Wade Plaintiff Was Paid to Switch Sides, Documentary Says."

Norma had not, in fact, been paid to become pro-life. She'd simply been paid to give speeches after her conversion—just as she'd been paid to speak before it. Despite the headlines, she'd said nothing to the contrary. The filmmaker, however, had asked Norma if her pro-life turn had been "an act," and Norma had answered yes—one more improvisation in a life that for so long had been a sort of performance art.

Pro-life leaders, those many Christians who had both embraced and exploited Norma, found themselves in the impossible position of having to vouch for her authenticity, while the pro-choice, from Alexandria Ocasio-Cortez to the president of NARAL, saw in what Norma had called her "deathbed confession" the immorality of the right, of they who had bought off Jane Roe.

As evidence, the film presented an IRS form that showed the large sum of $456,911. But that sum was the gross receipts of Norma's Roe No More ministry over nine years. The number hadn't even appeared on an IRS form. The film made it appear as if it had, to obscure what Norma had been paid in speaking fees, compensation that averaged $20,458 annually before the ministry folded in 2007.

In one sense, though, the film was true to Norma. For what had long marked her, alas, was not simply an indifference to truth and a need for attention but a deep desire to get even, to hit back; her spectacular conversion was nothing if not a rebuff of the pro-choice who had rebuffed her. (As she told the filmmaker Meghan O'Hara: "That was just like a big slap in the face, like hey, fuck you!") Now, from the grave, Norma had turned on the pro-life too, her last lie taking root as no doubt she imagined it would. When once I pointed out to Norma that she had just lied, she'd replied with a smile: "They'll take anything you say."

Norma enjoyed telling stories. She had endeavored, over the years, to fashion a life story worthy of her pseudonym. But if she'd not been raped or had a child kidnapped or been made to reassemble aborted babies, she had been forced by law to birth a child she did not want. That one inarguable trauma had done nothing to lessen her struggles. It was no easy thing to be Jane Roe—or, for that matter, to be the plaintiff in any famous suit. "The individual's life and what it means can get lost in these cases," observed Angela Bonavoglia, the journalist dispatched by Gloria Steinem to interview Norma back in 1989. "They become sacrificial lambs in a way."

———

THE NOVELIST JODI PICOULT observed that "sharing DNA does not make you fast friends." And four years after the three daughters born to Norma first met in 2013, Melissa wished they were closer. Jennifer lifted her up but rarely got in touch. And Shelley again retreated. Reading through the letters Shelley had written her back in 1993, Melissa took in the painful fact that, a quarter-century later, she and Shelley had never had the relationship Melissa desired. Says Melissa: "I just hoped it would be so different."

Melissa had hoped for a different relationship with her mother, too. She had wanted a mother who wanted her. Norma had wanted the same from Mary. And Mary, decades before, had been made by her mother, Bertha, to surrender her firstborn.

Melissa had vowed to stop that cycle. She had vowed to love and mother her two girls without condition or pause. So she had. When, in late 2017, her daughter Jordan married and had her late father's widow—one of Kerry's many affairs—officiate the ceremony, Melissa kept her hurt to herself. "Just trying to get through it best I can," she said after the ceremony, crying quietly over a whiskey sour.

The year that followed was difficult. Melissa was beset by anxiety and high blood pressure. She had surgery on her wrist and stopped working. Then, when she wanted a job, she couldn't find one and collected one paycheck in fourteen months. Eric, meantime, was struggling to find work as well, and the couple was soon months behind on the mortgage. They had begun selling off their stuff—furniture, tools, clothing—when, in August 2019, Melissa landed a job administering vaccines for people planning trips abroad. She loved the work. But in March 2020, as she and Eric began to pay off their bills, the coronavirus ground travel to a halt and Melissa was soon again out of a job and facing foreclosure.

Melissa was distraught. But Eric found steady work doing sheetrock and painting, cabinetry and tiling, in a mansion right there in Katy. He and Chloe remained at her side. And after her marriage quickly ended, Jordan drew close to Melissa, too. Here was a family.

———

MONTHS AFTER NORMA DIED, Jennifer turned fifty. She was in a good place. She loved her partner, Lisa helping her to care for her two grandchildren three or four nights a week. She loved her job and had the respect of two dozen subordinates who called their key-jangling boss "warden." Her son and daughter were overcoming their addictions. And she had peace of mind from having found her biological family, her sisters and father and mother.

Jennifer was not sentimental. She did not mourn Norma. She'd known her birth mother little more than three years when she died. In the end, Jennifer had gotten from Norma what she wanted—less a relationship than information. She'd wanted the same from her father, and Pete had introduced Jennifer to his family. But she had since reduced their relationship to occasional texts. "A nice guy and all," says Jennifer, "but I don't have that connection with him."

Jennifer felt differently about her sisters. It pained her that Shelley had pulled away. And work was the reason she so rarely saw Melissa. It left her exhausted; she worked nights and spent so many hours on her feet that she lost some twenty pounds. But that was poised to change. In 2019, Jennifer lost her mother and inherited money. She began to think about retirement, about buying a piece of land with Lisa and spending time on it with her son and daughter. That she might see more of her big sister excited her, too.

Jennifer also hoped to see more of her little sister. But the death of Norma had done nothing to indicate that Shelley wanted the same. After Shelley phoned Jennifer to ask about the memorial, she had said little. And then, says Jennifer, "she went on her merry way."

NEARLY THIRTY YEARS BEFORE, in 1988, a marine recruit had phoned Shelley on a leave from boot camp to say that he would one day marry her. But when he next got in touch, in 2009, twenty-one years had passed, and he was married for the third time to someone else.

Todd Peterson had always loved being with Shelley. They had met at a picnic the summer before ninth grade, two skinny kids with blue eyes and fathers who drank. Their talks had helped him through Highline High. In the years since, he'd wanted to reach out to her many times— to tell, for example, of the marital infidelities he had suffered, and of the daughter he had lost touch with, and of his suicide attempt that had come from that estrangement. But it wasn't until he'd retired from the marines and was working for the National Guard in suicide prevention that he finally got in touch.

Shelley told Todd that she was married. Still, they spoke intermittently. "My wife would get jealous," he says. In 2016, after Shelley told him that she had separated from Doug, Todd confided that he was thinking of separating, too. One year later, Shelley phoned. "She said," recalls Todd, "you need to make a decision right now."

There was little keeping Todd in Seattle. He was retired with two pensions. A few months later, Shelley took a few days off from her job at a car dealership to welcome him to Tucson, the old friends driving in his 1971 Nova to San Diego. A month or so later, Shelley invited her new boyfriend to move in.

Todd had known Shelley before she learned of *Roe*. This was a comfort to them. "We can go back to that time," he later reflected. "We were both happy then." They were happy now too; Shelley felt unbound and got her first tattoo—a ball of yarn and knitting needles on her right forearm. In late 2017, five months into their relationship, Todd proposed. Shelley said yes.

Still, Shelley was not at peace. She struggled to get past the unalterable fact that her birth mother had let her go. "It's a daily process of why wasn't I good enough for this person," she says. That her birth mother had turned out to be Norma McCorvey remained a second trauma.

Decades before, her lawyer had drummed into Shelley the need to keep the identity of her birth mother secret. But if Shelley was scared to let it out, she hated keeping it in. And she had begun, in recent years, to tell her family about Norma—her aunts and uncles and cousins and daughters and, now, Todd as well. Sharing her secret was empowering. Says Shelley: "I want everyone to understand that this is something I've *chosen* to do."

The public, meantime, continued to speculate about the *Roe* baby. A novel called *Jane's Baby* suggested that she had become the president of the United States. And, setting aside *Roe*, those who googled Norma searched above all for "Norma McCorvey Daughter." Google, though, hadn't a clue. Says Shelley: "Nobody was ever close to where I was."

That people looked made sense; it was hard to imagine a better argument against abortion than the *Roe* baby. "This person," wrote a minister in Ohio, "is in many ways a tangible representative of the state of abortion in America." After Norma died, pro-life leaders tried to find her. Allan Parker and Patrick Mahoney and others phoned Melissa and me for information.

Shelley feared being found. Still, she took a certain pride that it was she—and not her sisters—being looked for. "She's not the *Roe* baby," Shelley said of Melissa. "She's not the one people are gonna come knocking on her door and say, 'How do you feel about abortion?' No one cares. They care about me."

If Shelley was one of three, she was thus also alone. And it now seemed to her, looking back, that she'd only cared to know her missing siblings as a young child. But, in fact, Shelley had been in her twenties when the prospect of a sister had filled her with joy. As she wrote then to Melissa: "Please God, let it be true."

———

ANOTHER ANNIVERSARY OF *ROE* had come and gone when, in early 2019, Shelley again wished to make clear that she was in no way connected to the ruling. "My association with *Roe*," she said, "started and ended because I was conceived."

Shelley was right that her conception was bound to *Roe*; Justice Blackmun had alluded to her gestation in his aside on mootness. But conception is never an end. It is only a beginning. The cell created when sperm and egg conjoin will become a person. That person will grow in step with the DNA of the man and woman who conceived it. And that Shelley—against the will of her mother—had grown from single cell to woman had turned her (or the notion of her) from the mere impetus of a lawsuit into a symbol.

Shelley wanted no part of it. Ever since she'd been made to confront both Norma and *Roe* at the age of eighteen, she had sought to minimize their influence on her life. "I have no attachments to [Norma]," Shelley said. "I have no attachments to this case."

Shelley did her best to make those statements true; she had so thoroughly distanced herself from *Roe* that, come 2019, she had yet to hear of Justice Blackmun or Operation Rescue. But it was harder to detach from Norma. Norma was half her biology. Two years after Norma's death, Shelley reflected upon why she had never confirmed that fact.

"Reality is a cruel, cruel thing," she said in late February, seated on an olive couch in a hotel lobby in Tucson. "There's a certain romanticism about the things you don't know."

Shelley was dressed in gray and pink and black, her nails painted blue. Her fiancé Todd was at her side, and she continued her thought. "If you're fine with the family you grew up with and the stories they've told . . . why mess with it? Let your father be Elvis Presley and your mother be Ann-Margret. There's nothing wrong with it. You don't need to have all the answers." Added Shelley: "My parents are Billy and Ruthie Thornton. I grew up in Houston, Texas . . . That's my reality."

Thirty years after learning of Norma, Shelley wished that she hadn't. "It's not a secret that I had to ever know about," she'd reflected a few months before.

And yet, on this winter afternoon, Shelley was pondering the sad fact that she and Norma had never come to détente. "The prospect of me being in her life . . . probably scared the living daylights out of her," she said. "Norma was not the type of person who could handle any kind of burden like that."

Shelley was speaking with unusual calm. And she was right. Every life is of infinite consequence. That Norma had wished but failed to prevent her child's birth had traumatized them both—Shelley left to confront a mother who had desired her extirpation, Norma to wonder if the life her unwanted child was living had proved, in the words of Yeats, "a compensation for the pang of his birth."

"If I had allowed her to be part of my life," reflected Shelley, "given everything I'd overcome, I think that would have caused her more guilt. Look at this massive impressive thing that I tried to destroy. Where would the world be if that had happened?"

Still, sitting on that olive couch, Shelley felt for Norma. "I've always empathized with her," she said. "That doesn't mean I forgive her, that I absolve her. But it makes me sad she lived her life like that."

The life Shelley lamented was a life centered on abortion. For abortion in America consumes those who give themselves to it. And Norma had surrendered to her suit as wholly as Shelley had run from it. That suit had pitted Norma against the fetus Shelley had been. Fifty years later, the tens of millions of Americans pledged to choice or life were no less irreconcilable. They were bound only by Norma, the matriarch of a family as fractured as her own: the Family Roe.

———

BEFORE *ROE* WAS A FLASHPOINT, a law that polarized the people and politics of this country like little else, it was the desperate attempt of a woman to end her third pregnancy. She had not been allowed to. In June 2020, the child she birthed turned fifty.

Not long after her birthday, Shelley broke up with Todd. They were back together in the fall—Shelley, like both of her sisters, engaged yet with no real plan to marry. Relationships were hard. But she loved

Todd. And for the first time in her life, she began to truly commit to a relationship with one of her sisters, she and Jennifer speaking several times a week. "It's really helping me," Shelley reflected. "She's pretty terrific, that sister of mine."

Shelley then decided to connect with the family of her biological father, too.

In 2015, I had told Shelley that I'd very likely found her father. The office of the Dallas County district clerk had unearthed for me the record of a Bill Wheaton who, decades before, had been arrested for driving drunk in Dallas. I then learned from his children that he'd lost part of a finger, just as Norma had recollected. He'd died in 1998.

For years, Shelley was not prepared to meet those children. But, soon after turning fifty, she suddenly was, and spoke over Zoom to a retired librarian in Virginia named Wendy. Shelley shared with her that she was not the first half-sister she'd met late in life. "You're a braver person than I am," said Wendy. "I would just cut my phone off and not talk to anybody." Shelley laughed. "I've already done that," she said.

The conversation turned to their father, to his abuse and drinking. Wendy confided that she was still working at sixty-eight to accept the hard fact that she'd been born to him. Shelley understood the struggle to accept a birth parent, and offered sympathy. "It's really nice to know," continued Wendy, "that a lovely person is related to me who has no direct relationship to [him]." Shelley smiled, thankful for her new sister, and also to learn more about her father, no matter how deep his flaws. "I'm able to put all of the puzzle together," Shelley told her sister. "Now I have a finished piece."

A THOUSAND MILES east of Shelley, at home in Katy, Texas, Melissa moved the ceramic urn on her bedroom dresser to her kitchen table. She had long wished to share Norma's ashes with Jennifer and Shelley, and had invited her sisters to her house to do so. But Shelley had no desire to possess any of the pulverized bone that almost four years before had been her mother. As Shelley texted Jennifer: "I just have no personal connection with her."

And so, on October 21, 2020, Jennifer alone stood beside Melissa as she dipped a Chinese soup spoon down into ash. "If Shelley ever decides she wants some," said Melissa, "I'll give her some too."

Melissa dropped the ash into a small black velvet bag that Norma had used for holy water and pot. "She kept her stash in there," she said. The sisters laughed and Jennifer said that she would set the bag in her den beside the mixed remains of her parents and cats. "I have the family in a mason jar," she said. The sisters laughed again.

Melissa had long wished to sprinkle Norma's remains in a body of water. And one week later, she drove east with her daughters to Simmesport, the Louisiana town where both Norma and the Atchafalaya were born.

The river was voracious. It would have captured the Mississippi had the U.S. not built floodgates. "Atchafalaya," wrote John McPhee. "The word will now come to mind more or less in echo of any struggle against natural forces."

The river was thus a fitting resting place for Jane Roe. Carrying her ashes, Melissa drove to the levee beside which Norma had lived as a toddler. But the levee had been raised, and the river was not near. So Melissa and her daughters drove to a park beside a bayou just off the river.

The park was untended. A fallen cypress lay on the ground, and a swing set, Norma's totem, stood bent and rusted. But the park had a dock. And minutes after three, as Melissa walked to the water together with her daughters, Jordan in flannel, Chloe in a leopard top, a light rain began to fall.

The rain heralded a hurricane named Zeta that was bound this October night for the Louisiana coast. And here in Yellow Bayou, the brown pool that reflected a canopy of bald cypresses and red oaks began to ripple. "I know this water isn't the cleanest," Melissa said, addressing the plastic baggie of ash in her hand. "But I know you loved Louisiana and your people and we all loved you."

Melissa extended the bag over the water. She turned it over and shook it, and a gray diagonal mist, long as Norma, settled into the brown water.

The water was low, some six feet below the dock. But the tide would

rise. The bayou would flow and carry that gray mist into another bayou
and then another until, more than a hundred miles south, it would enter
Bayou Chene. There, the remains of Norma would join the Atchafalaya, to be carried another fifteen lonesome miles toward the edge of
America.

Author's Note

Thirty years ago, I knew nothing of *Roe v. Wade* when someone handed me a book titled *Abortion and Divorce in Western Law*. The author was a pro-life law professor named Mary Ann Glendon. She criticized America for not doing more to help pregnant women and mothers, and quoted an author who observed of abortion that "each side views its cause as sacred, and both are right." And yet, she barely presented the pro-choice point of view; one reviewer marveled at the "astonishing" one-dimensionality of her arguments. Still, I was twenty and had a column to fill for my college paper. So I blithely echoed the passages in the book that the reader had underlined. Abortion law in the U.S. was extreme, I wrote. It was indifferent to unborn life, and had begotten an industry marked by profit.

Looking back, it is hard for me to understand those words. Setting aside that I disagree with them, I now see, as the sociologist Kristin Luker noted, that such simplicities preclude "coming to terms with real human dilemmas." Those dilemmas run through this book, "giving voice," as the legal scholar Laurence Tribe once wrote that we must, "to the human reality on each side of the 'versus.'"

TO WRITE ABOUT ABORTION is to invite accusations of bias. Tripwires abound, beginning with language. As Luker noted: "a choice of words is a choice of sides." And how even to label those sides?

There are many possibilities. The Associated Press stylebook recommends "anti-abortion" and "pro-abortion rights." I chose instead "pro-life" and "pro-choice." I did so because those terms are familiar and because they're what the two sides call themselves—even though, as Luker notes, both sides consider the terms "a mockery" of what the other is actually about.

Of course, the two sides also disagree on what to call the unborn. To the pro-life, they are, from the moment of conception, *children*. To my mind, however, a fertilized egg is not a child, even if it will become one. And so, when writing of that growing body which will either be aborted or born, I generally use the word *fetus*, mindful, as the writer Katha Pollitt notes, that two-thirds of abortions occur by the eighth week of pregnancy, when the abortus is in fact an embryo.

It will thus be said that I have chosen a side. And, indeed, I am pro-choice. But I am not an advocate—a distinction the pro-choice academic Katie Watson made when she wrote a book about abortion. I am a journalist. And writing this book, I strove to be as sympathetic to the pro-life as the pro-choice.

———

THE REALIZATION THAT Jane Roe had not had an abortion—that somewhere there was a *Roe* baby—was what led me into this book. My interest, however, quickly spread from that one child to all three children Jane Roe had borne. From them it grew to include Jane Roe herself, *Roe v. Wade*, and the whole of abortion in America.

I could not tell that larger story through Norma McCorvey and her daughters alone. And so, I found three people in Texas who would enable me to do so: the abortion provider Curtis Boyd, the lawyer Linda Coffee, and the pro-life advocate Mildred Jefferson. Their lives, alongside Norma's, reach into every corner of what abortion in America has become.

Dozens more characters entered the book, beginning with the movement leaders who worked with Norma on both sides of *Roe*. They were a difficult lot. Sarah Weddington would not speak with me. Randall Terry called me "a criminal." I told myself that if Norma could handle them, so could I.

When I met Norma in 2013, she was sixty-six years old. Her memory was faded, and also obstructed by the various stories she had told. But, in time, she welcomed my interest in her life. And she tried to help, thrilled, for example, when the name of the deceased man who had fathered her youngest came to mind.

I was helped as well by a thrilling find: in early 2011, I discovered Norma's private papers in the garage of the home where she'd lived with Connie. After Connie gave them to me, I asked Norma if she wanted them. She did not. She sold them to me instead, and after she died, I engaged a broker to sell them (along with other documents I uncovered in my research), to a research library at Harvard. After I finished the book, I gave the net proceeds of the sale to Norma's daughters.

Those three women were active participants in the book. Delighted that I had brought them together—her "happiest moment in life," reflected Jennifer on Facebook—they wished to help me write their stories. So they invited me to important events from weddings to memorials, and communicated with me hundreds of times. Shelley, meantime, mindful of her secret, instructed me to speak to no one about her without her prior consent, and I complied. Ultimately, she wanted it known that the decision to tell her story was her own. "I want everyone to understand," she told me in 2019, "that this is something I've *chosen* to do." When the book was done, I asked the sisters to review with me the passages in which they appeared. They did so to differing degrees, and offered up a handful of emendations, which I incorporated. Each blessed the book, and said it was "accurate." "You've done great," Melissa added kindly. They were ready to step forward.

―――

BEFORE THIS BOOK, people knew, of course, who Norma McCorvey was. They knew, too, that Linda Coffee filed *Roe*, and that Mildred Jefferson and Curtis Boyd fought on either side of it. But if people knew something of their work, they knew next to nothing of *them*. Among much else, they didn't know that Coffee was not only brilliant and feminist but gay and destitute, living in a heatless house in East Texas. Or that Boyd—sixty years after seeing a schoolmate ruined by an unwanted pregnancy—had come to determine that the law must *never* force a pregnant woman to birth a child. Or that it was prejudice, more even than conviction, that had led Jefferson to leave medicine for abortion— racism and misogyny so overt that she who publicly safeguarded the unborn had come, privately, to consider this world too unjust to bear a child of her own.

It took me time to uncover these things. People reveal themselves gradually, the dead too; though I'd come to know Jefferson through her papers at Harvard, what brought her to life were her FBI file and divorce record and ex-husband, sources it took me years to find. It took years to find Coffee, too. She had given just one in-depth interview since speaking with a student at Baylor in 1973. And even after I found her in Mineola, Texas, another fifteen months passed before we spoke. The night before we met in 2014, her partner presented me with a sheaf of papers, among them the personals ad that had brought Coffee to her, and the sad record of Coffee's arrests.

I thus saw again and again that if *Roe* was "undoubtedly the best- known case" the Supreme Court had ever adjudicated, as the legal phi- losopher Ronald Dworkin wrote, its protagonists remained unknown. Secrets, in fact, abounded. Some were small: the mistaken memory of a passage in a book that inspired Nellie Gray to found the March for Life. Some were not so small: the lie Sarah Weddington told, that Norma had carried her pregnancy to term so as to protect *Roe*. Some were important: the memo, written in 1991 by a Supreme Court clerk, that prefigured the 5-4 *Casey* ruling, and had not been quoted before. And one was deeply affecting.

———

I FOUND THE BIRTH DATE of the *Roe* baby in those papers Norma had left behind. But Norma's child did not yet wish to meet with me when, in late 2011, I readied to board a flight to Dallas to look for Norma's mother. I didn't know where in Dallas Mary was. But my research assis- tant, Susannah Brooks, knew from property tax records that, a few months previously, Mary had been living in a Dallas trailer park. Mary was no longer there, and I guessed that she'd moved to an assisted-living facility. Susannah gave me the names of twenty-nine such facilities in

Dallas that took Medicaid or Medicare. Awaiting my flight, I made my way down the list, phoning each facility to ask if it housed a woman named Mary Sandefur. Number twenty-three did: the Renaissance at Kessler Park.

Mary didn't tell me that she'd borne another daughter besides Norma. But three years later, that other daughter did, Velma recalling over seafood in Simmesport that Mary had phoned her back in 1983. "She said," Velma told me in early 2015, "'I'm your mama.'"

Velma and I drove from the restaurant to her home. There, on a bank of the Atchafalaya, she handed me the marriage certificate of the grandparents who had raised her. Bertha had wed Emar on July 15, 1922—six months before she gave birth to Mary. The document thus revealed another family secret: Bertha was pregnant at the altar, the first of three generations redirected by unwanted pregnancy, by the irreconcilability of sex and religion.

It was helpful to view Norma within the context of her family. And yet, her life resisted rendering. She had cloaked it in lies; her two autobiographies were fiction. Among much else, she wrote that a nun raped her, that a cousin raped her, that a trio of strangers raped her, that her husband beat her, that her mother kidnapped her child, that she went to an illegal clinic to get an abortion only to find it caked in blood, that she became Jane Roe because her lawyers got her drunk and didn't tell her what an abortion was, that she was shot at because she was Jane Roe, that she helped to perform unsafe abortions. None of it was true.

In writing Norma's story, I searched always for her earliest interview; before conjuring that bloody abortion clinic, for example, she revealed, in the early 1980s, that she'd found an illegal abortion provider but was scared to go to him. I searched as well for credible witnesses to her life, finding a few dozen people who, like her friend Andi Taylor, told me what Norma did not—that, for example, Norma had just birthed her second child, not her third, when a nurse accidentally handed the baby to her. It was hard to find these people. Andi happened to be at Cherries, a gay bar in Dallas, when, in 2012, the bartender read aloud a note I'd placed in a gay paper asking anyone who'd known Norma to get in touch. Thus did Norma's sixty-nine years take shape in these pages.

In October 2020, almost four years after I alerted the country that

Jane Roe had died, her daughter Melissa phoned me in New Jersey to say that she would soon sprinkle Norma's ashes in Louisiana. I wanted to be there. But I did not want to fly; the country was steeped in Covid. (It would soon take the lives of Norma's half-sister and brother-in-law, Velma and Robert having fallen sick beside the Atchafalaya.) And so, on a Monday morning at dawn, I backed out of my driveway, off to drive 2,800 miles in five days. The next night, in a trailer park in Mississippi, I read online that a hurricane was bearing down on the Gulf Coast.

I could only laugh. I had been at work on the book for almost eleven years, and none of it had been easy. It had, in fact, exhausted me. But I would do it again. As the great Neil Sheehan reflected to his wife upon completing his opus about the Vietnam War: "I saw more of our daughters than most fathers do, and I wrote the book I wanted to write."

New Jersey

June 2021

Acknowledgments

Writers normally thank their partners at the end of their acknowledgments. But I don't want to wait. Thank you, Shuly.

When we met in 2013, I had been researching this book off and on for three years. But I had not yet begun to write it. And though you're a person who believes things when she sees them, you believed in this book. You believed in me. You never asked me when I would finish writing. Instead, you made sacrifices so that I would. Thank you. We made it! And we have two kids to boot.

Ella, Eden—to have you in my life, to work with you at my feet, is a dream come true. It's helped me too. "I used to not be able to work if there were dishes in the sink," Anne Lamott wrote. "Then I had a child and now I can work if there is a corpse in the sink."

This book was difficult. Everything about it was fraught: The secret that drew me to it. Norma. Roe. People don't want to return your calls when you're calling about abortion.

Still, over eleven years, hundreds did. Their words fill more than five thousand (large blank Moleskine notebook) pages. And I am indebted to them: those who helped me get to know Norma, and those many others—the authors and publicists, genealogists and professors, librarians and civil servants, activists and archivists—who helped me get my arms around abortion in America. David Garrow, Sheree Havlik, Stanley Henshaw, Ronda Mackey, Michael Stoller, Charlotte Taft, Daniel Vinzant, and Rebecca Wind were especially good to me.

So were the people whose lives form the heart of this book. Thank you, Norma, for helping me tell the truth about your life even though you preferred your "version." Thank you, Curtis Boyd, Linda Coffee, and—though we did not meet—Mildred Jefferson. Thank you, Melissa, Jennifer and Shelley. I did my very best to merit your trust.

———

THANK YOU TO MY AGENTS, Sarah Chalfant and Rebecca Nagel. I am so lucky to be in your care. Thanks to my editor, Tom Mayer. You wanted this book and helped me realize its potential. And thank you, Karen Blumenthal. I miss our conversations about *Roe*. I am so sorry for your family.

More thank-yous. To professor Johanna Schoen, who read the manuscript, and Professor Daniel Williams, who read several chapters. To Andy Young and Allegra Huston, who fact-checked and copyedited the book. To Andrew Kent, who answered many, many questions about the law. And to Meir Feder, who answered even more, and read the manuscript, and provided endless direction.

Then there were the Dubler-Furmans. Ilan helped me with endnotes, while Ariela and Jesse explained to me the due process clause and judicial overreach, read the manuscript and saw to it that my family and I had a safe place to live when Covid hit. Thank you, Victoria Moran-Furman, for providing that safe place. We will never forget your kindness.

Thank you to Susannah Brooks, who helped me locate a hundred needles in a hundred haystacks. To my cousins Mark and David Kaminsky, who gave me different sorts of help. To Mara Certic, who did it all—transcription, endnotes, bibliography—with laughter and aplomb. To Cullen Murphy and Paul Steiger, who always know what a journalist should do. To Stuart Karle and David Schulz, for measured advice. To Michael Train and Dassi Zeidel for finishing touches. To 23andMe, for helping a broken family fill the void. And to my wonderful friends and relatives who've helped me fill one, too.

Thanks also to Toya Delgado, who nurtured me and my family when the finish line was not in sight. Thank you, Joan Covici and Michael Jewell, for housing me on the night I found Norma's papers. And a final thank-you to Walther Hetzer and Ellen Lewis, for your home in Provence where, on February 7, 2010, this book began.

Notes

ABBREVIATIONS:

NMP: Norma McCorvey Papers. In Joshua Prager Collection on Norma
      McCorvey and *Roe v. Wade*, 1926–2018, Schlesinger Library on the His-
      tory of Women in America, Radcliffe Institute for Advanced Study,
      Harvard University.
MJP: Papers of Mildred Jefferson, 1947–2010, MC 696, Schlesinger Library
      on the History of Women in America, Radcliffe Institute for Advanced
      Study, Harvard University.
HABP: Harry A. Blackmun Papers, Manuscript Division, Library of Congress.

PROLOGUE

1 **"free of interference"**: *Roe v. Wade*, 410 U.S. 113 (1973), Section X.

1 **feminist icon Ruth Bader Ginsburg**: Ruth B. Ginsburg, "Some Thoughts
  on Autonomy and Equality in Relation to *Roe v. Wade*," *University of North
  Carolina Law Review* 63, no. 375 (1985).

1 **others applauded *Roe*'s logic**: A group of nearly nine hundred American law
  professors filed a brief for the 1989 case of *Webster v. Reproductive Health Services* affirming the legal right to abortion "as delineated . . . in *Roe v. Wade*."
  Stephen L. Carter, "Abortion, Absolutism, and Compromise," *Yale Law
  Journal* 100, no. 8 (1991): 2747–66.

1 **the Senate did not even ask**: U.S. Senate, Committee on the Judiciary, On the
  Nomination of John Paul Stevens to be an Associate Justice of the Supreme
  Court, 94th Cong., 1st sess., 1975.

2 **"undoubtedly the best-known"**: Ronald Dworkin, *Life's Dominion: An Argument About Abortion, Euthanasia, And Individual Freedom* (New York: Vintage, 1993), 102.

2 **"Any victory"**: Mary Ziegler, *Abortion in America: Roe v. Wade to the Present* (Cambridge: Cambridge University Press, 2020), 212.

2 **"exposure to the raw"**: Harry A. Blackmun, preamble, *Roe v. Wade*, 410 U.S. 113 (1973).

2 **unhappily pregnant**: Sally Blackmun wrote of her pregnancy in the introduction to the book by Gloria Feldt and Laura Fraser, *The War on Choice: The Right-Wing Attack on Women's Rights and How to Fight Back* (New York: Bantam, 2004), xv.

2 **"the normal 266-day"**: *Roe v. Wade*, Section IV A.

2 **The Federal Rules**: Rule 10a of the Federal Rules of Civil Procedure states: "The title of [a] complaint must name all the parties."

3 **"Despite the use"**: *Roe v. Wade*, Section IV A.

3 **I read an article**: Margaret Talbot, "A Risky Proposal," *New Yorker*, January 7, 2010.

PART I: SEX AND RELIGION

7 **"in the fifteenth century"**: Bryan P. Piazza, *The Atchafalaya River Basin: History and Ecology of an American Wetland* (College Station: Texas A & M Press, 2014), 17.

7 **beginning in 1755**: Carl A. Brasseaux, *Acadian to Cajun: Transformation of a People, 1803–1877* (Jackson: University Press of Mississippi, 1992), xi, 4.

7 **Africans working their fields**: Brasseaux, *Acadian to Cajun*, 5.

7 **five thousand Acadians**: Carl A. Brasseaux, email to the author, September 22, 2020.

7 **French names**: Carl A. Brasseaux, email to the author, January 13, 2021.

7 **forty-nine Acadians**: Brasseaux, *Acadian to Cajun*, 7.

8 **Some deserted**: Brasseaux, *Acadian to Cajun*, 66–67.

8 **a derisive variant**: Brasseaux, *Acadian to Cajun*, 101–2.

8 **named Amand Gautreaux**: *Diocese of Baton Rouge Catholic Church Records*, vol. 1a, revised, *The Registers of St. Charles Aux Mines in Acadia, 1707–1748*, 3rd edition (Baton Rouge: Diocese of Baton Rouge, 1999). Judy Riffel, emails to the author, March 13–14, 2015.

8 **He arrived in Louisiana**: Jacqueline K. Vorhies, *Some Late Eighteenth-Century Louisianians: Census Records of the Colony, 1758–1796* (Lafayette: University of Southwestern Louisiana, 1973), 441–86. Judy Riffel, emails to the author, March 13–14, 2015.

8 **generations of his progeny**: Vorhies, *Some Late Eighteenth-Century Louisianians*, 463. Judy Riffel, emails to the author, March 13–14, 2015.

8 **daughter named Bertha**: Velma Gross, interview with the author, January 27, 2011.

8 **married just six months**: Amar Gourthreau and Bertha Chenvert, certificate of marriage, July 15, 1922, Marksville, LA. Courtesy of Velma Gross.

9 **A Pentecostal preacher**: Velma Gross, interview with the author, January 23, 2015.

9 **while the children hid**: Velma Gross, interview with the author, January 23, 2015.

9 **"Many illegitimacies"**: Pete Daniel, *Deep'n As It Come: The 1927 Mississippi River Flood* (Fayetteville: University of Arkansas Press, 1996), 120.

9 **American Social Hygiene Association**: Daniel, *Deep'n As It Come*, 119.

9 **"We hope this"**: Daniel, *Deep'n As It Come*, 120.

9 **"too poor to notice"**: Brasseaux, *Acadian to Cajun*, 75.

9 **"You wouldn't even say"**: Sandra Guilbeau, interview with the author, January 9, 2015.

9 **"when a girl"**: Velma Gross, interview with the author, January 23, 2015.

10 **"English, and no other"**: Theodore Roosevelt, *American Ideals* (Springfield, IL: Collier, 1897), 26.

10 **Louisiana banned French**: *Constitutions of the State of Louisiana: Text of the Constitution Adopted June 18, 1921, With Text of Corresponding Articles in All of the Constitutions of the State, Including All Amendments*. Compiled by Huey P. Long, Governor. Article XII, Section 12, 377–78. Judy Riffel, email to the author, March 13, 2015.

10 **spoke French and were illiterate**: U.S. Census, 1940, Pointe Coupee Parish, Louisiana, Ward 1, ED 39-1, sheets 6B–7A, family 122, line 73.

10 **"against sickness"**: Victor Simon, letter to Emar Gautreaux, November 16, 1936. Courtesy of Sandra Guilbeau.

10 **"outgoing, laughing"**: Julia Anderson, née Saucier, interview with the author, February 16, 2015.

10 **brothers were also in the fields**: Sandra Guilbeau, interview with the author, January 29, 2015.

11 **"burn our legs"**: Sandra Guilbeau, interview with the author, January 29, 2015.

11 **"It makes you"**: Sandra Guilbeau, interview with the author, January 9, 2015.

11 **On April 25, 1940**: U.S. Census, 1940.

11 **It cost four dollars**: U.S. Census, 1940.

11 **Brother Deshotels**: Velma Gross, interview with the author, January 27, 2015.

12 **"If a girl"**: Julia Anderson, née Saucier, interview with the author, February 16, 2015.

12 **Mildred went off**: Julia Anderson, née Saucier, interview with the author, February 16, 2015.

12 **Emar and Bertha met them**: Velma Gross, interview with the author, January 23, 2015.

12 **"I can tell you"**: Velma Gross, interview with the author, October 14, 2016.

12 **Velma's biological father:** Mary told Velma the name of her biological father: Earl Pendarvis. Pendarvis died in 1975 having never met his daughter. He was fifty-six and estranged from his wife and their five children. They did not know of Velma but did know of at least two other children Earl had fathered out of wedlock. Velma Gross, interview with the author, January 23, 2015. Earl Pendarvis Jr., interview with the author, May 3, 2021.

12 **in the Good Book:** Wavia Ital, interview with the author, January 28, 2015.

12 **Emar kept the Bible**: Sandra Guilbeau, interview with the author, January 29, 2015.

13 **"That pregnancy changed"**: Velma Gross, interview with the author, January 23, 2015.

13 **a job waitressing**: Velma Gross, interview with the author, January 23, 2015.

13 **His father William**: Buck Graves, interview with the author, May 5, 2015.

13 **Alma was readying to marry**: Alma married William Nelson, then Charlie Warren, then Otis Horton, then Kimble McAuley, the last in December 1943. Dallas County District Court records.

13 **wed Mary**: "Double Wedding Is Celebrated on Saturday," *State Times Advocate* (Baton Rouge), March 10, 1943.

13 **the Atchafalaya would capture**: John McPhee, "Atchafalaya," *New Yorker*, February 23, 1987, 39.

13 **"always wondered why"**: Velma Gross, interview with the author, January 23, 2015.

14 **Norma Lea Nelson was born**: Norma Lea Nelson, certificate of birth, September 22, 1947. Division of Public Health Statistics, Louisiana State Department of Health.

14 **Mary would never forget**: Melissa Mills, interview with the author, January 25, 2015. "Another Storm Is Approaching Florida Coast," *State Times Advocate* (Baton Rouge), September 22, 1947.

15 **"We just heard"**: Julia Anderson, née Saucier, interview with the author, February 16, 2015.

15 **trees were straight**: Norma McCorvey, interview with the author, March 23, 2015.

15 **To be a Jehovah's Witness**: The sect believed that the end of days was to come before the last of those alive in 1914 had died. Previously, it had determined that God would establish a new kingdom on earth in 1914. When this did not happen, it changed its teachings. It would do so again in 2013, determining that 1914 simply marked the beginning of the "last days" on earth.

15 **will spare 144,000 non-sinners**: The teaching is taken from Revelation 14:1–4 (KJV).

16 **"that's where they would sit"**: Sandra Guilbeau, interview with the author, January 9, 2013.

16 **"resented the teachings"**: Mary Nelson, interview with the author, October 5, 2011.

16 **"She was the opposite"**: Norma McCorvey, interview with the author, November 5, 2013.

16 **"a stupid little imp"**: Norma McCorvey, interview with the author, June 29, 2015.

16 **"always sad"**: Norma McCorvey, interview with the author, November 4, 2013.

17 **Wavia suggested**: Velma Gross, interview with the author, January 13, 2015.

17 **"He said 'no!'"**: Velma Gross, interview with the author, January 13, 2015.

17 **"I felt a bond"**: Velma Gross, interview with the author, September 14, 2020.

17 **"kept house"**: Velma Gross, interview with the author, January 13, 2015.

18 **her grades**: Elementary Pupil's Cumulative Record, Dallas Independent School District.

18 **twelfth percentile**: The test was the California short-form test of mental maturity. Elementary Pupil's Cumulative Test Record, Dallas Independent School District.

18 **"absent on slightest excuse"**: Elementary Pupil's Cumulative Test Record, Dallas Independent School District.

18 **"Norma was a handful"**: Velma Gross, interview with the author, January 22, 2013.

18 **"lay out with men"**: Norma McCorvey, interview with the author, February 4, 2014.

18 **God was punishing**: Norma McCorvey, interview with the author, June 29, 2015.

18 **"that I tried"**: Norma McCorvey, interview with the author, February 4, 2014.

18 **"a delinquent child"**: Clerk's File Docket and Civil Fee Book, Juvenile Court, Dallas County, no. 60–1993–Juv, October 31, 1960.

18 **her father paid**: Clerk's File Docket and Civil Fee Book, Juvenile Court, Dallas County, no. 60–1993–Juv, October 31, 1960.

18 **a Polynesian peasant**: Norma McCorvey, interview with the author, November 5, 2013.

18 **raped in a shower**: Norma McCorvey, interview with the author, November 4, 2013.

19 **But there never**: Sister Yolanda Martinez (Mount St. Michaels), interview with the author, March 25, 2015.

19 **an older student**: "Norma McCorvey a.k.a. Jane Roe," unpublished reminiscence written by Norma and Alyssa Lenhoff, undated. NMP.

19 **Mary and Olin divorced**: Certificate of divorce, February 21, 1961. Dallas County District Court records.

19 **"She lost all control"**: Norma McCorvey, interview with the author, February 4, 2014.

19 **shaved her eyebrows**: Norma McCorvey, interview with the author, June 29, 2015.

19 **"committed to an institution"**: Permanent Census Card, Dallas Independent School District.

19 **"one of the best"**: Texas Youth Council, Report to the Governor, 1964.

19 **"The pre-Christian world"**: Geoffrey Stone, *Sex and the Constitution* (New York: Liveright, 2017), 4.

20 **the Apostle Paul**: 1 Corinthians 7 (KJV).

20 **"man by his very nature"**: Augustine, *The City of God* (*De civitate Dei*), translated by John Healey (London: Griffith, Farran, Okeden & Welsh, 1890), 14, 17.

20 **"helped shape traditional American"**: Stone, *Sex and the Constitution*, 20.

20 **three dots inked**: The tattoo has been associated with various Southeast Asian gangs.

20 **"It was explained to me"**: Norma McCorvey, interview with the author, March 24, 2015.

20 **"mi cuata"**: In her autobiography, McCorvey misspelled the nickname as "mi quita." Norma McCorvey and Andy Meisler, *I Am Roe: My Life, Roe V. Wade, and Freedom of Choice* (New York: HarperCollins, 1994), 39.

21 **"what's been going on"**: Norma McCorvey, interview with the author, November 4, 2013.

21 **"She drank"**: Mary Nelson, interview with the author, October 5, 2011.

21 **"I beat"**: Mary Nelson, interview with the author, October 5, 2011.

21 **"soft and gentle"**: Norma McCorvey, interview with the author, November 4, 2013.

21 **"furburger"**: McCorvey and Meisler, *I Am Roe*, 42.

21 **"Back in Brooklyn"**: Carol, interview with the author, October 9, 2015. She does not wish to have her surname used.

21 **her mother had sent**: Carol, interview with the author, October 9, 2015.

22 **"they got rid"**: Anthony McCorvey, interview with the author, December 22, 2014.

22 **"Woody" was "hotheaded"**: Anthony McCorvey, interview with the author, December 22, 2014.

22 **"It was overkill"**: Norma McCorvey, interview with the author, June 29, 2015.

22 **Norma loved to perform**: Melissa Mills, interview with the author, March 24, 2015.

23 **"I wanted to be the first"**: Norma McCorvey, interview with the author, November 4, 2013.

23 **confided in a reporter**: Monika Maeckle, "The Double Life of Norma McCorvey," *Westwood Magazine* (supplement of *Dallas Times Herald*), October 18, 1981.

23 **"to excess"**: Norma McCorvey, interview with the author, June 29, 2015.

23 **at 6:27 a.m.**: Melissa Renee Sandefur, certificate of birth, May 25, 1965, Bureau of Vital Statistics, Texas Department of Health.

24 **Louisianan named Lodo Jeansonne**: Lodo Chenevert lived from March 28, 1882, to June 27, 1966.

24 **"We took good care"**: Mary Sandefur, interview with the author, October 5, 2011.

24 **a judge decreed**: Court of Domestic Relations, Dallas County, no. 65–4906–DR/2, September 30, 1965.

24 **he got married**: Elwood John McCorvey and Norma married on June 17, 1964, and divorced on September 30, 1965. He married Joyce Ann Weeks on October 15, 1965. Texas Divorce Index, 1968–2002.

25 **"She was real cute"**: Glenda Diane Watrous, interview with the author, March 25, 2015.

25 **"We went on a honeymoon"**: Glenda Diane Watrous, interview with the author, March 25, 2015.

25 **they moved into an apartment**: Glenda Diane Watrous, interview with the author, March 25, 2015.

25 **second attempt at a diploma**: Notes of reporter Joseph N. Bell. Courtesy of Bell's widow, Sherry Angel.

26 **shots from an osteopath**: Glenda Diane Watrous, interview with the author, March 25, 2015.

26 **"Ms. Sandefur wanted"**: Glenda Diane Watrous, interview with the author, March 25, 2015.

26 **"Norma wasn't very responsible"**: Glenda Diane Watrous, interview with the author, March 25, 2015.

26 **"Norma wanted"**: Glenda Diane Watrous, interview with the author, March 25, 2015.

26 **"Mary adopted her"**: Velma Gross, interview with the author, January 22, 2015.

26 **"intense pressure"**: Maeckle, "Double Life," 36–43.

26 **"kidnapped"**: McCorvey and Meisler, *I Am Roe*, 70.

27 **"I was always flirting"**: Pete Aguilar, interview with the author, March 31, 2015.

27 **looking at men**: Pete Aguilar, interview with the author, March 31, 2015.

27 **Ciudad Acuña**: Pete Aguilar, interview with the author, March 31, 2015.

27 **"I was going"**: Pete Aguilar, interview with the author, March 31, 2015.

27 **"She knew all the right"**: Pete Aguilar, interview with the author, March 31, 2015.

27 **She cut up his clothes**: Glenda Diane Watrous, interview with the author, April 1, 2015.

27 **"I dodged it"**: Pete Aguilar, interview with the author, March 31, 2015.

28 **up to twenty Coors**: Andi Taylor, interview with the author, November 8, 2012.

28 **twelve husbands**: Andi Taylor, interview with the author, June 30, 2015.

28 **a bar called Mercy Mary's**: Andi Taylor, interview with the author, August 3, 2015.

28 **"We couldn't tell anyone"**: Andi Taylor, interview with the author, June 30, 2015.

28 **"What'd we do"**: Andi Taylor, interview with the author, November 5, 2013.

28 **"If it was a feminine"**: Andi Taylor, interview with the author, November 8, 2012.

28 **She phoned back**: Pete Aguilar, interview with the author, March 31, 2015.

28 **"I've heard of a way"**: Norma McCorvey, interview with the author, July 8, 2016.

29 **"I would deliver the baby"**: Richard Lane, interview with the author, June 7, 2012.

29 **Dr. Wonderful**: Jennifer Ferguson, interview with the author, December 27, 2013.

29 **she was drinking more**: Norma McCorvey, interview with the author, June 29, 2015.

29 **"I can never recall"**: Norma McCorvey, interview with the author, November 5, 2013.

29 **The baby weighed**: Dallas Osteopathic Hospital discharge records, October 11, 1967. Courtesy of Jennifer Ferguson.

29 **"she fucked up"**: Norma McCorvey, interview with the author, November 4, 2013.

29 **"I never been"**: Andi Taylor, interview with the author, November 8, 2012.

30 **"She told me she had a little"**: Pete Aguilar, interview with the author, March 31, 2015.

30 **"I wonder"**: Pete Aguilar, interview with the author, March 31, 2015.

31 **"Their integrity"**: Mr. and Mrs. Hillary Messimer, letter to Henry McCluskey. Courtesy of Jennifer Ferguson.

31 **Four days after:** Jennifer Ferguson, interview with the author, October 26, 2015.

31 **"She was like"**: Cindy Kebabjian, interview with the author, March 4, 2013.

31 **her biological father**: Jennifer Ferguson, interview with the author, October 26, 2015.

32 **"I remember the name"**: Donna Kebabjian, interview with the author, June 11, 2012.

32 **The river no longer**: Piazza, *Atchafalaya River Basin*, 157–74.

32 **"didn't follow through"**: Sandra Guilbeau, interview with the author, February 12, 2015.

33 **"I will let you"**: Velma Gross, interview with the author, January 22, 2013.

33 **"It was real peaceful"**: Melissa Mills, interview with the author, March 11, 2013.

33 **"It was fun"**: Norma McCorvey, interview with the author, July 8, 2016.

33 **"I started seeing her"**: Patti Milford, interview with the author, February 10, 2015.

33 **"It's one of those things"**: Andi Taylor, interview with the author, February 10, 2015.

34 **"I'm not denying it"**: Norma McCorvey, interview with the author, March 23, 2015.

34 **"Valium was the answer"**: Norma McCorvey, interview with the author, November 4, 2013.

34 **"Why the hell"**: Norma McCorvey, interview with the author, June 29, 2015.

34 **hang it from a rope**: Norma McCorvey, interview with the author, June 29, 2015.

34 **William Kenneth Wheaton**: These paragraphs on Wheaton are drawn from a series of conversations and emails with his children Ken Wheaton and Wendy Craig, August and September 2015.

35 **claim to the family**: Wendy Wheaton, interview with the author, May 3, 2015.

35 **Daughter Wendy grabbed**: Wendy Wheaton, interview with the author, May 3, 2015.

35 **on grounds of "desertion"**: Commonwealth of Virginia Report of Divorce, State File Number 68 004935.

35 **Wheaton wed again**: Application for marriage license, State of Ohio, license no. 434717.

35 **cut off at the joint**: Jay Helfert, interview with the author, January 14, 2015.

35 **Norma took note**: Norma McCorvey, interview with the author, October 24, 2013.

35 **"All I knew"**: Norma McCorvey, interview with the author, February 10, 2015.

36 **"When you're in a hurry"**: Norma McCorvey, interview with the author, July 8, 2016.

36 **douching was protection enough**: Angela Bonavoglia, ed., *The Choices We Made: 25 Women and Men Speak Out Against Abortion* (New York: Random House, 1991), 138.

36 **"to turn my body"**: Lloyd Shearer, "This Woman and This Man Made History," *Parade*, May 8, 1983.

36 **"They were so highfalutin"**: Norma McCorvey, interview with the author, October 24, 2013.

36 **"I think he had been married"**: Norma McCorvey, interview with the author, October 24, 2013.

36 **"I really wanted"**: Norma McCorvey, interview with the author, October 24, 2013.

36 **"so that we could drink"**: Norma McCorvey, interview with the author, October 24, 2013.

36 **Wheaton had been arrested**: Ken Wheaton recalls that his father had numerous DUIs which led to the suspension of his license. Texas Department of Public Safety, Arrest Record for DUI, February 14, 1980. Ken Wheaton, email to the author, May 10, 2015.

36 **"I remember her"**: Melissa Mills, interview with the author, December 23, 2014.

38 **except to save**: Texas Penal Code § 1196 (1961).

38 **Alaska, Hawaii**: Centers for Disease Control, "Abortion Surveillance Report," 1970, Table 21.

38 **not explicitly illegal**: In November 1969, in the case of *United States v. Vuitch*, 402 U.S. 62 (1971), a federal district judge named Gerhard Gesell declared DC's anti-abortion statute unconstitutional.

38 **The doctor Hippocrates**: The Hippocratic Oath was long mistranslated as a general proscription of abortion. Much of the pro-life community continues to see it as such. But John M. Riddle, in *Contraception and Abortion from the Ancient World to the Renaissance* (Cambridge, MA: Harvard University Press, 1992), makes clear that the oath merely proscribes the use of pessaries, a type of vaginal or uterine suppository, to cause abortion. In reviewing Riddle's book, Professor James Mohr confirmed this translation with Owsei Temkin, a medical historian and scholar of classical language who was then director emeritus of the Johns Hopkins Institute of the History of Medicine. See James C. Mohr, "Sexuality, Reproduction, Contraception, and Abortion: A Review of Recent Literature," *Journal of Women's History* 8, no. 1 (Spring 1996): 9–10.

38 **"When couples have children"**: Aristotle, *Politics* (Chicago: University of Chicago Press, 2013), ch. 16.

38 **"The Bible contains"**: Richard B. Hays, *The Moral Vision of the New Testament* (San Francisco: HarperOne, 1996), 448.

39 **the book of Exodus**: Exodus 21:22: "If men fight, and hurt a woman with child, so that she gives birth prematurely, yet no harm follows, he shall surely be punished accordingly as the woman's husband imposes on him; and he shall pay as the judges determine" (NKJV).

39 **"as a tort"**: Daniel Schiff, *Abortion in Judaism* (Cambridge: Cambridge University Press, 2002), 27.

39 **rabbinic consensus**: Schiff, *Abortion in Judaism*, 4.

39 **"fully formed"**: Translation by Dr. David Ratzan, email to the author, January 27, 2021.

39 **"non formatum puerperium"**: St. Augustine of Hippo, *Writings on the Old Testament*, translated by Joseph T. Lienhard and Sean Doyle (New York: New City Press, 2016), 131.

39 **writing of a priest**: *Corpus Iuris Canonici*, ed. Aemilius Friedberg, 2nd ed. Aemilius Ludovicus Richteri, vol. 2: *Decretalium Collectiones* (Leipzig: Bernard Tauchnitz, 1881), 794. Translation by Dr. Michael Stoller, email to the author, January 22, 2021.

39 **three of the next 658 years:** In 1588, Pope Sixtus V issued a papal bull stating that abortion was "true homicide" whether the fetus was "formed or unformed." Three years later, his successor reinstated the canonical distinction between abortions early and late. Wrote Pope Gregory XIV: "We forever reduce the penalties for procuring the abortion of an inanimate fetus." Laerzia Cherubini, et al., *Magnum bullarium Romanum, a Beato Leone Magno usque ad S. D. N. Benedictum XIV*, 2nd ed. (Luxembourg: H.-A. Gosse & Soc., 1742), 2:702–03, 766–67. Translation by Dr. Michael Stoller, email to the author, January 22, 2021.

39 **Pope Pius IX**: Pope Pius IX, *Apostolica Sedis Moderationi*, October 12, 1869.

39 **lawyer named Thomas Carr**: The phrase used by Pope Pius is "Procurantes abortum effectu sequuto," which means "Procuring an abortion subsequently accomplished." Translation by Dr. Michael Stoller, email to the author, January 25, 2021.

40 **"animatus" and "inanimatus"**: Rev. Thomas J. Carr, "The Constitution 'Apostolicae Sedis Moderationi' Explained," *Irish Monthly* 7 (1879): 390-391.

40 **codification of canon law**: *Codex Iuris Canonici Pii X Pontificis Maximi iussu digestus Benedicti Papae XV autoritate promulgates* (Rome: Typis Polyglottis Vaticanis, 1918).

40 **"The life of each"**: The Vatican does make two exceptions, allowing abortion in cases of ectopic pregnancy and when the uterus becomes cancerous. Pope Pius XI, *Casti Connubii*, encyclical, December 31, 1930.

40 **"quick with child"**: Conn. Stat., tit. 22, § 4 (1821).

40 **Texas made no such**: Professor James Mohr, author of *Abortion in America: The Origins and Evolution of National Policy, 1800–1900* (New York: OUP, 1978), the foundational history of American anti-abortion laws, says that although the Texas law did not mention quickening, it was still the case that

only through quickening could a court determine if a woman was pregnant. James Mohr, interview with author, February 18, 2021. Texas Laws 1854, c. 49, § 1, set forth in H. Gammel, The Laws of Texas (1822–1897), vol. 3 (Austin: Gammel Book Co., 1898).

40 **"death and publicity"**: Leslie Reagan, *When Abortion Was a Crime: Women, Medicine, and Law in the United States, 1867–1973* (Berkeley: University of California Press, 1997), 125.

40 **died having abortions**: Reagan, *When Abortion Was a Crime*, 125.

40 **two to three thousand annually**: Christopher Tietze, MD, "Abortion as a Cause of Death," *American Journal of Public Health* 38, no. 10 (October 1948): 1434–41. Dr. Tietze reported that, according to the Census Bureau, there were 2,677 abortion-related deaths in 1933, 2,774 in 1934, 2,769 in 1935, 2,481 in 1936, 2,113 in 1937, 1,816 in 1938, and 1,786 in 1939. The numbers include deaths not only from illegal abortions but from "unintentional" ones, i.e. miscarriages, and "therapeutic" ones, i.e. that category of abortion permitted by law. According to Stanley Henshaw, a sociologist who did abortion research at the Guttmacher Institute for decades, owing to stigma, many alleged miscarriages that resulted in death were in fact abortions, and many deaths by abortion were attributed instead to septicemia, poison and other causes. As a result, he says, the true number of abortion-related deaths was "significantly higher" than what the Census Bureau reported.

40 **a naturopath named Ruth Barnett**: Barnett estimated that between 1918 and 1968, she performed forty thousand abortions. In 1959, the author Don James, writing under the pseudonym James Donner, profiled Barnett in his book *Women in Trouble.* James did not name Barnett but confided to a classroom of his students at Portland State University that Barnett was the subject of his book. Barnett later wrote an autobiography titled *They Weep on My Doorstep.* Marlene Howard, interview with the author, December 26, 2020.

40 **three blocks of brownstones**: Courtney Ryley Cooper, *Designs in Scarlet* (New York: Little, Brown, 1939), 213.

40 **"There is a significant disparity"**: Herbert L. Packer and Ralph J. Gampell, "Therapeutic Abortion: A Problem in Law and Medicine," *Stanford Law Review* 11 (1959): 417.

40 **"push for maternity"**: Reagan, *When Abortion Was a Crime*, 163.

41 **90 percent**: Mary Steichen Calderone, MD, "Illegal Abortion as a Public Health Problem," *American Journal of Public Health* 50, no. 7 (July 1960): 948–54. Dr. Calderone cites the 90 percent figure, which was the conclusion of a 1955 conference on abortion sponsored by the Planned Parenthood Federation of America and the New York Academy of Medicine.

41 **George Timanus in Maryland**: At a 1955 conference sponsored by Planned Parenthood, Dr. Timanus stated that between 1920 and 1951, he had performed 5,210 abortions on women referred to him by 353 doctors. George Lotrell Timanus, "Abortion in the U.S.," *Time*, June 2, 1958.

41 **the first American**: Diane Bernard, "How a Miracle Drug Changed the Fight Against Infection during World War II," *Washington Post*, July 11, 2020.

41 **284 confirmed deaths**: Thomas W. Hilgers, Dennis J. Horan and David Mall, eds., *New Perspectives on Human Abortion* (Frederick, MD: Aletheia Books, University Publications of America, Inc., 1981), 82. While the number of abortion-related deaths dropped steadily through the decades, they rose between 1956 and 1961, from 221 to 324.

41 **owing to stigma**: Stanley Henshaw, interview with author, June 17, 2019.

41 **133 abortion-related deaths**: Hilgers, Horan and Mall, *New Perspectives on Human Abortion*, 82.

41 **a thousand clergymen**: The network was called the Clergy Consultation Service on Abortion. Arlene Carmen and Howard Moody, *Abortion Counseling and Social Change* (Valley Forge, PA: Judson Press, 1973).

41 **activist Lawrence Lader**: Lader compiled his list of states with "skilled abortionists" in 1964. Lawrence Lader, *Abortion* (Indianapolis: Bobbs-Merrill, 1966), 54–55.

41 **"Our society"**: Tom C. Clark, "Religion, Morality, and Abortion: A Constitutional Appraisal," *Loyola of Los Angeles Law Review* 2, no. 1 (1969).

41 **"extremely frustrated"**: Plato, *Timaeus*, 91c: "A woman's womb or uterus, as it is called, is a living thing within her with a desire for childbearing. Now when this remains unfruitful for an unseasonably long period of time, it is extremely frustrated and travels everywhere up and down her body. It blocks up her respiratory passages, and by not allowing her to breathe it throws her into extreme emergencies, and visits all sorts of other illnesses upon her." J. M. Cooper and D. S. Hutchinson, eds., *Plato: Complete Works*, translated by Donald J. Zeyl (Indianapolis: Hackett, 1997), 1290.

42 **"chaperones, veils, wigs"**: Thomas B. Edsall, "Why the Fight Over Abortion Is Unrelenting," *New York Times*, May 29, 2019.

42 **excluded women**: Founded in 1846, the AMA did not begin to admit women until 1915.

42 **"Abortion was murder"**: Kristin Luker, "The War Between Women," *Family Planning Perspectives* 16, no. 3 (March/April, 1984): 105–10.

42 **now safer than birth**: According to the abortion researcher Stanley Henshaw, the mortality risk of legal induced abortion in 1972 was 4.1 per 100,000. That same year, the mortality risk of pregnancy and childbirth was 15.2 per 100,000 live births. (This estimate excludes deaths from ectopic pregnancy and induced abortion, and is based on data reported by the CDC.) The figures for 1970, writes Henshaw, are less accurate because the CDC had not begun collecting abortion mortality data. Stanley Henshaw, email to the author, July 5, 2020.

42 **illegal abortion accounted for**: In 1972, there were thirty-nine deaths from illegal abortions, twenty-four from legal. Lisa M. Koonin, Jack C. Smith, Merrell Ramick and Clarice A. Green, "Abortion Surveillance – United States, 1992," *Morbidity and Mortality Weekly Report* 45, no. SS-3 (May 3, 1996): 1–36.

43 **"The contraceptive was faulty"**: Lawrence Lader, "Cases of Non-Hospital Abortion," 1966–69, Woman #144, Lawrence Lader Papers, New York Public Library.

43 **"All the doctors"**: Lader, "Cases of Non-Hospital Abortion," Woman #144.

43 **"They were getting illegal abortions"**: Frank Bradley, interview with the author, August 1, 2012.

43 **American Law Institute**: The American Law Institute, a body of lawyers, professors and judges, proposed the reform of abortion law in 1959. In 1967, Colorado became the first state to adopt its guidelines.

43 **AMA now changed course**: Linda Greenhouse and Reva B. Siegel, *Before Roe v. Wade: Voices that Shaped the Abortion Debate Before the Supreme Court's Ruling* (New Haven: Yale Law School, 2012), 26.

PART II: THREE TEXANS

47 **Mildred Jefferson was born**: Mildred Fay Jefferson, standard certificate of birth, Texas Department of Health, Bureau of Vital Statistics.

47 **wedding in Waco**: Gurthie Lee Roberts and Millard F. Jefferson, certificate of marriage, June 16, 1926, DOC128S29111, McLennan County Marriage Book, 160A.

47 **the family farm**: Fannie Lou Roberts Thompson, interviews with the author, March 24, 2016, and April 28, 2016.

48 **"She had *nerve*"**: Fannie Lou Roberts Thompson, interview with the author, March 24, 2016.

48 **"Why don't you?"**: Esther Guilfoy, "Brilliant Woman Surgeon Joins VA Hospital Staff," *Manchester Union Leader*, November 4, 1955.

48 **after reading of Elizabeth**: Application for admission to Harvard Medical School, October 22, 1946. Courtesy of the Harvard Medical School Registrar.

48 **"When they killed"**: Fannie Lou Roberts Thompson, interview with the author, March 24, 2016.

48 **snipping with a scissors**: Fannie Lou Roberts Thompson, interview with the author, March 24, 2016.

48 **"I'm going to be a doctor"**: Fannie Lou Roberts Thompson, interview with the author, March 24, 2016.

48 **"They had a bulletin board"**: Fannie Lou Roberts Thompson, interview with the author, March 24, 2016.

48 **"I would be down there"**: Fannie Lou Roberts Thompson, interview with the author, March 24, 2016.

48 **visited from his pulpits**: Eleanor Roberts, "Dr. Mildred F. Jefferson Knew What She Wanted," *Boston Post*, July 15, 1951.

48 **"she knew God"**: Fannie Lou Roberts Thompson, interview with the author, March 24, 2016.

48 **no one spoke of abortion**: Kirthel Roberts, interviews with the author, February 23, 2016, and March 24, 2016.

49 **"I always wanted"**: Mildred Jefferson, "A New Iconoclast: You might not like what she says, but Mildred Jefferson speaks her mind," *Chicago Tribune*, July 22, 1990.

49 **her 138 IQ**: Roberts, "Dr. Mildred F. Jefferson Knew What She Wanted."

49 **5 feet 3¾ inches**: Application for admission to Harvard Medical School, October 22, 1946.

49 **"If you told her"**: Fannie Lou Roberts Thompson, interview with the author, March 24, 2016.

50 **group of Methodist ministers**: Texas College, "Mission & History," texascollege.edu.

50 **"You'd never say"**: Otile McManus, "Dr. Jefferson and her Fight Against Abortion," *Boston Sunday Globe*, December 3, 1976.

50 **"No other medical school"**: Roberts, "Dr. Mildred F. Jefferson Knew What She Wanted."

50 **Her father had enrolled**: *Plainsdealer* 46, no. 27 (July 9, 1943): 5.

50 **heading to South Korea**: Roberts, "Dr. Mildred F. Jefferson Knew What She Wanted."

50 **"a jewel too costly"**: Roberts, "Dr. Mildred F. Jefferson Knew What She Wanted."

50 **A's at Tufts**: Roberts, "Dr. Mildred F. Jefferson Knew What She Wanted."

50 **"all mankind"**: Application for admission to Harvard Medical School, October 22, 1946.

50 **first black woman**: Harvard acceptance letter, January 21, 1947.

50 **Read a headline**: "Harvard Admits Race Woman to Medical School," *Cleveland Herald*, May 31, 1947.

50 **because she was black**: The grant was from the Lt. Hirschel Gutman Fund, which was created "for the advancement of American ideals." "Establish Fund in Honor of Lt. Gutman," *Newton Graphic*, February 8, 1945.

51 **"most revolting"**: "Gutman Grant Sends Negress to Harvard Med," *Jewish Advocate*, May 29, 1947.

51 **"Americans are coming to realize"**: "Gutman Grant Sends Negress to Harvard Med."

51 **ballet and bridge**: Roberts, "Dr. Mildred F. Jefferson Knew What She Wanted."

51 **top third of her class**: FBI case file for Mildred Fay Jefferson, no. 161–HQ-9379, 28. Interview with A. J. A. Campbell, March 13, 1973.

51 **surgical internship**: Roberts, "Dr. Mildred F. Jefferson Knew What She Wanted."

51 **writing in breathless prose**: Roberts, "Dr. Mildred F. Jefferson Knew What She Wanted."

51 **"a willing of the right thing"**: Roberts, "Dr. Mildred F. Jefferson Knew What She Wanted."

51 **"in the interest of science"**: Roberts, "Dr. Mildred F. Jefferson Knew What She Wanted."

51 **was now a captain**: Roberts, "Dr. Mildred F. Jefferson Knew What She Wanted."

51 **Hattie Carnegie, Ceil Chapman**: Roberts, "Dr. Mildred F. Jefferson Knew What She Wanted."

51 **took out a small loan**: Charlestown Savings Bank loan, February 1, 1955. MJP, Box 3, Folder 4.

52 **"the first real defeat"**: Mildred Jefferson, letter to Dr. Carl W. Walter, October 15, 1955. MJP, Box 16, Folder 9.

52 **"serious personal problems"**: Mildred Jefferson, letter to Dr. Carl W. Walter, October 15, 1955. MJP, Box 16, Folder 9.

52 **"It may be that"**: Mildred Jefferson, "Dissonance," *Bulletin*, September 1955. MJP, Box 22, Folder 13.

52 **"girlish whims"**: Dr. Carl W. Walter, letter to Mildred Jefferson, October 11, 1955. MJP, Box 4, Folder 9.

52 **"too precious to waste"**: "Positive approach to life needed: MD," *Ottawa Citizen*, November 5, 1973.

52 **"she would run into problems"**: FBI case file for Mildred Fay Jefferson, no. 161–HQ-9379, 29. Interview with A. J. A. Campbell, March 13, 1973.

52 **Mildred had black friends**: Shane Cunningham, email to the author, May 5, 2020.

52 **The Progressives**: Shane Cunningham, email to the author, May 5, 2020.

52 **accepted fellowships**: Mildred Jefferson, letter to Dr. Morris Cohen, October 18, 1962. MJP, Box 16, Folder 9.

52 **a job in cancer research**: Mildred Jefferson, letter to Dr. Morris Cohen, October 18, 1962.

52 **"a superb doctor"**: FBI case file for Mildred Fay Jefferson, no. 161–HQ-9379, 57. Interview with Sidney Farber, March 9, 1973.

52 **research on tissue transplant**: FBI case file for Mildred Fay Jefferson, no. 161–HQ-9379, 57. Interview with Sidney Farber, March 9, 1973.

53 **A block away**: Raymond Roberts, interview with the author, February 18, 2016.

53 **She didn't join them**: Raymond Roberts, interview with the author, February 18, 2016.

53 **he was smitten**: Shane Cunningham, interviews with the author, February 19, 2016, and June 3, 2016.

53 **"As with everything"**: Anne Fox, interview with the author, February 23, 2016.

53 **"My Muse"**: Shane Cunningham and Mildred Jefferson letters. MJP, Box 3, Folder 15.

53 **"Our relationship"**: Shane Cunningham, interview with the author, June 3, 2016.

53 **"The term was moral turpitude"**: Shane Cunningham, interview with the author, June 3, 2016.

54 **miscegenation was**: Peter Wallenstein, *Tell the Court I Love My Wife: Race, Marriage, and Law— an American History* (New York: Palgrave Macmillan,

2002), 254. In 1957, South Dakota and Colorado repealed laws against interracial marriage, lowering the number of states with such laws to twenty-four. In most of those states, interracial marriage was a felony. In a few, it was not criminalized but was prohibited in-state.

54 **matter of will**: Roberts, "Dr. Mildred F. Jefferson Knew What She Wanted."

54 **"extreme unfairness"**: Shane Cunningham, interview with the author, October 28, 2016.

54 **"She would have been"**: Shane Cunningham, interview with the author, February 19, 2016.

54 **refused even to wire**: Mildred Jefferson, letter to John Jones, September 14, 1961. MJP, Box 2, Folder 11.

54 **"It is still traditional"**: Mildred Jefferson, letter to Kivie Kaplan, March 22, 1962. MJP, Box 16, Folder 9.

55 **she volunteered nothing**: Jefferson, "A New Iconoclast."

55 **"If a newspaper went unread"**: Shane Cunningham, interview with the author, February 19, 2016.

55 **"partly because she was a woman"**: FBI case file for Mildred Fay Jefferson, no. 161–HQ-9379, 61. Interview with Claude Welch, March 12, 1973.

55 **"I was aware"**: Mildred Jefferson, interview with Jennifer Donnally, October 22, 2007. Interviews of Jennifer M. Donnally, 2007–2012, MC1059, Box 60, CD 6. Schlesinger Library, Harvard University.

56 **She listened quietly**: Dr. Barbara Rockett, interview with the author, September 8, 2017.

56 **"Her manners were tops"**: FBI case file for Mildred Fay Jefferson, no. 161–HQ-9379, 58. Interview with Sidney Farber, March 9, 1973.

56 **choked with papers and belongings**: Shane Cunningham, affidavit, 1980. NMP.

56 **"There would be little aisles"**: Shane Cunningham, affidavit, 1980.

56 **"How can you live"**: Shane Cunningham, interview with the author, August 14, 2019.

56 **"If you are subconsciously"**: Shane Cunningham, interview with the author, August 14, 2019.

56 **"part of her intellectual"**: Shane Cunningham, interview with the author, February 19, 2016.

57 **"the voice of God"**: Shane Cunningham, interview with the author, June 4, 2016.

57 **"only my father"**: *Vital Concerns*, television program, Boston Neighborhood Network, October 1, 2009.

57 **remained "profound"**: Shane Cunningham, interview with the author, June 4, 2016.

57 **"The male parent"**: Mildred Jefferson, "Abortion: Self-Defeat Solution," *Centerscope* 5, no. 1–5 (March/April 1972): 9.

57 **"I was amazed"**: Dr. Barbara Rockett, interview with the author, June 3, 2016.

58 **Theirs was a country life**: Curtis Boyd, interview with the author, November 2, 2015.

58 **called black people**: Curtis Boyd, interview with the author, July 27, 2012.

59 **fell for Virginia**: The name Virginia is a pseudonym to protect her identity.

59 **"My great suggestion"**: Curtis Boyd, "The Morality of Abortion: The Making of a Feminist Physician," *St. Louis University Public Law Review* 13, no. 1 (1993–94): 303–14.

59 **"The fact that"**: Curtis Boyd, interview with the author, July 27, 2012.

59 **"Virginia was a sinner"**: Curtis Boyd, interview with the author, November 2, 2015.

59 **"Every act of intercourse"**: Curtis Boyd, interview with the author, January 21, 2015.

59 **"Most Courteous"**: *Life Matters: The Story of an Illegal Abortionist*, film, directed by Kyle Boyd, Grayscale, 2002. Available at: https://www.pbs.org/independentlens/lifematters/film.html.

59 **"how we should live"**: Curtis Boyd, interview with the author, January 21, 2015.

59 **carhop named LaMerle**: LaMerle Boyd, email to the author, October 24, 2016.

59 **"I learned that he"**: LaMerle Boyd, email to the author, July 30, 2016.

60 **"God came down"**: Curtis Boyd, interview with the author, November 2, 2015.

60 **"We were both devout"**: *Life Matters*, film.

60 **peddling hardbound Bibles**: Curtis Boyd, interview with the author, October 27, 2016.

60 **he became a Unitarian**: Curtis Boyd, interview with the author, October 27, 2016.

61 **"I was embarrassed"**: Curtis Boyd, interview with the author, September 1, 2016.

61 **looked for a doctor to perform:** Curtis Boyd, interview with the author, November 2, 2015.

61 **"He was the native son"**: *Life Matters*, film.

61 **"the problem that"**: Betty Friedan, *The Feminine Mystique* (New York: Norton, 1963), 63.

61 **"something more"**: Friedan, *The Feminine Mystique*, 78.

61 **"a simple, young"**: Curtis Boyd, interview with the author, January 21, 2015.

62 **"just sort of moved"**: Curtis Boyd, interview with the author, January 21, 2015.

62 **an abortion referral network**: In 1967, in New York, a minister named Howard Moody began the Clergy Consultation Service on Abortion. It spawned other clergy referral networks, including the Clergy Consultation Service on Problem Pregnancy in Chicago and another group by the same name in Texas, which Boyd joined.

62 **Twenty-nine states**: Lawrence Lader, *Abortion* (Indianapolis: Bobbs–Merrill, 1966), 54–55. Lader compiled his list of states with "skilled abortionists" in 1964, three years before the formation of the Clergy Consultation Service.

62 **Boyd agreed to help**: Glenna Boyd, interview with the author, January 5, 2021.

62 **"I knew it was illegal"**: Curtis Boyd, interview with the author, July 27, 2012.

62 **"strike a blow"**: *Life Matters*, film.

63 **"you get charged"**: Curtis Boyd, interview with the author, July 27, 2012.

63 **"If the death"**: Texas Penal Code § 1194.435 (1961).

63 **"Do not have complications"**: Curtis Boyd, interview with the author, August 9, 2016.

63 **"I became quite a master"**: Curtis Boyd, interview with the author, September 1, 2016.

63 **a young Sioux woman**: Reminiscences of Dr. Curtis Boyd, Physicians for Reproductive Choice and Health Project, 2001, 11. Oral History Archives, Columbia University.

63 **"It was scary"**: Curtis Boyd, interview with the author, January 21, 2015.

63 **"The second-trimester"**: Curtis Boyd, interview with the author, September 1, 2016.

63 **"the days of honest abortion"**: Norman Mailer, *The Prisoner of Sex* (New York: Little, Brown, 1971), 140.

64 **"this is fabulous"**: Curtis Boyd, interview with the author, September 1, 2016.

64 **"I was the only one"**: Curtis Boyd, interview with the author, January 21, 2015.

64 **some six hundred**: Reminiscences of Dr. Curtis Boyd, 92.

64 **Such men were "scoundrels"**: Curtis Boyd, interview with the author, August 9, 2016.

64 **"they couldn't take"**: Curtis Boyd, interview with the author, April 4, 2019.

64 **earned some $100,000**: Curtis Boyd, interview with the author, November 5, 2015.

64 **he took in cash**: Eva Cox, interview with the author, November 10, 2016.

64 **"It was too painful"**: Curtis Boyd, interview with the author, June 30, 2016.

64 **"Once you start"**: Curtis Boyd, interview with the author, November 2, 2015.

65 **two to five years**: Texas Penal Code § 1191 (1961).

65 **"The town went wild"**: LaMerle Boyd, email to the author, October 24, 2016.

65 **"I believe in this"**: Eva Cox, interview with the author, August 1, 2016.

65 **"You're sitting in"**: Eva Cox, interview with the author, October 11, 2016.

65 **"I didn't understand"**: Eva Cox, interview with the author, August 1, 2016.

66 **a newspaper ad**: Eva Cox, interview with the author, October 11, 2016.

66 **"He used the word"**: Eva Cox, interview with the author, August 1, 2016.

66 **"how to draw blood"**: Eva Cox, interview with the author, August 1, 2016.

66 **"It's all over"**: Reminiscences of Dr. Curtis Boyd, 69.

67 **"Oops!"**: Norma McCorvey, interview with the author, November 5, 2013.

67 **to fight the sodomy**: McCluskey was counselor of record in *Buchanan v. Batchelor*, 308 F. Supp. 729 (N.D. Tex. 1970).

68 **"Something real physical"**: Linda Coffee, interview with the author, February 6, 2014.

68 **"I needed to participate"**: Linda Coffee, interview with the author, February 5, 2014.

68 **"When I had to call"**: Linda Coffee, interview with the author, February 7, 2014.

68 **"to do something fun"**: Linda Coffee, interview with the author, February 6, 2014.

68 **"pretty chaste"**: Linda Coffee, interview with the author, February 6, 2014.

69 **"women to control"**: Linda Coffee, interview with the author, February 6, 2014.

69 **"I was beginning"**: Linda Coffee, interview with the author, February 7, 2014.

69 **twenty-eight teens**: "Dallas Senior Ready for New Zealand Trip," *Dallas Morning News*, February 6, 1960.

69 **Ford Foundation grant**: Kay Crosby, "The Law Clerks Are Girls," *Dallas Morning News*, September 2, 1968.

69 **"failed a typing test"**: Linda Coffee, interview with the author, February 5, 2014.

69 **"I sort of did it"**: Linda Coffee, interview with the author, February 5, 2014.

69 **Human Rights Research Council**: Crosby, "The Law Clerks Are Girls."

69 **"the protection of individual"**: HRCC ad, *Austin American–Statesman*, April 13, 1975.

70 **"My voice"**: Linda Coffee, interview with the author, February 5, 2014.

70 **"Her tone changed"**: Linda Coffee, interview with the author, February 5, 2014.

70 **"was most satisfactory"**: Linda Coffee, interview with the author, February 5, 2014.

70 **"Oh, we'd only hire"**: Diane Jennings, "Legal Eagle: The woman who helped make history with Roe," *Dallas Morning News*, July 29, 1990.

70 **"Just overt discrimination"**: Linda Coffee, interview with the author, February 5, 2014.

71 **"We didn't have to have friends"**: Barbara McCluskey Gouge, interview with the author, January 10, 2011.

71 **the young McCluskey**: Barbara McCluskey Gouge, interview with the author, April 10, 2014.

71 **"that he was hoping"**: Linda Coffee, interview with the author, February 5, 2014.

71 **"I wanted to get experience"**: Linda Coffee, interview with the author, February 5, 2014.

71 **since 1860**: *Texas General Laws, 8th Session 1859-60*, ch. 6, p. 97.

71 **binding in 1879**: Dale Carpenter, *Flagrant Conduct: The Story of Lawrence v. Texas* (New York: Norton, 2012), 9.

72 **"You have the government"**: Linda Coffee, interview with the author, February 5, 2014.

72 **"I wasn't about to"**: Linda Coffee, interview with the author, February 5, 2014.

72 **McCluskey had graduated**: Program, memorial service for Henry McCluskey, July 12, 1973. Courtesy of Barbara McCluskey Gouge.

72 **"The clerk was desperate"**: Linda Coffee, interview with the author, February 5, 2014.

72 **"I analyzed it right"**: Linda Coffee, interview with the author, February 5, 2014.

72 **"somewhere between friendly"**: Linda Coffee, interview with the author, February 5, 2014.

73 **"it seemed that"**: Linda Coffee, interview with the author, February 5, 2014.

73 **"a live and let live"**: UPI, "Texas Lawyer Makes Dent in Male-Dominated Jobs," *Wichita Eagle*, February 11, 1972.

73 **"due process"**: Linda Greenhouse explained that the "due process" clause calls for "specificity, so that a citizen can know precisely what is or is not within the law." The California law, meantime, was unspecific, permitting abortions "necessary to preserve her life." Linda Greenhouse, "Constitutional Question: Is There a Right to Abortion?," *New York Times*, January 25, 1970.

73 **"I just thought"**: Linda Coffee, interview with the author, February 5, 2014.

73 **"some important fundamental"**: "Oral Memoirs of Linda Coffee," Patricia Duke, interviewer, April 17, 1973, 6. Collection: Special Project: *Roe v. Wade*, Baylor University Institute for Oral History.

73 **Women for Change**: "Oral Memoirs of Linda Coffee," 22.

73 **"something that held women back"**: Linda Coffee, interview with the author, February 6, 2014.

73 **"if a woman self-aborted"**: Linda Coffee, interview with the author, February 7, 2014.

73 **Roy Lucas would file**: "State Abortion Curb Challenged in Suit as a Violation of Rights," *New York Times*, October 1, 1969.

74 **"I couldn't figure out"**: Linda Coffee, interview with the author, February 5, 2014.

PART III: ROE V. WADE

77 **"like she got out"**: Norma McCorvey, interview with the author, November 5, 2013.

77 **"she looked really pregnant"**: Linda Coffee, interview with the author, February 5, 2014.

77 **estimates could be off**: Curtis Boyd, interview with the author, June 2, 2020.

77 **"We weren't using"**: Frank Bradley, interview with the author, May 27, 2020.

77 **only in Oregon**: 1969 Oregon Senate Bill 193.

77 **and in California**: California law mandated that "in no event shall the termination be approved after the 20th week of pregnancy." Cal. Health & Safety Code 25953.

77 **law in DC**: The case was *United States v. Vuitch*, 402 U.S. 62 (1971). The appellee was a doctor named Milan Vuitch. According to his son, a pathologist named Frank Vuitch who worked in his clinic a few years later in 1973, "in all likelihood, he did go beyond twenty weeks . . . I don't think he had a cutoff." He adds that his father had learned to do surgical abortions in Yugoslavia, where it was legal. Frank Vuitch, interview with the author, August 13, 2020.

78 **"It was my opinion"**: "Oral Memoirs of Linda Coffee," Patricia Duke, interviewer, April 17, 1973, 10. Collection: Special Project: *Roe v. Wade*, Baylor University Institute for Oral History.

78 **"There were fairly established"**: Linda Coffee, interview with the author, February 5, 2014.

78 **"I remember saying"**: Linda Coffee, interview with the author, February 5, 2014.

78 **"likely had no idea"**: Linda Coffee, interview with the author, February 5, 2014.

78 **"I could tell she didn't"**: Linda Coffee, interview with the author, February 5, 2014.

78 **"It had to be"**: Philip Brasher, "'Roe still doesn't rue her fight for abortion rights," *Chicago Tribune*, January 22, 1983.

79 **a 1959 lawsuit**: The case was *Buxton v. Ullman*. See David J. Garrow, *Liberty and Sexuality: The Right to Privacy and the Making of Roe v. Wade* (Berkeley: University of California Press, 1998), 154.

79 **"I considered her"**: Linda Coffee, interview with the author, February 5, 2014.

79 **a group of women in Austin**: Victoria Foe, interview with the author, September 24, 2020.

79 **"would open and aboveboard"**: Garrow, *Liberty and Sexuality*, 393.

79 **"I have received"**: Sarah Weddington, interview with Jeannette B. Cheek, March 12, 1976, 2. Schlesinger–Rockefeller Oral History Project, Sophia Smith Collection of Women's History, Smith College.

79 **Delta Gamma sorority**: Weddington, interview with Cheek, 5.

80 **a clinic south of the border**: It was not until 1992, with the writing of her memoir *A Question of Choice* (London: Penguin, 1993), that Weddington revealed she'd had an abortion.

80 **"could do whatever"**: Weddington, interview with Cheek, 2.

80 **soloing in the church**: Weddington, interview with Cheek, 2–3.

80 **"with research and secretarial"**: Weddington, *A Question of Choice*, 50.

80 **she phoned Linda Coffee**: Garrow, *Liberty and Sexuality*, 393.

80 **"Would you consider"**: Linda Coffee, letter to Sarah Weddington, December 4, 1969. Courtesy of Rebecca Hartt.

81 **all belly and blue jeans**: This is the only scene in the book I was unable to satisfactorily verify. Norma, Coffee and Weddington all recalled at various times that the meeting took place as described here. But on September 23, 1971, Weddington wrote, in a letter to the abortion reformer Virginia Whitehill: "Meeting Jane Roe was fascinating." It would thus seem that she had not first met Norma twenty months before at Columbo's. In 1992, the historian David Garrow pressed Weddington on this point. Responded Weddington: "I can tell you what I remember. I can't tell you what was true or not." What I know to be true is that Norma honestly recalled meeting Weddington on this evening. (She recalled doing so as early as 1981 in conversation with the *Dallas Times Herald*.) If Norma did not meet her then,

the conversation she recounted with Weddington took place at another time. Coffee had told Garrow that she wasn't certain the lawyers met with Norma together before filing *Roe*, and that her recollection of a meeting at the restaurant was fuzzy. But asked about it in 2019 by the author Karen Blumenthal, she recalled it as described here. She added that it was Marsha and David King (soon to be Mary and John Doe) who suggested the restaurant, and that they were present too. Asked about the meeting in 2020, Marsha King said that she did not recall it. Garrow, *Liberty and Sexuality*, 862. Linda Coffee, interview with Karen Blumenthal, August 16, 2019. Courtesy of Karen Blumenthal. Kaki King, email to the author, December 18, 2020.

81 **"She was wholesome"**: Norma McCorvey, interview with the author, November 5, 2013.

81 **"I'm not saying"**: Norma McCorvey, interview with the author, November 5, 2013.

81 **"in desperate situations"**: Victoria Foe, email to the author, June 14, 2020.

81 **"American [Airlines]"**: Sarah Weddington, recorded interview with Luz Moreno-Lozano, *Austin American–Statesman*, June 16, 2019. Courtesy of Karen Blumenthal and Luz Moreno-Lozano.

82 **"solely for the benefit"**: "ABA 2018 Edition Compendium of Professional Responsibility Rules and Standards," ABA Model Code of Professional Responsibility, Disciplinary Rule (DR) 5–101: "Refusing Employment When the Interests of the Lawyer May Impair His Independent Professional Judgment." The Model Code was approved by the ABA House of Delegates on August 12, 1969. Rule 5–101 (A) reads: "Except with the consent of his client after full disclosure, a lawyer shall not accept employment if the exercise of his professional judgment on behalf of his client will be or reasonably may be affected by his own financial, business, property, or personal interests."

82 **"the collective interests"**: Kevin C. McMunigal, "Of Causes and Clients: Two Tales of *Roe v. Wade*," *Hastings Law Journal* 47, no. 3 (1996): 811.

82 **An abortion in Mexico**: Garrow, *Liberty and Sexuality*, 393.

82 **to see *Swan Lake***: Norma McCorvey, interview with the author, November 5, 2013. The performance, by the American Ballet Theater, was on February 21, 1970. *Dallas Morning News*, February 1, 1970.

83 **"the right to be let alone"**: Thomas M. Cooley, *Cooley on Torts, Or, A Treatise on the Law of Torts*, 2nd ed (Chicago: Callaghan and Co., 1888), 29.

83 **Brandeis then championed**: Samuel D. Warren and Louis D. Brandeis, "The Right to Privacy," *Harvard Law Review* 4, no. 5 (December 15, 1890).

83 **"the most comprehensive"**: *Olmstead v. United States*, 277 U.S. 438 (1928) (Justice Brandeis, dissenting).

83 **"the sacred precincts"**: *Griswold v. Connecticut*, 381 U.S. 479 (1965).

83 **"penumbras"**: *Griswold v. Connecticut*.

84 **"At that time"**: Linda Coffee, interview with the author, February 5, 2014.

84 **Coffee described Roe**: "Facts," March 3, 1970, p. 11, *Roe v. Wade*, 410 U.S. 113 (1973).

84 **"You almost had to argue"**: Linda Coffee, interview with the author, February 6, 2014.

84 **"Sarah didn't want"**: Linda Coffee, interview with the author, February 7, 2014.

85 **his phone number listed**: Kim Wade, email to the author, June 21, 2016.

85 **seek thirty death sentences**: Wolfgang Saxon, "Henry Wade, Prosecutor in National Spotlight, Dies at 86," *New York Times*, March 2, 2001.

85 **his older brother**: Kim Wade, email to the author, June 21, 2016.

85 **"My father was open-minded"**: Kim Wade, interview with the author, January 22, 2015.

85 **"I don't think"**: Kim Wade, interview with the author, January 22, 2015.

85 **would confide in his son**: Kim Wade, interview with the author, January 22, 2015.

85 **"was not anti-abortion"**: Kim Wade, interview with the author, March 5, 2014.

86 **ought to have named**: On May 22, 1970, during the *Roe* hearing in federal district court, a judge named Irving Goldberg raised this point to Coffee and Weddington. "We goofed," acknowledged Weddington. The mistake would prove academic as the district court would eventually decline to grant an injunction against Wade even as it found the law unconstitutional. Moreover, the Texas attorney general, Crawford Martin, had his office take over the case from Wade.

86 **her suit would not end**: Barbara Milbauer, *The Law Giveth: Legal Aspects of the Abortion Controversy* (New York: Atheneum, 1983), 12.

86 **"all other women"**: Plaintiff's First Amended Complaint, April 16, 1970, *Roe v. Wade*, 410 U.S. 113 (1973).

86 **Its central claims**: Affidavit of Jane Roe in Support of Plaintiffs' Motion for Summary Judgment, May 21, 1970, p. 56, *Roe v. Wade*, 410 U.S. 113 (1973).

87 **Judge John R. Brown**: Garrow, *Liberty and Sexuality*, 436.

87 **"very much opposed"**: John Tolle, interview with the author, June 17, 2016.

87 **"She thought she had"**: John Tolle, interview with the author, June 28, 2016.

88 **"We knew that baby"**: John Tolle, interview with the author, June 28, 2016.

88 **jurisdiction and standing**: Linda Coffee, interview with the author, February 5, 2014.

88 **the *Dallas Morning News***: Earl Golz, "Jurist Panel Rules Texas Abortion Law Void," *Dallas Morning News*, June 18, 1970.

88 **"Quite a victory"**: Martha Liebrum, "The Young Lawyers in the Abortion Battle," *Houston Post*, June 23, 1970.

88 **Coffee petitioned the judges**: "Judges Asked to Air Abortion Law Ruling," *Dallas Morning News*, November 26, 1970.

88 **Coffee told the press**: "Judges Asked to Air Abortion Law Ruling."

89 **6:51 a.m.**: Shelley Thornton, email to the author, December 30, 2012.

89 **Coffee explained to Weddington**: Linda Coffee, interview with Karen Blumenthal, August 16, 2019.

89 **"Never in a million years"**: Linda Coffee, interview with the author, February 5, 2014.

89 **At least eight times**: Linda Greenhouse and Reva B. Siegel, *Before Roe v. Wade: Voices that Shaped the Abortion Debate Before the Supreme Court's Ruling* (New Haven: Yale Law School, 2012), 124.

89 **"the mother's life"**: "An Act to establish a code of law for the District of Columbia," Section 809, approved March 3, 1901, amended in DC Code, Section 22–201.

89 **agreed to hear Roe**: in *No. 808 Roe et al. v. Wade, District Attorney of Dallas County*, the Court issued an order on May 3, 1971, noting "probable jurisdiction postponed to hearing of case on the merits." The proper citation for the order is 402 U.S. 941.

89 **Weddington exulted**: Weddington, *A Question of Choice*, 90.

89 ***Johnston v. Luna***: Coffee filed *Johnston v. Luna* on December 17, 1971, and won the case on January 20, 1972. Earl Golz, "Filing Fee Law Voided," *Dallas Morning News*, January 21, 1972.

89 **"They were embarrassed"**: Peggy Clewis, interview with the author, September 13, 2016.

89 **"She was younger"**: Linda Coffee, interview with the author, February 6, 2014.

90 **moot courts and mirrors**: Weddington, interview with Cheek, 21.

90 **"Linda worked with me"**: Weddington, interview with Cheek, 20.

90 **footing many bills**: Bowers donated $10,000, Cabot $15,000. Garrow, *Liberty and Sexuality*, 500.

90 **"vehicles for presenting"**: Weddington, *A Question of Choice*, 67.

90 **Lucas made clear**: Weddington, *A Question of Choice*, 110.

90 **"The clients in a case"**: Weddington, *A Question of Choice*, 110.

90 **"Sarah got in touch"**: Norma McCorvey and Andy Meisler, *I Am Roe: My Life, Roe V. Wade, and Freedom of Choice* (New York: HarperCollins, 1994), 139.

90 **"respond in a personal way"**: Weddington, interview with Cheek, 22.

90 **"She was rather attractive"**: Betty Wells, interview with the author, August 13, 2019.

91 **"large blond hair"**: Harry Blackmun, note, December 15, 1971, "No. 70–18–ATX," HABP, Box 152, Folder 2.

91 **"Since I wasn't arguing"**: Linda Coffee, interview with the author, February 6, 2014.

91 **"elegant opinions"**: Linda Coffee, interview with the author, February 6, 2014.

91 **that same amendment**: Weddington, *A Question of Choice*, 104.

91 **"to determine the course"**: Sarah Weddington, oral argument, December 13, 1971, *Roe v. Wade*, 410 U.S. 113 (1973).

91 **C+**: Blackmun, "No. 70–18–ATX."

91 **eighth in twelve months**: From June 20, 1970, up to (but not including)

December 13, 1971, sixteen women (Doris Bray, Eleanor Piel, Anna Lavin and Maria Marcus, Brenda Soloff, Malvine Nathanson, Doris Friedman Ulman, Elizabeth B. DuBois, Louise H. Renne, Mary Carol Los, Sybil H. Landau, Louise Korns, Elizabeth Roediger Rindskopf, Dorothy T. Beasley, Beatrice Rosenberg and Christine Y. Denson) presented a total of eighteen arguments at the Supreme Court. Marlene Trestman, "Women Advocates Before the Supreme Court, October Terms 1880 Through 1999," table, Supreme Court Historical Society—History of Oral Advocacy, http://supremecourthistory.org/history_oral_advocates.html.

91 **"When a man argues"**: Jay Floyd, oral argument, December 13, 1971, *Roe v. Wade*, 410 U.S. 113 (1973).

91 **"is no longer pregnant"**: Floyd, oral argument, *Roe v. Wade*.

91 **"squarely built"**: Blackmun wrote "sq, nice lookg." His secretary Wanda Martinson, versed in his shorthand, guessed that "sq" stood for "squarely built." Wanda Martinson, email to the author, September 7, 2016.

91 **five of the seven**: Garrow, *Liberty and Sexuality*, 532.

92 **"I'd give my eyeteeth"**: Nancy Blackmun, interview with the author, September 9, 2014.

92 **"Dad saw at close range"**: Nancy Blackmun, eulogy for Harry A. Blackmun, March 9, 1999, https://www.c-span.org/video/?121702–1/justice-blackmun-memorial-service.

92 **"She was a single mom"**: Nancy Blackmun, interview with the author, September 9, 2014.

92 **dropped out of school**: Linda Greenhouse, *Becoming Justice Blackmun* (New York: Times Books, 2005), 76.

92 **"in the treatment"**: Harry A. Blackmun, testimony, U.S. Senate, Committee on the Judiciary, On the Nomination of Harry A. Blackmun to be an Associate Justice of the Supreme Court, 91st Cong., 2nd sess., 1970.

92 **"a lawyer in Washington"**: Harold Koh, eulogy for Harry A. Blackmun, March 9, 1999, https://www.c-span.org/video/?121702–1/justice-blackmun-memorial-service.

93 **Burger assigned both cases**: "I suspect that about age five or six we were packed off to Sunday School by our respective mothers and that's where we first learned to know each other." The Justice Harry A. Blackmun Oral History Project, Harold H. Koh, interviewer, 49. HABP.

93 **"The insider speculation"**: George Frampton, interview with the author, October 5, 2016.

93 **"Would your well-stocked library"**: Harry A. Blackmun, letter to Thomas E. Keys, December 17, 1971. HABP, Box 152, Folder 2.

93 **"Apparently, we're free"**: Dave McNeely, "Wade to Continue Abortion Trials," *Dallas Morning News*, June 19, 1970.

93 **"Don't bet your safety"**: Curtis Boyd, interview with the author, June 30, 2016.

93 **"A police car"**: Curtis Boyd, interview with the author, June 30, 2016.

94 **One was New Mexico**: Greenhouse and Siegel, *Before Roe v. Wade*, 121–22.

94 **to wear something red:** Eva Cox, interview with the author, August 1, 2016.

95 **"he was meticulous":** Eva Cox, interview with the author, August 1, 2016.

95 **perforated her uterus:** Curtis Boyd, interview with the author, August 9, 2016.

95 **"the women were gone":** Eva Cox, interview with the author, August 1, 2016.

95 **Blackmun liked to work:** John Rich (Justice Blackmun's clerk), interview with the author, November 17, 2014. Wanda S. Martinson, Justice Blackmun's secretary, interview with the author, November 28, 2014. Nancy Blackmun, interview with the author, November 29, 2014.

95 **"to throw some question":** Nancy Blackmun, interview with the author, September 9, 2014.

96 **"You people":** Nancy Blackmun, interview with the author, September 9, 2014.

96 **"insufficiently informative":** Harry A. Blackmun, cover letter to his fellow justices regarding *Roe v. Wade*, May 18, 1972. HABP, Box 151, Folder 3.

96 **"a first and tentative":** Blackmun, cover letter to his fellow justices.

96 **"a disposition":** William Brennan, note to Harry A. Blackmun, May 18, 1972. Potter Stewart Papers, MS 1367, Box 268, Folder 3194. Yale University Library.

96 **"The *Roe* case":** John Rich, interview with the author, September 16, 2015.

96 **about the Fifth:** John Rich, "Communist Registration and the Fifth Amendment," *University of Florida Law Review* 15, no. 435 (1962).

96 **a judge whose work:** Judge David L. Bazelon served on the United States Court of Appeals for the District of Columbia Circuit.

97 **bench memo:** "Bench Memo: Roe v. Wade." HABP, Box 151, Folder 9, 164437.

97 **another memo:** The memo is numbered through page 13 but there are two pages numbered 11. Harry A. Blackmun, "No. 70–18—Roe v. Wade. Notes on Proposed Opinion." HABP, Box 151, Folder 9, 165540.

97 **"requires only nutrition":** Greenhouse and Siegel, *Before Roe v. Wade*, 240.

97 **"to serve as an incubator":** Greenhouse and Siegel, *Before Roe v. Wade*, 234.

97 **far from the law:** George Frampton, interview with the author, October 5, 2016.

97 **"nice, modest, sweet":** George Frampton, interview with the author, October 5, 2016.

97 **"You write the legal":** George Frampton, interview with the author, October 5, 2016.

98 **Blackmun was off:** Blackmun biographer Melissa Nathanson found the dates of his drive in handwritten notations in his 1972 desk diary (July 21: "en route home"; July 22: "en route home"; July 23: "arrive Roch."). HABP, Box 60, Folder 9.

98 **"the criminalization":** Greenhouse, *Becoming Justice Blackmun*, 92.

98 **"I didn't want them":** George Frampton, interview with the author, October 5, 2016.

98 **"he took that"**: George Frampton, interview with the author, October 5, 2016.

98 **"the decision to have"**: The percentages of Republicans, Democrats and Catholics that agreed with that sentence were 68, 59 and 56 percent, respectively. George Gallup, "Abortion Seen Up To Woman, Doctor," *Washington Post*, August 25, 1972.

98 **"intelligent, educated men"**: Rena Pederson, "Woman's Views," *El Dorado Times*, February 7, 1972.

98 **"I could not bear"**: Weddington, *A Question of Choice*, 91.

99 **charged with manslaughter**: David Westin, "Citizen Lewis Powell," *Washington and Lee Law Review Online* 72, no. 1 (2015).

99 **"The life of the law"**: Oliver Wendell Holmes, Jr., *The Common Law* (Boston: Little, Brown, 1881), 1.

100 **Justice Tom Clark**: Tom C. Clark, "Religion, Morality, and Abortion: A Constitutional Appraisal," *Loyola of Los Angeles Law Review* 2, no. 1 (1969). "Others . . . believe that abortion should be legal until the baby is viable, i.e., able to support itself outside the womb."

100 **lawyer named Cyril Means**: Means wrote that "after 24 weeks . . . more and more foetus become viable." Cyril C. Means, Jr., "The Phoenix of Abortional Freedom: Is a Penumbral or Ninth-Amendment Right About to Arise from the Nineteenth-Century Legislative Ashes of a Fourteenth-Century Common-Law Liberty?," *New York Law Forum* 17, no. 2 (1971): 390.

100 **"Viability seemed"**: George Frampton, interview with the author, October 5, 2016.

100 **Jon O. Newman**: *Abele v. Markle*, 351 F. Supp. 224 (1972). At least two other nations had previously connected viability to abortion law. In 1929, the Infant Life (Preservation) Act in England outlawed aborting "a child capable of being born alive." And in 1935, Germany (under Nazi rule), amended its Law for the Prevention of Hereditarily Diseased Progeny to allow abortions on eugenic grounds until "the foetus is already capable of independent life." See Michael Burleigh and Wolfgang Wippermann, *The Racial State: Germany 1933–1945* (Cambridge: Cambridge University Press, 1991), 140–41.

100 **"the 'compelling' point"**: Harry A. Blackmun, opinion, *Roe v. Wade*, 410 U.S. 113 (1973).

100 **complimentary even in dissent**: William Rehnquist, letter to Harry A. Blackmun, "Re: Abortion Cases: No. 70–18 – Roe v. Wade and No. 70–40 – Doe v. Bolton," November 24, 1972. HABP, Box 151, Folder 4.

100 **"It will be"**: Blackmun notepad. HABP, Box 151, folder 8: 171622.

101 **decrying abortion in a debate**: Paul Harrington, letter to Mildred Jefferson, July 28, 1970. Rev. Paul V. Harrington Papers, Box 1, Folder 2, Archdiocese of Boston archive. The folder is titled "Abortion, 1968–1970."

101 **"Instead of simply rehashing"**: Daniel K. Williams, *Defenders of the Unborn: The Pro-Life Movement Before Roe v. Wade* (New York: Oxford University Press, 2016), 133.

101 **1.5 million copies**: Greenhouse and Siegel, *Before Roe v. Wade*, 99.

102 **"the Catholic Bishops"**: Paul Harrington, letter to Mildred Jefferson, July 28, 1970.

102 **"not so much 'against abortion'"**: Mildred Jefferson, letter to Paul Harrington, September 14, 1970. Rev. Paul V. Harrington Papers, Box 1, Folder 2, Archdiocese of Boston archive.

102 **"their destruction"**: Michael Shea, "Fetal Rights & Traditional Values," *The Heights* 51, no. 13 (December 7, 1970): 11.

102 **"sought for economic"**: "Value of Life Committee, Inc. brochure." MJP, Box 15, Folder 6.

102 **"educated rhythm"**: Judy Klemesrud, "Abortion in the Campaign: Methodist Surgeon Leads the Opposition," *New York Times*, March 1, 1976.

102 **"presented women as victims"**: Williams, *Defenders of the Unborn*, 150.

102 **"The woman who arranges"**: Jefferson, "Abortion: Self-Defeat Solution," 9.

102 **"Society's efforts"**: Jefferson, "Abortion: Self-Defeat Solution," 9.

102 **"scientific evidence"**: Jefferson, "Abortion: Self-Defeat Solution," 8.

103 **"20–tooth smile"**: Mildred Jefferson, memo to Nancy Southworth, NRSC, January 29, 1982. MJP, Box 19, Folder 2.

103 **"he had to accompany her"**: Shane Cunningham, interview with the author, June 4, 2016.

103 **"singleness of purpose"**: "Harvard Graduates First Negro Woman Doctor," *Boston Globe*, June 22, 1951.

103 **"a black female"**: FBI case file for Mildred Fay Jefferson, no. 161–HQ-9379, 41. Interview with John J. Byrne, March 14, 1973.

103 **"refused to do so"**: FBI case file for Mildred Fay Jefferson, no. 161–HQ-9379, 67. Interview with Richard H. Egdahl, March 12, 1973.

103 **"I have found"**: Otile McManus, "Dr. Jefferson and her Fight Against Abortion," *Boston Sunday Globe*, December 3, 1976.

104 **"the essence and reasons"**: Mildred Jefferson, interview with Jennifer Donnally, October 22, 2007. Interviews of Jennifer M. Donnally, 2007–2012, MC1059, Box 60, CD 6. Schlesinger Library, Harvard University.

104 **"I believe that biology"**: McManus, "Dr. Jefferson and her Fight."

104 **"right-to-life organizations"**: Mildred Jefferson, testimony, U.S. Senate, Committee on the Judiciary, Subcommittee on Constitutional Amendments, hearing on "Abortion," August 21, 1974. 93rd Cong., 2nd sess.

104 **gained little traction**: Williams, *Defenders of the Unborn*, 4.

105 **"We need to make"**: On February, 24, 1969, Bush spoke in the U.S. House of Representatives regarding H.B. 4207. 91st Cong., 1st sess. *Congressional Record* 115, part 4, 4207.

105 **"No American woman"**: Richard M. Nixon, "Special Message to the Congress on Problems of Population Growth," July 18, 1969. Available at the American Presidency Project, https://www.presidency.ucsb.edu/documents/special-message-the-congress-problems-population-growth.

105 **Nixon would soon sign**: Nixon enacted his plan through Title X of the Public Health Service Act.

105 **rich in political opportunity**: Linda Greenhouse and Reva B. Siegel, "Before (and After) *Roe v. Wade*: New Questions About Backlash," *Yale Law Review* 120 (2011): 2028. In the 1969 book *The Emerging Republican Majority* (New York: Arlington House, 1969), Republican strategist Kevin P. Philips identified northern Catholics as a voting bloc ripe for picking.

105 **prompted by a memo**: On March 24, 1971, Pat Buchanan suggested in a memo to Richard Nixon that he "publicly take his stand against abortion, as offensive to his own moral principles." Cited in report of the U.S. Senate, Select Committee on Presidential Campaign Activities (the Watergate Committee), June 27, 1974, p. 4150.

105 **"unwanted fertility"**: John D. Rockefeller III, letter concerning the report of the Rockefeller Commission on Population Growth and the American Future, "Rockefeller Commission Report," March 27, 1972.

105 **"Abortion on demand"**: Richard Nixon, "Statement About Policy on Abortions at Military Base Hospitals in the United States," April 3, 1971. Available at the American Presidency Project, https://www.presidency.ucsb.edu/documents/statement-about-policy-abortions-military-base-hospitals-the-united-states.

105 **defeat all twenty-five**: Williams, *Defenders of the Unborn*, 2.

105 **judicial rulings legalized**: Williams, *Defenders of the Unborn*, 195, and Daniel Williams, email to the author, August 12, 2016.

105 **church funded ads**: John T. McGreevy, *Catholicism and American Freedom: A History* (New York: Norton, 2003), 277.

106 **"Right to life"**: Greenhouse and Siegel, *Before Roe v. Wade*, 33.

106 **"to legislate"**: Jefferson, "Abortion: Self-Defeat Solution," 9.

106 **"the perfect, the privileged"**: UPI, "Right to Life Committee Criticizes Abortion Ruling," *Sunday News* (Ridgewood, NJ), March 11, 1973.

106 **"no snippets of autobiography"**: Williams, *Defenders of the Unborn*, 172.

106 **"to get rid of the boy"**: "Advocates, Should Women Be Permitted Abortion on Demand?" WGBH, December 14, 1972. Available at http://americanarchive.org/catalog/cpb-aacip_15–79v15v8h.

106 **"This makes a mush"**: "Advocates; 311."

107 **"The alternative"**: "Advocates; 311."

107 **"feels she simply cannot"**: "Advocates; 311."

107 **"Having a baby"**: "Advocates; 311."

107 **"Their impact"**: Garrow, *Liberty and Sexuality*, 579.

107 **"I remember watching"**: Philip Moran, interview with the author, September 7, 2017.

107 **the governor of California**: The debate aired in Sacramento on December 14, 1972. *Sacramento Bee*, December 14, 1972 (TV listing).

107 **"humanitarian goals"**: Korman, "Gov. Reagan To Sign New Abortion Bill."

107 **Reagan had not thought**: Seymour Korman, "Gov. Reagan To Sign New Abortion Bill," *Chicago Tribune*, June 14, 1967.

108 **"I had to tell you"**: Ronald Reagan, letter to Mildred Jefferson, January 17, 1973. Courtesy of National Right to Life Committee.

109 **"The abortion issue"**: Harry A. Blackmun, statement. HABP, Box 151, Folder 3.

109 **"the deep and seemingly"**: Blackmun, statement. HABP, Box 151, Folder 3.

109 **"embarrassment to my family"**: Gloria Feldt and Laura Fraser, *The War on Choice: The Right-Wing Attack on Women's Rights and How to Fight Back* (New York: Bantam, 2004), xvi.

110 **"the health of the pregnant woman"**: Blackmun, statement, Box 151, Folder 3.

110 **participate in 3,874 rulings**: Greenhouse, *Becoming Justice Blackmun*, xii.

110 **A team of printers**: Supreme Court Historical Society, "De Minimus, or Judicial Potpourri," Yearbook 1977, 96–98.

110 **"a major contribution"**: "Respect for Privacy," *New York Times*, January 24, 1973.

110 **"wise and sound"**: "Abortion: Out of the 19th Century," *Washington Post*, January 31, 1973.

110 **"struck a reasonable balance"**: "Abortion and Privacy," *Wall Street Journal*, January 26, 1973.

110 **"the right of a [public]"**: *Lochner v. New York*, 198 U.S. 45 (1905) (Justice Holmes, dissenting).

110 **"the counter-majoritarian"**: Alexander M. Bickell, *The Least Dangerous Branch: The Supreme Court at the Bar of Politics* (New Haven: Yale University Press, 1986), 16.

111 **"from Congress and States"**: *Griswold v. Connecticut*, 38 U.S. 479 (1965) (Justice Black, dissenting).

111 **"an exercise of raw"**: *Roe v. Wade* (Justice White, dissenting).

111 **"Picketed!"**: "Chronology of Significant Events" (handwritten lists for each Supreme Court term). HABP, Box 1548, Folder 4.

111 **"morally indistinguishable"**: Williams, *Defenders of the Unborn*, 206, footnote.

111 **William Buckley**: "Court Decides When Life Begins," *Omaha World–Herald*, February 1, 1973.

111 **"for paganism"**: "Abortion and the Court," *Christianity Today*, February 16, 1973.

111 **"erroneous, unjust"**: Administrative Committee of the National Conference of Catholic Bishops, "Pastoral Message on Abortion," February 13, 1973.

111 **"Liebesleid"**: The piece was written for violin by Friedrich Kreisler. Nancy Blackmun, eulogy for Harry A. Blackmun, March 9, 1999, https://www.c-span.org/video/?121702–1/justice-blackmun-memorial-service.

111 **eighty thousand letters**: Feldt and Fraser, *The War on Choice*, xx.

111 **recalling decades later**: U.S. Supreme Court 1995 oral history interview, the Justice Harry A. Blackmun Oral History Project, HABP.

111 **initially to void the Texas law**: Harry A. Blackmun, cover letter to his fellow justices regarding *Roe v. Wade*, May 18, 1972. HABP, Box 151, Folder 4.

112 **"wise and courageous"**: Lawrence Van Gelder, "Cardinals Shocked—Reaction Mixed," *New York Times*, January 23, 1973.

112 **"this ruling will mean"**: Roberta Brandes Gratz, "Never Again," *Ms.*, April 1973.

112 **"It's all over"**: *Life Matters: The Story of an Illegal Abortionist*, directed by Kyle Boyd, Grayscale, 2002. Available at: https://www.pbs.org/independentlens/lifematters/film.html.

112 **"we walked around"**: Eva Cox, interview with the author, August 1, 2016.

112 **a doctor in Texas**: Weddington, *A Question of Choice*, 185.

112 **the first legal clinic**: Curtis Boyd, "The Morality of Abortion: The Making of a Feminist Physician," *St. Louis University Public Law Review* 13, no. 1 (1993–94): 303–14.

112 **"Preachers were preaching"**: *Life Matters*, film.

112 **"My commitment was"**: Curtis Boyd, interview with the author, June 30, 2016.

112 **"He would not agree"**: LaMerle Boyd, email to the author, July 30, 2016.

113 **The IRS made**: Associated Press, "Cost of Abortions, Vasectomies and Pills Ruled Tax Deductible," *New York Times*, April 11, 1973.

113 **insurance companies included**: "Most Insurers Are Paying for Abortions," *American Medical News*, March 26, 1973.

113 **thirty-four states**: Christopher Tietze, "Provisional Estimates of Abortion Need & Services in the Year Following the 1973 Supreme Court Decisions: United States, each state and metropolitan area," Guttmacher Institute, 1975, 88.

113 **745,000 women**: "The Unmet Need for Abortion Services in the U.S.," *Family Planning Perspectives* 7 (1975): 224–30.

113 **"to put a contract"**: Mildred Jefferson, "For Life—Against Abortion," *Encore*, March 1973.

113 **"photo-postcards"**: Martha Hume, "Abortion in Texas," *Texas Monthly*, March 1974.

113 **"an extermination complex"**: Mildred Jefferson, "The Biology and Morality of Abortion," February 4, 1973, 16. MJP, Box 22, Folder 11.

113 **"to provide abortion"**: National Conference of Catholic Bishops, statement of the Committee for Pro-Life Affairs, January 24, 1973.

113 **"almost no public hospitals"**: Lawrence Lader, letter to Alan Reitman, April 23, 1973, National Abortion Rights Action League. Records of the National Abortion Rights Action League 1968–1976, Carton 8. Schlesinger Library, Harvard University.

113 **"human life amendments"**: Rep. Lawrence J. Hogan (R–MD), January 30, 1973. The amendment resolved that the Fourteenth Amendment would protect the personhood of the fetus "from the moment of conception."

113 **"there are no cases"**: Weddington, *A Question of Choice*, 105.

114 **sixteen state legislatures**: Planned Parenthood, "Could the Supreme Court Abortion Decisions Be Lost? Yes!," April 1973. Wilda Scott Heide Papers, Box 11, Folder 12. Schlesinger Library, Harvard University.

114 **"effectively redefined the movement"**: Williams, *Defenders of the Unborn*, 215.

114 **carried representatives**: Darla St. Martin (co-executive director of NRLC), interview with the author, September 27, 2016.

114 **NRLC elected Mildred**: Mildred Jefferson, interview with Darla St. Martin. On June 8, 1973, Mildred is listed as the vice-chair of the NRLC board.

114 **wished to appoint her**: The name of the board was the Board of Regents of the Armed Services Medical College.

114 **"all . . . comment favorably"**: L. Patrick Gray III, letter to Alexander P. Butterfield, March 19, 1973. FBI case file for Mildred Fay Jefferson, no. 161–HQ-9379, 80.

114 **"a superior woman"**: FBI case file for Mildred Fay Jefferson, no. 161–HQ-9379, 59. Interview with Sidney Farber, March 9, 1973.

114 **"possible resentment"**: FBI case file for Mildred Fay Jefferson, no. 161–HQ-9379, 59. Interview with Sidney Farber, March 9, 1973.

114 **"We will consider"**: "30,000 at life rally in St. Louis." *National Right to Life News* 1, no. 1 (November 1973): 2.

114 **"I am not willing"**: Charlene Prost, "Thousands in March Against Abortion," *St. Louis Dispatch*, October 22, 1973.

115 **An article she wrote**: W. Kenneth Waller and Mildred F. Jefferson, "Prevention and repair of stricture of the extrahepatic bile ducts," *Surgical Clinics of North America* 5, no. 5 (October 1973): 1169.

115 **abortion cases were pending**: Weddington, *A Question of Choice*, 79.

115 **spoke first of LBJ**: Weddington, *A Question of Choice*, 159.

115 **flooded her office with flowers**: Weddington, *A Question of Choice*, 158–59.

115 **"who submitted the class"**: Louise Cook, "Abortion Ruling Reaction Mixed," *Pittsburgh Post–Gazette*, January 23, 1973.

115 **"I don't particularly care"**: Linda Coffee, interview with the author, February 6, 2014.

115 **"she was proud"**: Robert O'Brien, interview with the author, October 20, 2016.

115 **"the emotional, mental and physical"**: Southern Baptist Convention, "Resolution on Abortion," June 1, 1971.

115 **she felt the law**: Said Coffee: "I haven't decided whether it's possible to really protect the fetus or not . . . I do think that we don't need any law in the second trimester." "Oral Memoirs of Linda Coffee," 11.

115 **"would have little personal sympathy"**: Robert O'Brien, "Abortion Decision Leaves Moral Responsibility to Individual," *Baptist Standard*, January 31, 1973. The article ran in slightly different form with slightly different quotes a few days prior in the Baptist Press, the news service of the Southern Baptist Convention.

116 **"is essentially a matter"**: Linda Coffee, interview with the author, February 7, 2014.

116 **did not have that faith**: Rebecca Hartt, interview with the author, February 5, 2014.

116 **supported Shirley Chisholm**: UPI, "Texas Lawyer Makes Dent in Male-Dominated Jobs," *Wichita Eagle*, February 11, 1972.

116 **Gonzalez, the manager**: Notes of Joseph N. Bell. Courtesy of Bell's widow, Sherry Angel. Over the years, Norma would tell and write a different story, namely that Connie had been working in that market when she spotted Norma shoplifting. But Norma's first account of their meeting,

told to Bell in 1973, was different. In his article for *Good Housekeeping* ("A Landmark Decision," June 1973), Bell noted that days after Gonzales hired Norma, she calmed her down after three drunk men scared her at the register.

116 **"my little boy"**: Melissa Mills, interview with the author, February 24, 2017.

116 **their fifth surviving child**: Consuela Gonzalez, certificate of birth, February 5, 1931, Bureau of Vital Statistics, Texas Department of Health.

117 **Father Antonio**: Mary Helen Sandoval, interview with the author, October 14, 2016.

117 **never got pregnant again**: Mary Helen Sandoval, interview with the author, October 14, 2016.

117 **"She was seen in public"**: Mary Helen Sandoval, interview with the author, October 14, 2016.

117 **"I told her"**: Consuela Gonzales, interview with the author, June 29, 2010.

117 **selling an underground newspaper**: Transcript of meeting between Norma McCorvey and Allan Parker and other members of the Texas Justice Foundation, February 14, 2000. NMP.

117 **"mostly downers"**: Norma McCorvey, interview with the author, November 4, 2013.

117 **tried to kill herself**: Norma McCorvey, interview with the author, November 4, 2013.

117 **"It was clean"**: Norma McCorvey, interview with the author, November 4, 2013.

118 **"I always felt"**: Transcript of meeting between Norma McCorvey and Allan Parker et al.

118 **"rough as a cob"**: Dan Matise, interview with the author, November 23, 2018.

118 **earned twenty dollars**: Saundra Clark (building manager), interview with the author, November 21, 2018.

118 **"poison parties"**: Norma McCorvey, interview with the author, November 5, 2013.

118 **she was the plaintiff**: Monika Maeckle, "The Double Life of Norma McCorvey," *Westwood Magazine* (supplement of *Dallas Times Herald*), October 18, 1981. The next year, Norma told the *Dallas Morning News* that she learned of the *Roe* ruling from a newspaper delivered to her front door. Mimi Eckstein, "Plaintiff Has No Regrets," *Dallas Morning News*, January 22, 1982.

118 **"It's great to know"**: The Baptist Press did not come out Saturday or Sunday, so O'Brien, wanting to get his story out immediately, shared his scoop with the Associated Press, which ran it on Saturday, January 27. The Baptist Press ran the story on Monday, January 29, a week after *Roe*. Robert O'Brien, interview with the author, November 21, 2018. Associated Press, "Abortion Reformer Sheds 'Jane Roe,'" *Dallas Morning News*, January 27, 1973. Robert O'Brien, "Abortion Case Plaintiff Sheds 'Jane Roe' Identity," Baptist Press, January 29, 1973.

118 **"It's hard to determine"**: Associated Press, "Abortion Reformer Sheds 'Jane Roe.'"

119 **the *Dallas Morning News***: Associated Press, "Abortion Reformer Sheds 'Jane Roe.'"

119 **The Blackmun opinion**: *Roe v. Wade*, Section IV A: "Jane Roe. Despite the use of the pseudonym, no suggestion is made that Roe is a fictitious person. For purposes of her case, we accept as true, and as established, her existence; her pregnant state, as of the inception of her suit in March 1970 and as late as May 21 of that year when she filed an alias affidavit with the District Court; and her inability to obtain a legal abortion in Texas."

119 **Jane Roe had delivered**: Associated Press, "Abortion Plaintiff Had Baby," *Chicago Tribune*, January 23, 1973.

119 **"to avert the possibility"**: Associated Press, "Abortion Plaintiff Had Baby."

119 **her red plastic datebook**: Undated. Courtesy of Melissa Mills.

119 **Norma lied**: Joseph N. Bell, "A Landmark Decision," *Good Housekeeping*, June 1973.

119 **wondering how many months**: Rehnquist wrote: "a necessary predicate for such an opinion is a plaintiff who was in her first trimester of pregnancy at some time during the pendency of her law-suit." In other words, for a suit to have merit, the plaintiff needed to file it during her first trimester. Norma filed her case in early March, at roughly the start of her third trimester.

120 **"illegitimate" child**: Item number four mentions "the social stigma attached to the bearing of illegitimate children in our society." Affidavit of Jane Roe in Support of Plaintiffs' Motion for Summary Judgment, May 21, 1970, p. 56, *Roe v. Wade*, 410 U.S. 113 (1973).

120 **"who looked ten feet tall"**: Bell, "A Landmark Decision."

120 **she had no idea**: Bell, "A Landmark Decision."

120 **"Neither Linda nor I"**: Weddington, *A Question of Choice*, 273.

120 **two fishermen found her friend**: "Extradition to Begin on Hovila," *Dallas Morning News*, August 13, 1973.

120 **"salacious"**: Linda Coffee, interview with the author, February 5, 2014.

120 **"a bachelor"**: George Proctor, "'State Has Right to Kill Me,' Hovila Says in Death Penalty Murder Trial," *Dallas Morning News*, February 22, 1974.

120 **the men had been lovers**: Rob Wood, "Huntsville Death Row Inmate Wants to Die," *Eagle* (Bryan, TX), May 24, 1978.

121 **149 clients**: Barbara Gouge McCluskey, interview with the author, January 12, 2011.

PART IV: "THE RAW EDGES OF HUMAN EXISTENCE"

125 **"We already had adopted"**: Donna Kebabjian, interview with the author, June 11, 2012.

125 **Ruth could not conceive**: Shelley Thornton, interview with the author, December 14, 2012.

125 **"deadbeat, thin, narrow moustache"**: Billy Thornton, interview with the author, October 9, 2013.

125 **"In that neighborhood"**: Billy Thornton, interview with the author, April 9, 2013.

125 **the two of them ran off**: Shelley Thornton, interview with the author, November 7, 2013.

126 **"You ain't never seen"**: Billy Thornton, interview with the author, December 5, 2012.

126 **"felt it was important"**: Shelley Thornton, interview with the author, December 14, 2012.

126 **"dolls and books"**: Shelley Thornton, interview with the author, December 14, 2012.

126 **the little girl happy**: Shelley Thornton, interview with the author, December 14, 2012.

127 **"You could never see"**: Shelley Thornton, interview with the author, January 14, 2014.

127 **"I had tea parties"**: Shelley Thornton, interview with the author, February 26, 2019.

127 **Billy and Ruth married**: Billy Thornton, interview with the author, October 9, 2013.

127 **"Everything was Shelley"**: Billy Thornton, interview with the author, October 9, 2013.

127 **"they would split up"**: Shelley Thornton, interview with the author, December 14, 2012.

127 **"it was just"**: Shelley Thornton, interview with the author, November 7, 2013.

127 **"I would go"**: Shelley Thornton, interview with the author, March 14, 2013.

128 **"we had to lock"**: Cindy McMinn, interview with the author, December 11, 2013.

128 **"hyperactive"**: Cindy McMinn, interview with the author, December 11, 2013.

128 **"It was always mass destruction"**: Jennifer Ferguson, interview with the author, February 13, 2013.

128 **"I was the favorite"**: Jennifer Ferguson, interview with the author, February 13, 2013.

129 **"a ho"**: Jennifer Ferguson, interview with the author, November 11, 2012.

129 **judged herself unkindly**: Jennifer Ferguson, interview with the author, December 17, 2012.

129 **"looked at females"**: Jennifer Ferguson, interview with the author, December 17, 2012.

130 **"I was like, fuck you"**: Jennifer Ferguson, interview with the author, October 25, 2013.

130 **"I think he tried"**: Jennifer Ferguson, interview with the author, February 13, 2013.

130 **"I was hating life"**: Jennifer Ferguson, interview with the author, February 13, 2013.

130 **so much older and detached**: Melissa Mills, interview with the author, March 11, 2013.

130 **"we played under"**: Melissa Mills, interview with the author, January 24, 2015.

131 **"I always wanted"**: Melissa Mills, interview with the author, January 24, 2015.

131 **"Melissa was a happy"**: Velma Gross, interview with the author, January 22, 2013.

131 **"We both cried"**: Velma Gross, interview with the author, January 22, 2013.

131 **"I would say"**: Melissa Mills, interview with the author, March 11, 2013.

132 **"I felt filthy"**: Melissa Mills, interview with the author, March 6, 2016.

132 **"I thought I was evil"**: Melissa Mills, interview with the author, November 10, 2012.

132 **"You have the *genes!*"**: Melissa Mills, interview with the author, March 28, 2013.

132 **report on drugs**: Melissa Mills, interview with the author, March 6, 2016.

132 **"be in the history"**: Melissa Mills, interview with the author, March 28, 2013.

132 **"He looked just like"**: Melissa Mills, interview with the author, March 28, 2013.

133 **"Stabbed her"**: Melissa Mills, interview with the author, March 28, 2013.

133 **"He got us out"**: Melissa Mills, interview with the author, March 28, 2013.

133 **"I was with everybody"**: Melissa Mills, interview with the author, November 27, 2012.

133 **"hardship license"**: Melissa Mills, interview with the author, November 27, 2012.

134 **"Everything Norma stood for"**: Melissa Mills, interview with the author, December 17, 2013.

134 **her grandmother reassured her**: Melissa Mills, interview with the author, January 24, 2015.

135 **"I gave them a chance"**: Norma McCorvey, interview with the author, November 4, 2013.

135 **"Almost every day"**: Lloyd Shearer, "This Woman and This Man Made History," *Parade*, May 8, 1983.

135 **six hundred such women**: The article reviewed the findings of twelve studies of a total of 625 women. Hollie A. Askren and Kathleen C. Bloom, "Postadoptive Reactions of the Relinquishing Mother: A Review," *Journal of Obstetric, Gynecologic, and Neonatal Nursing* 28, no 4 (July/August 1999): 395–400.

135 **"Grief is an amputation"**: David Mitchell, *Slade House* (New York: Random House, 2015).

135 **"My mother never taught"**: Norma McCorvey, interview with the author, July 11, 2013.

136 **"That's just the feeling"**: Norma McCorvey, interview with the author, November 4, 2013.

136 **"I loved having an affair"**: Norma McCorvey, interview with the author, November 4, 2013.

136 **"That's all we had"**: Andi Taylor, interview with the author, June 30, 2015.

136 **"She's a lesbian"**: Judith Hower, interview with the author, March 12, 2017.

136 **She told Milbauer**: Milbauer interviewed Norma on September 20, 1980. Barbara Milbauer, *The Law Giveth: Legal Aspects of the Abortion Controversy* (New York: Atheneum, 1983), 330.

136 **the *Dallas Times Herald***: Monika Maeckle, "The Double Life of Norma McCorvey," *Westwood Magazine* (supplement of *Dallas Times Herald*), October 18, 1981.

137 **Norma felt guilty**: Debbie Nathan, "The Death of Jane Roe," *Village Voice*, April 30, 1996.

137 **"the problem of bringing"**: *Roe v. Wade*, 410 U.S. 113 (1973), Section VIII.

137 **"my law"**: Lianne Hart, "Neighbors—in Name Only," *Los Angeles Times*, May 29, 1995.

137 **"Freedom Lady"**: George Howe Colt, "Save My Law," *Life*, May 1989.

137 **first time to a meeting**: Norma went to her first NOW meeting in Dallas in June 1981. Maeckle, "Double Life."

137 **Norma began to volunteer**: Maeckle, "Double Life."

137 **"connected with regrets"**: Charlotte Taft, interview with the author, December 13, 2016.

138 **"She needed to find"**: Charlotte Taft, interview with the author, December 13, 2016.

138 **she told one journalist**: Norma McCorvey, unpublished interview with Claudia Dreifus, July 7, 1984. Courtesy of David Garrow.

138 **"I like my version"**: Norma McCorvey, interview with the author, March 24, 2015.

138 **"what I recall"**: Charlotte Taft, interview with the author, December 13, 2016.

138 **the *Dallas Morning News***: James Dunlap, "Humanist, Idealist, Herb Croner Remembers 84973," *Dallas Morning News*, October 28, 1975.

138 **Croner had been born**: The facts of Croner's life in Germany recounted here were assembled by the historians Christiane Jungblut and Gunhild Ohl-Hinz in a book about the victims of the Nazis in St. Pauli, a district in Hamburg. *Stolpersteine in Hamburg–St. Pauli: biographische Spurensuche* (Hamburg: Landeszentrale für Politische Bildung, 2009).

139 **a wisp of a man**: Jennie Hoskins, interview with the author, December 7, 2019.

139 **"had not one free day"**: Jungblut and Ohl-Hinz, *Stolpersteine*.

139 **telling the *Pittsburgh Press***: "Survivor of Horror Camps Seeks U.S. Citizenship," *Pittsburgh Press*, June 27, 1946.

139 **He was not a Jew**: Jennie Hoskins, interview with the author, December 22, 2019.

139 **a doctorate in philosophy**: Jennie Hoskins, interview with the author, December 8, 2019.

139 **he was a counselor**: Jennie Hoskins, interview with the author, December 7, 2019.

139 **"He didn't have"**: Jennie Hoskins, interview with the author, December 7, 2019.

139 **"just elsewhere"**: Jennie Hoskins, interview with the author, December 7, 2019.

140 **a black newspaper**: Jennie Hoskins, interview with the author, December 7, 2019.

140 **hospitalized after the second**: Jungblut and Ohl-Hinz, *Stolpersteine*.

140 **"into account my feelings"**: Herbert Croner, letter to Monica Maeckle, July 11, 1981. Courtesy of Marilyn Croner.

140 **"She'd call him"**: Charlotte Taft, interview with the author, December 13, 2016.

140 **"strongest champions"**: Molly Ivins, "Justice Lost a Champion with the Death of Herb Croner," *Dallas Times Herald*, February 23, 1984.

140 **"Broken people find"**: Jennie Hoskins, interview with the author, December 7, 2019.

140 **"She said she was Norma"**: Patricia Pinkusiewicz, interview with the author, December 16, 2016.

141 **paid five dollars**: Norma McCorvey, interview with Angela Bonavoglia, September 22, 1989. Courtesy of Angela Bonavoglia.

141 **Abortion Providers of America**: Norma McCorvey, interview with Claudia Dreifus, July 7, 1984. Courtesy of David Garrow.

141 **"She had a name"**: Norma McCorvey, interview with Angela Bonavoglia, September 22, 1989.

141 **interviewed in 1982**: KXAS-TV (Fort Worth, TX), January 22, 1982, https:// texashistory.unt.edu/ark:/67531/metadc968710/. University of North Texas Libraries, Special Collections.

141 **she drank before them**: Norma McCorvey, interview with the author, November 4, 2013.

141 **Norma was literally shaking**: Ruth Friendly, interview with the author, January 26, 2017.

141 **"as an important person"**: Norma McCorvey and Andy Meisler, *I Am Roe: My Life, Roe V. Wade, and Freedom of Choice* (New York: HarperCollins, 1994), 176.

141 **"who were out"**: circa 1984. NMP.

141 **politics of birth control**: Michael Manheim, email to the author, December 20, 2016.

141 **met movie stars**: McCorvey and Meisler, *I Am Roe*, 177.

142 **"wishes to make"**: John Alan Goren, letter to Linda Coffee, June 10, 1985. NMP.

142 **told the press**: Rene Stutzman, "'Jane Roe' Still Faces Backlash from Landmark Abortion Battle," UPI, September 29, 1985.

142 **sticker on the bumper**: Nathan, "The Death of Jane Roe."

142 **"That's what I call murder"**: Undated. NMP.

142 **Weddington who rewrote the speech**: Norma kept a copy of her speech with Weddington's handwritten edits, dated July 27, 1989. NMP.

142 **"The nomination of Robert Bork"**: Dan Shomon, "'Jane Roe' Calls Bork Nomination an Insult," UPI, August 3, 1987.

142 **the journalist Carl Rowan**: Kenneth B. Noble, "Key Abortion Plaintiff Now Denies She Was Raped," *New York Times*, September 9, 1987.

142 **"A little bit of hell"**: Charlotte Taft, interview with the author, June 2, 2012.

143 **"No fact was ever presented"**: UPI, "Woman lied in key abortion case," *Record* (Hackensack, NJ), September 9, 1987.

143 **The author Milbauer wrote**: Milbauer, *The Law Giveth*, 35.

143 **she first became aware**: Linda Coffee, interview with Karen Blumenthal, August 16, 2019. Karen Blumenthal, *Jane Against the World: Roe v. Wade and the Fight for Reproductive Rights* (New York: Roaring Brook Press, 2020), 144.

143 **Norma, though, told Milbauer**: Barbara Milbauer, interview with the author, January 10, 2021.

143 **"As a result of McCorvey's lie"**: Jack D. Nunn, "The Untold Story," letter to the editor, *Greensboro News & Record*, October 8, 1987.

143 **"This false information"**: Mary Ann French, "Setting Record Straight Is Hard but Necessary for 'Jane Roe,'" *St. Petersburg Times*, September 12, 1987.

143 **"I was getting tired"**: French, "Setting Record Straight."

144 **The Supreme Court dissolved**: David J. Garrow, *Liberty and Sexuality: The Right to Privacy and the Making of Roe v. Wade* (Berkeley: University of California Press, 1998), 608.

144 **Roe appeared as secure**: U.S. Senate, Committee on the Judiciary, On the Nomination of John Paul Stevens to be an Associate Justice of the Supreme Court, 94th Cong., 1st sess., 1975.

145 **"I do not look"**: Mildred Jefferson, testimony, U.S. Senate, Committee on the Judiciary, Subcommittee on Constitutional Amendments, hearing on "Abortion," August 21, 1974. 93rd Cong., 2nd sess.

145 **she had no expertise**: Kenneth C. Edelin, *Broken Justice: A True Story of Race, Sex and Revenge in a Boston Courtroom* (Martha's Vineyard, MA: Pondview Press, 2007), 169–70.

145 **"definition of terms"**: Edelin, *Broken Justice*.

145 **the ruling put it**: *Roe v. Wade*, Section IX B: "Viability is usually placed at about seven months (28 weeks) but may occur earlier, even at 24 weeks."

145 **technology would one day**: In her dissent in the 1983 case *City of Akron v. Akron Center for Reproductive Health*, O'Connor wrote: "It is certainly reasonable to believe that fetal viability in the first trimester of pregnancy may be possible in the not too distant future. . . . The Roe framework, then, is clearly on a collision course with itself."

145 **"without major morbidity"**: B. J. Stoll, N. I. Hansen, E. F. Bell, et al., "Trends in Care Practices, Morbidity, and Mortality of Extremely Preterm Neonates, 1993–2012," *Journal of the American Medical Association* 314, no. 10 (2015): 1048.

146 **"Once the placenta"**: Edelin, *Broken Justice*, 178.

146 **"can exhort for an hour"**: William P. Maloney, "The Owl in the Saguaro: Report to Officers and Board of Directors of the Right to Life Committee of New Mexico," January 23, 1974. American Citizens Concerned for Life, Inc., Records, Box 7, Gerald R. Ford Presidential Library.

146 **"inoculate himself"**: Edelin, *Broken Justice*, 168.

146 **pledging to help the cause**: Ronald Reagan, letter to Mildred Jefferson, February 15, 1973. Ronald Reagan Presidential Library.

146 **"social conservatives"**: reprinted in Linda Greenhouse and Reva B. Siegel, *Before Roe v. Wade: Voices that Shaped the Abortion Debate Before the Supreme Court's Ruling* (New Haven: Yale Law School, 2012), 215, 216.

146 **"The interrupting of pregnancy"**: Alice Hartle, "Reagan Likes HLA, Gives Views on Abortion, Euthanasia," *National Right to Life News*, December 1975, 1.

146 **"changed the partisan equation"**: Daniel K. Williams, *Defenders of the Unborn: The Pro-Life Movement Before Roe v. Wade* (New York: Oxford University Press, 2016), 232.

147 **"turning abortion into"**: Judy Klemesrud, "Abortion in the Campaign: Methodist Surgeon Leads the Opposition," *New York Times*, March 1, 1976.

147 **"enactment of a constitutional amendment"**: "Women," Republican Party platform, 1976. Available at the American Presidency Project, https://www.presidency.ucsb.edu/documents/republican-party-platform-1976.

147 **Never before had either political party**: According to John T. Woolley, co-director of the American Presidency Project website at UC Santa Barbara, the Democratic platform first mentioned "family planning" in 1968. The libertarian platform mentioned "birth control" in 1972. John T. Woolley, email to the author, January 9, 2017.

147 **"undesirable"**: "Civil and Political Rights," Democratic Party platform, 1976. Available at the American Presidency Project, https://www.presidency.ucsb.edu/documents/1976-democratic-party-platform.

147 **would flip too**: Daniel Williams, email to the author, January 26, 2017.

147 **"supported abortion on demand"**: Otile McManus, "Dr. Jefferson and her Fight Against Abortion," *Boston Sunday Globe*, December 3, 1976.

147 **"helped to polarize"**: Jennifer Donnally, "The Politics of Abortion and the Rise of the New Right," PhD diss., University of North Carolina at Chapel Hill, 2013, 22.

147 **"party of life"**: Williams, *Defenders of the Unborn*, 233 and 328, n. 75.

147 **2,800 chapters**: Williams, *Defenders of the Unborn*, 217.

147 **army of middle-income Americans**: Klemesrud, "Abortion in the Campaign."

148 **vendors servicing the NRLC**: Philip Moran, interview with the author, February 22, 2016.

148 **"absolute refusal to bend"**: Shane Cunningham, interview with the author, June 4, 2016.

148 **"I was unable"**: Shane Cunningham, interview with the author, August 14, 2019.

148 **"He'd call into the office"**: Judie Brown, interview with the author, March 24, 2017.

148 **Mildred stayed at the L'Enfant Plaza**: Philip Moran, interview with the author, March 13, 2017.

148 **"You know what"**: Thea Rossi Barron, eulogy for Mildred Jefferson, November 26, 2010. Courtesy of Thea Rossi Barron.

148 **"the long, tiring work"**: "NRLC President Takes Sen. Kennedy to Task," *National Right to Life News* 2, no. 8 (August 1975): 1. Cited in Donnally, "The Politics of Abortion," 130.

148 **leaders of the New Right**: "Congressional Liaison Group Holds its Initial Meeting," *National Right to Life News* 2, no. 10 (October 1975): 2.

149 **a matter of civil rights**: Thea Rossi Barron, interview with the author, June 30, 2019.

149 **"the people we risked"**: Thea Rossi Barron, interview with the author, June 30, 2019.

149 **"We kept tabs"**: Thea Rossi Barron, interview with the author, June 30, 2019.

149 **"I stand before you"**: "Convention Sidelights . . .," *National Right to Life News* 3, no. 8 (August 1976): 6. Cited in Donnally, "The Politics of Abortion," 167.

149 **congressman took Mildred's hand**: Donnally, "The Politics of Abortion," 167.

149 **"informed, articulate"**: Thea Rossi Barron, "Hyde Amendment Big Victory; Fight Goes On," report, National Right to Life Committee, Inc., January 1977, 1.

149 **"as a matter of conscience"**: Jesse Jackson, telegram to Thea Rossi Barron, September 6, 1977. Courtesy of Thea Rossi Barron.

149 **one in four women**: S. K. Henshaw et al., *Restrictions on Medicaid Funding for Abortions: A Literature Review* (New York: Guttmacher Institute, 2009).

149 **"to wring more"**: William Robbins, "Abortion Foes Look to Ultimate Victory," *New York Times*, June 19, 1977.

149 **conservative strategists began**: The first was called National Pro-Life, a PAC founded in Illinois by a Dominican priest. Williams, *Defenders of the Unborn*, 233.

150 **Among them was a PAC**: The PAC was called the Life Amendment Political Action Committee. Donnally, "The Politics of Abortion," 220.

150 **did not oppose abortion absolutely**: Since 1994, the Hyde amendment has contained three exceptions: allowing the use of federal dollars to end pregnancies that result from rape or incest as well as pregnancies endangering the life of the mother.

150 **"You can't give the individual"**: "A Fighter for Right to Life," *Ebony*, April 1978.

150 **"no abortions, ever"**: "A Fighter for Right to Life."

150 **absolute opposition to abortion**: They were Judie Brown, Nellie Gray and Margie Montgomery. Philip Moran, interview with the author, March 13, 2017, and Judie Brown, email to the author, March 26, 2017.

150 **blamed Mildred**: Caroline Gerster, "We Sought to Bring Life," *National Right to Life News* 7, no. 7 (June 16, 1980): 9.

150 **"No abortion-advocate's attacks"**: Mildred F. Jefferson, MD, "Lifelines from the President's desk," *National Right to Life News* 4, no. 3 (March 1977): 9.

150 **he headed a faction**: Andrew H. Merton, *Enemies of Choice: The Right-to-Life Movement and Its Threat to Abortion* (Boston: Beacon Press, 1982), 160. Philip Moran, interview with the author, March 13, 2017.

150 **"They had a concerted plan"**: Judie Brown, interview with the author, March 24, 2017.

150 **one of her eight**: Mildred Jefferson was joined in her votes by a doctor named Robert Krebsbach. "Shakeup Reported Among Leaders Of 'Right-to-Life' Movement," *Alexandria Daily Town Talk*, April 22, 1978.

151 **"She got far too much"**: Judie Brown, interview with the author, March 24, 2017.

151 **"opposes violence"**: *The MacNeil/Lehrer Report*, PBS, March 21, 1978.

151 **"She went into"**: Philip Moran, interview with the author, February 22, 2016.

151 **"In the heat of battle"**: Mildred F. Jefferson, MD, "Lifelines from the President's Desk," *National Right to Life News* 4, no. 3 (March 1977): 9. Cited in Donnally, "The Politics of Abortion," 219.

151 **"unbridled and unbossed"**: Doug LeBlanc, "Jefferson Fighting for Rights of the Unborn," *Sunday Advocate* (Baton Rouge), October 6, 1983.

151 **"a platform to accept"**: Judie Brown, interview with the author, March 24, 2017.

151 **more than $250,000**: Laurie Johnston, "Abortion Foes Gain Support as They Intensify Campaign," *New York Times*, October 23, 1977.

151 **"It's not me"**: Johnston, "Abortion Foes Gain Support."

152 **He sued**: Mary Ziegler, *Abortion in America: Roe v. Wade to the Present* (Cambridge: Cambridge University Press, 2020), 62.

152 **teamed up with Mildred**: The Right to Life Crusade was incorporated on February 6, 1979.

152 **her mother, Gurthie, and husband, Shane**: Robert Mears, "An Interview with Dr. Mildred Fay Jefferson," *New England Correspondent* clipping, 1984. MJP, Box 21, Folder 12.

152 **"very selfish"**: Otile McManus, "Dr. Jefferson and her Fight Against Abortion," *Boston Sunday Globe*, December 3, 1976.

152 **"violated the rights"**: Shane Cunningham, interview with the author, August 14, 2019.

152 **Eight years had passed**: Shane Cunningham, interview with the author, August 14, 2019.

152 **he had begun an affair**: Shane Cunningham, interview with the author, June 4, 2016.

152 **"a blow both personally"**: Mears, "An Interview with Dr. Mildred Fay Jefferson."

152 **unable to conceive**: Judie Brown, interview with the author, March 24, 2017.

152 **"that Christ was with me"**: Mears, "An Interview with Dr. Mildred Fay Jefferson."

152 **"The things I'm saying"**: Mears, "An Interview with Dr. Mildred Fay Jefferson."

153 **never discussed God**: Shane Cunningham, interview with the author, August 14, 2019.

153 **"genocide"**: "A Fighter for Right to Life."

153 **"extinction"**: David Newton, "Speaker: Abortions Threaten Civilization," *Greensboro Daily News*, November 13, 1977, B1.

153 **the annual total had doubled**: "Number of Abortions by State of Occur-

rence 1973–2017," graph, Guttmacher Institute, https://data.guttmacher.org/
states/trend?state=US&topics=66&dataset=data.

153 **roughly three abortions:** Of 100 pregnancies ending in abortion or live
birth, 29.6% ended in abortion and 70.4% ended in birth. Rachel K. Jones
and Kathryn Kooistra, "Abortion Incidence and Access to Services in
the United States," *Perspectives on Sexual and Reproductive Health* 43, no. 1
(March 2011): 43.

153 **a political scientist named Greg Adams:** Greg D. Adams, "Abortion: Evidence of an Issue Evolution," *American Journal of Political Science* 41, no. 3
(1997): 722.

153 **another decade:** Adams, "Abortion: Evidence of an Issue Evolution," 731.

153 **a trio of conservative strategists:** The strategists were Richard Viguerie, Howard Phillips and Paul Weyrich. Michele McKeegan, *Abortion Politics: Mutiny
in the Ranks of the Right* (New York: Free Press, 1992), 21.

153 **the Moral Majority:** The official Moral Majority platform would be "pro-life,
pro-traditional family, pro-moral and pro-America." Jerry Falwell, *Strength
for the Journey: An Autobiography* (New York: Pocket, 1988), 363.

153 **"the connection between easy abortion":** William Willoughby, "The Easy
Abortion Trend: Has Its Course Changed?," *Evening Star* (Washington, DC),
March 13, 1971.

153 **"encourage permissiveness":** White House Tapes, Old Executive Office, 407–
018, January 23, 1973. Richard M. Nixon Presidential Library.

153 **"A girl doesn't have to":** White House Tapes, Old Executive Office, 407–018.

154 **"The abortion issue":** Clarence Page, "How Abortion Helps the New Right,"
Chicago Tribune, January 25, 1987.

154 **also opposed to welfare:** McManus, "Dr. Jefferson and her Fight."

154 **the proposed Equal Rights Amendment:** Charles B. Fancher, Jr., "Much in
Common but Worlds Apart," *Philadelphia Inquirer*, April 23, 1978.

154 **agreed with in principle:** Mildred Jefferson, testimony, U.S. Senate, Committee on the Judiciary, Subcommittee on Constitutional Amendments, hearing on "Abortion," August 21, 1974, p. 14. 93rd Cong., 2nd sess.

154 **confused and dehydrated:** Anne Fox, interview with the author, February
23, 2016.

154 **dressed in navy wool crêpe:** photo, https://www.reaganlibrary.archives.gov/
archives/audiovisual/contactsheets/C256.jpg.

154 **a gathering of pro-lifers:** The meeting with Ford and pro-life leaders was held
on January 22, 1976. A White House memo five days later noted that Mildred Jefferson was "unable to attend." Judie Brown, who was then director
of public relations for the NRLC, recalled in an email on May 23, 2017, that
Mildred missed the meeting owing to a speaking engagement. When, on
September 24, 1976, Brown wrote the White House asking if the president
would meet with Mildred, the president declined on the advice of associate
counsel Bobbie Greene Kilberg, who warned that the NRLC argued for passage of a pro-life amendment. James Cannon Papers, Abortion (2), Gerald
R. Ford Presidential Library.

154 **dedicated to world population**: The board was the National Commission for the Observance of World Population Year 1974. Press release, July 11, 1974. Richard M. Nixon Presidential Library.

154 **"NOT EVER"**: Richard Nixon Presidential Library, WHCF: Alphabetical Name File, Box 79, Folder Jefferson M, p. 64.

154 **"There was an electricity"**: Judie Brown, interview with the author, March 24, 2017.

154 **"from 1970 through Reagan"**: Judie Brown, interview with the author, March 24, 2017.

154 **"She was the architect"**: Robyn Claridy and Susan Taft, "ET Native, Anti-Abortion Physician Dies," *Longview News–Journal*, October 19, 2010.

154 **fight for civil rights**: Richard S. Myers, "Pro-Life Litigation and the American Civil-Rights Tradition," in *Abortion and the Constitution: Reversing Roe v. Wade Through the Courts*, edited by Dennis J. Horan, Edward R. Grant, and Paige C. Cunningham (Washington, DC: Georgetown University Press, 1987), 23–46.

155 **"an aging Ken doll"**: James J. Drummey, "Mildred Jefferson: An Exclusive Interview with the Distinguished Boston Surgeon Who Has Thrown Her Hat in the Ring Against Ted Kennedy," *Review of the News* 18, no. 11 (March 17, 1982).

155 **photo of herself and Reagan**: "Woman Surgeon Will Seek GOP Run Against Kennedy," *Providence Journal–Bulletin*, February 6, 1982.

155 **"the symbol"**: Massachusetts Citizens for Life, letter to supporters, May 9, 1984. MJP, Box 6, Folder 10.

155 **"influential adversaries"**: Mears, "An Interview with Dr. Mildred Fay Jefferson."

155 **"IT SHOULD NEVER"**: Mildred Jefferson, undated note. MJP, Box 2, Folder 9.

155 **abortion and unwed mothers**: The White House invited her on April 23, 1984, to a discussion with religious leaders titled "Alternatives to Abortion and Help for Unwed Mothers."

155 **printed an essay**: "Reagan Beginning to Get Top Billing in Christian Bookstores for Policies," *New York Times*, September 28, 1984. The essay originally appeared in *The Human Life Review*.

155 **"with jaw set"**: "Reagan Beginning to Get Top Billing."

155 **"a champion of all"**: "Reagan Beginning to Get Top Billing."

156 **held a press conference titled**: In 1984, the AUL held a conference by the same name. Three years later, it published the papers in a book. Dennis J. Horan and Edward R. Grant, *Abortion and the Constitution: Reversing Roe v. Wade Through the Courts* (Washington, DC: Georgetown University Press, 1987), xi.

156 **"a series of steps"**: Horan and Grant, *Abortion and the Constitution*, 207.

156 **issuing a quartet of opinions**: The four rulings were issued between 1977 and 1980: *Maher v. Roe*, *Beal v. Doe*, *Poelker v. Doe*, and *Harris v. McRae*.

156 **minor girls**: *Planned Parenthood v. Danforth*, 428 U.S. 52 (1976), and *Bellotti v. Baird*, 443 U.S. 622 (1979).

156 **fetal remains**: *Planned Parenthood Assn. v. Ashcroft*, 462 U.S. 476 (1983), *City of Akron v. Akron Center for Reproductive Health, et al.*, 462 U.S. 416 (1983), and *Thornburgh v. American College of Obstetricians and Gynecologists*, 476 U.S. 747 (1986).

156 **"dancing to the tune"**: "National Affairs," *New York Times*, July 4, 1976.

156 **spoken forty-nine times**: U.S. Senate, Committee on the Judiciary, On the Nomination of Sandra Day O'Connor to be an Associate Justice of the Supreme Court, 97th Cong., 1st sess., 1981.

156 **"wholly unjustifiable"**: Robert Bork, testimony, U.S. Senate, Subcommittee on the Separation of Powers, hearing on the Human Life Bill (S.B. 158), June 1, 1981. 97th Cong., 1st sess.

156 **"Robert Bork's America"**: *Congressional Record* 133, part 14, 18519 (July 1, 1987). 100th Cong., 1st sess.

156 **divide along party lines**: Adams, "Abortion: Evidence of an Issue Evolution."

157 **Congressmen voted their party lines**: Adams, "Abortion: Evidence of an Issue Evolution," 724.

157 **The public was similarly divided**: Adams, "Abortion: Evidence of an Issue Evolution," 731.

157 **"both the marker"**: Kristin Luker, "The War Between Women," *Family Planning Perspectives* 16, no. 3 (March/April 1984): 105–10.

157 **majority of activists**: Luker, "The War Between Women," 106. Luker interviewed more than 200 women in California active on both sides of the abortion debate. Writes Luker: "More than 80 percent of those people identified in their communities as highly involved on either side of the abortion issue are women."

157 **"Since the core issue"**: Luker, "The War Between Women," 110.

157 **Closed: 99 Ways**: Joseph M. Scheidler, *Closed: 99 Ways to Stop Abortion* (San Francisco: Ignatius Press, 1985), laid out all manner of attack from "sidewalk counseling" to "blitzes of abortion clinics."

157 **bombed and set fire**: National Abortion Federation, "Provider Security," October 1982–October 1987, https://prochoice.org/our-work/provider -security/. Accessed November 28, 2020.

157 **"a domestic war"**: "All Over but the Legislating," *New York Times*, January 25, 1998.

158 **"Their fight legitimized"**: Nina Totenberg, "Robert Bork's Supreme Court Nomination 'Changed Everything, Maybe Forever,'" *All Things Considered*, NPR, December 19, 2012.

158 **"The Bork fight"**: Joe Nocera, "The Ugliness Started with Bork," *New York Times*, October 21, 2011.

159 **"never wanted to make"**: Shearer, "This Woman and This Man Made History."

159 **design a framed print**: Contract between Norma McCorvey and Tom Goff, Sarah McCallister and Gus Clemens, January 18, 1988. NMP.

159 **"my part was"**: Sarah Gallagher, interview with the author, February 27, 2017.

160 **"We believed Norma"**: Sarah Gallagher, interview with the author, February 27, 2017.

160 **"I think it's accurate"**: Gus Clemens, interview with the author, November 2, 2012.

160 **Holly Hunter visited Norma**: Michelle Green and Lois Armstrong, "The Woman Behind Roe v. Wade," *People*, May 22, 1989.

160 **nineteen rewrites**: Bill Carter, "Television; Crafting 'Roe v. Wade': Tiptoeing on a Tightrope," *New York Times*, May 14, 1989.

160 **three bullets pierced her home**: Associated Press, "Gunshots Fired at Abortion Activist's House," *New York Times*, April 6, 1989.

160 **of shortchanging her**: Norma McCorvey, interview with the author, November 4, 2013.

160 **FBI concluded the shot**: Melissa Nathanson (Blackmun's biographer), email to the author, November 22, 2016.

160 **"Someone was out"**: Gloria Feldt and Laura Fraser, *The War on Choice: The Right-Wing Attack on Women's Rights and How to Fight Back* (New York: Bantam, 2004), xx–xxi.

160 **"the incident was symbolic"**: Associated Press, "Gunshots Fired at Abortion Activist's House."

160 **she never responded**: FBI report, "UNSUB(S); NORMA NELSON MCCORVEY, aka Jane Roe—Victim," May 10, 1989, file # DL 44A-10755.

161 **"Hello," she said**: George Howe Colt, "Save My Law," *Life*, May 1989.

161 **"We don't know"**: Steven Waldman, "Attacking the Real 'Jane Roe,'" *Newsweek*, April 17, 1989.

161 **"The movie is essentially"**: NARAL, "Talking Points for May 15 House Parties," May 5, 1989. Cited in William Saletan, *Bearing Right: How Conservatives Won the Abortion War* (Berkeley: University of California Press, 2003).

161 **Famous attendees greeted**: Colt, "Save My Law."

161 **"she just came right up"**: Sarah Gallagher, interview with the author, February 27, 2017.

161 **Allred knew firsthand**: Laurie Winer, "The Avenger," *New York Times*, June 18, 2010.

161 **"trotting her out"**: Sue Reilly, "26 Years Later, 'Roe' a Celebrity," *Augusta Chronicle*, April 30, 1989.

161 **"Women's freedom"**: Andrew Rosenthal, "Reporter's Notebook; 'Jane Roe' Has Part in a Drama of High Emotion," *New York Times*, April 9, 1989.

162 **"Say Versus rather than V"**: The firm was called Ready for Media. NMP.

162 **"the Jane Roe Foundation"**: Gloria Allred, press conference, *NBC News*, April 26, 1989.

162 **paid a hundred dollars a plate**: Associated Press, "Celebrity Fund-Raiser Planned to Help Abortion Law Figure Jane Roe," April 20, 1989. Reilly, "26 Years Later."

162 **"How can somebody"**: Deborah Hastings, "Jane Roe Fund-Raiser Profits Unaccounted For," *Los Angeles Herald Examiner*, October 4, 1989.

162 **"wouldn't raise money"**: Gloria Allred, interview with the author, December 12, 2012.

162 **"I never thought"**: Norma McCorvey, interview with the author, November 4, 2013.

163 **ascended the staircase**: Philip Benham, press conference, *NBC News*, April 26, 1989.

163 **"it was beautiful"**: Wrote Norma, "The Supreme Court today. It was beautiful." Undated. NMP.

163 **"her career a long study"**: Leslie Bennetts, "A Woman's Choice," *Vanity Fair*, September 1992.

163 **"I did have some real"**: Amy Wilson, "Weddington v. History," *Orange County Register*, January 13, 1998.

163 **been made to resign**: Paul Taylor, "Weddington Resigns as Lobbyist for Texas," *Washington Post*, April 18, 1985.

163 **the title of best college speaker**: The National Association for Campus Activities named Weddington best college lecturer in 1990. Sarah Weddington, *A Question of Choice* (London: Penguin, 1993), 254.

163 **"My name is Sarah Weddington"**: Sarah Weddington, testimony, U.S. Senate, Committee on the Judiciary, On the Nomination of Clarence Thomas, to be an Associate Justice of the Supreme Court, 102nd Cong., 1st sess., 1991.

163 **Weddington had had a co-counsel**: Rick Johnston, interview with the author, September 14, 2016.

164 **the quiet counsel had contributed**: Whitehill spoke of Coffee to the author Marian Faux for her 1988 book *Roe v. Wade*. She told me on March 5, 2014, that her doing so angered Weddington. "She fell out with me because I talked with Marian Faux. I told her that I also thought Linda had done a lot. [Weddington] thought she was Joan of Arc."

164 **"Sarah's the frosting"**: Virginia Whitehill, interview with the author, March 5, 2014.

164 **"I mentioned to her"**: Margaret Whitehill, interview with the author, January 15, 2016.

164 **"not a people person"**: Peggy Clewis, interview with the author, September 13, 2016.

164 **"Delinquent Notice"**: State Bar Registration Card, Linda Nellene Coffee – Bar Card #4483000. Courtesy of State Bar of Texas.

164 **becoming a judge**: UPI, "Texas Lawyer Makes Dent in Male-Dominated Jobs," *Wichita Eagle*, February 11, 1972.

164 **Coffee told stories**: Martha Liebrum, "The Young Lawyers in the Abortion Battle," *Houston Post*, June 23, 1970. Laura Allen, "'Lady Lawyers' Handle the Defense," *Dallas Morning News*, July 13, 1975.

164 **she wore dresses**: UPI, "Texas Lawyer Makes Dent in Male-Dominated Jobs."

164 **spoke on a panel**: "Discrimination Seminar Planned," *Plano Daily Star-Courier*, April 16, 1974.

164 **a young girl who wished:** Don Hancock, "Carrie Wants to Stay in Cub Scouts," *Denton Record–Chronicle*, April 14, 1974.

165 **passed over because of her sex:** *Carter v. Shop Rite Foods, Inc.*, 463 F. Supp. 777 (N.D. Tex. 1977).

165 **Coffee worried about Roe:** "Abortion—What goes on here?," *Dallas Times Herald*, January 20, 1974. Julia Wallace, "Dallas Abortion: Unregulated but not unprofitable," *Dallas Times Herald*, 1983. Ann Zimmerman, "Decade-old Abortion Case Still Debated," *Dallas Times Herald*, January 22, 1983.

165 **confided to a student:** "Oral Memoirs of Linda Coffee," Patricia Duke, interviewer, April 17, 1973, 19. Collection: Special Project: Roe v. Wade, Baylor University Institute for Oral History. Said Coffee: "I know one of Sarah's bills even provided that under the age of fourteen, the only consent required is the parents' consent, and I really think I disagree with that." The bill—Texas H. B. 148, 63rd R. S. (1973)—was not enacted. See https://lrl.texas.gov/LASDOCS/63R/HB148/HB148_63R.pdf.

165 **"no moral or theological":** Baptist Press, "Over Abortion Clinic," May 5, 1976.

165 **the SBC joined them:** Southern Baptist Convention, "Resolution on Abortion," June 1, 1980.

165 **"fetal life":** Southern Baptist Convention, "Resolution on Abortion," June 1, 1971.

165 **"developing human being":** Southern Baptist Convention, "Resolution on Abortion," June 1, 1980.

165 **"a living individual":** Southern Baptist Convention, "Resolution on Abortion," June 13, 1984.

165 **"deviant moral behavior":** Southern Baptist Convention, "Resolution on Homosexuality," June 1, 1977.

165 **"I thought it was":** Linda Coffee, interview with Karen Blumenthal, August 16, 2019. Courtesy of Karen Blumenthal.

165 **"For a long time":** Linda Coffee, interview with Barbara Milbauer, September 19, 1980. Milbauer, *The Law Giveth*, 33.

166 **"LESBIAN SEEKS":** Personal ad, *Dallas Observer*, December 1–14, 1983. Courtesy of Rebecca Hartt.

166 **Hartt leaned left:** Rebecca Hartt, interview with the author, February 6, 2014.

166 **"My idea of happiness":** Rebecca Hartt, interview with the author, February 5, 2014.

166 **"I did not use":** Linda Coffee, interview with the author, February 7, 2014.

166 **happy ones for the couple:** Rebecca Hartt, interview with the author, February 6, 2014.

166 **"I got people registered":** Rebecca Hartt, interview with the author, February 6, 2014.

167 **belt came off:** Rebecca Hartt, interview with the author, December 16, 2013.

167 **$125 an hour:** Maria McFadden, "The Norma McCorvey Story: Woe is Roe," *Human Life Review* 20, no. 4 (Fall 1994): 27–39.

167 **"I remember feeling jealous"**: Darwin Payne, *Indomitable Sarah: The Life of Judge Sarah T. Hughes* (Dallas: Southern Methodist University Press, 2004), 401.

167 **'I did the case'**: Linda Coffee, interview with the author, February 7, 2014.

167 **"Sarah came on real strong"**: Linda Coffee, interview with the author, February 7, 2014.

167 **lawyers would each be paid**: Linda Coffee, interview with the author, February 6, 2014.

167 **indicted on charges of fraud**: Michael Totty, "Federal Grand Jury Indicts Dallas Lawyer in Fraud Case," *Dallas Times Herald*, April 5, 1989.

167 **faced five years**: Bill Lodge, "Bankruptcy Lawyer, Ex-Partner Charged with Fraud," *Dallas Morning News*, April 5, 1989.

167 **The indictment was big news**: The headlines of the two articles read "Abortion-Case Figure's Home Fired On" and "Federal Grand Jury Indicts Dallas Lawyer in Fraud Case." *Dallas Times Herald*, April 5, 1989.

167 **"I spent about two weeks"**: Linda Coffee, interview with the author, February 7, 2014.

167 **His name was Kim Wade**: Linda Coffee, interview with the author, February 7, 2014.

167 **Coffee would help**: Kim Wade, interview with the author, March 5, 2014.

167 **"brilliant and very forthright"**: Kim Wade, interview with the author, March 5, 2014.

168 **"She felt she'd not done"**: Kim Wade, interview with the author, March 5, 2014.

169 **jumped 27 percent**: Susan B. Hansen, "State Implementation of Supreme Court Decisions: Abortion Rates Since *Roe v. Wade*," *Journal of Politics* 42 (1980): 378.

169 **illegal ones fell**: Willard Cates, Jr., and Roger Rochat, "Illegal Abortions in the United States: 1972–1974," *Family Planning Perspectives* 8, no. 2 (1976): 87.

169 **The number of deaths**: Lisa M. Koonin, Jack C. Smith, Merrell Ramick and Clarice A. Green, "Abortion Surveillance – United States, 1992," *Morbidity and Mortality Weekly Report* 45, no. SS-3 (May 3, 1996): 1–36.

169 **"an improvement"**: Leslie Reagan, *When Abortion Was a Crime: Women, Medicine, and Law in the United States, 1867–1973* (Berkeley: University of California Press, 1997), 246.

169 **Roe had "disappeared"**: Hannah Smothers, "What It Was Like to Perform Abortions Before Roe v. Wade," *Cosmopolitan*, November 2, 2016.

170 **that he add "M.D."**: Curtis Boyd, interview with the author, September 1, 2016.

170 **"They thought, oh"**: Curtis Boyd, interview with the author, September 1, 2016.

170 **"hard and closed"**: Curtis Boyd, interview with the author, January 21, 2015.

170 **"a greater serenity"**: Curtis Boyd, interview with the author, September 1, 2016.

170 **"in low gentle tones"**: Eva Cox, interview with the author, September 5, 2016.

170 **"My friends and their mothers"**: Glenna Boyd, email to the author, April 16, 2017.

171 **hesitated to approve him**: Eva Cox, interview with the author, September 5, 2016.

171 **"emotionally exhausted"**: Curtis Boyd, interview with the author, September 1, 2016.

171 **"I was trying"**: Curtis Boyd, interview with the author, March 7, 2017.

171 **the number of hospitals**: "Number of Abortion Providers 1973–2017," graph, Guttmacher Institute, https://data.guttmacher.org/states/trend?state=US& topics=66&dataset=data.

172 **"Just because it's legal"**: Curtis Boyd, interview with the author, May 3, 2017.

172 **"take a little more risk"**: Curtis Boyd, interview with the author, September 1, 2016.

172 **"It was just a matter"**: Curtis Boyd, interview with the author, May 3, 2017.

172 **doctors in Scotland**: Barbara Rubin, "Laminaria Digitata: A Checkered Career," *Economic Botany* 31, no. 1 (1977): 66–71.

172 **"to disarticulate the fetus"**: Curtis Boyd, interview with the author, May 3, 2017.

173 **"I began to identify"**: Curtis Boyd, interview with the author, September 1, 2016.

173 **"It was a horrible experience"**: Curtis Boyd, interview with the author, September 1, 2016.

173 **"murderer"**: Curtis Boyd, interview with the author, September 1, 2016.

173 **human life amendment died**: The amendment, SJR 3, sponsored by Senators Orrin Hatch and Thomas Eagleton, fell seventeen votes short of the required two-thirds majority and was defeated in the Senate 49–50 on June 28, 1983.

173 **Reagan remained vigorously pro-life**: On July 30, 1987, Reagan announced that family planning clinics which "provide counseling and referral for abortion services" would not receive federal funds.

174 **withholding federal funds**: On June 17, 1984, Reagan announced the "Mexico City policy," which withheld U.S. funding from nongovernmental organizations that "perform or actively promote abortion."

174 **some $150,000**: Curtis Boyd, interview with the author, May 23, 2019.

174 **"I'll campaign for you"**: Curtis Boyd, interview with the author, March 7, 2017.

174 **"The service has to speak"**: Curtis Boyd, interview with the author, March 7, 2017.

174 **"Surviving a Holy War"**: G. J. Halvorson Boyd, "Surviving a Holy War: How health care workers in U.S. abortion facilities are coping with antiabortion harassment," PhD diss., Fielding Institute, 1990.

174 **sending a letter of blessing**: The mother and daughter were named Ruby Menard and Kathren Simmons. Susan Schneider, "The War on Sex," *Mademoiselle*, April 1986.

175 **one in three performed**: "Abortion, Harassment and RU 486," editorial, *New York Times*, January 10, 1990.

175 **steady at 1.58 million**: "Number of Abortions, U.S. vs Alabama 1973–2017," graph, Guttmacher Institute, https://data.guttmacher.org/states/trend?state =US+AL&topics=66&dataset=data.

175 **the declines would continue**: "Number of Abortion Providers 1973–2017," graph, Guttmacher Institute, https://data.guttmacher.org/states/trend?state =US&topics=71&dataset=data.

175 **a handwritten death threat**: Karen Tumulty, "Clinics Avoided; Abortion: Few Doctors at the Front," *Los Angeles Times*, August 14, 1989.

175 **nearly 24 million abortions**: Guttmacher Institute data on the annual number of abortions from *Roe* through the 1980s is missing three years: 1983, 1986 and 1989. Not counting those years, the sum total of abortions is 19,101,360. Including the estimates for those years, the sum total of abortions from 1973 to 1989 is 23.8 million.

175 **"abortion restrictions"**: Ellen R. Wiebe, Lisa Littman, Janusz Kaczorowski and Erin L. Moshier, "Misperceptions About the Risks of Abortion in Women Presenting for Abortion," *Journal of Obstetrics and Gynaecology Canada* 36, no. 3 (March 2014): 223–30.

175 **"voiced anti-choice attitudes"**: E. R. Wiebe, K. J. Trouton, S. L. Fielding, J. Klippenstein and A. Henderson, "Anti-Choice Attitudes to Abortion in Women Presenting for Medical Abortions," *Journal of Obstetrics and Gynecology Canada* 27, no. 59 (2005): 63.

175 **"in all or most cases"**: R. G. Thomas, A. Norris and M. F. Gallo, "Anti-Legal Attitude toward Abortion among Abortion Patients in the United States," *Contraception* 96 (2017): 357–64.

175 **intentional killing**: Interviewed on KVUE on November 6, 2009, Curtis Boyd said: "Am I killing? Yes, I am. I know that."

176 **have a right to know**: Rule 10a of the Federal Rules of Civil Procedure states: "The title of [a] complaint must name all the parties."

176 **grant a plaintiff pseudonymity**: The case, *Poe v. Ullman*, 367 U.S. 497 (1961), concerned women in Connecticut who sought contraception to avoid a medical threat posed by pregnancy. The Supreme Court of Errors of Connecticut, in the 1959 case *Buxton v. Ullman*, 147 Conn. 48 (1959), granted them pseudonymity owing to "the intimate and distressing details" of their suit, and the Supreme Court extended the courtesy owing to "the special circumstances" of the case.

176 **"irrelevant"**: "Our Bodies, Our Law – Q and A with Vicki Quade," *Barrister* 13 (Summer 1986).

176 **Weddington would later confide**: *From Danger to Dignity: The Fight for Safe Abortion*, film, directed by Dorothy Fadiman, KTEH, 1995.

176 **"to explain"**: Wilson, "Weddington v. History."

176 **one in every 2.3 women**: Stanley K. Henshaw, "Unintended Pregnancy in the United States," *Family Planning Perspectives* 30, no. 1 (January/February 1998): 28. Data from three cycles of the National Survey of Family Growth.

176 **"contact theory"**: Gordon Allport, *The Nature of Prejudice* (New York: Addison-Wesley, 1954).

176 **"see how elastic"**: Herman Melville, *Moby-Dick; or, The Whale* (London: Richard Bentley, 1851), ch. XI.

177 **2,887 women recalled**: Sarah E. Burns, "2,887 Women Who Have Had Abortions et al.," Brief as Amicus Curiae, *Webster v. Reproductive Health Services*, 492 U.S. 490 (1989).

177 **"to take responsibility"**: Adrienne Rich, *On Lies, Secrets, and Silence: Selected Prose 1966–1978* (New York: Norton, 1995), 260.

PART V: UNDUE BURDEN

181 **"When someone's pregnant"**: Shelley Thornton, interview with the author, July 8, 2016.

181 **"Everything I learned"**: Shelley Thornton, interview with the author, July 8, 2016.

182 **"was *so not* Texas"**: Shelley Thornton, interview with the author, November 7, 2013.

182 **"I could rock"**: Shelley Thornton, interview with the author, February 28, 2019.

182 around **"everything"**: Shelley Thornton, interview with the author, November 9, 2013.

182 **"sleepy and sad"**: Shelley Thornton, interview with the author, November 7, 2013.

183 **"blindsided"**: Shelley Thornton, interview with the author, November 7, 2013.

183 **"She was the one"**: Todd Peterson, interview with the author, March 5, 2019.

183 **"I started drinking"**: Jennifer Ferguson, interview with the author, February 13, 2013.

184 **"mature enough to deal"**: Jennifer Ferguson, interview with the author, December 17, 2012.

184 it was **"scary"**: Jennifer Ferguson, interview with the author, August 31, 2017.

184 **"My mom"**: Jennifer Ferguson, interview with the author, February 13, 2013.

184 her adoption records: Cindy McMinn, interview with the author, December 11, 2013.

185 **"I was nothing"**: Jennifer Ferguson, interview with the author, December 17, 2012.

185 **"cold-cocked me"**: Jennifer Ferguson, interview with the author, December 27, 2013.

186 pick her grandmother up from jail: Melissa Mills, interview with the author, August 1, 2019.

186 shout aloud: Melissa Mills, interview with the author, October 27, 2013.

186 **"There was a mom"**: Melissa Mills, interview with the author, March 23, 2016.

186 **"Where are you from"**: Melissa Mills, interview with the author, March 15, 2013.

187 **"Reminded me of Norma"**: Melissa Mills, interview with the author, July 31, 2017.

187 **"Watching all the sex"**: Melissa Mills, interview with the author, December 23, 2014.

187 **"I always wanted"**: Melissa Mills, interview with the author, January 25, 2015.

187 **"Why don't you leave"**: Melissa Mills, interview with the author, December 17, 2013.

188 **drew her a bath**: Melissa Mills, interview with the author, December 17, 2013.

188 **"He was always"**: Melissa Mills, interview with the author, December 17, 2013.

188 **"It raised my endorphins"**: Melissa Mills, interview with the author, December 17, 2013.

188 **"freak out"**: Melissa Mills, interview with the author, December 23, 2014.

188 **"Everything Norma stood for"**: Melissa Mills, interview with the author, December 17, 2013.

188 **"Norma gave everybody up"**: Melissa Mills, interview with the author, December 17, 2013.

189 **"I don't know nothing"**: Melissa Mills, interview with the author, December 31, 2013.

190 **outside the small cabin**: Judith Hower, interview with the author, March 14, 2017.

190 **"a lesbian who was raped"**: Judith Hower, interview with the author, March 12, 2017.

190 **"I'm gay"**: Judith Hower, interview with the author, March 14, 2017.

191 **"Without a blink"**: Judith Hower, interview with the author, March 14, 2017.

191 **"there was more"**: Judith Hower, interview with the author, August 2, 2017.

191 **"little hippie"**: Judith Hower, interview with the author, August 2, 2017.

191 **"Pixie could not handle"**: Judith Hower, interview with the author, March 14, 2017.

191 **"They saved my life"**: Judith Hower, interview with the author, March 12, 2017.

192 **"See you whenever"**: Notes of reporter Joseph N. Bell. Courtesy of Bell's widow, Sherry Angel.

192 **"She was not happy"**: Judith Hower, interview with the author, May 25, 2017.

192 **"a vast educational difference"**: Judith Hower, interview with the author, March 14, 2017.

192 **"We were trying to find"**: Judith Hower, interview with the author, March 15, 2017.

193 **"It wouldn't have occurred"**: John Rich, interview with the author, September 16, 2015.

193 **"unwilling mother"**: Barbara Milbauer, *The Law Giveth: Legal Aspects of the Abortion Controversy* (New York: Atheneum, 1983), 14.

193 **"of its singular place"**: Milbauer, *The Law Giveth*, 14.

193 **"I would much rather"**: Rene Stutzman, "'Jane Roe' Still Faces Backlash from Landmark Abortion Battle," UPI, September 29, 1985.

193 **"wondering is my son"**: Steven Waldman, "Attacking the Real 'Jane Roe,'" *Newsweek*, April 17, 1989.

193 **Jane Pauley asked her why**: *Today*, NBC, April 25, 1989.

193 **"What this is all about"**: *Today*, NBC, April 25, 1989.

194 **to suicide**: Jeffrey Hanft, interview with the author, January 14, 2021.

194 **"they had torn underwear"**: Jeffrey Hanft, interview with the author, September 5, 2017.

194 **"a cold reunion"**: Jonah Hanft, interview with the author, December 10, 2013.

194 **"Her big thing"**: Jonah Hanft, interview with the author, December 10, 2013.

194 **"It was almost underworld"**: Jonah Hanft, interview with the author, December 10, 2013.

194 **found more than six hundred**: Valerie Richardson, "Child of 'Jane Roe' Identified in Seattle," *Washington Times*, June 29, 1989.

194 **"the *National Enquirer*"**: Richardson, "Child of 'Jane Roe' Identified."

195 **She opposed abortion**: Richardson, "Child of 'Jane Roe' Identified."

195 **"This was the one thing"**: Jonah Hanft, interview with the author, December 10, 2013.

195 **thirty-seven girls born**: 1970 Summary Birth Index. Texas Department of State Health Services, Vital Statistics Unit.

195 **"Oh my God!"**: Jonah Hanft, interview with the author, December 10, 2013.

195 **she flew north**: Ruth Ann Price's notes on conversation with Toby Hanft. Courtesy of Shelley Thornton.

195 **Wow!**: Shelley Thornton, interview with the author, November 10, 2013.

195 **"her mother was famous"**: Rochelle Sharpe, "Search May Have Found 'Roe' Child," *Burlington [VT] Free Press*, June 26, 1989, 4a.

195 **"connected to a national case"**: Shelley Thornton, interview with the author, November 10, 2013.

196 **a pioneering pathologist**: Reginald Heber Fitz, 1843–1913.

196 **he took a job**: Julie Yamamoto, "No Apologies for Checkbook Journalism," *Unity News*, July 29, 1994.

196 **"Even at his funeral"**: Joan Hart, interview with the author, December 28, 2014.

196 **Norma had appeared in *Star***: Anne Eaton, "Mom in Abortion Case Still Longs for Child She Tried to Get Rid Of," *Star*, April 25, 1989.

196 **"I want to find out"**: Michelle Green and Lois Armstrong, "The Woman Behind Roe v. Wade," *People*, May 22, 1989.

196 **"We don't believe"**: Sharpe, "Search May Have Found 'Roe' Child."

196 **"Unfortunately"**: Sharpe, "Search May Have Found 'Roe' Child."

196 **"I was very upset"**: Shelley Thornton, interview with the author, January 14, 2014.

197 **"She looked at it"**: Sharpe, "Search May Have Found 'Roe' Child."

197 **"My mom"**: Shelley Thornton, interview with the author, November 10, 2013.

197 **"They kept asking me"**: Shelley Thornton, interview with the author, December 30, 2012.

197 **"All I wanted to do"**: Shelley Thornton, interview with the author, December 30, 2012.

197 **"pro-life"**: Sharpe, "Search May Have Found 'Roe' Child."

197 **"We left the restaurant"**: Shelley Thornton, interview with the author, December 30, 2012.

197 **"Here's my chance"**: Shelley Thornton, interview with the author, November 10, 2013.

198 **"What is she going to say"**: Lisa Belkin, "Woman Behind the Symbols in Abortion Debate," *New York Times*, May 9, 1989.

198 **"I knew I couldn't"**: Shelley Thornton, interview with the author, November 10, 2013.

198 **"would love to show"**: Christie Chavez's notes on conversation with Toby Hanft. Courtesy of Shelley Thornton.

199 **"begged and pleaded"**: Ruth Ann Price, interview with the author, February 21, 2011.

199 **"the race was on"**: Courtesy of Shelley Thornton.

199 **"What a life"**: Courtesy of Shelley Thornton.

199 **"I'd look down"**: Norma McCorvey, unpublished interview with Claudia Dreifus, July 7, 1984. Courtesy of David Garrow.

199 **Shelley wrote a list**: Courtesy of Shelley Thornton.

199 **"to tuck her away"**: Shelley Thornton, interview with the author, November 10, 2013.

199 **"My darling be re-assured"**: Undated. Courtesy of Norma McCorvey.

200 **"in conjunction"**: Christie Chavez, notes on conversation with Toby Hanft. Courtesy of Shelley Thornton.

200 **"Thanks to the *National Enquirer*"**: "Roe/McCorvey Story exclusive to the National Enquirer." Prepared statement, undated, never printed. Courtesy of Norma McCorvey.

200 **its scoop on the cover**: Reginald Fitz and Steve Grenard, "Roe vs. Wade Abortion Shocker—Enquirer Finds Jane Roe's Baby," *National Enquirer*, June 20, 1989.

200 **"I'm glad to know"**: Fitz and Grenard, "Roe vs. Wade Abortion Shocker."

200 **"This nineteen-year-old"**: Richardson, "Child of 'Jane Roe' Identified."

200 **had not tested her DNA**: Richardson, "Child of 'Jane Roe' Identified."

202 **"a chill wind blows"**: *Webster v. Reproductive Health Services*, 492 U.S. 490 (1989) (Justice Blackmun, concurring/dissenting).

202 **"a triumph"**: Mildred Jefferson, "Statement on U.S. Supreme Court's 'Webster' Decision by Dr. Mildred F. Jefferson," press release, July 24, 1989. MJP, Box 10, Folder 9.

202 **"it was a legacy"**: Judith Hower, interview with the author, March 14, 2017.

203 **"the Rosa Parks"**: William J. Choyke, "'Jane Roe' Looks for Child She Tried to Abort in 1970," *Anniston Star*, April 27, 1989.

203 **"I thought, wow"**: Judith Hower, interview with the author, March 15, 2017.

203 **"I would say, 'Look, Pixie"**: Judith Hower, interview with the author, March 15, 2017.

203 **copied out a poem**: The name of the poem was "Because We're Women." *A History of International Women's Day in Words and Images* (Pennington, Australia: IWD Press, 1985), 46–51. NMP.

203 **"all women today"**: NMP.

203 **had a senator telephone**: The Senator was Diane Watson. Judith Hower, interview with the author, March 15, 2017.

203 **"Gloria was asking"**: Judith Hower, interview with the author, March 14, 2017.

204 **"I feel we were a bit"**: Judith Hower, interview with the author, March 14, 2017.

204 **"an opportunity to get"**: NARAL, "Talking Points for May 15 House Parties," May 5, 1989, as cited in William Saletan, *Bearing Right: How Conservatives Won the Abortion War* (Berkeley: University of California Press, 2003), 80.

204 **resigned her job**: Alyssa Lenhoff-Briggs, interview with the author, July 24, 2017. Alyssa Lenhoff, "Hearts Belong to Dad," *Contra Costa Times*, June 18, 1989.

204 **"There was pressure"**: Alyssa Lenhoff-Briggs, interview with the author, July 24, 2017.

204 **"a decades-long project"**: Jia Tolentino, "A Woman's Work," *New Yorker*, October 2, 2017.

204 **the reason her client had struggled**: NBC Universal Archives, April 26, 1989, SN17C9249–004–89WA6393_1.

204 **Lenhoff let her stay**: Alyssa Lenhoff-Briggs, interview with the author, July 24, 2017.

204 **"circular conversations"**: Alyssa Lenhoff-Briggs, interview with the author, July 24, 2017.

205 **told Norma she was done**: Alyssa Lenhoff-Briggs, interview with the author, July 24, 2017.

205 **who'd fought for decades**: Martin and Lyon began their activism in 1955 when they founded the Daughters of Bilitis, an organization that fought for the rights of lesbians.

205 **prominent lesbian lawyer**: In 1977, Hitchens founded the Lesbian Rights Project, a legal body later renamed the National Center for Lesbian Rights.

205 **three strong gay women**: Letter from Donna Hitchens to Norma McCorvey, Judith Hower, Del Martin and Susan Kennedy, November 16, 1989. NMP.

205 **"I couldn't believe"**: Judith Hower, interview with the author, March 14, 2017.

205 **"There was no note"**: Judith Hower, interview with the author, March 14, 2017.

206 **inscribed to her with everlasting**: Photo courtesy of Judith Hower.

206 **a student of marine biology**: Joseph N. Bell, "Jane Roe Settles into New Life of Her Own," *Los Angeles Times*, June 28, 1990.

206 **the women talking**: Barbara Ellis, interview with the author, July 23, 2018.

206 **"radicalized" her**: Barbara Ellis, interview with the author, July 23, 2018.

207 **"It was hilarious"**: Barbara Ellis, interview with the author, July 23, 2018.

207 **"I do not promote"**: Angela Dash, "Pro-Abortion Rally Draws 400 to Gym," *Laney Tower* 27, no. 9 (February 1, 1990): 1.

207 **"It was phenomenal"**: Barbara Ellis, interview with the author, July 23, 2018.

207 **seeking her endorsement**: Pat Keeble, "Feminist Heroine of 'Roe' Case Enters East Bay Politics," *Contra Costa Times*, July 14, 1990.

207 **saw her own face**: Barbara Ellis, interview with the author, July 23, 2018.

207 **Oprah Winfrey flew the women**: Barbara Ellis, interview with the author, July 23, 2018. The show was filmed on January 14, 1991.

208 **a job making lattes**: Barbara Ellis, interview with the author, August 14, 2018.

208 **after Norma propositioned**: Barbara Ellis, interview with the author, July 23, 2018.

208 **leaving nothing behind**: Barbara Ellis, interview with the author, July 23, 2018. Joseph N. Bell, who wrote about Norma in 1990 for the *Los Angeles Times* (having profiled her in 1973 for *Good Housekeeping*), did not mention in his article her breakup with Bragg (whom he called Diane). But he did so in his notes. Courtesy of Bell's widow, Sherry Angel.

208 **"barely acknowledged"**: Notes of reporter Joseph N. Bell.

208 **"became complacent"**: Kevin Fagan, "Abortion Rights Leader Returns to Texas," *Oakland Tribune*, June 23, 1991.

208 **"They seriously shunned"**: Barbara Ellis, interview with the author, July 23, 2018.

208 **"high status"**: Barbara Ellis, interview with the author, July 23, 2018.

208 **to stand beside Norma**: S. J. Diamond, "Where Are They Now?: A drifter, a deadbeat and an intensely private doctor," *Los Angeles Times*, August 30, 1992.

209 **"polish that old diamond"**: Notes of reporter Joseph N. Bell.

209 **"I LIKE / LOVE HER"**: Norma's datebook, June 24, 1989. NMP.

209 **its list of donors**: Notes of reporter Joseph N. Bell.

209 **"on a butcher table"**: Joni James, "'Jane Roe' Steps Out of Shadow," *Register-Guard* (Eugene, OR), May 5, 1991.

209 **"also was at the conference"**: James, "'Jane Roe' Steps Out of Shadow."

209 **"hard to go"**: James, "'Jane Roe' Steps Out of Shadow."

209 **"It was sudden"**: Barbara Ellis, interview with the author, July 23, 2018.

209 **lapis to ground**: Kathleen Donnelly, "The Real Roe," *Miami Herald*, July 2, 1994.

210 **"The fact is"**: Matt Zoller Seitz, "Rough Roe," *Dallas Observer*, August 15, 1991.

210 **soon had a 900 number**: Seitz, "Rough Roe."

210 **Dr. Robinson paid her bills**: Notes of reporter Joseph N. Bell.

210 **"I'm really not"**: Notes of reporter Joseph N. Bell.

210 **"She doesn't need"**: Notes of reporter Joseph N. Bell.

210 **"to get off their"**: Jessie Mangaliman, "'Roe': It's Time to Act," *New York Newsday*, July 1, 1992.

210 **wasn't able even to pay**: Norma McCorvey, letter to Donna Hitchens, December 10, 1991. NMP.

210 **"he found out he couldn't"**: Norma McCorvey, interview with the author, November 4, 2013.

211 **"unfairness in the world"**: Janie Bush, interview with the author, July 11, 2018.

211 **"was messing with her"**: Janie Bush, interview with the author, July 11, 2018.

211 **to the juvie officer**: Janie Bush, interview with the author, July 11, 2018.

211 **"the temperament"**: Janie Bush, interview with the author, July 11, 2018.

211 **"Norma wanted to be"**: Janie Bush, interview with the author, July 11, 2018.

211 **"her accidental place"**: Janie Bush, interview with the author, July 11, 2018.

211 she had been patronized: Norma McCorvey, interview with the author, November 4, 2013.

212 lines of cocaine: Norma McCorvey, interview with the author, November 4, 2013.

212 **Norma got half**: Norma McCorvey, interview with the author, November 4, 2013.

212 **"It all sounded plausible"**: Andy Meisler, interview with the author, November 14, 2012.

212 **"Of my many sorrows"**: Norma McCorvey and Andy Meisler, *I Am Roe: My Life, Roe V. Wade, and Freedom of Choice* (New York: HarperCollins, 1994), 3.

212 **"that she loves me"**: Fitz and Grenard, "Roe vs. Wade Abortion Shocker."

212 the pretty girl in the photograph: Shelley Thornton, interview with the author, December 14, 2012.

212 **"As long as I had"**: Shelley Thornton, interview with the author, November 7, 2013.

213 **"he didn't like"**: Shelley Thornton, interview with the author, November 9, 2013.

213 **"He was just like"**: Shelley Thornton, interview with the author, November 9, 2013.

213 **"I have no feelings"**: Shelley Thornton, interview with the author, December 14, 2012.

213 **"of American history"**: Audrey Lavin, letter to Shelley Thornton, February 12, 1990. Courtesy of Shelley Thornton.

213 **"It was like, oh God!"**: Shelley Thornton, interview with the author, November 10, 2013.

213 **"had us freaking scared"**: Shelley Thornton, interview with the author, December 14, 2012.

214 **"not at all"**: Shelley Thornton, interview with the author, November 9, 2013.

214 **"I guess I don't"**: Shelley Thornton, interview with the author, January 14, 2014.

214 **"a bunch of religious fanatics"**: Shelley Thornton, interview with the author, January 14, 2014.

214 **"There wasn't any choice"**: Shelley Thornton, interview with the author, November 9, 2013.

214 **"Yeah, we're really great"**: Shelley Thornton, interview with the author, November 10, 2013.

215 **"He was like a god"**: Melissa Mills, interview with the author, February 8, 2014.

215 **"We were penny-poor"**: Melissa Mills, interview with the author, January 3, 2014.

216 **"Dear Cheryl"**: Letter from Shelley Thornton to Melissa Mills, September 1, 1993. Courtesy of Melissa Mills.

216 **"I want to be with you"**: Letter from Shelley Thornton to Melissa Mills, September 17, 1993. Courtesy of Melissa Mills.

216 **"She had the love"**: Melissa Mills, interview with the author, January 3, 2014.

217 **"She's admitting"**: Letter from Shelley Thornton to Melissa Mills, September 28, 1993. Courtesy of Melissa Mills.

217 **"was all in my head"**: Melissa Mills, interview with the author, January 3, 2014.

217 **"he looked disappointed"**: Melissa Mills, interview with the author, January 3, 2014.

217 **"a marriage, a family"**: Melissa Mills, interview with the author, January 3, 2014.

218 **"You need to submit"**: Melissa Mills, interview with the author, January 3, 2014.

218 **were Doug to cheat**: Melissa Mills, interview with the author, January 28, 2014.

218 **"other family"**: Shelley Thornton, interview with the author, December 30, 2012.

218 **a watershed study**: Corinne H. Rocca, Katrina Kimport, Sarah C. M. Roberts, Heather Gould, John Neuhaus and Diana G. Foster, "Decision Rightness and Emotional Responses to Abortion in the United States: A Longitudinal Study," *PLOS One*, July 8, 2015.

218 **"increased risk"**: Henry P. David, "Born Unwanted: Mental Health Costs and Consequences," *American Journal of Orthopsychiatry* 81, no. 2 (2011): 184–92.

218 **spoken to one reporter**: Norma McCorvey, unpublished interview with Claudia Dreifus, July 7, 1984. Courtesy of David Garrow.

219 **"How could you possibly"**: Notes of reporter Joseph N. Bell.

219 **"discreet"**: Shelley Thornton, interview with the author, November 17, 2013.

219 **"How am I going to explain"**: Shelley Thornton, interview with the author, November 17, 2013.

219 **"I was like, what?!"**: Shelley Thornton, interview with the author, November 18, 2012.

219 **"I told her I would never"**: Shelley Thornton, interview with the author, November 9, 2013.

219 **"Norma gave me up"**: Shelley Thornton, interview with the author, November 17, 2013.

219 **to work at Planned Parenthood**: Melissa Mills, interview with the author, March 16, 2013.

219 **"I told Melissa"**: Shelley Thornton, interview with the author, November 17, 2013.

219 **"She's still my mom"**: Melissa Mills, interview with the author, January 3, 2014.

219 **"I was shocked"**: Melissa Mills, interview with the author, February 8, 2014.

220 **"I love you"**: Letter from Shelley Thornton to Melissa Mills, May 28, 1994. Courtesy of Melissa Mills.

220 **"I wanted the baby"**: Jennifer Ferguson, interview with the author, January 19, 2018.

220 **"I followed everything"**: Jennifer Ferguson, interview with the author, December 7, 2013.

221 **"throwing up"**: Jennifer Ferguson, interview with the author, December 7, 2013.

221 **"I'm a lesbian"**: Jennifer Ferguson, interview with the author, January 5, 2014.

222 **"You're what?!"**: Jennifer Ferguson, interview with the author, January 5, 2014.

222 **nicknamed her "bitch"**: Jennifer Ferguson, interview with the author, January 5, 2014.

222 **"I was always the bad"**: Jennifer Ferguson, interview with the author, January 5, 2014.

222 **"if there was anybody"**: Jennifer Ferguson, interview with the author, January 5, 2014.

222 **"Homosexuals, in my opinion"**: Letter, May 20, 1994. NMP.

222 **Norma wrote her a note**: circa 1994. NMP.

222 **"a compelling exploration"**: *Kirkus Reviews*, April 1, 1994.

223 **"Norma McCorvey's powerful account"**: "Notable Books of the Year," *New York Times*, December 4, 1994.

223 **"It was a pack"**: Judith Hower, interview with the author, March 12, 2017.

223 **had sought to abort her**: McCorvey and Meisler, *I Am Roe*, 104.

223 **"Why didn't my mother"**: circa 1993. NMP.

224 **asked her former counsel**: Linda Coffee, interview with the author, February 6, 2014.

224 **"I wanted to make sure"**: Kim Wade, interview with the author, March 5, 2014.

224 **"Some of the jurors"**: Linda Coffee, interview with the author, February 7, 2014.

224 **taken no classes**: Notes of reporter Joseph N. Bell.

224 **acquitted her**: The judge issued a Rule 29 judgement of acquittal. Lee Hancock, "2 Lawyers Cleared of Fraud," *Dallas Morning News*, August 16, 1989.

224 **"was just gone"**: Linda Coffee, interview with the author, February 7, 2014.

225 **"It was a travesty"**: Rebecca Hartt, interview with the author, February 6, 2014.

225 **"She became less"**: Peggy Clewis, interview with the author, September 13, 2016.

225 **"She didn't want to see"**: Virginia Whitehill, interview with the author, March 5, 2014.

225 **"she looked tore-up"**: Kent Frank Brooks, interview with the author, February 20, 2018.

225 **"she was muttering"**: Kent Frank Brooks, interview with the author, February 20, 2018.

225 **American public disapproved**: Geoffrey Stone, *Sex and the Constitution* (New York: Liveright, 2017), 394.

226 **"appears to have provoked"**: Ruth B. Ginsburg, "Some Thoughts on Autonomy and Equality in Relation to *Roe v. Wade*," *University of North Carolina Law Review* 63, no. 2 (1985): 375.

226 **"halted a political process"**: Ruth B. Ginsburg, Madison Lecture, NYU School of Law, March 9, 1993.

226 **"set off a cycle"**: David Brooks, "Roe's Birth, and Death," *New York Times*, April 21, 2005.

226 **"extremely strict"**: John Rich, interview with the author, September 6, 2015.

226 **"liberalization efforts"**: Linda Greenhouse and Reva B. Siegel, "Before (and After) Roe v. Wade: New Questions About Backlash," *Yale Law Review* 120 (2011): n. 169.

226 **"Political realignment"**: Linda Greenhouse and Reva B. Siegel, "Backlash to the Future? From Roe to Perry," *UCLA Law Review* 60, Discourse 240 (2013).

226 **"nationalized the anti-abortion"**: News Service, "Abortion: The Battle Lines are Drawn," *St. Louis Review*, February 9, 1973.

226 **"Roe was wrongly"**: Al Kamen, "White House Asks Court to Overturn Roe v. Wade," *Washington Post*, October 14, 1989.

227 **"the pristine exemplar"**: O. Carter Snead, *What It Means to Be Human: The Case for the Body in Public Bioethics* (Cambridge, MA: Harvard University Press, 2020), 106.

227 **"a domestic war"**: David Garrow, "All Over but the Legislating," *New York Times*, January 25, 1998.

227 **"a holy war"**: G. J. Halvorson Boyd, "Surviving a Holy War: How health care workers in U.S. abortion facilities are coping with antiabortion harassment," PhD diss., Fielding Institute, 1990.

227 **"an emotional"**: Roger Rosenblatt, "How to End the Abortion War," *New York Times Magazine*, January 19, 1992.

227 **"hating the idea"**: Anna Quindlen, "Hers," *New York Times*, March 13, 1986.

227 **wished to preserve the right**: Roger Rosenblatt, *Life Itself: Abortion in the American Mind* (New York: Random House, 1992), 8.

227 **"permit but discourage"**: Rosenblatt, *Life Itself*, 177.

227 **"less necessary"**: "A New Covenant with the American People," Democratic Party platform, 1992. Available at the American Presidency Project, https://www.presidency.ucsb.edu/documents/1992-democratic-party-platform.

227 **"right to life"**: This sentence first appeared in the Republican Party platform in 1984. "The Vision Shared: The Republican Platform, Uniting Our Family, Our Country, Our World," Republican Party platform, 1992. Available at the American Presidency Project, https://www.presidency.ucsb.edu/documents/1992-republican-party-platform.

227 **a tiny organization**: Mary Jacksteit, interview with the author, April 24, 2017.

227 **reveal an aborted female fetus**: Connie Paige, *The Right to Lifers: Who They Are, How They Operate, And Where They Get Their Money* (New York: Summit, 1983), 106–9.

227 **"one of those subjects"**: Katha Pollitt, *PRO: Reclaiming Abortion* (London: Picador, 2014), 44.

227 **"all wrong"**: Linda Bird Francke, "Running Scared on Abortion," *New York Times*, May 6, 1978.

227 **"with no real good"**: Mildred Jefferson, interview with Jennifer Donnally,

October 22, 2007. Interviews of Jennifer M. Donnally, 2007–2012, MC1059, Box 60, CD 6. Schlesinger Library, Harvard University.

228 **"A great number of Americans"**: Dworkin, *Life's Dominion*, 124.

228 **"Who decides?"**: Saletan, *Bearing Right*, 69.

228 **even at eighty-three**: Wanda Martinson, email to the author, March 5, 2018.

228 **"because it is bad"**: John Hart Ely, "The Wages of Crying Wolf: A Comment on *Roe v. Wade*," *Yale Law Journal* 82, no. 920 (1973).

228 **"In the entire opinion"**: Robert Bork, *The Tempting of America: The Political Seduction of the Law* (New York: Simon and Schuster, 1990), 112.

228 **fourteen cases**: *Roe v. Wade*, 410 U.S. 113 (1973), Section VIII, first two paragraphs.

228 **"the Wandering Jew"**: Richard Posner, *Overcoming Law* (Cambridge, MA: Harvard University Press, 1995), 180.

228 **"as delineated"**: Brief for a Group of American Law Professors as Amicus Curiae in Support of Appellees, p.1, *Webster v. Reproductive Health Services*, 109 S. Ct. 3040 (1989).

228 **proved a valuable precedent**: Mary Ziegler, "*Roe v. Wade* Was About More than Abortion," *New York Times*, January 21, 2018. *In re Quinlan* was a 1975 case concerning the right to die, and *State v. Saunders* was a 1977 case concerning the crime of fornication, which the judge termed "an act of illicit sexual intercourse by a man, married or single, with an unmarried woman."

229 **would hire female clerks**: Mark R. Brown, "Gender Discrimination in the Supreme Court's Clerkship Selection Process," *Oregon Law Review* 75, no. 2 (Summer 1996): 381.

229 **"fundamental constitutional right"**: *Webster v. Reproductive Health Services*, 492 U.S. 490 (1989) (Justice Blackmun, concurring/dissenting).

229 **"a moving absence"**: Janet Malcolm, "The Art of Testifying," *New Yorker*, March 13, 2006.

229 **to live without fuss**: David Garrow, "Justice Souter Emerges," *New York Times*, September 25, 1994.

229 **would be "inappropriate"**: David H. Souter, testimony, U.S. Senate, Committee on the Judiciary, On the Nomination of David H. Souter to be an Associate Justice of the Supreme Court, 101st Cong., 2nd sess., 1990.

229 **"I tremble for this"**: Molly Yard, testimony, U.S. Senate, Committee on the Judiciary, On the Nomination of David H. Souter to be an Associate Justice of the Supreme Court, 101st Cong., 2nd sess., 1990.

229 **"thought and cared more deeply"**: Dahlia Lithwick, "Justice Heartbreaker," *Slate*, May 1, 2009.

229 **"a mockery"**: Senator Dennis DeConcini, opening statement, U.S. Senate, Committee on the Judiciary, On the Nomination of David H. Souter to be an Associate Justice of the Supreme Court, 101st Cong., 2nd sess., 1990.

230 **"extremely significant issues"**: "Excerpts from Senate's Hearings on the Souter Nomination," *New York Times*, September 15, 1990.

230 **Just one argued**: Edward Lazarus, *Closed Chambers: The Rise, Fall, and Future of the Modern Supreme Court* (New York: Penguin, 1999), 468.

230 **"Roe implicates"**: Justice David Souter clerk memo, July 12, 1991.

230 **"undue burden"**: O'Connor used the phrase "undue burden" in her dissent in the 1983 case *Planned Parenthood v. Ashcroft*, 462 U.S. 476 (1983). It had been used in service of abortion cases before, most recently by President Reagan's solicitor general, Rex Lee, who, in a 1982 amicus brief (filed in the case of *City of Akron v. Akron Center for Reproductive Health*), put forward a standard of "unduly burdensome."

230 **concluded the opposite**: Lazarus, *Closed Chambers*, 467.

231 **"abhorrence of abortion"**: Sandra Day O'Connor, testimony, U.S. Senate, Committee on the Judiciary, On the Nomination of Sandra Day O'Connor to be an Associate Justice of the Supreme Court, 97th Cong., 1st sess., 1981.

231 **"some stable, defensible middle ground"**: Lazarus, *Closed Chambers*, 471.

231 **"Rehnquist and Scalia"**: David Savage, "The Rescue of Roe vs. Wade," *Los Angeles Times*, December 13, 1992.

231 **"essential holding"**: "The Supreme Court; Excerpts from the Justices' Decision in the Pennsylvania Case," *New York Times*, June 30, 1992.

231 **"Even in the earliest stages"**: *Planned Parenthood of Southeastern Pa. v. Casey*, 505 U.S. 833 (1992).

231 **"The ability of women"**: *Planned Parenthood of Southeastern Pa. v. Casey*.

232 **ought to undergird Roe**: Ruth B. Ginsburg, "Some Thoughts on Autonomy and Equality in Relation to *Roe v. Wade*," *University of North Carolina Law Review* 63, no. 2 (1985): 375. Ginsburg suggested that *Roe* ought to have been rooted not in the due process clause but in the equal protection clause. Blackmun would allow that he thought the criticism "valid" but that he wouldn't have gotten the five votes he needed for *Roe* with that line of reasoning. As he told his former clerk, Professor Harold Hongju Koh, on June 2, 1995: "William O. Douglas was dead set against approaching the case on that ground, and he would have had enough agreement on the Court that five votes to that effect would never have been achieved." The Justice Harry A. Blackmun Oral History Project, HABP, 202.

232 **"among the most memorable"**: Garrow, "Justice Souter Emerges."

232 **"The court is not asked"**: *Planned Parenthood of Southeastern Pa. v. Casey*.

233 **Blackmun recalled**: In a statement on April 7, 1994, Norma praised Blackmun and said: "I'd like to shake his hand and chat with him." The Justice Harry A. Blackmun Oral History Project, Harold H. Koh, interviewer, September 9, 1994, 40. HABP.

PART VI: BORN AGAIN

237 **"I did not imagine"**: Charlotte Taft, interview with the author, December 13, 2016.

237 **"It smelled like death"**: Terry Gross, *Fresh Air*, NPR, June 9, 1994.

238 **She grew surly**: Debbie Nathan, "The Death of Jane Roe," *Village Voice*, April 30, 1996.

238 **"Run-down, depressed"**: Nathan, "The Death of Jane Roe."

238 **six-plus dollars an hour**: Helen Thorpe, "Roe v. World," *Texas Monthly*, July 1995.

238 **"How far along"**: Thorpe, "Roe v. World."

238 **"I can give you"**: Thorpe, "Roe v. World."

238 **"This issue"**: Associated Press, "Violence at clinics scares 'Roe,'" *Augusta Chronicle*, January 4, 1995.

238 **"If abortion killed"**: Daniel K. Williams, *Defenders of the Unborn: The Pro-Life Movement Before Roe v. Wade* (New York: Oxford University Press, 2016), 263.

239 **"acting like it's murder"**: Randall A. Terry, *Operation Rescue* (New Kensington, PA: Whitaker House, 1988), 194.

239 **"I was conceived"**: Susan Faludi, *Backlash: The Undeclared War Against American Women* (New York: Crown, 1991), 416.

239 **born again**: James Risen and Judy L. Thomas, *Wrath of Angels: The American Abortion War* (New York: Basic Books, 1998), 224–26.

239 **"sobbed convulsively"**: Risen and Thomas, *Wrath of Angels*, 232. The film was titled *Whatever Happened to the Human Race?*

239 **bombing an abortion clinic**: Risen and Thomas, *Wrath of Angels*, 237.

239 **the Terrys convinced a woman**: Randall Terry, interview with the author, December 4, 2018. The Terrys adopted the two children in 1994.

240 **"It's for Jesus"**: Risen and Thomas, *Wrath of Angels*, 253.

240 **kidnapped an Illinois provider**: The name of the abortion provider was Dr. Hector Zevallos. Alesha Doan, *Opposition and Intimidation: The Abortion Wars and Strategies of Political Harassment* (Ann Arbor: University of Michigan Press, 1997), 109.

240 **from Jeremiah to Luke**: Jeremiah 1:5: "Before I formed you in the womb I knew you. Before you were born I sanctified you" (KJV). Luke 1:44: "For indeed, as soon as the voice of your greeting sounded in my ears, the babe leaped in my womb for joy" (KJV).

240 **"We must obey"**: Terry, *Operation Rescue*, 95.

240 **the Apostle Peter**: Acts 5:29 (KJV).

240 **"violence" and "force"**: Susan Faludi, "The Antiabortion Crusade of Randy Terry," *Washington Post*, December 23, 1989.

240 **"ethically legitimate"**: Randall Terry, interview with the author, January 30, 2019.

240 **destroy the crematoria**: Randall Terry, interview with the author, January 30, 2019.

240 **"Tyrannicide"**: Randall Terry, interview with the author, January 30, 2019.

240 **"When I, or people like me"**: Skipp Porteous, "OR Founder Calls for 'Christian Nation,'" *Freedom Writer* (newsletter of the Institute for First Amendment Studies), September 1995.

240 **"We have bullets"**: Thorpe, "Roe v. World."

241 **four of them dead**: NARAL, "Anti-Choice Violence and Intimidation Fact Sheet," January 1, 2017.

241 **"you sow blood"**: Randall Terry, interview with the author, February 1, 2019.

241 **burst into his clinic**: Curtis Boyd, "The Morality of Abortion: The Making of a Feminist Physician," *St. Louis University Public Law Review* 13 (1993–94): 303–14.

241 **tires slashed**: Boyd, "The Morality of Abortion."

241 **the pressures exerted**: David E. Anderson, "Doctors, Patients, Assess Abortion Ruling," UPI, March 15, 1990.

241 **"What we end up getting"**: Sheryl Stolberg, "More Like War than Medicine," *Los Angeles Times*, March 20, 1993.

241 **just 12 percent**: J. Steinauer, J. Turk, T. Pomerantz, K. Koenemann, K. Simonson and U. Landry, "Abortion Training in U.S. Obstetrics and Gynecology Residency Programs," *Obstetrics and Gynecology* 130, supp. 1 (2017): 44S–45S. According to Lois Backus, executive director of Medical Students for Choice, hospitals that didn't provide abortion training were either Catholic, or were responding to pro-life pressure, or no longer felt the need to do so because nearby clinics were performing abortions. Lois Backus, interview with the author, January 11, 2018.

241 **forced to mandate**: In 1995, the Accreditation Council for Graduate Medical Education introduced abortion into its program requirements for obstetrics and gynecology. It wrote: "Experience with induced abortion must be part of residency training, except for residents with moral or religious objections . . ." "Abortion training to Be Required in Standard Ob/Gyn Curriculum," *Reproductive Freedom News* 4, no. 4 (February 24, 1995): 6–7. That language would evolve. In 2017, Section IV.A.6.d of the ACGME Program Requirements for Graduate Medical Education in Obstetrics and Gynecology stated: "Programs must provide training or access to training in the provision of abortions, and this must be part of the planned curriculum."

241 **"conscience clause"**: The first such clause was a rider to the Public Health Services Act, June 18, 1973.

241 **"It was my Christian values"**: Jon O'Brien, "Why I Am Prochoice," *Conscience* 34, no. 3 (September 22, 2013): 14.

242 **spoke out against**: *All Things Considered*, NPR, March 11, 1993.

242 **"injure, intimidate or interfere"**: Freedom of Access to Clinic Entrances & Places of Religious Worship Statute, 18 U.S.C. § 248, a1.

242 **"toward symbolic action"**: Carol Mason, *Killing for Life: The Apocalyptic Narrative of Pro-Life Politics* (Ithaca, NY: Cornell University Press, 2002), 102.

242 **"We knew"**: Philip Benham, interview with the author, January 31, 2018.

242 **"anything to overcome"**: Philip Benham, interview with the author, January 31, 2018.

242 **he suggested**: Philip Benham, interview with the author, January 31, 2018.

242 **invited him**: Jim Henderson, "Bio: Flip Benham," *Houston Chronicle*, May 31, 1998.

242 **"I said, 'Oh my gosh!'"**: Philip Benham, interview with the author, January 31, 2018.

243 **"church would be"**: Philip Benham, interview with the author, January 31, 2018.

243 **"fat and soft"**: Nathan, "The Death of Jane Roe."

243 **"preacher started praying"**: Norman Mailer, "By Heaven Inspired," *New Republic*, October 12, 1992.

243 **he merely prayed**: Philip Benham, interview with the author, February 9, 2018.

243 **"keep doing"**: Philip Benham, interview with the author, January 31, 2018.

243 **"When that check"**: Philip Benham, interview with the author, January 31, 2018.

243 **"I think it comes"**: Johanna Schoen, email to the author, August 26, 2020.

244 **"It was just"**: Philip Benham, interview with the author, January 31, 2018.

244 **"moral Americans"**: Jerry Falwell, *Listen America!* (New York: Doubleday, 1980), 252.

244 **homosexuality was an evil**: Philip Benham, interview with the author, January 31, 2018.

244 **"It's sin"**: Tamar Lewin, "Death of a Doctor: The Moral Debate," *New York Times*, July 30, 1994.

244 **"You ought to be ashamed"**: Norma McCorvey and Gary Lee Thomas, *Won by Love: Norma McCorvey, Jane Roe of Roe V. Wade, Speaks Out for the Unborn as She Shares Her New Conviction for Life* (Nashville: Thomas Nelson, 1997), 51–52.

244 **"In essence"**: U.S. House of Representatives, Subcommittee on Regulation, Business Opportunities and Energy, "Investigation and Hearing on Bogus Abortion Clinics: The Role of False, Deceptive and Misleading Telephone Directory Advertisements and Listings; State Enforcement Efforts and the Extent of Federal Consumer Protection Jurisdiction," May 24, 1991, p. 67. 102nd Cong., 1st sess.

244 **"attempted physical restraint"**: Wyden, "Investigation and Hearing on Bogus Abortion Clinics," 2.

245 **accused of strong-arming**: Marc Cooper, "Robbing the Cradle," *Village Voice*, July 26, 1994.

245 **"These woman-centered strategies"**: Kimberly Kelly, "In the Name of the Mother: Renegotiating Conservative Women's Authority in the Crisis Pregnancy Center Movement," *Signs* 38, no. 1 (Autumn 2012): 203–30.

245 **Supreme Court would defend**: *National Institute of Family and Life Advocates v. Becerra* 585 U.S. ___ (2018)

245 **for promoting abstinence**: The reporter Eliza Griswold noted that CPCs received federal funding under both President Clinton, whose 1996 welfare reform law included $50 million annually for abstinence education, and President George W. Bush, who in 2003 allotted an additional $33 million for abstinence education. Eliza Griswold, "The New Front Line of the Anti-Abortion Movement," *New Yorker*, November 11, 2019.

245 **two thousand or so**: Wyden, "Investigation and Hearing on Bogus Abortion Clinics," 1.

245 **CPCs far outnumbering**: Amy G. Bryant and Jonas J. Swartz, "Why Crisis Pregnancy Centers are Legal but Unethical," *AMA Journal of Ethics* 20, no. 3 (2018): 269–77.

245 **"we could talk to moms"**: Philip Benham, interview with the author, January 31, 2018.

245 **"horrified"**: "Operation Rescue Moves in Next to Clinic," *Los Angeles Times*, April 1, 1995.

245 **helped to shutter A to Z**: "A to Z Women's Clinic Closes Suddenly," *Aware* 3, no. 3 (March 1995): 4.

245 **"At the killing center"**: "Operation Rescue Moves in Next to Clinic."

245 **Norma stopped working weekends**: Barry Shlachter, "Between Battles, 2 Opponents Connect," *Fort Worth Star–Telegram*, May 18, 1995.

246 **"She was really upset"**: Rene Nevarez, interview with the author, July 12, 2018.

246 **saw *The Silent Scream***: The film was made in 1984 by Jack Dabner and Dr. Bernard Nathanson. It used ultrasound to show an abortion being performed. Many dismissed the film, and with it the reactions ascribed to the fetus, as grossly misleading. Planned Parenthood said it was "riddled with scientific, medical, and legal inaccuracies as well as misleading statements and exaggerations." Planned Parenthood Federation of America, "The Facts Speak Louder Than the 'Silent Scream,'" 1985.

246 **"By the time we got"**: Rene Nevarez, interview with the author, July 12, 2018.

246 **"She wanted to make sure"**: Rene Nevarez, interview with the author, July 12, 2018.

246 **"a great evil"**: Rene Nevarez, interview with the author, July 12, 2018.

246 **"I remember thinking Flip's approach"**: Rene Nevarez, interview with the author, July 12, 2018.

247 **"Opening up a conversation"**: Rene Nevarez, interview with the author, July 12, 2018.

247 **"He yelled at me"**: Rene Nevarez, interview with the author, July 12, 2018.

247 **offered to divine his future**: Shlachter, "Between Battles."

247 **"She was looking"**: Philip Benham, interview with the author, November 20, 2012.

247 **her fiancé's parents**: Ronda Mackey, interview with the author, December 11, 2017.

248 **"I wasn't afraid"**: McCorvey and Thomas, *Won by Love*, 208.

248 **"need Jesus too"**: Ronda Mackey, interview with the author, December 11, 2017.

248 **"as long as they're not killing"**: Ronda Mackey, interview with the author, December 11, 2017.

248 **"I wanted her to go"**: Emily Blewett, interview with the author, December 11, 2017.

248 **"I had viewed"**: McCorvey and Thomas, *Won by Love*, 106.

248 **"a child, not a problem"**: McCorvey and Thomas, *Won by Love*, 106.

248 **"She began to see me"**: Philip Benham, interview with the author, November 20, 2012.

248 **"operating open saloon"**: Norma was arrested on November 4, 1971. Texas Department of Public Safety records.

248 **"She kind of reminded"**: Jamie Cackler Bennetts, interview with the author, March 5, 2017.

249 **O'Hara cold-called her**: Meghan O'Hara, interview with the author, January 16, 2018.

249 **"I literally dropped"**: Meghan O'Hara, interview with the author, January 16, 2018.

249 **"Nobody wanted to hear"**: Meghan O'Hara, interview with the author, January 16, 2018.

249 **ran on the front page**: Shlachter, "Between Battles."

250 **"I was lonely"**: Norma McCorvey, interview with the author, November 4, 2013.

250 **"I still haven't met"**: Susan Swartz, "The Real Jane Roe," *Press Democrat* (Santa Rosa, CA), October 1, 1989.

250 **"looking for a spiritual"**: *Today*, NBC, June 17, 1995.

250 **"a leader"**: NOW spokeswoman Sheri O'Dell as quoted in Steven Waldman, "Attacking the Real 'Jane Roe," *Newsweek*, April 17, 1989.

251 **"be the first girl"**: Norma McCorvey and Andy Meisler, *I Am Roe: My Life, Roe V. Wade, and Freedom of Choice* (New York: HarperCollins, 1994), 124.

251 **"They didn't really lead me"**: Angela Bonavoglia, ed., *The Choices We Made: 25 Women and Men Speak Out Against Abortion* (New York: Random House, 1991), 139.

251 **"a wonderful person"**: Barbara Milbauer, *The Law Giveth: Legal Aspects of the Abortion Controversy* (New York: Atheneum, 1983), 13. Norma was interviewed by Milbauer on September 20, 1980.

251 **wrote in a memoir**: Sarah Weddington, *A Question of Choice* (London: Penguin, 1993), 16.

251 **explained away that discomfort**: Associated Press, "Abortion Plaintiff Had Baby," *Chicago Tribune*, January 23, 1973.

251 **"A decision had to be made"**: Weddington spoke on February 28, 1976. Bonnie Andrikopoulos and Warren M. Hern, eds., *Abortion in the Seventies: Proceedings of the Western Regional Conference on Abortion, Denver, Colorado, February 27–29, 1976*, (New York: National Abortion Federation, 1977), 279. Weeks later, on March 12, 1976, Weddington told the same story to Jeannette Bailey Cheek, former director of the Schlesinger Library at Radcliffe. Said Weddington: "She chose to carry the pregnancy to term because at that point the law regarding abortion was in a nebulous enough state that we were afraid that the Supreme Court, if it wanted to, could duck the issue by saying that it was moot because she had been able to get an abortion. So we thought if we showed the court that she'd actually had to go through the pregnancy, that that would give us the best kind of standing. We explained

all that to Jane Roe and told her if she wanted to go [out of state for an abortion], we would help her. But I think even then, she had in some ways a sense of the historic proportion of the case." Sarah Weddington, interview with Jeannette B. Cheek, March 12, 1976, 24–25. Schlesinger–Rockefeller Oral History Project, Schlesinger Library, Harvard University.

252 **"I think they're embarrassed"**: Dana Rubin, "Roe Redux," *Texas Monthly*, February 1993.

252 **"I don't have"**: Tammye Nash, "'Jane Roe' Goes Public with New Book," *Dallas Voice*, July 1, 1994.

252 **"The Vassar girls"**: Philip Benham, "Hallelujah! Jesus is Alive!," Operation Rescue newsletter, August 25, 1995.

252 **Rosaura Jimenez**: David S. Cohen and Carole Joffe, *Obstacle Course* (Berkeley: University of California Press, 2020), 84.

252 **"With the national organizations"**: Elizabeth Dias and Lisa Lerer, "How a Divided Left Is Losing the Battle on Abortion," *New York Times*, December 1, 2019.

253 **"to be a woman"**: Dias and Lerer, "How a Divided Left."

253 **filled with the Holy Spirit**: Morris Sheats, interview with the author, January 29, 2018.

253 **"it bothered me"**: Morris Sheats, interview with the author, January 29, 2018.

253 **"tired of living"**: McCorvey and Thomas, *Won by Love*, 159.

253 **"immoral"**: On July 22, 1995, the clinic A Choice for Women in Dallas, Texas, sent employees a "confidential memo." Courtesy of Ronda Mackey.

253 **"I want to go up"**: Ronda Mackey, interview with the author, December 11, 2017.

253 **"all warm inside"**: Nathan, "The Death of Jane Roe."

254 **Norma quit the clinic**: Lianne Hart, "Neighbors—in Name Only," *Los Angeles Times*, May 29, 1995.

254 **Norma called Miss Ronda**: Ronda Mackey, interview with the author, December 11, 2017.

254 **"a lady I can trust"**: Philip Benham, interview with the author, January 31, 2017.

255 **"I honestly have to say"**: Norma McCorvey, interview with Peggy Wehmeyer, *ABC News*, August 8, 1995.

255 **"They genuinely love me"**: Norma McCorvey, interview with Wehmeyer.

255 **"I just wonder"**: Norma McCorvey, interview with Wehmeyer.

255 **"What if your new church"**: Norma McCorvey, interview with Wehmeyer.

255 **"She kept saying"**: *Roe vs. Roe: Baptism by Fire*, film, directed by Meghan O'Hara, Cinemax, 1997.

256 **"God's poem"**: "Norma's Baptism," *ABC News*, August 8, 1995.

256 **"the sinful desires"**: "Norma's Baptism," *ABC News*.

256 **"the ultimate convert"**: Frank Bruni, Ross Douthat and Michelle Goldberg, "The Argument, Credibility and Converts: Revisiting Tara Reade and Jane Roe," *New York Times*, May 28, 2020.

256 **"I baptize you"**: "Norma's Baptism," *ABC News*.

256 **"hedge of protection"**: "Norma's Baptism," *ABC News*.

257 **"It involves the woman"**: *ABC World News Tonight*, August 10, 1995.

257 **crucifix refashioned by Benham**: Philip Benham, interview with the author, July 18, 2017.

257 **the *New York Post***: "Jane Roe flip-flops on abortion: 'I'M PRO-LIFE,'" *New York Post*, August 11, 1995.

257 **President Clinton**: Knight-Ridder, "Ripples from McCorvey's Baptism Wash across Country," *Southern Illinoisan*, August 13, 1995, 18.

257 **"God has given Norma"**: Philip Benham, interview with Peggy Wehmeyer, *ABC News*, August 8, 1995.

258 ***The 700 Club***: Steven Waldman and Ginny Carroll, "Roe v. Roe," *Newsweek*, August 21, 1995.

258 **"Jesus won"**: Joe Maxwell, "Driving Miss Norma," *World*, August 26–September 2, 1995.

258 **"The poster child"**: Ellen Goodman, "Ambivalent Poster Child," *Washington Post*, August 16, 1995.

258 **"a person who has"**: Bob Mahlburg and Barry Shlachter, "'Jane Roe' Switches Sides," *Fort Worth Star–Telegram*, August 11, 1995.

258 **"She got to be right"**: Charlotte Taft, interview with the author, June 2, 2012.

258 **"It's a career choice"**: Gloria Allred, interview with the author, May 7, 2012.

258 **"All they ever wanted me"**: *Roe vs. Roe*, film.

258 **"She lied to me"**: *ABC News Nightline*, ABC, August 10, 1995.

258 **"What she does"**: "'Jane Roe' New Position Reaction," August 10, 1995. CONUS Video Archive.

258 **"All Jane Roe did"**: Waldman and Carroll, "Roe v. Roe."

258 **"There is a moral responsibility"**: Religion News Service, "Reaction swift and strong to 'Roe' conversion to anti-abortion side," August 11, 1995.

259 **"Norma McCorvey should be seen"**: Naomi Wolf, "Our Bodies, Our Souls," *New Republic*, October 16, 1995.

259 **"What if they try"**: *ABC News Nightline*, August 10, 1995.

259 **"dying to reconcile"**: CNN, August 11, 1996.

259 **no more public comments**: Bill Minutaglio and Monica Soto, "Effect of McCorvey Baptism Unclear in Abortion Debate: Benham denies that he orchestrated timing of event," *Dallas Morning News*, August 12, 1995.

259 **"I'm not pro-choice"**: Al Baker and Jane Furse, "'Jane Roe' Is Pro-Herself Doesn't Want A Role in Abortion Debate," *New York Daily News*, August 12, 1995. I had not yet discovered this sentence when in 2013, I wrote a similar one in *Vanity Fair*. ("But in truth McCorvey has long been less pro-choice or pro-life than pro-Norma.") I then found yet another similar sentence in *Newsweek*: "This is not pro-choice, it is not pro-life. It is pro-Norma" (Waldman and Carroll, "Roe v. Roe").

259 **"I wouldn't leave Connie"**: Baker and Furse, "'Jane Roe' Is Pro-Herself."

259 **owned a saloon**: Mahlburg and Shlachter, "'Jane Roe' Switches Sides."

259 **"Norma will be set free"**: Associated Press, "Jane Roe's 'Conversion' Took Just 4 Months," August 12, 1995.

260 **"He's the devil"**: Associated Press, "Jane Roe's 'Conversion.'"

260 **many women wished**: Pat Keeble, "Feminist Heroine of 'Roe' Case Enters East Bay Politics," *Contra Costa Times*, July 14, 1990.

260 **"Dear Lord"**: Norma McCorvey, undated note. Courtesy of Ronda Mackey.

260 **"she was talking"**: Philip Benham, interview with the author, May 29, 2018.

260 **"to be as articulate"**: Dan Donehey, interview with the author, April 22, 2018.

261 **"God used the child"**: Press release for *Reversing Roe*. Courtesy of Ronda Mackey.

261 **one in six Americans**: In January 1998, 17 percent of respondents in a Gallup poll said that abortion ought to be illegal in all circumstances. Gallup, "Abortion," September 25, 2020, https://news.gallup.com/poll/1576/abortion.aspx.

261 **"compromise"**: "Miss Norma has experienced a real turn around," Operation Rescue newsletter, October 25, 1995.

261 **a passage in Corinthians**: 1 Corinthians 6:11 states of homosexuality: "and that is what some of you were" (KJV). The past-tense "were" indicated, said Benham, that homosexuality could be left behind.

261 **homosexuality could be vanquished**: Philip Benham, interview with the author, May 1, 2018.

261 **"The couple assured me"**: Philip Benham, interview with the author, November 20, 2012.

261 **"The love is still there"**: *Roe vs. Roe*, film.

261 **"I still have"**: *Roe vs. Roe*, film.

261 **quit her job**: Nathan, "The Death of Jane Roe."

261 **"He never could get"**: *Roe vs. Roe*, film.

261 **baptized by Benham**: Philip Benham, interview with the author, January 31, 2018.

262 **curb the sinful desires**: Philip Benham, interview with the author, May 29, 2018.

262 **"success rate"**: Wyatt Buchanan, "Report: 'Ex-Gay' Therapy Claims Deceptive," *San Francisco Chronicle*, March 3, 2006.

262 **Chambers left to apologize**: Alan Chambers, "I Am Sorry," Exodus International blog, June 19, 2013. https://exodusinternational.org/2013/06/i-am-sorry/. Accessed November 30, 2020.

262 **"I could just tell"**: Sheree Havlik, interview with the author, April 30, 2018.

262 **"I said, 'Norma'"**: Sheree Havlik, interview with the author, April 26, 2018.

262 **occasional night with a stranger**: Norma McCorvey, interview with the author, October 17, 2013.

262 **"She was a sexual being"**: Meghan O'Hara, interview with the author, December 19, 2017.

262 **would long recall her prowess**: Pete Aguilar, interview with the author, March 30, 2015. Diane Hyman, interview with the author, March 25, 2015.

262 **"I never have found"**: Rene Stutzman, "'Jane Roe' still faces backlash from landmark abortion battle," UPI, September 29, 1985.

262 **"a delinquent child"**: Clerk's File Docket and Civil Fee Book, Juvenile Court, Dallas County, No. 60–1993–Juv, October 31, 1960.

262 **"healing Norma"**: Jan Jarboe Russell, "No Choice," *Texas Monthly*, October 29, 1995.

263 **"rearticulated her"**: Christianna K. Barnard, "Jane Roe Gone Rogue: Norma McCorvey's Transformation as a Symbol of the U.S. Abortion Debate," MA thesis, Sarah Lawrence College, 2018.

263 **"coded herself as straight"**: Barnard, "Jane Roe Gone Rogue."

263 **"[If] I know"**: Angelia Wilson, *Below the Belt: Religion, Sexuality and Politics in the Rural South*. (New York: Bloomsbury, 1999), 105.

263 **"from all appearances"**: Philip Benham, interview with the author, May 1, 2018. 1 Thessalonians 5:22 (KJV).

263 **200,000 miles**: Jeff Hooten, "Roe No More," Focus on the Family's *Citizen* magazine, January 20, 1997.

263 **"I couldn't finish"**: *Roe vs. Roe*, film.

263 **"I wept . . ."**: *Roe vs. Roe*, film.

263 **"like a prophet"**: *Roe vs. Roe*, film.

263 **let go of her hatred**: Norma wrote of the comfort Morris Sheats provided her in a note she titled "Passing of a Parent/Friend," January 4, 1996. NMP.

263 **"could stand before God"**: Associated Press, "'Roe' Switches Faiths and Joins Catholic Church," October 19, 1998.

264 **"This is my home"**: *Roe vs. Roe*, film.

264 **"Flip had a fit"**: Associated Press, "'Roe' Switches Faiths."

264 **only to rehire them**: Jessie Anne Nobles, interview with the author, April 25, 2018.

264 **"It was his way"**: Ronda Mackey, interview with the author, December 11, 2017.

264 **"in the fountain"**: Operation Rescue newsletter, January 27, 1996.

264 **"Norma has repented"**: *Roe vs. Roe*, film.

264 **"I was thinking principally"**: Rob Schenck, interview with the author, July 27, 2018.

265 **"Everybody wanted"**: Rob Schenck, interview with the author, July 27, 2018.

265 **abortion providers executed**: In September 1995, Terry spoke to a gathering of the radical right U.S. Taxpayers Alliance. Said Terry: "When I, or people like me, are running the country, you'd better flee, because we will find you, we will try you, and we'll execute you." Porteous, "OR Founder."

265 **a choreographed kiss**: Rob Schenck, interview with the author, July 27, 2018.

265 **"We forgive you"**: *Reversing Roe*, film, directed by Dan Donehey, Donehey & Associates, 1996.

265 **she proclaimed Jane Roe dead**: Associated Press, "'Jane Roe' in D.C. to Mark Heated Anniversary," January 22, 1996.

265 **"Glory!"**: Operation Rescue newsletter, February 15, 1996. Courtesy of Sheree Havlik.

265 **"Hallelujah!"**: Associated Press, "'Jane Roe' in D.C."

265 **"her bargain clothes"**: Nathan, "The Death of Jane Roe."

265 **"Miss Norma McCorvey"**: Nathan, "The Death of Jane Roe."

265 **coined one year prior**: The phrase "partial-birth abortion" was coined in 1995 by three people: congressman Charles Canady, congressional lawyer Keri Harrison, and Douglas Johnson, policy adviser of the National Right to Life Committee. See Cynthia Gorney, "Gambling with Abortion," *Harper's Online*, January 1, 2005.

265 **"Lord, use my body"**: The sentence is from Norma's poem "Empty Playgrounds."

266 **"to find Jesus"**: Jason Sickles and Todd Bensman, "Roe vs. Wade Figure Accused of Pushing Worker at Clinic," *Dallas Morning News*, March 16, 1996.

266 **"under wraps"**: Philip Benham, interview with the author, May 23, 2018.

266 **Norma simply knelt**: "Norma McCorvey Remarks," April 30, 1996. CONUS Video Archive.

266 **"bought by the blood"**: *Roe vs. Roe*, film.

266 **"Miss Norma"**: Hooten, "Roe No More."

266 **two hundred dollars**: Philip Benham, email to the author, November 20, 2020.

266 **the landlord had agreed**: Philip Benham, interview with the author, May 4, 2018.

266 **"I wrote my own ticket"**: Norma McCorvey, interview with the author, November 4, 2013.

267 **"You start dealing"**: Frank Pavone, interview with the author, May 12, 2018.

267 **Department of Motor Vehicles**: Frank Pavone, email to the author, January 22, 2021.

267 **"the most important moral issue"**: Frank Pavone, interview with the author, May 12, 2018.

267 **"I was being called"**: Frank Pavone, interview with the author, May 12, 2018.

268 **"Never discount anyone"**: Frank Pavone, interview with the author, May 12, 2018.

268 **"I'd love to be able"**: Frank Pavone, interview with the author, November 30, 2012.

268 **"the de facto chaplain"**: Rob Schenck, interview with the author, August 16, 2018.

268 **"it was not a focus"**: Frank Pavone, interview with the author, May 18, 2018.

268 **"to a past relationship"**: Frank Pavone, interview with the author, May 12, 2018.

268 **"a gospel issue"**: Philip Benham, interview with the author, May 23, 2018.

268 **"a battle over"**: Philip Benham, interview with the author, May 29, 2018.

268 **"You go to confession"**: Philip Benham, interview with the author, November 20, 2012.

269 **"such a thing"**: Frank Pavone, interview with the author, May 12, 2018.

269 **presidential nominee Bob Dole**: Dole had proposed that Republicans soften the language on abortion in their platform. He backtracked.

269 **"excommunicated"**: Troy Newman, interview with the author, June 5, 2018.

269 **pledged himself**: Troy Newman, interview with the author, June 5, 2018.

269 **gone to Planned Parenthood**: Troy Newman, interview with the author, June 5, 2018.

269 **"I look at these children"**: Leigh Sales, "Troy Newman: the American anti-abortion campaigner facing deportation from Australia," *ABC News Australia*, December 1, 2015.

270 **"to tell them"**: Troy Newman, interview with the author, June 7, 2018.

270 **"permissible theologically"**: Troy Newman, interview with the author, June 7, 2018.

270 **"The mom put the baby"**: Troy Newman, interview with the author, June 4, 2018.

270 **"feeling very uneasy"**: Philip Benham, interview with the author, January 26, 2021.

270 **veered from the script**: Troy Newman, interview with the author, June 4, 2018.

270 **"There was crying"**: Troy Newman, interview with the author, June 4, 2018.

270 **"He would trot Norma out"**: Troy Newman, interview with the author, June 4, 2018.

270 **accepted an invitation**: Troy Newman, interview with the author, June 4, 2018.

270 **"cut out"**: Gary Thomas, "Roe v. McCorvey," *Christianity Today*, January 12, 1998.

270 **"He's too tough"**: Norma McCorvey, letter to Ronda Mackey, August 29, 1996. Courtesy of Ronda Mackey.

271 **"I wanted a closer walk"**: Janet Thoma, interview with the author, May 3, 2018.

271 **a book by Jerry Falwell**: Jerry Falwell, *If I Should Die Before I Wake* (Nashville: Thomas Nelson, 1986).

271 **it was a sin**: Hooten, "Roe No More."

271 **Connie was now straight**: "Conservative corner exclusive interview!" January 22, 1997. McCorvey papers.

271 **"I chose to be a lesbian"**: Melanie Schurr, "The Lord Turned My Life Around," *Lookout*, March 16, 1997.

271 **"I took . . . the McCorvey"**: Janet Thoma, interview with the author, May 3, 2018.

271 **$80,000**: Philip Benham, interview with the author, January 31, 2018.

271 **Norma use the money**: Philip Benham, email to the author, November 22, 2018.

271 **fixed up the house**: Melissa Mills, interview with the author, November 26, 2018.

272 **his job was not**: Janet Thoma, interview with the author, May 3, 2018.

272 **worked the phones**: Thorpe, "Roe v. World." Hart, "Neighbors—in Name Only."

272 **"that he would not"**: McCorvey and Thomas, *Won by Love*, 187.

273 **"he was a father"**: Meghan O'Hara, interview with the author, January 19, 2018.

273 **"I started loving you"**: Norma McCorvey, letter to Ronda Mackey, undated. Courtesy of Ronda Mackey.

273 **"You are not only"**: Norma McCorvey, letter to Ronda Mackey, undated. Courtesy of Ronda Mackey.

273 **had helped to enlist**: Ronda Mackey, interview with the author, December 11, 2017.

273 **"I just couldn't believe"**: Norma McCorvey, letter to Ronda Mackey, October 9, 1997. Courtesy of Ronda Mackey.

273 **"If I didn't show up"**: Ronda Mackey, interview with the author, October 7, 2018.

273 **"I'm sad"**: Norma McCorvey, letter to Ronda Mackey, undated. Courtesy of Ronda Mackey.

274 **"strive in the name"**: Rev. Mel McGinnis, "Legacy After Roe Redemptively Lives On," letter to the editor, *Post–Journal* (Jamestown, NY), January 27, 2018.

274 **"It's an industry"**: Philip Benham, interview with the author, May 23, 2018.

274 **did not promote Norma's film**: Dan Donehey, interview with the author, April 22, 2018.

274 **thirty-nine states**: Jan Crawford Greenburg, "Roe vs. Wade at 25: America's Great Divide," *Chicago Tribune*, January 19, 1998.

274 **"What hurt the most"**: Philip Benham, interview with the author, May 23, 2018.

274 **"Her theology"**: Waldman and Carroll, "Roe v. Roe."

275 **write to a friend**: "Praise the Lord!," she wrote. Norma McCorvey, email to Meghan O'Hara, May 7, 1998. NMP.

275 **"A still, small voice"**: McCorvey and Thomas, *Won by Love*, 233.

275 **turned her away**: Roe No More newsletter, December 1997. Courtesy of Philip Benham.

275 **soon on air with Pavone**: The episode of *Defending Life* that featured Norma was filmed in August 1997 and aired in 1998. Eternal World Television Network, 1998.

275 **"You've got to be compassionate"**: Gary Thomas, interview with the author, May 3, 2018.

276 **at the Senate**: U.S. Senate, Committee on the Judiciary, Subcommittee on the Constitution, Federalism, and Property Rights, "Examining the Status of the Supreme Court Decision *Roe v. Wade* 25 Years Later," January 21, 1998. 105th Cong., 2nd sess.

276 **"She lied to me"**: U.S. Senate, Committee on the Judiciary, Subcommittee on the Constitution, Federalism, and Property Rights, "Examining the Status of the Supreme Court Decision *Roe v. Wade* 25 Years Later," January 21, 1998. 105th Cong., 2nd sess.

276 **"I wish"**: Carl Weiser, "'Jane Roe': Rape, incest don't justify abortions," *News Journal* (Wilmington, DE), January 18, 1998.

276 **"The lesbian nurse"**: Mason, *Killing for Life*, 179.

276 **"We get the lesbian"**: Carol Mason, interview with the author, June 4, 2018.

276 **confided to a friend**: Barbara Ellis, interview with the author, July 23, 2018.

277 **"Wouldn't it be horrible"**: Norma McCorvey, interview with the author, October 17, 2013.

277 **"sister in Christ"**: Melissa Mills, interview with the author, November 10, 2012. McCorvey and Thomas, *Won by Love*, ix.

277 **"I don't care"**: *Roe vs. Roe*, film.

277 **"YOUR THE REASON"**: Norma McCorvey, letter to Connie Gonzalez, January 16, 1998. NMP.

277 **favoring vodka**: Norma McCorvey, interview with the author, November 4, 2013.

277 **"She would throw"**: Ronda Mackey, interview with the author, December 11, 2017.

277 **Christian network was so angry**: Moody Radio, fax to Ronda Mackey, March 11, 1998. Courtesy of Ronda Mackey.

277 **publisher was angry, too**: Thomas Nelson, Inc., fax to Ronda Mackey, March 11, 1998. Courtesy of Ronda Mackey.

277 **"I started having"**: Ronda Mackey, interview with the author, December 11, 2017.

277 **"I know God wants"**: Ron Mackey, letter to Norma McCorvey, February 27, 1998. Courtesy of Ronda Mackey.

278 **"to seek God"**: Ron Mackey, letter to Morris Sheats, March 1998. Courtesy of Ronda Mackey.

278 **"of going full blast"**: Ron Mackey, letter to Norma McCorvey, February 27, 1998. Courtesy of Ronda Mackey.

278 **"I'M LOOKING"**: Norma McCorvey, letter to Ronda Mackey, March 18, 1998. Courtesy of Ronda Mackey.

278 **"If I see Ronda again"**: Ron Mackey, letter to Morris Sheats, March 1998. Courtesy of Ronda Mackey.

278 **"I Love You"**: Ronda Mackey, letter to Norma McCorvey, March 17, 1998. Courtesy of Ronda Mackey.

278 **"insatiable yearning"**: Nathan, "The Death of Jane Roe."

278 **"I recall hearing Norma"**: Fonda Lash, interview with the author, July 30, 2018.

279 **to stand outside Norma's clinic**: Daniel Vinzant, interview with the author, July 5, 2018.

279 **"hedge of protection"**: "Norma's Baptism," *ABC News*, August 8, 1995.

279 **"laughter and scripture"**: Daniel Vinzant, interview with the author, July 9, 2018.

279 **read it through twice**: "Daniel Vinzant: Former Southern Baptist Minister," *The Journey Home*, television program, Coming Home Network International, September 25, 1998.

279 **awoke in a sweat**: Daniel Vinzant, interview with the author, July 5, 2018.

279 **"the contrast"**: Daniel Vinzant, interview with the author, July 5, 2018.

279 **"spear"**: Daniel Vinzant, interview with the author, July 9, 2018.

279 **stealing away on Sunday mornings**: Daniel Vinzant, interview with the author, July 5, 2018.

280 **"picking up the liturgy"**: Daniel Vinzant, interview with the author, July 9, 2018.

280 **privately confiding**: Daniel Vinzant, interview with the author, July 9, 2018.

280 **with Catholic dogma**: Daniel Vinzant, interview with the author, July 9, 2018.

280 **"She got to feel"**: Frank Pavone, interview with the author, May 31, 2018.

280 **how to pray**: Frank Pavone, interview with the author, May 31, 2018.

281 **"The decision is in"**: Norma McCorvey, email to Frank Pavone, May 21, 1998. NMP.

281 **"Praise the Lord!!!"**: Norma McCorvey, "Coming Home to Rome," Roe No More Ministries press release, June 15, 1998. NMP.

281 **"tell him I love him"**: Norma McCorvey, email to Frank Pavone, May 22, 1998. NMP.

281 **"The work He wants"**: Frank Pavone, email to Norma McCorvey, May 27, 1998. NMP.

281 **"by coming home"**: Peter Sonski, "McCorvey to Enter Catholic Church," *National Catholic Register*, June 21, 1998.

281 **okayed "every word"**: Frank Pavone, email to the author, April 20, 2021.

281 **"He would do that"**: Jenn Morson, interview with the author, October 27, 2020.

281 **"extremely hot"**: McCorvey and Thomas, *Won by Love*, 158–60.

281 **"I clearly heard"**: McCorvey, "Coming Home to Rome."

282 **"full flowering"**: Catholic News Service, "'Jane Roe' Says She'll Become Catholic," *Catholic Advance*, June 26, 1998.

282 **the catacombs in Rome**: Edward Robinson, email to Norma McCorvey, June 19, 2007. NMP.

282 **crucifixion of St. Peter**: Norma McCorvey with Frank Pavone, "My Journey into the Catholic Church" (New York: Priests for Life, 1999).

282 **"Father said"**: Bill Howard, "Norma Received into the Catholic Church," Catholic News Service, August 27, 1998.

282 **become her "sponsor"**: Lynn Mills, interview with the author, June 26, 2018.

282 **"all the babies"**: Frank Pavone, "Fr. Frank Pavone Receives Norma McCorvey into the Catholic Church," video, YouTube, February 27, 2017.

282 **37 million legal**: Rachel K. Jones and Kathryn Kooistra, "Abortion Incidence and Access to Services in the United States 2008," *Perspectives on Sexual and Reproductive Health* 43, no. 1 (March 2011): 43, table 1.

283 **"like having my own children"**: McCorvey with Pavone, "My Journey into the Catholic Church."

283 **"abandoning"**: Monika Maeckle, "The Double Life of Norma McCorvey," *Westwood Magazine* (supplement of *Dallas Times Herald*), October 18, 1981.

PART VII: REPERCUSSION

287 **"terrified"**: Shelley Thornton, interview with the author, December 4, 2012.

287 **"to run and hide"**: Shelley Thornton, interview with the author, March 13, 2016.

287 **"He has his opinions"**: Shelley Thornton, interview with the author, November 9, 2013.

287 **"To hear that someone"**: Shelley Thornton, interview with the author, December 4, 2012.

288 **"How can I come"**: Shelley Thornton, interview with the author, December 4, 2012.

288 **"knowing who you are"**: Shelley Thornton, interview with the author, December 4, 2012.

288 **"I knew what"**: Shelley Thornton, interview with the author, November 10, 2013.

288 **To speak of her birth**: Shelley Thornton, interview with the author, November 10, 2013.

288 **"this big huge secret"**: Shelley Thornton, interview with the author, November 10, 2013.

288 **buy a pair of shoes**: Shelley Thornton, interview with the author, November 7, 2013.

288 **"I am done"**: Shelley Thornton, interview with the author, November 10, 2013.

288 **"You know how she"**: Shelley Thornton, interview with the author, December 4, 2012.

288 **"I hate that I am"**: Shelley Thornton, interview with the author, November 10, 2013.

289 **"in a dark"**: Shelley Thornton, interview with the author, November 10, 2013.

289 **"always there"**: Shelley Thornton, interview with the author, November 10, 2013.

289 **"I would be like, you"**: Shelley Thornton, interview with the author, November 9, 2013.

289 **"I don't like"**: Shelley Thornton, interview with the author, November 9, 2013.

289 **"For purposes"**: *Roe v. Wade*, 410 U.S. 113 (1973), Section IV A.

290 **in legal terms**: A terminated pregnancy constitutes an *exception* to mootness that the law classifies as "capable of repetition, yet evading review."

290 **"claimed to regret"**: Johanna Schoen, *Abortion After Roe* (Chapel Hill: University of North Carolina Press, 2015), 149.

290 **"Does he know"**: Holly B. Hampton, "Is 'Ms. Roe' thinking about her child's life?," letter to the editor, *Tennessean*, August 16, 1995.

290 **The first question**: Norma McCorvey and Gary Lee Thomas, *Won by Love: Norma McCorvey, Jane Roe of Roe V. Wade, Speaks Out for the Unborn as She Shares Her New Conviction for Life* (Nashville: Thomas Nelson, 1997), 49.

290 **she was bound for hell**: Shelley Thornton, interview with the author, March 16, 2013.

290 **"secular"**: Shelley Thornton, interview with the author, November 9, 2013.

290 **"very dull"**: Shelley Thornton, interview with the author, November 10, 2013.

290 **"It could be something"**: Shelley Thornton, interview with the author, November 10, 2013.

291 **her tubes tied**: Jennifer Ferguson, interview with the author, January 13, 2014.

291 **"cold-cocked me"**: Jennifer Ferguson, interview with the author, January 5, 2014.

291 **"I just couldn't"**: Jennifer Ferguson, interview with the author, December 7, 2013.

291 **'Yup, I'm gay'**: Jennifer Ferguson, interview with the author, January 5, 2014.

292 **her ex went to prison**: Jennifer Ferguson, interviews with the author, December 17, 2012, and January 13, 2014.

292 **"She would be gone"**: Jennifer Ferguson, interview with the author, January 13, 2014.

292 **"she started drinking"**: Jennifer Ferguson, interview with the author, January 13, 2014.

293 **"She was like, 'Oh'"**: Jennifer Ferguson, interview with the author, January 13, 2014.

293 **"She choked me"**: Jennifer Ferguson, interview with the author, January 13, 2014.

293 **"I didn't have shit"**: Jennifer Ferguson, interview with the author, January 13, 2014.

294 **vowed to rid herself**: Jennifer Ferguson, interview with the author, January 13, 2014.

294 **"Either we get"**: Lisa Gipson, interview with the author, January 13, 2014.

294 **"It was always"**: Lisa Gipson, interview with the author, January 13, 2014.

294 **"it kept me so flat"**: Melissa Mills, interview with the author, January 3, 2014.

294 **"I felt like"**: Melissa Mills, interview with the author, January 3, 2014.

294 **"he might not come"**: Melissa Mills, interview with the author, January 3, 2014.

295 **"I had no crying"**: Melissa Mills, interview with the author, January 3, 2014.

295 **"He'd grab me"**: Melissa Mills, interview with the author, February 8, 2014.

295 **"he'd done wrong"**: Melissa Mills, interview with the author, February 8, 2014.

295 **"I thought I was crazy"**: Melissa Mills, interview with the author, February 8, 2014.

295 **"Everybody knew"**: Melissa Mills, interview with the author, September 6, 2018.

296 **"I wanted him"**: Melissa Mills, interview with the author, February 8, 2014.

296 **Jordan came out**: Jordan Mills, interview with the author, September 9, 2018.

296 **"He wanted to beat"**: Melissa Mills, interview with the author, February 8, 2014.

296 **blamed Melissa**: Melissa Mills, interview with the author, February 8, 2014.

296 **his horribleness**: Melissa Mills, interview with the author, March 2, 2014.

296 **"purity of soul"**: *Lake of Fire*, film, directed by Tony Kaye, Anonymous Content, 2008.

296 **made Melissa cry**: Melissa Mills, interview with the author, November 11, 2012.

297 **"I love children"**: Norma McCorvey, email to Judy Wiggins, July 21, 2009. Courtesy of Judy Wiggins.

297 **"I was looking"**: Melissa Mills, interview with the author, February 8, 2014.

297 **"He was a dog"**: Melissa Mills, interview with the author, February 8, 2014.

297 **"I couldn't think"**: Melissa Mills, interview with the author, March 2, 2014.

298 **"I wanted to meet"**: Melissa Mills, interview with the author, March 2, 2014.

298 **What moved him**: Eric Heumann, interview with the author, March 2, 2014.

299 **"I've tried to fill"**: Melissa Mills, interview with the author, August 8, 2013.

300 **her talking points**: NMP.

300 **publishing a booklet**: Norma McCorvey with Frank Pavone, "My Journey into the Catholic Church" (New York: Priests for Life, 1999).

300 **"unsure of the details"**: Catholic News Service, "'Jane Roe' Says She'll Become Catholic."

300 **"I liked it so much"**: McCorvey with Pavone, "My Journey into the Catholic Church."

300 **"The Catholics are nonviolent"**: Richard N. Ostling, "Roe Reconverts," Associated Press, October 10, 1998.

301 **"that we had lost"**: Rob Schenck, interview with the author, August 16, 2018.

301 **"We all knew"**: Rob Schenck, interview with the author, July 27, 2018.

301 **roughly doubled donations**: Rob Schenck, interview with the author, August 16, 2018.

301 **"It would be extremely"**: Rob Schenck, interview with the author, July 27, 2018.

301 **"condemned before God"**: Ralph Ovadal, *More Than These: A History of How the Pro-Life Movement Has Advanced the Cause of the Roman Catholic Church: A Call for Reformation* (Monroe, WI: Heart of Matter Publications, 2004), 199.

301 **"as an evangelical"**: "How Does the Christian World View the Pope's Pilgrimage to the Holy Land?," *Larry King Live*, CNN, March 22, 2000.

301 **"as close to an ecumenical"**: N. E. H. Hull and Peter Charles Hoffer, *Roe v. Wade: The Abortion Rights Controversy in American History* (Lawrence: University Press of Kansas, 2010), 339.

301 **"Glorify God"**: Len Bartlett of Premiere Speakers, email to Norma McCorvey, October 13, 1998. NMP.

301 **cashed her checks**: Andy Meisler, interview with the author, November 14, 2012.

301 **"She was destitute financially"**: Ron Allen, interview with the author, April 22, 2018.

301 **more than quadruple**: Jennifer Gonnerman, "Father Frank's Crusade," *Village Voice*, May 22, 2001.

302 **"NO ONE WILL 'CONTROL'"**: Norma McCorvey, email to Ron Mackey, July 28, 1998. NMP.

302 **"We never know"**: Bill Hampton, email to Norma McCorvey, August 25, 1998. NMP.

302 **to a speaking firm**: The firm was called Interact Client Marketing. NMP.

302 **Pavone himself helped**: Frank Pavone, interview with the author, May 31, 2018.

302 **"for any complicity"**: Ostling, "Roe Reconverts."

302 **depression was clinical**: Medical notes of Dr. Ramon Garcia, April 21, 1999. NMP.

302 **"another million deaths"**: Allan Parker, speaking in *A Cold Day in Hell: The Conversion of Norma McCorvey*, film, directed by Randall Terry, Victorious Lady Films, 2017.

302 **"They were over-scheduling"**: Sheree Havlik, interview with the author, April 30, 2018.

302 **"National Day of Death"**: NMP.

303 **wrote that God**: Ruth Lasseter, email to Norma McCorvey, August 3, 1999. NMP.

303 **"Lord Jesus Christ"**: Steven Waldman and Ginny Carroll, "Roe v. Roe," *Newsweek*, August 21, 1995.

303 **"little Christians"**: Norma McCorvey, interview with the author, November 4, 2013.

303 **"I'd put my hands"**: *A Cold Day in Hell*, film.

303 **"We're pregnant"**: *A Cold Day in Hell*, film.

303 **"shadow lesbian"**: Rob Schenck, interview with the author, July 27, 2018.

303 **support abortion in just one instance**: Benham made the comment to Angelia R. Wilson, a professor of politics at the University of Manchester. Cynthia Burack, *Tough Love: Sexuality, Compassion and the Christian Right*. (Albany: State University of New York Press, 2014), 60.

303 **"Instead of building"**: Philip Benham, "Homosexuality vs. Christianity . . . Should we build bridges or storm the gates?," Operation Rescue newsletter, December 1999.

303 **"homosexuals and lesbians"**: Randall A. Terry, *The Judgement of God: Terrorism, Flood, Droughts and Disasters* (Windsor, NY: Reformer Library, 1995), 49.

303 **"abortion and homosexuality"**: Jim Schneider, *Crosstalk*, radio program, Voice of Christian Youth, July 9, 2015.

303 **"spell of lesbianism"**: "Father Frank Pavone," *Daily Catholic*, http://www.dailycatholic.org/pavonbio.htm.

303 **amendment to bar gay marriage**: "Head-to-head: Should the U.S. Constitu-

tion bar gay marriage? Rev. Rob Schenck and Kevin Cathcart," *BBC News,* February 26, 2004.

304 **"Nobody was going to"**: Rob Schenck, interview with the author, July 27, 2018.

304 **"anxious and claustrophobic"**: Karen Garnett, interview with the author, July 19, 2018.

304 **"King Herods I have"**: Norma McCorvey, fax to Frank Pavone, January 10, 2000. NMP.

304 **"Miss Norma"**: *A Cold Day in Hell,* film.

304 **the plains of Oklahoma**: Allan Parker, interview with the author, January 17, 2020.

304 **"I was kind of"**: Allan Parker, interview with the author, January 17, 2020.

305 **"major scientific theories"**: Allan Parker, interview with the author, January 17, 2020.

305 **"alone with God"**: Allan Parker, interview with the author, January 17, 2020.

305 **"So what?"**: Allan Parker, interview with the author, January 17, 2020.

305 **including the International Covenant**: Article 6(5) of the 1966 International Covenant on Civil and Political Rights states: "Sentence of death shall not . . . be carried out on pregnant women." International Covenant on Civil and Political Rights, United Nations General Assembly, December 16, 1966.

306 **life began at conception**: Article 4(1) of the 1969 American Convention on Human Rights states: "Every person has the right to have his life respected. This right shall be protected by law and, in general, from the moment of conception." American Convention on Human Rights, Inter-American Specialized Conference on Human Rights, November 22, 1969.

306 **"to tell people"**: Allan Parker, interview with the author, January 17, 2020.

306 **founded a local organization**: The organization was called the Christian Conciliation Service of San Antonio.

306 **lawyers collected affidavits**: *Elizabeth Herrera, et al. v. The State of Texas, et al.,* Cause No. 2002–02958, 125th Judicial District Court of Harris County, Texas.

306 **Baby M adoption case**: *In re Baby* M, 109 N.J. 396, 537 A.2d 1227 (1988).

306 **Cassidy was readying**: The case was *Santa Marie v. Whitman.* (It was later named *Marie v. McGreevey.*) Frank Pavone, "Interview with Harold Cassidy, an attorney who is bringing a lawsuit that may challenge Roe v. Wade concerning the rights and well-being of women," *Life and Choice,* Catholic Family Radio, October 31, 1999.

306 **more than nine in ten**: G. Sisson, L. Ralph, H. Gould and D. G. Foster, "Adoption Decision Making among Women Seeking Abortion," *Women's Health Issues* 27, no. 2 (March/April 2017), 136–44.

306 **millions in China alone**: In 2013, data from the Chinese health ministry revealed that since 1971, when China began to introduce policies to curb the population, doctors had performed 336 million abortions. The number of those that were forced was not known. In some parts of the country, the government mandated that women have intrauterine devices implanted after giving birth, and forced sterilizations and abortions were common, some in the third trimester. Mei

Fong, author of *One Child* (Boston: Houghton Mifflin, 2015), estimates that the number of forced or coerced abortions is easily in the millions. Mei Fong, interview with the author, August 27, 2020. Simon Rabinovitch, "Data Reveal Scale of China Abortions," *Financial Times*, March 15, 2013.

306 **Cassidy's client had too**: Rick Marschall, "The Man Who Would Reverse *Roe v. Wade*," *Rare Jewel Magazine*, January/February 2005.

307 **"He was talking about"**: Karen Garnett, interview with the author, July 19, 2018.

307 **"the lie that abortion"**: "Important Supreme Court News from Allan Parker," Prayer Surge Now blog, November 12, 2015.

307 **"post abortion survivor syndrome"**: P. G. Ney, C. Sheils and M. Gajowy, "Post Abortion Survivor Syndrome," *Journal of Prenatal and Perinatal Psychology and Health* 25 (December 2010): 107–29.

307 **"post-abortion men"**: C. T. Coyle and R. Enright, "Forgiveness Intervention with Postabortion Men," *Journal of Consulting and Clinical Psychology* 65, no. 6 (1997): 1042–46.

307 **"crankery"**: David Tell, "Planned Un-Parenthood: Roe v. Wade at Thirty," *Weekly Standard*, January 27, 2003.

307 **"no association"**: National Cancer Institute, summary report: early reproductive events and breast cancer workshop, 2003. Available at: https://www.cancer.gov/types/breast/abortion-miscarriage-risk.

307 **Mother Teresa wrote**: "Mother Teresa Attacks Abortion," *Miami Herald*, June 30, 1986, 5.

308 **born in 1948**: Vincent Rue, interview with the author, February 10, 2021.

308 **"Psychologically and biologically"**: Nancy Knaak, "The Psychology of Women, or No Rose, By This or Any Other Name," *Educational Horizons* 52, no. 3 (1974): 123–34.

308 **"the true identity"**: Liz McGuinness, "Should Women Be Educated to Compete with Men in Business?" *Los Angeles Times*, December 2, 1964.

308 **presented a paper**: Vincent M. Rue, "A U.S. Department of Marriage and the Family," *Journal of Marriage and the Family* 35 (November 1973): 689–98.

308 **"The DMF"**: "Uncle Sam, Marriage Counselor," *Human Behavior* 3, no. 7 (July 1974): 42–43.

308 **activist named William Brennan**: Vincent Rue, interview with the author, February 10, 2021.

308 **"so-called science"**: Vincent Rue, interview with the author, February 10, 2021.

309 **"abortion counseling"**: Vincent Rue, interview with the author, February 10, 2021.

309 **"brought up abortion"**: Vincent Rue, interview with the author, February 10, 2021.

309 **twenty-four of its effects**: Vincent Rue, testimony, U.S. Senate, Committee on the Judiciary, Subcommittee on the Constitution, "Constitutional Amendments Relating to Abortion: Hearings on S.J. Res. 17, S.J. Res. 18, S.J. Res. 19, and S.J. Res. 110," November 4, 1981, p. 329–39. 97th Cong., 1st sess.

309 **"It's a type"**: Vincent Rue, interview with the author, October 31, 2018.

309 **woman named Olivia Gans**: Olivia Gans, "When the Mothers Found Their Voice: The Emergence of the Post-Abortion Presence in America," National Right to Life Committee, January 1998, https://www.nrlc.org/outreach/ava/.

309 **spoke of PAS**: Tamara Henry, "Koop Discusses Abortion," UPI, March 16, 1989.

309 **write up a report**: Ellie J. Lee, "Post-Abortion Syndrome: Reinventing Abortion as a Social Problem," in Joel Best, *How Claims Spread: Cross-National Diffusion of Social Problems* (New York: Aldine de Gruyter, 2001), 55.

309 **Dr. Koop reviewed**: Henry, "Koop Discusses Abortion."

309 **"flawed methodologically"**: Letter from C. Everett Koop, U.S. Surgeon General, to President Ronald Reagan, January 9, 1989, reprinted in *Family Planning Perspectives* 21 (January/February 1989): 31–32.

309 **"He's afraid"**: Martin Tolchin, "Koop's Stand on Abortion's Effect Surprises Friends and Foes Alike," *New York Times*, January 11, 1989.

310 **"always been able"**: Tolchin, "Koop's Stand."

310 **"relatively rare"**: N. E. Adler, H. P. David, B. N. Major, S. H. Roth, N. F. Russo and G. E. Wyatt, "Psychological Responses After Abortion," *Science* 248, no. 4951 (April 6, 1990): 41–44.

310 **more likely to express relief**: Adler et al., "Psychological Responses After Abortion."

310 **indicate much the same**: A 2008 report by the American Psychological Association found "no evidence sufficient to support the claim that an observed association between abortion history and mental health was caused by the abortion per se, as opposed to other factors." Brenda Major, Mark Appelbaum, Linda Beckman, Mary Ann Dutton, Nancy Felipe Russo and Carolyn West, "Report of the Task Force on Mental Health and Abortion," American Psychological Association, 2008, Washington, DC.

310 **The Turnaway Study**: Corinne H. Rocca, Katrina Kimport, Sarah C. M. Roberts, Heather Gould, John Neuhaus and Diana G. Foster, "Decision Rightness and Emotional Responses to Abortion in the United States: A Longitudinal Study," *PLOS One*, July 8, 2015.

310 **"no link between receiving"**: Diana Greene Foster, email to the author, July 1, 2020.

310 **"There is no evidence"**: Nada L. Stotland, MD, "The Myth of the Abortion Trauma Syndrome," *Journal of the American Medical Association* 268, no.15 (1992): 2078–79.

310 **"Abortion is a right"**: Sarah Bustain, "Choice Language," *American Prospect*, November 22, 2004.

310 **"Abortions will not"**: Gwendolyn Brooks, "the mother," in *Selected Poems* (San Francisco: Harper and Row, 1963).

310 **"overwhelming," "minuscule"**: U.S. House of Representatives, Committee on Government Operations, "Medical and Psychological Impact of Abortion," March 16, 1989, p. 241. 101st Cong., 1st sess.

310 **has no greater impact**: The study concluded that "severe negative reactions [to abortion] are rare, and they parallel those following other normal life

stresses." Nancy E. Adler et al., "Psychological Factors in Abortion: A Review," *American Psychologist* 47, no.1194 (1992): 1202–03.

311 **"possible detrimental"**: *Planned Parenthood of Southeastern Pa. v. Casey*, 505 U.S. 833 (1992).

311 **"informed consent"**: Lee, "Post-Abortion Syndrome," 63.

311 **"You can't repent"**: Emily Bazelon, "Is There a Post-Abortion Syndrome?," *New York Times Magazine*, January 21, 2007.

311 **"I am so scared"**: Norma McCorvey, email to Nathan Macklin, December 1, 2003. NMP.

311 **convert Oprah**: Transcript of meeting between Norma McCorvey and Allan Parker and other members of the Texas Justice Foundation, February 14, 2000. NMP.

312 **"The women"**: Transcript of meeting between Norma McCorvey and Allan Parker et al.

312 **"I am particularly interested"**: Transcript of meeting between Norma McCorvey and Allan Parker et al.

312 **"Me too"**: Transcript of meeting between Norma McCorvey and Allan Parker et al.

312 **"a couple of pitchers"**: Transcript of meeting between Norma McCorvey and Allan Parker et al.

312 **Norma had been unequivocal**: Norma later recalled that she learned the word "abortion" from a nurse while pregnant with her second child. Norma McCorvey, interview with the author, July 8, 2016.

312 **"built upon false"**: Brief for Norma McCorvey as Amicus Curiae, *Donna Santa Marie, et al. vs. Christine Todd Whitman, et al.*, Civil Action No. 99–2692 (GEB), March 15, 2000.

312 **"God is going to overturn"**: Transcript of meeting between Norma McCorvey and Allan Parker et al.

313 **"the most important"**: "Statement of Norma McCorvey," March 2000, Texas Justice Foundation. NMP.

313 **"at least gives the mother"**: "Statement of Norma McCorvey," Texas Justice Foundation.

313 **"even more painful"**: Marian Faux, *Roe v. Wade: The Untold Story of the Landmark Supreme Court Decision That Made Abortion Legal* (New York: Cooper Square Press, 1988), 119.

313 **"at risk for long-term"**: The article reviewed the findings of twelve studies, representing a total of 625 women. Hollie A. Askren and Kathleen C. Bloom, "Postadoptive Reactions of the Relinquishing Mother: A Review," *Journal of Obstetric, Gynecologic, and Neonatal Nursing* 28, no. 4 (July/August 1999): 395–400.

313 **"We're not animals"**: Monika Maeckle, "The Double Life of Norma McCorvey," *Westwood Magazine* (supplement of *Dallas Times Herald*), October 18, 1981.

313 **disseminating an instruction sheet**: "Instructions for Completing Affidavit and Authorization Form," Texas Justice Foundation, 2000. NMP.

313 **"The plan"**: Kathleen Cassidy, "Post-Abortive Women Attack Roe v. Wade," *At the Center*, January 2001.

313 **"For a long time"**: "History in the Making: 'Roe' Files Motion to Re-open Roe v. Wade, the Landmark Case Legalizing Abortion," Sermonindex.net, June 17, 2003.

313 **"Severe depression"**: "History in the Making."

314 **catastrophes God would bring**: Allan Parker, "Message to Pastors: Warning Something Big Is Coming," Christian Newswire, July 17, 2015.

314 **"It is my duty"**: Parker, "Message to Pastors."

314 **verses from Isaiah**: Isaiah 28:17–18: "Also I will make justice the measuring line, And righteousness the level; Then hail will sweep away the refuge of lies And the waters will overflow the secret place. Your covenant with death will be canceled, And your pact with Sheol will not stand" (NKJV).

314 **when God planted in him**: Karen Garnett recalled that Parker spoke of his plan to collect affidavits before his return to Dallas. Karen Garnett, interview with the author, July 19, 2018. Marschall, "The Man Who Would Reverse Roe v. Wade." "PSN 11/14 with John Robb," Prayer Surge Now.

314 **Pavone maintained his ties**: Email exchange between Norma McCorvey, Frank Pavone and Janet Morana, January 7, 2002. NMP.

314 **she was the keynote speaker**: Reception program, "Life In the West II," Justice Foundation, June 29, 2002. NMP.

315 **"applying [the decision] prospectively"**: "Grounds for Relief from a Final Judgment, Order or Proceeding," Federal Rules of Civil Procedure, Rule 60b.

315 **"You have to show"**: Marschall, "The Man Who Would Reverse Roe v. Wade."

315 **"a woman now has"**: Marschall, "The Man Who Would Reverse Roe v. Wade."

315 **he and Norma announced**: "History in the Making."

315 **"What if *Roe v. Wade*"**: Patrick J. Buchanan, "A Decision Based on Deceit," American Cause, June 23, 2003, theamericancause.org.

316 **knew this to be untrue**: Philip Benham, interview with the author, May 23, 2018. Frank Pavone, interview with the author, May 31, 2018.

316 **Parker insists**: Allan Parker, email to the author, January 25, 2021.

316 **lie at the heart**: Affidavit of Norma McCorvey, June 11, 2003, *McCorvey v. Hill*, Civil Action No. 3:03–CV-1340–N (formerly 3–3690–B and 3–3691–C) (N.D. Tex. Jun. 19, 2003).

316 **"the link between"**: "New Developments in the Battle to Overturn Roe v. Wade & Doe v. Bolton," Justice Foundation, undated. NMP.

316 **nearly three thousand women**: Sarah E. Burns, "2,887 Women Who Have Had Abortions et al.," Brief as Amicus Curiae, *Webster v. Reproductive Health Services*, 492 U.S. 490 (1989).

316 **"respond with support"**: Just 26.8 percent of disclosures, wrote Cowan, "received a negative reaction." Sarah K. Cowan, "Enacted Abortion Stigma in the United States," *Social Science & Medicine* 177 (March 2017): 259–68.

316 **42 million**: "Induced Abortion, Facts in Brief 2000," Guttmacher Institute,

https://web.archive.org/web/20020312193042/http:/www.guttmacher.org/
pubs/fb_induced_abortion.html. The total number of legal abortions performed between 1973 and 2000 was slightly more than 39 million. To this
number I added the roughly 2.6 million performed in 2001–02.

316 **the only photo**: Elizabeth Gumport, "Our Bodies, Ourselves, Our Anger,"
New York Times, April 29, 2018.

316 **stigma so intense**: The National Association for the Repeal of Abortion Laws
became NARAL Pro Choice America.

317 **"sad anti-choice"**: "Roe v. Roe? Too Late, Texas Judge Says," *National Catholic Register*, June 29, 2003.

317 **not a single brief**: Lynn M. Paltrow, "Missed Opportunities in *McCorvey v.
Hill*: The Limits of Pro-Choice Lawyering," *NYU Review of Law and Social
Change* 35, no. 194 (2011): 197.

317 **"a stunning non-response"**: Paltrow, "Missed Opportunities."

317 **"The pro-choice"**: Paltrow, "Missed Opportunities."

317 **"was certainly final"**: Lisa Falkenberg, "Court Dismisses Request to Reconsider Roe v. Wade," *Austin American–Statesman*, June 21, 2003.

317 **"The implication"**: Jeannie Suk, "The Trajectory of Trauma: Bodies and
Minds of Abortion Discourse," *Columbia Law Review* 110, no.1193 (2010):
1195–97.

317 **Buchanan compared him**: Buchanan, "A Decision Based on Deceit."

317 **Dick and Betsy DeVos**: The Dick and Betsy DeVos Family Foundation
donated $25,000 to the Justice Foundation in 2003, the year Parker filed
McCorvey v. Hill. See https://www.documentcloud.org/documents/4488372
-Dick-and-Betsy-Devos-Family-Foundation-2003.html.

317 **the Covenant Foundation funded him**: The Covenant Foundation funded
the Justice Foundation for five years, starting in 2000 when Parker
first partnered with Norma. It donated a total of $870,000. See https://
www.influencewatch.org/non-profit/covenant-foundation-inc/.

317 **"mouth-peace"**: Norma McCorvey, email to Allan Parker, 2005. NMP.

317 **"vital to be more jealous"**: Robert Cooley, letter to Philip Benham, August
11, 1995. NMP.

318 **a Catholic pro-life group**: The Catholic Pro-Life Committee of North Texas.

318 **poinsettias and bird food**: Edward Robinson, email to Norma McCorvey,
December 14, 1998. NMP.

318 **"a little clutch purse"**: Daniel Vinzant, interview with the author, July 5,
2018.

318 **"She was alone"**: Daniel Vinzant, interview with the author, July 5, 2018.

318 **"I was always comfortable"**: Daniel Vinzant, interview with the author, July
11, 2018.

318 **"I just loved"**: Daniel Vinzant, interview with the author, July 5, 2018.

318 **"pure gossip"**: Daniel Vinzant, interview with the author, November 22,
2020.

318 **"perverse result"**: Steven Kreytak, "Roe v. Wade remains closed," *Austin
American–Statesman*, September 15, 2004.

319 **let a woman die**: Henry Morton Robinson, *The Cardinal* (New York: Abrams, 1950), 88.

319 **the baby had died**: Megan Rosenfeld, "Waging the New War of the Roses," *Washington Post*, January 3, 1979.

319 **"No exceptions"**: Emily Langer, "Nellie Gray, March for Life founder, dead at 88," *Washington Post*, August 14, 2012.

319 **"They are trying"**: "'March for Life' Rally," CSPAN, January 24, 2005.

319 **Parker clapped wildly**: "'March for Life' Rally."

319 **"if one woman"**: Muriel Rukeyser, "Käthe Kollwitz," in *The Speed of Darkness* (New York: Random House, 1968).

319 **"change the abortion"**: David Reardon, *Making Abortion Rare: A Healing Strategy for a Divided Nation* (Irvine, CA: Acorn, 1996), x.

320 **proposed a ban**: "We find the testimonies of these women an important source of information about the way consents for abortions are taken, as well as many other matters relevant to the mandate given to this Task Force by HB 1233." Report of the South Dakota Task Force to Study Abortion – Submitted to the Governor and Legislature of South Dakota, December 5, 2005, Section II.A, 22.

320 **"While we find"**: *Gonzales v. Carhart*, 127 S. Ct. 1610, 1634 (2007).

320 **a Parker amicus brief**: The specific brief Kennedy cited was filed on behalf of Sandra Cano, the born-again Mary Doe of *Doe v. Bolton*, whom Parker represented along with Norma.

320 **"was a development"**: Linda Greenhouse, "Adjudging a Moral Harm to Women from Abortions," *New York Times*, April 20, 2007.

320 **"The [Operation] Outcry"**: Reva B. Siegel, "The Right's Reasons: Constitutional conflict and the spread of women-protective antiabortion argument," *Duke Law Journal*, April 2008, 1641.

320 **"Norma McCorvey is patient"**: Mary Ziegler, "What McCorvey Believed Matters," *Atlantic*, May 31, 2020.

321 **"the logical culmination"**: Schoen, *Abortion After Roe*, 20.

322 **the committee pay Mildred**: Thea Rossi Barron, letter to David W. O'Steen, November 22, 1989. Courtesy of Thea Rossi Barron.

322 **There were robocalls**: Mildred Jefferson, robocall recording. MJP, Box 22, Folder 4.

322 **"If he is not a child"**: Commercial transcript. MJP, Box 22, Folder 4.

322 **There was a booklet**: Robert L. Krebsbach, *Abortion: Have We the Right?* (Right to Life Crusade, Inc., 1984), vii.

322 **"Only rarely does pregnancy"**: Right to Life Crusade, Inc., flier, undated. Courtesy of Kathleen Bothell.

323 **"matriarch"**: Louis Prisock, "'If You Love Children, Say So': The African American Anti-Abortion Movement," *Public Eye*, October 1, 2003.

323 **"to limit our population"**: Spoken by Xavier Suarez, a Cuban-born activist, who sat on the panel beside Jefferson, Erma Craven, a black social worker, and Constance Redbird Uri, a Native American doctor. Their press con-

ference was at the 1976 NRLC convention. "Leaders Answer Questions at Press Conference," *National Right to Life News* 3 (August 1976).

323 **"racial overtones"**: Harry A. Blackmun, preamble to *Roe v. Wade*.

323 **"Enforced motherhood"**: Margaret Sanger, "Suppression," *Woman Rebel* 1, no. 4 (June 1914).

323 **Fears of overpopulation**: Wrote Sanger: "We who advocate Birth Control . . . lay all our emphasis upon stopping not only the reproduction of the unfit but upon stopping all reproduction when there is not economic means of providing proper care for those who are born in health." Margaret Sanger, "Birth Control and Racial Betterment," *Birth Control Review*, February 1919.

323 **"well-born"**: Francis Galton, *Inquiries into Human Faculty and Its Development* (London: Macmillan, 1883).

323 **"Society has no business"**: Letter from Theodore Roosevelt to Charles Davenport, January 3, 1913, http://eugenics.us/letter-by-theodore-roosevelt-to-charles-davenport-society-should-not-permit-degenerates-to-reproduce-their-kind/176.htm.

323 **"criminals, idiots, imbeciles"**: Laws of Indiana, 1907, Chapter 215, 377–78.

323 **Two dozen states followed**: Paul A. Lombardo, *Three Generations, No Imbeciles* (Baltimore: Johns Hopkins University Press, 2010), 294, Appendix C.

323 **"It is better for all"**: *Buck v. Bell*, 274 U.S. 205–207 (1927). It is important to note that the ruling was never overturned.

324 **granted the U.S. eugenicist**: Harriet Washington, *Medical Apartheid: The Dark History of Medical Experimentation on Black Americans from Colonial Times to the Present* (New York: Doubleday, 2007), 194.

324 **"in the silence"**: Paul Lombardo, interview with the author, August 1, 2019.

324 **would be robbed of the ability**: Professor Lombardo notes that there are few official state tallies of the sterilizations. They were compiled by a political scientist in New York state named Julius Paul, who collected his findings in an 840–page unpublished manuscript titled "Three Generations of Imbeciles Are Enough: State Eugenic Sterilization Laws in American Thought and Practice." The total number of sterilizations that Paul presented, 65,370, was a conservative estimate. Lombardo, "Three Generations," 293–94.

324 **cited the Holmes opinion**: "Karl Brandt defense documents," 1946–47, Nuremberg Trials Project, no. 53, 122. Harvard Law School Library.

324 **"seeking to assist"**: Sanger, "Birth Control and Racial Betterment."

324 **"the feeble-minded"**: Sanger, "Birth Control and Racial Betterment."

324 **"Sanger did not tie"**: Dorothy E. Roberts, *Killing the Black Body: Race, Reproduction, and the Meaning of Liberty* (New York: Vintage, 1999), 81.

324 **"fed, nurtured, and sustained"**: Roberts, *Killing the Black Body*, 81.

324 **"about six out of ten"**: DeNeen L. Brown, "Civil rights crusader Fannie Lou Hamer defied men—and presidents—who tried to silence her," *Washington Post*, October 6, 2017.

324 **experimental surgeries**: Sims performed the surgeries on approximately

eleven women who had vesicovaginal fistulae. Washington, *Medical Apart-heid*, 64.

324 **appropriation of black bodies**: Washington, *Medical Apartheid*, 115–42.

324 **its notorious study of syphilis**: DeNeen L. Brown, "'You've got bad blood': The horror of the Tuskegee syphilis experiment," *Washington Post*, May 16, 2017.

324 **doctors could provide contraception**: The case, *United States v. One Package of Japanese Pessaries*, 86 F.2d 737 (2d Cir. 1936), was decided in 1936.

325 **"We do not want word"**: Letter from Margaret Sanger to Dr. Clarence Gamble, December 10, 1939. Margaret Sanger Papers, Sophia Smith Collection, Smith College.

325 **"The mass of ignorant Negroes"**: W. E. B. DuBois, "Black Folk and Birth Control," *Birth Control Review*, June 1932, 166.

325 **"race suicide"**: Julian Lewis, "Is Birth Control a Menace to Negroes?," *Jet*, August 19, 1954.

325 **from Langston Hughes**: Langston Hughes, "Population Explosion," *New York Post*, December 10, 1965.

325 **to Dick Gregory**: Dick Gregory, "My Answer to Genocide," *Ebony*, October 1971.

325 **"black genocide"**: The resolution passed at the 1967 National Conference on Black Power in Newark, NJ. Nathan Wright, "Black Power vs. Black Genocide," *Black Scholar*, December 1969.

325 **"the unborn Black baby"**: Erma Clardy Craven, "Abortion, Poverty and Black Genocide, Gifts to the Poor?," in T. W. Hilgers and D. J. Horan, eds., *Abortion and Social Justice* (New York: Sheed and Ward, 1972), 231.

325 **birth control programs**: William A. Darity and Castellano B. Turner, "Fears of Genocide Among Black Americans as Related to Age, Sex, and Religion," *American Journal of Public Health* 63 (1973): 1029.

325 **"male rhetoric"**: Shirley Chisholm, *Unbought and Unbossed* (Boston: Houghton Mifflin Harcourt, 1970), 108.

325 **80 percent of black women**: Donald J. Bogue, "Family Planning in Negro Ghettos of Chicago," *Milbank Memorial Fund Quarterly*, April 1970, part 2, 283.

325 **"Negroes don't want children"**: Hannah Lees, "The Negro Response to Birth Control," *Reporter* 34 (May 19, 1966): 46. Cited in Washington, *Medical Apartheid*, 200.

326 **twelve times more likely**: Rachel Benson Gold, "Lessons from Before *Roe*: Will Past Be Prologue?," *Guttmacher Report on Public Policy* 6, no. 1 (2003): 10.

326 **almost triple that**: The number of white women, per 1,000 women in the population, having abortions was 11.9 in 1972, 13.7 in 1973, 15.6 in 1974, and 17.3 in 1975, while the corresponding number of nonwhite women having abortions was 21.9 in 1972, 32.7 in 1973, 41.9 in 1974, and 50.2 in 1975. "White" includes white Hispanics and "nonwhite" includes black and other races. But the effect on the data is negligible, says the abortion researcher Stanley Henshaw, because there were relatively few Hispanic women and women of other races in the U.S. in the 1970s. The CDC was the source for

the total number of abortions in 1972, and the Guttmacher Institute was the source for the other years. The distribution by race was provided by the CDC. The rates for 1972 and 1975 are from Table 101 of the 1980 Statistical Abstract of the United States, and those from 1973 and 1974 were calculated by Henshaw.

326 **"The people who are fewer"**: Charles B. Fancher, Jr., "Much in Common but Worlds Apart," *Philadelphia Inquirer*, April 23, 1978.

326 **Mildred continued to speak**: Black History Month Symposium poster, 1985. MJP, F+D1.

326 **"I refuse to represent"**: Mildred Jefferson, interview with Jennifer Donnally, September 22, 2010. Interviews of Jennifer M. Donnally, 2007–2012, MC1059, Box 60, CD 7. Schlesinger Library, Harvard University.

326 **"bitterness"**: FBI case file for Mildred Fay Jefferson, no. 161–HQ-9379, 36. Interview with Ruth Marin, March 13, 1973.

327 **"a political apartheid"**: Renee Loth, "Jefferson in GOP Bid for Senate," *Boston Globe*, February 12, 1990.

327 **"Social programs are killing"**: Jefferson, "A New Iconoclast."

327 **"self-indulgent"**: Otile McManus, "Dr. Jefferson and her Fight Against Abortion," *Boston Sunday Globe*, December 3, 1976.

327 **"I like someone else to carry"**: McManus, "Dr. Jefferson and her Fight."

327 **"the principle"**: Mildred Jefferson, testimony, U.S. Senate, Committee on the Judiciary, Subcommittee on Constitutional Amendments, hearing on "Abortion," August 21, 1974, p. 14. 93rd Cong., 2nd sess.

327 **"ERA means abortion"**: Phyllis Schlafly, "ERA means abortion and population shrinkage," *The Phyllis Schlafly Report*, December 1974.

327 **many first-wave feminists**: On July 8, 1869, on page 4 of the *Revolution*, a weekly feminist newspaper published by Susan B. Anthony and Elizabeth Cady Stanton, an article titled "Marriage and Maternity" wrote of abortion: "no matter what the motive, love of ease, or a desire to save from suffering the unborn innocent, the woman is awfully guilty who commits the deed." The next year, on October 8, 1870, *Woodhull & Claflin's Weekly*, a newspaper published by Victoria Woodhull and her sister Tennessee Claflin, also decried abortion. "The truth of the matter is," read an editorial on page 11, "that it is just as much a murder to destroy life in its embryonic condition, as it is to destroy it after the fully developed form is attained, for it is the self-same life that is taken." The editorial indicated, however, that were abortion possible before the embryonic heart began beating, it would *not* be murder. This, though, was not possible, it asserted, as "modern science" taught that the heartbeat began at conception. We now know that the fetal heartbeat does not begin until twenty-two days after conception.

327 **"unearthed the political gold"**: Tanya Melich, *The Republican War Against Women: An Insider's Report from Behind the Lines* (New York: Random House, 2009).

327 **"These two issues"**: Jill Lepore, *These Truths* (New York: Norton, 2018), 647.

328 **"a gray world"**: Mildred Jefferson, "Lifelines from the President's Desk," *National Right to Life News* 4 (August 1977).

328 **"terrorists"**: "Excerpts from Dr. Jefferson's Speech at Houston," *National Right to Life News* 5 (January 1978).

328 **"the essence and reasons"**: Mildred Jefferson, interview with Jennifer Donnally, October 22, 2007.

328 **unlike 84 percent**: In 1990, 84 percent of women at the end of their childbearing years had given birth. Gretchen Livingston, "They're Waiting Longer, but U.S. Women Today More Likely to Have Children Today Than a Decade Ago," *Pew Research Center Analysis of Current Population Survey*, January 18, 2018.

328 **"I wanted to ask her"**: Russell Gary Heikkila, interview with the author, July 19, 2017.

328 **children would impede**: Anne Fox, interview with the author, August 22, 2019.

328 **she'd been unable**: Judie Brown, interview with the author, March 24, 2017.

328 **threatened to bring shame**: Dr. Joseph Stanton, letter to Mildred Jefferson, November 10, 1993. MJP, Box 4, Folder 5.

328 **the word "formerly"**: Dr. Joseph Stanton, letter to Mildred Jefferson, November 10, 1993. MJP, Box 4, Folder 5.

328 **turned personal**: For more on the split between Dr. Jefferson and Dr. Stanton, see Mary Ziegler, *After Roe: The Lost History of the Abortion Debate* (Cambridge, MA: Harvard University Press, 2015), 279, n. 67.

328 **"It is all too obvious"**: Dr. Joseph Stanton, letter to Mildred Jefferson, November 10, 1993. MJP, Box 4, Folder 5.

328 **a working surgeon**: "Black Conservatives Meet in Houston," *Issues and Views*, Fall 1994.

328 **"I do what I do"**: Judy Klemesrud, "Abortion in the Campaign: Methodist Surgeon Leads the Opposition," *New York Times*, March 1, 1976.

329 **$9,071**: Check from Mildred Jefferson to Cambridge French Trust, May 15, 1995. MJP, Box 3, Folder 8.

329 **Mildred had inherited**: Kirthell Roberts (Mildred Jefferson's cousin), interview with the author, August 23, 2019.

329 **to cover some of her rent**: Anne Fox, interview with the author, August 22, 2019.

329 **parsing public data**: Janet Pearson, "PCs Revolutionize Political Campaigning," *Tulsa World*, October 26, 1992.

329 **wrote her landlord a check**: Check from Mildred Jefferson to Cambridge French Trust, May 15, 1995. MJP, Box 3, Folder 8.

329 **"I don't like"**: RealAmerican93, "Can the Republic Be Saved—Dr Mildred Jefferson—Part 1," YouTube, December 4, 2010.

329 **statement on abortion**: Various, "The America We Seek: A Statement of Pro-Life Principle and Concern," *First Things*, May 1996.

330 **a convention in Tampa**: "American Life League Brings Pro-Life Leaders to Tampa Celebration," American Life League, press release, October 8, 1997.

330 **steadily dropping**: R. K. Jones, E. Witwer and J. Jerman, *Abortion Incidence and Service Availability in the United States, 2017* (New York: Guttmacher Institute, 2019), https://www.guttmacher.org/report/abortion-incidence-service-availability-us-2017.

330 **"somewhat more serious"**: Molly Ivins, "'This Right of Privacy,'" *Texas Observer*, February 16, 1973.

330 **Roe to 0.5**: Tara C. Jatlaoui et al., "Abortion Surveillance—United States, 2015," *Morbidity and Mortality Weekly Report* 67, no. SS-13 (2018): 1–45, Table 23.

330 **ended with just a few pills**: Eric A. Schaff, Stephen L. Fielding, Carolyn Westhoff et al., "Vaginal Misoprostol Administered 1, 2, or 3 Days After Mifepristone for Early Medical Abortion," *Journal of the American Medical Association* 284, no. 15 (October 18, 2000).

330 **slept just three hours**: Robert Mears, "An Interview with Dr. Mildred Fay Jefferson," *New England Correspondent* clipping, 1984. MJP. Box 21, Folder 12.

330 **"more devastating to the U.S."**: American Life League, press release, January 22, 2002.

330 **"ASK FOR MONEY"**: Mildred Jefferson, notes, undated. MJP.

330 **third most admired**: Mildred trailed only Phyllis Schlafly and Nancy Reagan. Ira R. Allen, "Poll Says Reagan No Longer Most Admired Conservative," UPI, September 22, 1981.

330 **nominated her for a position**: Henry Louis Gates, Jr., and Evelyn Brooks Higginbotham, eds., *African American Lives* (Oxford: Oxford University Press, 2004), 448. The committee was the Secretary's Advisory Committee on Human Research Protection. Michael McCarthy, "US Human Research Committee Draws Fire," *Lancet* 361, no. 9352 (January 11, 2003).

331 **"Many aspects"**: Gates and Higginbotham, *African American Lives*, 447.

331 **"She wanted to keep"**: Kathleen Bothell, interview with the author, February 7, 2017.

331 **told a pro-life organization**: "Mildred Fay Jefferson, MD," *American Feminist: Remarkable Pro-Life Women III* 10, no. 2 (Summer 2003): 12.

331 **"on self-assigned sabbatical"**: Mildred Jefferson, fax to the American Life League, August 4, 2003. MJP, Box 2, Folder 9.

331 **opposition to affirmative action**: Mildred Jefferson, fax to the American Life League, August 4, 2003. MJP, Box 2, Folder 9.

331 **"American ideals"**: "Establish Fund in Honor of Lt. Gutman," *Newton Graphic*, February 8, 1945.

331 **"served the equivalent"**: Mildred Jefferson, fax to the American Life League, August 4, 2003. MJP, Box 2, Folder 9.

331 **a chain of newspapers**: Doug LeBlanc, "Jefferson Fighting for Rights of the Unborn," *Sunday Advocate* (Baton Rouge), October 6, 1985.

331 **or be the dean**: Jefferson, "A New Iconoclast."

331 **"she was very eager"**: Brendan O'Connell, interview with the author, August 2, 2019.

332 **repeat her own opinion**: McManus, "Dr. Jefferson and her Fight."

332 **"Those seven men"**: Roger Resler, *Compelling Interest: The Real Story Behind Roe v. Wade* (Escondido, CA: eChristian, 2012), 136.

332 **landlord wrote to Mildred**: Rene Mugnier, letter to Mildred Jefferson, October 27, 2003. MJP, Box 3, Folder 10.

332 **"the newspapers were piled up"**: Dusty Maguire, interview with the author, October 31, 2019.

333 **"We all came to the conclusion"**: Philip Moran, interview with the author, September 3, 2019.

333 **"We thought she"**: Amy Baum, interview with the author, August 14, 2019.

333 **"The only consolation"**: Philip Moran, email to Anne Fox, June 8, 2007. MJP, Box 6, Folder 1.

333 **"She wasn't interviewing"**: Brendan O'Connell, interview with the author, August 14, 2019.

334 **"the whole family"**: *Vital Concerns*, television program, Boston Neighborhood Network, October 1, 2009.

334 **"no nuances"**: Anne Fox, interview with the author, August 22, 2019.

335 **"I went to Public"**: Dusty Maguire, interview with the author, October 31, 2019.

335 **"I don't think anyone"**: Mildred Jefferson, interview with Jennifer Donnally, September 22, 2010.

335 **"literally, literally, literally"**: Mildred Jefferson, interview with Jennifer Donnally, September 22, 2010.

335 **"genes from the plains"**: *Vital Concerns*, television program, Boston Neighborhood Network, October 7, 2010.

335 **"There is nothing dignified"**: *Vital Concerns*, television program, Boston Neighborhood Network, November 5, 2009.

336 **"like a leaf"**: Anne Fox, interview with the author, August 22, 2019.

336 **"a beautiful, articulate, educated"**: Thea Rossi Barron, eulogy for Mildred Jefferson, November 26, 2010. Courtesy of Thea Rossi Barron.

336 **"the perfect, the privileged"**: Dennis Hevesi, "Mildred Jefferson, 84, Anti-Abortion Activist, Is Dead," *New York Times*, October 18, 2010.

337 **traded to Harvard**: Anne Fox, email to the author, October 2, 2019.

337 **"books, papers, periodicals"**: Divorce ruling, January 16, 1981. NMP.

337 **heart disease the probable cause**: "Probable Cardiac Dysrhythmia Medical Due to Atherosclerotic Cardiovascular Disease." Certificate of death: Mildred Fay Jefferson, filed October 26, 2010, Commonwealth of Massachusetts Dept of Public Health Registry of Vital Records and Statistics, R 351456.

338 **its highest award**: Cynthia Gorney, "Abortion Providers Meet to Honor Peers," *Washington Post*, May 9, 1990.

338 **Boyd simply rescheduled:** Curtis Boyd, "The Morality of Abortion: The Making of a Feminist Physician," *St. Louis University Public Law Review* 13 (1993–94): 303–14.

338 **"a good and moral"**: "Prepared Statement of Curtis Boyd, M.D., Santa Fe,

NM," in *Hearings Before the Subcommittee on Civil and Constitutional Rights of the Committee on the Judiciary House of Representatives: One Hundred First Congress, First and Second Sessions.* (Washington: Government Printing Office, 1994), 83.

339 **law review article**: Boyd, "The Morality of Abortion."

339 **"I don't like"**: Henry Eisenberg and Howard Eisenberg, *Night Calls: The Personal Journey of an Ob-Gyn* (New York: Berkley, 1988), 129.

339 **"rare"**: Bill Clinton, remarks accepting the presidential nomination at the Democratic National Convention in Chicago, August 29, 1996. Available at the American Presidency Project, https://www.presiden cy.ucsb.edu/documents/remarks-accepting-the-presidential-nomination -the-democratic-national-convention-chicago.

339 **"I have often paused"**: *Voices of Choice: Physicians Who Provided Abortions Before Roe v. Wade*, film, created by Physicians for Reproductive Health, Fly on the Wall Productions, 2003.

339 **"the potential to become"**: Curtis Boyd, interview with the author, September 1, 2016.

339 **"There is no possibility"**: Warren M. Hern and Billie Corrigan, "What About Us? Staff Reactions to D & E," *Advances in Planned Parenthood* 15, no. 1 (1980): 7.

339 **"a small arm"**: Cynthia Gorney, *Articles of Faith: A Frontline History of the Abortion Wars* (New York: Simon and Schuster, 2000), 300.

339 **"blind spot"**: "A Weekend Without War Over the Abortion Issue," *New York Times*, June 3, 1996.

339 **"in order to terminate"**: Christopher Hitchens, "Minority Report," *Nation*, April 24, 1989.

340 **"freedom to abort"**: Judith Wilt, *Abortion, Choice, and Contemporary Fiction* (Chicago: University of Chicago Press, 1990), xii.

340 **"abortion is always"**: Andrew Sullivan, "Life Lesson," *New Republic*, February 7, 2005.

340 **"I have always frankly"**: Camille Paglia, "Fresh Blood for the Vampire," *Salon*, September 10, 2008.

340 **"Intellectually, I thought"**: Curtis Boyd, interview with the author, February 13, 2019.

340 **"She has the ultimate right"**: Curtis Boyd, interview with the author, February 13, 2019.

340 **carried the additional horrible risk**: Dena Kleiman, "When Abortion Becomes Birth: A Dilemma of Medical Ethics Shaken by New Advances," *New York Times*, February 15, 1984.

340 **"I love my work"**: Gorney, "Abortion Providers Meet to Honor Peers."

340 **"I really had arrived"**: Curtis Boyd, interview with the author, September 1, 2016.

340 **"You have to always"**: Curtis Boyd, interview with the author, May 3, 2017.

341 **"You were either"**: Joffe interviewed Boyd in 1988. Carole E. Joffe, *Doctors of Conscience: The Struggle to Provide Abortion Before and After Roe v. Wade* (Boston: Beacon Press, 1995), 153.

341 **give him a pseudonym**: Joffe called Boyd "David Bennett."

341 **Two companies on Wall Street**: The companies were Diversified Medical Corp. and Comprehensive Education Systems, Inc. Howard Eisenberg, "The Mad Scramble for Abortion Money," *Medical Economics*, January 4, 1971, 991–97.

341 **upped by a third**: Eisenberg quotes one doctor saying: "By the way, my fee is no longer $200—it's now $275." Eisenberg, "The Mad Scramble for Abortion Money."

341 **capped the cost**: Eisenberg, "The Mad Scramble for Abortion Money."

341 **cost three or four times**: Curtis Boyd, interview with the author, March 7, 2017.

341 **$200,000**: Curtis Boyd, interview with the author, May 23, 2019.

341 **his larger clinics**: Curtis Boyd, interview with the author, April 4, 2019.

341 **threat to her mental health**: Both *United States v. Vuitch*, 402 U.S. 62 (1971), and *Doe v. Bolton*, 410 U.S. 179 (1973), defined "health" to include both physical and psychological well-being. *Roe v. Wade*, Section X, allowed third-trimester abortions.

341 **seven states**: Those seven states are Alaska, Colorado, New Hampshire, New Jersey, New Mexico, Oregon and Vermont.

342 **died in a plane crash**: Judy L. Thomas and David Klepper, "Life Experiences Shaped Tiller's Career," *Wichita Eagle*, June 7, 2009.

342 **to take it over**: David Barstow, "An Abortion Battle, Fought to the Death," *New York Times*, July 25, 2009.

342 **"The only [thing] worse"**: Reminiscences of Dr. George Tiller, Physicians for Reproductive Choice and Health Project, 2001, 3. Oral History Archives, Columbia University.

342 **His patients explained**: Judy Lundstrom Thomas, "Tiller: Tired but Determined," *Wichita Eagle*, September 8, 1991.

342 **"equal in magnitude"**: Reminiscences of Dr. George Tiller, 6.

342 **"I can remember the terror"**: Reminiscences of Dr. George Tiller, 7.

343 **vowed to be better prepared**: Reminiscences of Dr. George Tiller, 7–8.

343 **"It is that invitation"**: Reminiscences of Dr. George Tiller , 26.

343 **"My practice just went"**: Reminiscences of Dr. George Tiller, 10.

343 **used a baseball**: Cathy Reavis, interview with the author, March 8, 2019.

343 **"He did say"**: Cathy Reavis, interview with the author, March 8, 2019.

343 **"particularly with fetal abnormality"**: Reminiscences of Dr. George Tiller, 10.

343 **"He started ordering"**: Cathy Reavis, interview with the author, March 8, 2019.

343 **"I can't do it"**: Curtis Boyd, interview with the author, February 13, 2019.

343 **injecting into the fetal heart**: Among the doctors pioneering the use of digoxin was Dr. Paul Wright of Oakland. Dr. Warren M. Hern was among the first to use urea as described in his paper "Serial multiple laminaria and adjunctive urea in late out-patient dilation and evacuation abortion," *Obstetrics and Gynecology* 63 (1984): 543–49.

344 **"The concept that you"**: Charlotte Taft, interview with the author, March 13, 2019.

344 **"even if it's ironic"**: Charlotte Taft, interview with the author, March 13, 2019.

344 **more humane**: JoAn Armentrout, interview with the author, March 8, 2019.

344 **using an ultrasound machine**: Cathy Reavis, interview with the author, March 8, 2019.

344 **"The patient wasn't maimed"**: Reminiscences of Dr. George Tiller, 10.

344 **using the forty-week model**: Katie Watson, *Scarlet A: The Ethics, Law, and Politics of Ordinary Abortion* (Oxford: Oxford University Press, 2018), 149.

344 **"The *Roe* framework"**: Justice O'Connor wrote in dissent in the case *City of Akron v. Akron Center of Reproductive Health*, 462 U.S. 416 (1983).

344 **"initially desired"**: Barbara Vobejda and David Brown, "Harsh Details Shift Tenor of Abortion Fight," *Washington Post*, September 17, 1996.

345 **"Dr. George Tiller"**: Minutes, Meeting of the Medical Advisory and Education Committee of the National Abortion Federation, Dallas, TX, March 16, 1985. Takey Crist Papers (series "Abortion"), Sally Bingham Center for Women's History and Culture, file NAF 1985, Duke University.

345 **to refer complaints**: Minutes, Meeting of the Medical Advisory and Education Committee of the National Abortion Federation.

345 **do not recall**: Glenna Boyd, interview with the author, March 15, 2019.

345 **"public perception"**: Charlotte Taft, interview with the author, March 13, 2019.

345 **"He just felt"**: JoAn Armentrout, interview with the author, March 8, 2019.

345 **"If I'm not"**: Reminiscences of Dr. George Tiller, 15.

345 **an arrest for driving drunk**: Tiller did his rehab at the Ridgeview Institute in Smyrna, Georgia. David Barstow, "An Abortion Battle, Fought to the Death," *New York Times*, July 25, 2009.

345 **four days**: Devin Friedman, "Savior vs. Savior," *GQ*, January 8, 2010.

346 **"ministry"**: Reminiscences of Dr. George Tiller, 30.

346 **at that point**: Lundstrom Thomas, "Tiller: Tired but Determined."

346 **"Nature makes mistakes"**: Lundstrom Thomas, "Tiller: Tired but Determined."

346 **Two in five abortions**: Carole Joffe, "Working with Dr. Tiller: Staff Recollections of Women's Health Care Services of Wichita," *Perspectives on Sexual and Reproductive Health* 43, no. 3 (September 2011): 199–204.

346 **"readily treatable"**: Barstow, "An Abortion Battle."

346 **"many were perfectly healthy"**: Barstow, "An Abortion Battle."

346 **a second doctor**: 2006 Kansas Code – 65-6703.

346 **"Babies and families"**: Lundstrom Thomas, "Tiller: Tired but Determined."

346 **"personalize the struggle"**: Risen and Thomas, *Wrath of Angels*, 320.

346 **"the nation's pre-eminent"**: Barstow, "An Abortion Battle."

347 **"Dr. Tiller was"**: JoAn Armentrout, interview with the author, March 8, 2019.

347 **NAF honored Tiller**: The Christopher Tietze Humanitarian Award.

347 **one in a thousand**: In 1992, 0.1 percent of abortions were performed in the third trimester. Gina Kolata, "In Late Abortions, Decisions Are Painful and Options Few," *New York Times*, January 5, 1992. Because the numbers of third-trimester abortions are so small, they're typically reported collec-

tively by the CDC as all abortions performed at 21 weeks or later. As of 2018, the most recent year for which data are available, exactly 1 percent of abortions occurred after 20 weeks. Tara C. Jatlaoui et al., "Abortion surveillance – United States, 2018," *Morbidity and Mortality Weekly Report* 69, no. SS-7 (2020): 1–29, Table 9.

347 **including Randall Terry**: "It's a matter of self-defense," he says. Randall Terry, interview with the author, January 28, 2019.

347 **agreed that a woman**: 75 percent of people surveyed in 2003 (and in 2018) believe abortion ought to be legal even in the third trimester when a woman's "life is endangered." Lydia Saad, "Trimesters Still Key to U.S. Abortion Views," Gallup, June 13, 2018.

347 **half the country agreed**: 48 percent of people surveyed in 2003 (and in 2018) believe abortion ought to be legal even in the third trimester when a child will be "born with a life-threatening illness." Saad, "Trimesters Still Key."

347 **nine had had nothing wrong**: David Brown, "Late Term Abortions," *Washington Post*, September 17, 1996.

347 **"everything that was right"**: JoAn Armentrout, interview with the author, March 24, 2019.

347 **patient was the woman**: Reminiscences of Dr. George Tiller, 11.

347 **"simply want non-judgmental"**: Reminiscences of Dr. George Tiller, 22.

347 **with the alcoholic**: Reminiscences of Dr. George Tiller, 24.

348 **more easily delivered**: Kolata, "In Late Abortions."

348 **disbursed it widely**: Vobejda and Brown, "Harsh Details Shift Tenor."

348 **"as close to infanticide"**: Vobejda and Brown, "Harsh Details Shift Tenor."

348 **the fetus fell into a coma**: Dr. McMahon stated in a letter to the House Judiciary Subcommittee on the Constitution, June 23, 1995, that, owing to the anesthesia given the woman, "a medical coma is induced in the fetus" which in turn causes "a neurological fetal demise." U.S. House of Representatives, debate on Senate Amendments to the Partial-Birth Abortion Ban Act of 1997, H.R. 1833, March 27, 1996. 104th Cong., 2nd sess. *Congressional Record* 142, part 44.

348 **minor relief of pain**: Dr. Norig Ellison stated in a letter to the Senate Judiciary Committee, November 22, 1995, that the anesthesia administered to the woman "will provide no-to-little analgesia to the fetus." U.S. House of Representatives, debate on Senate Amendments to the Partial-Birth Abortion Ban Act of 1997, H.R. 1833, March 27, 1996. 104th Cong., 2nd sess. *Congressional Record* 142, part 44.

348 **"That's what changed"**: Curtis Boyd, interview with the author, September 1, 2016.

349 **"woman as womb"**: Adrienne Rich, *Of Woman Born: Motherhood as Experience and Institution* (New York: Norton, 1976).

349 **Justice Byron White lamented**: *Planned Parenthood v. Danforth*, 428 U.S. 52 (1976) (Justice White, dissenting).

349 **John Willke spoke**: John Willke, memo to NRLC, February 21, 1978. Cited

in Rosalind Pollack Petchesky, "Antiabortion, Antifeminism, and the Rise of the New Right," *Feminist Studies* 7, no. 2 (Summer 1981): 221.

349 **sign of a protester**: Eleanor Mayfield, "Focus on . . . Curtis Boyd, MD," *World: The Journal of the Unitarian Universalist Association* 6 no. 2 (March/April 1992): 43.

349 **Albuquerque clinic ablaze**: T. J. Wilham, "Arson Fire Damages Doctor's Office," *Albuquerque Journal*, December 8, 2007. Scott Sandin, "2 Sentenced in Abortion Clinic Torching," *Albuquerque Journal*, June 11, 2009.

349 **"I don't know what"**: *From Danger to Dignity*, film, directed by Dorothy Fadiman, Concentric Media, 1995.

349 **"arbitrary" cutoff**: Curtis Boyd, interview with the author, September 1, 2016.

349 **"artificial barrier"**: Curtis Boyd, interview with the author, February 13, 2019.

349 **"Last week"**: Curtis Boyd, interview with the author, February 13, 2019.

349 **"I felt philosophically"**: Curtis Boyd, interview with the author, April 4, 2019.

350 **"I thought I'd"**: Curtis Boyd, interview with the author, April 4, 2019.

350 **"Dr. Warren Hern and myself"**: Reminiscences of Dr. George Tiller, 41.

350 **one and a half million**: Barstow, "An Abortion Battle."

350 **38 percent**: Barstow, "An Abortion Battle."

350 **"The most famous person"**: Friedman, "Savior vs. Savior."

350 **he was also despised**: "The Tiller Report II: A Shocking Exposé on America's Most Infamous Late-Term Abortionist," Operation Rescue report, 2006.

350 **Nazi doctor**: Stephanie Simon, "Protestors who Push the Limits," *Los Angeles Times*, February 17, 2004.

351 **"execut[e] convicted murderers"**: Wrote Newman: "When moms, dads, abortionists are added together, well over 100,000,000 people bear personal bloodguilt for at least one abortion. The doctrine of community bloodguilt found in Scripture further implicates the entire nation. The perpetrators are far too numerous and the bloodguilt has spread too far. We deserve God's judgment.

"In addition to our personal guilt in abortion, the United States government has abrogated its responsibility to properly deal with the bloodguilty. This responsibility rightly involves executing convicted murderers, including abortionists, for their crimes in order to expunge bloodguilt from the land and people." Troy Newman, *Their Blood Cries Out* (Wichita, KS: Restoration Press, 2003), 165–66.

351 **"that his conduct"**: Troy Newman and Cheryl Sullenger, "Execution of Paul Hill Nothing Less than Murder," Operation Rescue West and California Life Coalition, press release, September 3, 2003.

351 **"violence will never, never"**: Simon, "Protestors who Push the Limits."

351 **"pain and unpleasantness"**: Scheidler spoke at a pro-life convention in Appleton, WI, which convened April 11–13, 1985. *Holy Terror*, film, directed by Victoria Schultz, Hudson River Productions/Helsinki Films, 1986.

351 **a House subcommittee**: Abortion Clinic Violence: Oversight Hearings

before the Subcommittee on Civil and Constitutional Rights of the Committee of the Judiciary House of Representatives, 99th Cong., May 6, 1985.

351 **"from the guy"**: Kimberley Sevcik, "One Man's God Squad: Troy Newman's plan to stop abortions in Wichita, Kansas," *Rolling Stone*, July 29, 2004.

351 **"I want these employees"**: Sevcik, "One Man's God Squad."

351 **"If I could get my hands"**: Bill O'Reilly, "George Tiller Update," *The Radio Factor with Bill O'Reilly*, Fox News Radio, November 6, 2006.

351 **"What I found out"**: Amy Goodman, "Dr. George Tiller (1941–2009): Murdered Abortion Provider Remembered for Lifelong Dedication to Women's Reproductive Health," *Democracy Now*, WBAI, June 1, 2009.

352 shot him dead: David S. Cohen and Krysten Connon, *Living in the Crosshairs: The Untold Stories of Anti-Abortion Terrorism* (Oxford: Oxford University Press, 2016), 1.

352 lunch with Troy Newman: Amanda Robb, "Not A Lone Wolf," *Ms.*, June 4, 2010.

352 **"Something like if"**: Robb, "Not A Lone Wolf."

352 would liken Tiller: Roeder wrote the post on September 3, 2007, on the Operation Rescue site ChargeTiller.com. Judy L. Thomas, "Suspect in Tiller's Death Supported Killing Abortion Providers, Friends Say," *Kansas City Star*, May 31, 2009.

352 **"justice had not been served"**: Laura Bauer and Judy L. Thomas, "Operation Rescue Adviser Helped Tiller Suspect Track Doctor's Court Dates," *Kansas City Star*, June 3, 2009.

353 Barack Obama: The president issued a two-sentence statement: "I am shocked and outraged by the murder of Dr. George Tiller as he attended church services this morning. However profound our differences as Americans over difficult issues such as abortion, they cannot be resolved by heinous acts of violence." Barack Obama, "Statement from the President on the Murder of Dr. George Tiller," May 31, 2009. Office of the Press Secretary, White House Archives.

353 **"George Tiller was a mass-murderer"**: Matthew Hay Brown, "Killing of George Tiller: Faith-Based Reactions," *Baltimore Sun*, June 1, 2009.

353 **"an angry post-abortive man"**: Brown, "Killing of George Tiller."

353 police pulled him over: Thomas, "Suspect in Tiller's Death."

353 a piece of paper: Bauer and Thomas, "Operation Rescue Adviser Helped."

353 **"justifiable defensive action"**: Newman and Sullenger, "Execution of Paul Hill Nothing Less than Murder."

353 **"peaceful and legal"**: "Operation Rescue Statement Regarding Suspect in Tiller Killing," Christian Newswire, June 1, 2009.

353 didn't recall: Robb, "Not a Lone Wolf."

353 **"abortion fatigue"**: Robin Abcarian, "Slain Abortion Doctor George Tiller's Clinic to Close," *Los Angeles Times*, June 10, 2009.

353 bloodied carpet: Friedman, "Savior vs. Savior."

353 widow sang a prayer: David Barstow, "Kansas Doctor Remembered as Devoted to Family and Women," *New York Times*, June 6, 2009.

353 **moved to a vault**: Underground Vaults & Storage, Hutchinson, KS.

353 **'What are we going to do'**: Curtis Boyd, interview with the author, April 18, 2019.

354 **"miscalculation"**: Curtis Boyd, interview with the author, February 13, 2019.

354 **"pleading"**: Curtis Boyd, interview with the author, May 23, 2019.

354 **"induced anxiety"**: Curtis Boyd, interview with the author, April 18, 2019.

354 **"You're thinking"**: Curtis Boyd, interview with the author, April 18, 2019.

354 **"you got to twenty-seven"**: Curtis Boyd, interview with the author, February 13, 2019.

354 **"represented an inconsistency"**: Curtis Boyd, interview with the author, April 18, 2019.

355 **"I think the reason"**: *After Tiller*, film, directed by Martha Shane and Lana Wilson, Code Red Pictures, 2013.

355 **"Appointments for late abortions"**: Robin Abcarian and Michael Haederle, "Abortion Doctors Filling in for Tiller," *Los Angeles Times*, March 16, 2010.

355 **"late-term abortion capital"**: "Abortion Capital: Boyd & Co. Turn Albuquerque into the Late-term Abortion Capital of the World," Operation Rescue report, April 27, 2010.

355 **to stand outside**: Leslie Linthicum, "Anti-Abortion Group Targets New Mexico," *Albuquerque Journal*, November 21, 2010.

355 **among the four largest**: Curtis Boyd, interview with the author, April 18, 2019.

355 **urged Congress to codify**: U.S. House of Representatives, 93rd Cong., 1st sess., January 3, 1973.

355 **"to the extent"**: *Roe v. Wade*, Section X.

356 **"there were rumors"**: Ivins, "'This Right of Privacy.'"

356 **passed fifty-eight bills**: Donald T. Critchlow, *Intended Consequences: Birth Control, Abortion, and the Federal Government in Modern America* (Oxford: Oxford University Press, 2001), 200.

356 **restrictions that ranged**: Elizabeth Nash, Senior State Issues Manager, Guttmacher Institute, email to the author, September 20, 2019.

356 **"an open invitation"**: The ruling, *Webster v. Reproductive Health Services*, 492 U.S. 490 (1989), upheld a state ban on the use of public resources for abortion. Roger Rosenblatt, *Life Itself: Abortion in the American Mind* (New York: Random House, 1992), 13, 14.

356 **two of eighty-four**: Brian D. Sweany, "A Long and Bitter Fight," *Texas Monthly*, March 2014.

356 **nearly triple the number**: "Laws Affecting Reproductive Health and Rights: 2011 State Policy Review," Guttmacher Institute, 2012, https://www.guttmacher.org/laws-affecting-reproductive-health-and-rights-2011-state-policy-review.

356 **"in terms acceptable"**: Hilgers and Horan, eds., *Abortion and Social Justice*, ix.

356 **asserting the personhood**: Charles E. Rice, Brief of Americans United for Life as Amicus Curiae in Support of Appellee, *Roe v. Wade*, 410 U.S. 113 (1973).

356 **"that the unborn child"**: Illinois Abortion Law of 1975 (720 ILCS 510/).

356 **"There's a spectrum"**: Clarke Forsythe, interview with the author, May 16, 2019.

357 **brought to the House floor**: Mimi Swartz, "Mothers, Sisters, Daughters, Wives," *Texas Monthly*, August 2012.

357 **0.6 deaths per 100,000**: E. G. Raymond and D. A. Grimes, "The Comparative Safety of Legal Induced Abortion and Childbirth in the United States," *Obstetrics and Gynecology* 119, no. 2, part 1 (February 2012): 215–19.

357 **"legally, financially, emotionally"**: Carol Sanger, *About Abortion: Terminating Pregnancy in Twenty-First-Century America* (Cambridge, MA: Harvard University Press, 2017), xi.

357 **only hospitals**: The Woman's Right to Know Act, Texas Health & Safety Code § 171.004.

357 **must have admitting privileges**: Sweany, "A Long and Bitter Fight."

357 **point of pride**: Curtis Boyd, interview with the author, May 3, 2017.

358 **would shutter more than half**: Caitlin Gerdts et al., "Impact of Clinic Closures on Women Obtaining Abortion Services After Implementation of a Restrictive Law in Texas," *AJPH Research* 106, no. 5 (May 2016): 857.

358 **philosophical arguments**: See Watson, *Scarlet A*, ch. 4.

358 **Court should have fixed**: Much of the pro-life community has advocated an abortion ban at twenty weeks—when, they assert, the fetus begins to feel pain. Their claims rest on the research of Dr. Kanwaljeet Anand, a professor at Stanford University Medical Center, but the American Congress of Obstetricians and Gynecologists has stated that the fetus is unlikely to feel pain until the start of the third trimester, at roughly twenty-nine weeks. The scientist Carl Sagan proposed that abortion remain legal until roughly thirty weeks, when, he wrote, "the beginning of characteristically human thinking becomes barely possible." But others, including the prominent Swedish pediatrician, Dr. Hugo Lagercrantz, have written that the fetus is "potentially conscious" at roughly twenty-four weeks with "the activation of the cortex by thalamocortical connections." Annie Murphy Paul, "The First Ache," *New York Times Magazine*, February 10, 2008. Olga Khazan, "When Did Fetal Pain Become Pro-Life Strategy," *Atlantic*, November 18, 2013. Carl Sagan, *Billions and Billions: Thoughts on Life and Death at the Brink of the Millennium* (New York: Random House, 2011), 212. Nelly Padilla and Hugo Lagercrantz, "Making of the Mind," *Acta Paediatrica* 109, no. 5 (May 2020): 883–92.

358 **"the right to life"**: Judith Jarvis Thomson, "A Defense of Abortion," *Philosophy and Public Affairs* 1, no. 1 (1971): 47–66.

358 **"have an acceptable"**: Curtis Boyd, interview with the author, February 13, 2019.

358 **"LATE-TERM: REFUSE"**: The folder is viewable in one scene of the film *After Tiller*.

359 **performed nearly every**: Curtis Boyd, interview with the author, April 18, 2019.

359 **"trying to reconcile"**: Curtis Boyd, interview with the author, April 4, 2019.

359 **"With breath"**: Curtis Boyd, interview with the author, February 13, 2019.

359 **"I am in the extreme"**: Curtis Boyd, interview with the author, January 21, 2015.

359 **philosopher Porphyry**: *Porphyry: To Gaurus on How Embryos Are Ensouled and On What Is in Our Power*, translated by James Wilberding (London and New York: Bloomsbury Academic, 2011), 31–56.

359 **"The pregnancy"**: Curtis Boyd, speech in Bogotá, October 9, 2014. Courtesy of Curtis Boyd.

360 **"historical footnote"**: Diane Jennings, "Legal Eagle: The woman who helped make history with Roe," *Dallas Morning News*, July 29, 1990.

360 **"hostile"**: Notes of reporter Joseph N. Bell. Courtesy of Bell's widow, Sherry Angel.

360 **"She hid her brilliance"**: Molly Bartholow, interview with the author, February 18, 2018.

360 **"Linda and Sarah Weddington"**: Molly Bartholow, interview with the author, February 16, 2018.

361 **a violation of rule**: The rule reads: "A lawyer shall not engage in the practice of law when the lawyer is on inactive status or when the lawyer's right to practice has been suspended or terminated, including but not limited to situations where a lawyer's right to practice has been administratively suspended for failure to timely pay required fees or assessments or for failure to comply with Article XII of the State Bar Rules relating to Mandatory Continuing Legal Education."

361 **A spokesperson for the Bar**: Claire Reynolds, Public Affairs Counsel, Office of the Chief Disciplinary Counsel, State Bar of Texas, interview with the author, September 22, 2020.

361 **Coffee had fallen behind**: Rebecca Hartt, interview with the author, January 23, 2014.

361 **filed for Chapter 13**: U.S. Bankruptcy Courts, case number 3:93bk35699.

361 **"They came in"**: Rebecca Hartt, interview with the author, February 5, 2014.

361 **"I would just be"**: Dr. Kazia Luszczynska, psychiatric assessment of Linda Coffee, Metrocare Services, September 18, 2007. Courtesy of Rebecca Hartt.

362 **"She talked to herself"**: Peggy Clewis, interview with the author, September 13, 2016.

362 **"She was almost"**: Molly Bartholow, interview with the author, February 18, 2018.

362 **named Weddington its Humanitarian**: Robert Miller, "Planned Parenthood Luncheon Is Today," *Dallas Morning News*, January 23, 2003.

362 **"a wife is to submit"**: Southern Baptist Convention, "The Baptist Faith and Message," 1998. Hamil R. Harris, "Baptist Call for Submissive Wives Criticized," *Washington Post*, June 12, 1998.

362 **"pathological, abnormal"**: Southern Baptist Convention, "Resolution on Homosexual Marriage," June 1, 1996.

363 **"a human being"**: Southern Baptist Convention, 2005c "Statement on Sanctity of Life," 2010.

363 **"I have always considered"**: Rebecca Hartt, interview with the author, February 5, 2014.

363 **at odds with a car dealer**: Lacinetta Coxson, interview with the author, June 12, 2019. The case was *Ebbets Partners II, Ltd. v. Derrick Coxson and Lacinetta Lynn Johnson AKA Lacinetta Lynn Coxson*, Case no. GC-2005–00531. Filed March 18, 2005, Texas District Court, Denton County.

363 **"fundamental human freedom"**: Sarah Weddington, *A Question of Choice* (London: Penguin, 1993), 72.

363 **Hartt drank too much**: Police report, Dallas Police Department, July 26, 2006. Courtesy of Rebecca Hartt.

363 **"harassed Linda"**: Peggy Clewis, interview with the author, September 13, 2016.

363 **"slow to anger"**: Police report, Dallas Police Department, July 26, 2006. Courtesy of Rebecca Hartt.

363 **"economics"**: Linda Coffee, interview with the author, February 6, 2014.

363 **"assaulted" Hartt**: *State of Texas v. Linda Coffee*, Cause no. M06–720–60, "Notice of State's Intent to Use 404(B) Evidence."

363 **assault her partner twice**: Police reports, Dallas Police Department, July 17, 2006, and July 26, 2006. Courtesy of Rebecca Hartt.

363 **"I'm a lesbian"**: Mary Carter, interview with the author, May 28, 2019.

363 **"no food, no electricity"**: Police report, Dallas Police Department, July 26, 2006. Courtesy of Rebecca Hartt.

363 **her mother had likened**: June Hartt, letter to Rebecca Hartt, August 26, 1989. Courtesy of Rebecca Hartt.

364 **"possible underlying psychopathology"**: Dr. Kazia Luszczynska, psychiatric assessment of Linda Coffee, Metrocare Services, September 18, 2007. Courtesy of Rebecca Hartt.

364 **an oil painting they found**: The painting was *Winds on the Lake, Lake Michigan* by Miles Jefferson Early. Rebecca Hartt, interview with the author, February 6, 2014.

364 **Coffee and her sister**: *Dallas County et al. v. Linda Nellene Coffee, et al.*, Suit no. TX-07–30734.

364 **answered an ad**: Linda Coffee, interview with the author, February 7, 2014.

364 **"hard stick"**: Linda Coffee, interview with the author, February 6, 2014.

364 **Coffee did so**: Linda Coffee, interview with the author, February 6, 2014.

364 **"Here is the Roe"**: Rebecca Hartt, interview with the author, January 23, 2014.

364 **"braggadocio"**: Linda Coffee, interview with the author, February 7, 2014.

364 **"With very little resources"**: Linda Coffee, interview with the author, February 6, 2014.

365 **"I think it would have raised"**: Terry Woster, "Abortion fight keys on S.D.," *Argus Leader* (Sioux Falls, SD), November 9, 2008.

365 **eighty-six dollars**: Royalty check from NBC. Courtesy of Rebecca Hartt.

365 **He and his mother**: Scott Jackson, interview with the author, May 31, 2019.

365 **dubbed her "banker"**: Rebecca Hartt, interview with the author, February 4, 2014.

365 **She and Hartt got by**: Rebecca Hartt, interview with the author, January 23, 2014.

365 **Home in their little**: Rebecca Hartt, interview with the author, January 23, 2014.

366 **"the sister and Linda"**: Rebecca Hartt, interview with the author, February 5, 2014.

366 **kept her bloodied shirt**: Lifting the shirt, Hartt said: "This is my blood, my trophy for being a loyal person." Rebecca Hartt, interview with the author, February 6, 2014.

366 **"little love"**: Rebecca Hartt, interview with the author, January 23, 2014.

366 **a long hike**: Rebecca Hartt, letter to the author, November 2014.

366 **preparing eggplant and lamb**: Rebecca Hartt, interview with the author, February 6, 2014.

366 **an absentee ballot sent from**: "pd pol ad Conservative Republicans of Texas," February 2014. Courtesy of Rebecca Hartt.

366 **her face in a mural**: *Equal Justice Under Law* by J. William Myers.

366 **"She asked me"**: Linda Coffee, interview with the author, February 6, 2014.

367 **"Though the fig tree"**: Rebecca Hartt, interview with the author, February 5, 2014. Habakkuk 3:17–18 (NKJV).

368 **"masochistic"**: Charlotte Taft, interview with the author, December 13, 2016.

368 **the same mental space**: *Roe vs. Roe*, film.

368 **occasional public appearance**: "Canticle Talks . . . with Norma McCorvey," *Canticle*, Winter 2000.

368 **"are very unstable"**: Norma McCorvey, letter to the Resource Center of Dallas, July 8, 1999. Courtesy of Janie Bush.

369 **"the hardest thing"**: Norma McCorvey, interview with the author, November 4, 2013.

369 **Norma still avoided weddings**: Sheree Havlik, interview with the author, April 30, 2018.

369 **the turpitude of men**: Sheree Havlik, interview with the author, April 26, 2018.

369 **raising a fourth**: Sheree Havlik, interview with the author, October 25, 2018.

369 **people only cared to know**: Sheree Havlik, interview with the author, December 6, 2018.

369 **to look after Norma**: Sheree Havlik, interview with the author, December 6, 2018.

369 **"deep, deep depression"**: Sheree Havlik, interview with the author, August 20, 2020.

370 **showed Havlik the razor**: Sheree Havlik, interview with the author, December 6, 2018.

370 **"Christian principles"**: Articles of Incorporation of Roe No More Ministry, Inc., Article IV.1, November 12, 1997. NMP.

370 **"acted gay"**: Sheree Havlik, interview with the author, April 26, 2018.

370 **decades with Connie**: Sheree Havlik, interview with the author, April 26, 2018.

370 **Norma was at the wheel**: Sheree Havlik, interview with the author, December 6, 2018.

370 **her "goddaughter"**: North Dallas Rehabilitation Hospital, Discharge Instructions, July 30, 2004. NMP.

370 **"needs to hurry up"**: Utah Foster, interview with the author, February 1, 2019.

370 **"She started drinking"**: Sheree Havlik, interview with the author, December 6, 2018.

370 **$62,000**: IRS communications, 2001, 2002, 2003. NMP.

371 **a temporary bump**: IRS communication, 2004. NMP. Norma earned $34,000 in 2004.

371 **"The Lord came upon"**: Hector Ferrer, interview with the author, July 25, 2018.

371 **"I'm hanging it up"**: Hector Ferrer, interview with the author, July 25, 2018.

371 **"one hundred percent"**: Hector Ferrer, interview with the author, July 25, 2018.

372 **"I lost it"**: Hector Ferrer, interview with the author, July 25, 2018.

372 **$15,000 all year**: In 2005, Norma reported income of $14,827. NMP.

372 **food stamps**: NMP.

372 **"We've got a little"**: Katie Fairbank, "For 'Roe,' Trials Out of Court: Dallas plaintiff in '73 abortion case struggles to make ends meet," *Dallas Morning News*, January 12, 2006.

372 **Connie's family was aghast**: Mary Helen Sandoval (Connie's niece), interview with the author, October 4, 2011.

372 **Norma *believed* they were hungry**: Sheree Havlik, interview with the author, December 6, 2018.

372 **"Whether I was right"**: Michelle Green and Lois Armstrong, "The Woman Behind Roe v. Wade," *People*, May 22, 1989.

372 **"I just started"**: Sheree Havlik, interview with the author, December 6, 2018.

373 **Connie refused to leave**: Sheree Havlik, interview with the author, December 6, 2018.

373 **hundreds faced off in Jackson**: Sarah Olson, "Last Stand for Choice in Mississippi," *Making Contact*, October 25, 2006.

373 **and a Koran**: Jean Gordon, "Anti-Abortionists' Burning of Quran Called 'Hateful,'" *Clarion–Ledger* (Jackson, MS), July 20, 2006.

373 **"the majority of abortionists"**: WVIT, "Connecticut News-makers," July 16, 1989. Cited in Susan Weidman Schneider, "The Anti-Choice Movement: Bad News for Jews," *Lilith*, Summer 1990.

373 **"the words and deeds"**: Terry first wrote of Islam in 2001 in a booklet he titled "The Crescent Terror." In the course of earning an online masters degree in 2011 from Norwich University, in both diplomacy and international terrorism, he wrote a paper titled "Words and Deeds of Muhammad" in which he argued, he says, that "Islamic terrorists . . . are imitating the example and following the orders of [Islam's] founder, Muhammad." Randall Terry, interview with the author, January 30, 2019.

373 **boycott of Disney**: Lesley Clark and Lenny Savino, "Disney Protest Brings 3 Arrests," *Orlando Sentinel*, December 30, 1997.

373 **white supremacist newspaper**: *The Jubilee* was a bimonthly based in Midpines, CA.

373 **"overtly anti-Semitic"**: Carol Mason, *Killing for Life: The Apocalyptic Narrative of Pro-Life Politics* (Ithaca, NY: Cornell University Press, 2002), 185.

373 **"Is it not likely"**: "An Association of Priests for the Pro-Life Cause," Priests for Life, cited in Catholics for a Free Choice, "Faithless Politics: Priests for Life Defies Constitution and Conscience," August 2006.

374 **secured fifteen men**: Joshua Mercer, "Father Pavone Eyes Pro-life Religious Order," *National Catholic Register*, June 11–17, 2000, cited in Catholics for a Free Choice, "Faithless Politics."

374 **Cardinal Edward Egan**: "Father Pavone Asked to Leave Priests for Life," *EWTN Pro-Family News*, September 10, 2001. Cited in Catholics for a Free Choice, "Faithless Politics."

374 **"We are shocked"**: "Father Pavone Asked to Leave."

374 **"continuing to negotiate"**: "Father Pavone Asked to Leave."

374 **to back the Iraq war**: Catholics for a Free Choice, "Faithless Politics."

374 **if he found a bishop**: Daniel Burke, "Priest Scraps Plans for Anti-Abortion Society of Priests," Religion News Service, September 24, 2008.

374 **$130 million seminary**: Karen Smith Welch, "Records Reveal Growing Tensions Between Pavone, Bishop," *Amarillo Globe–News*, October 15, 2011.

374 **where forty-nine parishes**: Terry Mattingly, "Texas Priest Speaks for Life," *Knoxville News–Sentinel*, January 28, 2006. Cited in Catholics for a Free Choice, "Faithless Politics."

374 **"guerilla group"**: George McKenna, "Criss-Cross: Democrats, Republicans, and Abortion," *Human Life Review*, Summer/Fall 2006.

374 **"He's naive"**: Norma McCorvey, interview with the author, November 4, 2013.

374 **"She walked away"**: Frank Pavone, interview with the author, May 31, 2018.

374 **God Himself**: "Canticle Talks . . . with Norma McCorvey."

374 **"the catalyst"**: "Fr. Frank A. Pavone: National Director, Priests for Life and Missionaries of the Gospel of Life," priestsforlife.org.

374 **"not to be seen"**: Norma McCorvey, email to Karen Garnett, March 18, 2004. NMP.

375 **beseeching them**: Norma McCorvey, email to Karen Garnett, March 18, 2004. NMP.

375 **"no one who is pro-life"**: "Statement from Bishop Patrick J. Zurek," Roman Catholic Diocese of Amarillo, November 8, 2016.

375 **the realities of Roe**: Catholic News Service, "Father Pavone Affirms Continuing Pro-Life Involvement," *National Catholic Register*, December 9–15, 2001. Cited in Catholics for a Free Choice, "Faithless Politics."

375 **what lay before her**: Patricia McEwen, interview with the author, January 14, 2019.

376 **transporting aborted fetuses**: Patricia McEwen, interview with the author, January 14, 2019.

376 **"in a matter"**: Charlotte Taft, interview with the author, February 1, 2019.

376 **90 percent**: S. K. Henshaw and J. Van Vort, eds., *Abortion Factbook, 1992 Edition: Readings, Trends and State and Local Data to 1988* (New York: Alan Guttmacher Institute, 1992), Table 5.

376 **they wished to be transparent**: Charlotte Taft, interview with the author, February 1, 2019.

376 **pathology labs**: According to Taft, only in rare instances of fetal abnormality did abortion clinics pay pathology labs to examine fetal tissue. Otherwise, the clinics simply paid the labs to incinerate the tissue or send it to a waste management company. Charlotte Taft, interview with the author, February 1, 2019.

376 **"To hold a memorial"**: UPI, "Fetus Memorial Service Is Endorsed by Reagan," *New York Times*, May 27, 1982.

376 **Court of Appeals agreed**: Gene Blake, "Appeal Court Bars Disputed Plan to Bury 16,000 Fetuses," *Los Angeles Times*, July 3, 1984.

377 **"16,000 Faces"**: Bob Baker, "Several Hundred Anti-Abortionists Attend Service for Fetuses," *Los Angeles Times*, May 20, 1985.

377 **ordered that the embryos**: T. W. McGarry, "County Orders Burial of Controversial Fetuses," *Los Angeles Times*, August 28, 1985.

377 **"Just as the terrible toll"**: T. W. McGarry, "Fetuses Buried—With Hymns, Prayers," *Los Angeles Times*, October 7, 1985.

377 **staged funerals**: Schoen, *Abortion after Roe*, 155–57.

377 **a blackened fetal body**: Jack Jones and Andrea Ford, "350 Arrested for Abortion Protest," *Los Angeles Times*, March 24, 1989.

377 **pieced it back together**: Ronda Mackey, interview with the author, January 29, 2019.

377 **"bizarre and fetishistic"**: Carol Vinzant, "Fetus Frenzy," *Spy*, May 1993.

377 **"transformed remains"**: Schoen, *Abortion After Roe*, 159, 160.

377 **an aborted male fetus**: Patricia McEwen, interview with the author, January 16, 2019.

377 **"reminded me that"**: Patricia McEwen, interview with the author, January 19, 2019.

378 **"He had a source"**: Patricia McEwen, interview with the author, January 14, 2019.

378 **"figure out"**: Patricia McEwen, interview with the author, January 14, 2019.

378 **photograph of the priest**: Pavone welcomed me to his office on January 2, 2013.

378 **"They'd welcome me"**: Patricia McEwen, interview with the author, January 16, 2019.

378 **"medical specimen"**: Patricia McEwen, interview with the author, January 14, 2019.

378 **"They didn't know"**: Patricia McEwen, interview with the author, January 14, 2019.

378 **"Who was this baby"**: Patricia McEwen, interview with the author, January 14, 2019.

378 **"Very often a baby"**: Patricia McEwen, interview with the author, January 14, 2019.

378 **how many minutes**: Patricia McEwen, interview with the author, January 14, 2019.

378 **"was like holding"**: Patricia McEwen, interview with the author, January 14, 2019.

378 **"Father Frank had charge"**: Patricia McEwen, interview with the author, January 14, 2019.

378 **Pavone disputes**: Frank Pavone, email to the author, January 16, 2021.

379 **bury it, months later**: Joshua Cogswell and Leah Rupp, "Abortion Protestors Hold Memorial for Fetus at Park," *Clarion–Ledger* (Jackson, MS), July 20, 2006.

379 **She did not attend**: Cogswell and Rupp, "Abortion Protestors Hold Memorial."

379 **continued to partner**: "Sam Brownback Features Norma McCorvey from Abortion Case at Straw Poll," LifeNews.com, August 8, 2007.

379 **weepily rue *Roe* in films**: *Whatever Happened to Jane Roe?* was a 2006 documentary made by the Veritas Forum, a Christian nonprofit serving college students.

379 **"the one thing"**: Frank Di Bugnara, interview with the author, January 14, 2019.

379 **"about adult things"**: Frank Di Bugnara, interview with the author, February 24, 2019.

379 **approached the altar**: The church was St. Maria Goretti in Scottsdale.

379 **approached and prophesied**: Frank Di Bugnara, interview with the author, February 24, 2019.

379 **"an instrument of positiveness"**: Frank Di Bugnara, interview with the author, February 24, 2019.

380 **just $11,000**: IRS communication, 2007. NMP.

380 **"enraptured"**: Daniel Vinzant, interview with the author, July 11, 2018.

380 **"unconscious cruelty"**: Fred Bronson, *The Billboard Book of Number One Hits*, fifth edition (New York: Billboard Books, 2003), 229.

380 **native Mississippian**: Margie Casey, interview with the author, June 26, 2018.

381 **four abortions**: Judy Wiggins, interview with the author, July 12, 2018.

381 **"that the source"**: Judy Wiggins, interview with the author, July 12, 2018.

381 **"I want to apologize"**: Judy Wiggins, interview with the author, July 12, 2018.

381 **she phoned Vinzant**: Daniel Vinzant, interview with the author, August 26, 2020.

382 **It was a climax**: Hector Ferrer, interview with the author, July 25, 2018.

382 **word of the event spread**: Christian Newswire, "Norma McCorvey Former 'Roe' in Roe vs. Wade Will Be Making a Special Appearance in Wayne, NJ," October 8, 2007.

382 **"frantic"**: Hector Ferrer, interview with the author, January 22, 2019.

382 **"Much Love"**: Norma McCorvey, letter to Connie Gonzalez, August 24, 2007. NMP.

382 **"I did get a couple"**: Sheree Havlik, interview with the author, December 7, 2018.

382 **police came**: Judy Wiggins, interview with the author, July 12, 2018.

382 **"She would always say"**: Daniel Vinzant, interview with the author, July 11, 2018.

383 **"She looked like"**: Debbi Caldwell, interview with the author, July 11, 2018.

383 **"to witness to all"**: Debbi Caldwell, interview with the author, July 11, 2018.

383 **"Most people downplayed that"**: Judy Wiggins, interview with the author, July 12, 2018.

383 **"She personified"**: Judy Wiggins, interview with the author, July 12, 2018.

384 **Norma paid**: Debbi Caldwell, interview with the author, July 11, 2018.

384 **'I have to get out'**: Troy Newman, interview with the author, June 4, 2018.

384 **"It had the fetus"**: Judy Wiggins, interview with the author, July 12, 2018.

385 **to be where Dorothy**: Father Robinson, email to Norma McCorvey, July 13, 2007. NMP.

385 **"because it's January"**: Troy Newman, interview with the author, June 4, 2018.

385 **titled *American Holocaust***: The film was later retitled *Blood Money*. Directed by David K. Kyle, TAH, 2010.

385 **"Seeing the famous folks"**: Judy Wiggins, interview with the author, July 12, 2018.

385 **"Norma was never given"**: Judy Wiggins, interview with the author, July 12, 2018.

386 **"She really wanted"**: Judy Wiggins, interview with the author, June 25, 2019.

386 **"the former Jane Roe"**: Newman, *Their Blood Cries Out*.

386 **"I was just trying"**: Troy Newman, interview with the author, June 4, 2018.

386 **"She was very jealous"**: Judy Wiggins, interview with the author, July 12, 2018.

386 **"She just went through"**: Judy Wiggins, interview with the author, July 12, 2018.

387 **"If you brought"**: Sheree Havlik, interview with the author, December 7, 2018.

387 **"Even after she had"**: Utah Foster, interview with the author, January 29, 2019.

387 **"It was reckless"**: Frank Di Bugnara, interview with the author, October 4, 2018.

387 **"make money"**: Randall Terry, interview with the author, January 28, 2019.

387 **"righteous testosterone"**: Porteous, "OR founder calls for 'Christian nation.'"

388 **"pathetic males"**: Randall Terry, *The Judgement of God*, 49.

388 **"repeated sinful relationships"**: Hanna Rosin, "Randall Terry Censured by Church," *Washington Post*, February 12, 2000.

388 **"only had sex"**: Rosin, "Randall Terry Censured by Church."

388 **"Now you see"**: Dan Barry, "Icon for Abortion Protestors Is Looking for a Second Act," *New York Times*, July 20, 2001.

388 **additional snickering**: Michael Powell, "Family Values," *Washington Post*, April 22, 2004.

388 **Terry moved to Nashville**: Barry, "Icon for Abortion Protestors."

388 **"resumed ministry"**: Barry, "Icon for Abortion Protestors."

388 **"The movement has gone"**: Jacqueline L. Salmon, "Old Mission, New Life," *Washington Post*, July 15, 2009.

388 **he'd paid her**: George Basler, "'Jane Roe' Backs Terry," *Press & Sun–Bulletin* (Binghamton, NY), October 25, 1997.

388 **in his bid for Congress**: Randall Terry, interview with the author, January 28, 2019.

388 **sold more than five hundred**: Randall Terry, interview with the author, January 28, 2019.

388 **the two would meet up**: Randall Terry, interview with the author, January 28, 2019.

389 **fake blood he bought**: Salmon, "Old Mission, New Life."

389 **Terry invited her**: Salmon, "Old Mission, New Life."

389 **heckling the judge**: Kate Phillips, "About One Abortion Protester at Sotomayor Hearing," The Caucus (blog), *New York Times*, July 13, 2009.

389 **dumping pink plastic fetuses**: Marie Magleby, "'Jane Roe' to Nancy Pelosi: 'Don't Put Abortion in Health-Care Reform Bill,'" CNSNews.com, July 28, 2009.

389 **"so unstable"**: Frank Di Bugnara, interview with the author, October 4, 2018.

389 **she arrived home**: Daniel Vinzant, interview with the author, July 11, 2018.

PART VIII: THE FAMILY ROE

393 **"She never had the abortion"**: Margaret Talbot, "A Risky Proposal," *New Yorker*, January 7, 2010.

393 **Connie had not spoken**: Sheree Havlik, interview with the author, December 7, 2018.

394 **"Please!"**: Connie Gonzales, interview with the author, June 29, 2010.

394 **under $15,000**: Warranty Deed from Darla Rayburn to Connie C. Gonzales, July 25, 1967 (filed July 28, 1967), Dallas County Texas County Clerk, vol. 67147, p. 1059. Also Deed of Trust from Jack Keller to Connie C. Gonzales, filed July 28, 1967, Dallas County Texas County Clerk, vol. 67147, p. 1004.

394 **more than $80,000**: The house was four years old when Connie bought it in 1967. According to the deed, Connie assumed what was left of both its original $13,550 mortgage and a $900 vendor's lien. According to the Dallas Central Appraisal District, the total market value of the home in 2001 was $80,460.

394 **Connie had to agree**: Peter J. Parenti, letter to Norma McCorvey, December 4, 2004. NMP.

394 **Connie did not**: Peter J. Parenti, interview with the author, October 29, 2019.

394 **borrowing $92,000**: Brice, Vander Linden & Wernick, P.C., letter to Norma McCorvey and Connie Gonzalez, April 15, 2010. Courtesy of Sheree Havlik.

394 **she owed $4,000**: Brice, Vander Linden & Wernick, P.C., letter to Norma McCorvey and Connie Gonzalez, April 15, 2010. Courtesy of Sheree Havlik.

394 **a hardship loan**: Sheree Havlik, interview with the author, October 4, 2019.

394 **Norma refused**: Sheree Havlik, interview with the author, October 4, 2019.

394 **"ORDER FOR FORECLOSURE"**: Brice, Vander Linden & Wernick, P.C., letter to Norma McCorvey and Connie Gonzalez, April 15, 2010. Courtesy of Sheree Havlik.

395 **They agreed**: Connie Gonzales and Linda Tovar, interview with the author, January 13, 2011.

395 **found the birthdate**: Peter Sonski, "McCorvey to Enter Catholic Church," *National Catholic Register*, June 21, 1998.

395 **She said that she had**: Ruth Price, interview with the author, February 21, 2011.

395 **hire a private investigator**: Lisa Gipson, interview with the author, January 13, 2014.

396 **Jennifer had not heard**: Jennifer Ferguson, interview with the author, November 9, 2012.

396 **"I think it's interesting"**: Jennifer Ferguson, interview with the author, November 9, 2012.

396 **"happiest moment"**: Jennifer Ferguson, Facebook post, November 10, 2012.

396 **"I always wondered"**: Melissa Mills, interview with the author, November 10, 2012.

396 **"I can't believe"**: Melissa Mills, interview with the author, November 10, 2012.

396 **"You do look"**: Author's notes on conversation between Melissa Mills and Jennifer Ferguson, November 11, 2012.

396 **"She's just a very"**: Author's notes on conversation between Melissa Mills and Jennifer Ferguson, November 11, 2012.

397 **"It's answered a lot"**: Author's notes on conversation between Melissa Mills and Jennifer Ferguson, November 11, 2012.

397 **"Y'all like"**: Author's notes on conversation between Mary Sandefur and Jennifer Ferguson, November 11, 2012.

397 **"it's always going"**: Shelley Thornton, interview with the author, November 18, 2012.

397 **"THAT I REALLY DO"**: Jennifer Ferguson, email to Shelley Thornton and the author, November 27, 2012.

398 **"Anonymity combined"**: Dwight Garner, "A Dive into the Abyss in the Anonymous 'Incest Diary,'" *New York Times*, July 19, 2017.

398 **"Secrets and lies"**: Shelley Thornton, interview with the author, December 14, 2012.

398 **"It's exhausting"**: Shelley Thornton, interview with the author, December 14, 2012.

398 **"It's helping me"**: Shelley Thornton, interview with the author, December 30, 2012.

398 **"I would like"**: Shelley Thornton, interview with the author, December 14, 2012.

399 **"purity of soul"**: *Lake of Fire*, film, directed by Tony Kaye, Anonymous Content, 2008.

399 **"I get mixed up"**: Melissa Mills, interview with the author, January 8, 2013.

399 **"Jennifer kind of got"**: Shelley Thornton, interview with the author, November 10, 2013.

399 **its biological father**: Affidavit of Norma McCorvey, June 11, 2003, *McCorvey v. Hill*, 385 F.3d 846.

399 **began to regulate**: In 1851, Massachusetts passed the Adoption of Children Act, which required judges to determine if adoptive parents were fit to rear children.

399 **roughly four times more likely**: In 1972, there was an estimated total of 716,760 abortions performed in the U.S.: 586,760 legal, and an estimated 130,000 illegal. "Abortion Surveillance, 1972, 1974," Family Planning Evaluation Division, Centers for Disease Control, no. 74–8205. Willard Cates, Jr., and Roger W. Rochat, "Illegal Abortions in the United States: 1972–1974," *Family Planning Perspectives* 8, no. 2 (March/April 1976): 86–92. In 1970, there were 175,000 adoptions in the U.S. Marianne Bitler and Madeline Zavodny, "Did Abortion Legalization Reduce the Number of Unwanted Children? Evidence from Adoptions," *Perspectives on Sexual and Reproductive Health* 34, no. 1 (January/February 2002): 25–33.

400 **All were pro-choice**: Shelley Thornton, interview with the author, November 10, 2013. Jennifer Ferguson, interview with the author, November 11, 2012. Melissa Mills, interview with the author, November 10, 2012.

400 **"I've always been pro-choice"**: Melissa Mills, interview with the author, November 10, 2012.

400 **"My boobs are"**: Author's notes on conversation between Shelley Thornton and Jennifer Ferguson, March 14, 2013.

400 **"This is where"**: Author's notes on conversation between Jennifer Ferguson and Shelley Thornton, March 15, 2013.

402 **she drove on**: Daniel Vinzant, interview with the author, November 13, 2019.

402 **"I said, Norma McCorvey"**: Adena Lewis, interview with the author, November 12, 2019.

402 **in "the perfect place"**: Adena Lewis, interview with the author, November 12, 2019.

403 **"The state park"**: Daniel Vinzant, interview with the author, November 13, 2019.

403 **"talk about what"**: Lauren Nailen, interview with the author, July 13, 2018.

403 **"It wasn't a religious"**: Peter Mackenzie, interview with the author, August 6, 2018.

403 **"there better not"**: William Goldman, *Boys and Girls Together* (New York: Simon and Schuster, 1964), 583.

404 **"bloody realism"**: Annie Finch, ed., *Choice Words: Writers on Abortion*, (Chicago: Haymarket, 2020), xv.

404 **writing of soaked slippers**: Sharon Olds, "The End," in *The Dead and the Living* (New York: Knopf Doubleday, 1984).

404 **"it's really an awfully simple"**: Ernest Hemingway, "Hills Like White Ele-phants," in *Men Without Women* (New York: Charles Scribner's Sons, 1927).

404 **"the very thought"**: Richard Yates, *Revolutionary Road* (New York: Little, Brown, 1961).

404 **rare was the script**: Gretchen Sisson and Katrina Kimport, "Facts and Fic-tions: Characters seeking abortion on American television, 2005–2014," *Contraception* 93, no. 5 (May 2016): 446–51. "Majority of TV abortion plot lines reinforce myths about the procedure," Advancing New Standards in Reproductive Health, ansirh.org.

404 **$25,000**: Peter Mackenzie, interview with the author, November 12, 2019.

404 **"complicated, protective and cerebral"**: Hollie McKay, "Roe v. Wade Plaintiff Norma McCorvey Makes Acting Debut in New Film 'Doonby,'" *Fox News*, May 13, 2011.

404 **"pitchforked into fame"**: Peter Mackenzie, interview with the author, August 6, 2018.

405 **"I think people forget"**: Erin Way, interview with the author, October 9, 2012.

405 **"She just liked"**: Jeannie Ralph, interview with the author, June 13, 2018.

405 **ten or so Bud Lights**: Susan DeVine, interview with the author, September 15, 2018.

405 **who remained thankful**: Susan DeVine, interview with the author, Septem-ber 15, 2018.

405 **"I could have"**: Henry Lee Taylor, interview with the author, June 12, 2018.

406 **"Having similar bruises"**: Henry Lee Taylor, interview with the author, June 12, 2018.

406 **"scorned, rejected, snubbed"**: Barbara Ellis, "Norma," 1995, draft of article submitted to newsletter of the National Women's Political Caucus, Alameda North branch. NMP.

406 **"Which is it Fr. Frank"**: Norma McCorvey, email to Frank Pavone, February 2, 2009. Courtesy of Judy Wiggins.

406 **"She feels at the end"**: Erin Way, interview with the author, October 9, 2012.

406 **"On the pro-choice side"**: Melissa Mills, interview with the author, May 19, 2020.

406 **publicly stating her position**: Days after *Roe*, Norma told the reporter Robert O'Brien: "I wouldn't want to wait over three months for any abortion, because I might be ending a human life after that time." And days after her conversion, she told Ted Koppel that she felt abortion ought to be legal through the first trimester. Associated Press, "Abortion Reformer Sheds 'Jane Roe,'" *Dallas Morning News*, January 27, 1973. *ABC News Nightline*, ABC, August 10, 1995.

407 **"the mushy middle"**: Steven Waldman and Ginny Carroll, "Roe v. Roe," *Newsweek*, August 21, 1995.

407 **a poll would soon reveal**: Lydia Saad, "Majority of Americans Still Support Roe v. Wade Decision," Gallup, January 22, 2013.

407 **"a microcosm of America"**: "Justice Foundation Press Conference, Subject: Petition for Supreme Court to Reverse Decisions in Roe v. Wade and Doe v. Bolton," Federal News Service, January 18, 2005.

407 **drunk and pole dancing**: Norma McCorvey, text message to Henry Taylor, September 23, 2010. Courtesy of Henry Taylor.

407 **"I like my life"**: Rhys Blakely, "How Woman Behind U.S. Pro Abortion Law Changed her Mind," *The Times* (London), August 1, 2011.

408 **she came to believe**: Rosie Lopez, interview with the author, December 3, 2019.

408 **"Religion wounded her"**: Rosie Lopez, interview with the author, November 25, 2019.

408 **praying for a husband**: Norma McCorvey, text message to Henry Taylor, February 7, 2011. Courtesy of Henry Taylor.

v **"I'm dating men now"**: Ronda Mackey, interview with the author, December 11, 2017.

408 **"I thought you'd be proud"**: Ronda Mackey, interview with the author, December 11, 2017.

408 **cut her off too**: Judy Wiggins, interview with the author, July 12, 2018.

408 **the man she had wed**: Daniel Vinzant, interview with the author, July 11, 2018.

408 **"I was in deep"**: Frank Di Bugnara, interview with the author, October 4, 2018.

409 **was wholly unaware**: Frank Di Bugnara, interview with the author, October 4, 2018.

409 **"They gave us"**: Linda Tovar, interview with the author, August 2021.

409 **so as to better picture**: Lianne Hart, "Neighbors—in Name Only," *Los Angeles Times*, May 29, 1995.

410 **the blood of millions**: Daniel Vinzant, interview with the author, November 13, 2019.

410 **Norma hung up**: Peter Mackenzie, interview with the author, August 6, 2018.

410 **"I obeyed"**: Paul Bond, "Woman at Center of Roe v. Wade Stars in Abortion-Themed Movie," *Hollywood Reporter*, May 4, 2011.

410 **"heart has been low"**: Norma McCorvey, text message to Henry Taylor, August 28, 2010. Courtesy of Henry Taylor.

410 **the accompanying photographer**: The photographer was Bob Daemmrich. Blakely, "How Woman Behind U.S. Pro Abortion Law."

410 **85 percent of them**: Diana Greene Foster, *The Turnaway Study: Ten Years, a Thousand Women, and the Consequences of Having—or Being Denied—an Abortion* (New York: Scribner, 2020), 126.

410 **"There was a disconnect"**: Susan DeVine, interview with the author, November 10, 2019.

411 **did not support it**: Peter Mackenzie, interview with the author, August 6, 2018.

411 **"moving and thought-provoking"**: Gianfranco Grieco, "'Doonby' to open in the United States," *L'Osservatore Romano*, February 12, 2012.

411 **"painful regrets"**: Grieco, "'Doonby' to open."

411 **arranging a screening**: Peter Mackenzie, interview with the author, November 12, 2019.

411 **mismanagement of funds**: David Gibson, "Priests for Life in Financial Trouble," *National Catholic Reporter*, September 26, 2011.

411 **"good standing"**: David Gibson, "After a Year of Exile, Anti-Abortion Priest Frank Pavone Is Back," *National Catholic Register,* October 16, 2012.

411 **"I had a lot"**: Heidi Erwin, interview with the author, August 27, 2018.

411 **have children too**: 59 percent of women who have abortions are already mothers. Millions more women, like Erwin, have children after their abortions. Jenna Jerman, Rachel K. Jones and Tsuyoshi Onda, "Characteristics of U.S. Abortion Patients in 2014 and Changes Since 2008," Guttmacher Institute, 2016.

412 **"She was withdrawing"**: Heidi Erwin, interview with the author, June 14, 2020.

412 **"had a permanent"**: Frank Di Bugnara, interview with the author, October 4, 2018.

412 **"Do not vote"**: "Norma McCorvey – Jane Roe of 'Roe v Wade' on Randall Terry for Congress Commercial," YouTube, February 18, 2017.

412 **"a piece of pizza"**: Lauren Nailen, interview with the author, July 13, 2018.

412 **"mass murderer"**: Blakely, "How Woman Behind U.S. Pro Abortion Law."

412 **had instructed her to reassemble**: Norma McCorvey, interview with Peter Mackenzie, July 24, 2014. Courtesy of Peter Mackenzie.

412 **"in a dangerous place"**: Daniel Vinzant, interview with the author, July 5, 2018.

414 **"to save our souls!"**: Angie Heiter, interview with Mater Dei Latin Mass Parish, May 21, 2016, https://materdeiparish.com/2016/05/parish-life-series-rosary-makers/.

414 **"I was cranking"**: Norma McCorvey, interview with the author, November 4, 2013.

414 **the plastic Jesus**: Norma McCorvey, interview with the author, November 4, 2013.

415 **"This whole roe anniversary"**: Nancy Hokamp, email to Sue Cyr, January 23, 2013. Courtesy of Sue Cyr.

415 **"What she desperately needs"**: Nancy Hokamp, email to the author, January 23, 2013.

415 **"She offers her sufferings"**: Angie Heiter, email to Sue Cyr, February 16, 2013. Courtesy of Sue Cyr.

415 **"the one I want"**: Norma McCorvey, interview with the author, November 4, 2013.

415 **"There's something about"**: Norma McCorvey, interview with the author, November 4, 2013.

415 **"you have no impact"**: Shelley Thornton, interview with the author, March 16, 2013.

416 **"COLD AND NONCHALANT"**: Jennifer Ferguson, email to Shelley Thornton and the author, November 27, 2012.

416 **"I always wanted"**: Author's notes on conversation between Shelley Thornton and Melissa Mills, March 16, 2013.

416 **"I was totally being treated"**: Shelley Thornton, interview with the author, March 24, 2013.

416 **found it difficult**: Melissa Mills, interview with the author, March 28, 2013.

416 **was also taken aback**: Jennifer Ferguson, interview with the author, May 29, 2013.

417 **"I now see a certain genius"**: Rob Schenck, interview with the author, July 27, 2018.

417 **her very last function**: Norma McCorvey, interview with the author, November 27, 2014.

418 **"I'm not ready"**: Shelley Thornton, interview with the author, October 15, 2013.

418 **"nigger lover"**: Melissa Mills, interview with the author, November 10, 2012.

418 **"fornicating homosexual"**: Jordan Mills, interview with the author, October 18, 2013.

418 **could possibly forgive**: Mary Sandefur, interview with the author, October 5, 2011.

418 **"You can't trust her"**: Mary Sandefur, interview with the author, October 5, 2011.

418 **"Kind of a traditional"**: Author's notes on conversation between Daniel Schramm and Melissa Mills, October 17, 2013.

419 **long gone drinking**: Author's notes on conversation between Norma McCorvey and Melissa Mills, October 17, 2013.

419 **"He's brought me"**: Author's notes on conversation between Melissa Mills and Norma McCorvey, October 17, 2013.

419 **paid her a thousand dollars**: Norma McCorvey, text message to the author, August 10, 2012.

419 **"to meet all my daughters"**: Author's notes on conversation between Norma McCorvey and Melissa Mills, October 17, 2013.

420 **"built up hatred"**: Jennifer Ferguson, interview with the author, November 17, 2013.

420 **"I fucking hate you"**: Jennifer Ferguson, interview with the author, November 17, 2013.

420 **Jennifer felt joy**: Jennifer Ferguson, interview with the author, November 17, 2013.

420 **"You and mommy dearest"**: Author's notes on conversation between Lisa Gipson and Jennifer Ferguson, October 18, 2013.

421 **busy studying**: Jennifer Ferguson, interview with the author, May 25, 2020.

421 **"It's been mind-fucking"**: Jennifer Ferguson, interview with the author, October 25, 2013.

421 **"She's blocked"**: Jennifer Ferguson, interview with the author, October 25, 2013.

421 **"look at her"**: Jennifer Ferguson, interview with the author, November 17, 2013.

421 **'How would you feel'**: Melissa Mills, interview with the author, October 27, 2013.

421 **"The whole kit"**: Shelley Thornton, interview with the author, December 17, 2013.

421 **she felt loved**: Shelley Thornton, interview with the author, January 14, 2014.

421 **"I didn't know *how*"**: Shelley Thornton, interview with the author, February 14, 2021.

421 **"If I say no"**: Shelley Thornton, interview with the author, March 2014.

421 **"I can't get close"**: Melissa Mills, interview with the author, February 8, 2014.

422 **"You don't get a break"**: Jennifer Ferguson, interview with the author, March 16, 2013.

422 **tying a bandanna**: Norma McCorvey and Andy Meisler, *I Am Roe: My Life, Roe V. Wade, and Freedom of Choice* (New York: HarperCollins, 1994), 117.

422 **"I let politics run"**: Norma McCorvey, interview with the author, November 5, 2013.

422 **"I can understand a woman"**: Norma McCorvey, interview with the author, November 5, 2013.

422 **"It's really a lot harder"**: Norma McCorvey, interview with the author, November 5, 2013.

422 **"Because I'm scared"**: Shelley Thornton, interview with the author, January 14, 2014.

422 **"She's very, very fragile"**: Valerie Richardson, "Child of 'Jane Roe' identified in Seattle," *Washington Times*, June 29, 1989.

422 **"The emotional similarities"**: Shelley Thornton, interview with the author, November 10, 2013.

423 **"I wasn't going"**: Shelley Thornton, interview with the author, November 10, 2013.

423 **"Shelley thinks"**: Norma McCorvey, interview with the author, February 4, 2014.

423 **"very taboo"**: Norma McCorvey, interview with the author, February 1, 2014.

423 **"We skirted around"**: Shelley Thornton, interview with the author, August 15, 2018.

423 **"My first instinct"**: Shelley Thornton, interview with the author, March 13, 2016.

423 **"just to let her know"**: Melissa Mills, interview with the author, July 27, 2014.

423 **"ready to go see Grandma"**: Shelley Thornton, interview with the author, March 13, 2016.

423 **"I couldn't talk"**: Shelley Thornton, interview with the author, February 14, 2021.

424 **"Please let me know"**: Melissa Mills, text message to Shelley Thornton, December 23, 2014. Courtesy of Melissa Mills.

424 **"just like Norma"**: Melissa Mills, interview with the author, September 1, 2014.

424 **"I'm tired of bleeding"**: Norma McCorvey, interview with the author, May 31, 2014.

424 **"I raised hell"**: Norma McCorvey, interview with the author, June 2, 2014.

424 **"My family can't"**: Melissa Mills, interview with the author, June 25, 2014.

424 **"It just really hurt"**: Melissa Mills, interview with the author, December 13, 2013.

425 **"I've seen it too often"**: Melissa Mills, interview with the author, December 13, 2013.

425 **moving her to a nursing home**: Frank Pavone, interview with the author, June 26, 2014.

425 **only word from Pavone**: Norma McCorvey, interview with the author, November 27, 2014.

425 **"I can't live"**: Melissa Mills, interview with the author, January 24, 2015.

425 **"She's too fucking nice"**: Jennifer Ferguson, interview with the author, November 10, 2016.

426 **tried to stab**: Glenda Diane Hyman, interview with the author, March 25, 2015.

426 **a half-dozen partners**: Pete Aguilar, interview with the author, March 31, 2015.

426 **"We were having a threesome"**: Pete Aguilar, interview with the author, March 31, 2015.

427 **"When you have something"**: Pete Aguilar, interview with the author, March 31, 2015.

427 **had come to see**: Pete Aguilar, interview with the author, June 30, 2015.

427 **"You look so much"**: Author's notes on conversation between Pete Aguilar and Jennifer Ferguson, June 30, 2015.

428 **He was too controlling**: Shelley Thornton, interview with the author, March 13, 2016.

428 **"were vulnerable enough"**: Shelley Thornton, interview with the author, February 26, 2019.

428 **"For me, family"**: Shelley Thornton, interview with the author, March 13, 2016.

429 **"I will die"**: Norma McCorvey, email to Judy Wiggins, September 4, 2008. Courtesy of Judy Wiggins.

429 **calling her "mother":** Norma McCorvey, interview with the author, March 23, 2015.

429 **"a good hard prick"**: Norma McCorvey, interview with the author, March 23, 2015.

429 **"sex and religion"**: Norma McCorvey, interview with the author, March 23, 2015.

429 **given away the silver ring**: Sheree Havlik, interview with the author, April 30, 2018.

429 **"a rough life"**: Norma McCorvey, interview with the author, June 29, 2015.

430 **"absent and unfaithful"**: Norma McCorvey, interview with the author, February 14, 2020.

430 **"He's short"**: Author's notes on conversation between Melissa Mills and Ray McCorvey, September 19, 2015.

430 **one time she'd met him**: Author's notes on conversation between Melissa Mills and Ray McCorvey, September 19, 2015.

430 **For only they**: Melissa Mills, interview with the author, May 17, 2020.

431 **her rise at Walmart**: Jennifer Ferguson, email to the author, January 26, 2016.

431 **"My stomach is in knots"**: Melissa Mills, interview with the author, April 26, 2016.

432 **"a Medicaid bed"**: Author's notes on conversation between Eric Heumann and Melissa Mills, March 6, 2016.

432 **"You have to be"**: Melissa Mills, interview with the author, March 6, 2016.

432 **"The movement"**: Kass McMahon, interview with the author, July 22, 2018.

432 **"They didn't do nothing"**: Melissa Mills, interview with the author, February 8, 2016.

432 **annual budget in the millions**: Catholics for a Free Choice, "Faithless Politics: Priests for Life Defies Constitution and Conscience," August 2006.

432 **Pavone refused in 2014**: David Gibson, "Cardinal Timothy Dolan Cuts Ties with Anti-Abortion Crusader Frank Pavone," *National Catholic Reporter*, December 15, 2014.

432 **turned to the Texas case**: The case was *Whole Woman's Health v. Hellerstedt*. By a vote of five to three, the Supreme Court ruled that various regulations at Texas abortion clinics constituted an undue burden on women and were thus unconstitutional.

432 **"Women have been doing"**: Author's notes on conversation between Norma McCorvey and Melissa Mills, March 6, 2016.

432 **paid her $3,000**: Melissa Mills, interview with the author, May 2, 2016. Norma also alerted Father Pavone that Sweeney paid her. "I charged of course so I'll have some bucks at the end," she wrote. Norma McCorvey, text message to Frank Pavone, May 24, 2016. Courtesy of Frank Pavone. Sweeney later said that "Norma was not paid to participate in the documentary" beyond licensing fees of her personal archive. "Documentary Reveals Norma McCorvey, 'Jane Roe', Was Paid to Reverse Abortion Stance," *American Voices with Alicia Menendez*, MSNBC, May 23, 2020.

433 **Melissa was furious**: Melissa Mills, interview with the author, May 2, 2016.

433 **"I should had abort you"**: Norma McCorvey, text message to Melissa Mills, May 9, 2016. Courtesy of Melissa Mills.

433 **"She's vindictive"**: Melissa Mills, interview with the author, April 26, 2016.

433 **"She's probably mad"**: Author's notes on conversation between Shelley Thornton and Eric Heumann, July 7, 2016.

433 **"I went through"**: Author's notes on conversation between Shelley Thornton, Melissa Mills and Jennifer Ferguson, July 8, 2016.

434 **Norma got booted**: Melissa Mills, interview with the author, May 17, 2020.

434 **lungs were profusely damaged**: Melissa Mills, interview with the author, July 26, 2016. A recent test had revealed that her FEV1 score, the amount of air she could exhale in a second, was 34 percent.

434 **Norma was "performing"**: Melissa Mills, interview with the author, October 6, 2016.

434 **"to learn to love"**: Jennifer Ferguson, interview with the author, May 25, 2020.

435 **"I'm dying"**: Shelley Thornton, interview with the author, February 15, 2017.

435 ***"Fils de putain"***: Author's notes on conversation between Norma McCorvey and Melissa Mills, February 16, 2017.

435 **"going the right way"**: Melissa Mills, interview with the author, February 17, 2017.

436 **"Hey, sweet lady"**: Author's notes on conversation between Chloe Mills and Norma McCorvey, February 17, 2017.

436 **"Jell-O"**: Author's notes on conversation between Norma McCorvey, Melissa Mills and Chloe Mills, February 17, 2017.

436 **"I'm here now"**: Author's notes on conversation between Melissa Mills and Norma McCorvey, February 18, 2017.

438 **legalized gay marriage**: *Obergefell v. Hodges*, 576 U.S. 644 (2015).

438 **"The Supreme Court has"**: Transcript of Record at 3095, *Perry v. Schwarzenegger*, 704 F.Supp.2d 921 (N.D. Cal. 2010), no. C:09cv02292.

438 **twelve times less likely**: Robert Green, Adam Rosenblatt, "C-SPAN / PSB 2018 Research Supreme Court Survey," CSPAN, PSB, August 13–15, 2018.

438 **"No other nation"**: Michael Kinsley, "What Abortion Debate?," *Slate*, November 19, 2005.

438 **one of fifty-eight countries**: Angelina Theodorou and Aleksandra Sandstrom, "How Abortion Is Regulated Around the World," Pew Research Center, October 6, 2015.

438 **"was enough to settle"**: "The War that Never Ends," *Economist*, January 16, 2003.

439 **"justify abortion"**: "The War that Never Ends," *Economist*.

441 **"individualism and libertarianism"**: Mary Ann Glendon, *Abortion and Divorce in Western Law: American Failures, European Challenges.* (Cambridge, MA: Harvard University Press, 1989), 52.

439 **Christopher Hitchens**: Christopher Hitchens, "Fetal Distraction," *Vanity Fair*, February 2003.

439 **"preoccupation with evil"**: Roger Rosenblatt, *Life Itself: Abortion in the American Mind* (New York: Random House, 1992), 106.

439 **"reproduce themselves by fission"**: Rosenblatt, *Life Itself*, 131.

439 **"take abortion out"**: Michael Kilian, "Specter Joins '96 Field, Targets GOP Far Right," *Chicago Tribune*, March 31, 1995.

439 **"The unborn child"**: "The Vision Shared: The Republican Platform, Uniting Our Family, Our Country, Our World," Republican Party platform, 1992. Available at the American Presidency Project, https://www.presidency.ucsb.edu/documents/1992-republican-party-platform.

439 **only developed country**: Mona Siegel, "The Forgotten Origins of Paid Family Leave," *New York Times*, November 29, 2019.

439 **"weakness of the Republican Party"**: Ross Douthat, Michelle Goldberg and David Leonhardt, "The Abortion Debate," The Argument (podcast), *New York Times*, February 7, 2019.

439 **"The pro-life cause"**: Daniel K. Williams, *Defenders of the Unborn: The Pro-*

Life Movement Before Roe v. Wade (New York: Oxford University Press, 2016), 267.

440 **"psychological harm"**: *Roe v. Wade*, 410 U.S. 113 (1973), Section VIII.

440 **as Blackmun had written:** In 2007, in explaining why the Court had upheld the federal ban against certain late-term abortions, Justice Anthony Kennedy wrote of the "severe depression and loss of self-esteem" that abortion can occasion. *Gonzales v. Carhart*, 127 S. Ct. 1610, 1634 (2007).

440 **"the Court has spoken"**: Lee Gidding, to the board of the National Abortion Rights Action League, February 7, 1973. Records of the National Abortion Rights Action League 1968–1976, Carton 1, 1973–1974, Executive Committee Folder. Schlesinger Library, Harvard University.

440 **"started to lose ground"**: Rebecca Traister, "Warning: Abortion's Deadly DIY Past Could Soon Become its Future," *New York Magazine*, January 9–22, 2017.

440 **"When we women"**: Ursula K. Le Guin, *Dancing at the Edge of the World: Thoughts on Words, Women, Places* (New York: Harper and Row, 1989): 147–60.

441 **a 1978 book:** Linda Bird Francke, *The Ambivalence of Abortion* (Sydney: Penguin Australia, 1978).

441 **1989 amicus brief:** Sarah E. Burns, "2,887 Women Who Have Had Abortions et al.," Brief as Amicus Curiae, *Webster v. Reproductive Health Services*, 492 U.S. 490 (1989).

441 **publications begun in 2000:** Abortion Conversation Project records. David M. Rubenstein Rare Book and Manuscript Library, Duke University.

441 **abortions they'd had *before***: Johanna Schoen, *Abortion After Roe* (Chapel Hill: University of North Carolina Press, 2015), 15.

441 **Ali MacGraw:** Ali MacGraw, "When Abortion Was Illegal," *People*, August 5, 1985.

441 **Whoopi Goldberg:** Angela Bonavoglia, ed., *The Choices We Made: 25 Women and Men Speak Out Against Abortion* (New York: Random House, 1991), 137.

441 **"no celebrity"**: Susan Dominus, "The Mysterious Disappearance of Young Pro-Choice Women," *Glamour* 103, no. 8 (August 2005).

441 **two documentaries:** *Speak Out: I Had an Abortion*, film, directed by Gillian Aldrich, Speak Out Productions, 2005. *The Abortion Diaries*, film, directed by Penny Lane, 2005.

441 **"the dread secret"**: Lawrence Lader, *Abortion* (Indianapolis: Bobbs-Merrill, 1966), 1.

441 **"cramps are getting"**: Patty Lee, "Angie Jackson Live-Tweets her Abortion to 'Demystify' Procedure, Receives Death Threats," *Daily News* (New York), February 26, 2010.

441 **"a bold new movement"**: Elizabeth Kissling, *From a Whisper to a Shout: Abortion Activism and Social Media* (London: Watkins Media, 2018), 18.

442 **"to start thinking"**: Katha Pollitt, *PRO: Reclaiming Abortion* (London: Picador, 2014), 27.

442 **"a good and moral choice"**: "Prepared Statement of Curtis Boyd, M.D., Santa

Fe, NM," in *Hearings Before the Subcommittee on Civil and Constitutional Rights of the Committee on the Judiciary House of Representatives: One Hundred First Congress, First and Second Sessions* (Washington, DC: Government Printing Office, 1994), 83.

442 **95 percent**: Corinne H. Rocca, Katrina Kimport, Sarah C. M. Roberts, Heather Gould, John Neuhaus and Diana G. Foster, "Decision Rightness and Emotional Responses to Abortion in the United States: A Longitudinal Study," *PLOS One*, July 8, 2015.

442 **if women learned of abortion**: Joey Peters, "A Moral Choice," *Santa Fe Reporter*, July 19, 2017.

442 **more than half of the clinics**: Owing to HB2, the number of clinics in Texas had dropped in fifteen months from forty-one to nineteen. Caitlin Gerdts et al., "Impact of Clinic Closures on Women Obtaining Abortion Services After Implementation of a Restrictive Law in Texas," *AJPH Research* 106, no. 5 (May 2016): 857.

442 **abortion providers had been falling**: There were 1,558 abortion providers in the U.S. in 1973, 2,908 in 1982, and 1,587 in 2017. "Number of Abortion Providers 1973–2017," Guttmacher Institute, https://data.guttmacher.org/states/trend?state=US&topics=71&dataset=data.

442 **Five states**: The five states were Kentucky, Mississippi, North Dakota, South Dakota and West Virginia. See https://www.guttmacher.org/sites/default/files/report_downloads/abortion-incidence-service-availability-us-2017-tables.pdf.

442 **accounted for nearly one in three**: In 2016, according to the Guttmacher Institute, there were 874,080 abortions in the United States. Of those, 140,700 were performed in California and 110,840 in New York, comprising 28.7 percent of the total. R. K. Jones, E. Witwer and J. Jerman, *Abortion Incidence and Service Availability in the United States, 2017* (New York: Guttmacher Institute, 2019), https://www.guttmacher.org/report/abortion-incidence-service-availability-us-2017.

442 **down by nearly half**: There were 1,590,750 abortions in the U.S. in 1988 and 862,320 in 2017. "Number of Abortions by State of Occurrence 1973–2017."

442 **rate of abortion**: R. K. Jones, E. Witwer and J. Jerman, "Abortion Incidence and Service Availability in the United States, 2017" (New York: Guttmacher Institute, 2019), https://www.guttmacher.org/report/abortion-incidence-service-availability-us-2017.

443 **regulations had helped**: For more on the causes of the decline in pregnancy rates and abortion rates, see Geoffrey Stone, *Sex and the Constitution* (New York: Liveright, 2017), 429–33.

443 **between sixteen and twenty-nine**: Katie Watson, *Scarlet A: The Ethics, Law, and Politics of Ordinary Abortion* (Oxford: Oxford University Press, 2018), 31. Watson explains in a footnote that her calculation assumes that a woman will begin having sex at seventeen, which is the national average, and not at fifteen, which is the age at which fertility starts (245).

443 **roughly one in five**: 18 percent of pregnancies (excluding miscarriages) ended

in abortion in 2017. R. K. Jones, E. Witwer and J. Jerman, *Abortion Incidence and Service Availability in the United States, 2017* (New York: Guttmacher Institute, 2019), https://www.guttmacher.org/report/abortion-incidence -service-availability-us-2017.

443 **in an amicus brief**: Brief for National Abortion Federation as Amici Curiae, *Whole Woman's Health v. Hellerstedt*, 579 U.S. __ (2016).

443 **fourteen in France and Germany**: German law states that abortion is legal through the twelve weeks following conception, which is equivalent to fourteen weeks from the last menstrual period.

443 **none of the countries**: Nicolas Boring and Jenny Gesley, foreign law specialists at the Law Library of Congress, emails to the author, February 22, 2021.

444 **"We would happily trade"**: Douthat, Goldberg and Leonhardt, "The Abortion Debate."

444 **could not provide a single instance**: *Whole Woman's Health v. Hellerstedt*, 579 U.S. ___ (2016), IV.

444 **"great for the women"**: Curtis Boyd, interview with the author, June 30, 2016.

444 **"very pro-choice"**: *Meet the Press*, NBC, October 24, 1999.

444 **he was pro life**: *The Laura Ingraham Show*, Talk Radio Network, February 9, 2011.

444 **had supported a ban**: David Brody, "Brody File Exclusive: Donald Trump Comes Out in Support of 20 Week Abortion Ban," CBN News, July 22, 2015.

444 **opposition to abortion was complete**: *Meet the Press*, NBC, August 16, 2015.

444 **"some form of punishment"**: Tom Kertscher, "In Context: Transcript of Donald Trump on punishing women for abortion," *Politifact*, March 30, 2016.

444 **"The woman is the same"**: Troy Newman, *Their Blood Cries Out* (Indiana: Restoration Press, 2003), 81.

445 **found not guilty**: *Keeler v. Superior Court*, 2 Cal. 3d 619, 87 Cal. Rptr. 481, 470 P.2d 617 (1970).

445 **according to a report**: Lynn Paltrow and Jeanne Flavin, "Arrests of and Forced Interventions on Pregnant Women in the United States (1973–2005): The implications for women's legal status and public health," *Journal of Health Politics, Policy and Law* 38, no. 2 (2013): 299.

445 **"These laws"**: "The Feticide Playbook, Explained," editorial, *New York Times*, December 28, 2018.

445 **Eight states decreed**: The states are Arizona, Delaware, Idaho, Kentucky, Oklahoma, South Carolina, Nevada and Utah. Courtesy of National Advocates for Pregnant Women.

445 **a variety of offenses**: Courtesy of Lynn Paltrow, National Advocates for Pregnant Women. Regarding self-abortion, see for example *Commonwealth of Virginia v. Michelle Roberts* in 2017 (CR17F00844-01). Regarding abuse of a corpse, and concealing a birth, see *State v. Anne Bynum* in Arkansas in 2018 (CR-16-879). Regarding murder, see for example *State v. Latice Fisher* in Mississippi in 2018 (2018-0028-CRH).

445 **"abortion opponents blame"**: Pollitt, *PRO: Reclaiming Abortion*, 35.

445 **"The woman is a victim"**: Matt Flegenheimer and Maggie Haberman, "Donald Trump, Abortion Foe, Eyes 'Punishment' for Women, Then Recants," *New York Times*, March 30, 2016.

446 **"pick Mike Pence"**: Isobel Yeung, "Consent," *Vice on HBO*, Vice Media/HBO, September 28, 2018.

446 **"the 24–karat-gold model"**: "Consent," *Vice on HBO*.

446 **"sent to the ash heap"**: *Congressional Record* 157, part 2, H1156 (February 17, 2011). 112th Cong., 1st sess.

446 **"That'll happen automatically"**: Aaron Blake, "The final Trump–Clinton Debate Transcript, Annotated," *Washington Post*, October 19, 2016.

446 **"These Supreme Court nominations"**: Jeffrey Toobin, "Still Standing," *New Yorker*, November 28, 2005.

446 **"proxies on *Roe*"**: David A. Kaplan, *The Most Dangerous Branch* (New York: Random House, 2018), 201.

446 **just two of the votes**: Republican Lincoln Chafee voted against confirming Samuel Alito, and Democrat Benjamin Nelson voted against confirming Elena Kagan.

446 **"Constitutional law"**: Kaplan, *The Most Dangerous Branch*, 247.

447 **meeting with groups of evangelicals**: The meeting with Newman and Benham was convened by the Southern Baptist lobbyist Tony Perkins. Troy Newman, email to the author, April 22, 2020.

447 **"Here before me"**: Barbie Latza Nadeau, "Why Catholics Crucified Clinton," *Daily Beast*, November 9, 2016.

447 **"Hillary Clinton and the Democratic platform"**: Sarah Pulliam Bailey, "A Catholic Priest Put an Aborted Fetus on the Altar in an Appeal for Donald Trump," *Washington Post*, November 7, 2016.

447 **"Everyone who respects"**: Ed Mechmann, "A Political Desecration," Archdiocese of New York, November 7, 2016, https://archny.org/a-political -desecration/.

447 **"be reserved for divine"**: Code of Canon Law, c. 1239 §1.

447 **"no one who is pro-life"**: Patrick J. Zurek, "Statement from Bishop Patrick J. Zurek," Roman Catholic Diocese of Amarillo, November 8, 2016.

447 **despite Pavone's claims**: Mary Pezzulo, "Frank Pavone Throws Down the Gauntlet, and I Respond," *Patheos*, April 22, 2020.

447 **no longer a priest in good standing**: Robert Aranda, a deacon at the Amarillo diocese, said that when asked about Father Pavone, "we don't ever issue a letter of good standing." Robert Aranda, interview with the author, August 10, 2020.

447 **video generated press**: Rhina Guidos, "Diocese Investigating Priest over Political Video of Fetus, Altar Use," Catholic News Service, November 9, 2016.

447 **declared that Obama**: Manny Fernandez, "A Texas Candidate Pushes the Boundary of the Far Right," *New York Times*, March 12, 2016.

447 **84 percent**: "Seeing Red: County goes big for GOP," *Wood County Monitor*, November 16, 2016.

447 **among the 69 percent**: Hannah Fingerhut, "About seven-in-ten Americans oppose overturning Roe v. Wade," Pew Research Center, January 13, 2017.

448 **"Trump on abortion"**: Danielle Paquette, "What People Really Wanted to Know about Trump on Election Day," *Washington Post*, November 8, 2016.

448 **thousands gathered in protest**: The North Texas March for Life is sponsored by Texans for Life, the Catholic Pro-Life Committee/Pro-Life Dallas and the Diocese of Fort Worth.

448 **constitutional originalist**: Neil Gorsuch, "Judge Neil Gorsuch: Why Originalism Is the Best Approach to the Constitution," *Time*, September 6, 2019.

448 **"American liberals"**: Neil Gorsuch, "Liberals 'N' Lawsuits," *National Review*, February 7, 2005.

448 **"that all human beings"**: Neil Gorsuch, *The Future of Assisted Suicide and Euthanasia* (Princeton: Princeton University Press, 2006), 4.

448 **"Gee, might that principle"**: Ed Whelan, "Misguided 'Pro-Life' Attack on Trump Supreme Court Candidate Neil Gorsuch," *National Review*, November 30, 2016.

448 **"pablum posing as humility"**: Kaplan, *The Most Dangerous Branch*, 82.

449 **had passed sixty-three**: Elizabeth Nash, Rachel Benson Gold, Lizamarie Mohammed, Zohra Ansari-Thomas and Olivia Cappello, "Policy Trends in the States, 2017," Guttmacher Institute, January 2, 2018.

449 **"the Great White Whale"**: Kaplan, *The Most Dangerous Branch*, 202.

449 **rise in breast cancer**: Joel Brind, "Abortion and Breast Cancer: Evidence Mounts: Laws Pass; Medical Media Stay in Denial," *National Right to Life News*, November 30, 1995, 22. According to the American Cancer Society, "the scientific evidence does not support the notion that abortion of any kind raises the risk of breast cancer or any other type of cancer"; see https://www.cancer.org/cancer/cancer-causes/medical-treatments/abortion -and-breast-cancer-risk.html.

449 **drop in crime**: John J. Donohue III and Steven D. Levitt, "The Impact of Legalized Abortion on Crime," *Quarterly Journal of Economics* 116, no. 2 (May 2001): 379–420. Steven Pinker assails the theory in his book *The Better Angels of Our Nature: Why Violence Has Declined* (New York: Viking, 2011), 119–21.

449 **"women or unborn children"**: William Saletan, *Bearing Right: How Conservatives Won the Abortion War* (Berkeley: University of California Press, 2003), 188.

449 **"is the most consequential"**: Jack Goldsmith, "Justice Kennedy's Retirement Leaves the Future of U.S. Constitutional law Entirely up for Grabs," *Washington Post*, June 27, 2018.

449 **"the firewall for abortion rights"**: Julie Hirschfeld Davis, "Departure of Kennedy, 'Firewall for Abortion Rights,' Could End Roe v. Wade," *New York Times*, June 27, 2018.

450 **concerned a Mexican teenager**: *Garza v. Hargan*, 874 F.3d 735 (D.C. Cir. 2017).

450 **"a new right for unlawful"**: *Garza v. Hargan*.

450 **"The constitutional right to abortion"**: Mark Joseph Stern, "The End of *Roe*," *Slate*, June 27, 2018.

451 **"the appellant's case"**: *Roe v. Wade*, Section IX.

451 **"Abortion Is Unconstitutional"**: John Finnis, "Abortion Is Unconstitutional," *First Things*, no. 312 (April 2021): 29–38.

451 **rejected the notion of a personhood**: Clarke Forsythe, *Politics for the Greatest Good: The Case for Prudence in the Public Square* (Downers Grove, IL: InterVarsity Press, 2009), 190.

451 **Trump advocated**: Oriana Schwindt, "Donald Trump's '60 Minutes' Interview: 12 Biggest Takeaways," *Variety*, November 13, 2016.

451 **"she makes her choice"**: Jay Floyd, oral argument, December 13, 1971, *Roe v. Wade*, 410 U.S. 113 (1973).

451 **illegal in at least twenty-four**: Center for Reproductive Rights, "What If Roe Fell?," 2019, https://reproductiverights.org/what-if-roe-fell.

451 **sixteen illegal, thirty-four legal**: Clarke Forsythe, email to the author, May 4, 2020.

451 **below the federal poverty level**: The proportion of abortion patients who are poor or low-income is growing. As of 2014, 49 percent were living below the federal poverty level. Jenna Jerman, Rachel K. Jones and Tsuyoshi Onda, "Characteristics of U.S. Abortion Patients in 2014 and Changes Since 2008," Guttmacher Institute, May 2016.

452 **"have higher earnings"**: Kate Bahn, Adriana Kugler, Melissa Mahoney, Danielle Corley and Annie McGrew, "Linking Reproductive Health Care Access to Labor Market Opportunities for Women," Center for American Progress, November 21, 2017.

452 **sharp rise in *medical* abortions**: Michelle Oberman, "What Happens When Abortion Is Banned," *New York Times*, May 31, 2018.

452 **"Law enforcement will"**: Oberman, "What Happens When Abortion Is Banned."

452 **"actually reinforce the power"**: Susan Sontag, "The Third World of Women," *Partisan Review*, Spring 1973, 204. Originally published in the October 1972 issue of *Libre*, a Spanish quarterly in Paris, in a translation by Juan Goytisolo.

452 **"I don't think"**: David Crary and Carla K. Johnson, "Overturning Roe v. Wade wouldn't turn back the clock to 1973," Associated Press, May 27, 2019.

453 **"If abortion becomes"**: Michael Kinsley, "What Abortion Debate?," *Slate*, November 18, 2005.

453 **"litigation addiction"**: Gorsuch, "Liberals 'N' Lawsuits."

453 **"would probably ignite"**: Jeffrey Rosen, "The Day After Roe," *Atlantic*, June 2006.

453 **"reflect the popular will"**: Rosen, "The Day After Roe."

453 **first trimester only**: According to a 2018 Gallup poll, 60 percent of Americans believe abortion should be legal through the first trimester. That percentage drops to 28 for the second trimester, and 13 for the third. Lydia Saad, "Trimesters Still Key to U.S. Abortion Views," Gallup, June 13, 2018.

453 **"I wanted it louder"**: NMP.

453 **"To overrule an important precedent"**: Robert H. Jackson, "Decisional Law

and Stare Decisis," *American Bar Association Journal* 30, no. 6 (June 1944): 334.

453 **"to presume that bedrock"**: *Vasquez v. Hillery*, 474 U.S. 254 (1986), Section V.

454 **"major precedents"**: Dan Keating, Brittany Renee Mayes and Kevin Schaul, "How Often Does the Supreme Court Overturn Precedents like Roe v. Wade," *Washington Post*, May 21, 2019.

454 **"unduly upset"**: *Ramos v. Louisiana*, 590 U.S. ___ (2020). (Justice Kavanaugh concurrence), Section I.

454 **Archibald Cox . . . defended**: Wrote Cox: "Constitutional rights ought not to be created under the Due Process Clause unless they can be stated in principles sufficiently absolute to give them roots throughout the community and continuity over significant periods of time, and to lift them above the level of the pragmatic political judgements of a particular time and place. . . . The failure to confront the [abortion] issue in principled terms leaves the [*Roe*] opinion to read like a set of hospital rules and regulations . . ." Archibald Cox, *The Role of the Supreme Court in American Government* (Oxford: Oxford University Press, 1976), 113–14.

454 **"the most compelling interest"**: Cox, *The Role of the Supreme Court*, 53.

454 **"that the Court's reversal"**: Justice David Souter clerk memo, July 12, 1991.

454 **"*Roe* was wrongly decided"**: Robin Toner, "Cold Paper Trail Leads Some to Scrutinize Nominee's Past Words on Abortion," *New York Times*, July 21, 2005.

455 **"doorjamb by doorjamb"**: Al Kamen, "Supreme Court Restricts Right to Abortion, Giving States Wide Latitude for Regulation," *Washington Post*, July 4, 1989.

455 **"rape, incest, and me"**: Ellen Goodman, "Abortion the Wobbly Majority," *Washington Post*, April 15, 1989.

455 **found to have pressured various partners**: Mike DeBonis, "Rep. Tim Murphy Resigns from Congress after Allegedly Asking Woman to Have Abortion," *Washington Post*, October 5, 2017. Peter Holley, "Congressman who Advised Ex-Wife to Seek Abortion Votes for Late-Term Abortion Ban," *Washington Post*, May 16, 2015.

455 **Alabama's bill**: The Human Life Protection Act (H.B. 314), enacted May 15, 2019.

455 **identified the embryo as "Baby Roe"**: Ashley Remkus, "Judge Tosses 'Baby Roe' Abortion Lawsuit Filed against Huntsville Clinic," AL.com, August 31, 2019.

455 **Oregon and Vermont**: "Abortion Policy in the Absence of Roe," Guttmacher Institute, May 1, 2020.

455 **the Women's Health Protection Act**: Melissa Jeltsen, "Lawmakers Reintroduce Bill to Protect Abortion Access Nationwide," *Huffington Post*, May 23, 2019.

456 **"setting the tone"**: Maggie Astor, "On Abortion Rights, 2020 Democrats Move Past 'Safe, Legal and Rare,'" *New York Times*, November 25, 2019.

456 **"the truth that the best"**: Caitlin Flanagan, "The Things We Can't Face," *Atlantic*, December 2019.

456 **"A deliberative democracy"**: Emma Green, "Science Is Giving the Pro-Life Movement a Boost," *Atlantic*, January 18, 2018.

456 **National Women's Political Caucus**: Luz Moreno-Lozano, "Roe v. Wade attorneys revisit case, look to future," *Austin American–Statesman*, June 16, 2019.

456 **after I noted in an article**: Joshua Prager, "Roe v. Wade's Secret Heroine," *Vanity Fair*, January 19, 2017.

456 **suggested Coffee join her**: Cynthia Montgomery, interview with the author, July 2, 2019.

456 **"We realized that nobody"**: Sarah Weddington, recorded interview with Luz Moreno-Lozano, *Austin American–Statesman*, June 16, 2019. Courtesy of Karen Blumenthal and Luz Moreno-Lozano.

456 **"Hold it like a lollipop"**: Sarah Weddington, recorded interview with Luz Moreno-Lozano.

457 **"sort of obsolete"**: "Oral Memoirs of Linda Coffee," Patricia Duke, interviewer, April 17, 1973, 20. Collection: Special Project: Roe v. Wade, Baylor University Institute for Oral History.

457 **"the sanctity of . . ."**: Southern Baptist Convention, "Resolution on Abortion," June 1, 1971.

457 **a bronze bust of Mildred**: Meredith Shamburger, "Bust Unveiling Ceremony of Dr. Mildred F. Jefferson Held," *Panola Watchman*, February 23, 2018.

457 **"You either had to not"**: Reminiscences of Dr. Curtis Boyd, Physicians for Reproductive Choice and Health Project, 2001, 54. Oral History Archives, Columbia University.

457 **250,000 abortions**: Curtis Boyd, interview with the author, June 2, 2020. Boyd estimated that he had personally performed 200,000–250,000 abortions, and that his clinics had performed 400,000–500,000.

458 **went into cardiac arrest**: Claire Chretien, "Woman Dies after Late-Term Abortion at Shady Clinic with History of Abuse," LifeSite, lifesitenews.com, August 23, 2017.

458 **"It doesn't make it"**: Curtis Boyd, interview with the author, June 2, 2020.

458 **a backslidden minister**: Christian Newswire, "Former Tiller Abortionists Make Albuquerque the New Late-Term Abortion Capital," March 17, 2010.

458 **Trump spoke again and again**: Donald Trump, "Remarks by President Trump at the 47th Annual March for Life," White House Archives, January 24, 2020.

458 **"baby body parts"**: Marsha Blackburn, "An Investigation in Defense of Life," *U.S. News and World Report*, November 10, 2015.

458 **The Texas governor**: Greg Abbott signed Senate Bill 8 on June 6, 2017.

458 **attorney general exonerated Boyd**: Matthew Reichbach, "AG Finds No Law Broken over Fetal Tissue Donations," *NM Political Report*, January 5, 2018.

458 **state abortion ban unconstitutional**: Maggie Astor, "Texas Abortion Law Is Unconstitutional, Federal Judge Rules," *New York Times*, November 22, 2017.

458 **filed suit**: *Whole Woman's Health v. Paxton*, 17–51060 (5th Cir. 2020).

458 **all the way to the Supreme Court**: Astor, "Texas Abortion Law Is Unconstitutional."

458 **mired in more litigation**: *Planned Parenthood Center for Choice, et al. v. Greg Abbott, as Governor of Texas, et al.*, case 1:20–cv-323 (USDC, W. D. Tex. 25 Mar 2020).

458 **Texas attorney general banned**: Raga Justin, "No Abortions in Texas Unless the Mother's Life Is in Danger, Texas Attorney General Says as Coronavirus Spreads," *Texas Tribune*, March 23, 2020.

459 **"There are more important"**: Justine Coleman, "Texas Lt. Governor on Reopening State: 'There are more important things than living,'" *The Hill*, April 21, 2020.

459 **Texas lifted its abortion ban**: Shannon Najmabadi, "Texas Clinics Resume Abortion Services as State Acknowledges Ban Is No Longer in Place," *Texas Tribune*, April 22, 2020.

459 **"We made it through"**: Curtis Boyd, interview with the author, June 2, 2020.

459 **FBI list**: Anna North, "Forty Years After Roe, Abortion Doctors Still Fear for Their Safety," *Buzzfeed*, January 18, 2013.

459 **"It's not your normal"**: Reminiscences of Dr. Curtis Boyd, 50.

459 **"It never left me"**: Curtis Boyd, interview with the author, June 2, 2020.

459 **"Too narrow a front"**: "Getting God's Kingdom Into Politics," *Christianity Today*, September 19, 1980.

459 **81 percent**: Molly Worthen, "A Match Made in Heaven," *Atlantic*, May 2017.

459 **"Can we say"**: Mark Galli, "Trump Should Be Removed from Office," *Christianity Today*, December 19, 2019.

459 **"this goddamn loser Biden"**: Mary Pezzulo, "Diocese of Amarillo: Disregard and Pray for Pavone," *Patheos*, September 17, 2020.

459 **would not grant absolution**: Roman Catholic Diocese of Amarillo, "Diocese of Amarillo Issues Statement Regarding Father Frank Pavone," September 16, 2020.

460 **"pray for Father Pavone"**: Roman Catholic Diocese of Amarillo, "Diocese of Amarillo Issues Statement."

460 **"We ask you Father"**: "Guillermo Maldonado Prays for President Donald Trump during Evangelical Rally in Miami," *Miami Herald*, YouTube, January 3, 2020.

460 **Ginsburg had co-founded**: The journal was the *Women's Rights Law Reporter* at Rutgers School of Law in Newark, NJ.

460 **"This is something central"**: "The Supreme Court; Excerpts from Senate Hearing on the Ginsburg Nomination," *New York Times*, July 22, 1993.

460 **"It's time to put an end"**: Colby Itkowitz, "Barrett Signed Ad in 2006 Decrying 'Barbaric Legacy' of Roe v. Wade, Advocating Overturning the Law," *Washington Post*, October 1, 2020.

460 **she joined a dissent**: Associated Press, "A Look at Judge Amy Coney Barrett's Notable Opinions, Votes," September 26, 2020.

460 **"a vapid and hollow charade"**: Elena Kagan, "Confirmation Messes, Old and New," *University of Chicago Law Review* 62, no. 2 (Spring 1995).

460 **"that no justice"**: Amy C. Barrett, Precedent and Jurisprudential Disagreement, *Texas Law Review* 91, no. 1711 (2012–13).

461 **"My most fervent wish"**: Matthew Choi and Josh Gerstein, "Ginsburg's Wish: 'I will not be replaced until a new president is installed,'" *Politico*, September 18, 2020.

461 **the trio of Trump justices**: The case was *FDA v. American College of Obstetricians and Gynecologists*, 592 U.S. ___ (2021). Adam Liptak, "Supreme Court Revives Abortion-Pill Restriction," *New York Times*, January 12, 2021.

461 **the first two**: *June Medical Services LLC v. Russo*, 591 U.S. ___ (2020).

461 **Two hundred and seven members**: The two Democratic congressmen who signed the amicus brief were Collin Peterson of Minnesota and Daniel Lipinski of Illinois.

461 **"an excellent vehicle"**: Ed Whelan, "Best Opportunity the Supreme Court Will Ever Have to Overturn Roe," *National Review*, November 9, 2020.

461 **"That little Richie Rich"**: Norma McCorvey, interview with the author, February 5, 2017.

462 **had any final wishes**: Author's notes on conversation between Jennifer Ferguson and Melissa Mills, February 18, 2017.

462 **drawn in a white carriage**: Norma McCorvey, text message to Henry Taylor, September 8, 2010. Courtesy of Henry Taylor.

462 **"She had so many"**: Author's notes on conversation between Melissa Mills and Jennifer Ferguson, February 18, 2017.

462 **obituary was online within minutes**: Emily Langer, "Norma McCorvey, Jane Roe of Roe v. Wade Decision Legalizing Abortion Nationwide, Dies at 69," *Washington Post*, February 18, 2017.

462 **"She didn't want you"**: Author's notes on conversation between Melissa Mills and Jennifer Ferguson, February 18, 2017.

462 **"I was like, 'Okay'"**: Shelley Thornton, interview with the author, February 25, 2019.

463 **"like now you can start"**: Shelley Thornton, interview with the author, February 25, 2019.

463 **"in the middle"**: Shelley Thornton, interview with the author, February 25, 2019.

463 **in a profile I'd written**: Joshua Prager, "The Accidental Activist," *Vanity Fair*, February 2013.

463 **she'd worried to her sisters**: Shelley Thornton, text message to Jennifer Ferguson and Melissa Mills, January 25, 2017. Courtesy of Melissa Mills.

463 **a London tabloid**: The *Daily Mail* assigned Ben Ashford to the story. He emailed me on February 20, 2017, noting that I would be "properly compensated" for any tips.

463 **"Roe's baby"**: The ad was created by Ryan Bomberger, Chief Creative Officer of the Radiance Foundation, http://www.radiance.life/roe.

463 **get a DNA sample**: Frank Di Bugnara, interview with the author, February 24, 2019.

463 **obituary was true to Norma**: Langer, "Norma McCorvey."

463 **"bickered over"**: Andy Klein, "Abortion for Grins," *Dallas Observer*, March 6, 1997.

463 **words of a master's thesis**: Barnard, "Jane Roe Gone Rogue."

463 **"It would have been nice"**: Keri Blakinger, "Norma McCorvey: Abortion Case's 'Roe' Dies at 69; Texan behind landmark decision 'at peace at end,'" *Houston Chronicle*, February 19, 2017.

464 **"My mom just wasn't"**: Kaki King, interview with the author, July 31, 2012.

464 **portrait Annie Leibovitz had taken**: Annie Leibovitz and Susan Sontag, *Women* (New York: Random House, 1999), 138.

464 **"when she died"**: "Terry Hopes Docu Sets the Record Straight on McCorvey," *Defend Life*, July/August 2017.

464 **"It was like, no!"**: Melissa Mills, interview with the author, February 20, 2017.

464 **he was noncommittal**: Melissa Mills, interview with the author, February 20, 2017.

464 **pay for police, catering**: Karen Garnett, interview with the author, February 22, 2017.

465 **Shelley had called**: Shelley Thornton, interview with the author, February 21, 2017.

465 **"I'm thinking"**: Shelley Thornton, interview with the author, February 21, 2017.

465 **"start a new chapter"**: Melissa Mills, text message to Shelley Thornton and Jennifer Ferguson, February 24, 2017. Courtesy of Melissa Mills.

465 **"It doesn't matter"**: Author's notes on conversation between Melissa Mills and Eric Heumann, February 24, 2017.

465 **"She came out good"**: Author's notes on conversation between Melissa Mills and Eric Heumann, February 24, 2017.

465 **would be in touch**: Melissa Mills, interview with the author, February 24, 2017.

466 **"In my fifty years"**: Henry Taylor, interview with the author, February 24, 2017.

466 **"I no longer believe"**: Rob Schenck, *Costly Grace: An Evangelical Minister's Rediscovery of Faith, Hope, and Love* (New York: Harper, 2018), 324.

466 **"People were exasperated"**: Rob Schenck, interview with the author, July 27, 2018.

466 **Melissa had said no**: Melissa Mills, interview with the author, February 20, 2017.

468 **Melissa set a blue**: Melissa Mills, interview with the author, May 19, 2020.

469 **"about me being the face"**: Melissa Mills, interview with the author, July 26, 2018.

469 **"I don't know how"**: Melissa Mills, interview with the author, February 28, 2017.

469 **"a childhood of almost unrelenting"**: "Roe v. Wade, Part 1: Who Was Jane Roe?" The Daily (podcast), *New York Times*, July 23, 2018.

469 **a *Times* headline**: Jenny Gross and Aimee Ortiz, "Roe v. Wade Plaintiff Was Paid to Switch Sides, Documentary Says," *New York Times*, May 19, 2020.

469 **Alexandria Ocasio-Cortez**: Tweet, May 19, 2020: "Wow: Norma McCorvey (aka "Roe" of Roe v Wade) revealed on her deathbed that she was paid by right-wing operatives to flip her stance on reproductive rights. So, like many right-wing operations, it turns out a huge part of the anti-choice movement was a scam the entire time."

469 **the president of NARAL**: Ilyse Hogue, tweet, May 19, 2020, 2:10 pm. "Jane Roe's (Roe v. Wade) conversion to become anti-abortion was all a paid act according to a new documentary. This is an extreme example of precisely why we do not base rights on individual experiences and feelings. Norma McCorvey had a very troubled life and was exploited for a far-right agenda in deeply immoral ways. The architects of the anti-choice movement depended on these kinds of strategies to weaponize abortion access and stop social progress."

469 **compensation that averaged**: Ron Allen, Norma McCorvey's accountant, email to the author, May 25, 2020.

470 **"That was just like"**: *Roe vs. Roe*, film.

470 **"They'll take anything"**: Norma McCorvey, interview with the author, March 24, 2015.

470 **"The individual's life"**: Angela Bonavoglia, interview with the author, August 10, 2018.

470 **"sharing DNA"**: Jodi Picoult, *Handle with Care* (New York: Atria, 2009), 379.

470 **"I just hoped"**: Melissa Mills, interview with the author, August 1, 2019.

471 **"Just trying to get through it"**: Melissa Mills, interview with the author, December 10, 2017.

471 **"warden"**: Jennifer Ferguson, interview with the author, July 8, 2016.

471 **"A nice guy"**: Jennifer Ferguson, interview with the author, November 10, 2016.

472 **"she went on"**: Jennifer Ferguson, interview with the author, May 18, 2017.

472 **he'd wanted to reach out**: Todd Peterson, interview with the author, March 5, 2019.

472 **"My wife would get"**: Todd Peterson, interview with the author, March 5, 2019.

473 **"We can go back"**: Todd Peterson, interview with the author, February 27, 2019.

473 **"It's a daily process"**: Shelley Thornton, interview with the author, February 25, 2019.

473 **"I want everyone"**: Shelley Thornton, interview with the author, February 26, 2019.

473 **A novel called**: Christopher Bauer, *Jane's Baby* (Rosaryville, MD: Intrigue, 2018), 275.

473 **"Norma McCorvey Daughter"**: Google Trends, accessed May 18, 2020.

473 **"Nobody was ever"**: Shelley Thornton, interview with the author, February 28, 2019.

473 **"This person"**: Christopher Signil, *Race, Faith, and Politics: The Dilemma, the Deal Breakers and the New Direction* (Lake Mary, FL: Charisma Media, 2012), 105.

473 **"She's not the *Roe* baby"**: Shelley Thornton, interview with the author, August 25, 2018.

473 **she'd only cared to know**: Shelley Thornton, interview with the author, February 26, 2019.

474 **"Please God"**: Shelley Thornton, letter to Melissa Mills, September 1, 1993. Courtesy of Melissa Mills.

474 **"My association with *Roe*"**: Shelley Thornton, interview with the author, February 28, 2019.

474 **"I have no attachments"**: Shelley Thornton, interview with the author, February 28, 2019.

474 **not heard of Justice Blackmun**: Shelley Thornton, interview with the author, February 26, 2019.

474 **"Reality is a cruel"**: Shelley Thornton, interview with the author, February 26, 2019.

474 **"If you're fine"**: Shelley Thornton, interview with the author, February 26, 2019.

475 **"It's not a secret"**: Shelley Thornton, interview with the author, August 15, 2018.

475 **"The prospect of me"**: Shelley Thornton, interview with the author, February 26, 2019.

475 **"a compensation for the pang"**: W. B. Yeats, "Among School Children" (1928), in *The Poems of W.B. Yeats* (New York: Macmillan, 1933).

475 **"If I had allowed"**: Shelley Thornton, interview with the author, February 26, 2019.

475 **"I've always empathized"**: Shelley Thornton, interview with the author, February 26, 2019.

476 **"It's really helping me"**: Shelley Thornton, email to the author, January 7, 2021.

476 **"a braver person"**: Wendy Craig, Zoom call with the author, and Shelley Thornton, February 17, 2021.

476 **"I just have no personal"**: Shelley Thornton, text message to Jennifer Ferguson, September 2020. Courtesy of Jennifer Ferguson.

477 **"Atchafalaya"**: John McPhee, "Atchafalaya," *New Yorker*, February 23, 1987, 39.

477 **"I know this water"**: Melissa Mills, interview with the author, October 28, 2020.

AUTHOR'S NOTE

479 **Abortion and Divorce**: Mary Ann Glendon, *Abortion and Divorce in Western Law: American Failures, European Challenges.* (Cambridge, MA: Harvard University Press, 1989).

479 **"each side views"**: Gilbert Yale Steiner, *The Futility of Family Policy* (Washington, D.C.: Brookings Institute Press, 1981), 71.

479 **"astonishing" one-dimensionality**: Lauren Robel, review of *Abortion and Divorce in Western Law* by Mary Ann Glendon, in *Constitutional Commentary* 6 no. 115 (1989): 135.

479 **blithely echoed:** Glendon wrote that U.S. abortion law was marked by a "studied rejection of efforts to preserve the fetus," and that "Only in America has a vast profit-marking industry grown up around abortion." Mary Ann Glendon, *Abortion and Divorce in Western Law: American Failures, European Challenges.* (Cambridge, MA: Harvard University Press, 1989), 20, 22.

479 **"coming to terms with real"**: Kristin Luker, *Abortion and the Politics of Motherhood* (Berkeley: University of California Press, 1985), 2.

479 **"giving voice"**: Laurence H. Tribe, *Abortion: The Clash of Absolutes* (New York: Norton, 1992), 6.

479 **"a choice of words"**: Luker, *Abortion and the Politics of Motherhood*, 2.

480 **"a mockery"**: Luker, *Abortion and the Politics of Motherhood*, 2.

480 **Katha Pollitt notes**: Katha Pollitt, PRO: *Reclaiming Abortion*, (London: Picador, 2014), 14.

480 **Katie Watson**: Katie Watson, *Scarlet A: The Ethics, Law, and Politics of Ordinary Abortion*, (Oxford: Oxford University Press, 2018), 9.

480 **"a criminal"**: Randall Terry, *Voice of Resistance*, "Episode 1019: Does Anyone Care about Norma McCorvey?," YouTube, May 11, 2017.

481 **"happiest moment"**: Jennifer Ferguson, Facebook post, November 10, 2012.

481 **"I want everyone"**: Shelley Thornton, interview with the author, February 26, 2019.

481 **it was "accurate"**: Jennifer Ferguson, interview with the author, January 14, 2021. Shelley Thornton, interview with the author, February 14, 2021. Melissa Mills, interview with the author, April 8, 2019.

481 **"You've done great"**: Melissa Mills, interview with the author, April 11, 2021.

482 **"undoubtedly the best-known"**: Ronald Dworkin, *Life's Dominion: An Argument About Abortion, Euthanasia, And Individual Freedom* (New York: Vintage, 1993), 102.

483 **'I'm your mama'**: Velma Gross, interview with the author, January 23, 2015.

484 **"I saw more of our daughters"**: Susan Sheehan, "When Will the Book Be Done?," *New York Times Magazine*, April 15, 1990.

ACKNOWLEDGMENTS

485 **"I used to not"**: Anne Lamott, "bird by bird with annie," *Independent Lens*, PBS, October 8, 1999.

486 **preferred your "version"**: Norma McCorvey, interview with the author, March 24, 2015.

Bibliography

This bibliography includes scholarly articles and books, but does not include newspaper and magazine articles or the blizzard of documents referenced in the notes, such as court cases, polls, press conferences, newsletters, political party positions, congressional records, private emails and letters, census data, birth and marriage and divorce and death certificates, FBI and police records, etc.

Adams, Greg D. "Abortion: Evidence of an Issue Evolution." *American Journal of Political Science* 41, no. 3 (1997).

Adler, Nancy, et al. "Psychological Facts in Abortion: A Review," *American Psychologist* 47, no. 1194 (1992).

Adler, N. E., H. P. David, B. N. Major, S. H. Roth, N. F. Russo and G. E. Wyatt. "Psychological Responses After Abortion," *Science* 248, no. 4951 (April 6, 1990):41-44.

"America We Seek, The: A Statement of Pro-Life Principle and Concern," *First Things*, May 1996.

American Psychological Association. "Report of the Task Force on Mental Health and Abortion." Washington, DC, 2008.

Andrikopoulous, Bonnie, and Warren M. Hern, eds. *Abortion in the Seventies: Proceedings of the Western Regional Conference on Abortion, Denver, Colorado, February 27–29, 1976.* New York: National Abortion Federation, 1977.

Askren, Hollie A., and Kathleen C. Bloom. "Postadoptive Reactions of the Relinquishing Mother: A Review." *Journal of Obstetric, Gynecologic, and Neonatal Nursing* 28, no. 4 (July/August 1999): 395–400.

Augustine, Saint. *The city of God (De civitate Dei).* Translated by John Healey. London: Griffith, Farran, Okeden & Welsh, 1945.

————. *Writings on the Old Testament*. Translated by Joseph T. Lienhard and Sean Doyle. New York: New City Press, 2016.

Bahn, Kate, Adriana Kugler, Melissa Mahoney, Danielle Corley and Annie McGrew. "Linking Reproductive Health Care Access to Labor Market Opportunities for Women." *Center for American Progress*, November 21, 2017.

Balkin, Jack. *What Roe v. Wade Should Have Said: The Nation's Top Legal Experts Rewrite America's Most Controversial Decision*. New York: NYU Press, 2005.

Barnard, Christianna K. "Jane Roe Gone Rogue: Norma McCorvey's Transformation as a Symbol of the U.S. Abortion Debate." MA thesis, Sarah Lawrence College, 2018.

Bauer, Christopher. *Jane's Baby*. Rosaryville, MD: Intrigue, 2018.

Bickell, Alexander M. *The Least Dangerous Branch: The Supreme Court at the Bar of Politics*. New Haven: Yale University Press, 1986.

Bitler, Marianna, and Madeline Zavodny. "Did Abortion Legalization Reduce the Number of Unwanted Children? Evidence from Adoptions." *Perspectives on Sexual and Reproductive Health* 34, no. 1 (January/February 2002): 25–33.

Blumenthal, Karen. *Jane Against the World: Roe v. Wade and the Fight for Reproductive Rights*. New York: Roaring Brook Press, 2020.

Bogue, Donald J. "Family Planning in Negro Ghettos of Chicago." *Milbank Memorial Fund Quarterly*, April 1970.

Bonavoglia, Angela., ed. *The Choices We Made: 25 Women and Men Speak Out Against Abortion*. New York: Random House, 1991.

Bork, Robert. *The Tempting of America: The Political Seduction of the Law*. New York: Simon and Schuster, 1990.

Boyd, Curtis. "The Morality of Abortion: The Making of a Feminist Physician." *St Louis University Public Law Review* 13, no. 1 (1993–94): 303–14.

Brands, H. W. *Reagan: The Life*. New York: Anchor, 2015.

Brown, Mark R. "Gender Discrimination in the Supreme Court's Clerkship Selection Process." *Oregon Law Review* 75, no. 2 (Summer 1996).

Bryant, Amy G., and Jonas J. Swartz. "Why Crisis Pregnancy Centers are Legal but Unethical." *AMA Journal of Ethics* 20, no. 3 (2018): 269–77.

Buchanan, Patrick J. "A Decision Based on Deceit." The American Cause, June 23, 2003.

Burack, Cynthia. *Tough Love: Sexuality, Compassion and the Christian Right*. New York: State University of New York Press, 2014.

Burleigh, Michael, and Wolfgang Wippermann. *The Racial State: Germany 1933–1945*. Cambridge: Cambridge University Press, 1991.

Bustain, Sarah. "Choice Language." *American Prospect*, November 22, 2004.

Calderone, Mary S. "Illegal Abortion as a Public Health Problem." *American Journal of Public Health* 50, no. 7 (July 1960): 948–54.

"Canticle Talks . . . with Norma McCorvey." *Canticle*, Winter 2000.

Carmen, Arlene, and Howard Moody. *Abortion Counseling and Social Change*. Valley Forge, PA: Judson Press, 1973.

Carpenter, Dale. *Flagrant Conduct: The Story of Lawrence v. Texas*. New York: Norton, 2012.

Carter, Stephen L. "Abortion, Absolutism, and Compromise." *Yale Law Journal* 100, no. 8 (1991): 2747–66.

Cassidy, Kathleen. "Post-Abortive Women Attack Roe v. Wade." *At the Center*, January 2001.

Cates, Willard, Jr., and Roger Rochat. "Illegal Abortions in the United States: 1972–1974." *Family Planning Perspectives* 8, no. 2 (1976).

Catholics for a Free Choice. "Faithless Politics: Priests for Life Defies Constitution and Conscience." In "Opposition Notes: An Investigative Series on Those Who Oppose Women's Rights and Reproductive Health," 2006.

Center for Reproductive Rights. "What if Roe Fell?" 2019. https://reproductiverights.org/what-if-roe-fell.

Centers for Disease Control. "1980 Statistical Abstract of the United States."

————. "Abortion Surveillance Report, 1970."

————. "Abortion Surveillance Report, 1972."

Chisholm, Shirley. *Unbought and Unbossed*. Boston: Houghton Mifflin Harcourt, 1970.

Clark, Tom C. "Religion, Morality, and Abortion: A Constitutional Appraisal." *Loyola of Los Angeles Law Review* 2, no. 1 (1969).

Clermont, Betty. *The Neo-Catholics: Implementing Christian Nationalism in America*. Los Angeles: SCB Distributors, 2010.

Cohen, David S., and Carole Joffe. *Obstacle Course*. Berkeley: University of California Press, 2020.

Cohen, David S., and Krysten Connon. *Living in the Crosshairs: The Untold Stories of Anti-Abortion Terrorism*. Oxford, UK: Oxford University Press, 2016.

Congressional Research Service, *Exceptions to Mootness: Capable of Repetition, Yet Evading Review*. Constitution Annotated. https://constitution.congress.gov/browse/essay/artIII_S2_C1_1_7_3_3_3/.

Cooley, Thomas M. *Cooley on Torts, or A Treatise on the Law of Torts*. 2nd ed. Chicago: Callaghan, 1888.

Cooper, Courtney Ryley. *Designs in Scarlet*. New York: Little, Brown, 1939.

Cowan, Sarah K. "Enacted abortion stigma in the United States." *Social Science and Medicine* 177 (March 2017): 259–68.

Cox, Archibald. *The Role of the Supreme Court in American Government*, Oxford: Oxford University Press. 1976.

Coyle, C. T., and R. Enright. "Forgiveness intervention with postabortion men." *Journal of Consulting and Clinical Psychology* 65, no. 6 (1997).

Craig, Barbara Hinkson, and David M. O'Brien. *Abortion and American Politics*. London: Chatham House, 1993.

Critchlow, Donald T. *Intended Consequences: Birth Control, Abortion and the Federal Government in Modern America*. Oxford: Oxford University Press, 2001.

Darity, William A., and Castellano B. Turner. "Fears of Genocide Among Black Americans as Related to Age, Sex, and Religion." *American Journal of Public Health* 63 (1973).

David, Henry P. "Born Unwanted: Mental Health Costs and Consequences." *American Journal of Orthopsychiatry* 81, no. 2 (2011): 184–92.

Doan, Alesha. *Opposition and Intimidation: The Abortion Wars and Strategies of Political Harrassment.* Ann Arbor: University of Michigan Press, 1997.

Donnally, Jennifer. "The Politics of Abortion and the Rise of the New Right." PhD diss., 2013, University of North Carolina at Chapel Hill.

Donner, James. *Women in Trouble.* Derby, CT: Monarch, 1959.

Donohue, John J., III, and Steven D. Levitt. "The Impact of Legalized Abortion on Crime." *Quarterly Journal of Economics* 116, no. 2 (May 2001): 379–420.

DuBois, W. E. B. "Black Folk and Birth Control." *Birth Control Review,* June 1932.

Dworkin, Ronald. *Life's Dominion: An Argument About Abortion, Euthanasia, and Individual Freedom.* New York: Vintage, 1993.

Edelin, Kenneth C. *Broken Justice: A True Story of Race, Sex and Revenge in a Boston Courtroom.* Martha's Vineyard, MA: Pondview Press, 2007.

Eisenberg, Henry and Howard Eisenberg. *Night Calls: The Personal Journey of an Ob-Gyn.* New York: Berkley, 1998.

Eisenberg, Howard. "The Mad Scramble for Abortion Money." *Medical Economics,* January 4, 1971.

Ely, John Hart. "The Wages of Crying Wolf: A Comment on *Roe v. Wade.*" *Yale Law Journal* 82, no. 920 (1973).

Faludi, Susan. *Backlash: The Undeclared War Against American Women.* New York: Crown, 1991.

Falwell, Jerry. *If I Should Die Before I Wake.* Nashville: Thomas Nelson, 1986.

———. *Listen America!* New York: Doubleday, 1980.

———. *Strength for the Journey: An Autobiography.* New York: Pocket, 1988.

Faux, Marian. *Roe v. Wade: The Untold Story of the Landmark Supreme Court Decision that Made Abortion Legal.* New York: Cooper Square Press, 1988.

Feldt, Gloria, and Laura Fraser. *The War on Choice: The Right-Wing Attack on Women's Rights and How to Fight Back.* New York: Bantam, 2004.

Finch, Annie, ed. *Choice Words: Writers on Abortion.* Chicago: Haymarket, 2020.

Finnis, John. "Abortion is Unconstitutional," *First Things,* no. 312 (April 2021): 29–38.

Forsythe, Clarke. *Politics for the Greatest Good: The Case for Prudence in the Public Square.* Downers Grove, IL: InterVarsity Press, 2009.

Foster, Diana Greene. *The Turnaway Study: Ten Years, a Thousand Women, and the Consequences of Having—or Being Denied—an Abortion.* New York: Scribner, 2020.

Francke, Linda Bird. *The Ambivalence of Abortion.* Sydney: Penguin Books Australia, 1978.

Friedan, Betty. *The Feminine Mystique.* New York: Norton, 1963.

Galton, Francis. *Inquiries into Human Faculty and its Development.* London: MacMillan, 1883.

Garrow, David J. "How Roe v. Wade Was Written," *Washington and Lee Law Review* 71, no. 2 (Spring 2014): 893–924.

Garrow, David J. *Liberty and Sexuality: The Right to Privacy and the Making of Roe v. Wade.* Berkeley: University of California Press, 1998.

Gates, Henry Louis, Jr., and Evelyn Brooks Higginbotham, eds. *African American Lives*. Oxford: Oxford University Press, 2004.

Gerdts, Caitlin, et al. "Impact of Clinic Closures on Women Obtaining Abortion Services After Implementation of a Restrictive Law in Texas." *AJPH Research* 106, no. 5 (May 2016).

Ginsburg, Ruth B. Madison Lecture, NYU School of Law, March 9, 1993. http://law.nyu.edu/sites/default/files/ECM_PRO_059254.pdf.

———. "Some Thoughts on Autonomy and Equality in Relation to *Roe v. Wade*." *University of North Carolina Law Review* 63, no. 375 (1985): 375–86.

Glendon, Mary Ann. *Abortion and Divorce in Western Law: American Failures, European Challenges*. Cambridge, MA: Harvard University Press, 1989.

Gold, Rachel Benson. "Lessons from Before Roe: Will Past Be Prologue?" *Guttmacher Report on Public Policy* 6, no. 1 (2003).

Goldman, William. *Boys and Girls Together*. New York: Simon & Schuster, 1964.

Gorney, Cynthia. *Articles of Faith: A Frontline History of the Abortion Wars*. New York: Simon & Schuster, 2000.

Gorsuch, Neil. *The Future of Assisted Suicide and Euthanasia*. Princeton: Princeton University Press, 2006.

Greenhouse, Linda. *Becoming Justice Blackmun*. New York: Times Books, 2005.

Greenhouse, Linda, and Reva B. Siegel. "Backlash to the Future? From Roe to Perry." *UCLA Law Review* 60, Discourse 240 (2013).

———. "Before (and After) Roe v. Wade: New Questions About Backlash." *Yale Law Review* 120, no. 2028 (2011).

———. *Before Roe v. Wade: Voices that Shaped the Abortion Debate Before the Supreme Court's Ruling*. New Haven: Yale Law School, 2016.

Guttmacher Institute. "Abortion Policy in the Absence of Roe." May 1, 2020.

———. "Laws Affecting Reproductive Health and Rights: 2011 State Policy Review."

Halverson Boyd, G. J. "Surviving a Holy War: How health care workers in U.S. abortion facilities are coping with antiabortion harassment." PhD diss., Fielding Institute, 1990.

Hansen, Susan B. "State Implementation of Supreme Court Decisions: Abortion Rates Since Roe v. Wade." *Journal of Politics* 42 (1980).

Hays, Richard B. *The Moral Vision of the New Testament*. San Francisco: HarperOne, 1996.

Henshaw, S. K. "Unintended Pregnancy in the United States." *Family Planning Perspectives* 30 no. 1 (January/February 1998).

———, and J. Van Vort, eds. *Abortion Factbook, 1992 Edition: Readings, Trends and State and Local Data to 1988*. New York: Guttmacher Institute, 1992.

———, et al. *Restrictions on Medicaid Funding for Abortions: A Literature Review*. New York: Guttmacher Institute, 2009.

Hern, Warren M. "Serial multiple laminaria and adjunctive urea in late outpatient dilation and evacuation abortion." *Obstetrics and Gynecology* 63 (1984): 543–49.

———, and Billie Corrigan. "What About Us? Staff Reactions to D & E." *Advances in Planned Parenthood* 15, no. 1 (1980).

Hilgers, Thomas W., and Dennis J. Horan, eds. *Abortion and Social Justice.* New York: Sheed & Ward, 1972.

———, and David Mall, eds. *New Perspectives on Human Abortion.* Frederick, MD: Altheia Books, University Publications of America, 1981.

Hirschman, Linda. *Sisters in Law: How Sandra Day O'Connor and Ruth Bader Ginsburg Went to the Supreme Court and Changed the World.* New York: Harper Perennial, 2016.

Hogue, Ilyse, and Ellie Langford. *The Lie That Binds.* Washington, DC: Strong Arm Press, 2020.

Holmes, Oliver Wendell, Jr. *The Common Law.* Boston: Little, Brown, 1881.

Horan, Dennis J., and Edward R. Grant. *Abortion and the Constitution: Reversing Roe v. Wade Through the Courts.* Washington DC: Georgetown University Press, 1987.

Horrocks, Thomas L. *Beyond the Binaries: The Complexity of Abortion and What to Do About It.* Coppell, TX: Thomas Horrocks, 2020.

Hull, N. E. H., and Peter Charles Hoffer. *Roe v. Wade, The Abortion Rights Controversy in American History.* Lawrence: University Press of Kansas, 2010.

Jackson, Robert H. "Decisional Law and Stare Decisis." *American Bar Association Journal* 30, no. 6 (June 1944).

Jatlaoui, T. C., et al. "Abortion Surveillance—United States, 2015." *Morbidity and Mortality Weekly Report* 67, no. SS-13 (November 23, 2018).

———."Abortion surveillance – United States, 2018," *Morbidity and Mortality Weekly Report* 69, no. SS-7 (2020).

Jefferson, Mildred. "Abortion: Self-Defeat Solution." *Centerscope* 5, no 1–5 (March/April 1972).

Jefferson, Mildred. "Dissonance." *Bulletin,* September 1955.

Jefferson, Mildred. Interviews with Jennifer Donnally. Schlesinger Library on the History of Women in America, Radcliffe Institute for Advanced Study, Harvard University.

Jerman, Jenna, Rachel K. Jones and Tsuyoshi Onda. *Characteristics of U.S. Abortion Patients in 2014 and Changes Since 2008.* New York: Guttmacher Institute, 2016.

Joffe, Carole E. "Working with Dr. Tiller: Staff Recollections of Women's Health Care Services of Wichita." *Perspectives on Sexual and Reproductive Health* 43, no. 3 (September 2011): 199–204.

Joffe, Carole E. *Doctors of Conscience: The Struggle to Provide Abortion Before and After Roe v. Wade.* Boston: Beacon Press, 1995.

Jones, Rachel K., and Kathryn Kooistra. "Abortion Incidence and Access to Services in the United States." In *Perspectives on Sexual and Reproductive Health.* New York: Guttmacher Institute, 2008.

Jones, Rachel K., E. Witwer and J Jerman. *Abortion Incidence and Service Availability in the United States, 2017.* New York: Guttmacher Institute, 2019.

Justice Foundation. "New Developments in the Battle to Overturn *Roe v. Wade* and *Doe v. Bolton.*" Undated.

Kagan, Elena. "Confirmation Messes, Old and New." *University of Chicago Law Review* 62, no. 2 (Spring 1995).

Kaplan, David A. *The Most Dangerous Branch.* New York: Random House, 2018.

"Karl Brandt defense documents." 1946–47. Nuremberg Trials Project no. 53, 122. Harvard Law School Library.

Kelly, Kimberly. "In the Name of the Mother: Renegotiating Conservative Women's Authority in the Crisis Pregnancy Center Movement." *Signs* 38, no. 1 (Autumn 2012): 203–30.

Kissling, Elizabeth. *From a Whisper to a Shout: Abortion Activism and Social Media.* London: Watkins Media, 2018.

Koonin, Lisa M., et al. "Abortion Surveillance — United States, 1992." *Morbidity and Mortality Weekly Report* 45, no. SS-3 (May 3, 1996).

Krebsbach, Robert L. *Abortion: Have We the Right?* Tulsa, OK: Right to Life Crusade, Inc., 1984.

Lader, Lawrence. *Abortion.* Indianapolis: Bobbs-Merrill, 1964.

Latimer, Heather. *Reproductive Acts: Sexual Politics in North American Fiction and Film.* Montreal: McGill–Queen's University Press, 2013.

Lazarus, Edward. *Closed Chambers: The Rise, Fall and Future of the Modern Supreme Court.* New York: Penguin, 1999.

Lee, Ellie J. "Post-abortion syndrome: reinventing abortion as a social problem." In *How Claims Spread: Cross-National Diffusion of Social Problems,* edited by Joel Best, 39–68. New York: Aldine de Gruyter, 2001.

Lees, Hanna. "The Negro Response to Birth Control." *Reporter* 34 (May 19, 1966).

LeGuin, Ursula K. *Dancing at the Edge of the World: Thoughts on Words, Women, Places.* New York: Harper & Row, 1989.

Leibovitz, Annie, and Susan Sontag. *Women.* New York: Random House, 1999.

Lepore, Jill. *These Truths.* New York: Norton, 2018.

Levine, Phillip. *Sex and Consequences: Abortion, Public Policy and the Economics of Fertility.* Princeton: Princeton University Press, 2007.

Lewis, Andrew R. *The Rights Turn in Conservative Christian Politics: How Abortion Transformed the Culture Wars.* Cambridge: Cambridge University Press, 2017.

Lewis, Julian. "Is Birth Control a Menace to Negroes?" *Jet,* August 19, 1954.

Lombardo, Paul A. *Three Generations, No Imbeciles.* Baltimore: Johns Hopkins University Press, 2009.

Luker, Kristin. *Abortion and the Politics of Motherhood.* Berkeley: University of California Press, 1985.

———. "The War Between Women." *Family Planning Perspectives* 16, no. 3 (March/April 1984): 105–10.

Mason, Carol. *Killing for Life: The Apocalyptic Narrative of Pro-Life Politics.* Ithaca, NY: Cornell University Press, 2002.

Mayfield, Eleanor. "Focus on . . . Curtis Boyd, MD." *World: The Journal of the Unitarian Universalist Association* 6, no. 2 (March/April 1992).

McCarthy, Michael. "US human research committee draws fire." *Lancet* 361 (January 11, 2003).

McCorvey, Norma, and Andy Meisler. *I Am Roe: My Life, Roe v. Wade, and Freedom of Choice.* New York: HarperCollins, 1994.

McCorvey, Norma, with Frank Pavone. "My Journey into the Catholic Church." New York: Priests for Life, 1999.

McCorvey, Norma, and Gary Lee Thomas. *Won by Love: Norma McCorvey, Jane Roe of Roe v. Wade, Speaks Out for the Unborn as She Shares her New Conviction for Life.* Nashville: Thomas Nelson, 1997.

McFadden, Maria. "The Norma McCorvey Story: Woe is Roe." *Human Life Review* 20, no. 4 (Fall 1994): 27–39.

McGreevy, John T. *Catholicism and American Freedom: A History.* New York: Norton, 2003.

McKeegan, Michelle. *Abortion Politics: Mutiny in the Ranks of the Right.* New York: Free Press, 1992.

McKenna, George. "Criss-Cross: Democrats, Republicans, and Abortion." *Human Life Review* 34, nos. 3 & 4 (Summer/Fall 2006).

McMunigal, Kevin C. "Of Causes and Clients: Two Tales of Roe v. Wade." *Hastings Law Journal* 47, no. 3 (1996).

Means, Cyril C., Jr. "The Phoenix of Abortional Freedom: Is a Penumbral or Ninth-Amendment Right About to Arise from the Nineteenth-Century Legislative Ashes of a Fourteenth-Century Common-Law Liberty?" *New York Law Forum* 17, no. 2 (1971): 335–410.

Melich, Tanya. *The Republican War Against Women: An Insider's Report from Behind the Lines.* New York: Random House, 2009.

Merton, Andrew H. *Enemies of Choice: The Right-to-Life Movement and its Threat to Abortion.* Boston: Beacon Press, 1982.

Milbauer, Barbara. *The Law Giveth: Legal Aspects of the Abortion Controversy.* New York: Atheneum, 1983.

"Mildred Fay Jefferson, MD." *The American Feminist: Remarkable Pro-Life Women* III 10, no.2 (Summer 2003).

Mohr, James C. *Abortion in America: The Origins and Evolution of National Policy, 1800–1900.* New York: OUP, 1978.

———. "Sexuality, Reproduction, Contraception and Abortion: A Review of Recent Literature." *Journal of Women's History* 8, no 1 (Spring 1996): 9–10.

Nash, Elizabeth, Rachel Benson Gold, Lizamarie Mohammed, Zohra Ansari-Thomas and Olivia Cappello. "Policy Trends in the States, 2017." New York: Guttmacher Institute, 2018.

National Abortion Federation. "Provider Security." October 1982–October 1987.

National Cancer Institute. "Summary report: early reproductive events and breast cancer workshop." 2003.

Newman, Troy. *Their Blood Cries Out.* Wichita, KS: Restoration Press, 2003.

Ney, P. G., C. Sheils and M. Gajowy. "Post Abortive Survivor Syndrome." *Journal of Prenatal and Perinatal Psychology and Health* 25 (December 2010): 107–29.

O'Brien, Jon. "Why I am prochoice." *Conscience* 34, no. 3 (September 22, 2013).

Olasky, Marvin. *Abortion Rites: A Social History of Abortion in America.* Wheaton, IL: Crossway, 1992.

Olson, Sarah. "Last Stand for Choice in Mississippi." Making Contact, October 25, 2006.

Operation Rescue. "The Tiller Report II: A Shocking Exposé on America's Most Infamous Late-Term Abortionist." Wichita, KS: Operation Rescue, 2006.

Ovadal, Ralph. *More Than These: A History of How the Pro-Life Movement Has Advanced the Cause of the Roman Catholic Church: A Call for Reformation.* Murray, UT: Heart of the Matter, 2004.

Packer, Herbert L., and Ralph J. Gampell. "Therapeutic Abortion: A Problem in Law and Medicine." *Stanford Law Review* 11, no. 3 (1959).

Paige, Connie. *The Right to Lifers: Who They Are, How They Operate, and Where They Get Their Money.* New York: Summit, 1983.

Paltrow, Lynn M. "Missed Opportunities in *McCorvey v. Hill*: The Limits of Pro-Choice Lawyering." *NYU Review of Law and Social Change* 35, no. 194 (2011).

———, and Jeanne Flavin. "Arrests of and forced interventions on pregnant women in the United States (1973–2005): The implications for women's legal status and public health." *Journal of Health Politics, Policy and Law* 38, no. 2 (2013).

Pare, C. M., and H. Raven. "Follow-up of patients referred for termination of pregnancy." *Lancet* 1, no. 7648 (March 28, 1970).

Payne, Darwin. *Indomitable Sarah: The Life of Judge Sarah T. Hughes.* Dallas: Southern Methodist University Press, 2004.

Petchesky, Rosalind Pollack. "Antiabortion, Antifeminism, and the Rise of the New Right." *Feminist Studies* 7, no. 2 (Summer 1981): 206–46.

Pinker, Steven. *The Better Angels of Our Nature: Why Violence Has Declined.* New York: Viking, 2011.

Pius XI. *Casti Connubii.* Encyclical. December 31, 1930.

Planned Parenthood Federation of America. "Could the Supreme Court Abortion Decisions Be Lost? Yes!" April 1973.

———. "The Facts Speak Louder than the 'Silent Scream.'" 1985.

Pollitt, Katha. *PRO: Reclaiming Abortion.* London: Picador, 2014.

Porphyry. *Porphyry: To Gaurus on How Embryos are Ensouled and On What is in Our Power.* Translated by James Wilberding. New York and London: Bloomsbury Academic, 2011.

Porteous, Skipp. "OR founder calls for 'Christian nation.'" *Freedom Writer* (Institute for First Amendment Studies), 1995.

Posner, Richard. *Overcoming Law.* Cambridge, MA: Harvard University Press, 1995.

Prisock, Louis. "'If You Love Children, Say So': The African American Anti-Abortion Movement." *Public Eye*, October 1, 2003.

Raymond, E. G., and D. A. Grimes. "The Comparative Safety of Legal Induced Abortion and Childbirth in the United States." *Obstetrics and Gynecology* 199, no. 2 (February 2012): 215–19.

Reagan, Leslie. *When Abortion Was a Crime: Women, Medicine and Law in the United States, 1867–1973.* Berkeley: University of California Press, 1997.

Reagan, Ronald. *Abortion and the Conscience of the Nation.* Washington, DC: New Regency, 1983.

Reardon, David. *Making Abortion Rare: A Healing Strategy for a Divided Nation.* Irvine, CA: Acorn, 1996.

Resler, Roger. *Compelling Interest: The Real Story behind Roe v. Wade*. Escondido, CA: eChristian Books, 2012.

Rich, Adrienne. *Of Woman Born: Motherhood as Experience and Institution*. New York: Norton, 1976.

———. *On Lies, Secrets, and Silence: Selected Prose 1966–1978*. New York: Norton, 1995.

Riddle, John M. *Contraception and Abortion from the Ancient World to the Renaissance*. Cambridge, MA: Harvard University Press, 1994.

Risen, James, and Judy L. Thomas. *Wrath of Angels: The American Abortion War*. New York: Basic Books, 1998.

Robenalt, James. *January 1973: Watergate, Roe v. Wade, Vietnam, and the Month That Changed America Forever*. Chicago: Chicago Review Press, 2017.

Roberts, Dorothy E. *Killing the Black Body: Race, Reproduction and the Meaning of Liberty*. New York: Vintage, 1999.

Rocca, Corinne H., Katrina Kimport, Sarah C. M. Roberts, Heather Gould, John Neuhaus and Diana G. Foster. "Decision Rightness and Emotional Responses to Abortion in the United States: A Longitudinal Study." *PLOS One*, July 8, 2015.

Rosenblatt, Roger. *Life Itself: Abortion in the American Mind*. New York: Random House, 1992.

Rubin, Barbara. "Laminaria Digitata: A Checkered Career." *Economic Botany* 31, no. 1 (1977): 66–71.

Rubin, Eva R. *Abortion, Politics, and the Courts: Roe v. Wade and Its Aftermath*. Santa Barbara, CA: Praeger, 1987.

———. *The Supreme Court and the American Family*. New York: Greenwood Press, 1986.

Rukeyser, Muriel. "Käthe Kollwitz." In *The Speed of Darkness*. New York: Random House, 1968.

Saletan, William. *Bearing Right: How Conservatives Won the Abortion War*. Berkeley: University of California Press, 2003.

Sanger, Carol. *About Abortion: Terminating Pregnancy in Twenty-First-Century America*. Cambridge, MA: Harvard University Press. 2017.

Sanger, Margaret. "Birth Control and Racial Betterment." *Birth Control Review*, February 1919.

———. "Suppression." *Woman Rebel* 1, no. 4 (June 1914).

Schaff, Eric A., Stephen L. Fielding, Carolyn Westhoff et al. "Vaginal Misoprostol Administered 1, 2, or 3 Days After Mifepristone for Early Medical Abortion." *Journal of the American Medical Association* 284, no. 15 (October 18, 2000).

Scheidler, Joseph M. *Closed: 99 Ways to Stop Abortion*. Gastonia, NC: Tan, 1993.

Schenck, Rob. *Costly Grace: An Evangelical Minister's Rediscovery of Faith, Hope, and Love*. New York: Harper, 2018.

Schiff, Daniel. *Abortion in Judaism*. Cambridge: Cambridge University Press, 2002.

Schlafly, Phyllis. "ERA means abortion and population shrinkage." *Phyllis Schlafly Report*, December 1974.

Schoen, Johanna. *Abortion After Roe*. Chapel Hill: University of North Carolina Press, 2015.

Shea, Michael. "Fetal Rights & Traditional Values." *The Heights* 51, no. 13 (December 7, 1970).

Siegel, Reva B. "The right's reasons: constitutional conflict and the spread of women-protective antiabortion argument." *Duke Law Journal* 57, no. 6 (April 2008).

Signil, Christopher. *Race, Faith, and Politics: The Dilemma, the Deal Breakers and the New Direction*. Lake Mary, FL: Charisma Media, 2012.

Simon, James F. *The Center Holds*. New York: Simon & Schuster, 1995.

Sisson, Gretchen, and Katrina Kimport. "Facts and fictions: Characters seeking abortion on American television, 2005-2014." *Contraception* 93, no. 5 (May 2016): 446-51.

Sisson, Ralph, and Foster Gould. "Adoption Decision-Making Among Women Seeking Abortion." *Women's Health Issues* 27, no. 2 (March/April 2017): 136-44.

Snead, O. Carter. *What It Means to Be Human: The Case for the Body in Public Bioethics*. Cambridge, MA: Harvard University Press, 2020.

Solinger, Rickie, ed. *Abortion Wars: A Half Century of Struggle, 1950–2000*. Berkeley: University of California Press, 1998.

Solnit, Rebecca. *The Mother of All Questions*. Chicago: Haymarket, 2017.

Sontag, Susan. "The Third World of Women." *Partisan Review*, Spring 1973.

Stein, Marc. *Sexual Injustice: Supreme Court Decisions from Griswold to Roe*. Chapel Hill: University of North Carolina Press, 2013.

Steinauer, J., J. Turk, T. Pomerantz, K. Koenemann, K. Simonson and U. Landry. "Abortion training in U.S. obstetrics and gynecology residency programs." *Obstetrics and Gynecology* 130, no. 1 (2017).

Stevens, Joyce. "Because We're Women." In *A History of International Women's Day in Words and Images*. Pennington, S. Australia: IWD Press, 1985.

Stoll, B. J., N. I. Hansen, E. F. Bell et al. "Trends in Care Practices, Morbidity, and Mortality of Extremely Preterm Neonates, 1993-2012." *Journal of the American Medical Association* 314, no. 10 (2015).

Stone, Geoffrey. *Sex and the Constitution*. New York: Liveright, 2017.

Stotland, Nada L. "The Myth of the Abortion Trauma Syndrome." *Journal of the American Medical Association* 268, no. 15 (1992).

Suk, Jeannie. "The Trajectory of Trauma: Bodies and Minds of Abortion Discourse." *Columbia Law Review* 110, no. 1193 (2010).

Sullivan, Andrew. "Life Lesson." *New Republic*, February 7, 2005.

Terry, Randall A. *The Judgment of God: Terrorism, Flood, Droughts and Disasters*. Windsor, NY: Reformer Library, 1995.

———. *Operation Rescue*. New Kensington, PA: Whitaker House, 1988.

Theodoru, Angelina, and Aleksandra Sandstrom. "How abortion is regulated around the world." Pew Research Center, October 6, 2015.

Thomson, Judith Jarvis. "A Defense of Abortion." *Philosophy and Public Affairs* 1, no. 1 (1971).

Tietze, Christopher. "Abortion as a Cause of Death." *American Journal of Public Health* 38, no. 10 (October 1948): 1434–41.

———, et al. "Provisional estimates of abortion need & services in the year following the 1973 Supreme Court decisions: United States, each state and metropolitan area." New York: Guttmacher Institute, 1975.

Trestman, Marlene. "Women Advocates Before Supreme Court, October Terms 1880 through 1999." Table. Supreme Court Historical Society, History of Oral Advocacy.

Tribe, Laurence H. *Abortion: The Clash of Absolutes.* New York: Norton, 1992.

"Unmet Need for Abortion Services in the US, The." *Family Planning Perspectives* 7 (1975).

Wagner, Theresa R., ed. *Back to the Drawing Board: The Future of the Pro-Life Movement.* South Bend, IN: St. Augustine's Press, 2003.

Wallenstein, Peter. *Tell the Court I Love My Wife: Race, Marriage, and Law—an American History.* New York: Palgrave MacMillan, 2002.

Warren, Samuel D., and Louis D. Brandeis. "The Right to Privacy." *Harvard Law Review* 4, no. 5 (December 15, 1890).

Washington, Harriet. *Medical Apartheid: The Dark History of Medical Experimentation on Black Americans from the Colonial Times to the Present.* New York: Doubleday, 2007.

Watson, Katie. *Scarlet A: The Ethics, Law and Politics of Ordinary Abortion.* Oxford: Oxford University Press, 2018.

Weddington, Sarah. "Our Bodies, Our Law—Q and A with Vicki Quade." *Barrister* 13 (Summer 1986).

Weddington, Sarah. *A Question of Choice.* London: Penguin, 1993.

Weingarten, Karen. *Abortion in the American Imagination: Before Life and Choice, 1880–1940.* New Brunswick, NJ: Rutgers University Press, 2014.

Wiebe, E. R., K. J. Trouton, S. L. Fielding, J. Klippenstein and A. Henderson. "Anti-choice attitudes to abortion in women presenting for medical abortions." *Journal of Obstetrics and Gynecology Canada* 27, no. 59 (2005).

Williams, Daniel K. *Defenders of the Unborn: The Pro-Life Movement Before Roe v. Wade.* New York: Oxford University Press, 2016.

Wilson, Angelia. *Below the Belt: Religion, Sexuality and Politics in the Rural South.* New York: Bloomsbury, 1999.

Wilt, Judith. *Abortion, Choice, and Contemporary Fiction.* Chicago: University of Chicago Press, 1990.

Woodward, Bob, and Scott Armstrong. *The Brethren: Inside the Supreme Court.* New York: Simon & Schuster, 2005.

Wright, Nathan. "Black Power vs. Black Genocide." *Black Scholar,* December 1969.

Ziegler, Mary. *Abortion and the Law in America: Roe v. Wade to the Present.* Cambridge: Cambridge University Press, 2020.

———. *After Roe: The Lost History of the Abortion Debate.* Cambridge, MA: Harvard University Press, 2015.

Index